BEHIND THE SCREAMS

By Jason Norman

Behind the Screams
© 2016. Jason Norman All rights reserved.

All illustrations are copyright of their respective owners, and are also reproduced here in the spirit of publicity. Whilst we have made every effort to acknowledge specific credits whenever possible, we apologize for any omissions, and will undertake every effort to make any appropriate changes in future editions of this book if necessary.

No part of this book may be reproduced in any form or by any means, electronic, mechanical, digital, photocopying or recording, except for the inclusion in a review, without permission in writing from the publisher.

Published in the USA by:
BearManor Media
P O Box 71426
Albany, Georgia 31708
www.bearmanormedia.com

Printed in the United States of America
ISBN   978-1-62933-069-3 (paperback)

Book & cover design and layout by Darlene Swanson • www.van-garde.com

Contents

	Foreword..v
	Tribute..vii
Roy Abramsohn:	Escape from Tomorrow...................................1
Amanda Adrienne:	Savaged..9
Eva Allen:	Beyond the Black Rainbow...............................13
Leslie Andrews:	Sick Girl...16
Joseph Bishara:	Insidious..20
	The Lizzies of Borden!..................................25
Caroline Boulton:	Curse of the Witching Tree..............................30
Naté Bova:	Da Sweet Blood of Jesus................................33
Krew Boylan:	Primal..36
Raine Brown:	39
Sarah Butler:	I Spit on Your Grave series.............................44
George Buza/Joe Silvaggio:	A Christmas Horror Story...............................51
Roberto Campanella:	Silent Hill...55
Neve Campbell:	Scream series...59
Tonantzin Carmelo:	Imprint...65
Lauren Ashley Carter:	Jugface/The Woman...................................70
Ellie Church:	Time to Kill...75
Julie Cobb:	Salem's Lot...78
Tonya Crowe:	Dark Night of the Scarecrow............................81
Tim Curry:	It...84
Vicky Dawson:	The Prowler..91
Marcia de Rousse:	True Blood..94
Devin DeVasquez:	Society...97
Heather Donahue:	Blair Witch Project....................................100
Brad Dourif:	Child's Play series....................................106
Amy Everson:	Felt..113
Megan Franich:	30 Days of Night.....................................116
	The Story's Freaks....................................121
	Creatures of the Fright................................131
Jonathan Fuller:	Castle Freak..135
Marta Gastini:	The Rite/Dracula 3D..................................139
Geretta Geretta:	Demons..142
Rodleen Getsic:	The Bunny Game.....................................146
Leah Gibson:	The Devil's Ground...................................157
Buddy/Rick Giovinazzo:	Combat Shock..161
Angela Goethals:	Behind the Mask: The Rise of Leslie Vernon.............165
Carole Goldman:	Superstition..172

Macarena Gómez:	*Dagon*	176
Holter Graham:	*Maximum Overdrive*	179
Lynne Griffin:	*Black Christmas/Curtains*	184
Steffie Grote:	*Pawn Shop Chronicles*	187
Luke Hawker:	*Krampus*	191
Lindsay Hayward:	*R100*	195
Andrew Hubatsek:	*Pet Sematary*	200
Amy Huck:	*The Omen*	203
John Jarratt:	*Wolf Creek*	205
LEGEND ALERT	Caught in the Grip of *Jaws*	208
Tobias Jelinek/Kimberly Leemans:	*Fire City: End of Days*	221
Gene Jones:	*The Sacrament*	224
Slavitza Jovan/Alice Drummond:	*Ghostbusters*	230
Dan Kamin:	*Creepshow 2*	235
Andrew Kavadas:	*Monsterville: The Cabinet of Souls*	243
Daisy Keeping:	*Neverlake*	247
Sylva Kelegian:	*Desperation*	250
Nick King:	*Sinister 2*	252
Amelia Kinkade:	*Night of the Demons* series	255
James Kirk/Haley, Webb/Ellen Wroe:	*Final Destination*	259
Heather Langenkamp:	*Nightmare on Elm Street*	266
	The First and Second *Last*	279
Ramon Llao:	*The Green Inferno*	289
Jill Larson:	*The Taking of Deborah Logan*	291
Joan McCall:	*Devil Times Five/Grizzly*	295
Jennifer McKinney:	*Death Ship*	297
Teri McMinn:	*Texas Chain Saw Massacre*	301
Rachel Miner		305
Ingrid Mortimer/Bailey Spry:	*It Follows*	311
David Naughton:	*An American Werewolf in London*	315
Daniel Newman:	*Children of the Corn*	318
Stacey Nelkin:	*Halloween III: Season of the Witch*	323
Amber Perkins/Rachel Quinn:	*Megan is Missing*	327
LEGEND SPOTLIGHT:	Anthony Perkins/Janet Leigh: *Psycho*	334
Emily Perkins:	*It/Ginger Snaps*	344
Linnea Quigley		347
Duncan Regehr/Andre Gower:	*The Monster Squad*	351
Tristan Risk:	*American Mary*	356
Conrad Roberts:	*The Serpent and the Rainbow*	360
Debbie Rochon		363
Perla Rodriguez:	*The Cloth*	369

Victoria Sanchez:	*Wolf Girl*	374
James Sizemore:	*The Demon's Rook*	378
Stephan Smith Collins:	*Hellraiser: Revelations*	382
Sissy Spacek:	*Carrie*	388
Oakley Stevenson:	*The Convent*	399
Madison Stone:	*Evil Toons*	402
Dyanne Thorne:	*Ilsa* series	404
Samm Todd:	*Trick 'r Treat*	408
Mark Torgl:	*Toxic Avenger* series	412
Allan Trautman:	*Return of the Living Dead*	416
Baph Tripp:	*The Gate* films	423
Ana Turpin:	*Para Elisa*	426
Kevin Van Hentenryck:	*Basket Case* series	429
Debi Sue Voorhees:	*Friday the 13th V: A New Beginning*	432
Lara Vosburgh:	*Inner Demons*	435
Eileen Walsh:	*The Magdalene Sisters*	439
Dawn Wells:	*The Town That Dreaded Sundown*	442
Liz White:	*The Woman in Black*	447
Billy Wirth/Jamison Newlander:	*The Lost Boys*	453
Mary Woronov		457
Scary kids		461
Ella-Maria Gollmer:	*The Countess*	462
Lindsey Haun:	*Village of the Damned*	466
Gregor Hesse:	*Dead Again*	473
Bret Loehr:	*Identity*	476
Marc Marut:	*The Paperboy*	480
Heather Mazur:	*Night of the Living Dead*	484
Addy Miller/Madison Lintz:	*The Walking Dead*	487
Jake Thomas:	*The Cell*	492
	Epilogue	494
	References	496
	About the Author	506

Horror legend Linnea Quigley looks back and forth at her iconic career.

Foreword....

I NEVER EVER thought in a million years that I would be acting or be in a band.

I grew up as a very shy child. It wasn't until I moved from Davenport, Iowa, to Los Angeles that my life changed completely. I started working at a health spa and two girls I met there introduced me to acting. I started out doing extra work on films and also did modeling gigs. These two ingénues took me to meet their agent and my career launched from there.

Horror and I get along well because I never looked down on it. As a teenager, I always relished watching horror films, especially with my best friend Dawn. We loved watching "Creature Features" on Saturday nights, munching on pizza and pretending to be the characters we were watching: "I'm going to get you, Barbara!"

Jason Norman has given me the opportunity to talk about the journey of my career, which I truly appreciate. I've written a few books in my life, and Jason has inspired me to get busy and write another one! If you want to pursue acting, I say that it is so important to follow your passions and live your dreams: that way you will have no regrets with your own personal journey. The way that I prepare for my various roles in films is to just jump in with the material and absorb the character and the story.

I know that during my acting career I have had the opportunity to be a role model to some extent to others, as I have portrayed many fearless and courageous characters in my films. In my personal life,

I am very involved with animal rights and have a soft heart for rescue dogs. I try to be good to people and practice kindness.

I hope you have enjoyed some of the roles I have played as well as in my upcoming films and that you've learned something from this.

Here's to horror!

Screams, Linnea Quigley

Tribute

THAT'S A WORD I kept in mind all the way through both this book and its predecessor—and every such one that I'll knock out from here on. The interviews, the research, the writing, the editing, and everything else that went into taking so many ideas to transcription, and making my way through this book, it was about homage.

I am paying it to the people that terrified—and oftentimes adrenalized—so many of us, those that have been so frightening on the screen for so long. We've already run into one such lady back in the foreword—over the next few chapters, we'll meet many more from a genre that doesn't always get the respect it should (or so we believe!).

"Everything about the genre is appealing to me!" exclaims world-renowned scream queen Tiffany Shepis, a veteran of over a hundred such productions on screens of every size. "The genre is filled with so many different sub-genres: comedy, romance, suspense, thriller, and drama; horror films have it all, usually! Besides, at least for me, there is nothing cooler than getting to play a fun monster—or run from one."

But also to those that make the horror community the airtight-knit family that it truly is. The people that set the horror and sci-fi genres apart from the legions that check out other types. The ones that take the time not just to face down the films, but step into the world they create. Those that give the fear fans of the world a chance to meet their screen heroes at conventions and other events—and those that take part at doing so. The ones that come not just in costume, but character. Dressing up and being made up as their favorites, talking like them . . . for that brief period, *being* them.

A common sight myself at such events, I obtained much of the info here from people I'd found so scary in character—and throughout them, I realized that others like that deserved their own spot in the spotlight. You'll hear more than enough from me throughout this tome—let's listen to some other fans.

"Acting is acting, but you typically don't see people in horror movies going up for awards," one angry fan asserts. "Horror and thriller as a genre don't get the respect they're due. You have to be intelligent to enjoy it, or of a violent nature to enjoy it. You're in one or two or both groups. I think the best example of it was Dante: the road to hell is paved with good intentions."

"The one thing that's guaranteed in life is the one thing that scares us all: death," says another. "That's what horror movies are about—killing each other in all sorts of terrible, horrifying ways. That's what it's about. We see death every day. It's the one thing that everybody has to face. But what makes it less scary for me is to see it and know it's not real."

Many people see the realistic films as scariest because they are, in fact, just that: realistic. But under all the blood and gore, these films give a new, although unpleasant study in human nature, one fellow, decked out in Leatherface garb, testifies.

"It's the amount of thought and creativity," he explains. "It's not the shock value; it's the buildup. I want to think about something. I want to roll it over in my head. I know a lot of people get appalled by gory horror movies. They think, what would make a person be that way? But that isn't what draws me. What draws me is trying to get into the scenes and see the line of thought and understand it, not condemn it."

Of course, there's more than one category of horror films. But diversity is a huge key to appeal, the ability of horror to, even tied up with a small common thread, still manage to reach so many in such a special way.

"I have an abnormal fear receptor," one lady admits. "I don't have the normal reaction to fear that most people do. It takes a lot to scare me. I don't have a thing that makes me say 'Oh, that's horrifyingly creepy!' I'm not really sure why I am the way I am, but I don't have a set thing that sends chills down my spine. Fear is something you can't control. It's an observation thing for me."

Indeed, observation plays quite the role in horror fan-hood. But impersonation, as so many utilize, goes even farther.

"It's super fun to get gory and nasty and gory and nasty," explains one overly-articulate zombie fan, clad in *Walking/Living Dead* regalia. "We get to relive or reenact any kind of fantasies, bad days, or just fun. It brings out the beast in all of us!"

And there's a special other group that might just get some unexpected help at stepping over the line from reality to dream. Not just stepping over it, but erasing it entirely. Many of the people we'll hear from started out as fans, from the outside (or the audience) just looking in and on. Then, somewhere along the way, they decide to become a part of the world they admired so much, to put their names alongside the performers that had entertained them for so long. Some, probably most of them, heard at some point, "Why are you trying that? There's NO chance you'll make it!"

But they did. And the readers here may as well. Many people here were asked about advice to those looking to make it to the interviewees' level. Some were more detailed than others, but whatever worked for them can work for those looking to be the next explorer of cinema nightmares.

"I would just say, if you really love acting," advises Shepis, "just never give up. Also, don't think you'll have a second chance. If the opportunity comes, *take it*!"

Note—over a year has passed since I started out this work. During that time, this book found a new reason to be written, a new person to pay tribute to, but for causes much more serious and sad than we just heard. You'll hear his name throughout . . . the end of this tome will pay a greater thanks to someone who sadly will never get to read this.

Some unexpected Disney pain creeps up on Jim White (Roy Abramsohn) and his daughter in 2013's *Escape from Tomorrow*.

Roy Abramsohn:

Escape from Tomorrow

IS IT ALL just a dream, one that we welcome from keeping us from reality? All a façade that waves an image of magic and morality that gets yanked away from us when we realize that it's all just an image after all?

We could ask these questions about *Escape from Tomorrow* (2013). We could ask them about the film's main character. But after watching the film itself, we also might just have to ask them about the place that loves to remind us that it truly is "the happiest place on earth."

Disney. It's a Land or a World, depending on which side of the country we're on. But it's also supposed to be the place of wonder, the kingdom of magic. A place where fantasy and reality meet, and one welcomingly overtakes the other. More than anything else, it's intended as the place to visit when we need to be picked up just a bit.

And it's tough to imagine a fellow more in need than one in the mass of those that troop through Disney every day. Jim White's wife Emily is driving him nuts. His two kids are right there at that stage of brattiness. And with just one day left in the Magic Kingdom, he's just found out there's a slip of pinkness from work waiting for him back at home. All that Disney magic they came to search for looks like it's gone.

Far too many guys have been through that sort of thing. But this wouldn't be special enough for a book about horror film acting if there wasn't more to it, would it?

"Me being a father of two, dealing with all the strains and struggles of a marriage, (Jim) was a very relatable character," recalls Roy Abramsohn. "As an unemployed actor, I sure understood getting and losing jobs."

But if getting into Jim's mind wasn't overly challenging, the filming process itself certainly was, and long before Abramsohn was anywhere near the picture in any sense. For months before filming kicked off, Randy Moore and the rest of the *Tomorrow* crew staked out the Disney parks on both sides of the country to plot out one scene after another. Disney, known for protecting its privacy and copyrights with more tenacity than its villains Ursula, Jafar, and Scar put together, would never let anyone—particularly an unproven writer/director like Moore—drag their golden name through the mud, even in the fictional sense, let alone do so on the parks' own grounds. Everyone would have to do this on the serious downlow.

"The filmmakers went there nine times, Disney World and Disneyland, to check over the sun and lighting," Abramsohn says, "planning out where each shot was and where the light was going to be that day."

Charging from coast to coast, and then from ride to ride, the cast and crew tried to stay out of the security's spotlight—the same stealthy techniques coming in handy, as someone could only whisper, "Action!" Clipboards, grips, and huge cameras would have all gotten too much attention.

And so would stars from the A-, B-, or even C-list in Hollywood. Being a nobody came fast in handy for Abramsohn.

"They didn't want any stars in this," he says. "The way we filmed it, you couldn't. If I were Christian Slater or Noah Wyle walking around, I'd get recognized. Being an unknown completely paid off for me. After years and years of struggle, I'd finally gotten the lead in a feature film with a small budget."

Still, one misstep, one mistake, the wrong person (not even people!) seeing something could have ruined a ton of effort and blackened careers and names in an instant, and it almost did.

In one shot, Jim strolled through the turnstiles, ready to act out a day of fun. But one of the billion things that can cause a re-shoot happened, and he hurried back out, only to spin the stills again moments later.

This time, someone noticed.

"A security guy came up and said 'Sir, why did you enter the park twice in seven minutes?'" remembers Abramsohn. "I was like 'Oh shit, finally we're caught.'" The guard asked if he might be a celebrity, noticing that those apparently in the paparazzi business had been spending quite a bit of snapshots on him.

Abramsohn quickly spun a fairytale of his daughter misplacing her sunscreen and having to hurry back outside and grab it. Then he realized that the whole crew had placed different last names on the season passes they'd purchased. One wrong question could get him ejected, and perhaps worse.

As the rest of the cast and crew abandoned him, Abramsohn asked for a quick trip to the john.

"I had some sound equipment in my pocket, and I was ready to throw it in the trash," he says. Like most of the cast, he'd been carrying tape recorders around, getting everything on tape—yet still unable to pause and restart, which would play holy hell with the sound crew.

"Then I realized that I could have thrown out a few days' worth of work," he recalls. "I put it in my sock." He went back outside, waited until the guards weren't looking, and snuck away.

Now let's get back to the ultimate preparation process—how Jim led Moore, Abramsohn, and horror audiences from a land of wonder straight through to pitch black (and white) madness and death.

"Jim wasn't a hero," Abramsohn says. "It was complicated, and I didn't really understand it, and I kind of like things I don't understand well. At the same time, I totally understood this guy. He was missing his lost youth, and he was missing all the options he gets to have with women." More on that later—Abramsohn also checked back to his own Disney memories, not all so special from either perspective.

"I had been to Disney World as a child," he recalls. "My favorite memory of that was losing a ten-dollar bill my uncle had given me and weeping the whole time. I had an experience of the misery of waiting in line for an hour and fifteen minutes. The fact that you're a dad in the happiest place on earth, you have an expectation as a father, you try to give your kids the best time in the world, but by the time you find a place to park and take the shuttle to get in, you're tired already.

"I had been to Disneyland on a cold day with my son and daughter," he continues. "I remember leaving once with my real wife and saying 'This is the most miserable place on earth.' I didn't have to do any research; I had done it."

Still, we're in the realistic sense. It's time to finally escape into the new world. The dark world. The unreal, or at least *sur*real world. The true journey from dark comedy to out and out horror.

Trying to hide the fearful uncertainty the layoff has imposed, Jim and his family roll to the monorail, where two far-too-young girls give him the once-over and invitation. Even with them stuck in his mind, he can't stop seeing evil countenances on the legendarily-friendly smiles of Disney characters. Emily dangles her own supposed infidelity in his face, then gets a real attitude when he takes their son on Space Mountain (still, nothing in this film is even remotely as terrifying as the revelation that the crew had to ride "It's a Small World" about a dozen times in a row during filming!).

David Lynch is considered about the king of dark surrealism when it comes to film directing, but Moore's a new disciple in the field, and that's about to roar straight through. A quick visit to the park nurse to treat Jim's daughter's small injury reveals the presence of a local "cat flu," which asymptomatically sneaks up on its victims, never knowing until it's too late.

That's hardly all. Jim and his daughter meet a strange, enthralling beauty with a huge amulet necklace. One blackout later, Jim's suddenly below her in a bed, tied up as she has her way with him, his daughter just in the other room. He can only hope it's all a dream.

"It's like people that gamble and people that become alcoholics," Abramsohn says, "he's going into a dream world of fantasy because he can't stand his reality. When I saw the movie, I had a sinking feeling in the pit of my stomach, because I didn't realize the proximity of my daughter being in the other room while I was committing adultery would have such an effect on me."

In her first acting role in four years, Alison Taylor became the mysterious lady of allure.

Alison Taylor portrays the bombshell who mentally and sexually overpowers Jim (and the audience, it appears!) in *Escape from Tomorrow* (2013).

"I've always liked off-kilter roles," says Taylor, who, unlike the crew, got to do all her performing off park grounds, in hotels and studios. "I thought she was kind of dark and broken, and I liked that about her. She goes around seducing fathers and stealing little girls, a bit of a lost soul in a way. She was the dark side of everything. I play dark characters all the time anyway, so I just used that technique."

Things would get tougher, on both Abramsohn and Jim. Back at the hotel, Jim spies the two young girls from before. After fantasizing about this all day, he finally decides to make a move.

"One was fourteen, the other was twenty at the time," remembers Abramsohn. I told (Moore) that I thought it was creepy, and he said 'Roy, I *want* it to be creepy.' You want to do your best, but at the same time, you don't want to be known as this type of person."

Maybe Jim wasn't. Perhaps even after all the pain from in and out, emotional and physical, he still stuck to what was right. When one of his forbidden targets invites him to make his sad (and criminal) fantasy come true, it takes everything to say no.

She spits in his face. Later on, that will exponentially increase in disgust.

"He didn't like his wife that much," Abramsohn says. "He's trying to be a great father, but he's missing his youth. (The girls) are kind of sirens calling him to the other side. Then there's his nagging wife. Then there's this aging seductress. They're calling him to the other side."

No one has any idea how far a trip that would be, but Moore was determined to show us. After being jumped by security, Jim's suddenly trapped under an Epcot ride, detained and interrogated. An apparent gamester explains that Jim was a pet project since his first Disney visits back in youthhood. His ride difficulties, even the job loss, were all part of the plan.

Then an Epcot-shaped helmet appears from thin air and starts to scan Jim. But he's had about enough, escaping and smashing the questioner, found to be animatronic "himself."

He and his daughter escape from the woman who captured him earlier. Jim makes it back to the hotel room, and puts his children and wife to bed. Whatever the trauma was, and from where, it looks like this ending will be typical Disney fare.

But it won't. Jim begins to hack mysterious hairballs from his throat (they were actually corn silk and molasses, and spewing them up for an hour was one of Abramsohn's toughest tasks of filming). His digestive system suddenly at war, he can't move. By the time Emily wakes in the next morning, he's long gone, a macabre grin on his face and his eyes like cats'. The spitting he received earlier infected him with something far past a cold—the nurse's warning has come fatally true.

"He's rotting inside, his soul is rotting, and the only escape he has is to die," Abramsohn explains. "That's how he escapes his tomorrow and goes to the other side."

Apparently prepared, a cleaning crew rushes in, spruces the place up, and whisks him away in a plain white van. Can't have anything, even the loss of human life, darkening Disney's sunshine.

Still, it's not over. As Jim takes his final ride, another van arrives, and his exact double emerges, accompanied by a beautiful woman and their daughter, all set to experience the Magic.

What's going on? Was Jim a clone, a creation? Was it all a bunch of Hollywood-esque coincidences? Did any of it truly happen? If it was a dream, it certainly wasn't one this guy's heart was making!

In any case, Moore, again following in the tradition of Lynch, Kubrick, and so many other such filmmakers, will leave it to the audience to discuss forever. But in one last dirty joke to Disney, he has "The End" appear in the middle of the screen, the two young girls from before fluttering in from the side, wings included, to make it vanish.

In other words, Tinkerbell with an attitude.

Moore's secrecy didn't end after filming; to keep any leaks from reaching Disney, he did the editing in Korea. Still, even after *Escape* made its way to festivals and eventually homes across the nation, Disney stayed silent, perhaps fearing that responding would only create more publicity for a film already doing a bit of damage.

"People say the most important thing about it is how they filmed it," Abramsohn says. "I wasn't pretending to get it. I thought it was much more of an art film than when I had auditioned for the movie. It's a psychological drama."

Speaking of David Lynch, this guy is a master of scaring the hell out of viewers without allowing his films to slip into the genre of horror. *Blue Velvet*, *Twin Peaks*, these things were more terrifying than much we'll find in books like this.

Largely because they're based so much on the unknown. Lynch is like Stanley Kubrick when it comes to the whole "film ambiguity" thing, and it can be all kinds of scary when we're led through a cinematic world by a director who won't tell us where we're going, even when we get there.

Like in *Mulholland Drive* (2001). If you don't understand what the hell's going on, you're probably right.

"People should see the movie at least five times," recommends Bonnie Aarons. "Every time you watch it, you learn something new."

It twists, it turns, it goes in more directions than anyone could ever count. Some argue that everything is tied up in the end, others say no, perhaps hoping to guilt-trip Lynch into making a sequel!

"With David Lynch, you want anything!" exclaims Aarons, a huge *Twin Peaks* fan. "If he's doing something, you want to be in it. He's one of the greatest storytellers of all time. What an honor that was!"

On the title street in Los Angeles, a young beauty (Laura Harring) is suddenly kidnapped by her limo driver. Managing to escape, she collapses inside a nearby apartment. Meanwhile, hopeful actress, and full-blown cockeyed optimist, Betty Elms (Naomi Watts) arrives in town and happens upon her. Finding a ton of money and a blue key inside her purse, the pair set off to find out just who Harring's character really is. Elsewhere, a ton of other storylines start popping up.

But now let's meet Aarons' character.

At a small restaurant called Winkie's (can you imagine anyone ever saying, "I'm hungry. Let's eat at that Winkie's place"?), Dan (Patrick Fischler) describes in all kinds of detail a dream that won't stop tormenting him. It's the only world we can never hope to control, and it's terrifying him—an ominous demoness just waiting to make his pain real. One that just *happens* to live right outside this very restaurant!

"I had the face," Aarons remembers. "David was trying to find the most unusual face, and luckily enough, he thought it was mine. He said, 'You have the most incredible face I've ever seen!' He kept my green eyes. He didn't want one bit of features distorted or taken away. He just added to it." Quite a bit and not in a cosmetic way, we find.

Dan's friend insists there's nothing to worry about and follows him outside. We feel a parallel to Mommy and Daddy assuring us that there's no monster in the closet or under the bed, ready to grab us as we doze away.

They get closer and closer to the nearby alley, and it looks like he's right.

"I didn't know much about it until I got (to the set)," Aarons recalls. "There was a lot of makeup. It took hours, all day. I think I still have some of the stuff in my hair."

As Dan, his friend, and the viewers get right up to the corner, there's nothing there.

Until there is. Aarons' girl steps out.

Strangely, that's all she does. She doesn't say anything, doesn't motion towards him, only casts a knowingly-evil, Mona Lisa-like smile at her visitors. It's like she knew they were coming, and how they'd react if she showed.

Did she know Dan would keel over and die of shock? Maybe not, but that's what happens.

"David was specific, telling me what to do," Aarons remembers. "I was thinking about how much I love him."

Her face is so matted with grime and mud that we can hardly see her eyes and teeth. Her stained hair is like a pile of rough tree branches. Long ago, at least it probably seems so to her, this had been a lovely woman. But by now, she's just stopped trying. As joltingly frightening as her appearance is, it's also sad that she probably wouldn't have been here if just a few things had gone differently. That's a common feeling when encountering the homeless.

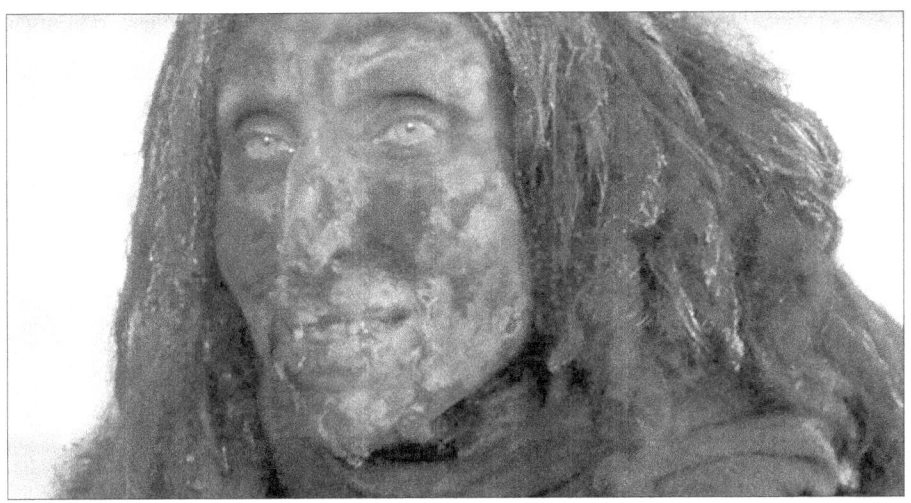

What dark secrets does this mysterious lady hold? Bonnie Aarons terrified us all in 2001's David Lynch thriller *Mulholland Drive*.

"David kept everything secret," Aarons remembers. "Only David would pick a woman to play this bum role. He wanted me to have a very evil look. I gave him a look like I loved him, and he said 'That's the look.'"

As complex as the film gets for the next two hours, it's easy to forget that little electrification. Betty and her friend have a sudden bed rendezvous, and Betty's declaration of love for someone she met that morning implies that this isn't real. Then Betty wakes up, only now her name is Diane, and she's the ex of Camilla, who Harring now becomes.

The new Diane is an actress whom Hollywood is phasing out, down with drugs and mental illness. She's at Winkie's, trying to coax a hitman into harming those that harmed her. Dan's standing there too, glancing at her like he just can't wait for her to mess up.

Normally, the piece might have stopped before this. *Mulholland* was originally scheduled to give Lynch another go-round at the small screen, his tale as the jumping-off point for a TV pilot. When that didn't happen, he decided to put an ending on *Mulholland*. Not a happy ending or even a remotely clear one, but an ending nonetheless.

We see Aarons' character again, off to herself, placing something inside a small bag. Two old people, who we've seen sprinkled through the film, come wandering out (by this point, reality is no kind of priority). They find a way inside Diane's apartment, chasing her, laughing wildly. Her career, her safety (after the hit), and her sanity gone, there's just one escape left, and it's the self-sacrifice. We see Aarons' blackened face one more time, and the film ends.

"She could have been a magical beast from another planet, another realm, another dimension," Aarons remarks of her lady. "Where else would she get such a beautiful box?"

So what the hell did we just see? Exactly what does Aarons' character represent? How much of any of it was real at all?

No answers. Well, tons of them, just nothing concrete. Lynch has never fully explained it, probably because it would still be up for personal opinion even if he did. His view is his view, everyone else's is theirs. It's frightening and more than a bit frustrating, but it also forces us to think a bit.

And enough people certainly were willing—*Mulholland* is considered one of Lynch's top films and nearly won him a directing Oscar.

"I think it had to do with parallel universes, parallel worlds," Aarons opinionates. "My character was manipulating the world. In Hollywood, things aren't what they seem to be, and my character was the one that switched the worlds. Maybe it all was real.

"I could be wrong. You could think about it in so many different ways."

How did her character get to that point? It would be interesting to write *that* backstory! But she might have started out just as the gal Aarons became a decade later for *The Fighter* (2011). She was Bonnie, a drug-using colleague of Dicky Eklund, whose portrayal won Christian Bale an Oscar.

"(Director) David (O. Russell) told me what he wanted, and then Christian directed me," she remembers. "It worked out really well. I'm lucky enough to work with the greatest storytellers of our time. The characters are in me; the directors pull them out." Living in Hollywood, she'd seen far too many people fall into similar traps.

"Just like alcoholism, it's a disease that people can't cut out," she says. "It's unfortunate that people waste their lives doing that."

Amanda Adrienne:

Savaged

THE STORY HAD been told before, several times over the course of a few decades. Woman is brutally assaulted by a group of sadist sex maniac men, only to find within a part of her she never knew existed to come back and violently give them back her pain, probably quintupled.

However, a slightly tweaked tale can become brand new, very quickly. We take what we have, and we make an addition there, a subtraction elsewhere. A small set of switches can move a legend to newness.

First you take the basics—a rape victim realizing the vengeful dream of every woman who's ever been through this horrific nightmare, and many of those who have had to help pick up the pieces.

Then you add a new challenge for both the character and the lady portraying her—the removal of senses that so many take for granted.

Finally, you put in some supernatural effects. Yep—give the heroine some assistance that can't be found in this boring, repetitive world of reality. That'll be sure to spruce things all the way up.

But back at the start of every film, there are still the same jumping-off spots that get every cinematic experience going, like some serious desire to get things done on the crew's part, and finding enough funding to put it all the way together. For 2013's *Savaged*, the first was much easier to locate than the second.

"Michael Ojeda is incredibly passionate and uncompromising in his vision," Amanda Adrienne recalls of the film's main man behind the camera (the film was marketed as *Avenged* in some areas). "As an actor, that kind of energy is inspiring to be around."

She'd start things out as Zoe, ready to take a big step in any young one's life: moving in with her beloved for the first time. It's an even bigger one for her than for most—first off, the fellow's states away.

Secondly, Zoe lacks the ability to hear. If something happens, she's not going to be able to call for help. Since this is a horror movie, she indeed gets caught by the worst of society, brutally assaulted in every sense, and left for dead. Not that this is anything new to these cretins or their genetics: their people have been wiping out the Apache for generations (just one of the neverending ways that Native Americans have lost the land they nurtured for about 1500 years).

Again, though, this *is* a horror movie. So we're not surprised—but hopefully inspired!—when Zoe recovers, sort of, and gets her bloodily-justified payback.

For a time, that was all Adrienne, Ojeda, and the rest would need; a trailer behind them, Ojeda and others went off to use his commercial to entice outside funding, while Adrienne searched for Zoe's character.

"I felt emotionally connected to Zoe," she says, "and knew on some kind of gut level that she could teach me something about myself. She was both familiar *and* surprising." For the nine months it took for the donated dough to arrive, she sharpened her archery skills and trained like crazy in the Chinese martial art wushu.

The legendary power of the Native American spirit helped
Amanda Adrienne's Zoe get some payback in 2013's *Savaged*.

And yes, she got ready to do everything while showing that Zoe couldn't hear any of it. Adrienne worked with a co-star on sign language and read some online blogs by the deaf, along with Helen Keller's writings. She also checked out a 2003 episode of MTV's documentary series *True Life* about a deaf participant.

"But being deaf is just a small aspect of who Zoe is as a person," Adrienne asserts. "Michael and I had discussions on how he saw her and her rebel spirit." That spirit, however, wouldn't be all Zoe's.

Sorry if that sounded a bit strange. With full filming finally under way, here's what happened, story-wise.

Finding the victim, a grandfatherly Native American tries to ritualistically resurrect her. It's both a great success and a terrifying mishap.

Zoe makes it back—but along with her comes the spirit of Mangas Coloradas, who spent a quarter century defending his Apache people from both Mexico and the United States. Just as the Civil War got going in the east, Mangas was captured and executed by military leaders in New Mexico. Even today, much like Geronimo and others, he's seen as a legend and martyr by Native Americans—and not enough others—across the country.

"I did a lot of research," Adrienne recalls. "I felt a great deal of obligation to learn his story and truth." With something past human stirring her fire, Zoe's back out for blood, and some of those that harmed her soon find their own red plasma and inner organs splattered across the ground, walls, and anywhere else unlucky enough to host their deaths (she even makes a meal of a guy's heart, letting everyone know just how far from human Zoe has gone).

Still, it wasn't all about physicality for the actress. Putting oneself in such a mindset, and staying there through filming, requires us to force our mentality into areas it normally wouldn't go near. Adrienne sent her memory back to some journaling techniques she'd learned in acting classes.

"I would basically meditate and get really relaxed," she explains. "Then I just let the hand flow without trying to censor thoughts. Sometimes nothing came up, and other times I would surprise myself with new understandings of how to enter the character. I believe in putting in detailed work and then letting go on set and just trying to trust that it's all there."

There's just one rapist still alive, and he just happens to be of the bloodline that killed Mangas. He's got a chainsaw, but she's armed with huge knife and tomahawk, along with a spirit that now has its own extra reason for vengeance. For her part, Adrienne *didn't* have a stunt double for most of her work.

"I worked with Michael on the body language of Zoe as the warrior, versus Zoe as Zoe," she says. "There is such a precision and athleticism required for those scenes in addition to bringing the emotional reality of the character. It can be a challenge to strike that balance." A squib on her chest broke during filming, Adrienne continues, sending her to the hospital.

Keeping with the horror movie tradition, Zoe (and Mangas) come out on top in the final battle. But possession has caused her resurrected body to degenerate too fast to come all the way back to health, and her boyfriend's forced into a spontaneous cremation, allowing both Zoe and her "visitor" a peaceful finale.

"Watching the movie and seeing how Michael edited the action sequences is quite magical," Adrienne remarks. "It's like I'm watching someone else, because I don't see myself as that badass in real life. (Performers should) know that their stories are valid to tell and should be heard. At least, that's what I've found most helpful for myself."

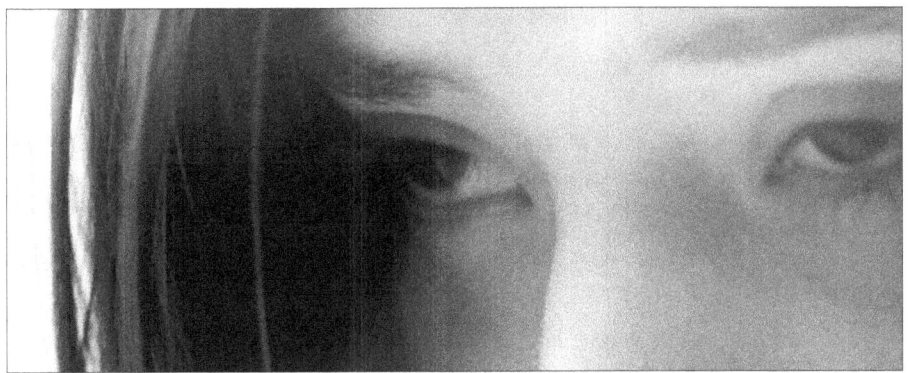

Eva Allen traveled *Beyond the Black Rainbow* in 2010 to find
a mental power greater than those that had harmed her.

Eva Allen:

Beyond the Black Rainbow

THE WORLD'S TOUGHEST labyrinth would probably be easier to negotiate. The strongest GPS device in the universe couldn't help us find our way through it, couldn't help us locate what we want so badly to find.

It's our mind. It's what's within. The carrier of our past, our pain, our ultimate uncertainty as to why we have so much trouble knowing what to do, where to go, how to heal. Leavenworth, Attica, and Alcatraz combined would never be as effective at blocking our way to freedom from the suffering that it's too often so cold as to grasp with iron.

We never stop trying to find a way to leave certain things behind, in our minds or those of others. And there's probably never going to be a surefire, uniform way for all of us to do that, but some things have worked for some people.

Typically for the villains in a horror movie, the cretins that run the show at Arboria Institute *say* that that's all they're looking for. They *proclaim* that their only objective is to help others find some sort of happiness, a cleansing of the mentality.

But they don't talk about the eggs that have to be broken to finish up the omelet, the innocent lady who's become their personal petri dish, her trapped inside for them to examine and experiment upon. If it works and their goals are located, great. If it doesn't, well, about eggs and omelets again. . . .

Beyond the Black Rainbow (2010) wouldn't just be Eva Allen's horror debut; it was her first time before a film's camera, away from the TV roles she'd done thus far. Acting is its own mysterious world, and being the lady lead so early in the game, Allan was feeling the burden.

"When we started filming, I realized how many people really were involved," she recalls of the 2010 flick, "and not only involved, but who had put everything into this film, and I put a lot of pressure on myself to succeed for them."

They were counting on her to carry off Elena, the human experiment herself. Allan couldn't give her character speech, with Elena's telekinetic ability keeping her under study at Arboria, its highers-up hoping that she, intentionally or otherwise, could lead them to the place's dream.

A prisoner there since her youth, it was the only home Elena had ever known. Allan had to find a way to feel as she'd been there for decades as well.

Being alone for so long, her only interactions with the guards and personnel, Elena had certainly spent much of her time ludicrously deep in thought. She'd undoubtedly wondered what existed beyond Arboria's walls, even if she may not have wanted to actually visit it. Allan took a few steps within as well, trying out one of the world's oldest (its effectiveness is a matter of debate) tactics at fighting back the suffering our mind and memory sometimes put us through.

"I meditated a lot," she remembers, "because I knew I would need to be able to be vulnerable, focused, and open to an extreme level during filming."

It's how Elena had found her place in the world, and how she eventually moves from it. It's how Allan located her. And, surprisingly, but certainly fortunately, it's a journey that ended with Allan herself finding the strength to slam a few doors from her own past, a task certainly tougher than anything she'd ever find in the acting world.

"The world and the characters and the imagery were so wild and strong," Allan recalls. "I just knew I had to book it."

With her only communication from the mind, Elena works her way through therapy sessions by silently asking where her dad might be. But that's not really important to the place's gatekeepers, and quickly enough, she's not the only one used as a variable.

Letting her know just who's running the show, a nurse destroys a photo of Elena's mom. But as she walks away, Elena peers up at her, sadly, seemingly hopeful for an apology.

Nope. The nurse turns around, appearing in pain. She begs Elena to stop, but we don't know what the young woman is doing. Will the nurse explode? Burst into flames?

Elena's just looking. She's not like Carrie White, punctuating her telekinetic actions with a wide-eyed glare that does everything but blast death rays from her pupils. There's very little emotion on her face at all. Perhaps this is nothing more than putting gas in the car or drinking a glass of water, another necessary task that all of us take for granted.

Then the nurse's head caves in from within, her body lifeless before it hits the ground. On a monitor, the place's doctor watches almost gleefully. Clearly, he knew what was going to happen, and things went as planned.

See, it's not just professional for him. Years ago, he went through a treatment looking to find his own inner heaven. But being jammed into a vat of black, tar-like liquid drove him over the edge, soon killing the wife of the man who put the place together to begin with.

She was Elena's mom. Elena was put in the black stuff too. She was an infant at the time, so she couldn't follow in his murderous footsteps.

But she still may. Left unattended, she finds a way out of the establishment, making her way past some non-human creatures that once might have looked like her.

She's out of the doctor's control, and soon everything else is as well. He kills his wife. He murders his boss. He even whomps two guys who just happen to be nearby. As Elena makes her way through the night, entranced by the newness of moonlight, grass, and bugs, he's in pursuit.

"The one thing I remember thinking when I read the script," Allan explains, "was that Elena was not a victim, and I loved seeing that in a young woman."

Her abilities still at work, Elena senses her captor behind her. More emotional than she's been all film, she starts to cry. Suddenly, he can't move; she's rooted him to the ground. Then he topples, and his temple loses the battle with a large sharp rock.

Elena makes her way toward a nearby town. Telling the story of her social integration might make a great sequel.

Her steps in the night represent not just an escape and evolution for Elena, but for the lady behind her as well.

"Thinking about it now, I believe I was also drawn to Elena," Allan explains, "because I had certain experiences in my life that I had not closed the chapter on. Being such an emotionally driven character, it allowed me to self-medicate in a way."

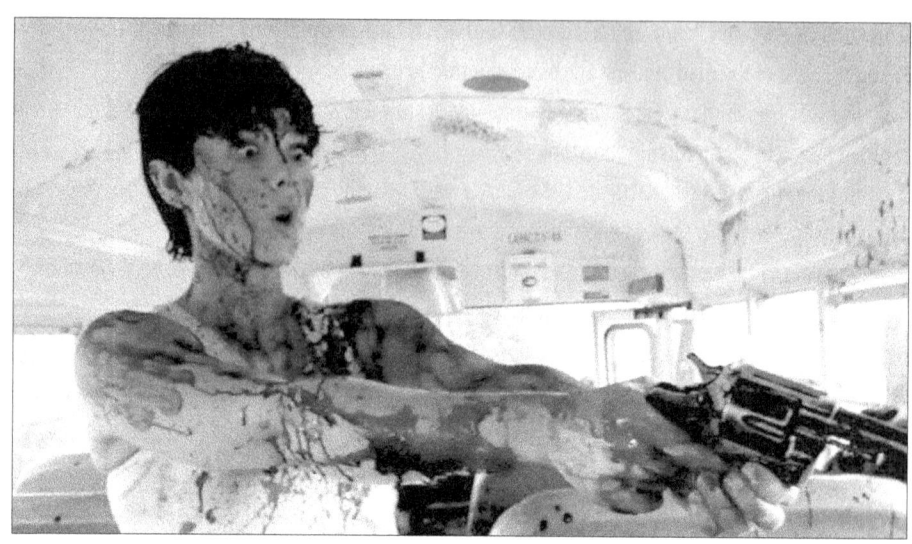

Leslie Andrews went all kinds of extra miles to personify the title role in 2007's *Sick Girl*.

Leslie Andrews:

Sick Girl

HEY, HORROR FANS! Quick trivia question here—what was the last horror movie you saw where a woman was the only villain?

Not the kingpin (or queenpin!), with underlings working for her. Not such an underling, working for the top bad guy. The sole one. Doing everything by herself, and usually succeeding before meeting a violent end. Pretty uncommon occurrence, now that we think about it.

Oh, it *has* happened, like when Betsy Palmer kicked off the *Friday the 13th* series in 1980, or Kathy Bates' Oscar-winning turn in *Misery* (1990), and Patty McCormick's trendsetting establishment of both the "evil female" and "terrifying kid" genres in *The Bad Seed* way *way* back when in 1956. So the territory's not entirely unexplored. But more people have been to the moon than have played a lone female slaughterer in American horror.

Why? Who knows? Perhaps filmmakers don't have the confidence that audiences will pay to see a lady do it all herself—abuse, torture, even kill . . . again and again. That if she had the power to do wrong, she wouldn't know how to use it, or would be afraid to. But maybe all those ladies who'd love to play the bad guy just need a chance—because back in 2007, we met one who showed what those who get one can do with it.

"It had always been a dream of mine to do a horror film," Leslie Andrews recalls, "and when reading the breakdown, I really liked the fact that Izzy wasn't a victim, and that she had all the power in the film."

Despite her laid-back moniker, Izzy's in the roughest of situations. Barely out of high school herself, she's left to raise her little brother Kevin alone: their parents are dead, their older brother Rusty overseas in the marine core.

Stressful as hell? That's more than an understatement. But what happens early on shows us that this one's going to go in a different direction than most horror tales of terror, and a hell of a lot farther at the same time.

"I thought she was an extremely complex girl with a lot of layers," Andrews explains of her "role model." "I also thought after reading the script of her as this larger-than-life character, kind of like a mixture of Marie in *Haute Tension* (a French flick that hit America in 2006 under the name *High Tension*) and then the lesbian comic strip *Hothead Paisan*, which I was really into in middle school."

By the way, the comic, one of the first to push homosexuality into the mainstream back in the early '90s, featured as its protagonist a self-proclaimed "Homicidal Lesbian Terrorist," who did as badly to men as anything Izzy would. The aforementioned Marie killed her female friend's parents, and some other people, to psychotically force her friend to move their relationship past plutonic.

Get where we're going with this? You will . . . all too soon.

Rather than building up to Izzy's badness, *Sick Girl* doesn't waste time at all showing exactly why she deserved to be the title character. Minutes into the action, Izzy's already beaten the hell out of a nun, stoically gutted one classmate, then terrified his friend into running away before chasing him down and bloodily taking him out too.

Before we can even react, though, things get even crazier; with a gun she found in the guys' car, Izzy destroys everyone on a bus, chases two girls off of it, kills one (casually dumping gasoline down the girl's throat), and captures the other. She's cleaning all the DNA off her skin, emotional as a statue.

"For me to become a character really starts with the appearance," Andrews says. "So I didn't fully feel like her until I chopped all my hair off into a boy cut, dyed it, and felt strong from working out with a trainer every day. Then I felt like I could be her and take her on and live inside of her."

Still, as rough as, well, *spree murder* was for Izzy, things get even worse; a flashback shows us Rusty telling her he's joining. She begs him to stay, saying they can raise Kevin, whom she affectionately names "Little Boots." But Rusty still feels this is best.

Then she tries to make out with him. Her own brother. Clearly, this lady's upstairs issues go farther than just violence—or, judging from her gleeful killing of several males, one builds all over the other.

Of course, there's an even more heartbreaking answer to the question of her violence, but we're not anywhere near that...

Just like in real life, even Izzy's cinematic colleagues aren't sure how to handle a woman born tougher than they'll ever be. Kevin's teacher has a pet rat that's gone missing, and some school bullies have it hidden, ready to let Little Boots be its next meal. But Izzy arrives, frees her little bro, and takes the rodent.

But she doesn't return it, not yet. Instead, Izzy marches straight up to Mr. Putski and lets him know in the most certain of terms that he'd better look after Kevin a bit better than he did the rodent. He, horrified, has no idea how to deal with this.

And considering his past, albeit not in the character sense, that's quite an accomplishment; Putski's none other than Stephen Geoffreys, who played wicked for both *Fright Night* (1985) and *976-Evil* (1988).

Still, it's time to give Izzy a little redemption, in some way. She rides up on Kevin's tormentors, soon forcing one to kill the other two. But he's not escaping; Izzy soon takes him straight back to the barn, where the guy and girl she kidnapped earlier still wait in confined terror.

"Izzy appealed to me because not only was she a strong female role," Andrews says, "but also because she had a code when it came to killing. It wasn't her going on a killing spree, but it was really about protecting her family. I wanted to make sure that although she might have been doing awful things, people would still want to hang out with her at the end of the day. I wanted people to root for her and like her despite what she was doing."

As Christmas draws in, things are getting even more out of control than Izzy can handle. Andrews had spent months shaping up with a personal trainer before filming, but keeping her own mentality under control was just as important and even more difficult.

The trainer, Andrews remembers, "got me into the fighter's mindset and helped me own my physical space. I think Izzy was very aware of the presence she held in dominating situations and the space around her." When someone invades it, however, even inadvertently, Izzy's dominance, the control she's been exuding throughout, slips right away. A simple recollection of seeing Rusty with his girlfriend causes her to flip out and crush the life from the woman, smothering her and beating her to death at the same time. She gives Kevin a gun for Christmas, hardly appropriate for a pre-teen.

It's time to take out her emotions one last time (remember, we still haven't gotten the whole story as to why she's so ticked). Out in the barn, she mutilates the male hostage by the manhood, then begins to rape the woman. Still no emotion on Izzy's face. It doesn't appear to be about gratification for her; it's as if she feels she's just doing what she should. Some say that rape is so much more about obscene power than sex, but it appears that Izzy's strength was here long beforehand.

But then a family friend unexpectedly walks in—and for the first time all film, Izzy's plans are wrenched out of her control. She's in a situation that isn't working out like she expected.

And her reaction is all that we could have ever expected; she hurls an axe into the fellow, with whom her family was longtime friends. But when he falls, something else appears: Kevin, standing right behind him, watching his sister do all these things. It's now Izzy who's lost it all.

Terrified, he charges into the house. Soon, he's pointing the gun at her, and she doesn't try to dissuade him.

But he can't. Instead, he turns it on himself.

Strangely enough, even after acting out some of the most disgusting acts ever, helping Izzy witness tragedy firsthand for the first time (that we know of) was Andrews' toughest job, she says.

"It was the first time I was working with guns on a set," she remembers, "and you just don't realize how loud and startling a gunshot is until it's next to you, so I just wasn't sure what it would be like until it happened, and I just remember going off in a corner and trying to be as calm and quiet as possible beforehand because it was also a really emotional scene."

Everything gone inside and outside, Izzy burns down the barn and walks away—and we finally see the reason she was over the edge to begin with.

One last flashback, this one with sad, eerie music as the only sound, shows two marines arriving at her door. We can't hear them, but she attacks them, two people she's never seen before.

Clearly, Rusty was killed in the war. He was dead before Izzy ever took over the school bus. Everyone she killed or hurt was paying for the death of probably the only man she ever loved.

Hey, let's not end this on such a downbeat note—because Izzy wasn't Andrews' only foray into fear. A few years later, she wrote herself into the female lead in the short of 2011's *Last Halloween*, a tale of a girlfriend and boyfriend whose post-Halloween party breakup takes a horrifying turn.

"I wasn't really auditioning as much as I would have liked at that time," Andrews says, "so I needed to create something to be in for myself. It was also a very personal project for me and I wanted to do a spin on a relationship-focused short and turn into horror. It was a way of dealing with things I was going through at the time and a way for me to turn it into art. I don't think there was a lot of prep in terms of getting into her mindset because I think we've all been betrayed at some point in our lives."

Then, in 2013, she got a call from David Baker. Like so many, he'd been terrifyingly wowed by Izzy. Now he was putting together his own tale and wanted Andrews on his team. His *Screen* (2013) told the story of a group of horror fans who tried to solve the mystery of why so many people suddenly dropped dead from fright in the middle of a drive-in movie. Getting ready for hardcore horror fan Carrie, Andrews' prep methods changed and stayed the same.

First off, she looked back at some of the improvisational training she'd picked up while training at the comedy sketch school Upright Citizens Brigade Theatre.

"To be able to really listen to your scene partner and be able to get where you need to go in a scene through improv can be a really scary thing," she admits, "but I felt really great about my performance." Another trip to the salon helped get her in character in the cosmetic sense, but physicality was left far behind this time around.

"I didn't work out at all," she says. "Carrie would have never been caught dead in a gym. I basically turned everything up to an eleven."

Just by appearing from nowhere, Joseph Bishara gave *Insidious* (2010) some of the most terrifying moments of the millennium.

Joseph Bishara:

Insidious

IT'S A BATTLE that every creative person faces all too often.

A wonderful thought comes rushing through your head like a lightning bolt. It's the greatest piece of art, music, acting, writing, anything your mind has ever happened upon, something sure to wow anyone lucky enough to see or hear your work.

Then you try to reach into your creativity and yank it out. Draw it on canvas, write it on paper, find the right notes to scale it . . . and you can't.

It's not a creative block, when your mind won't give you anything to work with. It's having a wondrous burst of creativity come out of nowhere, a trick our minds just *love* to play on us, and not being able to share it with others as we saw it within. Some say it's even more frustrating than the block. . . .

One artist may have a decent enough solution. Something that's aided him in more than one aspect of the performance arts.

Move. Don't try to control or even snare the blast. Just let it take over for the while it may take to get it from imagined to real.

Music has always played a strong role in horror. It's impossible to think too long about the *Jaws* or *Halloween* series without their tunes subliminally wafting through our heads, just as the sounds of the *Psycho* (1960) shower scene are themselves perhaps its scariest aspect.

Let's hear from one reason why the *Insidious* films, and many others, tend to lose something with the mute button pressed.

Checking over a film he's about to score out, explains Joseph Bishara, "I just hear it. It's like I get quiet inside, and whatever's looking back at me, I hear it and try to translate what I'm hearing. It's almost a take-down process of things I'm processing." But music wouldn't be the only time Bishara would terrify us in one of the most unexpectedly horrifying sagas of the 2010s.

"I've been into music and horror films since I was little," Bishara recalls. "Those were the kinds of things that drew me in, and I got pulled in the direction of both. Eventually, they just came together."

He slipped a foot through the movie tune door while helping put together a cover tune for the 1995 underrated action flick *Strange Days*. As he and others knocked out a new version of some sounds from The Doors, Bishara got some help from Ray Manserik, who'd pounded a keyboard right next to Jim Morrison himself.

"That led to more film work, and eventually into horror movies," Bishara recalls. He'd score the soundtracks of a couple of scarers in the first decade of the 2000s.

Over those years, he started hanging out with some other names looking to become more than a blip on the Hollywood radar.

"I was in a circle of Hollywood filmmakers in L.A.," he says. "It was a group of horror filmmakers that saw each other's work." He'd hang out with Darren Bousman, who'd soon put together some *Saw* films. Bishara helped his pal Mike Mendez with the tunes of *The Convent* (2000) and *The Gravedancers* (2006).

Along the way, Bishara also met a fellow named James Wan, but we'll hold off that for now. Let's talk about something else he got straight into that shows the true power of networking.

At these hangouts, especially during the last weeks of October, it wasn't at all uncommon for these folks to explore the dark side of cosmetology, particularly when makeup artists showed up to practice the trade that just might get them somewhere in entertainment.

"We did life-casts," Bishara says. "We'd dress like zombies for Halloween."

Eventually, he and Wan chatted about the director's new plans. Wan had launched the *Saw* series years before; now he was looking to make his horror a bit more family friendly (at least, as much as a PG-13 horror flick can be).

Insidious (2010) started the same as most flicks of the time: family moves to new house, only to find it's haunted with demonic forces that focus mainly on the kids. We'd seen that in *Amityville* and far too many of its clones. But this was something a bit different.

Young Dalton Lambert (Ty Simpkins) has been deep in a coma for months, and his parents Renai and Josh (Rose Byrne and Patrick Wilson) moved from one new place to another to help him and their other kids. But Josh's mom Lorraine (Barbara Hershey) has seen this before, and we're about to see something new.

The whole out-of-nowhere shock attempt in horror is a can of worms; we went through the ceiling when Glenn Close jumped out of the bathtub near the end of *Fatal Attraction* (1987), but it doesn't always work too well. But Wan had created an aura of terror in *Saw* (2004), about eighty percent of which took place in one room—the guy knew how to scare us.

"It was a really cool, rare kind of opportunity that I just happened to walk into," Bishara recalls.

"The conversation came about because he saw that I was very OK with getting into a lot of makeup, no stranger to getting life-casts or put into prosthetics."

There's a tense mother-son chat about a sick kid, never an easy conversation. But as Josh leans back, we and Lorraine see something that didn't come from nowhere—it came from another dimension. It's standing behind him, and that's about all we know for sure.

It's not entirely unlike a human, except it's red and black. Its small yellow eyes don't appear to be focused, but its open mouth seems ready to attack, jagged teeth at the ready. We have no clue how to respond, and, as is usually the case when that happens, fear inadvertently takes charge.

We were shocked and scared shitless. We'd just seen Bishara, after hours in the makeup chair.

Inspiration and preparation for the role, he explains, "came in a similar fashion to music. It was talking with James, coming up with ideas, then getting out of the way and letting ideas come through. I was hearing things in my head and letting it all grow together organically."

Some paranormal activists arrive, like Elise (Lin Shaye, who'd helped Wes Craven kick off the *Nightmare on Elm Street* phenomenon) and Specs (Leigh Whannell, who'd written *Saw*'s screenplay and then acted out his own words). Sensing something there, they transcribe a drawing—and it's a depiction of the same figure that just caused a collective and sudden bowel emptying amongst the audience.

It turns out that, like Mom, Elise is in familiar territory. Dalton's not in a coma; his mind just has the ability to travel to other spiritual paths far from this one. Now it's too far; his spirit's living in the land of the dead, and . . . things like the red creature are using it to get here and do some horrifying work.

Elise has seen it—in Josh, who gave his son the most unwelcome of inheritances. Now Josh is under spiritual sedation, looking for Dalton from the inside out. He finds him, but the demon's there, and he likes the whole "visiting Earth" thing, chasing them around their former attic.

"It's hard to relate it to things, but it's very consuming," Bishara says of getting ready and staying in character, even one so far from reality. "It's kind of a meditation, because it's about getting yourself out of the way. It's hard to tell what people will be scared by. You're just trying to let it come through clearly, and letting people show you how they'll respond. It's about looking at what it is, opening it up to the world, and letting it come through as clearly as possible." The men escape his demon, but something follows them back in Josh's body. . . .

Bishara stayed behind the camera for *Insidious 2* three years later, "only" scoring the film that told the tale of Josh's original possession by the spirit of a serial killer and the mother who tortured the hell out of him. Still, the same year, he scored and acted for Wan in *The Conjuring*, the true (well, in the dramatic sense, much like *The Exorcist*) tale of a husband-wife team that, fresh off solving the mystery of a demonic doll named Annabelle (keep reading!), now head to Rhode Island to meet a family tormented by the entity of the witch that used to own the place.

That broom-riding babe's name was Bathsheba, who'd eventually reach inside the wife before being whomped by the goodness of exorcism. "She" was Bishara.

The next years, a true believer in continuity, Bishara scored the story of *Annabelle* herself, the title

Insidious 3's The Man Who Can't Breathe (Michael Reid MacKay) attempts to charm his prey into her lungs.

character in the tale of "her" own creation and possession. He also acted out yet another demonic figure in the story.

"It's not very often that you get to grow the score and a character organically together," says Bishara. "Trying to define what it is while making it doesn't really enter into the equation. Comparing to something or asking if it's like this or that is not even part of it. It's about looking at what it is, and getting out of the way and making that and showing that."

Horror scripting had turned him into an instant household name with *Saw*, and scribbling down the first two *Insidious* flicks had reinforced Leigh Whannell's moniker in the screenplay world. He'd even acted out his own words in each series. Now it was time for something different.

After telling two tales of the Lambert family's fight with evil supernatural soul-stealers, Whannell was using the third *Insidious* (2015) to show just how these wars were started—namely, how his ghostbusting guy Specs and his friend Tucker (Angus Sampson) first hooked up with matriarchal medium Elise Ranier (Shaye) to establish the squad that came to help the Lamberts in the first films.

Insidious 3 rolled out with the story of young Quinn (Stefanie Scott) searching the spirit world for her mother, lost far too soon and suddenly. But even with the help of a reluctant Elise, she finds that punishments for trespassing in the afterlife carry much more than a citation.

And for the first time in his career, Whannell was pulling triple duty—acting, writing, and, newly, directing. Watching the tryouts for one of the youngster's top tormentors, his mind went backwards.

Like the legions of others lucky enough to check out *Se7en* nearly two decades before (yes, it's really been than long!), he'd been terrified at screaming volume by the film's sloth aspect. Acting out the sin of laziness, the victim had been tied to a bed for a full year until mercifully passing away just before he was discovered.

Except he hadn't. As *Se7en*'s detectives lean over the "corpse," he suddenly revives, screeching gibberish. Millions of viewers were probably doing the same thing. Now Whannell was having a flashback, albeit a much less emotional one.

He stepped toward one of the auditioners and let the fellow know how much he reminded Whannell of the person who'd turned sloth into a scream fest. Inside, Michael Reid MacKay figured he might just have his first acting role in a decade.

Sloth had been MacKay himself.

"I had to do a little research," recalls MacKay, unfamiliar with the first *Insidious* flicks before trying for the third one. "I auditioned for this character, called the Man Who Can't Breathe. I had to do some body movements and small, subtle movements with my eyes."

Unlike with the *Se7en* guy, this one could move around and go on the frightening offensive. But like with sloth, MacKay would be buried under makeup—and a mask!

"The special effects people designed the character with cancer in mind," MacKay says. "He represented cancer. They came up with the idea to have my skin all mottled, with a breathing apparatus on my face. After they completed everything, I could feel it in my marrow, which was really scary."

For three hours, he sat in a makeup chair, building up some energy to explode on the screen, just as he had for *Se7en*.

"I felt like this character had to be scary and powerful," MacKay explains. "I got into my little mode."

As the girl tries to understand why so many strange things are happening around her and her family, someone, or rather, some*thing* warns her to stay right back in reality. A demon, perhaps the same one that earlier told Elise to stay away, pounces on Quinn. He tricks her into getting hit with a car, then tries to yank her out a window. The mask, the furious eyes, the aggression he's forced to physicalize, unable to say it, he's as evil as Bishara's creation was, maybe more.

Elise finally steps up to fight, but it's Quinn who must lead the way to war. Still, just as the demon gets too strong for her, her mom's spirit shows up to save her, showing her the strength to send this demon back from whence he arrived.

Elise and the two guys are off on their new team venture. But in the final seconds, a familiar red and black face shows up next to the lady, reminding us that this was much more a beginning than an end.

"It was like a suddenness and a scariness when the acting came into play," MacKay remembers. "Here I am, this small guy, transforming into something so powerful and scary. I got all out and let loose and release all this power, and it's cool to be so small, but ten-foot-tall scary. It keeps the whole feeling of surprise.

"That's what acting's all about—why it's the ultimate!"

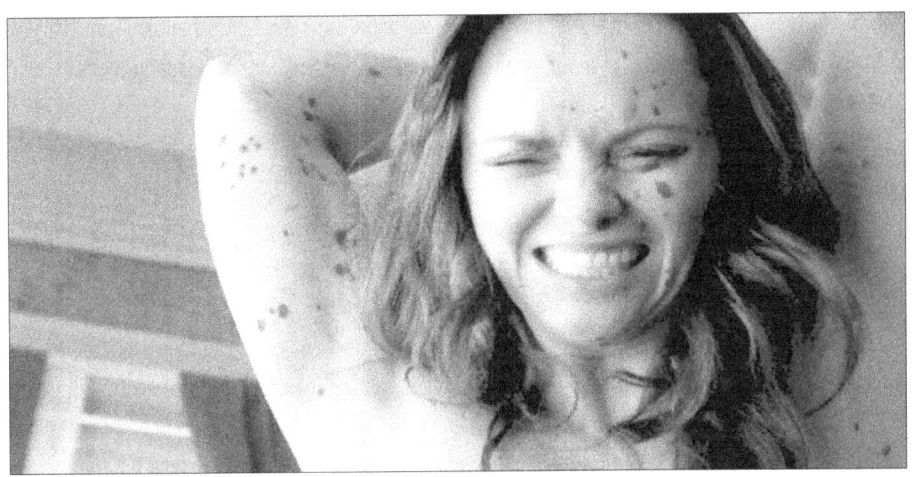
She personified true-life evil when Christina Ricci grabbed the title role in 2014's *Lizzie Borden Took an Axe*.

The Lizzies of Borden!

How to tell a tale told so many times before, and make it interesting? How to show audiences a story that generations have studied, and get them chomping to hear more? How can we make people want to hear what they probably already know?

Several books, plays, songs, and TV shows have asked and answered these questions about one of the most pitch-coal-midnight-black infamous moments in American history. Some have been more effective than others. But this sort of thing has never been remotely easy, and three actresses in particular grabbed their own ways—and their films' ways—of telling a "new" version of Lizzie Borden.

She had no alibi, but certainly a hell of a motive. She gave several different accounts of a story that was crucial to keeping her out of jail. She'd allegedly talked about getting rid of the victims before, and supposedly destroyed evidence afterward. There wasn't a shred of hard evidence against anyone else.

Pretty much what it all boiled down to was Lizzie's most obvious quality: she was, indeed, a woman. And women didn't do this sort of thing. Murder, particularly of this ludicrously violent type? Slaughtering two people, one of whom was her daddy? It just couldn't go that way.

That's pretty much the long, short, and medium of how things went for the jury that took just ninety minutes (and we thought O.J. Simpson's four-hour deliberation was quick!) to acquit the gal accused of brutalizing her father and stepmother that sweltering Massachusetts day in August 1892. If Lizzie had been Louis, she'd probably have gone to jail, and no way would we be still talking about this a century later. You wouldn't hear any rhymes about that time where Lizzie "took an axe, and gave her mother forty whacks. And when she saw what she had done, she gave her father forty-one" (first of all, it was her stepmother, not her mom, and secondly, the female victim took less than twenty blows, the papa just eleven).

As the crime neared its century-and-a-quarter anniversary, Borden's tale suddenly enveloped the acting world, and a trio of women became her—in one form or another.

Christina Ricci got to stay in realism. Amanda Baker was tossed into the supernatural. Danielle De Luca's work forced her to straddle the line between the two.

It was hardly Ricci's first foray into fear—she'll never fully leave Wednesday Addams behind, and I dare anyone who saw her there to even try to say they weren't chilled to the marrow. *Lizzie Borden Took an Axe* (2014) wasn't even Ricci's debut in real-life terror, as she played the girlfriend of murderess Alieen Wuornous (herself a history maker as America's first female serial killer) next to Charlize Theron's Oscar-winning work in 2003's *Monster*. But to be the bad girl herself, to actually act out the commission of this sort of crime, well, that was new.

"It was a real challenge," Ricci recalls of getting ready, "because the way the character was written was left up to interpretation and it's sort of difficult to play somebody who you're not necessarily sure what their mental state was at the time. We sort of had to come up with theories on our own."

Like her, De Luca got into scary performing in single-digit age.

"I've been obsessed with horror movies ever since I saw *Friday the 13th* as a little girl," she recalls. "I remember sneaking into the TV room late at night one weekend to watch Rhonda Shear's horror movie picks for the evening. I immediately burst into my mom's room afterwards and told her I was going to be a scream queen."

While Ricci's 2014 TV movie stuck mainly to the facts, De Luca had had to combine past and present for *The Curse of Lizzie Borden* (2006) a few years before.

In one of her first cinematic appearances after tons of theater, the actress felt the burden atop her. *The Curse* would reach her as young college student Cassy, who finds her personal interest in Lizzie's actions taking too much from her.

"Cassy started out as a young, naïve student," she recalls. "I didn't have a whole lot of work to do to prepare for her other than create her backstory and research women who experienced psychotic breakdowns. Totally relatable."

As is quite often the case with the new faces in acting, she didn't have much time to get ready, with less than two weeks between getting the call of winning the role and the first shout of "Action!" Helped along by Nine Inch Nails' dark, angry tunes, De Luca knocked the hell out of one Internet trek to Borden after another.

"I'm drawn to villains, dark psyches, unstable characters," she admits. "I'd do my research, imagine committing some of the most heinous crimes with my new prop (she bought the same kind of axe that Borden allegedly used), and treat myself at the end of the day with a much-needed horror movie fix.

The days began and ended with horror. But no real humans were murdered or harmed in the process!"

Audiences hadn't seen Baker do much frightening, but a certain small-screen group certainly knew her name and face; after four years of watching Alexa Havins play Babe Chandler on *All My Children*, Baker stepped into the role in October 2007. The switch between the two was truly one of the series' most surreal: Havins steps in to hug Babe's mom Krystal—when she steps back, Babe's become Baker.

"I knew since I was replacing the character of Babe there would be a lot of people wanting me to act like (Havins)," Baker says. "I had to stay true to who I was and take what I knew of Babe and make her my own." Over the next year, Babe would get involved in one erotic scandal after another before attempting to take over a cosmetics company, only to have her patented perfume found cluttered with toxins that nearly kicked off a nationwide pandemic, then be killed during a tornado attack.

"As she evolved, I really just relied on my instincts and try to experience every scene as realistically as I possibly could," Baker recalls. "I think about what the character would be feeling and thinking and try not to over-prepare and approach scenes naturally." As she stepped into the title role in 2012's *Lizzie*, that would be a tough task.

Her Lizzie Allen is battling night tormentors from hell, dreams brought on by a childhood trauma she can't fully remember. Back in the home where the nightmare began, Lizzie can't tell what's real and what's supernatural. The visions of a man named Andrew, dressed in 1890s attire, along with a little girl and a brunette whose face keeps changing from normal to demonic . . . is stability anywhere near?

Ricci's preparation may not have been advantageous compared to her colleagues', but it was certainly different, because, again, her story was the realistic side of what (probably) happened. She and the rest of the crew zealously launched into the endless mountains of research done on the case, then attempted to show what had been theorized so many different ways.

"I never tried to portray her as innocent," she remembers, "but I tried to portray her as someone who wanted to be thought of as innocent—someone who is playing a part. That gets into a whole thing because she had to in some ways believe she was innocent. You can't be so convincing that people are then confused—so you know it was complicated."

We see the murder aftermath, then Lizzie Borden at trial, proclaiming she didn't do it. By this point in the game, even Borden might have believed herself.

"She's a very deceptive character and there's so many layers, it's natural to look for what your character's truth is," Ricci says, "but with her, there's layer upon layer of deception: the truth she's trying to convince people of, that she maybe knows, maybe she's one of those people who's able to convince herself. There's so much ambiguity to the character that I spent most of my time sort of grappling with those sort of questions on a scene-by-scene basis."

Back at the *Curse*, Cassy and her friends visit a museum filled with possessions owned by the Bordens themselves. Soon enough, Cassy's got a job playing Lizzie on museum tours, wearing the same jewelry her idol once did.

Lizzie Borden's evilness lived on in Amanda Baker in 2012's *Lizzie*.

And the effects are the same; ax in hands, the new Lizzie kills the curator, along with the professor that turned her on to Lizzie and some of her friends. Her boyfriend is the only one to survive, and we finally see Cassy back in a mental hospital, whispering a certain nursery rhyme. Maybe the whole story took place in her addled brain.

"It was never proven that Lizzie murdered her father and stepmother," De Luca says. "But for the purposes of *The Curse of Lizzie Borden*, I needed to treat her as a villainous spirit. That's how that script portrayed her."

Checking over her own work, she felt a childhood dream come true.

"Watching the project in its final state gave me a sense of accomplishment," she says. "I had become an official scream queen."

As filming on *Lizzie* moved forward, Baker kept learning as she went along.

"I researched the story about Lizzie Borden even more so I could get a good grasp of what actually took place and have an idea of what Lizzie would have been haunted by," she recalls. "I didn't spend a lot of time preparing for the role because I wanted to discover who Lizzie was organically. I wanted to actually experience what she might have been feeling as we were filming."

One popular theory is that Lizzie indeed committed the murders, but did so during a blackout, natural or drug induced. As Baker's story wound down, it appeared her character, a big-time boozer, would end up the same way.

Stumbling to consciousness, she finds a friend brutally stabbed to death. Then her boyfriend, having suffered the same fate. Convinced she must have done it, Lizzie's got nothing left but the gun in her hand.

But it's not until after she uses it that the final question is answered. Andrew was the father that Lizzie Borden killed. The dark-haired lady was Lizzie Borden herself, in spirit form. And the little girl was Lizzie, a young version of the current version. The one who watched her mother, overtaken by Borden's murderous spirit, slaughter Lizzie's dad.

And the one that lives on, before the credits roll. Blood spattered on the wall behind her after a self-shot bullet though the mouth, Lizzie sits back up and evilly glances straight at us. Lizzie Borden's murderous work isn't finished yet: her spirit is now in the vessel of a woman that shared her name, and now her deeds.

"You are doing take after take and you have to continue intense emotions for quite some time," Baker says. "I remember leaving set that day with a bad headache and I was exhausted."

In a moment that would undoubtedly crash the Internet were it to occur today—much like the verdicts of Simpson and Casey Anthony, who may overtake Borden as America's most infamous acquitted murderess—Lizzie Borden was found not guilty on June 20, 1893. After getting some inheritance dough, she lived out a life in seclusion.

Once again, unlike her fellow performers, Ricci was the real-life Lizzie, and in the last moments, her film finally takes a stance. Blasting out as much rage as audience have ever seen from her, Ricci—now naked to keep away from blood evidence—takes Lizzie's axe and whacks away on everyone, showing us all what so many will always believe occurred.

Including her.

"I think she was guilty," admits Ricci, who parlayed her role into the short-lived small-screen venture *The Lizzie Borden Chronicles*. "There doesn't really seem to be any other explanation for it. From the evidence that was collected, the information we have now, who's to say that if they had the tools we have now that there wouldn't actually be more to consider?"

The power of the dead exploded inside Caroline Boulton's blindfolded beauty in 2015 for *Curse of the Witching Tree*.

Caroline Boulton:

Curse of the Witching Tree

MAYBE BECAUSE WE find a natural sense of sympathy. Perhaps our mind can't help but subliminally send us to her position, to imagine what life's like for her, someone lacking what we can't help but take for granted. Or it might just be our belief that arrives from nowhere that she's hiding something, and it must be specifically from us, and it's probably pretty scary.

Either ways, a blindfolded lady, especially in a horror movie, both creeps us out and makes us care just a bit at the same time, particularly if the eyes under the cloth don't work too well to begin with.

On the other hand, you'd think that by now, after decades' worth of horror films, that certain people would learn something by now. Namely, if you're born and raised in the luxuries of the big city, stay there, or head to another such city. Don't try to find yourself at a secluded home in the deep, dark boonies—because something's going to find you, living or otherwise.

That's what the Thorson family finds out the hard way in *Curse of the Witching Tree* (2015). The father clinging to life from a coma, the wife hoping against reality that he'll awaken, the daughter in typical teenage mode, and an undersized son as the perfect target for local ruffians, the group moves from well-to-do to much-to-do in their new wooded home.

And if the local bullying population isn't bad enough, there's evil spirits helping the roughhousers along, tormenting the kids, making them sick in the mind and the body. Soon enough, there's only one try left to make, one person left to whom to turn.

It's the local beauty with a bit of unwelcome experience at this sort of thing.

"Any good script sent to me in the horror genre gets me way too excited, to be honest," says Caroline Boulton, "and I nearly always say yes to working on it." Fresh off battling things out at hardcore war next to Dwayne Johnson in *Hercules* (2014), Boulton charged back to the frightening worlds she'd romped through in *Toothache* (2011) and other such flicks (quite a distance away from her standup comedy hobby!).

"I just couldn't put it down," she recalls of the *Tree* tome. "I read it late one night alone in bed and it terrified me so much I knew I had to work on it."

As it just happens to turn out, on the Thorson home land stands the title tree, which once inadvertently participated in a Salem-esque hanging, the noosing of a woman accused of witchery after the death of her son. But none of that subtle Pied Piper-type revenge shit here; she's cursing all kids around from here out, not leading them away.

And it's still working—the siblings' minds and dreams are going nuts. Fortunately, as, again, is quite often the case in these flicks, someone's around who's been there. She was Boulton's next conquest.

In her own youth, Eva saw her own mother give exorcism the old college try on her brother, an experience that made its way all the way into her brain and her visuals, which haven't worked since, hence the huge black blindfold covering two-thirds of her face.

But, armed with some candles and a Ouija board, she might just be able to get these evil entities to take their business elsewhere....

"The role of Eva was quite a challenge as I spend the whole film blindfolded and cloaked," Boulton recalls, "so my movement and facial expressions are very limited. I had to develop other ways to express her torment while so physically restricted." Indeed, it's not new for horror performers to be saddled with showing emotion without facial expressions *or* voices (how many have been hidden behind masks, hockey, William Shatner, or otherwise?), but to have one with a voice, but only part of a face? That's a whole separate challenge.

"We developed the style of movement she would have with impaired vision," Boulton says. "This was the foundation of the character of Eva as she has a type of half sight, so she can sense people but not see them. We needed to blend those two opposite elements together to create this sense of awareness within her so that the audience could read and understand Eva's character."

That would take some time, for those on and off the screen. Being a young exorcist and psychosomatically forced into blindness are some pretty notable traits, but Eva's moving toward her next quest at low speed and a voice that's soft, in an uber-eerily soothing sort of way.

"I naturally speak quickly," says Boulton, "but we felt she would be a lot more calm and relaxed as she is so thoughtful and so therefore would speak much slower. She chooses her words very carefully and doesn't waste time on anything, so I worked thoroughly on slowing my speech right down to reflect her mood."

Eva's mood, and, through her, Boulton's, would change quite soon. Eva looks to contact the spirits that no one wants to meet in person. So when she does, it's clear that not even she expected it to be this rough, though few would guess that spiritual mediums have anything easy.

Her voice rises higher than ever. Then plasma starts to pour from under her blindfold. The children victimized by the witch's curse are taking it out on her, but she's not even Eva anymore.

She grabs the son, and roars into the barn, killing the sister's boyfriend along the way. The blindfold comes off, but it's not her only visual obstacle; her eyes are sewn shut. She's become the mother who died so long ago, come to give a new little boy the same treatment.

But just in time, the sister all but forces Eva to reach back for control, just long enough for the brother to stab her.

She's soon dead. Sadly, so is the father. But the closing scenes show that another chapter in this story may one day be written. . . .

"It is so much fun to get covered in fake blood!" Boulton exclaims. "If you want to work in horror, I would advise you get used to the taste of fake blood and hours sat in the makeup chair for prosthetics! Eva is quite a calm but melancholic character when she's not possessed, and I feel her presence balanced the intense horror scenes out really well."

Her lovely smile belies Naté Bova's dark destiny to be bathed in *Da Sweet Blood of Jesus* (2014).

Naté Bova:

Da Sweet Blood of Jesus

FINDING NEW LOVE. Then holding on to it, adapting to it . . . these all sound like the most welcome problems one could ever face. And maybe they are, in reality, in the movies, everywhere. It sounds like it should be the greatest thing in the world. It's how we express it, how we live it, how we change ourselves for it, that brings up the questions it raises.

It's quite the understated issue in the vampire world: new members of the undead community often find their new perk to be quite a tough switch, even though, again, love is involved.

How does one survive if one is so suddenly and completely changed? Forget the whole "no-sun, plasma-diet" lifestyle. Just about every variation on the vampire legend takes one liberty or another with the rules being followed, and sexuality (in all specific fairness, omnisexuality) is a large part of a vampire's life. One goes both ways in the sexual sense when one joins the eternally fanged, especially in this version of the tale.

It's just one of many adjustments Naté Bova found herself yanked into and twisted about for her film debut.

"I've been a fan of horror for as long as I can remember," Bova explains. "I love movies about the 'undead.'"

By the time we snared the honor of seeing her, however, *Da Sweet Blood of Jesus* had already bathed us in all kinds of surprise—starting with the 2014 flick's opening credits.

After decades in the business, Spike Lee was going elsewhere.

Moving away from feature work to documentaries had almost (and damned well should have!) won him an Oscar for *4 Little Girls* (1997), but supernatural horror? That's a tough ground for anyone to cover—Scorsese? Stone? Even before and after winning the statuettes, it's an area they'd never hit. But Lee's never been one to follow the crowd.

Why? Doesn't matter. Maybe because he just wanted to try something new. Step outside the normal zone. In other words, do what so many in the acting business—before or behind the camera—find too frighteningly uncomfortable to even try. Something uber-admirable about that.

Not enough critics and fans gave *Jesus* the credit it should, but that's why books like this get written.

Decades before, Martha's Vineyard had backgrounded the cinematic creation of a shark with an addiction to human flesh; now Dracula's newest colleagues gave a similar portrayal in the same spot. As the *Blood* crew spread at high speed—filming lasted just over two weeks—Bova got ready for her debut.

After carving himself out, literally and figuratively, one hell of an anthropology career, Stephen Tyrone-Williams' Dr. Hess Green suddenly finds himself addicted to blood transfusions. Getting—it appears—fatally stabbed by a student puts him away, only to surprisingly discover himself alive again. It's just that now he can't consume anything but red-celled liquid, and doing so means murder. As millions read and saw the similar plight of Louis in both the cinema and literary versions of *Interview with the Vampire*, it's (new pun alert!) painful for him to swallow!

While her brother belted out one "Cut!" and "Action!" after another, Joie Lee helped Bova write her character's backstory. The two biographied the lifespan of Green's ex, angry at some scorn he'd dumped on her, and wanting perhaps not revenge, but at least explanation. They decided what she liked to do, what she wanted to own, where she wanted to visit. Putting her own mother's ring on her hand, Bova used it to connect to her character's past, along with other memories from her life.

"We also did some fantastic visualization/meditation techniques," she recalls. "We practiced screaming also!"

But every vampire story has an aspect of love, and the new attraction (romantic, sexual, and otherwise) to everyone that's the slightest bit strong on the eyes can be a frightening part of every new vampire's lifeline. Ganja (Zaraah Abrahams), the wife of Hess' attempted murderer, who himself became the doctor's first victim, shows up, only to find her heart and libido in his hands. She's soon his eternal soulmate and wife, but finds herself similarly pained by the realization that survival is slaughter for a vampire.

That's where Bova finally comes in. Her gorgeous Tangier was a part of Hess' past, and never learned exactly why he wanted it that way. Now he's invited her over, maybe helping his wife make a new friend.

And maybe more than that. Ganja's forced new sexual preferences have a new attraction in her heart, and Tangier's the type of gal whose looks might just make any hetero gal think about this sort of thing for only a few seconds. The two meet, getting close, moving a bit fast for newfound acquaintanceship (hey, maybe Tangier had her own secret fantasies all along!).

"What appealed to me about this character was her carefree and sensual nature," Bova explains. "I see a lot of me in her. To prepare for the role I dieted and worked out like a beast!"

She and Ganja share a dance that blasts sensuality like a volcano. Closer and closer. Who could resist either at this point? But it's all too good to be true. Clearly disliking her obligation, Ganja's forced to strangle the life from Tangier's body.

"The toughest scene to do was the choking scene," Bova says. "The stunt coordinator was very close by to coach us through making it look like Ganja was really choking and killing me. I had to hold my breath and strain to make a particular vein in my forehead pop out. We got what we needed in five or six takes, so overall it wasn't too painstaking."

But the two might just have one more shot. Green dies, a journey he wanted so badly to take. As *Blood* ends, we see Ganja walk back onto a beach.

And who should be there but Tangier herself, now in her natural state? Perhaps the two will follow the same journey as Louis and Lestat, and so many other couples from vampiric lore.

"Seeing myself on the big screen was quite an experience," Bova recalls. "I turned beet red and was slightly overwhelmed and then excited. An open mind is very important. Don't be scared and have fun with it. We laughed between most takes."

The evil forces of nature overtook innocent Mel to make her go full *Primal* (2010) on her friends.

Krew Boylan:

Primal

FOR ALL THE talk we hear about the human mind and body being the greatest of inventions, these tools can be tough to control. Athletes who train so hard for an event, only to have the body reach right out and cause them to choke at the most climactic moment. Students who memorize a textbook's worth of information, only to suddenly forget it all as soon as the exam arrives.

Then there are authors who sit in front of a blank screen, victimized by writer's block, wishing that somehow, somewhere, the mind would gift us with a strong enough burst of creativity to knock out an A-plus worthy essay or an effective book profile (speaking from *far* too many personal instances there!).

On the other hand, it's possible to go too far to the other side.

Getting turned feral might be quite stigmatized in the horror film world—those who do are often given to murderous, cannibalistic tendencies, their minds too addled to comprehend such complexities, forcing others to, per their beliefs, sadly put them out of their misery. But there is an upside; with the mind gone, the body often overcompensates into superhumanity in the physical sense. People shoved into undead mode become strong beyond belief, easily shrugging off blows that would have slaughtered them had they still been merely human.

Trying to act out the title adjective of 2010's *Primal*, Krew Boylan was faced with stunting her own work in her horror debut, including leaping over a tree (in a single bound! Take *that*, Superman!) to catch her fleeing friends.

The Sydney native had felt one adrenaline rush after another through years of dancing and figure skating, and hoped that one more would run up through her.

"I had to take this huge run up through the bush, hit the (trampoline), fly through the air and land on the mat, but not hit the tree," she explains. Charging toward the bouncing tool, she could feel her energy accelerating like a rocket.

But then it got a bit too high.

"I hit the (trampoline) so hard, I flew through the air, thinking I nailed it," Boylan recalls, "but I missed the mat and the tree. I flew straight over it. The whole crew gasped. I landed in the bush, off my face on adrenaline, bleeding but laughing hysterically."

She'd come a long way from being a common sight on the stages of Australian theaters, and even farther from voicing the bratty Grubby on *Dirtgirlworld*, the Emmy-winning TV series that taught kids about nature and recycling.

"In my head, (Grubby) was a seven-year-old cute bossypants with a lisp," Boylan remembers, "so that was wonderful to collaborate and really find the character through exploration. When preparing for any role, you have to do your homework, create the tools or find the tools you already have in your treasure chest box that sits next to your heart, and build from there."

For *Primal*, she'd have to look pretty hard. With a group of friends traipsing through the outback to peruse some paintings done before anyone knew what years were, Boylan's Mel takes a study break in a nearby pond, disregarding the inconvenience of a bathing suit. But she's not welcome in the waves; leeches feast upon her as she emerges, much more so than that landmark scene in *Stand By Me* (1985).

Normally, a sick lady in the woods in a horror film would be happened upon by Bigfoot, Leatherface, or something else far from society. But *Primal* follows into *Cabin Fever* (2002) territory; it's nature itself that's going to victimize Mel. Her teeth gone and replaced by fangs bigger than Dracula's, she's knocked back down the evolutionary scale, and anything that moves is fair game for consumption!

"There was no way anyone would cast me as the chick that turns into a monster and eats her friends," Boylan admits, "so I was out to prove myself wrong. The best part about playing any lead is that you get to drive the story, and it's the telling of a story that feels satisfying."

Super strength can certainly raise one's self-confidence, and Mel's got it in abundance. Not just that tree-hurdling we already talked about—she chases down a kangaroo and turns it into dessert, and bursts out of a trap her friends set. Meanwhile, one of her friends steps into the same water that turned Mel and starts to degenerate himself, and now he's on her team.

Mel's mental activity might have stepped out early on, but it was tough for Boylan to put hers aside—while chowing down on a colleague, however, who wouldn't be bothered?

"I had one scene towards the end of the shoot," she remembers, "where I was hunkered over, eating my friend, chomping on his gelatin intestines and heart. I was exhausted, wired and thinking, 'This is some messed up shit!' Other than that, it was a riot."

Sometimes, actually pretty often, we're victimized by things we can't control, as the *Primal* group was by nature. And, as we discussed earlier, it's our emotions and our bodies that sometimes appear to smack us down. As most performers with an appreciation for diversity do, Boylan's felt this sort of thing before, be it as Mel, Grubby, and in the theater, either acting out another's words or watching others do her own (she's written a few stage shows). She's felt the gain and loss of another uber-important quality that we wish would venture to us and stay forever.

"Confidence is a little sneaky, sneaky character," Boylan explains. "She can shimmy up on you and latch on for a solid hot forty-eight hours, and then dump you overnight, leaving you bereft and broken. Grab her by the nether regions daily and take control of her. Tell her where to sit and what to say. Keep her in a downward dog pose or something, to keep the ego in a healthy and humorous state until she is your compatriot. Go forth and be brilliant!"

Raine Brown blasted off like a meteorite to become one of horror's biggest new stars of the 2000s.

Raine Brown

IN THE HORROR performing world, there are quite a few ways to tell when someone is impressing some very important people.

First off, does she (as this particular profile is of a lady, we'll stick to the individual female perspective) manage to stay alive until the end, even getting to bump off the main bad guys in the climax? Letting someone *not die* all the way through the flick that we created and, at least early in the career years, probably paid for, shows that she's got a big chunk of our faith.

Even beyond that is a question that not enough women in horror have even been asked—can she be *the* villain? Not just *a* villain or even the main one, but the only one? That's a tactic that hasn't even been attempted enough in horror to have a clear response.

Raine Brown has been through just about all of it. From getting killed in the first milliseconds (2006's *Satan's Playground*) to getting chased down and caught (2003's *Horror*, 2005's *Aunt Rose*) to getting chased down and making it out (2007's *Barricade*, 2009's *Psycho Holocaust*) to helping the main bad guy do his thing (2007's *100 Tears*) to carrying the full evil weight herself (2009's *Sculpture*), Brown's career has run all kinds of gamuts.

Normally I start these stories with the character's main roles and work my way down, but, as it took Brown quite some time to work her way up to arguably her toughest and pride-instilling roles, we'll try that here.

After starting off in *Horror* and not escaping from *Rose*, Brown opened *Playground* by becoming an opening-minute victim of supernatural evil (longtime horror queen Felissa Rose was the "protagonist-ess" there). Then she and her friends stepped behind the *Barricade*. In true *Texas Chainsaw* fashion, her Nina and some friends are roughing it out in Germany when a cannibalistic family (not *too* far from the Scotlands that the infamous Bean family terrorized) shows up for an impromptu delicatessen. Inspired by her *Horror* work, the producers felt Brown could be the lead lady in distress—and, for the first time in her career, survive!

"That is how you know you're moving up in the horror world," Brown jokes, "you start living to the end! But it is so hard to really have things set in any specific way for film. You don't know what the location looks like. Most of the time you've never met the people. So I think you have to be open to letting a lot happen organically on set. This was a hard adjustment for me because, doing mostly theater before this film, you have tons of rehearsal and time to develop a course of action or flow for the character and script. With film often I find I have to really just familiarize myself with the dialogue and intentions and then just make choices the day of (being) on set as things develop."

Not long after that, she'd be back in the woods, fighting off another group of backward backwoods baddies in *Holocaust*. This time, she was Talina, battling for her friends, her husband, and the life inside her. In true new horror fashion, the crew zoomed through filming in mere days.

"I don't know how we got it done, but we did," Brown admits. "I loved the fact that (Talina) was just a normal girl: not a superhero, just someone who loved her friends, husband, and baby to be. She was put in a horrible nightmare, and how does she manage to survive it? That really attracted me, and again . . . I got to survive!"

A few other roles, however, would put her on the other side of *that* equation. . . .

It appears early on that *100 Tears* might be shaping as just another throwaway horror flick. There's a gaggle of youths chilling in a group home. Suddenly, a guy shows up with a butcher knife that's like a machete on steroids, and goes to work.

Some die fast, no time to fight back. Others battle and almost win, but it's too early to show the killer with weakness. Clearing out the home, he saunters over to a nearby gym and sends a few more six feet down.

He kills innocent people and a girl in a wheelchair, so we *know* he's just a horrible fellow with a heart of ice. By the way, he's also a clown.

Yeah, looks like this one might not have much to it. But a few local reporters, looking for the Pulitzer-snaring scoop, find the backstory to the person, whose pre-seen murders weren't his first.

No, he was once a proud man of the circus, there for the kids, families, and cheers. But a false rape accusation pushed him over the edge. Now trapped in the clown's mindset, his only remaining spot of cerebral stability, he's taking it all out on, well, everyone.

Soon enough, we see Brown show up as Christine, a lovely young lady who, like most of her age, can't understand why her mom won't let her just go out and live! Audiences as we are, we just know that she's going to wind up face to wildly made-up face before long, and that her DNA will be mixed in with that already on his blade.

But we're only half right. Indeed, the two indeed run into each other. However, it's not a bloodbath, but a reunion of sorts. She's his long-lost daughter—and soon enough, his partner in violent crime. Helping him continue the spree and putting some deranged entries in the column herself, we see that Christine's the best and worst kind of daughter. She slips just as far and even faster over the edge than her dad, and it's just the right place to be and thing to do.

"That was a character that was so great to play," Brown exclaims. "You think she is the blonde victim and then it turns out that she is as crazy and murderous as her killer clown dad! (I prepared by) just reviewing the script and motivation."

Whether playing the practitioner of evil or its victim, one's techniques don't differ very much, she continues.

"For horror," she tells upcoming scream queens and kings, "have your scream ready and access your ability to be frightened and venerable or evil and insane. Also, plan to spend a lot of your days covered in blood! I always think I have had an easy day on set if I get through without being doused in some sort of blood!"

And now it's time for the main focus of this profile—and judging from that criteria, Brown's work here must have been excruciating. In 2009, the same year she starred alongside horror legend Debbie Rochon in *Game Over*, Brown stepped farther into the spotlight than ever before, and couldn't wait to darken the hell out of it.

Sculpture starts out on an opposite track from *Tears*; a young girl hits the hometown for her dad's funeral, and it looks like this will be about her recovery from his loss—or maybe getting revenge on those who took him out.

A quick job at her brother's gym and a call from a local museum looking to show off Ashley's art bring her spirits up a bit, but we quickly find out why they've been down for so long. This isn't just about her dad dying; it's what he did while he was alive. What he did to her mom. What he did to her (i.e., the same things he did to mom when she was young). Things that no man has any right doing to a woman, let alone a child, let alone *his* child. Things that should have resulted in his death long ago.

"I loved the fact that Ashley was a true tortured soul," Brown says. "The script give her a strong backstory and emotional and psychological motivation to become what she does."

Let's go ahead and get to that. A moment of fury results in Ashley's ex-friend's violent, bloody death, and she realizes that she doesn't fully dislike the feeling its commission gave her. She gets alone with a fellow whose heart (not just lust) is in her hands, but looking into his eyes, she suddenly sees another pair staring back.

Her mind trapping her in a flashback, Ashley gives her dad what he long deserved, slaughtering him in the most painful of ways. It's not until things calm down that she sees what she's done.

But it's too late to turn back now. She can't give her father his own desserts; he's in the ground. But those in her position will take solace wherever they can find it, and this is suddenly a war against all those who represent her dad. In other words, the handsome young fellows at the local gym, those that would love to love Ashley in all kinds of ways. She's a seductress on a bloody mission: revenge and gratification combined.

"I really like the fact that the script was set up in a way to really make you, if not excuse her behavior, at least have empathy of where she is coming from," Brown recalls. "I had an acting coach with whom I was able to discuss hashing out (Ashley's) intentions and motivations, which was really helpful . . . I wanted to make the parts that were dramatic and touching as real as possible to give it a true solid heart, even with all the blood!"

Zipping through filming in weeks was tough enough, and being in just about every scene trapped Brown in Ashley's murderous mind for all of it.

"I had to be on and ready the whole time," she says. "At the same time, it was a fulfilling experience because I was doing what I love and the creative Zen was just flowing. I was really able to get into a zone and then just be able to go with whatever they threw at me."

As it has a tendency to do with most things, the killing gets easier as she goes. Bloodier, gorier, more drawn out to her demonic enjoyment. It even gets more creative.

"The scene where it is an overhead shot of me cutting a body on the bed was shot at like two in the morning after a long day of filming," she recalls, "and it was done in one take, so basically I was shooting straight for fifteen minutes, very physically cutting and reacting and it was just a crazy vibe because cast and crew was just watching, exhausted, and it just felt like something special was going on."

And when the secrets of Ashley's brother, who to this point seemed like a decent guy, find their way into Ashley's addled memory (he followed in Daddy's footsteps with her), things get even farther out of control than the mass murders she's rushing through.

"The last scene with my brother was pretty intense to film emotionally just because it is the breaking point for the character," says Brown, "and everything gets thrown out on the table and really dealt with. And I do think the final art show scene came out really well. When something works, it works, and it just seemed to come together."

She's been suffering her whole life, and they'll pay. But that's not enough—this sort of thing really deserves to be put all over public display: and remember, we learned early on that she had a great idea for an art exhibit. . . .

All along, in or out of horror (ironically, Brown's first acting job was on a *Sex and the City* episode), performing's been her true home. On the stages of which she spent quite a bit of time before the screens beckoned or before a camera, she's found her true town, even though it's about gutting someone like a fish.

"I always was attracted to performing and pretending and it's like it just bubbled out of me," she says. "When I started to perform, it was like something clicked, that I was supposed to be there and be doing that. It just felt right. And I do love that often the characters are off beat and strange. So that is always appealing. As a performer, to get the chance to explore such diverse and creative characters is always awesome."

Her body and mind almost ruined, Jennifer (Sarah Butler) came back for revenge in the 2010 *I Spit on Your Grave* remake, then for Part III in 2015.

Sarah Butler:

I Spit on Your Grave series

It wasn't an easy tale to sell, or even tell to begin with.

The story of a lady with power. Violent power that she decides to use and exude in high degree. Brutality towards those bigger, stronger than her. To use the qualities so often looked down upon in those of the female persuasion as full-blown weaponry.

But also to do what's right, in her own way. To hurt those who caused so much needless harm. To be the one who exacts justice, no matter the cost, instead of standing back and cheering for those that do so. To protect, if not oneself, then others from harm, pain, even death.

In other words, to be more of a man than many of us with two types of chromosome only dream of.

Film audiences tend to be a bit iffy about that sort of story. When Meir Zarchi put out *I Spit on Your Grave* several decades ago, it wouldn't have seemed more foreign to viewers if it had been in Latin.

A woman is violently raped by some gleeful cretins. But she doesn't call the cops. She doesn't go to her father, brother, boyfriend, whoever. She doesn't ask a man to do her dirty work. For one of the first and still one of the few times, this lady's going to do it all herself. And she's not done until they're begging for mercy, the few she left the ability to form a word or thought.

That's probably a big reason why the original didn't get much positive response from audiences when it came out, if any at all. But when Steven Monroe decided to remake the film in 2010 (Zarchi was a producer), he had a few advantages. First off, film audiences were at least a bit more cognizant, if not completely accepting, of women as violent in films. It's no longer uncommon to see gals getting down and bloody with men and each other in films of any kind.

That, and audiences of today are more liberal when it comes to acceptance of violence in films in general. After dozens of gory horror and action films per decade, there's little that hasn't been tried or seen before. Subtlety is quite the dirty word. Monroe could get away with letting his leading lass take a few more liberties with her vengeance.

But who would she be? Who would be the new main woman, Jennifer, in town, the role Camille Keaton had carried off in the '70s? Who could re-summon the energy to descend into murderous madness and take down as many human (subhuman, in this case) lives as Jason Voorhees or Freddy Krueger on a good outing? Who could not only act those things out, but accept that (hopefully!) millions of people would want to see her doing it?

When she first read the script, Sarah Butler knew the answer: absolutely not her.

"I cried and had nightmares," she recalls. "I was like, 'There's no way I can do this. I feel it too deeply.'"

Still, one of her representatives convinced her to take another gander at Jennifer.

"Normally, he'd protect me from stuff like this," she remembers, "but he said, 'No, Sarah, you've got to re-read it. It's really good! You get to come out on top, killing all of those guys.' So I decided to give it another read through and so I focused on that, instead of the violence." Though it usually involves the negative side of a person coming to light, often in response to the dark realities of adulthood, character development is always a strong attraction for actors. The chance to show a strong personal progression—again, even regressive—in a character is tough to pass up. With this in mind, Butler charged into the biggest role of her career, to that point.

"I just look at it for the role," she explains. "Since the character changes over the course of the film, it's an actor's dream. Besides the violence, it was a great role and a great opportunity for me at this point in my career, and after re-reading, I knew he was right. From then, I got more excited, and I wanted to do a film people will remember, something that grabs their attention, and I think this film is that."

The film starts out with the same obscene atmosphere as its predecessor: a lovely young novelist heads to her cabin for some private writing time, and some neighborhood cretins show up and do the worst of acts. When she escapes, however, this Jennifer does something new, finding a policeman who appears to want to help her make everything as better as possible. But back at her house, she finds that he's just like all the rest from the wood's neck, as he takes part in a second gang attack.

For the victim scenes, Butler recalls, "I tried not to prepare too much, because a human knows that when there's danger or pain coming their way, the natural instinct is to guard yourself from it, so I felt I'd be shooting myself in the foot to prepare myself to be tortured."

Now past the point of sanity and probably to no return, Jennifer wanders out of the house and onto a bridge. Naked, battered, and bruised, she jumps off, apparently intending to free herself from life's agony.

But, just as we've already found out for all the wrong reasons, the deception of looks can go the other way as well.

"I don't think (Keaton) and I approached it that differently," says Butler, who met her "role model," although she says they didn't really talk about the two films. "There are not really that many approaches you could have. It's like, you're a nice girl and people start doing bad things to you for no reason. And then you decide that you're not gonna let that happen and that you're gonna be the one with the last laugh." Keaton says she'd enjoyed the film remake, with Butler's performance as a highlight.

It's a month later, and the creativity that sparked Jennifer into the diverse career of authorship has now been turned into a deadly weapon, reminiscent of Jigsaw from the *Saw* films.

Just as with the first film, a noose becomes her first weapon, but the first victim(izer) isn't quite killed, just comatose for the time being. The second, however, won't be as fortunate; after immobilizing him with a bear trap in the woods, Jennifer pries his eyes open with fish hooks. But even she's not so sadistic as to keep that up for long—it's going to get *much* worse. The guts of a fish are spread across his eyes and face, and crows swoop in for a fatal meal (in one scene, the film pays tribute to both *Clockwork Orange* [1971] and *The Birds*! [1963]).

"This was such an honor, to be able to go to this extreme, and be able to portray that victim convincingly," Butler says, "to be crying, thinking I'm going to die, and saying, 'I'm going to kill myself.' Then going to that dark place, where I'm almost a monster." For her, it gets worse or better, depending on the viewers' personal opinions. For her rapists, however, there's no debate about fate's directions.

A convenient baseball bat to the skull temporarily puts down another, but it'll be a piece of cake compared to what comes next. He finds himself tied to a set of boards over a full bathtub, with Jennifer holding his head underwater. Drowning, however, is even too good for this guy; she dumps in a bag of lye and rips out one of the boards, leaving his ab strength as the only thing between him and facial disintegration.

All those situps he didn't do fail to pay off, as he slowly collapses into the deadly water, leaving him without a face . . . or a pulse.

Just as Keaton did with Jennifer, Butler makes her nearly devoid of emotion as her spree goes on. There's absolutely nothing else in her life right now, and if she never does anything else after this, that's perfectly OK.

"I think my goal was to make people straddle a fine line between 'Yeah girl! Get 'em! They deserve that!'" Butler says, "and like, 'Woah, who is the bad guy in this story?' I didn't want them to be able to settle on either side of that."

After putting a tire iron into the cerebellum of the fourth target (we get the feeling that Jennifer's backstory includes some self-defense or martial arts experience), Jennifer's got him tied up like the horse the men made her behave like early on. She rips out his teeth with pliers. She simulates fellatio by forcing a pistol into his mouth.

But that's not realistic enough for her; hedge clippers in tow, she chops off his manhood, jams it down his throat, and watches him bleed to death.

Aggression is one thing; this is horrific punishment. Aggression would be shooting them in the head and getting it over with. This is justified sadism. It's permitted torture. And it really makes a person wonder what would happen if this were to actually occur, if a woman had this happen to her, took this type of revenge, and then went to trial. What defense would be used? Would justifiable homicide or temporary insanity work? Something tells me that this would be a defense attorney's dream. Something also tells me it should be required viewing in prison and sex offender rehabilitation programs.

"It was actually, really satisfying doing those scenes in the end, when I got my revenge," recalls Butler. "It was like all that pain and fear that I had been through in the beginning, it was coming back, and it really was a good time. There was a lot to deal with. It was complicated. I had most of the dialogue, I had to control the scene, and I was dealing with prosthetics and special effects makeup. And I was feeling sorry for my co-stars that were tied up in weird positions and couldn't feel some of their appendages. Even for days after, a couple of the guys didn't have feeling in their arms for like three days to a week. I knew how uncomfortable they were, but I had to set that aside and just wreak havoc on them."

The first Jennifer would have been done at this point. She also seemed to be as recovered as one could be in the situation; Keaton's Jennifer appeared exhausted but triumphant as the final credits rolled, like an almost deadly weight had finally been lifted from her and that she was ready to build her life back again.

But for far too many rape victims, the pain never leaves. Not completely. It's never fully recovered from, and it certainly isn't forgotten. To one degree or another, depending on the woman, the situation, and about a million other things that can't be controlled or predicted, the experience and memory of rape leave a permanent black spot on one's psyche, if not her physical body.

That's something we see on Butler's creation; her Jennifer ends things differently. And not just yet—there's more death to cause.

"It's more of just allowing myself to go into a really dark, isolated place," Butler explains, "to someone who is a complete shell of a person, who's void of spirit."

After conning her way into the policeman's house and apparently stealing his daughter, Jennifer lures him to a park. Once again, her knockout capability is spectacular, as he's soon on the wrong side of consciousness. Like his partners, he's soon tied up and at her mercy.

With a shotgun up his ass.

There's a string around the trigger, and another tied to the former hanging victim, nearby and unconscious but still alive. One movement, however, will put a shotgun shell through the both of them.

Jennifer leaves them to their own device, and the spent fellow awakens. Never a rocket scientist to begin with, he instinctively shifts. Seconds later, there's a cannonball-like gutshot through the pair, and the girl's revenge is complete.

Well, at least on the outside. Back in the woods, Jennifer slowly sits on a fallen tree. Eerily reminiscent of Norman Bates' last chilling moments in *Psycho* (boy, the subtle tributes just keep coming here, don't they?), a small but evil grin starts to creep across her face.

Triumph? Relief? A thirst for more? The start of a quest to take revenge on those who have wronged other women, or hurt Jennifer herself in the past? Well, had Butler's flick gone bust, we might never have known.

It didn't, so we do. She stepped away for the first sequel in 2013; that was the tale of Jemma Dallander's young model Katie, terrorized by three brothers and their mom before coming back to kick ass on all four. But two years later, Butler brought Jennifer back for *I Spit on Your Grave 3: Vengeance is Mine*. Driven over the edge by the rape and murder of her friend, she goes for revenge on not only the perps of that crime, but others as well.

"There's that tinge that I'm a little crazy," Butler says. "When I look around, I'm in the middle of nowhere, and I could imagine how I would really be, with the anger, and that's what I'm trying to feel. This is what I think a lot of women who this happens to want to do—they have these fantasies of what they want to do to these men. They can't, because it's illegal, and we're all better people than that, but that's where this movie goes, and that's what I'm trying to be. This human woman who has been completely battered and broken in both and physical and spiritual way, and somehow she decides to survive, but she can never be the same woman again."

In similar film action, the 2012 flick might sound like a schoolyard Disney family comedy. *Girls Against Boys* wasn't even remotely close.

Like *Grave*, this one's got the female revenge thing going in dying color, most common being the dark-red shades of blood, but there's a slightly different spin—one that many fans of such films had seen before; but, just like back then, few of us saw it coming.

Looking on the wrong side on self-confident, the lovely young lady casts a confused, yet seemingly-determined look at the wall. Her sexy attire shows us what's coming, but it looks to be a new thing for her. She steps out of the bathroom, and it's a motel, with a cop sitting on the bed, waiting for her. Her mood slowly evolves into the take-charge sultriness that women in these films often use to hide something, and he, typical male, can't wait to let her take advantage.

Clearly never having seen this sort of film before, he doesn't realize that this is undoubtedly going to be too good to be true, even with the addition of handcuffs and a blindfold. With a cop as her prisoner, she takes out a gun. Someone's not leaving.

And a clue too easy to miss has already given something away.

After years of ballet and modeling, Nicole Laliberte was ready to move on from performing. "I was at a bit of crossroads," recalls the Manhattan native. "I was about to go to acupuncture school. I needed something to challenge me at every level." Lu would certainly give her that opportunity.

"That role was really colorful," Laliberte says. "It seemed like a great opportunity to do something I'd never done before." Not in real life, of course, although some probably wish they could. Her Lu was galpals with Danielle Panabaker's Shae, a young college student just hoping that her lover will leave his wife and daughter for her. It's just another trap that far too many naïve women have fallen into, too sweet-talked into seeing that the misogynistic pig just wants a new way to get laid.

But her colleague seems to have been here before, inviting Shae out to drink and dance—just as friends, of course (right?). If her adulterer boyfriend didn't represent the worst of his genre, the guy Shae meets certainly does, tricking her into taking him to her house and then doing the worst of the worst.

Lu (Nicole Laliberte) takes a longing, lustful glance at her latest victim in 2012's *Girls Against Boys*.

Lu convinces her to tell the cops, but these guys are the same dirtbags that too many rape victims run into, not taking her seriously at all. It's going to be up to Lu to create a new definition of justice.

With no one else seemingly seeing her, she casts some flirtatious looks and words towards the guy who blew Shae off. He's the one we saw back at the start. Soon, the two are hidden away, her in charge—and now that gun gets used, taking his most valuable downstairs section, and soon his life.

"I love the scenes with the policeman," says Laliberte. "Gearing up for this sexually, mentally, and physically empowered the shot that I was able to bring up for that." If she looked off-balance for her first kill—that we know of!—it becomes easy quickly. The pair heads to see the rapist's friends, and the cop's gun in Lu's hands takes care of them as well.

By now, Shae's starting to get into this herself. It almost becomes valid in the audience's mind. You're scared, but enthralled. You're intimidated, but you can't help but follow, in part because you want to see what's next, and maybe because you hope that one day you'll have the chance and the guts to do it yourself. The way a woman like Lu carries herself, the way she can do these acts without blinking? They're unthinkable to you, as to most people, but she does them as easy as drinking a glass of water.

How does she do it? It's a question whose answer has led many, maybe too many, to follow people like her.

"Acting really pushes all of my buttons," Laliberte explains. "It stresses me out and forces me to express myself. I came from a household where verbal expression was rare. We are all things, are we not?"

Enthralled with Lu's mindset herself, she'd had to look in and out to find it. Violent revenge-based films like *Romeo Must Die* (2000) and *Inside* (2007) had helped her out.

"I tend to not watch a lot of bloody horror films," she admits, "but I watched a lot of really scary films that I probably would not have watched if I had not been in this role. I also did a lot of writing. I went to some really dark, manipulative places." She and Shae go to some more. They knock out the rapist, and Lu uses a power saw to dismember him alive. The women kidnap Shae's lover, and Lu blasts his brains out.

Now Shae's starting to rediscover some humanity, even while watching the extermination of evil. But Lu's fine with it—no reason for her violence, it's just something she enjoys, or so she claims.

"I think that's the only way you can portray these people is to love them," Laliberte says. "There's always a reason why people do these things, and it's usually because they're hurt. It's not that hard to find compassion for these characters."

During filming, though, she'd taken some unusual methods to keep anyone else from finding any in Lu.

"I isolated myself a lot on the set," she remembers. "I stayed in character most of the day. That was a little tough, because I love socializing. I'm normally pretty bright, cheerful, pleasant, so that was tough. But I really loved playing her."

Back home, Shae hangs out with one of the first decent guys we've met all film. In the midst of a costume party, Lu catches him alone with a sword, and slashes him out. Clearly, her feelings for Shae are past plutonic.

Lu makes one more play, exuding the same sultriness that drove men to their knees and deaths. It doesn't work this time. Finding a strength within we never saw, Shae slashes her right across the stomach. But even as she falls, Lu can't help but gasp out a few more pleas of love. Perhaps it was strong enough to overcome her pain.

Little about this film has gotten anywhere near normal, but even this is pushing it. Shae now comforts another co-worker in the midst of man-trouble, but Lu's still behind her, just watching.

Now we recall that Lu never interacted with anyone while Shae was present. We never saw her do anything on her own without Shae being involved somehow. No one responded to her. No one has called her by name. No one asked Shae about her.

And if we remember back to the very beginning, when Lu left the bathroom for her first murder, she stepped before a mirror. But Shae's reflection had looked back.

Looks like is this another *Fight Club* sort of ending; the character with all the strength and charisma didn't actually exist—he (or she, in this film) was just a mental creation of the protagonist, a persona invented to live as who they wished they were. Like the *Grave* gals, Shae had indeed gotten some revenge on her own, just in a different form of herself.

"I'm the part of her psyche that became present after she was raped, to protect her," Laliberte explains. "I'm her protective spirit. Did these things happen or not? (At the end) I'm around, but I'm not in charge anymore. I'm not leading her down that path."

Santa Claus (George Buza) had a very heartbreaking Christmas in *A Christmas Horror Story* (2015).

George Buza/Joe Silvaggio:

A Christmas Horror Story

WE DON'T *WANT* this guy coming to town, tonight or otherwise. If we *were* to see him smooching Mommy, it might lead into some serious *Living Dead* action on her part. And maybe he really is the kind of guy that would order his four-legged antlered minions to run down our kindly grandmother after all!

Even the Claus man has a dark side. All those cookies and milk we've been leaving out for the guy for generations, and *for what?* Even at a time for giving, there's still a place for horror—and unlike the multitude of *Christmas Carol* versions, *A Christmas Horror Story* (2015) was not a scary tale with a spiritually happy conclusion.

"Christmas projects have become more attractive as I get older," explains George Buza, who's been churning out holiday tales for the past few years, "and I find sliding into a Santa Claus role rewarding and lots of fun. Feel-good movies rub off on the performers as well as the viewers." As we could tell as soon as we saw the title, however, *Horror Story* wasn't going that way.

Perhaps *Stories* would have been more appropriate, or maybe that's just my English professor side that won't shut up when I'm trying to write books. The flick was an anthology, made up of four stories with a wraparound throughout. Typical for this type of film, it had three men behind the camera, with Grant Harvey, Brett Sullivan, and Steve Hoban doing a director threeway. If those names sound familiar, it's because the trio helped put together the *Ginger Snaps* (2000) flicks of a few years before (there's another inside joke there, so please keep going). That, and a promise of a gruesome onscreen death, grabbed Joe Silvaggio straight by the attention span.

"I'm a big fan of *Ginger Snaps*," recalls Silvaggio, who'd already done the horror thing before as a zombie in 2004's *Resident Evil: Apocalypse*, as well as 2013's *Torment* alongside *Ginger* herself, Katharine Isabelle. "I love seeing myself on the big screen. I know some actors can't look at what they've done, which I find weird."

Back in 2011, Silvaggio and Buza showed up in *The Case for Christmas*, not entirely unlike something resembling *Miracle on 34th Street* (1947). *Horror Story* had them doing something more than slightly different.

But not at first. People still listen to the radio on Christmas, and DJ Dan had the job of entertaining them when he'd probably rather do . . . about *anything* else. Still, Dan gave film fans an unusual treat; between stories, we'd get to see William Shatner and his long-distinguishable voice in a rare horror appearance.

While Shatner's Dan droned away, we saw the story of a group of teens breaking into their high school (teens breaking *in* to school? Teachers' dreams come true after all!), only to end up against a ghost, who impregnates the girl and kills the guys. Then comes that one about the family that wanders into the forest to steal a Christmas tree, only to have their son get lost in the snow.

Oh, they find him, and bring him home. But this is a horror flick, so of course it's not really him, not inside. He was actually switched with a changeling; it's a word that doesn't quite sound scary, but certainly means it. It's like an evil spirit that possesses someone's body. That's what happens here, all the way to the child killing his daddy.

However, the ending's not all sad. Realizing that it's not her son's fault, Mom takes him back to the snowy worlds, and takes out the changeling's own owner, freeing the spirit, who, showing that even the much maligned aren't always all bad, frees the kid.

We didn't recognize him yet, but we'd just seen Silvaggio as the critter.

"A pleasure of mine was in prosthetics," he recalls. "It was the transformation: going from me, this human being, and five hours later, in a chair, in front of my own eyes, I became a new character. It takes you right into the character."

He'd be in another one soon, but not yet. Story three is of a family trying to con their rich auntie out of her green. It doesn't work, and payback is coming in the now-real fable of Krampus, here to punish those who dare misbehave during Christmas.

Looking like a half-dragon, half-goat on serious steroids, the creature demolishes the thieving family, except for the daughter, the only one who meant well—and we thought the Grinch had an attitude!

But in this version, the Krampus wasn't its own self; it was the aunt's caretaker, transformed into the creature by his pissiness toward the family.

Joe Silvaggio became a possessed elf out for Santa's blood in *A Christmas Horror Story* (2015).

The daughter kills him, but finds out the aunt was behind the whole matter. Furious at the old lady, the young gal starts to grow and change.

See, this Krampus isn't like the Incredible Hulk, who only overtakes one man's body. Anyone who gets too upset during the holiday can go into Krampus mode. The daughter does so, and the aunt's not getting out....

We'll see the Kramp thing again, but it's time to finally meet the new Santa, the one that Buza had to find a new spin around.

It's the North Pole's busiest time, and it's all that Santa and his wife Marta (Debra McCabe, so hot in this she almost melts the snow on looks alone!) can do to keep up. Fortunately, there's a group whose work ethic wouldn't fit inside their vertically-challenged bodies.

It's the elves, and Silvaggio is back in action as Jingles. But good doesn't last in horror films, and horror hits coldly home in a virus that's slowly mutating everyone into the undead, inside and out. Jingles is forced to go cannibalistic evil.

"I made a few different choices," Silvaggio recalls. "I was kind of innocent, 'Hi Santa, how are you doing?' Then I completed a really nice contrast when I created Jingles: Mach II. He turned into a rabid, snarling dog."

Somehow or other, Santa's ready, or at least equipped, to battle back those who turn on him. Hey, the guy's eternal, so it's easy to believe he might have picked up some brawling techniques along the way. Or perhaps Buza was channeling the spirit of the Beast, who he voiced through years of *X-Men* cartoons!

"Preparing for the role had several levels," he remembers, "first, physically, to be able to handle the numerous fight scenes, which meant many hours in a gym, and then the characters themselves." To an extent, he was certainly playing more than one person. Keep reading!

Santa bloodily fights off the new bad guys and gals, tossing Jingles into a saw along the way, only to heartbreakingly learn that his (much) better (looking!) half has become a victim as well.

Before he can escape, however, who/what should show up, but Krampus! Good and evil will battle for holiday supremacy!

"My favorite parts of the film were the action scenes, which were also the most demanding," Buza says. "As always in film, you do a scene multiple times from numerous angles over many hours before the scene is completed. The final scene with Krampus was shot in an unheated stable, the temperature at about -25 Celsius."

It looks like Santa might take it home, then visit some other homes for his one-night-a-year employment. But there's one more twist to take, and it's why this profile began by badmouthing Christmas' angel of goodness.

None of it was real at all. Santa's actually Norman, a weatherman back in modern times and places who's killed a multitude of innocent people. The zombies he slaughtered, like Jingles and Marta, were creatures created by his own warped mind. He's back at a mall, raining down the worst kind of realistic horror.

"The character of Santa was more of a Nordic version of St. Nick that played out as a hallucination in Norman the Weatherman's mind," Buza remembers. "It was appealing because it played on many levels and was a deviation from the traditional Santa roles in the past. All had to be played realistically, as in Norman's mind there was no separation of fantasy and reality."

Horror Story, along with *Krampus*, 2015's more cartoonish flick about the horned thing, might teach parents a new lesson about scaring their kids straight for the year's last month. The Krampus himself (herself, itself, whatever you believe) hasn't been spoken of much in America, but that might soon change: European parents have been using it for generations. If you act up, you won't get coal and switches from Santa . . . but you might get torn apart by something worse than your nightmares!

This could work!

As *Silent Hill* moved from the video game to the big screen in 2005, Roberto Campanella personified the Red Pyramid.

Roberto Campanella:
Silent Hill

WITH ALL THESE special effects, so much CGI, tough costuming, acting without speech, Roberto Campanella knew he'd have all kinds of difficulty with his next acting job.

But he couldn't have guessed that he'd end up in Hell!

OK, OK, that might have been a bit dramatic, or least requires just a BIT more explanation. Still, when Campanella arrived at the set of *Silent Hill* in 2005, he expected to start and finish his job without any official filming at all.

"I was there solely to be a dance coordinator on the film," he recalls of his first such job on the big screen. "I was teaching the others to dance, going through the movements." Nearby, director Christophe Gans and the rest of the crew cast the pieces together.

Moving a story from the video game world to the cinematic one has always been tough (What the hell happened with 1993's *Super Mario Bros*. mess?), but *Hill*'s crew could take some inspiration from the success that *Resident Evil* had found in both. Many gamers put *Evil* and *Hill* in the same bracket as far as challenges and storyline went, and the *Hill* group hoped they'd flock as much to the new creation as had Milla Jovovich's zombie-whacking work in *Evil*.

Hill would cut back on the violence, replacing it with all kinds of drama, even realism. At the core, it would be the story of a couple, desperately trying to help their adopted, troubled little girl adjust to her new surroundings, to push back the demons that still lived in her mind.

It's just that, in this case, the goddamned things were outside as well — and thirstier than dehydrated vampires.

With their adoptee Sharon (Jodelle Ferland) spending her nightmares wandering through the mysterious, but conveniently nearby, title area, Rose (Radha Mitchell) and Christopher (Sean Bean) take her there. An accident leaves the parents separated and Sharon gone, Rose and others searching for her. Christopher walks everywhere with a cop named Tom Gucci—back then, no one knew that Gucci portrayer Kim Coates would ride undead savagery to a household name in *The Walking Dead* (2010)!

Clearly, the plot here is *far* from the *Hill* games, the first helping to ring in 1999 and the second two years later. Not that Campanella minded much either way; as filming got rolling, he hadn't been much of the gaming type. Learning a group on the mysterious arts of inhabiting the undead was as much a challenge as anything he'd faced.

That's when he got hit as hard and fast as anyone who'd ever wandered through the *Hill* worlds, even with the use of controllers.

"We were trying to cast the Red Pyramid," he recalls. "I was going through the movements, when (Gans) turned to me and said, 'Why don't you do that?' I said sure."

The character would be modified on the inside and out; aside from changing Pyramid's looks, his mannerisms would be switched as well. The fellow didn't show up in the games until part two, and then, he spends much of the time stalking the main character and his lady friend through the game. Through the magic of reincarnation, he gets to kill the lady twice, only to take his own life.

And we thought that Mario having to find his way through eight levels of turtle-stomping to rescue a princess was diverse!

"I asked if it was possible to get as many clips as I could from the game sent to me," Campanella remembers. "I studied the video game. Some of my movements were from the game, and the others were invented by me and (Gans)." Along the way, he'd find some extra assistance from a very well-known, but probably unexpected for this sort of practice, source of info.

The cinematized *Silent Hill* was full of creatures formed from the darkness: not only from the coal mine flames that condemned the town so long ago, but the anger and hatred of the people that were ruined there—per usual for horror flicks, humanity is so much more evil here than anything sprung from the dark caverns of imagination.

And it was up to Campanella to help his troupe find a way to impersonate the non-human, the living-impaired creatures that terrified Rose and other visitors without really meaning much harm. So to find a new form of horror, he looked to a comedy. A very *Divine Comedy*.

"The key for me was mentioning Dante's *Inferno*," he explains of the epic poem that took Dante Alighieri himself over a decade to put together, the tale of a man making his way through Hell, all over Purgatory, then earning his right into the Almighty Kingdom.

"*The Divine Comedy* really lit a lightbulb and hit the spot for me," Campanella remembers. "(The creatures) were trapped in those little bodies, suffering, being punished. The whole *Inferno* idea was what made it for me. What helped the most was to listen to (Gans). He is something of a visionary. Everything has to look amazing, and the movement was so visible. There was no gray area there."

With a costume that took hours for Campanella to enter, the Red Pyramid's appearance in the first flick was mercifully quite brief, and fully villainous; as Rose and others make their way toward a church, he appears, rips off a woman's clothes, and then her skin. Later, with Rose trapped inside a dark basement, he reaches in to get her, only to have her blast his hand away.

But that wouldn't be Campanella's darkest acting in *Silent Hill*.

Surrounded by the cult that poisoned the church, and ultimately the town, Rose sees a flashback of her new child's past. Sharon was once part of young Alessa, accused of being dirty for being illegitimate, and bullied by her classmates.

She was also molested by a scumbag janitor. That was Campanella without the makeup.

In witch custom, Alessa was burned, and it was that fire that secretly turned into one the likes of which we'd never seen before, at least outside of Chicago. But she'll have revenge. And this is a horror movie, so we're going to see it one dismemberment at a time.

Rising from a puddle of Rose's blood, Alessa does her *Hellraiser* impression, firing barbed wire everywhere. People are literally torn to shreds. Alessa and Sharon fuse back together—but they and Rose can't get all the way out of Silent Hill. . . .

Yes, of course, it's sequel time.

It took six years, but *Silent Hill* finally had its own private *Revelation*—in *3D*. Her mom still trapped in the title town, Sharon was now Adelaide Clemens, having forgotten Alessa at all, on the run with Christopher (clearly, Bean was luckier here that he'd be years later in *Game of Thrones*!). They're trying to stay ahead of The Order, the cult that killed Hill, and nearly them.

Again, Campanella began as "just" the action coordinator.

For Pyramid Head, this time, "the director wanted a man over seven feet tall," Campanella says, "and I'm 6'1". I was coaching a bunch of people." Then new head cameraman Michael Bassett asked him to play the old character again—but this time, in a new kind of way.

As Sharon escapes from the group that stole her dad, she sees the Head man and hides away—and glancing at him, who exactly wouldn't? But later on, as her dad and friend are being held away by the Order leader, she calls on the Pyramid man himself, who shows his true colors, and skills with the sword he's been wielding for two films, honorably gutting hell out of the leader and helping the good guys escape.

And for those who stuck it out through the credits, we see him strolling as leisurely as such a being could through the Hill. Might we see the Pyramid man again someday?

"At some point, I had to let go of looking at the clips," Campanella explains. "There were a few things that had to be there. One was the heavy sword; when I would drag the heavy sword, I had to fake that, making it look heavy. It was how I'm interpreting what I just saw. It comes a vicious circle, trying to be an exact circle, trying to do exactly what was done. I added a limp. I actually used prosthetics. I was on stilts, and I asked if we could make one leg shorter. I played off that limp. The boot was made crooked. It was a combination of what the Pyramid was in the game, and my interpretation of it."

Neve Campbell turned Sidney Prescott and the *Scream* series into landmarks in the horror genre.

Neve Campbell:

Scream series

"WHAT'S YOUR FAVORITE *scary* movie?"

It was the line that adrenalized a genre that was stagnating at best, plummeting at worst. It cornerstoned chapter after chapter of a series with the guts to plot its own course in horror. It came to epitomize not just a film and its sequels, but an entire generation of horror fans.

And all too often, those who were ominously asked it over one phone after another throughout the *Scream* films had just moments to live.

Still, we can't give that line, nor any one thing or person in particular, *all* the credit for *Scream* success. There's many more players in the game. There was Drew Barrymore's series-opening performance, shocking not just because of its power, but because the biggest name in the acting credits was gone in the film's first tenth! Wes Craven's directing skills, the same ones that had helped him launch one legendary horror saga back with *Nightmare on Elm Street* (1984), now did again a decade later. Kevin Williamson's screenplays. Roger Jackson's vocal work to perfect the delivery of the (in)famous query.

And the lady who evolved from princess all the way to scream queen, whose name—in and out of character—landed quickly alongside (and, many feel, even above) so many other monikers throughout the horror franchise.

"I've had a lot of people ask me how I feel about the fact that *Scream* had such a huge effect on my career," Neve Campbell remembers. "I'm sure it affected my career in certain ways, but at the same time, it made my career. The films are so intelligent. They changed the horror genre in a huge way and did great things for my career. Of course, there are times when (horror is) all I get offered, but at the same time, it's the very reason that I get offers on films at all."

Where the soon-to-be series took its first steps in 1996, Campbell's star had just started to rise. She'd been on the small screen on *Party of Five* for a year, and horror fans had gotten a small look at her (a point further discussed shortly), but it's safe to say that Barrymore's and Craven's names probably sold the majority of the tickets that helped *Scream* rocket to the top of the box office in its debut.

"I remember us having this summer together and having a blast, and I remember thinking it was a good script," Campbell says. "I was lucky to be a part of it." In the midst of filming, she and co-star Skeet Ulrich got an extra boost of confidence when their recent witchcraft work *The Craft* (1996) cast a black magic spell across millions of viewers. Still, Campbell's work there had certainly been significant, but not leading. Sidney Prescott would be her first protagonist(ess) role.

Fortunately, she had a bit of help. Craven's skill in the department was hardly a matter of debate, and Williamson's screenplays formed enough development to make viewers want to follow Sidney. Even before the flick's storyline, the high-schooler had been through more turmoil than most of us ever face. The murder of her mother, and having to testify to put away the man that did it. Or at least, so she thought; nosy Woodward/Bernstein wannabe reporter Gale Weathers (Courtney Cox, though her looks and persona kept most of us from recognizing her until well into the film) couldn't leave well enough alone, poking around the mystery that many felt and certainly hoped had been solved, looking for her scoop to stardom.

The script also carried a fresh sense of self-reverence that managed to stay slightly above deprecation. "The first (*Nightmare*) was good, but the rest sucked!" Barrymore's character declares, Craven's nod and mocking glance at those that followed him in the *Elm Street* directing chair.

"You're starting to sound like something out of a Wes Carpenter movie!" Sid's friend Tatum (Rose McGowen) chides her. And so on and so forth.

But there were more violent murders to commit, and the killer's black costume and Ghostface mask, looking like a spiritual version of Munch's *The Scream* painting (oh, how appropriate!), doesn't quite lower our blood temperature.

At least, not as much as the voice that sets up the physical side of slaughter.

"I try to think happy thoughts!" ominous orator Jackson claims of prepping for the role, surprisingly. "The guy has to be interesting enough and sexy-sounding enough to keep her on the phone, get her interested, and draw her in a little before the cat springs the trap on the mouse. Somehow, I had to make it universal and different. Ghostface is the worst in each and every one of us." It's fortunate that *Scream* started when it did—had Caller ID been around when Barrymore answered the phone for the first time, the mystery would have been solved right then and there and the series would be over before it started!

As more and more friends die at Ghostface's hands and machete (though Campbell called Tatum's infamous dog-door noosing her favorite death of the series), the film keeps calling on one genre cliché after another. Sex and boozing don't *always* get you killed in horror, but the killer—and, per usual, it's not just one—*always* comes back for one last scare. Of course, by this point, as a soldier in battle will usually (albeit not fortunately) eventually be hardened into killing without blinking, as Sid's stoically-determined face just screams as she puts a bullet through Ulrich's murdering head.

American audiences of the early '90s hadn't been paying much attention—or money!—to the horror film world, and if *Scream* had been ignored, as so many others had been, it's tough to say how or if the genre would have recovered. But hey, why worry or argue about it now? What's important is that people responded as they hadn't in a while. Whatever made *Scream* work, hell, *it worked*! The old genre had found a new connection with fans; it had reached out a bottle and snared a bolt of lightning. Not just here, but everywhere; the flick yanked in nearly $200 million across the globe. And well before it hit that point, everyone knew that another chapter would be written by Williamson, directed by Craven, and acted out by Campbell, Jackson, and faces new and familiar.

Just a year later, it did. Just as the first one had, *Scream 2* (1997) opened with the bloody deaths of some household acting names, Omar Epps and Jada Pinkett the unlucky recipients this time around (if only they'd gone to see the Sandra Bullock film down the block! Actually, never mind; going by the release date, it would have to have been *Speed 2* [1997], which fell much farther short of its predecessor than the second *Scream*!). And yet again, the film reached out and yanked self-reference into the plot, full dialogue devoted to just how ten-feet-below-awful sequels are, even by definition—except for *Terminator 2* (1991) and *Godfather II* (1974), of course!

Still, Sidney manages to stay away from the bedroom gymnastics and the above-21 beverages, nor does she ever say, "I'll be right back." In horror, that's all you need to make it. Playing a college student, Campbell got ready by watching some of Craven's earlier work. And once again, she escapes the killer: Laurie Metcalf, a performance that stunned west *hell* out of *Roseanne* fans!

It took a bit longer to make the pair a trilogy, albeit nothing compared to what came a bit later in that department. Meanwhile, Campbell finally got her own chance to go on the dark offensive, revealed as the murderous mastermind mistress behind a plot that results in the violent deaths of several others and boatloads of money for herself in 1998's uber-erotic thriller *Wild Things*.

Two years later, Sidney was a crisis hotline counselor, helping others through stuff she'd somehow managed to escape.

"I was nervous about doing the film," Campbell admits. "It's tough to make three good films of anything. (Horror fans) give me faith about what we made. How do you make it better when we've done such a great job so far?"

With the dramatized version of the murders making it to the big screen in the storyline (Gale's showbiz dreams come true!), Ghostface and his ominous voice are back, and more people are dying. But why? Sid's ex-boyfriend, who'd killed her mom, was dead, and his own mom went down at the end of part two. The guy unfairly jailed for Mommy's murder gets whacked early in *Scream 3*; it's not him. Hopefully, it's not just some random nutcase killing people for the hell of it—avoiding that kind of superficiality was part of *Scream*'s appeal.

Williamson was gone for the time being, but Ehren Kruger (*almost* the same last name as

Freddy!) was there now. He'd pulled off a rare twist with the "bad guy wins and gets away" ending in the woefully underrated *Arlington Road* (1999), and eventually staked his final landmark in 2002 by penning *The Ring*. And, just as many part threes of the past had, this film walked in the footsteps of introducing a twist that turned around the series' entire storyline.

Subtlety is probably one of the last words anyone would ever associate with the slasher genre, but it became Campbell's mantra and art form as she kept introducing more and more layers of Sidney. Using the same techniques to get down and bloody with the bad guys and come out on top was working just fine, and she didn't want to mess up a good thing there, but giving a character a sense of individualism is what truly completes a scream queen's work. Just as Jamie Lee Curtis had with Laurie Strode and Heather Langenkamp with Nancy Thompson, Campbell had to reach deep and find all the sides of Sid's true bio. Where was she? Where had she been? Where was she going? What did she want?

Then she just went out and kicked the shit out of the bad guys.

"The challenge of playing Sidney was always trying to keep it interesting," she recalls. "The majority of the time, she was in fear, so what levels of fear could I show to keep it interesting to the audience in some way, considering the circumstances, and just trying to stay true to herself, considering the fact that she was growing? In the first one, she was a victim. In the second, she had learned to be a little stronger. By the third, she had gotten over being a victim. I think I learned who Sidney was in those stages. I could conceive of what she would be experiencing next."

Here's where things got personal again for Sidney. As it turned out, there was just one killer this time—the brother she never knew she had, the one that their mother had turned away for her own acting career. The guy who'd been all the way behind the mom's murder from the start. The fellow who'd been directing the film within a film, and acting out the real violence before it.

And now he was going to take out the sibling that stole his show.

That doesn't happen, but for the first time, Sidney makes it through a flick without killing anyone herself; David Arquette's daffy deputy Dewey blasts out the brother's brains.

As *Scream 3* ended, we saw Sidney and her friends doing what they'd been forced into too many times: helping each other recover from the same tragedies of blood, death, and murder. At Sidney's home, we and she saw a door behind her swing open as she was leaving a room. She glances at it, and everyone expects to see the fulfillment of yet another prediction *Scream* had shown: a killer rushing through it, armed with a gun, knife, or whatever else. Maybe Sidney would become the same victim so many of her friends and family had.

But it didn't. It was just the wind. No one was there, or would be.

It looked like a strong piece of wonderful symbolism, yet another area of film that horror rarely bothers with. Sidney was finally safe for good.

That's what we figured for the next decade. So when the sounds of *Scream 4* started leaking across the Internet in 2010, we were confused. What reason was there for a fourth round? What could be added to the Woodsboro nightmare? Why?

Or perhaps, just *maybe*, the *Scream* crew wanted Sidney to reach one more goal. They wanted her to do what *Halloween*'s Laurie, *Nightmare*'s Nancy, and all the gals from *Saw*, *Friday the 13th*, and every other multi-layered horror saga in American history didn't or couldn't.

They wanted her . . . to *survive four films*! Yeah, let's go with that. Sounds right, even if it's not.

"We went with a character that was incredibly strong and wasn't as huge a victim as many females in the genre," Campbell explains. "At this point, she's lost so many people that she had to be insane! Every single family member and every single friend and every single boyfriend had been slaughtered in front of her. She'd be in a straitjacket. But at the same time, how realistic is that? There's something wonderful that she's carried on, and that she's strong."

With Williamson, who'd also kicked off the *I Know What Did Last Summer* series in 1997, back hard at screenwriting work, the fourth flick starts with some inside jabs at the remakes and sequels that drowned the horror film world since the start of the millennium. We see a few clips of the next chapters of the films based on the local killings, only to find out that the last one was for real—and that Sidney, now back in town to promote her own authored memoirs, is in trouble once again.

Getting ready to take the scream queen throne at least one more time, Campbell watched her younger co-stars prepare by watching her own earlier Sidney exploits.

"It was interesting to go on the set and see the rest of the cast that was the age that we were when we did the first one," she recalls. "That was crazy—and wonderful. I was nervous about it. After so long, I was wondering if audiences would still be interested. And who would Sidney be at this point? She'd obviously grown up, so who would she be? I was happy with the author part of it. That made a lot of sense."

The killings begin again, and now it appears that someone's copying *Scream* itself, as the same film trivia that resulted in Barrymore's eventual death way back when causes more to feel her fate. Once again, there's two killers, and, again, family rivalry comes back at Sidney; as it turns out, one murderer is her cousin Jill (Emma Roberts), with motives similar to Roman's. Sidney got all the fame and fortune by making it through the first three episodes, and now Jill's going to steal her heroine-ism by any means necessary.

Just as we'd seen before, Jill takes out her fellow killer, and tries to do so to Sidney. But if Sid was truly going to take her final bow, Williamson and Craven would have made it a much bigger deal: she'd die taking a bullet for a child, or pushing a group of people out of the way of a speeding truck. Just stabbing her would have been far too subtle.

So when Jill and Gale face off in a hospital room, we're just waiting for Sidney to make her own final scare. And she does, with some brand new means, sending currents through Jill with a defibrillator. Then she uses the old reliable, one last bullet in Jill's most vital spot to end the threat forever.

Well, not to beat the whole *maybe* thing to death here, but, well . . . maybe. In 2015, MTV brought *Scream* to the small screen, as one of the too-common cyberbullying incidents causes murder in a small town. Williamson wrote the pilot, and Tracy Middendorf, who worked for Craven in 1994's *New Nightmare*, has a small role.

Want to hear something funny and ironic? Despite appearing (well, in a sense) in all four *Screams* together, Campbell and Jackson didn't meet until 2015, years after the saga was through.

"I never had the script until we were about to shoot, so I never knew who the killer was," Jackson recalls. "The voice stayed inside the mask the whole time. Wes definitely subscribed to the idea that the scariest monster is the monster you make with your own imagination."

In hindsight, we can find one last appeal to the *Scream* saga that gave more and more viewers a new reason to start caring about horror, or start doing so again. Long thought of as a man's world, full of violence and promiscuity, Campbell and Sidney's work, in both *Scream*'s violent and dramatic sides, showed fellow ladies around the world that a woman, even forced, could go straight on the offensive, and stay there until she came out on top, time and time again.

"I've had a lot of women come up to me," Campbell says, "and say they found strength as women, by seeing a female in a horror film not be the victim, but be the strong one. I don't know if it's feminist, but it shows the strength in women."

Oh, and by the way, now, for the first time (well, hopefully one of them), let's finally hear a personal answer to the query that launched the *Scream* series straight into the public eye and eventual icon-hood.

What is it, Ms. Campbell?

What's *your* favorite scary movie?

She hesitates . . . but it doesn't seem to be for lack of knowing. Perhaps proper wording is the issue here.

"*The Changeling*!" Campbell finally blurts, referring not to the 2008 Clint Eastwood/Angelina Jolie flick, but to 1980's supernatural horror flick with George C. Scott. "The wheelchair?! The ball down the stairs?! *Are you kidding me?*"

Shayla Stonefeather (Tonantzin Carmelo) faced back her Native American culture and supernatural evil in 2007's *Imprint*.

Tonantzin Carmelo:

Imprint

LOOKING OVER THE history books, it appears that the "Trail of Tears," though a horrifically accurate moniker, might actually have a greater application than it entails.

It's the official term for the route traveled by thousands of Native Americans away from their homes and families from the south to the unfamiliar lands of Oklahoma's still-undeclared area back in the early 1800s, a trip that thousands didn't survive, a knockout punch by the white government that had already been killing and stealing from the true Americans for decades.

But if you really think about it—not that many would be eager to—this land's Native American population has traveled a Trail of Tears ever since invaders landed here in the 1400s: anyone who thinks that Christopher Columbus was a) the first non-Native American to show up or b) anything but a slavemaster who helped start, if not complete, the slaughter of thousands, hasn't learned enough history. A population had established and maintained a healthy society for generations, only to have it stolen, their lives taken, their culture quashed to the extent that, even today, the first "settlers" of this land are considered at best an afterthought by far too many without Native American blood.

Still, no matter what tribe, no matter where they live, voluntarily or otherwise, there's also a positive trademark shared by the Native American people. It's one of strength. It's one of unity. It's the knowledge, or at least the hope, that one day in a hopefully very soon future, the people that kept this land together for a millennium will get the respect, the recognition that they never have.

And while your typical horror films don't finish up with a culturally-uplifting ending, Tonantzin Carmelo and the cast of *Imprint* (2007) gave it one, in the dreams that the film will live up to its name and, pulling together, Native Americans can truly make their mark on the culture they helped form. And if that starts with the cinematic world, well, it's as great a place as any.

But there was quite a bit of ground covered in Carmelo's entertainment career long before the big screens beckoned, like the native dancing that got things going, the theater career that carried her up and down the west coast, the CDs she's recorded, and the voice work as the evil Kendra Daniels on the multi-million-selling video game *Dead Space* (2008).

"When I was young, everyone thought I was too shy, as both my parents were dancers and performers," Carmelo recalls. "I was challenged to overcome my shyness. I have always been attracted to acting, though it seemed out of reach. As a dancer, I did a lot of traveling and got exposed to a lot of productions here and there, the making of pilots and other films. I realize that it intrigued me and made me want to be a part of it."

Starting out, performers can't afford to be picky with their choices; it's more about adding entries to a résumé and names to the network than anything else. But Carmelo's biggest role, to that point, was far past professional passion.

A six-hour miniseries (and you thought 1990's *Dances with Wolves* took its time!), produced by a fellow named Spielberg, that covered over half a century of North and Native American history, 2005's *Into the West* told the tale of America's growth toward the center and left side of today's nation back in the 1800s. In the midst of a cast of hundreds was the Lakota lady Thunder Heart Woman, who sees her husband killed and her daughter kidnapped by another tribe, which then sells her into slavery before she's rescued by story narrator Jacob (Matt Settle). Moving around the nation with her husband and growing family, she sees far too many pass away—the film depicts the Wounded Knee massacre in South Dakota, in which hundreds of Lakotas and dozens of soldiers were killed when a disarmament attempt by the military went tragically wrong—but makes it through to the end, the story finishing with her daughter teaching local children about her people's past.

Indeed, this was about far more than a résumé extension for Carmelo.

"I knew I would be great for it," she recalls, "and that it was the kind of amazing role that doesn't come along very often. It could make my career." Campaigning her way to audition as a complete unknown (and snaring a chance after impressing the casting director at a showcase), she managed to come out ahead of the tryout group.

"That role took a *lot* of preparation, because it's a serious piece," Carmelo remembers. "I remembered my grandmothers and looked to them for inspiration. We have a very strong oral history in our family, and I grew up hearing all kinds of stories in my family. I knew of my great- and great-great-grandmothers and their stories. They were legends in my family."

Herself of the background of the Tongva and Kumeyaay tribes, Carmelo stepped into a different culture of her heritage to find Thunder Heart's background.

"I had to learn Lakota," she says. "We're California Indians, and she was a Plains Indian, but the similarities are there. She was a survivor; she survived all these terrible tragedies that had happened to her and her people. As the actors, you get into this world, and it's a great place, because you get to step into someone else's shoes to observe their humanity."

It would be all but impossible for her to stand out; *West*'s cast reached past two hundred, like past Oscar nominee Tom Berenger and future nominee Josh Brolin, established names like Beau Bridges and Gary Busey, and lightning stars like Rachel Leigh Cooke and Keri Russell, not to mention household Native American performers Irene Bedard, Russell Means, and Wes Studi. Carmelo didn't even get the full role, so to speak; Sheila Tousey took over Thunder Heart's later years. But when all was said, done, and directed, something about the lady that many were seeing for the first time became the most unexpected and certainly welcome *West* highlights—of all of her co-stars and competition throughout the miniseries medium, Carmelo's work was the only one to garner a Screen Actor's Guild acting nomination (Helen Mirren won the 1998 statuette for *Elizabeth I*). The series also brought in a year-leading sixteen Emmy nominations and won a pair.

Carmelo had stood all the way out; two years later, she turned back to her heritage to horrify.

No matter how far we travel, no matter how much we change inside and out, one thing we can never leave all the way behind is our past. Our beginnings, our culture, no matter how much we might want to forget them, no matter how pain they still rain down on our psyche, they'll always be around. Not always a negative—suffering can work if we learn from it, even if we just figure out how not to be and what not to do.

And even in the supernatural and fantastical world of horror, sometimes our culture can show us that what we wanted to forget might be what we should carry on forever, especially for a member of the people that this very land tried to expel, if not exterminate.

Some had tried to escape the pain of their heritage's history and live a new life, far from their families and homeland. *Imprint* protagonist Shayla Stonefeather was one such person, engaged to a white man, a politician no less, taking the next step in her law career by prosecuting a young Native American fellow for murder, a move that, all too realistically, turned her into quite the pariah amongst her family.

"What I really liked about Shayla was that she lived in two worlds, and that she navigates them the best she can," Carmelo explains, "and I feel that, as an individual, you live culturally, for all of the people you grew up with, and, as in my case as an artist, you live in this other world that has all sorts of expectations of you, as they did of Shayla in her other world as a lawyer." She looked back on the law classes she'd taken on the way to a degree in environmental analysis and design (minoring in dance) from UC Irvine to fire up Shayla's legal passion.

Trying to convince herself that she's just the messenger of justice, Shayla heads to the home reservation, where her father is about finished. But someone's absent: her brother, and Shayla blames her dad.

"I had an idea of that world," Carmelo says of her character's mental mindset. "A small background can give you some standing, like going back to a small town, going back to a reservation."

Shayla's fiancé arrives and brings some tough news; the man she prosecuted has been killed, and his family's out to get her. And they're not alone—some visions are starting to show up all over the area, ghoulishly trying to tell Shayla a story, one that appears to be of her brother's death at her dad's hands.

"My sense of disbelief is very, very high, so I get scared very easily," Carmelo says, "especially from ghost stories."

Contact with the supernatural has long been a powerful part of her people's heritage, and Shayla tries to face it head on. Who are they? What are they saying? Not all of Carmelo's educational contact there was on screen, either.

"To me, acting is magic, letting out your magic," she says. "Main thing that an actor like me has to do is to know your lines very well—where you're at, what you're doing. It's like peeking at a picture, and imagining where you'd put yourself in that picture."

It takes a sad trip to the Wounded Knee area to get her some answers from a local medicine man, but she's not a patient woman, and this isn't a time to sit back and hear a story from others. The spirits are there to tell her the sad story of her brother's death, and she lets her dad have it, him passing during her verbal destruction. But this story can't end that way.

"I call it fast and loose shooting," Carmelo says. "It was all done very quickly. We shot some scenes in one day, very quick. I had to trust my instincts and I constantly had to ask 'What is my character doing at this moment?' The horse riding was a little tough for me. I know my way around horses, but when you have a camera on you and you have to go faster, over and over again, you feel the wear and tear on your body. It was about figuring things out and making them look good within the context of the story."

The spirits are still around, and Shayla's man isn't who she thought he was. Not only was he using her to further his career with a certain voting audience, he even framed her former defendant for murder. Shayla's ex, now a local cop, helps her find out a truth that's even more terrifying than she thought: not only was the fellow innocent and her brother alive, but the ghosts were trying to warn her of what just might happen if she didn't change. If she didn't get rid of her fiancé. If she forgot too much of her past and those that were desperate to get her to remember it.

"I didn't have to imagine too much," Carmelo says of Shayla's spiritual evolution. "I was in a house out in the middle of nowhere, and it was really scary to be out there, really on the creepy side sometimes. It was really fun to see the special effects. They pretty much paralleled what I was imagining." That past that she'd left behind, the same one that so many today, both Native American and otherwise, want to forget or at least ignore becomes her own message of hope, even if fear moved her into it.

"All of the experiences the characters goes through were pretty amazing to me, because she came full circle," she says. "I enjoy that about the film, and the audience enjoys that, making a character grow and change from one point to another. It has a lot of entertainment value, as well as emotional connection value."

Between the acting roles that have taken her onto screens and stages since, even to the animated world of *American Dad*, it's a connection that Carmelo—along with so many others in and out of Hollywood—hope to keep making with the rest of America's future. It's sad that a business, any business, needs governmental intervention to get to the now when it comes to diversification, although the acting world is one of the slowest there (think I'm wrong? Count the number of biopics of white folk against those of minorities). Carmelo discussed it with a U.S. Senate committee on Indian Affairs back in 2013.

"We talked about the images of native people in film and television," she recalls. "To begin with, there are really not too many Native Americans living in this country, and there's only a handful of Native actors. The Native American roles out there are so few and far between, it can kind of be like quicksand for your career if you are thought of one-dimensionally as an actor who plays Native roles. You have to diversify and do as many different roles as you can to survive as a working actor, to keep the ball up and keep it going and prove that you can do a lot of different roles."

The local supernatural starts to overtake Ada (Lauren Ashley Carter) in 2013's *Jugface*.

Lauren Ashley Carter:

Jugface/The Woman

IT'S TOUGH TO find in society today. It's never been easy to find in the horror genre.

In a nation run at high speed and volume, so many points made so often with everything but an atomic bomb, we're far more used to calamity than calm. With actions and reactions ruled much more with emotion than rationale, subtlety has become more of a dirty S-word than anything with four letters.

And, once again, in a genre that's all but legally required to overflow itself with emotion, mainly of the negative types of fear and anger, restraint is foreign. After all, it's just about giving people what they want, and what they're used to in and outside of the theater, right?

Usually, yes. Still, once in a while, even a horror film can sit back and create a world of obscene sexual escapades, child abuse, and sacramental murder . . . and make it seem normal. Get us to accept it, as the characters we see afflicted so long ago have.

That's the world that Lauren Ashley Carter and the rest of the team of *Jugface* created. They took a world that many of us wouldn't set a toe into for a billion dollars and showed us that it could work.

"It doesn't resemble normalcy," Carter admits, "but there's a lot of people in that situation, backwoods communities where people are uneducated and ignorant because of how they were brought up. I'm from a really small town in Ohio, and I knew families and communities like that, where they live off the grid. I could relate to (my character), and the story I understood. I saw these people in my head."

The 2013 film would be Carter's debut in the lead role, but she'd shown up in horror two years sooner with *The Woman*, one that took another route in horror that's rarely been blazed.

She was Peggy, the teenage daughter of a family who seemed to have it all: bonding, greenbacks, everything looking right from the outside.

Looks were at their utmost deception. Her father Chris was an abusive misogynist who'd beaten his wife—mentally and physically—into submission. He had the title character, Pollyanna McIntosh's savage tribeswoman who'd be gorgeous if she could spend an hour in a spa, confined in the barn, using her to train his son to be just as big a cretin as him.

But the woman wasn't his only victim. . . .

"I loved the whole family dynamic of the story," Carter recalls. "I was into Peggy's character. It's a painful character, because of the incest, the violence, the relationship with her father, and it was something I had a great respect for her and the situation. It was something I wanted to tackle because it's very far from who I am as a person. She's been abused, she's weak, she doesn't have much of a voice. It's very far from myself, so I knew it would be really challenging."

Don't think I'm trying to downplay anything here. See that quote above? Yes, she mentioned incest. Probably tired of his wife, Chris had traveled down the family tree to his own daughter, and it was getting disgustingly obvious.

"One of the big things is that she's starting to become visibly pregnant," Carter says, "and I'm about a hundred, 105 pounds on any given day. I gained twenty pounds so I'd be able to show that she was three months along and make it obvious she was hiding the pregnancy. I gained weight in my face."

Peggy was terrified. Not only because of what was happening to her physically, but the knowledge that no one would ever help her—right along with the fear that Chris might someday do the same to Peggy's little sister. As much as the saying about losing oneself in a character gets quipped in the acting world, Carter didn't want Peggy to have too much of herself.

"It's very difficult for me to stay in a head space like that for a long period of time," she recalls, "so it was better in between takes or not on set to relax and have conversations with other actors to get out of the head space for a while, because it can really start to weigh on you. All those feelings, you get stuck in a mood."

With her mom a scared shell and her sister too young to understand much, Peggy finally becomes the only one with a backbone (bigger balls than any man in her family!) to help out the woman. The escapee does what every woman in the world—and, of course, most men! —probably would love to do to every wife-beater, rapist, kiddie-fiddler, or any combo of the three.

As she chops his son in half, Chris has no clue what to do. No one stands up to him, let alone a lady. She's not going to give him a chance to so much as breathe, tearing the heart that we probably thought didn't exist from his chest.

The pathetic mom already dead, the woman looks over Peggy and her sister. Then she walks away.

Out of impulse or childish ignorance, the youngster follows. Then Peggy does as well—anything's better than what she's lived through.

"The woman inspired her to fight back when there was no other option," Carter explains. "Why does Peggy go off with her? I think it's more than inspiration; she respects the woman, and (the woman) does what she has to do for survival. She cares about the woman because she cares about people. At the end, she knows that there's no choice but to go with her. It's a combination of fear and respect."

Now let's get to the new and tough world of *Jugface*. Not a whole lot scary, or even unusual at first; we see Carter's Ada and a handsome fellow named Jessaby sneak off into the thick, ominous woods that surround their homestead for a little high-speed tryst action.

Then we learn of a large pit in the midst of the area, one that garners worship from the townsfolk. We meet local oddball Dawai (Sean Bridgers), a shaman in a computer nerd's body, who crafts clay pottery jars adorned with the face of he or she who must become the pit's next sacrificial meal.

Again, everyone in the film is used to this. Then, again in a laidback conversation that's easy to miss without a sharp pair of eyes and ears, we find that Ada is Jessaby's sister.

"The shamelessness that they had about it is very surprising, but it does exist," Carter says. "The way that I had to approach it was that there was this powerful connection between her and her brother. As much as she knew it was wrong, she cared so much for him and wanted to be with him. He was the only person that she could talk to. There's a missing sense of guilt that Ada has during the whole movie, something that she wasn't born with that makes her make the decisions that she does, and I had to do it with that blindness."

Rather than take the oft-traveled road of having a stranger from everyday society get lost somewhere and stumble into a new and terrifying world, and make the film about their perception (*Texas Chainsaw Massacre*, *Wrong Turn*, and about a billion others), *Jugface* hands itself to the people that are used to this sort of thing. It's new, horrifying, and far from anything we're used to, but it's not about us. The film is about looking from the inside out of those people and telling us who and why they work. We can like it or not, and it really doesn't matter. It's just about realizing that as different as some people, some worlds that might be nearby geographically, can seem, they're perfectly OK to those who don't know anything else—the same people who'd look at our world and call it a frighteningly foreign land. It doesn't tell anyone, like us viewers, that this is right or justified; it's just how they live, and live well, and always have.

"It's not until you get there and you're getting your schedule for the week," Carter recalls, "that you realize, 'I'm putting myself through hell right now!' A lot of actors like going to the dark places, because they're fun."

Ada's soon betrothed to another local, but the pit's resident kills him. Rather than pack up and run like hell, though, the community, if anyone could call it that, looks for a way to appeasement, and someone else becomes a willing victim; this is an honor code sort of thing.

Still, things stay as under control as they can. Ada realizes she's expecting her own nephew. Her mom Loriss (Sean Young) furiously inspects her womanhood, Ada pleading that she broke herself.

"The whole film was pretty tough," Carter says. "The moments with Sean Young were really difficult. It was hard for her, because she's a really gentle, loving woman, sensitive about what I'm going through. Those scenes were uncomfortable for both of us."

Jessaby becomes the next sacrifice, and Ada's falsely accused of an affair with Dawai. A whipping causes her a miscarriage, and her dad apologizes, even accepting that his son was the father. Soon after, he's killed, and Ada's got just one chance left at leaving with the same honor that so many others have carried off before her.

"The best thing for me to do is before I go in for a scene and shoot for a whole day, to only concentrate on that day," Carter explains. "I go back to old acting techniques: what are my givens? What happened before this? It's really important to me to match the intensity of each moment." But, as has been the case throughout the film, *Jugface*'s finale is notably lacking in much intensity at all.

With a chance to get away, Ada stays behind, knowing that Dawai will be killed if she runs off. As the locals arrive, led by Loriss, Ada's kneeling by the pit, ready to take responsibility for all of her mistaken misgivings.

"She's driven by impulse for the entire film, which is very strange, because she's such a quiet person," Carter says. "That's what makes her very unique and fascinating." Her mom, Dawai, and all the rest seem to feel the same way. A sharp blade is slowly drawn across her jugular, but Ada doesn't hardly blink. In a way that's just as unfounded and uncommon in horror as anything we've seen throughout the film, she's here to do what's right, just as so many other in the flick have, even if it means offering her own painful, bloody death as redemption.

Realism is something we don't always expect in horror, but inspiration is even less common. Ada leaves us feeling it.

"It was a learning experience for me to know I have to be *on* one hundred percent of the time," Carter recalls. "No matter how many takes there are, no matter how tired I am or what's going on, the focus is incredibly important."

Update: Literally days before this book went to press, I got word that Carter had just embarked on a new role, quite different than *Jugface*.

With the film not widely released at press time, Carter couldn't give away too much. Hopefully, by the time you're reading this, it will mean just a bit more.

She's in the title role as *Darling* (2016), a young lady who moves into an old mansion, unaware of the dark secrets it hides (perhaps a relative of the Overlook Hotel!). With Young back with her in a very different role, she finds herself being overtaken.

"(Director/writer) Mickey Keating and I developed it together," recalls Carter, who also helped produce the flick. "I kept begging him to come out to New York and do an apartment movie. I really wanted to play a villain."

Locating somewhere to put it on, however, would be as tough as any role preparation she'd ever have.

"It was very difficult to find a place," she admits. "Shooting a movie destroys a location." One day, she went to see the new home of a lady whose dog Carter previously took out for exercise.

"She had just bought a big house in Harlem," Carter remembers. "She said, 'Why don't you just shoot it here?'" She sent Keating a ton of photos to play with. The two rewrote the script. Carter lived in Darling's impromptu home during filming.

"It wasn't really an acting choice," she explains. "For insurance reasons, someone had to be there with the camera equipment, so I stayed. I felt that I knew the house backward. It was pretty organic and easy."

Filming was done without color, showing the madness that Darling can't fight off. To find a mindset so much darker than Peggy's, Carter looked over her own predecessors. Like the (so sadly!) late Zoe Lund, who'd been in the lead of 1981's *Ms. 45*, playing a mute driven by rape to a shooting spree against men. Or Catherine Deneuve, before Roman Polanski's cameras for *Repulsion* (1965) to tell the tale of a lady whose mind is wracked by visions of sexual violence that may or may not be all in her head.

Just as might just be the case with Darling. Getting ready for the aftermath of a particularly violent scene, Carter holed up in a room she'd come to know very well, for a very different reason.

"It was my first breakdown moment," she remembers. "I told everyone to give me five minutes.

"What does this have to be?" she recalls asking. "What is this moment? I had to imagine what this would be like, how psychotic and rage-filled and big I had to be to make this moment real. I just put myself in a room and went nuts."

Did it work? By the time of publication, that question will have an answer—and hopefully in the minds of so, so many!

With just twenty-four hours to live, *Time to Kill* (2014) protagonist Sara (Ellie Church, left) had nothing left to lose, and everything to try—and we mean *everything*!

Ellie Church:

Time to Kill

WE'VE SEEN THIS sort of story before—but never in this direction.

Terminal illness, finding out we only have X-amount of time left on this revolving ball of dirt . . . these tales have been told and filmed time and again. But they usually wind up as heartfelt dramas or comedies, stories of people healing old wounds and remaking friends and all sort of tear-jerking.

Yeah, not this one. Since this a book about horror, we know that the one we're about to discuss isn't heading that way. 2014's *Time to Kill* (no *A* at the beginning—Matthew McConaughey was nowhere near this one) did things with a verdict of death that few films have ever tried before . . . but have probably roamed through the minds of those who've been unlucky enough to get this sort of news.

Let's meet those behind it. Like too many potential acting success stories, Ellie Church believed that she was just too far from the game, in the geographic sense.

"I had always thought how much I would love to act," recalls the Indiana resident, "but didn't know there was a big pool of people in my area that made movies."

She may have been right, but the pool just needed a little deepening.

Back in the 1970s, a couple of filmmakers with little more than a dream and a set of guts—albeit not quite the amount that their films would spill!—put together a tiny studio that would soon be the headquarters for cult film royalty. Troma Studios became a haunted household name for the goriest, corniest, and campiest of horror films, roaring from the *Toxic Avenger* films to *Class of Nuke 'Em High* of 1986 to 2006's *Poultrygeist*, the epic of zombie chickens turning the tables on a fast-food place (yes, that really happened).

At the head of Troma is a fellow named Lloyd Kaufman, and an encounter with him showed Church that her dreams might not be all that far away.

"I was oblivious," she admits. "But through Lloyd, I met a ton of local directors, and I've made a lot of great connections."

Her first foray into film was a common story, and a very tough one—helping with 2013's *And Then YOU Die!*, Church worked behind the camera on the makeup, costumes, and special effects, then stepped in front of it play a lady named Tessa, the sad, angry adulteress of protagonist Sam (Chuck Smith), whose own torture from without leads him slam into a murderous rampage, a gory one-man death squad against those that made his own life hell.

A year later, Church followed in a few sets of footsteps.

First off, those of Kaufman and his producing buddies: she and her husband Brian Williams put together their (sort of misleadingly titled) company Mostly Harmless Productions. Brian's rough production values called up memories of action films of the '60s and '70s that were shockingly innovative back then, but seem so cheesy today. For Harmless' first turnout, Church would become something of a female Sam.

But, as with *YOU Die*, her part began long before acting—far from establishment, she and Brian ended up turning their home into the "on location" location.

"Putting the house and sets together in our home was definitely tough, but not near as tough as having to do it somewhere else," she says. "It was the most convenient way to build a set, but at the same time, sometimes it was in your way and not so convenient . . . there's only so many things you can build in a two-car garage."

Now for the film. Far from her past of drugs and strip club stages, young babe Sara heads to the doctor one morning, with no idea she's about to hear just about the worst news one can obtain from the medical profession. Apparently equipped with soothsaying abilities somewhere next to the Hippocratic Oath, her doc somehow knows that, by this time tomorrow, Sara's going to be sent skyward or downward.

Once again, at this point in this sort of film, characters usually focus on reuniting with the estranged, going places only dreamed of before, all kinds of things we do when reality is a bit too close and yet still so far away. But this film was *Time to Kill*, and it was time for Church to act upon it.

What MIGHT we do in that situation? Is it possible that we might just decide to exact all kinds of justice on those that deserve it? With nothing at all to lose, it's comprehensible that some of us might truly choose to go nuts and leave a pile of pain and bodies behind. What's the worst that can happen?

We get thrown in jail for . . . a few hours? It's not an unrealistic possibility.

And Sara doesn't hang around; back home, in the midst of an argument with her bratty sister, she decides that words aren't enough—and chops the woman's hand clean right off. Oh, but to not have to worry about laws and "justice" for awhile!

Indeed, it shows her that there's no reason to be scared anymore, and some people deserve to go down with her. First off is a disgusting scumbag she sees abusing a lovely lady on the side of the road. With machetes in both hands and a spiked bra for attire, Sara does what so many abused women dream of, putting a deep mouth under the guy's chin.

"I think I sound like the badass I am supposed to be in that scene!" she exclaims. More and more bodies fall.

Sara's destination's clearly in mind, but we're not certainly sure what she's going to do upon arrival; there's quite a bit to see beforehand; like, say, a *very* close bubble bath encounter with her gorgeous new friend—perhaps something else Sara'd always wanted to try, and finally has occasion (the lady in question was played by Church's real-life friend Charlie Moon, also new to the acting business)! There's also a mantra of pitch-black hilarious intermission commercials, complete with added scratches to the "film," remember, this is, after all, partly a tribute to films of generations past! After spending almost a year putting the film together, and even starting without a completed script, the *Kill* cast was coming all together.

"Preparing for the role was really me trying to transform myself into a cold-hearted badass, when I'm kind of a nervous, shy person," Church admits. "I would record my lines on my phone, and lay in the bath for long periods of time, and try to make my lines sound less and less like myself (the girl who is worried about everything and is wondering what to make for dinner) and more like Sara (who doesn't have anything left to lose and was out for blood)."

Finally, they arrive at Sara's old employed spot. Even for a strip joint, this place is rough (but hey, keep in mind that it's really Church and Williams' garage!). But that also makes it even more realistic; what better place would there be for the king of the underworld to hide!

That's right; Sara's target all along has been the object of faithful evil, her former boss. Sara's life may be over, but there's one chance left for her to stay on earth: taking this guy out. Blood will need to flow, gore will spew, and there's only going to be one left. . . .

We live, we die, and what's in between is up to the person. But when we head out for the first and last time (assuming there's nothing to that reincarnation stuff), the toughest, saddest part is not being able to do so on the terms we set for ourselves. Sara indeed has resources that don't really exist outside of the horror film world, but she's doing what far more of us probably would if we could than are willing to admit it.

Still, "The toughest thing for me, surprisingly enough, was the voiceover recording that I did for the very last scene in the movie," Church recalls. "I had to have a different demeanor than I had in most of the film, and it was hard for me to switch that. But what really ended up working for me was putting headphones in and listening to the song that was going to be playing in the scene. After I did that, I got it in one take."

Adulterous jezebel Bonnie Sawyer (Julie Cobb) tries to lie her way out of trouble in *Salem's Lot* (1979).

Julie Cobb:

Salem's Lot

IT'S A COMMON belief that we don't always realize what we have until it goes away, and that conviction usually has a certain stigma of sadness attached to it, as it's typically associated with missing something.

Still, that's not always the case. Sometimes, the realization comes from not being certain what one had to begin with. Sometimes, the realization can lead to a very pleasant surprise.

That's how Julie Cobb and the rest of the *Salem's Lot* group felt after seeing their work go from set to screen back in 1979. But we'll get to that shortly, because someone else in her family felt a bit differently about another piece of legendary horror work.

The acting trade was running through Cobb's genetics before she was born. Her grandparents were in the theater occupation for a while, and her mom was Yiddish actress Helen Beverley. Before she was out of grade school, Cobb's father, the late great Lee J. Cobb, had racked up an Oscar nomination in 1958 for *The Brothers Karamazov* and showed up next to Marlon Brando four years before in *On the Waterfront* (he was also one of the legendary *12 Angry Men* of the 1957 masterpiece).

Acting, Cobb recalls, "was my family business. It came by naturally. I was endowed by my parents with creativity and imagination, and surrounded by creative people. It was a natural choice for me." As it turned out, the tradition would follow her through marriage and motherhood.

When her dad grabbed the role of Lt. Kinderman in *The Exorcist* (1973), he, just like everyone else, obviously couldn't know the phenomenon the film would become, blasting across worldwide horror cinema and still standing as a landmark in the genre nearly half a century later. However, the elder Cobb got a few surprises from his film as soon as it hit, and not in a great way; the directions that director William Friedkin and the rest of the crew had taken led to a whole new area for Cobb.

"He was shocked at the effects," says Cobb, who appeared with her dad on a 1974 episode of *Gunsmoke*. "He expected it to be more of a thriller, and less of a vomit-fest. He had no idea that the production values would be so graphic. My father was a very brilliant, artistic man, and he didn't expect the special effects to be so exploitative."

A few years later, Cobb, an admitted non-horror fan, got a shot at bringing a relatively new author's book to the small screen. It was only his second book, after *Carrie*, but many still see *Salem's Lot* as his finest output. As would be the case with *It* (1991), *The Tommyknockers* (1993), *The Stand* (1994), and other literary creations later on, King's work would first be seen in small-screen miniseries form.

"*Salem's Lot* was just a job like other jobs," Cobb remembers. "It was during a time in my career where I was working quite a bit. It was a wonderful project, and I was lucky enough to get cast in it."

Her role wasn't huge, but the part was important. Still, there's a backstory to be told first. David Soul is Ben Mears, a writer who comes back to his homeland of the Maine title town to transcribe the tale of the house that terrified him through his youth. But someone else has already rented it out: a weird-looking guy named Richard Straker (James Mason), who recently opened an antique shop with his partner, Kurt Barlow, still out of town.

A recent widower, Ben gets to know local beauty Susan Norton (Bonnie Bedelia, who'd bring another of King's work to the visual world over a decade later, starring in 1993's *Needful Things*). Meanwhile, Straker hires trucker Cully Sawyer (George Dzundza) to grab a crate arriving by boat and bring it to the house.

But Cully's got other plans; his wife Bonnie works for Straker's landlord Larry Crockett (Fred Willard), and the two have been getting awfully close lately. Making up a fake work outing for his missus, Cully catches the pair *in flagrante*.

"She was the perfect character," Sawyer says of becoming Bonnie. "She was the victim of circumstances, the victim of men in her life, and I empathized with her quite a bit. She was innocent. She was fun, and saw the best in people."

Outsized by Larry, Cully might be outclassed if things went to fisticuffs. However, the rifle in his hands shifts the odds toward him. Ignoring his wife's false bleating about sexual assault victimization, Cully takes his boxers-clad prisoner into the living room.

"I may have read the book when I got the part," Cobb recalls. "They lightened my hair; I was a brunette at the time. The costumes were wonderful. I looked at her and had the characterization."

Forcing his hostage to place the gun barrel in his mouth, Cully pulls the trigger. But before Larry's life can flash before his eyes, they open—no bullets in the barrel.

Larry flees. But in the darkest of ironies, there's something outside waiting for him even more frightening; something unseen grabs him, and Susan and Mears later find him dead in his car.

As it turned out, the crate contained Barlow himself (late great Reggie Nalder, made up to resemble the legendary Count Orlok of *Nosferatu* fame). Before long, he and Straker are taking charge of the Lot, forcing many either out of town or into early graves (Cully and Bonnie left early). But Mears is able to take both out—unsurprisingly, a stake through the heart turns Barlow to dust—then burn down the vampires' house, taking out the infected. But even after he bolts to Mexico, someone's still in pursuit, and he's forced to whack his love Susan as she degenerates.

Unlike the gung-ho nature of blood and gore (and language!) he'd been able to inject into *Texas Chain Saw Massacre* (1974) a few years earlier, keeping *Lot* on the small screen forced Tobe Hooper to scare his audience in some cleaner ways. However, not until the screening did Cobb and the rest of the group find out just how effective those mannerisms truly had been.

Just as her dad had been by *The Exorcist*, Cobb was shocked by *Lot*—but this time in a great way.

"We were blown away," she says. "We were together in the theater so it had that group dynamic. It was terrifying. People were very amazed by the way Tobe Hooper pulled it off. It wasn't gory, just scary, and that's more of an art form. We were scared and delighted."

A quarter-century after the first *Lot*, a new version came back to cable. The town was the same, but that was about all—the story was updated to modern times, and Mears' character, now in Rob Lowe's persona, doesn't make it through—along with quite a few other changes.

One was that Barlow was Rutger Hauer, and he could now speak. Another was that Bonnie wasn't retained; Crockett, now played by Robert Grubb, is a sick scumbag sexually abusing his daughter (we actually *see* him become the vampires' dinner this time).

Here's another switch—the book and first flick had local faith man Father Callahan as a warm, albeit weak fellow who gives in to the vampires' power to save others. The new version made him their willing servant, killed by Mears.

The 2004 Callahan was played by James Cromwell, Cobb's then-husband.

"I didn't see the new version," Cobb says. "The adaptation that we had was pretty top-notch."

Marylee Williams (Tonya Crowe) starts to form her revenge plan against local evil in 1981's *Dark Night of the Scarecrow.*

Tonya Crowe:

Dark Night of the Scarecrow

CHANCES ARE, IF somebody murdered us, we'd be pretty pissed off at them, wouldn't we?

Yeah, taking your life gives you quite a legitimate reason to want to have words with somebody. Maybe even to get revenge. Imagine looking down from above on some SOB that took us out and saying, "Man, I hope I can get reincarnated the right way to go back down and fire off the business!"

Horror's darkly magical world has given several a chance to snare what we can't in reality; it's usual to see someone come back, albeit in a different, typically superhuman (if human at all) way to find their own form of justice.

And there might just be someone else still there, a person who cared for them pre-death and just might see them as a chance to exact some new redemption of their own. . . .

We've already given away *part* of 1981's *Dark Night of the Scarecrow*, so let's not take all the meat off its bones just yet. It's about a fellow a little below average in the IQ field (but above so in the compassion sense, usually the case in reality), his life taken by heartless neighborhood bullies with the nerve to hide under the vigilante label, who comes back, in a sense, to pay them back with fatal interest. It's also about the person who's there to help him out; per usual, said character is the last one anyone outside of the horror fan world would predict.

"My preparation is using my imagination and creating a whole story around who I think this character is before going on set," explains Tonya Crowe. "It wouldn't be based only on how the line sounded, but more about what I could bring to every scenario. I could make any line that they give me real, because I already had a method to that character."

Right in front of an audience of millions, Crowe made the switch from child to grownup star, moving from elementary school age to adulthood over a decade of playing Olivia Cunningham on the *Dallas* spinoff of *Knots Landing*. From 1980 to 1990, Olivia battled drug addiction, almost went to jail for her boyfriend's murder (she didn't do it), married a mobster, and disappeared down to Florida for the show's last few years.

"It wasn't hard for me to get lines down, even as a young girl," says Crowe, whose televised acting debut came on a 1976 episode of *Charlie's Angels*. "I have a very good memory. Now I look back on it as an adult, and I go, wow, I really had a lot of my own methodology. I used a lot of my imagination. I would imagine, create a life for myself out of the script, and I would make opinions about what I liked to do or who my friends were. By the time I was saying the lines, I already had a history, a past in my imagination. That's what made my work the caliber that it was. I never sounded like somebody just saying lines."

Two years into *Landing*, Crowe got a shot at horror that waited a while to put the "super" in front of natural. *Scarecrow* started off more sad than scary; in a precursor to his Emmy-winning work as Benny Stulwicz on *L.A. Law* later in the decade, Larry Drake played Bubba, whose heart of gold couldn't quite overcome his mental disabilities.

At least, in the eyes of most of the southern town, just waiting for him to make a disastrous mistake. But Crowe's Marylee Williams was too young to see the negatives they felt, legitimately or otherwise. Still, when she's nearly killed by a psychotic dog, Bubba's blamed and brutally taken down by an impromptu firing squad, led by Charles Durning's heartless postman Otis.

The justice system doesn't come through (and if it did, the movie wouldn't be made!), but one of the men sees a scarecrow watching over his field. Problem is, he didn't put it there.

Later on, it's suddenly gone. He'll be following suit very soon.

Bubba's back, now as the title character. One villain falls into a wood chipper and doesn't come out alive, or even whole. Otis gets in Marylee's face, but she tells him where to shove it (well, not quite—this was, after all, a TV movie).

"That's the first time you see that there's a dry sensibility that's pulled together," Crowe recalls. "I'm not like most little girls. There's this other side to me. There's glimpses that make you say 'That's a little off for a little girl.' Exploring the duality and the complexity of shooting, I just thought that was a really unique opportunity."

Bubba's scaring form continues his dark work from beyond, innovatively burying another of his killers in a suffocating mountain of grain. Otis kills Bubba's mom, heartlessly blowing up her house, then takes out his last conspirator to keep his mouth shut.

But Olivia is still around. Now convinced that it's actually the little lady behind it all—drunken logic for you—Otis chases her into a pumpkin patch.

"There was a *lot* of night shooting," remembers Crowe. "With tractors coming at me, it was a little bit eerie and creepy, and added to the ability to play that. It wasn't hard to play scared when you are cold and running. It's also super exciting. Any time you're in an unnatural environment, it's always exciting. There were different elements to contend with."

But nothing as dangerous as her pursuer did; Bubba's night-black magic fires a plower to life, and Otis loses his last few seconds to sheer terror.

"It was almost like a movie that was filmed in my imagination," Crowe says. "There are no boundaries of reality. It was one of my first (acting) experiences, and it matched my own version of my imagination. It didn't have the classic, realistic boundaries."

Yes, what of Marylee? We've seen several die violently, albeit justifiably. Rationale and morality aren't really traits of typical horror. Are *all* nearby people going to die? Will the blind desire for revenge keep the scarecrow from remembering one of the few who cared all along?

Or is there something to this that we didn't think of for the film's first 99.9 percent?

The frightened little girl slowly walks out from her hiding spot in the patch. The scarecrow approaches her. She glances up. . . .

And smiles. Then she slyly informs Bubba of her new idea about a "chasing game."

Was it her all along? If part two were to be made (as of 2016, it hasn't), would it be her, pulling Bubba's strings to get back at those that had hurt *her*?

"There are so many parts to her that I love," Crowe says (Drake sadly passed away in March 2016). "Is she good or is she bad? The whole time you're reading the script, you think she's just some sweet girl, and then you get to the end, and you're like, what? Is she the one that's pulling the strings to this vendetta, this avenging murderer?"

Pennywise (Tim Curry) traumatized millions against clowns in 1991's *It*.

Tim Curry:

It

I'M VERY ASHAMED of me.

I can't believe that I worked on a book about horror for years, and didn't think of this until now. Why did I need to write a profile about one crazy-ass clown (the Sid Haig piece in *Welcome to our Nightmares*) to remind me of the guy that absolutely set the role's standard? After being too terrified to forget the character for almost a decade, how could it have possibly taken me so long to include it here?

Well, let's go ahead and remedy the error. Let's talk about the fellow we'd often disliked, but never really feared. Let's talk about a role he played that instilled a new kind of terror, and what he *didn't* have to work with while doing so.

Oh, *It* wasn't first or last time Tim Curry played a bad guy, by the longest of shots. He was on the wrong side in *Annie (1982)*, *Three Musketeers (1993)*, the *Ferngully* cartoon flick (1992), the end of the criminally underrated 1985 comedic *Clue, and just about everything else* (hell, he was even a jerk during a few cameos on TV in 1993 on *Roseanne*!).

"The fact is that the bad guys are always much better written than the good guys," Curry says, "and they're kind of irresistible to play, because they're so much more fun."

But those were mostly light and oftentimes comedic, and there's a big difference between playing a bad guy who's a bumbling and/or a harmless idiot, someone to laugh at when things go the wrong way, and playing someone who absolutely scares the living shit out of you. Someone who gets into your psyche, digs in, and hangs out.

A fear of clowns is common enough that there's an official diagnosis for it (coulrophobia) but I will guaran-goddamn-tee you that *many* people who saw *It* still, over twenty-five years later, still can't look a circus performer in the eye, even those who'd never had an issue before. There's a reason why, according to a longtime rumor that during filming of the 1991 miniseries, even Curry's co-stars were too freaked out to be around him (it turned out to not be true, but you sure as hell can believe it!).

In a TV movie, especially a *non-cable* TV movie, there's much less you can get away with. No major cussing, little blood, hardly gore, very little to see. There's also a smaller budget than films have to kick around—less dough for fancy special effects (horror film trendsetter George Romero, with whom longtime friend King had worked on *Creepshow*, nearly directed the flick before Tommy Lee Wallace got the final nod).

And yet, even with all those hurdles to jump over, Curry managed to drop a gallon-jug of black paint all over our collective subconscious! Whether the word clown is written as a noun or a verb, it's supposed to imply humor, jokes, laughter, etc., and this one took all of those and gunned them straight into the Disney dumpster. From something associated with laughter, he truly became, as Pennywise the evil clown snarled right into the horrified faces of the viewers (on and off the screen!), "Every nightmare you've ever had! *I'm everything you ever were afraid of!*"

"I think you have to be the guy they love to hate," Curry explains," and the fact is that all of us would like to behave badly, all of us would like to behave in an underhanded way, to have the kind of power the bad guys have, and it's important to show that it's *fun*!"

One of Stephen King's greatest strengths as a fiction-eer has always been taking common, everyday folk and putting them into suddenly frightening supernatural situations, as we saw in his writings of *Tommyknockers, Salem's Lot, The Stand, Pet Semetery*, and, most effectively according to me, *Needful Things*. *It* was another standout, as one child after another turned up violently slaughtered in the small Maine town of Derry (not Castle Rock, King's usual hangout). The book and the film both had a very unassuming title, probably because there aren't words to describe what happens in them. Simplicity works the best in situations like this.

As their neighborhood started to panic, a group of kids, outcasts from all but each other because of their (perceived) shortcomings (speech impediments, obesity, poverty, etc.), joined together to face it. One of them lost his little brother to the evil, and things are far past personal now. But this was far beyond anything even their nightmares could come up with. People have debated for decades how King continuously manages to reach into his own mind to come up with things like this, and there's never going to be an easy answer. It's just how some of us are wired.

Before the film's half an hour old, Pennywise has murdered two kids barely up to kindergarten age. But this is TV, and we can't show much. As is almost always the case, the pain, the suffering, the agony, all of it only gets formed and take place in their minds of the audience. Maybe that's why these things are so hard to forget—when we're forced to create something ourselves, to bring something new into our own mind, it might be even tougher to get it to leave.

Focusing in on the few that are getting an idea as to what he's up to, the clown goes straight to their terror. He morphs into a girl's abusive father and a boy's deceased one. He becomes a werewolf for another.

Still, he lets them live, at least for now. Perhaps the ones that died violently, albeit quickly, were the luckiest. Physical torture and murder weren't enough for this horror; this is about destruction from the inside out. Our minds are the only thing we can never really run away from, and what's stuck inside there never goes away, unless we can find a way to let it.

"He's completely irredeemable," Curry says. "He's the kind of chap that's entirely without charm."

But even after the group appears to win, to take out the bad guy, he comes back. He's given them a few decades to recover, to try to forget, but this evil isn't dead. After most of them have moved on to move forward, he comes back for more. Children start to die again. There's one Loser still around, and it's up to him and the rest of the group to put everything they're doing aside and come back for one last (they can only pray) war with everything they've ever feared. It's a battle some don't return from.

Pennywise is back inside and out. He stalks one returnee through a library, another at a movie theater. He shows up at the grave of a young man's brother, the one he helped fill to begin with. He even becomes a gorgeous woman, nearly seducing a man to murder.

That's another reason Pennywise is so horrifying: he can't be killed by conventional means. He can't be shot, stabbed, beaten, etc. Because they are making him. They are feeding him. And when they give the evil he represents a bit too much space, it's now his for the short eternity he gifts them with.

That all of this is associated with the most child-friendly of images just pounds it a little farther into our minds. To do all of this, Curry had to take pleasure all the way to the other side, all the way past wariness, past fear, all the way to lasting terror.

And as a footnote, what's so often and easily glossed over is that Curry's role isn't all that visible. Even in a four-hour miniseries (well, less if we remove the commercials), Pennywise is actually around for less than a fifth of it. We don't see him much during the movie (and when we do, he's hardly in the same shots as his co-stars, indicating much of his filming may have been done separately), but we'll remember him more than anyone else. Just one more bridge Curry had to sneak up on and cross while getting ready for the role.

"Pennywise turns out not to be that physical—it's mostly mental cruelty," Curry explains. "What's fun about him is that a clown is traditionally a very cozy, comforting kind of image, and Pennywise is none of these. I think of him as a smile gone bad."

The clown's pitch-black smile was the first we saw of him before the credits even finished rolling out the opening. A storm rolling slowly toward Derry, a young girl rides her trikey up to her house, crooning out one of childhood's top tunes.

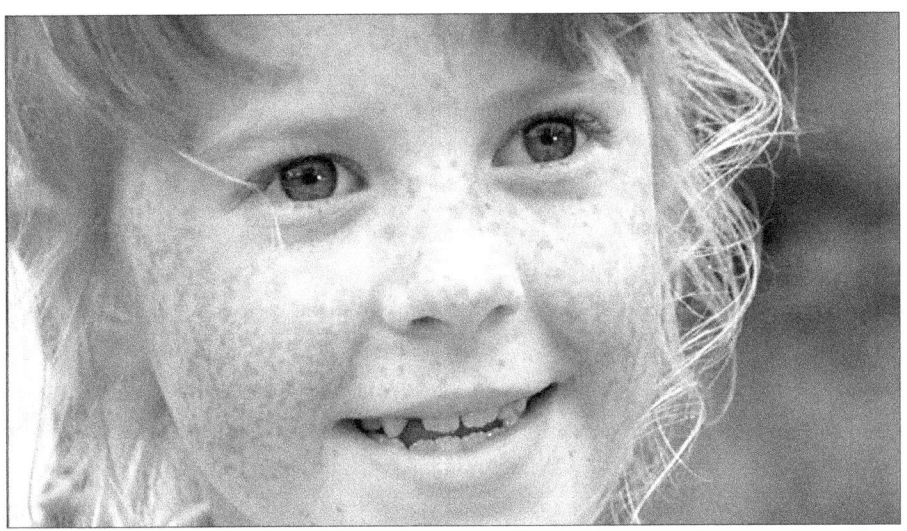

Laurie Ann (Chelan Simmons) casts an uncertain smile as she becomes *It*'s first victim (1991).

"I was at a table reading with the whole cast," remembers Chelan Simmons. "I thought, should I sing?"

One impromptu rendition of the legendary "Itsy Bitsy Spider" later, she got a huge ovation from the *It* In-crowd.

As her Laurie Ann makes her way toward the house, Simmons acted out Wallace's guidance to pretend she'd seen something scary. Through the wind-blown bedsheets on the clothesline, an ominous voice cackles its way into her attention.

Pennywise appears and vanishes, grinning at the child too young to understand what's happening. Then we see him again, and his face isn't so gleeful.

Laurie Ann's own smile starting to fade, something advances on her in slow motion. The scene goes black. When we make it back, her mom will be the only eyewitness to this horrific aftermath. Just knowing that a child was just brutally killed is more than enough to implant it in our minds like a jackhammer.

Even after her short job, Simmons hadn't actually seen Curry in character. But as she walked away from the set, the real Pennywise came to her to say hello.

"Thank God we didn't shoot with him!" recalls Simmons. Later, she'd evolve into adult horror, dying in *Final Destination 3* (2006), *Tucker and Dale vs. Evil* (2010), and the 2002 *Carrie* TV movie, just to name a few.

"A couple of other times, I saw the actors do death scenes, and I couldn't handle it," she recalls of *It* (just to reiterate, she was in elementary school at the time, so she shouldn't have been expected to want to see the full film). "I'm terrified of horror movies in general, unless they're my own and I'm in them."

Curry's Pennywise was full-blown evil, proclaiming his lust for destruction and making not the first bones about any of it, neither human nor remotely humane. Haig's Captain Spaulding was a bit different—murderous, yes, but in a cool sort of way, and certainly of a caring nature toward his family (then again, Charles Manson's family probably felt the same way about old Charlie!). 2014's *Clown* handed us a tug of war between decency and darkness, and Andy Powers was the eager rope.

"The role of Kent really intrigued me because ultimately I was playing two characters: Kent and Clown," Powers recalls of his horror debut. "I have always found the everyman nice guy really challenging. I've always gravitated to crazy or damaged roles."

His Kent was the true man's man, a real estate agent with a pretty good job, a devoted wife, one kid here and another on the way. Unfortunately, that's exactly the type that possessive demons just *love* to reach right out and corrupt, maybe because they just like the challenge of dirtying up the clean!

But this isn't an *Exorcist*-esque entity; rather than just possessing someone for the, pun intended, *hell of it*, the title critter hides inside a clown costume Kent stumbled into to brighten up his boy's birthday party.

It works. But the next day, the wig, the nose, and especially the outfit, won't come off Kent. Eventually, it gets under his skin to his mind, enticing him to carry on the work that it began long, long ago, a job that meant the slaughter of the same youth that clowns, most good clowns, try so hard to entertain at circuses and parties every day.

"Kent is a likable hardworking guy," Powers says. "He loves his family. He wants to live the American dream. Juxtapose that against an ancient demon out to eat children. It's pretty interesting."

Charging into tryouts, Powers was ready to show the dark side of his last name. But it wasn't quite good enough, at first.

"After my first read in the initial audition," Powers recalls, "(Casting director) Billy (Hopkins) said to me, 'That was good, Andy. Do it again and this time, I'm not going to say where, find a spot to be *super evil*.'"

How does one reach such an elevation? Powers wasn't certain.

"I laughed and said, 'Super evil?'" he remembers. "And without missing a beat, he said passionately, 'Super EVIL!'" Powers got his malevolent level to the extreme, and got a shot at Kent.

It's certainly common and very effective to use previous film work as one's preparation, but it's highly unlikely that Powers' pair of "assisters" in this regard have ever been even remotely associated with each other. One's considered pretty legendary in the horror/sci-fi world; the other is one of the many epitomes of guilty pleasure.

"I referred to (David) Cronenberg's *The Fly*," Powers recalls of the 1986 flick. "It wasn't just this monster growing beneath the skin; it was also the invasion into the mind that affected, and altered, motives and instincts."

And the second story? The one that, like with *Kick-Ass* (2010), *Death to Smoochy* (2002), and many others, most people probably secretly enjoyed, but didn't like publically admitting as much?

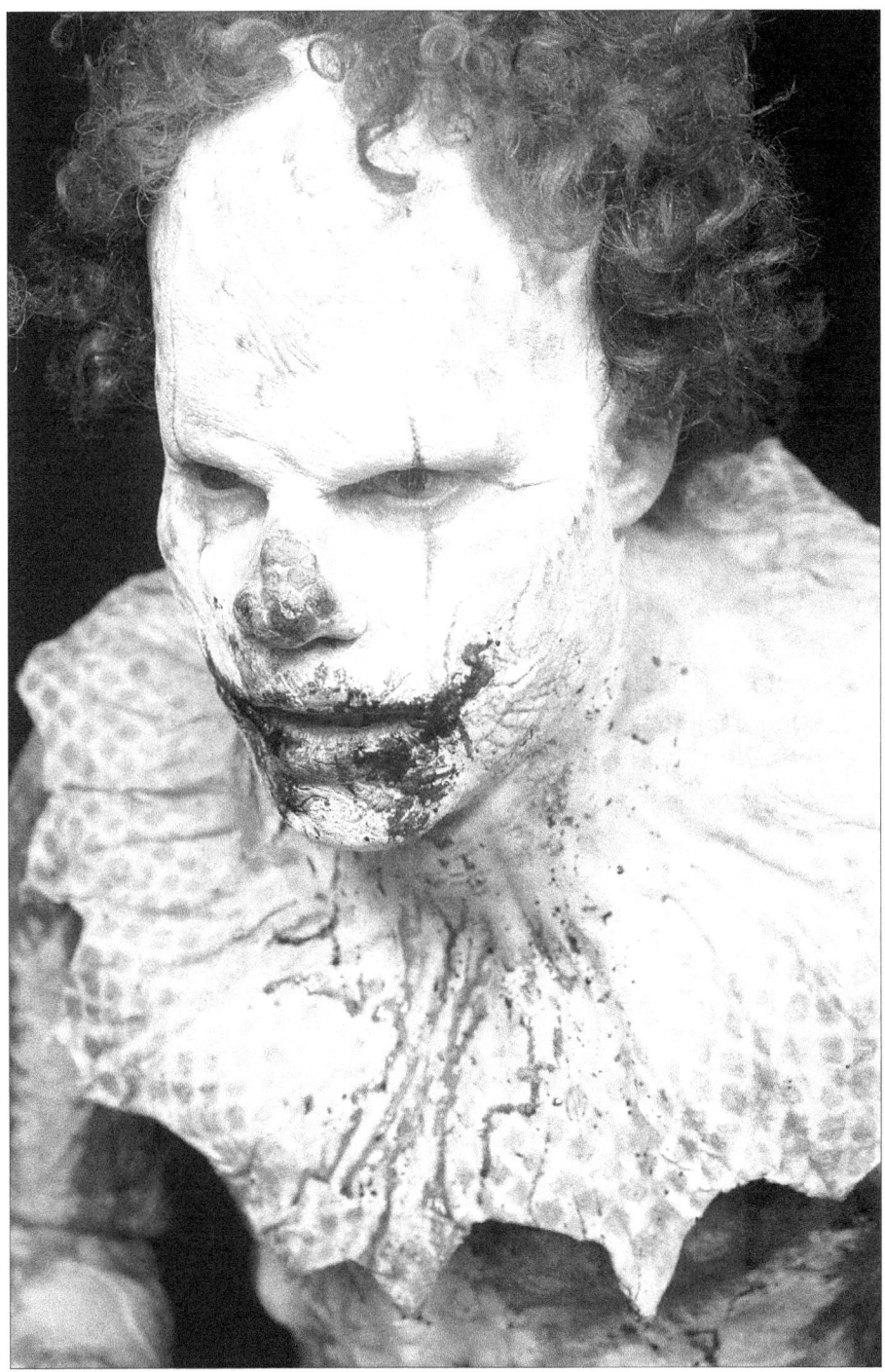

Coulrophobia-causing evil overtakes Andy Powers in the title role of 2014's *Clown*.

Powers and director John Watts discussed Jeffrey Jones' work as a scientist possessed by evil alien mentality in . . . that's right, 1986's *Howard the Duck*!

"I think we bonded there because we both loved that movie as kids," Powers recalls. "The rest of the audition was he and I one-upping each other doing our best 'demon' voices."

As the deadly urges take over, Kent tries to get away from it all, moving from his family and ready to take himself out to off the demon. But two suicide attempts fall short, and a youngster caught in the wrong place at the wrong time becomes his captor's first victim . . . and meal.

"They managed to find the cutest kid in Canada for a gruesome and completely undeserved death," Powers sadly recollects. "That, and the child actor was pretty frightened of my appearance to begin with. I'm pretty sensitive to kids, so it was rough to ignore that and be the thing he's frightened of."

More and more kids die. Kent's wife finds him, and, through the demonic voice that Powers worked so hard on, learns that just one more killing will mean satisfaction (and if you can't trust a demon, who *can* you trust, right?). She even thinks about helping it out. But when their home, their son, and the helpless life still unborn inside of her become the newest targets, there's no way to end this the right way.

Except one.

"Preparation was really laborious," Powers recalls. "I had to break down the script so specifically. It was all about assessing what was happening mentally and physically. Films are rarely shot in the order of the script so I had to keep track of when Kent was 'diminishing' and Clown was 'rising.' Once you're in that makeup, you are committed. To NOT go to an extreme would feel unnatural."

The climax would do so as well; Meg bashes her former hubby's head in with a sledgehammer, but evil doesn't even die that easily. Treating him just as he has so many youths up to now, she's forced to rip his head all the way off.

Ironically enough, as *The Fly* had helped Powers get into character, *Clown*'s ending mirrors the Cronenberg flick; just as Geena Davis' Veronica Quaife wept over the carcass of her love Seth Brindle, whose life she was forced to violently take after he degenerated into something else, something evil, now Kent's wife ends things the same way.

"I always see a role with total transformation as a gift from the gods," Powers says. "I see myself as an actor, not a horror actor. I've only done one horror movie and I think that may be it. But what an it, right?"

Pam McDonald (Vicky Dawson) tries to keep from becoming the next victim of *The Prowler* (1981).

Vicky Dawson:

The Prowler

HE'D KILLED BEFORE, and would love to do so again. Once mass murder's already been accomplished, its perpetrator's got nothing to lose. She had no idea what to do, where to go . . . anything at all. Hiding under a bed, hoping that the super senses her predator had appeared to develop during his years in the service wouldn't be strong enough to detect her, Pam McDonald was on the edge of sanity and safety.

And, as they so often do in the world of slasher flicks, things somehow got worse for the heroine of *The Prowler* (1981). Under the bed with her was a (probably not intentional) co-stalker. One with four legs and a terrible reputation, like its actions in the spreading of the Black Plague that had taken out seven or eight figures' worth of victims (depending on which source you believe) in England a half-millennium before.

Now it and some partners were using Pam as their exploratory land. In and out of character, this lady was terrified.

"The only thing I am afraid of is rats," remembers Vicky Dawson, "so the scene where they had to crawl over me while I was hiding under the bed was a personal challenge."

As slasher flicks stumbled into the American cinema's public eye back in late '70s (which gave us the first *Halloween*) and early '80s (when we first met Jason Voorhees and Freddy Krueger and ran back into

Michael Myers), Dawson took a jaunt away from the TV roles she'd been carrying thus far, all the way to a small New Jersey town, where one unsuspecting (but often promiscuous and/or substance-using) teen after another bloodily fell to the bayonet or pitchfork of a . . . thing in fatigues and military dress, perhaps having brought some demons home from the Vietnam War that America will never stop debating.

Pam would be Dawson's film debut, not just her first step into horror—but her prep methods didn't change.

"The writing and the words spoken need to be looked at over and over," she says of getting ready, "when I'm in different moods, different places. The same words will strike you in new ways and you will gain valuable insights." By the end of the film, Pam's friends could only wish that words were the only things striking them.

As the locals hold their first college graduation dance since some mysterious murders of decades before halted them, we start to find that time does not, in fact, heal all or even several wounds. The title character becomes a one-man invasion crew, jamming a bayonet and pitchfork through necks and chests. Perhaps he still thinks he's back on the battlefield, and, remember, this was *long* before anyone took the whole Post-Traumatic Stress Disorder issue very seriously!

"One of the hardest parts of this film shoot was that the story takes place in one night," Dawson recalls, "and most of the scenes were exterior. So, that means that for nearly two months, we were shooting outdoors, at night, dealing with the elements, etc. We all became nocturnal as our 'workday' took us from about 7 p.m. to 7 a.m. I started to get used to sleeping from about 10 a.m. to 4 p.m. It ended up taking its toll on me, and it was many months before I felt my regular sleep habits return."

With the small local law enforcement crew consisting of one sheriff who's out of town and a deputy who's never been near this sort of thing (not to mention a time *well* before cell phones and e-mails!), Pam's soon left alone with a scumbag looking to kill her from the outside and some rodents driving her nuts from within!

"I liked playing Pam because she was simple and sweet, but determined," Dawson explains. "I knew the audience would have sympathy for her, and, ultimately, her character would carry the movie to the end."

The impromptu detective that so many members of the prey team in horror often become, Pam just happens to fall onto some evidence that the murders of before her time were from a rejection of love, and that the resurrection of the dance caused a flashback in he (whoever he might be) who committed them way back when. Then it's just him and her—and the rats, of course!—in a room, and both won't be leaving.

As her fellow cast and crew members put together their *Prowler* parts, Dawson developed Pam's persona, one scene, one emotion, one mood morph into another at a time.

"As an actor you can never be too prepared," she says. "Sets are busy and distracting, and you need to be in charge of what you are bringing as an actor. As is the case, scenes are shot out of order, so I had to track where I was emotionally in each scene so it would flow naturally." Again, as slasher survivor gals are often forced to do, Pam moves from Sherlock Holmes to UFC champ, going toe to toe with a guy who'd killed so many and somehow coming out on top.

And revealing the reformed soldier's identity along the way: the sheriff, who'd overly avenged his broken heart after the Second World War with the first set of murders, and suffered a relapse from hell decades later. Still, it's the women who (almost!) always win in the end in horror, and Pam's shotgun blast separates his body and head, not too far from what happened to Ms. Voorhees the year before!

Like her, the sheriff doesn't come back. But unlike her, he didn't have any children to avenge him; at least, as of 2016, none had been discovered!

Marcia de Rousse gave her Dr. Ludwig a huge heart and bigger set of guts inside a small stature in *True Blood*.

Marcia de Rousse:

True Blood

DOING THIS SORT of thing to intentionally attract attention is one thing. Doing it to make the best of a sad fact of society is a separate issue.

"I always was a ham," admits Marcia de Rousse. "I loved getting a captive audience and doing things in front of everybody.

"But also, because I'm a little person and I'm different, I figured to just get in front of people, because they're going to look at me anyway."

Indeed, even in the 2010s, people still tend to look down on the little people in society, in every sense of the pun, far too many of us still turning them into unintentional standouts—as though the ghastly act of gawking makes anyone but the lookers look foolish.

But, as she pointed out, de Rousse knew that she'd always be getting the old triple-take from too many in society, so why not give them a reason? While she was at it, why not give the same reason to a few *million*—by stepping into one of TV's hottest series of the 2010s?

It didn't start out that way for de Rousse, whose first role actually came on the big screen; along with many of Hollywood's smallest population, she showed up in 1981's *Under the Rainbow*, a humorized version of the making of *The Wizard of Oz* (1939).

"I really loved to do comedy more than anything else," de Rousse says. "It was something I had born in me. It's been there, probably since a past life." That comment will gain a bit more weight a few paragraphs from now....

Coming off a stage production back in 2008, de Rousse got a phone call from her agent about HBO's new horror show.

"He said there was a cameo appearance on a show in the South about vampires called *True Blood*," de Rousse recalls. "I was going to try out for the role of Dr. Ludwig."

Unfamiliar with the storyline, she tore through Charlaine Harris' literary creations that told the story of a lovely young lady named Sookie Stackhouse, a half-faerie gal who finds herself in the midst of a world of bloodsuckers and realizes that they may not be as evil as people like Bram Stoker wrote. Patricia Ludwig (that's said "LOOD-wig," rather than like Beethoven's first name) was the medical matriarch of the story, apparently having seen something different in med school than her colleagues.

"I read the books and I couldn't be more different in description than Dr. Ludwig," de Rousse says. "She was three feet tall, dark complected, with dark hair."

Ironically enough, it wasn't the first time the four-and-a-half-footer had been above the maximum height for a role.

"I've had the problem of going into auditions and hearing someone say, 'You're too tall,'" remembers de Rousse, whose excessive (in this case) stature had kept her from an Ewok role in *Return of the Jedi*. "Seriously? I'm not too tall for second grade—how could I be too tall for this?"

She'd expected heavy competition, but only two other ladies showed up for the Ludwig tryout. De Rousse called up past and present to give things a shot.

"They wanted to know how I became so sarcastic," she says. "I said it was because I used to teach high school (she taught English, speech, and drama). It's self-preservation." Being from Missouri gave her the authentic Southern belle edge as well.

It was enough; de Rousse snared the role. But she wasn't finished getting ready, and someone else, someone quite unexpected (to most), gave her one last burst of inspiration. De Rousse's longtime friend Zelda Rubinstein, who made her own mark in horror in the legendary *Poltergeist* (1982), had recently passed away; were she still alive, de Rousse believes, Rubinstein might well have become Ludwig.

"I'm a psychic and a medium," de Rousse says. "I heard her saying she wanted me to have the role. She told me in spirit, and I believed her. I believed she helped me with this."

As the series' second season shot forward, Sookie (Anna Paquin) found herself the victim of a maenad, crazed lady followers of the mindset of madness and ecstasy, often pushed to brutal murder, assault, and sometimes even cannibalism. With a huge scratch down Sookie's back (the episode, the third of season two, was entitled "Scratches"), Ludwig arrives to help, nearly shoving Sookie's fanged friends Bill Compton (Stephen Moyer) and Eric Northman (Alexander Skarsgard) aside to bathe her wound in acid, then pull out a claw.

Punctuating her warp-speed medical knowledge with one obscenity after another, it's clear Ludwig isn't the slightest bit worried about working near those who must kill to live.

"In many ways, she was who I am," de Rousse says of her character. "I always believe in speaking my truth, but not as out and out as her. I don't use foul language. But in the script, I went a few steps farther. It was very liberating." Throwing an intimidated Northman a friendly "Fuck off!" as she leaves, Ludwig has made quite the impression—and her work, helped along by a sip of Bill's plasma, brings Sookie back to health.

Ironically, Sookie and Bill's relationship would transfer to Paquin and Compton themselves, who got together early in series filming and married in August 2010. A year later, midway through the fourth season, Ludwig was back, this time to help out one of the other main *Blood* gals.

Pam, Northman's bombshell protégé (i.e., she was a vamp because he'd initiated her) had been cursed by a witch, causing her body to rot from both the inside and out. Ludwig showed up to casually peel the skin from Pam's whole body, letting her know that lifelong injections are the only way to get back to looking good—oh, and staying alive, which appears to be secondary on Pam's priority list.

"The script was so well written that they made it pretty easy," de Rousse says. "I always saw (Ludwig) as being boastful and full of herself, kind of a braggart. I let my imagination go and brought a little of my high school teacher past into that. It was kill or be killed."

Still, even Ludwig had her own vulnerabilities, though we'd have to wait until the last month of *Blood* to find any. On August 3, 2014, in the seventh season's seventh episode, ironically entitled "May Be the Last Time," Bill finds himself in the deadly grip of Hep V, a blood disease as deadly to vampires as wooden stakes and sunlight.

Roaring into action in a black Hummer, Ludwig blasts away once again, peppering Bill and Sookie about how Bill's infection came about (after badmouthing Bill for pointing his fangs at her, of course). But as it turns out, Sookie's faerie lineage began with her grandfather (times a thousand, give or take), whose name plants a fear in Ludwig we may never have known even existed.

Charging from the room, Ludwig's quickly speeding away in the safety of her Hummer. As it turned out, Sookie's ancestors were known for brutally lowering the little people population.

"Her last appearance really culminated in who she was," de Rousse says. "She says what she wants and does what she wants, and walks into any situation with no fear. It's why people loved her. I developed those things with my inner dialogue."

It was Ludwig's farewell; three weeks later, the series came to an end, with Sookie delivering a mercy killing to Bill in one of the last moments.

"It felt like a piece of my life was gone," de Rousse says of the finale. "I cried. I knew I'd be sad, but not as much as I was. I was teary at leaving."

In a film jammed with monsters, zombies, cannibals, and who or whatever else, *Society* (1992) at least had the common decency to let Devin DeVasquez be one of its few normal (and above average!) looking folk.

Devin DeVasquez:

Society

SHE WAS A gorgeous woman—she knew it, and you'd damn well find out (and appreciate the hell out of it) *very* soon!

Speaking her mind, be it forcefully, flirtatiously, or otherwise, would *never* be an issue.

Even from the acting side, performing of the fearful type was a previously explored neck of the woods.

Still, when Devin DeVasquez had a chance for the biggest role of her career, to that point, it wasn't hard to see something new about the character, and the *Society* her gal Clarissa would be a part of.

"This movie was a dark comedy horror that I was drawn to because it was so different," DeVasquez recalls of the 1992 vehicle (actually filmed three years before). "Clarissa was also my first leading role, so she is indeed special for me."

Just about everyone who's made the journey through the mysterious and sometimes frightening world of high school can remember seeing certain people and think that when luck was being handed out, those guys and gals stole everyone else's share. That's probably how most of Bill Whitney's classmates felt about him. Rich family, high marks, impossible not to like if one could hammer back the jealousy. Still, as is probably often the case in reality—*this* issue is considerably rarer!—Bill had a few matters hidden away that lessened his self-awe.

However, they wouldn't stop him from snaring classmate babe Clarissa partway through *Society*. It's just that, when the film's creation kicked off, Clarissa wasn't DeVasquez.

"The role was given to another actress with way more experience than me at first," she recalls. "The director worked with this actress the first day on the set and decided she wasn't right even though they had already hired her. So they brought me back in and had me read every scene again and decided to fire her and hire me."

Society would be the first time filmgoers got to take a long, deep look at DeVasquez, although they'd had glimpses before. She'd been a part of a *Playboy* pictorial in 1981, then gotten an individual spread as Miss June 1985. *Star Search* fans had seen her win a spokesmodel contest. She'd had a small role in the horror flick *House II* of 1987, and used her sexual wiles to overwhelm everyman hero Al Bundy, going topless (from behind, of course), in a controversial 1989 episode of *Married... With Children*.

Bill's Billy Warlock had also started out in horror, with a brief part in 1981's *Halloween II*. *Society*, however, would be his own biggest role, and what a role it was.

Truly showing the film's age, Bill's friend gives him a *tape recording* of his family working its way through a cannibalistic orgy—and teens today think their parents are out there! Then the people around him start to die, and Bill gets the impression that everyone's in on this but him. However, he does take the time to do his thing with Clarissa, never minding her mom being a lunatic herself.

"Clarissa was cool," DeVasquez says. "I loved her lines like, 'Coffee, tea, or would you like me to pee in it?' She did the Sharon Stone open leg thing before *Basic Instinct* (1992)."

More and more die, but Bill's determined to find out the truth, and Clarissa's trying to hide her own secrets long enough to help him out. Back at his upper-upper-upper-class home, Bill lands in the midst of a party for those celebrating just how rich and important they truly are.

Then the final twist arrives. Bill learns that everyone he ever knew—including Clarissa—aren't his friends or family, or even human. Losing their clothes, they begin to act out the tape he heard before, mixing with each other and making meals out of the less "evolved."

Bill's about to be their next victim. But Clarissa, showing that her inside was as lovely as what we could see, helps him escape.

"I worked a month on *Society* and there was not much time to prepare as this was considered a low-budget film," DeVasquez says. "You had one, maybe two takes as an actor to get things right. So it was indeed a learning experience for me. I had to trust my instincts." Like many of its kind, *Society* hit a chord with a small but significant part of the film audience, roaring to cult classic status.

"Spitting in the face of another actor literally was difficult for me," DeVasquez remembers of her toughest scenes. "The special effects were rather cool given the genre. There is talk about a sequel now after twenty-five years." After Hurricane Katrina tore her Louisiana homeland apart, DeVasquez launched the aptly monikered Devin's Kickass Cajun Seasoning and knocked out a similarly themed cookbook to raise funds for victims of a slightly more realistic and certainly much more dangerous force than *Society* ever showed us.

"You never know what role is going to be that breakout role that may propel you to stardom," she recollects to future performers. "I would say work on your craft, your passion first and foremost, and be ready and prepared for the opportunities that may come your way."

Heather Donahue's tear-soaked face became one of horror's lasting images in 1999's The *Blair Witch Project*.

Heather Donahue:

Blair Witch Project

WHO COULD GUESS, have even remotely predicted, that a film with no big stars, no special effects, a budget that wouldn't get anywhere near the shoestring level, and so little else would revolutionize the entire film industry?

That with a little luck, a play on the gullibility of film audiences, and a tap into a newfound curiosity, three actors and a camera could open up a full new production vein in horror moviemaking, one that would never stop being imitated?

No, not 2007's *Paranormal Activity*; without a predecessor, that might never have come to the light, or the darkness. The first-person perspective seeds for that flick, as well as *Cloverfield* (2008), *Quarantine* (2008), and others had been sown long before.

For the female lead of 1999's *The Blair Witch Project*, it all started with a New York acting advertisement.

"An improvised feature film," it read, "shot in a wooded location. It is going to be hell and most of you reading this probably shouldn't come."

Outstanding PR work, isn't it?

But work's work for anyone in the acting field, especially those still knocking on the door to get in, so she went for it. But upon arrival, things didn't exactly clear up.

"They said, 'We want people who can behave completely naturally and can basically act in extreme circumstances,'" she recalls. "'If you don't like that, go away.'"

Uh, OK. Then a crew member came to her.

"He said, 'You've served seven years behind your sentence; why should we let you out on parole?'" she says. "And that was it. No monologue, no scene, no cold reading, just go up without creating the character or creating a story, without thinking for a second."

She made an impromptu impassioned plea for release, and won it (the crew saw something in her "obsessive and slightly psychotic")—straight into a strange new world that's been watched, debated, and, as we will see, taken far too seriously by certain members of the film viewing world.

Then came the tough part: without much of a script or storyline, she and a pair of other budding stars would be left to their improvisational wits to survive in the wilderness—both of the ominous woods of north central Maryland, and of the rough world of acting.

Less than two weeks later, their acting job was done. A year after, they, and their film, would hit Hollywood like a tornado unseen until *Paranormal* arrived.

Heather Donahue, Josh Leonard, and Mike Williams stepped into the story of three people trying to uncover the myth that had tormented the town of Burkittesville for centuries. Bickering amongst themselves almost from the time the last opening credit disappears, the trio eventually find themselves in the town woods, where much of their culprit's doings have been transpiring.

It's Donahue's project (the performers used their real names in the film, which she admits that in hindsight might have added a bit too much to its meanings), and the other two are there to help. She, of course, lets them know it throughout, wavering between classmate and drill sergeant. Rather than looking within for the role, Donahue based her work on a fellow actress whose identity, fortunately, is as secret as the witch's.

"She was one of those people, totally oblivious to the conditions and lack of necessities," she says. "She yelled at us for looking exhausted. I tried to think of my character as 'She has a job to do. She saved a lot of money for a very long time, and she's worked really hard to make this a reality. She wants it to come off well.' My job was just to go for it, get down and dirty. No holds barred, not even runny snot and splotchy cryface."

Perhaps hoping to get a glimpse of the creature, who might just be a Loch Ness-esque hoax after all, she tried to stay optimistic that they'd get in, film, and head back to the car in time to celebrate at the nearest bar with a couple of cold ones. But along the way, the trees seemed to get thicker. The paths became tougher to follow. When she looked behind her, familiarity didn't follow. Days stretched into nights. Food ran low. No matter where they went, everything kept looking different. There was no Internet, no maps, no cell phones, none of the technology of today that much of society would go blind, deaf, and completely insane without.

"I hadn't really thought about how nihilistic it was before," she says of *Blair*. "In a way you could look it as a way of identifying the existence of a greater governing force that punishes arrogance. If we had been less reliant on technology and the security that we enjoy in being divorced from what we used to know, maybe things would have turned out differently. The feeling that you can strip and paint nature bare—there's something very existentially dangerous about that."

As filming progressed, the group started to feel more and more alone in their new world, with the woods stretching farther and farther and something sinister closing in. The stars weren't in a much more stable position, as a GPS device led them to milk crates that the crew had positioned throughout the woods, filled with directions on what to banter back and forth about.

"We would open them up, read our notes, and try not to show them to each other," Donahue says. "So, as the day progressed, we would improvise about the story structure . . . From there we would come up with scenes. We could go beyond what (they'd) given us. We could create scenes and basically take these characters to places (we) didn't even think they would go. We would just go wherever we wanted. That was part of the appeal, was to me, initially, was that I saw an improvised feature. I mean, as an actor you just never get that kind of freedom." Mike's kicking the map into a river was unexpected, and Josh's and Heather's responses were truly those of people whose last link to safety and sanity had been shattered.

They'd get even closer to terrifying realism a few minutes later, as Heather and Mike wake up in their tents to find Josh gone. Their shock was genuine; while they'd figured that the group would be broken up in the film, they didn't know when or how.

"We knew someone would be leaving," she says. "We knew that somebody would have to go to alter the crew dynamic."

In Josh's place, however, his moans and cries of anguish ring darkly through the trees. Soon, Mike and Heather find a pile of twigs on the ground—with some extra additions.

"I went back and I opened them up and we do that whole scene," Donahue says, "and inside the twigs was hair, blood, and teeth. And it was actual teeth that they had brought from a Maryland dentist."

That's when things really start to slip away. Heather and Mike are in someone else's world now, and have been for a while. These woods aren't anywhere near their old lives, and, even if they make it out alive, they'll never be the people they once were.

"The thing that I thought at that time was it would be more effective for me, at that point because my life was already breaking down," Donahue says. "I thought that my character should really keep trying to hold things together and not give up yet. Because she had hope until that professional scene that they were going to find the car and get out there. I think that's then what sort of led into the confessional scene as well is that after trying to hold it together and not giving up hope for so many days, when you can finally just release it and let it go, you can open up those floodgates and they just won't close."

With the film and their journey nearing the end, its signature scene comes about. A tearful Heather, on the brink of at least hysteria and soon outright insanity, seems to know that she's not going to make it out alive. As her wide-eyed, tear-soaked face stares directly into the camera, an image that would be reproduced on the film's posters and home version boxes, she makes an impassioned plea for forgiveness, just in case the tape will be her last chance to say it.

"I just want to apologize to Josh's mom . . . and Mike's mom, and my mom," she stammers. "And I am so, so scared. I'm scared to close my eyes . . . I'm scared to open them."

"The note that I got for the confessional scene was that, basically, I was going to die and I had to make amends to all the people I had hurt," Donahue explains, "to try and die with as clear of a conscience as possible . . . I know a lot of actors draw on personal experience and things like that, but that's never really worked for me because it distracts me from the moment I'm supposed to be playing in and I probably meant being able to surrender to that, to the fictional circumstances when thinking, 'OK, you, now for the last six to eight days, have been holding it in, holding it in, holding it in, and holding it in.' And you just, 'AH!,' you know. All the words were mine."

Frantically trying to maintain some semblance of nature, she tries to stay in filmmaking mode, constantly carrying the cameras around (the three actors filmed the majority of the movie) as she and Mike roam blindly about for safety. Eventually, they make it to a small house, one spoken of in local legend, and dash inside, hoping for any kind of assistance.

But it's not there; Heather charges into a room to see Mike standing in a corner. The camera's suddenly knocked from her hands, and nothing moves again.

"The whole concept was based on that this is about you, your imagination," she explains. "What scares you? It's an imaginative horror film. You have to fill it in with your own thoughts, your own neurosis. Your own bogeyman. We didn't want to make it easy for you."

But what the witch—or whatever it was, as we never truly know—put Donahue through would be nothing compared to the shockwaves that the film would send into audiences when it arrived at America's box offices. It would become the top-ever grossing independent flick until *My Big Fat Greek Wedding* appeared in 2002 (it also set a record for profit margin; at a five-figure budget and grossing over $130 million, *Blair Witch* made thousands for every dollar it spent).

"The very first time that I saw this movie, my life just got altered," she says. "It went right from that first screening at Sundance (film festival) and then after Sundance came the onslaught where you've got to pick an agent, you've got to do this, you've got to get a manager and get a lawyer, have a family of people in nice suits around you who you never knew before. I think that looking at the image of performance on the big screen is not just about looking at the performance on the big screen. It's about everything that comes with that, which is a lot more stunning and in your face." For her, that meant spending an evening on Jay Leno's couch, showing up on an MTV awards show and in the pages of *Entertainment Weekly*, and other ventures.

But then, of course, there came an even darker side to the film than the nights that filming had taken up.

Phrases like "Inspired by actual events," and "Based on a true story," are usually just terms that filmmakers put out to give themselves the right to take creative licensing with their films, and the knowledge that these things are real ("real") gives horror fans just something extra to be scared of, like with the *Texas Chainsaw Massacre* series; basically, if *anything even remotely close to this storyline happened in real life, we can tell our audiences to watch out, because it might happen to them!*

To be fair, *Blair Witch* went a few steps farther. From the start, posters and other ads for the film blared that "Three student filmmakers vanished," and "A year later, their footage was found." And yes, tons of web sites popped up with "obituaries," describing the performers' horrific ends (it's credited as perhaps the first horror film to get a significant boost from Internet buzz). The three stayed out of the public eye to keep the mystique at full volume.

So, to an extent, we might have had reason to believe that there was more to the story than just imagination. But after seeing it, some people honestly continued to believe that it was more than just "based on" a true story.

In other words, there were actually those out there who truly felt that a) such a story could happen without the mainstream media going insane, instead waiting for the movie world to show it; that b) the obtained footage would just HAPPEN to occur in such a film-like order, getting more dramatic as it went along (perhaps the witch found it first, and edited it herself!); and that c) a distributor would be callous enough to put a film depicting the actual loss of human life into nationwide theaters. Those, and about a million other criteria that somehow didn't register in certain minds. "Hey, maybe it's JUST A MOVIE!"

So when things started to cool off for the film, and everyone admitted that it had all been for the show, some people reacted, say . . . less than positively. Some completely blew things out of proportion, as the public often does when it feels it's been lied to (James Frey, anyone?). It wasn't as if anyone had been hurt, but, as Donahue sadly had to find out, with such a large audience, there's bound to be a couple of morons that ruin it.

"I was chased once in my car," she recalls, "been confronted and called names on the street, driven off the road—it's been hard . . . There's a lot of numbness in the world now . . . the more information we have, the more fragmented things become, and the more gaps there are to be filled with fear and anxiety. All this technology for connection and what we really only know more about is how anonymous we are in the grand scheme of things. I don't know if I'm talking now about the success of the film or the fallout."

Many liked the film, and some didn't, and their dislike at the time may have extended to those who put on the show. But now, years later, when we hear Donahue's post-film speculations about its present and future impact, they sound like the definition of prophetic.

"I'm very proud of my performance in this movie," she says, "but I think the thing that I'm most proud of is that Hollywood just does not know what to make of this. That's a good thing for underdogs everywhere. It is possible by some. I mean, I'd believe I'd get struck by lightning better than me sitting here today talking about this, but, it happens anyway. Why? Who knows? Why think about it? Get out there and make your movie, if that's what you want to do. Better than being life or death, you know."

Stay with me for a moment here, but *The Blair Witch Project* actually ended up being one of 1999's most feel-good movies. Not so much because of the film itself, but because it gave hope to young filmmakers and performers everywhere. Sometimes, we can shock the world by having the guts to do what's never been done before, because too many thought it couldn't be. As simple as the self-filmed perspective that made the film so memorable may seem in hindsight, films were around for over a century before someone made it great, and that someone happened to be a person—or a few people—that no one had known beforehand, and that gave hope to those that one day, we all could find our own ground-smasher in films, before or in front of the camera.

Leonard kicked off a solid career in films, appearing in the 2000 Robert DeNiro/Cuba Gooding flick *Men of Honor*, with Kane Hodder in *Hatchet* (2006), and many other films, usually of the independent genre. Williams showed up on several different versions of *Law and Order* and on *CSI*. Donahue grabbed roles on *Without a Trace* (2003) and *It's Always Sunny in Philadelphia* (2005).

"I think it's always hard for actors whose first big movies become etched in people's memories," she says. "I think it was challenging for me to be seen as anything other than 'the girl from the *Blair Witch Project*.' For me, having people stuck in that one perception of me turned out to be a blessing, though it didn't feel that way at the time. It gave me the kick in the head I needed to move on from L.A. and acting. I was able to get back to writing with more commitment and discipline than I had when I was still auditioning. I was able to find a life I love.

"Most important? I learned how to let go. Have the courage to empty the cup, because it will fill again, with something more delicious. I guess it's that whole thing about nature abhorring a vacuum."

But was it actually NOT staged all along? Perhaps, just maybe, the story was true. Maybe the three who stepped into the woods never DID step out again, and only by some quick thinking on the government's behalf kept the story in the area of realistic fiction. Where's Jim Garrison when you need him?

"I'm actually not Heather Donohue," she admits. "I'm a bionic replica made to look and sound just like her—just cuter and more marketable!"

Brad Dourif has turned Chucky into everything but a Good Guy doll through decades of *Child's Play* films.

Brad Dourif:

Child's Play series

DONE RIGHT, A voice used as a horror weapon can reach straight into the psyche and send chills through a viewer's blood and right up their spine. As great an actor as Vincent Price was, his memory for many horror fans (and those of 1983's *Thriller!*) will always go first to his pitch-black vocals. Roger Jackson terrorized viewers through one diabolical speech after another in the *Scream* films, as did Tobin Bell throughout the legendary *Saw* saga.

In the late '80s, Brad Dourif got a vocal chance to add his own tone to horror for his genre debut, and save the category from the satirical campiness he feared it was entering.

"A horror film is not a horror film until you see it," explains Dourif. "It's just a damned movie that you're shooting. Most of the skill is trying to keep yourself present without being present, so that when it's time to go, you can go. It just feels like Halloween, because everyone's wearing some Halloween stuff. It's not real until you make it real, and that's only in front of the camera."

Well, not this time, not really. Most of this role would be behind the camera, before a microphone.

Once again, Dourif was one of many feeling a bit apprehensive about the direction horror was taking at the time, and his role, done incorrectly or inefficiently, could have easily pushed it farther down that road. Not that Dourif's ability was in question—he'd nearly been the top Supporting Actor of 1975 for his turn in the legendary *One Flew Over the Cuckoo's Nest*—but he'd be playing . . . a killer doll.

That's right; a child's plaything might just be the new addition to the world of Michael Myers and

Freddy Krueger! But, hey, this stuff could work: remember how terrifying Talky Tina was in that legendary 1963 episode of *The Twilight Zone*?

So a bit of groundwork had already been laid as Dourif searched for the character that would embody *Child's Play*, a darkly ironic title if horror'd ever seen one.

In the physical sense, getting ready for the role started off just as it would had Dourif had to actually be there and kill that. Rehearsing with his co-stars, Dourif thought about what his cosmetically created self would say if he ("he") were in the same situation as the spirit who'd end up staying within.

"I rehearsed with the actors to give everybody a feeling of what the presence of the guy was," he recalls, "and what I wanted it to be and how the director wanted it to be so we could do live, full-time rehearsals. By the end of that, I knew the lines pretty well."

Fans saw him up close and in dying color as the series started in 1988, as Dourif was Charles Lee Ray, a voodoo guru whose extensive experience in serial murder had earned him the moniker of the Lakeshore Strangler. Still, not even his faith could save him from the gun-wielding skills of detective Mike Norris (Chris Sarandon, stepping far from the villainous role he'd had in *The Princess Bride* a year before), who bumps him off shortly after the first credits.

But just as it looked like *Child's Play* would be one of the shortest films in history, Ray reached deep within and "medium-ized" his soul into the most unlikely of spots: a nearby doll in the Good Guy line of assembly.

Its name was Chucky. Now Dourif had to find a way a way to send fear straight through his voice box.

"I worked on a Chicago accent," he recalls (the storyline begins in the Windy City). "At that point, I had a lot of experience playing sociopaths. This was my first horror film, so I decided that Chucky enjoyed his job, and I would too."

With Chucky now far from a Good Guy, he searched for a way back inside a living being, and his new owner, young Andy (Alex Vincent), might just work. And nothing was going to stop him, even the people that fell victim to Ray's old killing skills.

But though it didn't seem clear, Chucky had a heart, and it ended up being his downfall, as Norris puts a bullet through it to take him out. Still, just as electricity in its natural form had once resurrected Jason Voorhees, a crazed current shoved Ray's entity and Dourif's voice inside Chucky again in 1990, and he came back for a third time the next year.

"When something is animatronic," Dourif explains, "you record the voice first, and the puppeteers use the recording to practice with it and bring the doll to life."

With *Bride of Chucky* in 1998, things started to get, say, a bit farfetched, even for a horror series about a killer doll. Impressing and depressing male fans across the world, Chucky managed to land Ray's gorgeous ex Tiffany (Jennifer Tilly), only to have her transfer into a doll. Not only that, but the two dolls would have an offspring, who got his own film six years later in *Seed of Chucky*.

"Every film is an event, and it has its own character and unique kind of life, and I have to find that,"

Dourif says. "Every story is different, and every concern of Chucky is different, from falling in love, in *Bride*, to becoming a father, in *Seed*."

Perhaps fearing that the comedic campiness of dolls having babies might call the credibility of a horror film too far into question, the *Child's Play* people finally went back to the same ideas that had made Chucky so scary to begin with in 2013. *Curse of Chucky* went back (well, mostly) to hardcore horror as Chucky went to work on the family of Sarah Pierce, Ray's revenge for her calling Norris on him way back when. Much less of Chucky's darkly humorous sarcasm and reproduction here; he was out for revenge instead of resurrection this time, taking out Sarah and other members of her family until it's down to him and her lovely daughter Nica.

And Ray comes back as well, for reasons both in the storyline and reality. Nica's a paraplegic, and we see that it's because Ray stabbed a pregnant Sarah, angry that he hadn't gotten to be the baby's father. And that was a bit more real for those that did a bit of research on the *Curse*; Nica was Fiona Dourif, Brad's real-life daughter.

"I normally do a great deal more preparation," Dourif admits, "but this time, I let Chucky find me—and he's been dogging me ever since!"

Two years to the day after Chucky first came out to play, he came right back, rebuilt by the company who nearly went out of business after its product became a pint-sized adorable serial killer. Andy's now a more convenient target, stuck in a foster home.

Fortunately for him, so was a new protector. Also fortunately for him (and probably Vincent in the bargain!), said newfound bodyguard just *happened* to be the type of gal that helped coin the whole "schoolboy crush" sort of terminology!

"How do you prepare for that?" Christine Elise recalls of her first acting gig. "I can't set up a scenario when I'd be chased around by a killer doll, so there's no way to prepare for it, nobody to speak to to find out what that's like. So you just have to play it like you're against anybody who would kill you."

A foster kid herself, her Kyle gave Andy the type of protection she'd never really had herself, even if it meant brawling with an undead toy.

"It was really, really exciting to get, and it was really fun to do it," Elise says. "I'm an actor and I wanted to work. I have never been an actress that has the luxury of picking and choosing. That is a misconception many have: that an actor's résumé reflects their taste in projects. That is only true for that handful of A-listers. The fact that I was never in *Twin Peaks* or *The Wire* or *Breaking Bad* does not mean I did not love those shows. It just means I never got that opportunity. So, especially in the beginning, I took every audition my agent gave me, and I took any job anyone offered me, unless it had nudity or was embarrassing. You have to take what you can get. That said, *Child's Play 2* was a huge score for me! I was really, really excited to get that part."

Chucky indeed tried to get back at his former prey, searching for a way to implant Ray's mind into a much smaller body. Elise got ready for the sequel by looking over his first bit of cinematic antics.

Christine Elise's Kyle tries to protect her friends from Chucky in 1990's *Child's Play 2*.

"Most of the jobs I've gotten in my career, you get hired, and you're working in just a couple of days," she says. "You get the job on Monday, you're working on Tuesday, sometimes. There is no time to prepare. But I have never had a role that required anything of me other than to convincingly portray another human—though sometimes in situations I had never experienced. I can't ever know what it is like to work in an ER or be a wounded firefighter, or be a doctor telling parents their child died. So—for me, I prepare for roles by just living a full life."

Chucky does his damnedest to ensure most around wouldn't get such a luxury. He kills Andy's teacher and foster parents, then some others. It's down to him and Andy way back where at the Good Guys factory, but Kyle's still around.

"Seven-year-olds don't always make good decisions," Elise says. "Kyle's handicap was having to take care of a seven-year-old, and that made it believable that she'd be vulnerable to a three-foot doll. Otherwise, she could just run away forever. But she was a foster kid herself and she understood being lost and unwanted. I think anybody would have protective instincts toward Andy, especially if they identified as being an unwanted kid."

However, Kyle's "dollistic" wars would come to be one of the easier portrayal aspects, she continues.

"It was difficult, because the doll took seven or nine puppeteers to work at the time," Elise says. "Alex Vincent was a minor, so he could only work short hours. We'd do the wide shots of scenes that involved all of us, and then Alex would go home. Then we'd shoot the doll and send the puppeteers home, and then they'd shoot me, the close-up stuff. If you don't see Alex or Chucky in the scene with me, they probably weren't there.

"I was reacting to tape," Elise recalls of her performance. "People would say '*That* red mark is Chucky, and *that* blue X is Alex!' There would be somebody by the camera reading the dialogue, and I'd have to act in a vacuum. That was challenging."

But the impromptu trio was certainly together for the end, as Kyle and Andy nearly drown (can a doll be drowned?) Chucky in wax, then use his head for overstuffing balloon practice, blowing it to bits with an air hose. Until the third film became a charm in 1991, of course.

Even with only his voice to work with, Dourif had at least had a physical jumping-off point to create his character: the form of the doll himself, which Dourif could look over and use to develop Chucky's situational emotion. For much of her earlier solely vocal work, Denise Poirier had as well, even if her role models were drawn.

"As for preparing for voice-over," she explains, "I think the key is to imagine oneself within the physicality of the character. I always imagine myself speaking from within that person's body, from their mouth even. Otherwise, it seems like you're adding a layer to the character that doesn't quite fit."

In 1995, a decade before Charlize Theron acted out the lady on the big screen for *Aeon Flux* (2005), Poirier had spoken for MTV's cartoon version of a secret agent that died in every episode (did *South Park* steal it when they started slaughtering poor Kenny McCormick on a weekly basis two years later?).

"With *Aeon*, I had a storyboard for every episode, which was so great," Poirier remembers. "The dialogue was sketched in along with the images. There were a lot of action sequences with *Aeon*; I had to be prepared to know which 'grunt' was which—was she throwing herself off the train, or getting hit by someone, or hitting someone?" She'd voice out another small-screen version of a film with the animated *Spawn* in 1997.

"When you're in a recording session, you often don't have a lot of time for direction, except for the specifics to that take," she says, "so it's hard to make major adjustments when you're in the booth. One has to rehearse a lot: get *really* familiar with the script. You also make lots of notes, and highlight words that are important, the 'music' of the sentence and paragraph. You need a good sense of how the lines flow, and what the point is—what, in the end, is the important part of this sentence/paragraph?"

Again, even for cartoons, most voice actors get at least *some* representation of he or she or it that will be speaking their words. *Deep Dark* (2015), through, presented an even tougher challenge for the actress.

Her character would be a hole in the wall. Literally, just a hole. One that speaks. Repeat: she'd be playing a hole with vocal capabilities.

And assuming the audience could get past that, she'd have to convince us, through only speech, that a hole could go evil—enough to entrance a new resident, and enough to literally kill another.

Basically, she'd be the blackhearted relative to the computer that Joaquin Phoenix's Theodore Twombly had fallen in love with two years before in *Her*, as Scarlett Johansson had voiced the caring machine through a screenplay that brought Spike Jonze a statuette.

"I've done narration and recorded audio-books and such, but this was on another level," Poirier says. "It seemed like it would be challenging and fun. Whenever you can find something that's interesting, and you like the people you're going to work with, it's just a win-win situation."

Winning is a pipe dream for film main man Hermann Haig (Sean McGrath). He's been a sculptor, at least in his own mind, his whole life, but no one takes him seriously. In a business where the difference between beauty and disgust lay almost solely on who is expressing an opinion (much like book writing!), no one wants Haig's name on their agent list or gallery.

He's full of hopes and dreams, but bill collectors and landlords don't accept that kind of currency. With nothing to do and no one to call, Haig collapses in despair in his new apartment.

Then he hears something. A voice pokes out of the ugly hole in the wall nearby.

Is it a neighbor, spying on him? A kid playing an idiotic joke? He hopes not, because it sounds like a lady: a very sultry type of lady. If she looks like she talks, he'd like to see her!

She, or "she," is the first to even *sound* friendly and encouraging. Even entities get lonely once in a while. But he's there now, and she might just be able to help him out. Others have lived here before, and she's watched them, chatted with them, learned from them. She might just be able to offer up some career advice.

The whole reality thing isn't working out too well for Haig, so why not try the unbelievable? She helps him put together some models that wow hell out of the local art community, including high-class agent Devora (Anne Sorce), impressed enough to possibly move their relationship past the professional level.

But the hole isn't having that. Haig's her first human contact in forever, and she's not giving up so easily. His career is because of her, and he owes her.

"It was kind of crazy getting into her mind," Poirier says. "The description was that she's an ancient, sinister being. She's from outside of his world, drawing him in." There's a neighbor who's into Haig. She disappears. Then in wanders a guy whose path to art success was clear and simple . . . until Haig and his not-so-holy-hole friend took things by storm.

The two men struggle, and the intruder's suddenly up against Poirier's mouthpiece. Then we see why he can't get away.

Something's being yanked from his back, and it looks pretty important. It gets all the way out, blood included, and he's down for good. We see the world through the hole's eye.

"It was interesting having a limited view of Haig's world," Poirier recalls. "With the camera angle looking out from the perspective of this creature. She has to draw him in, to pull his attention into her world, and only with the use of her voice, and seduction."

Perhaps truly believing that she's actually in a horror movie, Devora accepts Haig's confession of his unnatural relationship. But her blow to his head puts him down, and we see her against the wall too—but she's got a chainsaw, slicing away, the critter's blood pouring from the wood. She's going to make it her own impromptu assistant.

Well, no, she's not. Now she and Haig are at it, and perhaps the hole's got something to do here as well. They topple to the floor, and her tool just happens to cleanly remove all her fingers. No more art, check writing, even handshakes will ever be left to her again.

With her gone, Haig's not sure what to do. Should he attempt to destroy the thing that made him a success? Might he be the victim of the hole's fate? Is it worth taking a chance?

Of course. Why mess up a good thing? He hides his new friend with a photo. Looks like their work will continue as long as galleries appreciate it.

"The 'intimate' scenes are always tough," Poirier says. "One tries not to feel embarrassed while recording. The session really has to be a safe place—where you feel like everyone is respectful of what's happening—which absolutely happened with this project."

2015's *Felt* told us the sad, scary story of Amy, a woman who used her artistic interests to cope with her victimized past—until the demons simply grew too strong.

Amy Everson:

Felt

ONE WAY TO fight rape is to declare war on it. Anyone who calls that an overstatement probably hasn't had it happen to them. It may go right or wrong, but any other response has its risks as well. It's as good a tactic as any.

Maybe it's healthy and maybe it isn't. It might heal the ones it's hurt (a number that sadly increases probably every damned hour), it might not. But we don't need to worry about that. If it works for us, that's all that matters.

Those who saw 2015's *Felt* watched a lovely young lady do just that. Many wished they could do what she did.

And so did the lady who played her, who'd made her, who'd become her.

It's a film about rape. That's enough for horror. But *Felt* isn't about the act itself; we've seen that more than enough times. No, it's about someone who had to move on afterward.

She'd written the screenplay. Now Amy Everson was the female lead, in her first big-screen work.

The Amy she played carried more than a bit of Everson herself: not just because the two shared a moniker or some unusual tastes in art.

"It was an opportunity to share my experiences," Everson remembers. "I pulled from my own experiences and embellished on them. I pulled from my personal trauma and depression and the horrors of sexual violence."

"My life is a fucking nightmare," Amy sadly informs us off the bat, aimlessly walking around town, wearing only one of her strange hoodie-type artistic creations. She's been through something you never get past. Yeah, there's tons of people to talk to and places to go, but none of them give a rape victim a simple, effective way to recover. Women like her often become targets of the self-righteous who've never been through it, wondering why she can't just pick up the pieces and move on.

Well, maybe because no fucking rape victim ever has. Not right away.

Felt, at least at first, comes across very documentary-ish. Amy's narrating so much that we expect to see her speaking to the camera with a microphone in her shirt, punctuated by flashbacks in photos and videos. That doesn't become the case.

"While we were still brainstorming the film," Everson explains, "(director Jason Banker) followed me with a camera, and I was comfortable enough to live my life as he was following me, documentary style. I was able to show my emotional turmoil."

It didn't take long, and that wasn't fortunate for anyone.

"We jumped right into filming," Everson says. "On the day he arrived, I was having a rough time, crying and depressed, and I didn't hold back. He started shooting, and that kind of helped build the story. I was going through old journal entries, stories from my past, the majority of my experiences of sexual violence."

Amy finds as much solace as anyone in her position can in her art, often modeled after the human body, including some parts that women will never experience. She often drapes her entire body in it, in and out of public. We see her doing some reluctant modeling. The art she creates isn't just a hobby; it's a whole different world in which she becomes a whole different person. A lady who hasn't been through her pain. A woman who can approach a world where happiness and innocence still exist. It's who she once was and wishes she, in some strange way, could be again.

"I just pulled it from my life," she explains. "Body suits, underwear with genitalia, things I made several years before filming, just to make whatever comes to my mind with felt. I did some soul-searching through the course of filming. The art was me trying to take control over things that disturb me and find humor in them, to appropriate the male form and take control over things I have no control over. With introspection, I realize that the language was very crude and very sexual and realize now that it was a coping mechanism to find humor or make light of what my trauma was based on, to try to find control."

The new Amy, the inner creation the character finds, still knows how to be friendly, even flirtatious, even alone with a man. But she still hides herself, even seemingly trapping herself, wearing her art and nothing else.

"A lot of the film was improvised, from my life, relationships, therapy, addressing my past experiences," Everson says. "I tried to break down these experiences with a male co-star."

And along the way, she got some unexpected and totally unwelcome assistance.

"Being groped and catcalled by (a crew member) over the course of filming was very insensitive," she says. "Him following me with a camera, getting drunk, making sexual advances, mirrored a lifetime of experiences. The irony was that he capitalized on my anger toward him, but it was out there, and it resonated with him. It was weird, feeling that way."

It looks like Amy might just be ready to build a bridge between who she is and who she formulated. She's out with her guy friend. He's wearing some of her art. She's got a costume on. Per usual for the film, it includes a penis, and he doesn't seem (too!) creeped out.

But as we said back at the start, some people fight rape and the trauma it puts them through with violence. With war. And in every war, innocent people get hurt and killed.

Amy's experience sent her down the path of destruction of a gender. Most men consider rape to be the ultimate evil, but she can't be bothered with rules and their exceptions. One of *them* did this to her, so another's going to pay his price.

She goes nuts with a pair of scissors. Then she castrates him.

Then she plants his manhood on her costume and wears it as proudly as a medal.

"It made enough sense that there was an arc to the storyline, a woman traumatized and appropriating the male figure, taking control," Everson says. "Chopping off someone's dick has always been a joke of revenge on the people that have harmed me. It seemed appropriate: putting the penis on myself is what makes the film a tragedy. I become the monster."

The final scene probably shocked many into silence. But when rationale made its way back, *Felt*, admittedly by imposition, planted a damned good reason to bring rape to the public forefront.

"There is progress," Everson says, "but I've learned from conversations I've had since the reception of the film, and my personal experiences, that there is still a long way to go. Some people say thanks for speaking about my experiences with sexual violence, expressing the anger and pain, and tell me stories about their dramatic past. Others say they've never experienced it, so it's not true. The film is much more involved with the knowledge of sexual violence that affects so many people and relieving the silence of people from talking about it. We need to have a conversation about these issues."

Megan Franich played head vampire-ess Iris through *30 Days of Night* (2007).

Megan Franich:

30 Days of Night

FINDING THE NEXT character in our acting career often forces us to look deep within ourselves, and we might not expect what we locate there. However, it might still be the most pleasant of surprises—exactly what we need to become something far from ourselves, and, as we've seen throughout *Behind the Screams*, far from humanity.

"As an actor you have to probe your very makeup to find out what makes you tick, and then how to illicit certain emotional responses," explains Megan Franich. "You have to know, in essence, how to manipulate yourself. Actors have to do a lot of self-exploration. There is no manual because each person is so unique." And again, as we have seen so many times throughout this writeup, often the uniqueness of human minds, together or as one, can come up with more than enough creativity to find variations to ever degree on people, places, and surroundings to make performers busy for generations. It's what keeps performers like Franich so hard at work exploring some of the most diverse of artistic expression.

"In everyday life there is an acceptable spectrum of behaviors and emotions experienced day to day," she explains. "When I choose the role of a person who lives outside of that range, that's when I really get to play. Exploring how to genuinely feel and think things that I wouldn't usually is challenging and when it works can be exhilarating. Finding out how to shed my own skin and completely become another person is exciting." Even becoming the type of person ("person") that survives on mass murder, as we'll see!

If nature were charitable enough to allow more "polar nights" to run rampant, vacationers would have a blast. Basically, it's the term for days and nights that run for longer than twenty-four hours straight, and sometimes for weeks at a time. Going by sunsets and rising, we could play semantics into "three days, two nights" running all the way into months!

On the other hand, such an event would be carte blanche for horror's blood-guzzling population, something a group of Alaskans learned the fatal way in 2007's *30 Days of Night*. Five years after the country's comic-craving crews poured over panels and pages, the film hit the big screen. One such avid *Night* reader charged to the cinemas.

"I am a huge fan of fantasy," Franich says. "I loved that this film fell into the realm of the unreal. It's so intriguing to me."

As night and blizzard team up on the mere mortals of the area, the not-yet-dead of the area take advantage of Darkness Savings Time, feeding on one human after another. Heading up the pack is none other than Danny Huston's Marlow, with his lovely lass Iris right by his side, along with top lieutenant Arvin.

"I loved playing a character that started in such an extreme place," Franich says. "It was up to me to work out her backstory and what might have happened for her to get to that place."

It's a popular misconception than anyone bitten by a vampire becomes one; vampires would have taken over the world if that were the case (they'd also die out fast, as they can't feed off each other). As we've learned in *Interview with the Vampire* and other such tales, the "conversion" technique is quite different—most people chomped by vamps just die. There was a time when Iris had been just one of us, until someone, probably Marlow, saw something special inside.

"I created a history for Iris and worked with creating her life before becoming a vampire," Franich remembers, "what she was like as a person, her relationships, the situation of how she was turned, and how, eventually, she came to embrace that new 'life.' I explored how I would feel being in that situation: what it would feel like to lose everything and everyone I love and to then live with the creatures who took it from me, and to be one of them. What then would it take to accept that way of life? I imagined the scenarios necessary to get myself into the right frame of mind to be, literally, a bloodthirsty killer." She and Huston worked out their own pseudo-bio together, creating Marlow and Iris' eternal life and love to go with it.

Meanwhile, Andrew Stehlin turned himself into Arvin, out for blood in every sense of the saying.

"We went through some training with (Director) David (Slade)," Stehlin says. "He wanted these Vampires to movie different to the rest of the vampires that had come and gone . . . We started moving the way he showed us, then we screeched like Ringwraiths (the hooded Hobbit-stalkers from *Lord of the Rings*). The attack was intense as when we attacked our victims, we would go in like sharks and tear into their throats with violent movements, whipping our heads from side to side. It took awhile to get the movement to how David wanted it."

Even before Bram Stoker's original saga made it to the screen, Max Shrek portrayed the fanged count in *Nosferatu* (1922)—and did so years before talking on film was even innovated. Huston and Franich had similar issues to develop; Marlow used a tone similar to Bela Lugosi's Hungarian accent, with snippets of other languages far from Alaska. Iris didn't speak at all, merely cackling during her deeds and roaring in triumph afterwards.

"It was very liberating and taught me a lot," she remembers. "When you don't have words to express your emotions, body language has to do it for you. It also let me keep my energy a lot more centered. You can give away a lot of energy with your words, which is often a great thing, but it was nice to experiment with not doing that." Moving the vampires' eyes apart took hours a day in the makeup chair, Stehlin adds.

"We then put a little of our own characteristics in there, just to make it that little different from everyone," he says. "There's one scene where Arvin walks into the house that (the humans) were in, bunked in the attic. The head movement like a snake, I thought that would stand out, leading with the head and then the eyes follow."

Flick hero Eben (Josh Hartnett) braves the white stuff to lure his unwelcome trespassers to a nearby house—as everyone knows, *nothing* pisses a vampire off more than screaming, "Hey, motherfuckers!" at them. From high above on a nearby roof (perhaps they morphed into bat form and flew up when we were watching elsewhere!), Iris and her man scan the potential meal. Franich called the scene even tougher than acting out murder.

"I was getting a sense of vertigo being so high on a sloping surface, even though I was completely safe and was wired up," she recalls. "It was awesome to confront a fear and do that scene. I feel like I overcame my fear that day and haven't been afraid of heights since!"

We're not surprised to see Iris leading the attack on Eben. But he's ready now; equipped with an ultra-violent ultraviolet light, he blasts her away, burning her almost to death, and Marlow's forced to finish the job, a type of mercy and love that vampires rarely get to show. Arvin manages to take out Eben's friend, but meets his end at the blades of a shredder.

As an actress, Franich explains, "If you feel like you are doing everything you can to be the best you can be, it takes away so many of the other stumbling blocks towards achieving your dream . . . Your job, your *only* job, is to embody the character. When you are doing that to the best of your ability, not only does it take away any stress or distraction, you actually wind up having a lot of fun!"

Speaking of the gorgeous gals for a vamp man. . . .

All the "Draculas" throughout history have shown some fine taste in women, but it's only recently that *we've* come to know them. The bigamous fanged man's gals were little more than stunning statuettes when Bela Lugosi and Jack Palance played him, but Stoker had made them hardcore succubi in his book, and we finally saw this acted out in Francis Ford Coppola's 1992 version.

Dracula's guest Jonathan Harker (Keanu Reeves) wanders through the count's castle, led along by seductive voices here and there. He's soon happened upon by three gorgeous gals, who work him, and each other, over until the eternal realtor (Gary Oldman) shows up and takes over. He's actually their husband, and how he got so lucky is as big a mystery as anything else in the book (one such babe was

On behalf of their husband Dracula, Allera (Elena Anaya, left) and Verona (Silvia Colloca, right) prepare to turn Princess Anna Valerious (Kate Beckinsale) into lunch in 2004's *Van Helsing*.

Monica Bellucci, who'd star in the *Matrix* films and play Mary Magdalene in *The Passion of the Christ*).

Van Helsing had shown up in the backgrounds of several Dracula flicks in the past, usually armed with a cross and crossbow, but not until 2004 did he grab his own flick. Hugh Jackman's title character, on a mission from the Vatican higher-ups, shows up in Transylvania for his next assignment: to do what *many* men have done before and kill Dracula.

This Count's ladies, however, have much more than looks and sex appeal. Before we even see their man, the three of them swoop down upon the place's newcomer and the rest, ready to kill to protect.

"I have always appreciated the horror genre," remembers Silvia Colloca, "but I never thought I would end up in scary movies myself! I always wanted to be an actress, ever since I can remember." Her Verona, individualized by her flowing brunette mane, was the unofficial leader of the ladies, with Allera (Elena Anaya) and Josie Maran's Marishka behind her in battle.

The three are out to snare local leader Princess Anna Valerious (Kate Beckinsale), laughing off the arrows that Van Helsing fires through them. They even toss an innocent cow through a roof, showing how viscous they truly are! But just as Verona and Allera trap the princess in a room, fangs bared, the hunter guns one more arrow, punctuated with holy water, through their sister, leaving the two of them to depart in heartbreak (and the cow's seen OK!).

"I was very young and rather naïve when I was approached to audition for *Van Helsing*," Colloca says. "I was living in Rome and I had no experience of English language films, let alone Hollywood studio ones. So, I just went in for my screen test quite recklessly and perhaps it was because I was so relaxed that I was successful in winning the role." Her character would be in a much more emotional situation, as would her hubby the Drac man (Richard Roxburgh).

Trying to unleash their new arrivals upon the world, Dracula and his gals look for a new life force. Vampires having children has always been an iffy topic in the tales, but the spin here is that the kids are born dead, and must be fired up with someone else's "beingness." Anna's brother Velkan, himself a werewolf victim, becomes the unwilling guinea pig, and the brides lead their offspring straight back to battle in the village. But just as they're about to commit some induction attacks, things go wrong.

"When I signed on to do *Van Helsing*," Colloca remembers, "I had no idea I would be doing all my stunts! I wasn't very fit back then, rather skinny and with zero muscles, so that was a bit of a tough call. To top it off, I am scared of heights, which made most of my flying/jumping sequences really scary."

Just when the vampires have too many numbers, they're defeated from within. Before their moms' eyes and wings, the babies explode—Velkan didn't have enough life force to make them eternal. After losing her fellow bride and all of her kids in such a short time, it's tough not to feel sympathy for Verona.

"She appeared to be very worldly, like she had been around for a few centuries and would not be bothered by tedious things," says Colloca of her character, "and she would let the other two brides get their hands dirty instead! Verona is one classy vampire bride."

The girls have once chance left—steal the monster that some crazy doctor put together and use him to power up the little ones. But Van Helsing tricks Verona into opening up a carriage filled with explosives, which puts a quick end to her "eternal-ity." Aleera manages to grab Anna, but a stake through the heart makes Dracula a full-blown widower.

Ironically, Colloca and Roxburgh's relationship imitated fiction soon after the film's release; in November 2004, the pair wed.

"Life as an actor is challenging enough," Colloca claims, "(and) aiming for fame is not the sensible path to follow. Study hard, be always on time, be polite, and take in criticism. If you are desperate to be in horror film, work on your evil laughter or a killer scream!" Verona utilized both in abundance.

"In short, never take yourself seriously. But treat the profession with respect."

Ben Woolf's Meep takes center stage in *American Horror Story: Freak Show*, spurred on by strongman Dell (Michael Chiklis). Tragically, Woolf was killed in February 2015, shortly after the show's season ended.

The *Story's* Freaks

THERE WAS A time when "freak shows" were a part of American cultural entertainment. As much as the cotton candy, shooting gallery, and petting zoos, the freaks were the fairest of attractions.

Today, the world of the small-time traveling fair is about gone, and the freaky parts along with it. Most people seem pretty happy about this. After all, to them, these shows are about exploitation, the reason why greed is one of the seven deadly sins. Nothing but some cold ringmaster (or mistress) carting out the physically and mentally challenged to make a few extra bucks, then turn them out into the unforgiving open when people get tired of them!

Still, we don't hear much, not nearly enough, from the participants themselves. The ones that we (used to) pay to walk in and look at, to photograph, to stare at in awe and/or make snide comments towards. The freaks haven't gotten much of a chance to speak their own psyches.

If we did, we might just get a whole new perspective on these things, these events, these freak shows. What they mean to the most important ones of all.

His life hadn't even gotten a fair chance to start, and Ben Woolf was already faced with more tragedy than anyone deserves. The victim of an under-functioning pituitary gland, he was wracked by chemotherapy treatments that further stunted the hell out of his growth.

And even in a city that all but boasts of its diversity and acceptance, Woolf found himself looked down upon for reasons far past his lack of height.

"L.A. is kind of hard (to live in)," he remarked. "You don't think it would be. You think they'd be more accepting of people who are different. It's kind of the opposite. A lot of people don't treat me like an adult."

The fourth season of *American Horror Story* told us this story in 2014. It showed that, yes, while the public that Woolf described has always been around and perhaps even worse than it is today (the show took place in the 1950s), those that everyday folk call freaks find in their shows the only real place of acceptance. Not from the public that visits, but from each other.

Like many people who work in the business, Woolf had to eke out his living in an unfairly limited area.

"I'm a preschool teacher when I'm not acting," said Woolf, who'd briefly appeared on the *Story*'s first season as a resurrected fetus who went on a killing spree. "I love it, because when you're with children, you live in a different world that doesn't have any rules, that's more imagination. I relate acting to that, because I try not to censor myself or their thinking."

Again, *Freak Show* showed us one of the few areas that the unfairly afflicted can find someone who's sitting right next to them in the boat. It showed us the sibling-hood that all the participants share—and the loyalty that keeps existing after they have to say goodbye.

Freak Show started out just as its first three predecessors did: same performers, different characters. For the fourth straight year, Jessica Lange was heading things up, this time as Elsa Mars, the owner of the title escapade. A year after she and Lange won Emmys for the third season of *Story*, the witchery tale of *Coven*, Kathy Bates appeared as bearded babe Ethel. Evan Peters got a new kick at the *Story* can as freak man Jimmy, whose hands grew longer and larger than anything else on him (he was also Ethel's son, but we didn't know that until a bit later in the season).

Show veteran Sarah Paulson was also back, in a way *far* from she'd been before, playing two-headed twins Bette and Dot Tattler. Naomi Grossman was another returner, re-playing the pinhead Pepper that had been a hit two years earlier in *Horror Story: Asylum*.

And, of course, there would be Woolf's work as a scared young fellow named Meep—after the only syllable the character could say.

"Meep is a simple character who speaks in one word," Woolf explains. "When I play Meep, I want people to feel happy and realize that although he doesn't say a lot, that he's saying a lot in that one word."

Meep wouldn't be around long—and, tragically, neither would Woolf.

Right around the time *Freak Show* took place, storyline-wise, thousands of upcoming moms were using thalidomide to fight back their morning sickness, a drug they didn't even need a doctor's note to grab. Unfortunately, actually tragically, the drug caused defects in thousands of new babies, who were

From left, Amazon Eve (Erika Ervin), Ma Petite (Jyoti Amge), Jimmy (Evan Peters), and Paul (Mat Fraser) hope their show finds some new life in *American Horror Story: Freak Show* (2014).

themselves lucky enough to survive, unlike thousands of others. Blindness, deafness, heart defects, and other awful deformities were seen in thousands of kids across the world.

Including Mat Fraser. The medicine gave him phocomelia, which kept his arms from developing, leaving the British youth with hands that appeared attached to his shoulders.

"As a disabled guy, there was no one disabled on TV," he says, "no role model to aspire to or be like, except David Carradine's blind teacher on *Kung Fu* (1972). I was dissuaded by the notion that people were embarrassed by the notion of a disabled character on television." He went to a new brand of entertainment: grabbing hold of the crest of punk rock sweeping the world at the time, beating hell out of one band's drum set after another for the next few years.

Then, one day in the '90s, Fraser happened to catch a play featuring a group of others who hadn't allowed their disabilities to hold back their dreams of acting success.

"It wasn't embarrassing," he remembers. "It was really good, and I really enjoyed it. I realized that was what I wanted to do." He became a member of Europe's Graeae Theatre Company, created *Thalidomide! A Musical*, then put together *Sealboy: Freak*, the story of Stanislaus Berent, a fellow phocomelia sufferer who performed at Coney Island and other freak shows around the world for decades before his 1980 passing.

Just before helping put together the documentary *Born Freak*, which mentioned Berent, Fraser began performing in his own sideshows.

"I just loved the world of sideshow," he asserts. "It's immediate and brutal and honest and cuts all the crap. When I finally got the call, of course, I was surprised and delighted, but I also thought, finally it's happened." He was being asked to show up on *Freak Show*, playing the same persona that Berent had shown to so many for so long in the form of Paul, himself a drummer.

Like so many in the *Show*, Paul'd been shunned by society, both here and in his British homeland. Deciding he'd give those heartless gutless tools something to blither about, he'd covered almost his entire body in tattoos—much more stereotyped in the 1950s than today!

"I loved the way the tattoos looked," he says. "I love the tough-guy persona. The whole thing was a magical, once-on-a-lifetime experience."

Years before "Freak Show," even before *AHS* itself was about, Erika Ervin had created the persona of Amazon Eve, touring the world and tearing up the World Wide Web as a model and personal trainer.

"My earliest memories (are) of getting up in front of my third grade class acting like a ham," recalls the California native. "I decided while I was in college that I wanted to be an actor, (and) now I'm grateful I get to perform all over the world. It was a very long hard road."

When "Freak Show" first came about, the person that would become Eve was scheduled to be played by a guy, and Ervin, who transitioned (some might even say evolved!) in 2004 to female from her original gender and name of William, was ready.

"I auditioned for this role as a man and was fully prepared to play a man throughout the series," she recalls. "I told my manager we needed to think outside the box if we were going to get noticed. I've been preparing to be Amazon Eve for the last six years." Fortunately, she was allowed to incorporate both her name and identity into the character.

In 2011, Ervin (or Eve) scored the Guinness world record for tallest model. Later that year, Jyoti Amge was named the planet's smallest gal (even smaller than Meep!). "Freak Show" brought them together on and off the screen, as Amge and Ervin got close as Eve and Amge's Ma Petite.

"From my childhood, I (was) interested in TV shows and film, (to) pursue a career in acting," Amge says. "I love (the) Ma Petite role also, because Elsa, Naomi, and all actors (show) support and love to Ma Petite." Ma gave Pepper the shot at maternal love that she'd always wanted.

Still, another new and horribly mangled face wouldn't be shoving much love to anyone.

He'd hit psychological thriller as the warden in *Shutter Island* (2010) and in *Gothika* (2003), and true crime as a prime suspect in the mystery of *Zodiac* (2007), but John Carroll Lynch's new acting expedition took an even scarier step forward.

"When I think of straight horror, I think of *Friday the 13th* or *Halloween*, when the monster is a monster," Lynch says. "This was an aspect of horror I hadn't considered."

As the new and familiar start sharing the "Freak Show" screens, another manages to slip by everyone in about the only place in the world that no one would notice him.

It was a clown even more brutal—at least, in the physical sense—than even *It*'s Pennywise.

An evil clown with an innocent name, John Carroll Lynch took the next step in terrifying circus creation as Twisty in *American Horror Story: Freak Show* (2014).

Twisty the Clown, his face, as oversized as the rest of him, half-veiled by a mask of a demonic grin, punctuated by a pair of eyes that never seem to stop glaring, killed three people and imprisoned two more on a bus before the season's first episode (aired on October 8, 2014) came to a close.

"I got a sense of what the physical character looked like, because so much about what is terrifying about the character is the way the character looks," Lynch says. "In the process of getting a life cast made and costume fittings, there was a greater sense of what the physical character would look like."

Looks would give him quite a bit to work with for the first few episodes, for reasons that will be discussed shortly.

"I lost my voice a couple of times," Lynch says. "It was very helpful for me to vocalize under the mask. It was more of an intuitive process, and to take on the disfigurement under the mask as I worked was a big part of it."

The next episode would bring even more tragedy. Strong man Dell (Michael Chiklis) and his three-breasted beauty Desiree (Angela Bassett) arrive, only to have Dell frame Meep for the murder of a local cop (Jimmy actually did it when the cops tried to harass the freaks).

With some half-wits actually convinced that this guy could kill a cop, Meep's thrown into jail and terrifyingly beaten to death by inmates. But a sad solidarity soon arrives back at the show, as his body is returned for everyone to mourn over. Meanwhile, local brat Dandy (Finn Wittrock), spoiled by a mom who's given him an Oedipal complex that would creep out Norman Bates, tries to make friends with Twisty and help him hurt the kids, though Jimmy soon finds and frees them.

"I did some clowning work with a local street performer that the producers found," Lynch says, "which was really helpful in terms of the clown portion of the character. Clowning is obviously a millennium-long art form, and in and of itself as a performing genre, it's pretty complicated, so to do that in a couple of weeks is pretty intimidating."

Still, we'd learn why Twisty's the way he is, inside and out, and it was far worse than any freak show.

A flashback tells the terrible story of a former such event, where his co-stars couldn't deal with him being popular with the kids, branding him with the stigma of kiddy-fiddling and sending him over the edge. A suicide attempt with a shotgun didn't take his life, only his jaw and any semblance of sanity, hence both the mask and the killing spree.

"This guy is a crazy clown, and this is a straight horror thing," Lynch says, "but then it turns into something completely different, and it gets really richer with texture, not just for myself, but every single person in the cast, written so beautifully for pathos and pity. I really came to realize that in the course of doing it, that's really indicative of horror. You feel badly for Boris Karloff's monster. You feel sympathy for them."

But not for long; Elsa inadvertently calls out a demonic spirit to play his own Halloween prank, and things go wrong . . . sort of. Seeing that, somewhere within, Twisty still just wants all of his pain to end, the spirit takes him away from the living world.

Dandy and Dell (secretly Jimmy's dad) both face murderous urges and homosexual tendencies, with Dandy killing his maid, then his boyfriend, and stealing the twins. Denis O'Hare, also an *AHS* regular, shows up as con man Stanley, looking to steal a freak to sell to a museum.

"I don't consider any character a villain," says O'Hare. "I don't consider a character good or bad. I'm not being evasive; I just approach a character that way. I ask myself, what does the character want, where do they come from, how do they think? To me, the most important thing about being an actor is to be confident about what you're doing, and to have authority, like you own it. Because if you don't own it, you feel like a fraud. I figure out how a character walks, how they speak, if differently than I speak, if their metabolism is different than mine, faster or slower, if they have the same sense of humor that I have. Do they see the world to a length that I recognize?"

Guilt-tripped into helping him, Dell goes looking to jump Eve.

Big mistake. She whoops his ass.

"Learning how to do a fight scene is actually counter-intuitive to actual martial arts training," Ervin says, "so Michael Chiklis was so patient and kind enough to show me the ropes, during my fight scene."

But Chiklis' character couldn't be as nice; Dell recovers by bringing Ma Petite a new dress, then giving her a hug . . . until she breaks.

Conniving con man Stanley (Denis O'Hare) tries to charm his way into the heart, and eventually wallet, of Elsa on *American Horror Story: Freak Show* (2014).

Amge called it one of her toughest scenes.

"It's not easy to prepare for the scenes emotionally, for me, the non-American English speaker," says the India native. "Its pronunciation during any dialogue is also tough for me."

Along the way, Paul and Elsa were torridly having a secret affair, but lack of trust tore them apart, temporarily sending him into the arms of Grace Gummer's Penny, herself disfigured with tattoos by her asshole father.

"The world of the sideshow, how to be and how to act, was inherent in me," Fraser says. "I've been preparing for it for fifteen years. I just needed to add the historical and American aspects to what it would have been like in those days. It was a very personal set."

Ethel accuses Elsa of Ma Petite's death, and Elsa kills her in retaliation. Dandy kills his mom, his maid's daughter, and a group of women. The freaks find out that Dandy or Stanley will massacre them all,

Rose Siggins, who made Legless Suzi into a highlight of *American Horror Story: Freak Show* (2014), tragically passed away in December 2015.

Stanley to sell them to a museum (as he did Ma Petite) or Dandy just for the hell of it. Jimmy's arrested for Dandy's crimes, but Eve and Dell kill some bad cops to set him free. But Dell doesn't get redemption here; Elsa blasts his head off for killing her little friend.

And that's not the finale of the partnership that all stage workers at a freak show share, and why the departure of these shows was a loss to more than just the fans. And everyone took a look right back to one of the first pop culture events to spread the freak show word across America.

"Show Stoppers" opened the evening of January 14, 2015, with everyone welcoming Stanley to a friendly dinner and Elsa announcing a later showing of the 1932 horror-comedy *Freaks*, a tale of a group of sideshow performers that attack and transform a visiting jezebel, chanting, "Gooble, gobble!" all the while (one year after helming *Dracula*, Tod Browning lead the freaks). As Dandy buys the show, he stumbles upon their victim, Stanley's tongue, arms, and legs sliced off and dressed like the guy whose prison murder they all suffered through.

"Stanley was a classic American con man," explains O'Hare. "He was somebody who was trying to make his way into a landscape that was really challenging. All he had was his gift of gab. That's a true American type, somebody who can bullshit their way into your house, whether it's by selling a Bible, or steak knives, or encyclopedias. They can make you give them your money. He was out for himself. That's also kind of a traditional American theme: to be a self-made man out to make his fortune, but not taking any hostages." Stanley helped O'Hare grab his second Emmy nomination of his *Story* tenure (he'd also been nominated for the first season of "Murder House," but didn't win either).

"When horror is not successful is when you're making fun of it," O'Hare explains. "You can't make fun of it from the inside. It can be fun on the outside, but when we're doing it, we can't make fun of it. We have to be deadly serious." Those words would apply in bloody detail by the season's finale.

By that point, we'd had a certain degree of sympathy for everyone on board, even Dandy. But as the season's final episode, "Curtain Call," kicked off, that would be all gone.

The freaks are ready to give up their show, but Dandy takes away more than that, slaughtering almost everyone on the show, even Eve, who takes a fatal bullet for Desiree. But the twins finally drug him, and he's awakened in a water tank slowly filling with water. As things start, Dandy desperately searches for the trick that got Houdini out of this trap so many times.

It keeps going and going and going, and we're all just waiting for a fellow villain to show up and save him at the last second. But it doesn't happen—the water takes away Dandy's air for good. Rarely have audiences cheered so loudly at a death (except maybe Joffrey on *Game of Thrones*!).

Elsa's now a worldwide singing star, but she, like so many others who find fame, finds that there's a huge gap between expectation and reality, as she's still unhappy. Summoning the same apparition that killed Twisty, Elsa finds herself its last victim. But this afterlife isn't heaven or hell; she's just back to the supernatural form of her old show.

And everyone's there to greet her, even Ethel, Ma Petite, Meep, and everyone else whose death agonized us. She's finally married to Paul. With all of them on the stage and the crowd sold out, it's time for one last performance.

Because that's what so many of these show were always about; the performers finding solace with each other, a strange place that was the spot in which any of them felt safer than everything else.

"We're all freaks in our own way," Woolf said. "If there were no freaks, then everyone would be normal."

For a bit of time in a pair of *AHS* seasons, Woolf found as much acceptance as he ever did back home in the Golden State.

Tragically, he wouldn't get another chance; on February 19, 2015, just weeks after *Freak Show* ended, Woolf was hit by a car on a Hollywood street. Four days later, he took his own final curtain call.

"Uncertainty scares me, just not knowing what's there," he said shortly before. "I do what I can do to the best of my abilities. One goal I have is just to be successful in whatever I choose to do."

According to a co-star, that went far past the cameras.

"We became really close," Ervin recalls. "One time when we went out, I got to play his bodyguard and he got to play Mr. Big. We'd go into this pool hall, and I got to watch him clean the table on all these men that were playing pool that underestimated him. Our wrap party was in a pool hall, and I don't think anybody could beat him. What I am going to miss about him is that he was a sweet, sweet person. He was always happy. I've never seen him down."

Tragedy struck the *Freak Show* crew again in December 2015, as Rose Siggins, who lost her legs as a toddler and played the redundantly named Legless Suzi on the show, passed at age 43 following kidney surgery, leaving behind two small children.

"I couldn't imagine myself being normal, because this is my normal," Siggins said of her condition. "Legless Suzi is a very scared and frightened person. I can't imagine people treating you so poorly because of how you looked. Once you remove the legs, which is considered three-quarters of the body, mentally you start thinking of yourself as 'I'm not a whole person.' So of course she would have joined a circus too, because that was family."

"Rose was a fantastic woman and a great job to work with and be around," Fraser remembers. "I've never met such a down-to-earth, salt-of-the-earth type woman. I was really lucky to work with her."

Charley Brewster (William Ragsdale) found out the price of pissing off a vampire, incurring the wrath of Jerry Dandridge (Chris Sarandon) in *Fright Night* (1985).

Creatures of the *Fright*

EXPERIENCE. OUR NAMES out in the public open. Entries on our résumé. A chance at taking the difficult task of re-telling a centuries-old tale and finding a way to make it original. Make it *ours*.

Indeed, there are these and so many more reasons to grab the heroic (and heroine) lead in the world of horror, particularly at the star of a career.

Still, there's still more a little room for *personal* satisfaction in the business. Giving a hearty meal to one's own ego should never be the first reason to take a role, but nothing wrong with it being in the far background.

Hey, what young guy wouldn't want to see—probably along with his testosterone-fueled buddies—himself whomping all the bad guys, particularly those with the strengths of the undead, and saving the babe in distress at the same time? A *hell* of a thing to brag about, isn't it?

Same token, wouldn't a young lady in the same position take the shot at, even in character, becoming a modern-day Aphrodite, who all the men want and the ladies secretly want to become?

Fright Night (1985) gave a pair of acting newcomers those chances—and, considering the film's still running strong nearly three decades later, remakes and sequels abounding, it worked!

"Seeing yourself as an action hero, I would recommend it!" advises William Ragsdale, whose first named career role came as Charley Brewster, the average every-teen who can't understand why no one around believes that Charley's new next door neighbor is a colleague of Dracula.

"I had grown up on Dracula, so I knew the lore," Ragsdale remember. "For that role, it was about fun, this unlikely thing happening in your backyard."

The *thing* in question is Jerry Dandridge, the fellow next door whom Charley swears he saw sink his teeth into the neck of a lovely young lady, and not in a kinky way either. But, again, no one, not Charley's mom (Dorothy Fielding), the local cops, or even his girlfriend Amy (Amanda Bearse) take him with anything but salt grains.

"I wasn't a fan of horror," Bearse recalls. "It scared me to death. I used to have nightmares when I was a child about vampires. They had this human element. It wasn't so far off."

Even while charming Charley's mom, Jerry's trying to hide something from the youth himself, until the pair battle it out in Charley's room, a pencil through Jerry's hand bringing out his monstrous form before Charley's mom arrives. Still, he's able to guzzle holy water and pick up a crucifix, a pair of obstacles for the fanged group (depending, of course, on which version we read; 1994's *Interview with the Vampire*, for one, disregarded the cross issue).

However, his lack of mirror reflections helps drive the point home for the wonderers. But it's too

Amanda Bearse experienced the sexy, sultry side of vampirism in *Fright Night* (1985).

late; Jerry, noticing Amy's resemblance to his own lost love, soon has her captive in his home, starting the conversion process.

"The reason I got the part was because Amy has to transform, and it was a sexual experience," Bearse says. "There were a lot of seventeen-year-olds auditioning, but they didn't have a lot of life experience, and I did. I was twenty-six playing seventeen. There is obviously a very sensual undertone to what happened between Jerry and Amy."

As Amy starts to move over to the undead, the sexual power that vampires have been using as a deadly weapon since their own inception becomes hers as well, her looks moving from innocent loveliness to evil seduction.

"We did backstories for the characters," Bearse recalls. "I made it very present time for me: what was going on for Amy in school, how she felt about Charley. You start with some truthful things about yourself and then bring it into whatever situations the script is asking for. You keep it real. It was about reminiscing and remembering what it was like to be that age."

With Jerry and Amy on the attack, Charley manages to hold off the vampiress (Ragsdale broke his ankle during filming), then smashes a bunch of nearby windows to let welcome sunlight in, cooking Jerry to dust and releasing Amy from his grasp.

"My reality in the movie was an average American kid," Ragsdale recalls. "(Charley's) transition came from what happens to American teenagers."

1988 brought a sequel, in which Charley falls under the spell of a new vampiress, saved by his friends just before his own conversion. Didn't work as well.

"In the second one, they were trying to make more of an '80s movie with the music, the feel of it, bringing in a sexual feeling for Charlie," Ragsdale says. "It just didn't have the same pop as the first one. There's an innocence to (the first one) that everybody finds very accessible." He'd hit the other side of villainy in 2007's religious thriller *The Reaping*, while Bearse's name would get synonymous with comedy: she spent over a decade tormenting Al Bundy from next door as Marcie on *Married... With Children* (1987).

As has been a custom in Hollywood since the start of the new millennium, *Fright Night* got its remake in 2011. This time, it's Anton Yelchin as Charlie, Imogen Poots playing Amy, and Toni Collette as Charlie's mama. Colin Farrell's on the other side, in Jerry's role.

Equipped with more CGI abilities and larger budgets than its predecessor, the film culminates with Jerry attempting to blow up a house with everyone inside, then to the desert for a high-speed chase. Then the three heroes find themselves rear-ended by a fellow named Jay Dee.

Nostalgia time—it's Chris Sarandon himself, the original Jerry. And despite quickly being slaughtered at the *new* Jerry's hands and fangs, it's still a much easier job than the eight hours of makeup Sarandon endured to be the first *Fright* man.

"I read up on vampires—and *bats*!" Sarandon, a fan of old horror, recalls of getting ready for Jerry.

Just two years after *Fright Night*, Sarandon landed in another eventual cult classic as the cowardly Prince Humperdinck of *Princess Bride* (1987). The year after that, he'd be back in horror, battling a killer doll in the first *Child's Play*. And in the next decade, he'd give the younger crowds a chance to blend fear and wonder, voicing Jack Skellington, protagonist of 1993's wonderful *Nightmare Before Christmas*.

Fright Night, Sarandon recalls, "did fairly well at the box office, and it's had this endless life since then, first on video, on television, playing midnight shows, on DVD. Like *Princess Bride*, it's taken on a life of its own. It's a generational thing within families. People watch it with their parents, and when they get older, they watch it with their children—hopefully not *too* young!"

Even under tons of makeup, with no voice and hardly able to get around, Jonathan Fulller turned the title character of *Castle Freak* (1995) into one of the decade's most terrifying critters.

Jonathan Fuller:

Castle Freak

WHO IS THIS person? What is he doing in my world? Why is he trying to hurt me? And what the *hell* is going on with his horribly disfigured face and mangled body?

That's what the title character in 1995's *Castle Freak* must have been thinking. Moments before, he'd been lounging in his familiar time and place, the only world he'd ever had the chance to get any comfort in, and suddenly, some others—looking obscene and babbling some kind of gibberish that just *couldn't* have come from this planet—were on the invasive attack: trying to break in and take away his home, even his life, trespassing throughout and having the *nerve* to act shocked when he defended his own place.

How *dare* they?!

Well, just as the hunchback of Notre Dame, the phantom below an infamous opera, Leatherface and the rest of his pals down Texas way, and even the creature from the waves of that darkly colored lake, had found themselves the victims of trespassers of the worst order, this fellow wasn't putting up with it either. . . .

He hadn't expected it and certainly not trained for it—*Castle Freak* isn't the kind of role with which acting school instructors pepper their syllabi!—but Jonathan Fuller, like so many other fans of old-time horror, had found himself all but entranced with the work of a man named Lon Cheney (well, two, as junior followed senior into the business!), and that based on Cheney Sr.'s offerings themselves.

"One of my favorite influences was watching Lon Chaney Sr. films, and *Man of a Thousand Faces*," Fuller recalls, *Faces* being Chaney's 1957 biopic with James Cagney in the lead. "Stuart Gordon came back and told me he had this part, a six-hour makeup job, playing this horribly deformed person, like Quasimodo." The older Chaney had originated the hunchback role in 1929, and his son had nearly followed in his footsteps a decade later, with Charles Laughton ultimately snatching the 1939 sequel's lead.

Starting out in the theaters of Deep South Birmingham in his teenage years, Fuller had been to one of his homeland's first state-charted schools of the fine arts, then headed to Chicago to study at the Goodman School of Drama.

"In the '80s, I basically lived out of a suitcase, doing regional theater around the U.S., in New York and Los Angeles," Fuller recalls. Back in Chicago, he showed up at the Organic Theater Company, which Gordon had helped establish in the late 1960s. The director had splashed across the horror screen with his cinematic debut of *Re-Animator*, itself a darker rendition of the story of Frankenstein, in 1985. Six years later, he was putting an even more violent spin, this time on reality, with *The Pit and the Pendulum*.

"I went out to L.A. and got with Stuart," Fuller says. "He knew I was a good physical actor, good with swordfighting and rapier dagger work, and he had me audition to play Antonio."

Horror/action stalwart Lance Hendriksen showed Torquemada's reign of religious torture and slaughter across Spain, right around the same time countryman Christopher Columbus was leading an expedition over this way, then, long before the same fervor reached here to America in Massachusetts, had his opponent Maria (Rona De Ricci) imprisoned, using her outspokenness to accuse her of witchcraft.

Her husband Antonio isn't having it, breaking in to rescue her, but Torquemada catches him, then gives him a rough introduction to the title instrument.

"My first movie role was the lead," Fuller says of playing Antonio. "Running around in a castle in Italy, it was like being Errol Flynn, like a kid's dream come true."

A few years later, he'd return to Italy and to Gordon, this time for horror. Just as *Re-Animator* had, the director's new tale channeled the spirit of H.P Lovecraft for the terrifying tale of *Castle Freak*. Like his own literary hero Edgar Allen Poe, Lovecraft had struggled with mental and physical illness throughout a short life (he died of cancer at age 46 in 1937), and wasn't recognized for his writing talent until far too long after he was around to enjoy it.

Freak would be Gordon's version of Lovecraft's "The Outsider," published seven decades before, the story of a man who spends his life behind the thick walls of a castle, eventually breaking out to feel the sun's rays. Gordon's title character would follow the same objectives, albeit a bit more violently.

Years after they'd gone toe to toe as villain and heroine for the director in *Re-Animator*, Jeffrey Combs and Barbara Crampton would play John and Susan Reilly, a couple heading to John's recently inherited castle in Italy, visiting it as they attempt the impossible task of recovering from a car wreck that cost their son his life and their daughter Rebecca her eyesight.

But we've already seen the castle's original resident, and, for about the only time in the film, gained a bit of sympathy for him: the flick opened with a scene of his duchess mom beating the hell out of him with a whip, even if we haven't seen him yet.

We hear more about the castle and its residents from locals. We learn about the duchess and her servants. We get the secret tale of the children that she may or may not have had. One was named Giorgio, and he may still be living within the walls. His brother disappeared long ago.

"I'm classically trained, and that doesn't necessarily mean Shakespeare," Fuller says, "but I started so early. There are certain questions and things you address when you're entering any role. What is my overall desire in the film? What's in my way? How do I go about getting that? What are my limitations? What is my physicality like? What's my background like? You just put it together very methodically, or at least, that's what I do."

We won't see Giorgio for quite some time. Perhaps this gave Fuller some extra time to get ready for him.

"In the six weeks before filming, I did my best to lose as much weight as possible," he remembers. "I was eating maybe five or six hundred calories a day, and getting on a bike. I was still smoking at the time, and that was a good appetite killer." He'd spend about six hours a day in the makeup chair, getting worked on by John Vulich, whose work had helped *Babylon 5* win an Emmy the year before.

"The way the makeup was constructed," Fuller explains, "it kind of emphasized making my shoulder blades look bonier, with my hip pieces and chest piece. It gave me that skeletal look that they were going for." He also watched *Wild Child*, the 1970 French film based on the true story of a young boy who spent his first decade in a forest in the late 1700s, soon being brought to society and adjusting, a luxury Giorgio won't enjoy. Fuller checked out the 1963 British horror flick *The Haunting*, which, unlike its 1999 American remake with Liam Neeson and Catherine Zeta-Jones, didn't have all kinds of expensive special effects to help it scare.

"I had a horrendously long makeup job," Fuller says. "Six hours in, two hours out. I learned to nap in the makeup chair. Most of the days were twenty-hour days. I was basically acting through a wetsuit, which had its own challenges. I was tired all the time; most of my scenes started at about ten at night."

With Giorgio still unseen, a cat leads Rebecca (Jessica Dollarhyde—in her only film role, a HUGE loss to the acting world!) down to his lair. He doesn't grab her yet, but he kills the cat . . . and chews off his own thumb to escape from his cuffs!

"The film was kind of specific about things that happened to him from his mother's beating," Fuller says. "His left leg had been broken sideways. He had developed scoliosis in his back. He rips his thumb off to get out of the chain. Actors sometimes will take on an animal image to give our bodies a different rhythm and backbone to it. It reminded me of a praying mantis, and to go towards that to get into it."

John had to hit some tough places too, heading to the booze to recover from issues with his wife, then bringing a gorgeous prostitute back to the castle. But he's too hammered to take advantage, and the creature's the only one left to get her to earn her money. She can't; she gives him a friendly caress, only to find out that there's not enough equipment downstairs to finish the work. Then he kills her.

"We were addressing the cycle of abuse," Fuller says. "It was all that Georgio really knew, so anything that got into his way, he'd beat. He'd been chained to a wall since age five. The reveal is that this prostitute looks at his penis, and it's severed off. He still had testicles; he had a sexual drive, but nothing to do about it."

Covered in a sheet, the fellow tries to torment Rebecca, strapping down a lady who can't see inside the cell that kept him prisoner for far too long. But that's because it's his own caring spot, as he reveals his true full self for the first time. But unlike so many of those that have felt this torture before, like those we discussed early in this profile, the pain he causes her takes away any concern those on the outside might have had for him.

"I had to go to some pretty sick places," Fuller says. "It was supposed to be really appalling. Stuart did not want a sense of humor in this film."

Giorgio takes Rebecca, ready to visit on her the same concern that Mommy gave him—after all, it's the only care he's ever known. Susan shows up to save her daughter as a storm lands all over the outside, but Giorgio recovers and keeps "caring for" the ladies.

Then John, inadvertently helped by the local lawmen, realizes just how he got lucky enough to be gifted this building; he's the lost son of the duchess. Ticked because his dad left her for the U.S. of A., his mom brought him back her to meet his brother for the first time.

And now he's forced to fight his long lost and wishfully never found bro, Giorgio himself, on a rooftop, with fists, feet, and chains flying.

"Stuart wanted the castle to be a creepy thing in and of itself," Fuller says. "With the makeup itself, with all the foam rubber teeth on, I couldn't speak. The makeup was such that one eye was closed, and I had no depth perception. I had to be careful swinging that chain at someone. I was standing a few feet back, so I had plenty of clearance to swing the chain without hitting anybody." But everyone got hit quite hard during the finale: both brothers are yanked out of a window and land hard, too hard to ever do anything again.

Just as things had ended in the most violent, the most tragic sense for Quasi, the Phantom, and so many others, Giorgio will never again get to experience the magic of everyday society, the right to interact with and learn from others. The painful life he led will be the only existence he ever experienced, and all because a group of folk with the nerve to call themselves normal put their noses where they didn't belong.

"The way the Hollywood system works, they get major stars to do films like the hunchback," Fuller says. "This was my chance to do a Lon Chaney Sr. homage."

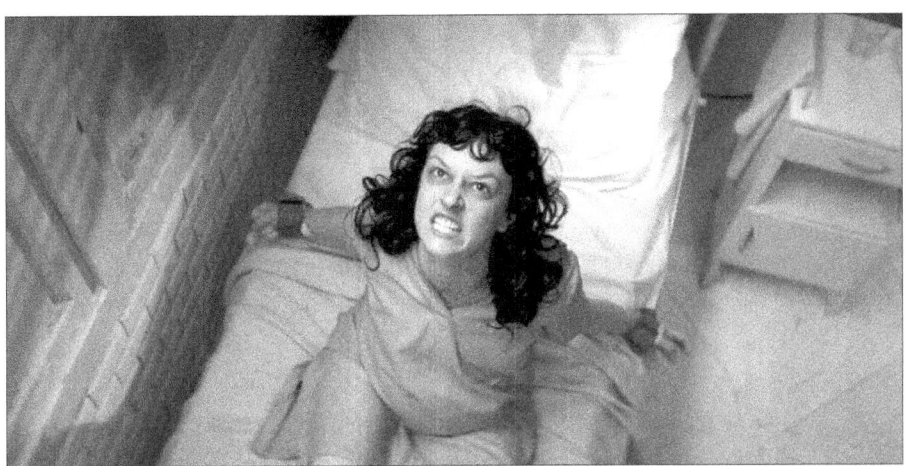

Rosaria (Marta Gastini) casts a furious look up at He (or She or It) who seems to have abandoned her in *The Rite* (2011).

Marta Gastini:

The Rite/Dracula 3D

SOME STORIES IN horror just never get too old. No matter how many different ways they're articulated, performers never stop searching for their own interpretations of (not quite) the same old stories, and audiences never tire of hearing them.

In the first two roles of her horror-performing career, Marta Gastini experienced both these feelings. One year after adding another notch to the layers of possession films that have flooded the category since *The Exorcist* (1973), Gastina got to be the next one to step into the terrifying world of a man named Bram Stoker and his gore-craving creations.

Like so many others in these books, Gastini spent most of her first two decades in the theater stages and acting classrooms.

"The reason I became an actress was my deep passion for the stage and a strong need to express my emotions," she remembers. "I started dancing ballet and contemporary dance when I was six; therefore I grew up in theaters. I developed my passion for acting throughout the years, especially thanks to my father, who was the first to believe in me and to support me to try and test my talent."

A high school acting workshop and some time at the New York Film Academy convinced her even more. So when Gastini came back home to Italy, it was time to embark on the oft-tedious task . . . of *auditioning*!

Fortunately for her, it didn't take long; small roles in TV and films came around rather quickly. Then, in 2011, she snared the chance to step right into America's eye on horror.

"I must say it was a surprise for me at first," Gastini remarks on this particular side of her career.

"I've never really been into horror films. I used to be very easily impressionable, but since I started acting in them I can now appreciate them and watch them with a more critical eye."

Ever since Linda Blair set the standard as Regan McNeil, critical eyes and minds have been dissecting every like performance. In 2011, Gastini added her name to the rank of victims, both of critics . . . and something just slightly darker.

Early in *The Rite*, Colin O'Donoghue's Michael Kovak, full of priesting potential but still searching for his own faith, visits Rome (the home of the Vatican, it's becoming more and more of a popular site for these films, perhaps because so many exorcists have been certified there) to learn the ins and outs of exorcism. It's here he runs into Father Lucas, as nonconformist as one in this business can be.

But he's not the concern just yet; more important is one of Lucas' patients, a young lady—another common practice for the genre—who appears to have encountered an unwelcome trespasser. But as amazing and heartbreaking as it sounds, the possession of Rosaria (apt name for a religion-based film!) isn't even the worst thing the teenager has been through.

She's pregnant. By her scumbag father.

"When I read the script and prepared for the audition," Gastini recalls, "my only thought was that I had to get the role given the fact that rarely as an actor you have the chance to play such an exciting, difficult, strong, crazy, extreme character and to work with one of the most brilliant actors of all time, Anthony Hopkins."

Oh yes, Hopkins does indeed show up as Lucas. But we're not there just yet.

Forced to convert Rosaria's natural Italian speech to English, and occasionally tongues, Gastini went hard to work with a dialogue coach. Physically, a stunt coordinator helped her get ready for the contortionistic practices the demon sent Rosaria through.

"I remember that the first day I arrived on set," Gastini says, "I started practicing how to run against a wall without hurting myself."

But even that was to step inside Rosaria's mind and, to the greatest possible extent, understand what it's like to witness the mental battle between pure evil and decency. One of over a dozen permitted exorcists in America, San Jose's Gary Thomas and his work became the role models for the film's jumping-off literary creation *The Rite: The Making of a Moden Exorcist*, for O'Donoghue, and, eventually, for Gastini as well.

After pouring through journalist Matt Baglio's 2009 book, the actress sat down with Thomas, who himself has witnessed about three figures' worth of possession cases.

"What really helped me understand my character and the suffering she was going through was the chance to go see real exorcisms," Gastini recalls "In that occasion I could speak with an exorcist and some of the people he is trying to cure and I could see with my eyes a suffering I have never experienced before, people who can't have a normal life in any way."

Clearly, Rosaria and her baby never could have either, no matter what happened, and they don't, as both die during childbirth. The demon, still around, sneaks inside Lucas (wow, maybe Hannibal Lecter should have used that as a defense!) before Kovak manages to yank it out, save everyone, and re-find his faith in the bargain.

The very next year, legendary Italian horror director Dario Argento followed in the footsteps of everyone in his colleague-hood from Murnau to Browning to Coppola, putting together the story of a fanged man from Transylvania. With the story in 3D and Thomas Kretschmann in the title role, Argento, who helped write the screenplay, took a new look at Dracula.

As Jonathan Harker wanders through the castle with the most gracious and ultimately menacing of hosts, he's suddenly nabbed and nipped by the ominous nobleman, and left to wonder what the hell's going on. Meanwhile, Harker's better half Mina shows up, along with family pal Lucy Kisslinger.

As is tradition for her dad's films, Argento's daughter Asia is Lucy. Gastini is Mina, whose resemblance to the vamp's past and late beloved steal his heart right away.

"Dracula is a timeless classic that can still be revisited and revived," Gastini says, "and Dario had an appealing vision of Dracula, revealing his human side, almost creating a romantic hero, tormented by his eternal life and moved by his eternal love for Mina . . . I could not resist."

Falling a hundred feet under Dracula's spell, Mina allows the count to lead her to a castle for his final battle with vampire-bashing icon Van Helsing (Rutger Hauer, in the job Hopkins did for Coppola back in 1992). Along the way, Mina and her mount suddenly find a new group of unwelcomes.

"A scene that was a little difficult to do was the one in the forest with the wolves in which I was riding a horse," she recalls. "I love animals and I love horses. I used to ride them but after a bad fall I became a bit scared of them. And if you add the wolves to the scene it all becomes quite scary! But of course everything was shot in absolute safety and I actually found the scene fun to do."

But fun certainly wasn't evident for Dracula near the end; most versions of the tale have him allowing Mina to take his life, knowing he's finally found peace after centuries of horror. But Argento and his story went a different way. During the final fight with the Van man, Mina shakes off Dracula's spell, picks up Van Helsing's gun, and blasts Drac to ash with a silver bullet.

"Mina is a well-educated, elegant young woman, sweet and careful towards Lucy, and in love with her husband, delicate, pure and affable," Gastini explains. "(Although) these characteristics might make her appear as the perfect victim for Dracula, Mina is actually very strong and combative. That's what I worked on when I was studying for the role."

The undead takes over Rosemary (Geretta Geretta) from outside the movie screens of *Demons* (1985).

Geretta Geretta:

Demons

INDEED, THAT TRULY is this performer's name—and the story of how it became so is just about as interesting as most of the acting preparation tales in this tome.

But Geretta Geretta isn't here just because of her unusual designation. Like everyone else, the horror performance tales come first (don't worry—we'll revisit the name tale by the end!).

"I started my career in New York," remembers the Portland native. "I was in *The Emperor's New Clothes* when I was seven or eight. I think the bug bit me then."

The daughter of a horror fan (it was actually her mom, usually the other way around), Geretta grew up learning tons about those who scare.

"As far as science fiction and horror go, they chose me," she says. "I was raised with the highest respect for these people's performances. They're scaring you with their thought processes. You have to believe in it, even if you're a member of the walking dead." Not *The Walking Dead* itself—that was a ways away. But soon enough, one of Geretta's biggest roles would come in a similar performance.

"I set out, like any actress, wanting to be a great actress, getting primary roles in all types of films," she says. "I don't think I ever sat down and said, 'Oh, I want to be a horror actress,' which I know people nowadays do. I'm a generation after, maybe a generation and a half after Blaxploitation films, so those where all when I was barely a teen. And the next time black women were hot again was the *Cosby Show*. Other than that and a very few other shows, there really wasn't enough work to go around, so all I wanted to do was get cast for anything: doctor, lawyer, nurse. If they were going to do a remake of *Roots*, I was ready."

Still, even after quite a bit of time in America's acting homelands of Los Angeles and New York, the big roles weren't really rolling her way. Geretta decided it was time for a reinvention—both of herself and her surroundings.

"People always ask me, why does your résumé say 'hooker, hooker, hooker, prostitute'?" she says. "Well, it's because that's all I could get until I went to Europe. In Europe, they didn't see a tall, thin black woman as a possible hooker with a heart of gold. They just saw me as a human being. That's how I got into horror."

Over the next decade, she'd help terrify legions of Italian film fans, and quite a bit of her work would find its way back to her home.

"I could act and hold a machine gun at the same time," she says. "There's something about my body type on camera that makes me look like I could kick some butt. I could jump, I could roll on the ground, I could do a couple of weak stunts. For a girl in my 20s, I could throw a punch pretty well. I just got called out on sets. I showed up on set, did the bit, shot some people, beat up some people, as you do." It was around this time that her name changes began . . . but again, we're not there just yet!

"I wasn't the only American actress in Rome," she says. "But I had developed a grab bag of techniques. I was used to working in Italian on bi-lingual sets. The bottom line is, you have to find what part in you that can become what you're trying to portray, and if you can't, you fake it. That's why it's called acting. I try to do a combination. I start with time, place, and breakdown of the essence. All you have to do is know that moment you're about to build. You know your lines before you get there, and you know what your character would do."

Ironically enough, the whole "streetwalking persona" act that she'd traveled around the globe to escape would bring Geretta some of her highest success. One year after battling crazed carnivorous four-legged beings in *Rats: Night of Terror* (1984), she stepped up to become the undead.

"I was called for an audition," Geretta remembers of the beginnings of 1985's *Demons*. "I'd been in the industry for a little bit, and realized it was a wonderful opportunity. There was no reason why I *wouldn't* want to be involved with it." One persuasive aspect from the positive side was the name on the production list. Long known as one of Europe's top horror filmmakers, Dario Argento had also helped director Lamberto Bava with the screenplay for over a year.

"I came prepared for anything on the set, and I had prepared myself," Gerreta says. "I was ready to do the training: what would it be, what would it feel like, how would I be if this actually happened to me, and how would I express that on camera?"

With a role like this one, questions like that are wide open and all up to individual interpretation.

As the lady lead makes her way to a new movie theater to check out the latest offering in local horror (*Demons* is set in Berlin), she and her friends see a pimp and his, ahem, *employees* checking out some props in the lobby. One such gal happens to be named Rosemary—who, like most, is a *hell* of lot easier on the eyes than most found wandering streets and overpasses of dark reality.

"Rosemary is a girl on her day off," Geretta says. "She wants to be the top hooker in her group. Already, we're not talking about someone in a crack house. She's pretty dressed up; she doesn't have a black eye. This isn't someone who has to work today. She's someone who's having a nice time on her day off."

But not for long: fiddling with a mask prop, the lady scratches her face with it. As the film gets going, amongst all the blood and guts of this flick within a flick, we see the same type of mask that cut Rosemary. We see a guy in the film put it on. Then we see him go psycho and slash his friends. Clearly, subtle foreshadowing is nowhere near the vocabulary of these filmers.

Stepping into the bathroom, Rosemary's horrified and helpless as her cut blasts open. Then her eyes and face degenerate at high speed, her teeth growing at the same rate.

"Most of the special effects were done on-camera," Geretta says. "We didn't have special effects. My face, all of that was makeup effects. When my face explodes, there were three men under the sink with gears and goo."

Her friend tries to help, but it's too late—she becomes the first victim in Rosemary's new bloodlust. Soon, the two are bringing the same terror they themselves saw on the screen to horrifying realism on the rest of the audience.

"All you think is that Rosemary is hooker number one, and she'll probably get slaughtered in the first five minutes," Geretta says. "But then she becomes immortal. The girl who's smoking whatever she's smoking in the theater at the beginning is not the same person who could rip off a woman's scalp about twenty minutes later. I'm hooker number one at the start, and by the end of the film, you know who I am. I am 'Rosemary.'"

Finding that the theater has trapped them inside, the audience is traumatized and transformed, person by person (as is tradition for Argento's films, he's got family in the cast, as one victim is played by his daughter Fiore). Just about everyone dies or is changed. The main man and woman escape, only to find that the title creatures have made it out and spread their infection across the city. A group of good-hearted gunmen just *happens* to drive by to take them to safety, but it's too late for the top girl, whose infection only waited a bit longer to change her. She's dead-blasted by another person, and the man is left alone.

"You can't act what's not real," Geretta says. "For some reason, there is humanity left in (Rosemary). People remember her name, although her name is said only once."

The tale that Italy knew and loved as *Dèmoni* roared to the cinema just before Halloween of 1985; the next summer, it found its way to Old Glory. Later that year, Argento's other daughter Asia would star in its sequel, this time with the title characters chasing humans around a high-rise apartment building.

Soon enough, Geretta found herself back home in America, finding her own diversity in the acting world, writing and directing shorts and commercials. But something back across the water snared her eyes and talent, and it was off to Ireland.

She and a group of other celebrities, mainly from the music world, put together *100 Voices Against Apartheid*, working towards integration. In 2001, she'd write and direct *Sweetiecakes*, which, in quite the unusual rom-com plot, had a woman trying to bridge the friendship gap between her husband and lover.

Five years later, Geretta would put a comedic spin on the integration aspect, stepping behind the cameras of *Whitepaddy* as Sherilyn Fenn, Lisa Bonet, and, in a departure from her usual horrifying work, the late great Karen Black, acted out Geretta's screenplay about white and black neighbors who can't stop winning each other's hearts.

"In the acting business," she explains, "it's a turkey shoot where you'll end up. Not everybody's going to be Brad Pitt-famous, but nobody's going to be completely unsuccessful. There's a lot of levels to this business, and you certainly don't know where you're going to end up. You don't get a choice as to where your career will go; you just get a choice to go out and do it, and it's a wonderful lifestyle, as long as you're not in it to be famous. But doing the work and enjoying it, meeting people, learning languages, getting out of your own skin and analyzing someone else's skin, frankly, I don't know anything better."

Still, she's never been able to leave horror totally behind; Geretta grabbed a small role in 2012's *Bloody Christmas*, playing a mom who tragically learns that her son has become the next victim of the child killer local cops are pursuing.

Now to step back to where we began—the evolution of Geretta's moniker. Like much else about her career, it was overseas when the changes arrived for the lady born Geretta Giancarlo.

"I was in a film directed by David Worth," she recalls of 1983's *Warrior of the Lost World*. "It was an American production being shot in Rome. My name gave it away that it wasn't shot in Los Angeles, because my first name looks Italian, even though it isn't—my first name is German, and my last name is Italian. The director asked if he could change my name for the poster. I said sure."

Audiences saw (and read) her as Janna Ryan. Geretta carried the name until she came back to the states a few years later.

"That's when I started getting my full name again," she says. "Then I went to Northern Ireland, and everybody got sick of my whole name. It was a tongue twister."

A different filmmaker tried to make it easier on everyone, announcing a double shot for her "new" name.

"I was re-Christened Geretta Geretta, and that stuck," she says. "It was a nickname that became my name. It starts a conversation very easily. Will I become Geretta Marie Giarcarlo again? We shall see!"

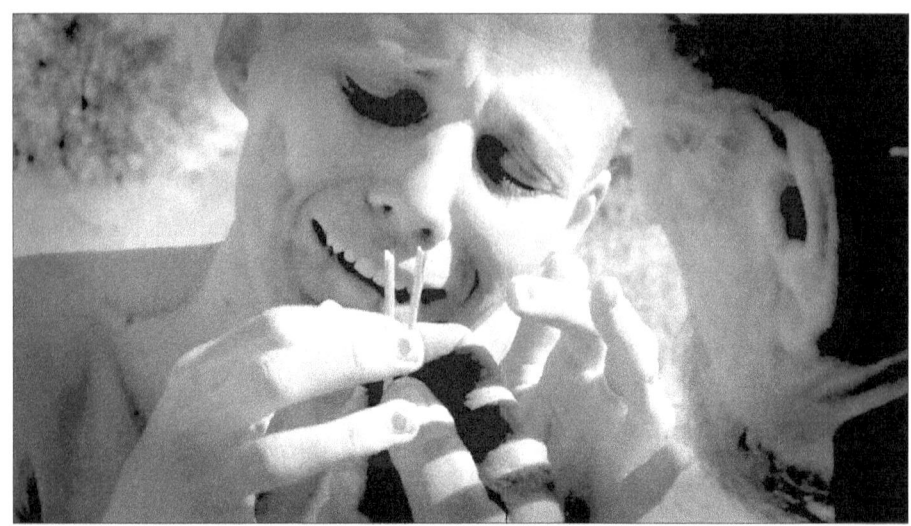

Sylvia Gray (Rodleen Getsic) can only hope for a merciful exit at her tormentor's hands in *THE BUNNY GAME* (2010).

Rodleen Getsic:

THE BUNNY GAME

WATCHING CERTAIN FILMS, sometimes you get really fucking angry.

The ones that show the darkness, the worst of people there are. Not those that have superpowers and can reincarnate at the call of a director's "Action!" We get scared of that stuff, but we know it's not real. But when we see the true, the cold, hard reality of the lives that so many suffer through, even on a screen in front of us, it just hurts so much more.

Life has always had both the tendency and the ability to throw a grenade into our stability just as we think we've got it all straightened out, and that can means all kinds of things.

THE BUNNY GAME (full caps intentional on the part of the film's creators) showed us some of the worst, but sadly, not at all unrealistic. We saw the commission of the pain and suffering that we only *think* is found in nightmares.

Why would someone make such a film? Well, that may have an easier answer, although not one we especially like to acknowledge. Perhaps because, as much as we'd like to dream they don't, people who do this sort of thing do exist. The world can be a scary and dangerous place, all too eager to remind us that good can't exist without evil, and one may have to hurt like hell in order to heal.

Although Rodleen Getsic had been pondering an acting career since single-digit age, her preparation for the lead role in BUNNY started long before she'd ever jump before a camera—maybe even before birth, as her dad was a photographer.

"It started from my childhood, wanting to do whatever I could to help the world," Getsic remembers. "There's a lot of darkness, but there's a lot of good people too."

As a kid, she leaped right into leading projects through her community. A career in politics seemed attractive. Then, in her last year before high school graduation, Getsic visited the nation's capital as part of a program designed to help those hoping to work there someday. She and the others got to sit down with some members of the staff of the first President Bush, just about at the end of his reign.

"I asked why our government focuses on war and helping other countries," Getsic recalls, "rather than on our own national internal problems: for instance, at the time, inner-city crime, violence, and homelessness."

A Bush cabinet member looked at her, and grinned at the naïve innocence of the query.

"That is very sympathetic of you," he responded, "but we are a World Power, and we need to maintain that status."

The man's name was Dick Cheney, although no one outside of DC would know who he was for a few more years. Getsic felt her heart break and her confidence in her government fall into a million little pieces.

"I was crushed," she says. "It was outrageous: the United States was standing by profiting and warring, meanwhile our beautiful country was deeply suffering, deteriorating from the inside out." Disillusioned of something she'd held to for years, it was time to take her first unwelcome gift of pain and do something with it. In her case, that something was creativity.

"I come from a family of musicians, yet up until that time I had not considered myself one," she says, "not until that summer of 1992, when songs and poetry began to emerge from my soul."

As with everything else Getsic has ever done, she went into things like a supersonic. She wrote and recorded hundreds of songs. She formed her own band. She played on stages across America. She appeared on MTV. She sang alongside Motley Crue's Tommy Lee and Bob Weir of the Grateful Dead.

Getsic kick-started a cartoon based on her life (probably not the type found on Saturday mornings). She had her own radio show for a few years.

When a huge landslide killed some of her friends in La Conchita, CA, early in 2005, Getsic spread the word about the area. She was there to help when Hurricanes Rita and Katrina did their awful work.

Then, in what seems to most of us an all-too-rare moment of slumber one night, Getsic had an encounter that guided her in a new direction. Spiritual forces have always played an important role in her life, but this was a markedly pivotal moment.

"One day, I had a dream, or a night vision, where my guardian angel appeared," she says. "He is a black man, and it was an all-white room, so his face stood out in the picture. But then I noticed what he was holding: linens. 'What are those for?' I asked. He said, 'They are for you. I will take you to your cell.'"

She'd go behind hypothetical bars unless she changed her career path. Singing had gone on long enough for now. It was time for something new.

"I was guided in dreamtime to focus again on being an artist; this time, an actress," she says. "I knew, because of who I am or was, I could make a bigger statement through art. It makes no sense to me, the lack of care for the common person. We are in crisis mode on our own homeland here, and yet our leaders continue to war around the world before picking up his own fellow man. America's flag is upside down in distress."

In 2000, she met Adam Rehmeier, a colleague on the music-making stages. As filling a jug with water one drop at a time, matters of BUNNY came about.

For years, the two kept skimming the water of filmmaking. Rehmeier filmed and photographed Getsic frolicking in a nearby forest, sightseeing over the Pacific, even performing a mourn in local graveyards.

Later on, Rehmeier mentioned his hopes of putting together *Horror, Horror*, which both of them hoped had the potential to be the scariest film ever made. But there were other matters aside from the title to attend to—like, say, the plot, the storyline, and the stars!

"For years, we had no idea what the film was really going to be about," Getsic says. "We allowed it to formulate itself. The storyline . . . came forward mysteriously for us through photo shoots and film experiments. We moved forward in faith in our work, knowing we were making an important film. When editing happened, Adam embedded our experiments into the film, expanding the depth of the plot by engulfing the present with the past through the framework of my character in milliseconds."

Back at cemetery called Hollywood Forever (the final resting place of Hollywood legend Cecil DeMille, Douglas Fairbanks, Jr. and Sr., Jayne Mansfield, Peter Lorre, and so many others), for a bit of brainstorming, the ideas suddenly began to evolve in Getsic. Rather, the memories.

Being abducted one night as a teenager before fortunately escaping. Almost becoming one more on a too-long list of rape victims.

"Sylvia Gray was born into me, her being merged within mine," Getsic says. "I took on Sylvia Gray as a figment, and she developed herself as time went along. I knew more about her. Who she was, in a fraction of myself, I became her. And as we got closer and closer to the production, especially in September and October prior to filming in 2008, I cultivated this new person inside of me."

It wouldn't be biographical in the least. The person she'd play—from the start, Getsic and Rehmeier knew she'd be in the lead—would be far from the upstanding citizen Getsic is.

"Sylvia Gray is a soul, combined maybe from several souls," Getsic explains. "We knew that she came to Hollywood with dreams that died, like so many. So sad. So desperate. She turned to drugs and prostitution. Homelessness. Survival. She became vulnerable to dark forces. We see actual characters like this in the world. We can have compassion for others, by relating to the 'what-ifs' that Sylvia Gray acts out in her real life on *BUNNY*. Sylvia Gray's soul is embedded into that film."

As has long been a custom of hers, Getsic went into a ritual fast before becoming Gray (though she couldn't get rid of the huge "Getsic" tattoo on her arm, not quite an inside joke as to the actress' true identity!).

"Fasting has always been a part of my life," she says. "It brings me closer to God, to my higher self and lets me have meditation. It quiets my body so the workings aren't working as hard, so my mind can be more clear." For nearly six weeks, Getsic forced her body to cleanse itself before she and Grey stepped into the dirtiest of worlds.

"It was intense, but it was also what it needed to be," she says of the fast. "Nothing that I couldn't handle. I was so in it, because I was having to become her, and it was a sacrifice."

Looking over the sad, nearly gothic nature of the black and white photographs he'd taken of her, Getsic found a blatant inspiration for Sylvia's atmosphere settling over her.

"The black and white is just really intense," she says. "It brings the story and the experience to the forefront. There's no color to look at. With the shades and white and black coming together, it makes you realize it even more. It's all about the light fighting with the dark. There's some symbolism there."

Even in her official debut as an actress, Getsic could feel an outside force inside her, slowly taking over. She became not a prisoner or captive in her own body, simply a passenger along for a ride of which neither she nor the director knew the ending.

"Beginning with ideas based on reality, based on the darkness that is ever-so-present in the world, *BUNNY* took on its own power," Getsic says. "Sylvia Gray informed me about who she is or was—through ways I cannot describe in words . . . The role of Sylvia Gray created itself. Adam filmed it as we went along, with the gut basis being vignettes in scenes, and games for the victim to play, forced by an evil master. It is all improvisational, truly riding the spirit. We invited the energy, dark and light, into this artistic platform of film to tell a story that needed to be told."

Even as filming got within sight, there was no script, not yet or maybe even ever. She and Rehmeier simply didn't feel the need to make one.

"This film was never written," she says. "*THE BUNNY GAME* is entirely an improvisation. Adam and I prepared by brainstorming bullet points, basically, games that the antagonist would play on the victim. The collaboration process between Adam and I is raw and spiritual. We don't even talk about it really. It just happens. Real encounters with evil are indeed what this film is based on."

OK, enough with the preliminaries. As stated before, Sylvia, like so many who head to Hollywood with dreams in their hearts and stars in their eyes, hit the harsh wall of reality early on, realizing that dreams of such so rarely come true. Like anyone in the world's oldest profession, she's now left to the unthinkable, offering herself on street corners.

"She's beautiful, tough, committed to getting by," Getsic says of Gray. "She lives on the streets of L.A. She does what she can, and she loves to get high. Her strange yearning for comfort, which I believe she never received as a child, led her out on to the streets searching. I would say soul searching, but this girl hadn't even gotten there yet. She is like (one) asleep. So, she is caught in the city, down and dependent, desolate. Then, she gets so lost in the drugs and desperation that she loses control of everything." Abuse of all kinds is commonplace to Gray, who doesn't so much as utter a syllable outside of cries of pain for nearly the first half hour of the film.

The world of prostitution is one of the saddest, and it's clear early on that Sylvia won't have the fairytale ending that Julia Roberts'"sex worker" got in *Pretty Woman* (1990), which Rehmeier demeans as "rubbish." But even her "colleagues" haven't gotten so caught up in what happens next, worse than anything Jack the Ripper ever did to a lady of the night.

Caught up with a customer who tries to get a little too close, she's suddenly and forcefully sedated, in the back of a truck. Virtually helpless. So begins a nightmare she will dream of waking up from.

The man beats her. Assaults her over and over again. That might be the worst, but it's not the end for Sylvia.

"I gave myself no choice but to become a slave to the story," she says. "My threshold for pain is enormous. The torture I experienced in *THE BUNNY GAME* was necessary, in that I needed to fulfill the 'what-ifs' for my character's reality . . . Through meditation, I was able to endure the horrific nature of the film. I take my art seriously. I take it all the way. When these scenes happened, I just did it." The character and the film were her life now, and what she'd gone through in the last thirty years seemed like a distant memory. This was her world now, and making the best of it was all she could ever hope for, because up against the wall of torture, one can fight, one can run, or one can lay down and eternally surrender.

In a perfect world, Sylvia would find a way out, or, better yet, suddenly get rescued by a handsome guy who'd immediately fall into eternal love with this tortured, gentle soul. But this film had been the darkest of pitch black again, and nothing was going to change.

"A big part of what I was tapping into during the filming of *THE BUNNY GAME* was the dark souls I have come into contact with here on Earth," she continues. "There are really people in the world that hurt others, and I have seen them. We all see them in our government, battlefields, torture prisons, video games, news, and then on the streets, or in your neighborhood, maybe even you, people who prey on innocence. This is real life. So, in order to display the fortune of someone who got caught in someone else's shadow, Sylvia Gray was at stake. And, because I was the one portraying her, I had to do what I had to do. I wasn't even sure what it all entailed. Because we, the crew, we were at the mercy of the monster. We were at the mercy of *THE BUNNY GAME*."

Mercy would be a word her captor had probably never been able to define. As his evil continues to override Sylvia in every sense, he starts to strip away her mentality as well.

He brands a symbol onto her back. He shaves her head.

And neither of those scenes were acting. Getsic actually allowed herself to be permanently marked and balded, all for the sake of character.

"The torture in *THE BUNNY GAME* did not hurt me," she claims. "My physical and mental endurance is one of the reasons I knew I could play the part. I knew I could take it to that extreme, because I had always been a tough girl, with mental toughness; a long distance runner and hiker; a fearless explorer in the world . . . The physical events that happened in the film were only skin deep. It was like an extreme obstacle course. I was in a deep state of meditation (concentration), and because of my high tolerance for pain (tattoos, brands, sports), the torture was not painful to me at all. So, the tears and screaming were enacted, though we consider it a 'real' response to the actual events taking place in the film."

All that anger I mentioned early on in this profile? Here's where we start to realize it's here for us as we watch (reiterate: it's been building since she was first taken, but only in the later scenes are we all but forced to *acknowledge* it!).

You get angry. You get frustrated. You get really pissed the hell off. Just like Sylvia, you feel it. She got hurt, she suffered, and for what? Exactly for what? Don't even try to think of an answer; it doesn't exist. But then, how many of us have been forced to ask these questions of our lives and others? Why do innocent women get raped? Why did so many serial killers torture and take the lives of those they had never seen before? Why can our loved ones suddenly get tossed into worlds of destruction and maybe death, and we're left to pick up the pieces and look for answers that don't exist?

THE BUNNY GAME takes the worst of humanity, puts on wide-open display the disdain that one person can have for another, the pain that people sometimes visit on each other, simply because they can justify it in their own twisted minds. And before we see it done to Sylvia, we might not have much regard for her. We might not like her at all, mostly because of how she makes a living. But in seeing all this horrible shit done to her, it's not just about sympathy, or caring. It's about having your body temperature rise to about 200 degrees, and not realizing it until you have to restrain yourself from putting your fist through the person who just stood in front of you for a little too long.

"*THE BUNNY GAME*," Getsic says, "is an expression of disaster, a consequence of the 'What-ifs,' and a fuck-you to the evil man. This film let me take it all the way, and even further. There is a freedom in this piece of art, energetically, succeeding to win . . . My role (in life) is to give everything all I got. From soul to soul, hear me roar. The world is awakening, and I am an artist put here to sound the bell."

With the film about at the climactic moment, we see the sad reason for its title—the man drapes Sylvia in a mask made from a rabbit's head, and forces her to play yet another disgusting game of agony.

"Nothing personal," he'd probably say, as serial killers and rapists so often do. We'd tell him to go fuck himself, and we'd be in the right. Visual displays tend to have a much stronger effect on their audiences than the spoken or written words; *THE BUNNY GAME* took evil and held it in front of our faces until we were forced to admit that it affected us, hurt us, made us angry.

THE BUNNY GAME asks us to find compassion for a person we don't know, perhaps don't like, based on little more than what we see. Without knowing anything about this woman other than that she screws for dollars, we see her go through all kinds of pain and suffering, and we still don't know hardly anything about her. But *THE BUNNY GAME* pushes the envelope with Sylvia's torture so much that it forces us to give a damn about someone we shouldn't really give a shit about to begin with. Driving down the street one night, seeing members of Sylvia's line of work on the corners, compassion doesn't exactly come to mind. But a person can only go through so much in front of our eyes before we start feeling . . . something.

"In my explorations as a youth, I was shown a vast array of reality," Getsic recalls, "conglomerates of wonderful and terrible. During these journeys, I did encounter some dangerous situations. But in the dangerous times, I live out the instinctual fight or flight method that comes with fear, and I eventually always got away. I'm alive today. I could write a whole book on my dances with the friends of the devil."

By now, there's no escape, and no return. Even if she gets out alive, Sylvia's never going to be right again. Too much pain, too much torture, too much darkness. The man even lets her out of the truck, and she escapes down the road, but there's nowhere to go. People don't come all the way back from things like this.

"We used our intuition, we used our higher guidance," Getsic says. "It was light and dark and all of the above. The intention was unknown, because it felt like something bigger. It was a spiritual experience for me, but my entire life is a spiritual experience."

As Sylvia ran blindly, no one knew where she'd end up, including the woman playing her or the man directing everything. The cast and crew weren't quite sure how this story should end. Hollywood, where she'd get saved, recover in seconds, or live happily ever after? Or reality, where she'd become just another victim.

As Getsic stumbled past a field, she saw a piece of wood that resembled a certain symbol, and the finale was set.

"It looked exactly like a cross," she says. "I just got right on it." Getsic lay down across it, and the cameras rolled for almost the last time.

"It was like the final sacrifice," Getsic says. "There were no more scenes to play. It was the end. I was ready to die, or ready to release, or let go. I had been through so much with the situation that I had to just let go, and that's why I was hysterical. I had to get to such a state of letting go, I was almost psychotic; it didn't matter if I won or lost anymore. I had to let go."

She was gone, but her torturer wasn't quite done. Another fellow drives up, and the two men load her body in the car and drive away. Staring off after the car as nothing happens for a few minutes, the same fury that grabbed hold of the audience for the past few hours degenerates into sadness, acceptance that this is how things tend to work out away from the movies.

Still, there were a few things that we didn't see, and few knew of . . . until now, of course.

Every scene in *THE BUNNY GAME* was recorded in the exact sequence of real time. On the morning of the last scene, Rehmeier was driving the van with Getsic laying in the back in preparation. "It was dark and alone," she says of being in the van. "My mind was quiet. We pulled into a gas station. I heard a bee buzzing, and I love bees so much. I love being stung by bees. I asked God, and prayed out loud in my mind that I would love to have a bee sting me."

God probably doesn't get many such requests . . . perhaps why this one was granted so quickly.

"Sure enough, that bee came, and landed right on my forehead," Getsic says. "It stung me, and flew off, then fumbled around and fell to the ground. That beautiful bee had given his life for me. It was perfect, in the right time at the right place."

The film took up two weeks. Now it was finally time for Getsic to step back into herself and ease Sylvia back out.

"Once it was over, she was dead," she says. "Sylvia Gray was dead, and I didn't have to be her anymore. I had to be tortured as Sylvia Gray, and it had to be real. None of it hurt me, physically or mentally. I can say that positively, now that I know what pain, torture, and suffering are." We'll talk more about that sad story in a few minutes. . . .

"I do. I act. I am. I become," she asserts. "When I experience life, I experience art happening. The way I create art is different every time. It is improv, just like my life. I do not script anything ahead. Sure, maybe I am open to memorizing a script, poem, or song of someone's, though I am only able to do this if I am deeply inspired at a soul level, and even then, it will come out in a unique, unexpected way, even to me, every time, because I am at the will of the All in All. Which is God, or whatever you call it. I am what I am: an artist who is free, not confined to any rules, other than that what I do may cause peace and awaken souls."

It was time to spread the work for Sylvia and the rest. As is all too often the case with this sort of thing, many (particularly outside of the indie film world) ignored Sylvia's story, not right away. Film critics aren't known for being especially independent and/or deep in their thinking. Typically, they looked at the pain Sylvia was forced through and the gleefulness of her tormentor and quickly labeled the film in reviews only as an overstated porno, an endorsement of the violent nature of sex, an exaltation for the sadomasochistic freaks of the world (keeping with the common motto of "to display is to glorify!"). Getsic wasn't at all surprised when the film was banned in the United Kingdom.

"That was all about control," she says of the censorship. "The people in power want to have control. We live in a free society, but when it comes down to it, it's not free at all. We're paying with our freedom, our livelihood. We're paying with our privacy. I hope it let people know that this is dangerous art, dangerous cinema, and not for the average bloke."

But *THE BUNNY GAME* is still around. Just as it took a very special individual to bring the story to the screen, it might take someone with the willingness to look under the surface to appreciate it. There's quite a bit more here than just a story of an innocent woman getting hurt and a dirtbag getting away with it.

"I don't know about other horror films, but I do know that we created this film in a spirit of complete submission to the piece," Getsic says. "The story being told was not ours to claim. We were slaves to the telling of it. My reaction in the film is completely intuitive and real. *THE BUNNY GAME* is a finished piece of art, its meaning evolves over time. It unfolds like a universe in its own revolution, destroying and building up, dying and being born . . . It is bigger than me. It is its own entity. I feel that its intention changes as it releases itself onto the earth. I feel it is a wakeup call.

"We were commissioned by Spirit to create the film, and we did it. One of my intentions is that

THE BUNNY GAME will cause some positive changes in people's behavior. That we can start waking up and making better choices in our society as a whole. Women and men are equal, but different, and we all need to be respected and loved."

She'd always have a right to be proud of becoming Sylvia, and walking away knowing that it had been an act that everyone had believed. But reality, once again, can get us no matter what precautions we take or where we go, and just as its darkest sides had reached out and trapped Sylvia, they'd get Getsic far too soon.

Because just as bad and even a million times worse, as painful as it had seemed becoming Sylvia had been for Getsic, as much as she'd hypothetically suffered before and while the camera rolled, it wouldn't be long before a new wave of misery hit her. One that fasting wouldn't prepare her for. One that a few days of rest wouldn't help her recover from.

On March 8, 2010, Getsic was dining at one of her favorite Hollywood restaurants. Walking across the floor, she suddenly slipped on a floor mat. She landed on her head, injuring her brainstem. In a flash, almost everything was gone.

After making it through years of her pushing intensity to the highest extreme, walking, thinking, normal activities that so many take for granted, became impossible chores. Life as she'd always known it was gone, almost certainly, it seemed, never to return.

This tragedy became her life. For four long years, Getsic endured a brain injury that worsened over time. No doctors could help her. Her body shut down, bedridden in indescribable pain. Eventually paralysis took over. Her entire body would go numb, and she was glad, as it was a relief from the pain.

If she and Rehmeier could turn this into a film, they might take a nicer route than *BUNNY*. They might just decide to go the full Hollywood route, where the good girls win, where the disease gets pushed aside, where human courage and decency are enough to triumph over any obstacle.

But this isn't the happy ending of Hollywood. As many strong, fast steps as the medical community takes nearly every day, it still can't answer every question, and for Getsic (and so many others who have been through this sort of thing), it's tough to find happy endings even in dreams. For the first time, all the energy, all the intensity, all the passion she ever showed before just . . . didn't seem to help.

God can be a funny guy sometimes. He (or She or It or whatever you want to believe) gets a great deal of credit for the good and the bad, and sometimes we pray after things we never wanted. Sometimes it can be tough to decide to whether someone who allows so much pain and suffering, particularly of the innocent, can truly be anywhere near all good. It would be much easier to believe that God's simply all powerful, but that would mean he's forcing us to get hurt and murdered, which sort of hurts his public appeal.

The Bible talks about finding messages in Someone's actions and having faith in them, knowing that, no matter what, it's all for the best, and that can be a tough truth to swallow. On the toughest journey of her life, Getsic keeps reaching out for the One she believes will always be there.

It's why she's suffering, but not scared. Always reminding herself of that familiar Biblical saying that so many used for inspiration, "Yea, though I walk through the Valley of the Shadow of Death, I will fear no evil." She, and so many others, continues to hold on to the hope and faith that something better is waiting on the other side, no matter how long it takes us to make it there.

"When I was young, I experienced the world fully," she says, "communicating with what some call God, questioning everything, discovering my soul in the calm of my own mind, exploring, taking chances, traveling alone, meeting new people. Life is a gorgeous whirlwind of yin and yang, dark and light. God is everywhere. To stay centered and out of shadow is key. Like at High Noon, where there is no shade, it takes a clear mind and wisdom to navigate in this world without getting caught in the abyss of darkness. Going through difficulties has taught me how to live right, how to survive."

Even still, Getsic maintains a spiritual faith in her journey that many of us can learn from. For four years after the ominous accident in that restaurant, she endured a deteriorating reality, an unfathomable, agonizing state of bedridden health.

Then, in 2014, Getsic received a miracle. She found some doctors who cared enough to look deeper, and, with state-of-the-art technology, received the proper imaging to further diagnose her injury. With the help of a world-renowned osteopathic neurosurgeon, she began the painful road of recovery.

And it's people like her that help you deal with the same feelings we've been discussing all profile. Yes, you probably spent *BUNNY* royally pissed.

And maybe it's affecting you too much. Maybe you have forgotten that it's *just a fucking* movie. But you don't think about that too much. Certainly not enough. Not enough to forget, at least not all the way, what you've just seen.

But while anger has quite the stigma attached to it, it doesn't *have* to lead to negativity, a bad outcome. Anger has won wars. Anger has battled injustice and discrimination. Good uses anger to take evil and beat it right back.

And it's exactly this about *BUNNY* that got it made, and what finally brings us full circle in the story of Sylvia Gray, whose terror, whose pain, whose sacrifice *could* push us in a better direction if we take the time and have the fortitude to think a little harder, learn a bit, and carry something away.

Asking film audiences to think and learn, and even to act on what they have seen in one's film isn't even a common question asked, particularly because it rarely gets an affirmative, especially in the horror sense. But just maybe Getsic's creation will become the next exception to the rule, with many more to follow.

"My film challenges its audience, offering some sort of a strange healing, a clearing, if you will, relatable in a dark punk avenue," she says. "This art helps move imperfect humans in a right direction. Perhaps as time moves forward, the intensity of this film will not affect the average individual in such a strong way . . . My film shows one person's microcosmic situation, and how she gets caught in the threshold of corruption. It is an indirect reflection of the whole world. It is a glimpse of caught events, naturally emulating the macrocosm of our current Earth status. Whore reckons with the World. Baby-

Ion! Punished, tortured, humiliated, submissive to man, abused, given to greed, ashamed, shamed."

We've got a chance to make things here in America right, or at least just a little better, one step at a time. Danger can create disaster, resulting in human emotion. Anger has led to positivity in the past, and it can entice strangers to come and work together. There isn't so much a common enemy to focus it on, but certainly one hell of a common goal.

Working together, putting aside all the reasons to discriminate and separate, we can save each other. We can prevent people like Sylvia from suffering these fates, and even stop people like her torturer from degenerating to his level. It's going to take time and work, but it can happen. If it's too much of a burden for our government to lead us to success, we'll have to make it there ourselves.

"People," Getsic implores, "all over the Earth, we have compromised our natural freedom. No one is to blame anymore except ourselves, as we stand watch. It is time to rise together on this planet in the name of Love and Truth. All religions and cultures can unite on this endeavor."

And if a person who, without any fault on her part, suddenly had nearly everything taken from her in a split second, can put that sort of pain aside during her years-long journey back to health, if she can put her personal suffering aside long enough to ask us all to worry about each other rather than ourselves, it's a source worth finding inspiration in and listening to. "In 1994, I was contacted by Archangel Gabriel," Getsic says. "He took me to the skies, to the edge of the Earth's orbit. There he explained to me the process by which I was born into the perfectly imperfect set of parental hosts, a childhood environment that enabled me to be born as a Light being on Earth. Others are born and being born, too, all throughout the planet, emanating brilliant blue rays of energy, white God energy, born into human beings. Our souls are crystallizing. By what Gabriel showed me, this powerful surge of light spreads, connects, then fills the entire face of the Earth, as more and more light beings are born. The God energy expands, encompassing the entire planet. You who are expecting a messiah, need to start looking within your own soul.

"This is where we are now: Unification in the name of God. Even if you are atheist, consider, that God is Everything, All in All, and you must believe that Everything exists."

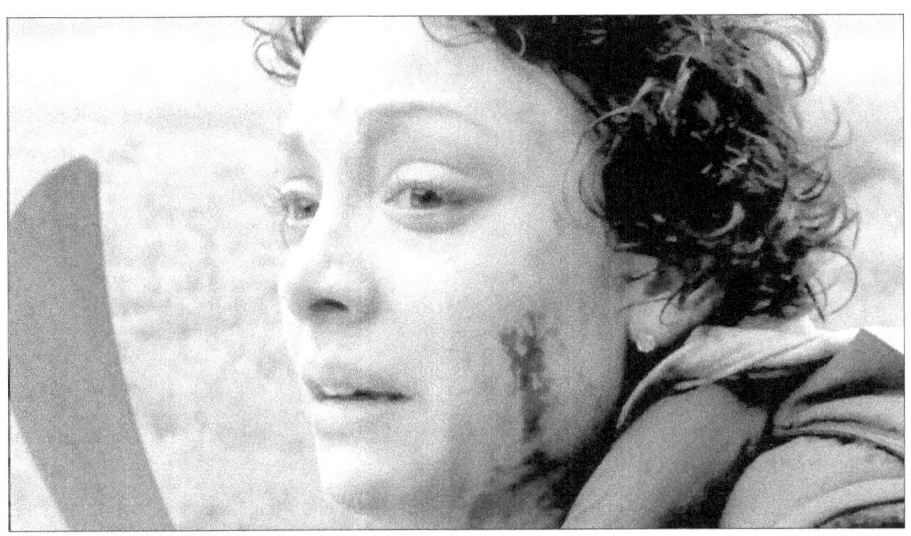

Up against the cold Pennsylvania wilderness, Amy Singer (Leah Gibson) prepares to walk *The Devil's Ground* (2009).

Leah Gibson:

The Devil's Ground

AS WITH JUST about any other profession, the first steps on the path to acting stardom are typically taken in the classroom. Many people in and out of this book will tell you that acting schools, lessons, classes, are all huge keys to success.

In that regard, Leah Gibson ended up as both the rule and the exception.

Indeed, Gibson got her start to acting in school—just not the type of study that most of her screen colleagues embark upon.

Growing up the British Columbia capital of Victoria, Gibson had dabbled in entertaining, dancing, and singing in the theatrical sense throughout her first two decades.

However, she remembers, "I always had this knock at my door, internally. Eventually, you just start to pay attention. There was just a point where I had to make the move."

She spent three years at the university, moving toward a degree in psychology. But before it arrived, Gibson couldn't wait any longer; she answered the door and decided to jump north up the BC province and a much stronger chance at acting than she could get back home.

"I moved to Vancouver," she says. "I didn't really know what I was doing, but it was something that I felt I had to do at this point in my life. It confused a lot of people in my life. My parents were supportive, but concerned. No one in my family, on either side of the expansion of my family, or close family friends are in the film industry. No one knew how to give me advice."

For the next half-year, she stumbled through auditions and agent searches, finally landing on one. But the roles weren't arriving, not yet.

"I'll never forget how foolishly naïve I was when I first started acting," Gibson laughs. "I said, 'I'm going to do this!' I had all my checklists, my goals ahead of me. I said 'I want to be the lead in a feature film one year from now!'"

It appeared for quite some time that her goal wouldn't become reality. But then the cast and crew of *The Devil's Ground* (2009) came calling.

"That movie was the greatest piece of work that had come my way in the beginning of becoming an actor," Gibson recalls. "It gave me kind of a romantic feeling in my heart: not only was it being a lead in a feature, but I'd be working on the outskirts of Prague, with Daryl Hannah. It was so, so special and challenging."

Over in the Czech Republic, she'd become Amy Singer, a college student on the search for a Pennsylvania burial ground to grab a few extra points for a class. But along the way, her friends are killed by a man with a mask and a huge knife, barely being saved by the welcome chance of Carrie's (Hannah) driving by. Of course, there's much more to this....

Gibson had been in pretty good physical shape her whole life. Finding Amy's panicked mindset, however, pushed her back to a more recent time—her college schooling.

"My approach with any part, I've been told, is very intellectual, which probably comes from my background in psych," she says. "I get really 'thinky' with my parts. I like to pour over research. (To become Amy) I watched other films that were relevant. I poured over the script from reading to filming, taking notes, writing connections, writing diagrams, just being very intellectual. I was journaling about the character's voice in certain situations, her backstory, the links between the relationships between her and the other people that she was working with. I just really connected to her fervent motivations."

We hear them right along with Carrie. Left the only one alive, Amy ran back to the gas station Carrie just left, only to have its former-friendly attendant call the very man who'd taken out her friends: it was Tobey, his brother. Just before Tobey finished his work, however, Amy managed to escape, when Carrie, almost literally, ran right into her.

"It's so demanding of certain qualities as an actor that you wouldn't do for other types of film," Gibson says. "For example, the time frame: we did it in thirteen days. That's very fast. You just go, and the crew works furiously, and you have to adapt to that pace. I remember how physically exerting that part was and all the tears I shed. Amy is constantly running and fighting and crying and living in a constant state of terror for that whole film. There wasn't a single day of filming Amy when I wasn't crying, when I wasn't in that emotional place."

And emotional is a very subtle way to describe the place that Carrie herself finally encounters. At a gas station, she desperately tries to call for help, but the cops don't believe her.

Not because they're lazy. Not because they're cold. Just because they've been here before. Amy's been here before.

She's been running down the same stretch for five years—on the anniversary of her own violent death on the same road. The Amy that we, and Carrie, fought so hard for didn't exist at all, not anymore.

As is usually the case when we're forced around that type of film twist, the villains do win: Tobey shows up and makes Carrie his next, and probably not last, victim.

Gibson had known how tough it would be to get into Amy's character. It had been even tougher to stay there—the film's creation time had seemed much longer than its near two weeks. But what she probably couldn't have predicted, at least until the experience of her first protagonist role has passed, was how difficult it may have been to leave Amy behind.

"Evening after wrapping the film in general, it's a very interesting process," she says, "the pain, the difficulties in shedding the skin of a character. Maybe not everybody is as weird about it as I am, but with regards to wearing the character like skin, you identify with the character's space and the emotional well-being, and you're in a very dark place with the emotion of horror. You want to bring that character's well-being to life, and that means manipulation of your thoughts and your personal and emotional well-being is sacrificed to pay homage to the character. To me, it's one of the most interesting things about the process. There's so much emphasis on feeling and believing in the voice and the thoughts and the mind of the character, and there is a process of shedding the mind of that character."

And, as she continued to realize in the next few days and weeks, from the physical side as well.

"I need to allow myself certain things when coming back to Leah," she says. "You have to honor the process of shedding the skin as much as you do stepping into it. It's emotionally exhausting, physically hard on the body. I needed a lot of rest, to come back to myself and be kind to myself and slowly put the character to rest."

The next year, she'd snare a much smaller role, albeit in a *slightly* larger-scale film. It was time to tell the third story of *Twilight*, and Gibson had a shot at finding the *Eclipse* in 2010 (she'd tried out for *New Moon* shortly before). She'd play Nettie, the Southern lass whose lust for power drove her away from her friends Maria (Catalina Moreno) and Jasper Whitlock (Jackson Rathbone), resulting in her death at Maria's inhuman hands and fangs.

"I went in a couple of times," Gibson recalls. "My last meeting was with (director) David Slade. He wanted me to play with Jasper as if he were a delicious piece of candy. I became animalistic, to use this great sexuality in regards to my appetite. Tasting on candy was fun and playful, a juicy thing to do. There was an element of play, a female creature preying on something delicious."

She didn't always get the same feelings from the *Twilight* crowd (*Twi-Hards*? Is that what they're called?). While the vampire films have been gold at the box office, they've been popular targets of scorn from fans and critics ever since the story of Edward, Bella, and the rest of the gang made its way to theaters.

"Along with the excitement comes a lot of hate," Gibson admits. "People would see my picture online and they'd say, 'Oh, she's not pretty enough,' or 'She looks this way or that way.' You just take that and find amusement in it. I've flown all over the world to meet with fans at conventions. I've never experienced anything close to that."

She keeps going, moving farther and farther into the mysterious and wonderful worlds of acting.

"The most giving side of the acting profession is complete submission to the character and the condition," Gibson explains, "and hopefully creating a piece of work that illuminates to all the people in the audience that we are all human beings with our struggles and that we're all doing the best we can. I like the chance to approach my work from that mentality. It's what drives my passion in this profession. I approach each role with the hunger to do as much research as possible with as many resources that are available to me, reading any kind of material in books and things that are relevant to the subject matter."

Fortunately, her education back home in Victoria gave her a special kind of preparation that not many enjoy, one that keeps prepping Gibson for "character-hood."

"I have always had a curiosity of the human condition," she says. "My background in psych is fueled by a lot of passion in trying to understand the human psyche, what makes us all the same and what makes us different. Understanding the human mind objectively is what I loved in psychology and how I went about my studies. It's where I continue to go as an actor. I want to understand my character inside and out to the best of my abilities objectively and be able to become completely different characters, to find out what I as Leah can understand about and relate to that and pay homage to that."

Buddy/Rick Giovinazzo:

Combat Shock

WE STEREOTYPE THE joy we only think, hope they feel. Those that fought through war and came back home, a journey that so many would never make, we on the outside might think them the luckiest people alive. We might believe that that's how they feel about themselves.

But those who actually made it home may disagree, and so might the families that watch those very ones return as different people. People unable to find any direction or stability, and descending (plummeting) straight into confused anger and violence, as such people too often do.

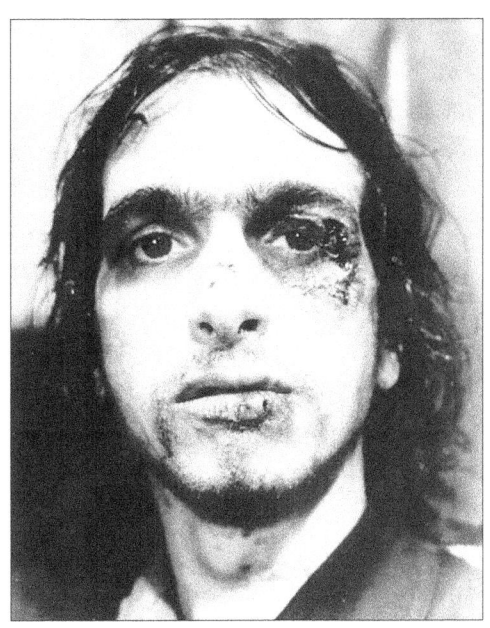

Like many Vietnam veterans, Frankie (Rick Giovinazzo) came back far from the same, we sadly saw in 1984's *Combat Shock*.

They find themselves yanked straight out of society, reprogrammed into cyborgs at boot camp, sent into combat, made to fight, forced to kill, used as target practice . . . then pulled back out and tossed back to their regular lives, the outsiders expecting them to re-adjust (or re-re-adjust) as quickly as a clothes change.

Some can do it. Most might (fortunately!) be a more accurate term, as many have gone to and come from battle, and ended up just as stable and productive as those who haven't, sometimes much more so.

But many don't. Many can't. Some find this "new" world just as ominous and painful as any battlefield. The homeland that housed them for decades is now dark and unwelcome, so they're mentally charged to believe. There's nowhere safe for them to be, no one they can trust, nothing they can do.

Some wind up on the wrong side of the law. Even they might be called lucky, by those that see their loved ones become causalities of a war that ended (in the physical sense) years ago.

No. It's estimated that, almost every single hour, another such life is lost—to its owner. Roughly six figures' worth of veterans have become their own casualties. You wish it was fictional horror, but it's just sad reality.

"*Combat Shock*," Buddy Giovinazzo recalls of his 1984 cinematic creation, "originally came from reading newspapers about war and soldiers. After a while, I realized that I was reading so many things about people that had freaked out, killed their families and killed themselves." And this was back in the early '80s.

Think the whole PTSD stuff is new? Wrong: as much attention as this horror has gotten publicly since it started affecting soldiers home from Iraq and Afghanistan over the past few years, it's been hitting veterans since the concept of war came about.

"I was fascinated by that," Buddy continues, "because it wasn't robbery, it wasn't greed. There was no reason why these violent crimes happened. The more I got involved with it, the more I realized that the people I was reading about were Vietnam veterans. What would happen if this took place, in one day?"

Sadly, that's happened, and not even rarely. Fortunately, for himself, Buddy hadn't gotten up close and personal with it, not a veteran himself. Way back in the ancient times of the '80s, he couldn't run up to a computer and Google out some tragic examples.

So he'd have to make it up on his own. No money, no experience, nothing but hope. But just as hope has managed to get many soldiers back home safe inside and out, it worked for him. Just not right away, per usual in the movie biz. Writing the screenplay took its own time. Now it was time to cast a cast that would work cheap (read: free) at a nanosecond's notice.

"Maybe six people auditioned," he remembers. "I needed someone I would have access to for two years." Then his brother Ricky showed up.

"He did great," Buddy says. "He'd never acted before, or since. I knew he'd be there."

Shock began by telling the story of Ricky's Frankie, running through the jungles of Vietnam. He actually hadn't had to travel too far for created combat.

"It was filmed all in Staten Island," says Buddy. "It was a lot of woods back then. I remember thinking when I was younger that it looked like Vietnam. The torture hunt was in my mother's backyards, shot from her roof. We waited until the grass grew for four or five months."

Shock, however, would be an *after* picture of war, not the *during* one that's been done on every single war, several times over. This was about Frankie's life back in the United area, not the scattered one that America only *thought* it could bring together with guns and bombs.

Frankie's awake, but reality is about a frightening as the nightmare he just had. He looks horribly unkempt, has no job to visit, has a pregnant wife that's ticked, an apartment they're about to lose, and a baby that. . . .

Well, for those wondering when the horror aspect will come in, it's right here (if the film being released by legendarily campy Troma Entertainment didn't give things away). Their baby looks like E.T.'s undergrown sibling, its cries something of a soprano with strep throat.

Was it Agent Orange's effects, as Frankie tries to convince himself? Maybe, but things are gonna get scary fast.

It's still the type of horror that former military men like Frankie face every day, however. He gets turned away at the employment office. He sees a junkie so desperate to be fixed that the guy cuts a hole in his arm with a coat hanger and dumps in the powder. He finds out that his dad, who thought Frankie was dead, is about to pass away himself, caught in cancer's inescapable grasp.

We can look at Frankie and know that this has been his daily life for a while. Hair all disheveled, eyes dancing around, head staring downward, voice tough to hear and comprehend. Getting such a look was one of his bro's toughest prep tasks, Buddy explains.

Ricky, says he, "is a crazily clean person. Then he plays this grungy character walking through swamp and garbage, His hair would never be greasy or dirty, and he'd never wear clothes like that. He just let himself go. (Frankie's) a guy who's deep down in life. He doesn't have hope, doesn't have anything."

Frankie's soon jumped, but gets revenge with a gun. His mind dragging him back to Vietnam, he remembers a land where people took their own lives to avoid the inevitable.

And now he will as well. This, sadly, has some precedence.

On July 31, 1966, the day before he committed (then) the largest mass shooting in American history, Charles Whitman wrote of his desire to relieve his loved ones from the suffering of today's world.

He began by killing his wife and mother. Then he went to the top of a tower at the University of Texas and started the sharpshooting skills he'd learned in the Marines. Before it was over, twelve people were dead, including an unborn baby (two others died later of their injuries), and over thirty were injured before Whitman was shot dead by police.

Still armed, Frankie heads back home.

"The graffiti everywhere helped him go into spirit of what the film is," Buddy says of Rick. "He let himself sink slowly into the role. (For the apartment) we rented the upstairs of a house. It was newly painted, and we had to fuck it all up, making it grimy, to look as bad as possible. It took a good two weeks to take a really nice apartment and dirty it up."

His wife's concerned about him, but Frankie's not so about himself. There's just nothing left for him, for her, for the baby that's here and the one who won't be.

"Everything that could go wrong for this guy goes wrong, even to the point of his shoelace breaking," Buddy says. "It's so dark, so depressing."

But it won't last. Frankie shoots his wife, over and over, demanding she die. Then he shoots his own child. Deformed or otherwise, it's a baby. His baby. And he just blasted it with a gun.

And if that's not enough, he now puts it in the oven and turns it on. The horror's hitting fast now.

Now it's all over. Of all the people that have died in the last few moments, Frankie's death will be the fastest. A bullet through his temple ends everything, including the film.

Another main man, fallen as the credits roll. *Scarface* had set that bar in 1983, but this is pretty good too.

"Killing himself was most disgusting scene because it was so bloody," Buddy says (the scene took hours to shoot). "He had to raise the gun and shoot himself without hurting himself. He was covered in blood, laying on the floor with blood pouring out of his head. The joke was that I put him through this hell of grime and blood, and had him laying in blood for four hours. We had to mop the floors and scrub the walls every time we shot the scene."

After shooting one piece after another for about a year, Buddy, Rick, and the rest of the *Shock*ers spent another calendar go-round knocking out the special effects, and Rick, already a composer, did the film score and music tracks.

Finally, with the Troma-tic name behind it, the film emerged in 1984. Marketed to the action crowd, it didn't hit too hard at first.

But, per usual for the group, once horror fans got wind of *Combat*, the Giovinazzos' flick burned straight to the accomplished lands of cult classic.

"You have this idea and you don't know if it's going to work," Buddy says. "You don't know if you can do it. You don't have the money to do it. At the time, we didn't know if it would work, and we didn't know if anyone would watch it. But it ended up being a really great feeling."

Taylor (Angela Goethals) hangs on to the hope that it's all a joke for Nathan Baesel's title character in 2006's *Behind the Mask: The Rise of Leslie Vernon*.

Angela Goethals:

Behind the Mask: The Rise of Leslie Vernon

WHAT DOES NORMAL mean for a serial killer?

We've spent this book discussing the preparation habits of performers, but what sort of planning and preparation go into the work of those that murder? Do they have rules, penalties, troubleshoots, even ethics?

Have you ever thought about how these guys feel about one another, what they might discuss if they could meet? Ever wonder what sort of coffee klatch Ted Bundy and Richard Ramirez would have, one they might actually be enjoying now in the underworld? Perhaps Jeffrey Dahmer, John Wayne Gacy, and Aileen Wuornos are in the booth next door, exchanging fraternal tales about who was truly the best man-killer. It's sort of like a fraternity of Satan.

Back in the 2000s, a film took a new look at some heavily explored territory, and even came up with some potential answers.

Many of us have probably dreamt of meeting some famous Hollywood stars, in or out of character, but there's one point where we'd need to be overly careful what we wished for. Imagine men named Krueger, Voorhees, or whoever else that have stretched their dirty work through one bloody sequel after another, strolling up to us and inquiring if we'd like to be the first to find out their secrets (and yes, Jason and Michael Myers didn't actually speak, but work with me here!).

In 2006's *Behind the Mask: The Rise of Leslie Vernon*, someone finally asked, and a young woman looking for a new spot before a camera (in and out of character) couldn't wait to say yes—to what exactly, no one could know just yet.

"I'm not a very brave soul when it comes to horror," admits Angela Goethals. "I don't really like to be scared, because I scare quite easily. (*Vernon*) was a true documentary that people were trying to make, creating an overlap to when the film becomes real, and suddenly instead of watching a horror film, you're being asked to suspend your disbelief even farther and think that this stuff really did happen. You're watching someone actually die or being pursued by whatever." She'd be Taylor, a budding news reporter leading her schoolmates through a documentary about the title character himself. Rumored to be following in the spirit of a man named Michael Myers, Leslie was kind enough to walk the crew through his meticulousness of getting ready to take out a huge group of youngsters with a single scythe.

Yeah, *sure* he was! Really, could there be any doubt that this gleeful fellow (Nathan Baesel) was anything but a high-class prankster, drawing everyone in too the limits of his dark sense of humor and imagination before pulling back and yelling, "Gotcha!"?

Could there be . . . please? There's a reason why *Vernon* came across as a pitch-black comedy through its first hour.

But let's keep things a bit lighter for now. Let's go back to the lead-ins for Goethals' first starring role.

Things got going for the New York, New York (repetition intentional) native in 1988, standing alongside fellow young acting newcomer Macaulay Culkin in *Rocket Gibraltar*. Two years later, the pair would be together again, and cinema lottery numbers would come up hard.

In the typical family youngster role, Culkin played a little brat that cruel family members just couldn't *wait* to tee off upon, including his older sister Linnie, practicing for the family's trip to France by referring to him as "*les incompétants*." But the morning of the trip, they're all frenzied to get out of the country on time, and Culkin's little fellow is left behind, easy prey for some dangerous new predators: a pair of burglars sweeping through the neighborhood.

But when they arrive, he's got tricks up his sleeve—and some irons and paint cans to drop on their heads, nails to pound through their feet, and a conveniently placed blowtorch to inflame an unsuspecting cranium.

Indeed, this is the story of 1990's *Home Alone*, which shocked everyone by becoming one of the highest-grossing films of all time.

Culkin was Kevin, and Goethals had been Linnie. But when the sequel arrived in Goethals' Big Apple homeland a few years later, she wasn't around.

"I felt like I wanted to stay in school," she explains of Linnie's disappearance, "to stay with my friends, and focus on some of my other extracurricular, and that decision was also enforced by the fact that Part Two was decidedly less interesting (for Linnie), because the character was not as compelling—there was less to play with."

Soon after, though, she'd roar into the small screen spotlight for the first time, becoming young tennis champ Angela Doolan in the too-short-lived comedy *Phenom* (1993).

"Other than being a dancer, which is very athletic, I never really played any team sports," Goethals recalls. "With *Phenom*, I was coached pretty rigorously before we started shooting the series, and during. I consider myself an active person (she'd eventually be on Vassar College's equestrian team), but in terms of sports or anything specific, other than dancing, I don't have any formal training."

The participation of minors in professional sports has been a controversial topic for decades, and Goethals and Angela (both of whom were still in their teenage years) could feel the pressure that's become too much for too many young athletes (the same could be said for children of the entertainment world). Training with professionals to develop Angela's skills would be tough enough; *Phenom* showed us her home life as well, filled with family issues and the oft-insufferable world of high school.

"It was definitely daunting," says Goethals, "specifically because one of the major focuses was this girl who, at a very young age, was incredibly gifted and talented. I wanted it to come off well for the people that truly know about the sport. It was really rewarding, because with the role, you get to learn a new skill or try to approach some kind of proficiency at something new. It's one of my favorite things about being an actor: that you're kind of a blank slate or canvas, and you get to experience these different things and learn these new skills, and often you're being coached or working with people who are at the height or their craft, their sport, their specialty. It's surreal, for sure."

Sports would lay the cornerstone for her next work as well, albeit in a less physical sense. Much like with Linnie, Goethals didn't get much screen time in *Jerry Maguire* (1996), but, again as with Linnie, we'd remember her.

Tom Cruise's title character is melting down; after committing the indefensible sin of recommending that his sports agency company focus less on the folding green and more on client humanity, he's out of a job. As his backstabbing colleagues steal one of his people after another, he's practically begging them to stick with the newly unemployed. Eventually, he finds one more of the underrated female clientele.

"The great thing was that (*Maguire* director) Cameron Crowe is a wonderful, collaborative sort," Goethals recalls. "Auditions can range from totally and completely painful to wonderfully inspiring and exciting, and fortunately, when I went in to read for the role, Cameron wanted to work. What could we build together in this room right now? That was a great gift."

She's athletic champ Kathy Saunders (her exact sport isn't revealed), and it just breaks her heart in *half* to leave the man who helped her reach the top of the sports endorsement world. Kathy's breaking down in tears, shattered at leaving him behind, she can't believe it's happening. . . .

And then her call waiting kicks in. Wiping away her emotions, Kathy clicks over, suddenly brighter than a sunrise. But Jerry's still on the line, and her tears are revealed as the crocodile sort.

"It was a short scene, but (Crowe) wanted to play with different interpretations," Goethals says, "and one thing we discovered while in the room was that Kathy starts as emotional, and then it dissolves into full-on tears. He really liked from minute one that she had an emotional quality to her voice, she's just barely holding it together, beside herself, because Jerry is a victim of this awful thing. We played with that, how far it got, how upset she got and ending up getting caught. How she says her name, how she answers the phone, it was a really awesome collaboration. When I got the role and arrived on set, a lot of the preparation had been done and the role already explored to a large extent."

It's almost time for *Vernon*. But before we get there, let's look at another of the actress' forays into fear, only this time she was the one causing the pain, and it was a bit more realistic.

As season five of *24* roared forth in 2005, central character Jack Bauer (Kiefer Sutherland) had just been canned by Los Angeles' Counter Terrorism Unit (CTU) director Erin Driscoll (Alberta Watson), who's then forced to reinstate him after a terrorist takes out one of her other colleagues.

As if an ongoing nuclear reaction crisis wasn't enough for Driscoll to handle, her daughter Maya arrives at the CTU clinic, Maya's schizophrenia becoming too strong for her.

To find Maya's dark world, Goethals turned to her colleagues, looking over Angelina Jolie's Oscar-winning work as a mental patient in 1999's *Girl, Interrupted*, and Jolie's *Girl* co-star Brittany Murphy's acclaimed performance as a similarly afflicted woman who torments Michael Douglas in *Don't Say a Word* (2001).

"It was disturbing and creepy, the detail and nuances that (Murphy) brought to that, and I aspired to a similar kind of attention to detail," says Goethals, who perused the Internet for more work on the disorder. "Some of the kinks, the frayed edges, the mannerisms. I put a patchwork together, and then the final element is getting set and getting with the other actors. That part, you can't prepare for, but luckily, on a show like *24*, you're surrounded by incredible actors. It's easy to draw from that."

With Driscoll hard at work, Maya's mind is too far gone; before the day is done, Driscoll finds her daughter has taken her own life.

The actual suicide was unseen, Goethals recalls, "so it was less hard for me and harder for Alberta, who had to come and discover me. You saw me before and after, but I imagine the 'during' would have been very intense and messy and traumatic. We didn't see the hardest part for Maya. But being zipped into a bodybag was an *awful* experience, profoundly disturbing. That really got to me: thirty seconds of terror." Such feelings would extend to hours for *Vernon*; let's get scary!

Once again, Taylor was looking for the most exclusive in a career that hadn't fully begun. Places like Crystal Lake, Haddonfield, and Elm Street may not exist, but they're welcome hangouts in the world of horror. In the similarly fictional Maryland town of Glen Echo, Taylor's learned the tale of Leslie Vernon, a fellow who, like Michael Myers, straddles the line between reality and horror. Is the tale tall, or real? We and she will find out soon.

"I fell in love with Taylor because of her earnestness," explains Goethals, "and because of her naïve sense of going out into the world and comporting herself always with this professionalism and focus, a very driven girl. I really loved being able to get inside the head space of someone on her first project, and she's going to just set the world on fire. I loved her ambition, her drive, her focus. She's young in a sweet way and curious and open, and the great fun of that is her then getting thoroughly messed with by Nathan's character."

Baesel was showing the rise, and unlike Jason and Michael, he not only discussed his crimes, but went into *all sorts* of detail! Desperate to be remembered amongst the ranks of superhuman killers, Leslie (who admits that he's just a man, and his last name's actually Mancuso, that Vernon's story was just an urban legend) plots out for his guests just what goes into such a spree.

In self-filmed *Blair Witch Project* (1999) style, Leslie discusses how he chooses his victims—usually some using teenagers with one tagalong who must be a) a very pretty girl, b) clean from the grime of booze and drugs, and c) a virgin.

He's targeted local waitress Kelly (Kate Lang Johnson), whom Taylor even helps prank, but not harm, early on. Leslie's even got some mentors in his work, a retired serial killer and the fellow's gorgeous wife, ready to give out pointers and pep talks.

Still, it all seems like one big joke. Why would anyone so openly brag about all this, especially before a camera, if they actually intended to do it? Taylor, her friends, and the viewers are waiting for a punch line.

"The dynamic of that was so fun to play with," Goethals says, "because here you have this kind of serious sort of dork (Taylor) coming up against this wackadoo (Leslie), and his funny, ironic personality that's larger than life, and it was fun to watch those two seesaw back and forth."

A few days before filming, Goethals, Baesel, director Scott Glosserman, and the rest of the cast and crew got together and rode around on location, trying to known Oregon's town of Portland and its neighbors.

"We got together and hung out, rehearsed a little bit, and hung out some more," Goethals says. "We walked around the old barn that got burned down at the end of the movie, and chased each other around a big open field, clowned around in a hayloft, went to Leslie's house, drove to the falls where the boy was tossed over the edge. Basically, we all spent time together, meeting the world of Glen Echo. There's something so powerful about being in the place (for filming), and it being a real place, not been built yesterday, not a set."

Over the next four days, the group learned of each other's ideas for themselves and one another as characters, and Glosserman discussed his shooting theories.

"It was profoundly helpful," Goethals says. "We felt like there wasn't much else that needed to be done. We got a sense of each other, of each other's styles as actors and people. It was the best jumping-off place, so when we got in front of the cameras, we were all together. We all knew what was what, and it felt really safe to jump in."

As the time for action draws closer, a few more folk of the unwelcome kind (to Leslie) arrive. *Poltergeist* veteran Zelda Rubinstein (in, sadly, her final film role) has a small part as a librarian that becomes his first victim, although it's not clear if her death is still part of the act. Then comes Dr. Halloran, whose psychiatric efforts to help Leslie failed, and now, just as Dr. Loomis was to stop Michael Myers, is ready to put his own life on the line to take down his former charge.

After portraying evil so many times as Freddy Krueger, Robert Englund now battled it as Halloran.

Still, even after Leslie lays out in overwhelming detail his plan to take out Kelly and her friends—enveloped in a night of drug-assisted passion—with the help of a scythe, Taylor and the gang still hope he's playing. Then, with them hidden in a closet, he brutally takes two lives. Here's where everyone finds out that this stuff is real.

"When Taylor realizes it's her he's after, that everything else has been a joke," Goethals says, "the one scene for me was one of those strange moments when you can't bring yourself back from the reality, even the created reality of the film."

With Taylor and her pals on the run outside, the viewers' view suddenly changes. No longer the self-filmed game being played, we're on the inside with them. Bravely stepping back inside the house, Leslie isn't to be found, but his targets are.

Including Kelly—and she's not the puritan Leslie described. With her soon dead and everyone else showing their own faults, we finally see who he had in mind all along.

The only true model of wholesomeness there, the faultless girl who found herself an innocent follower of fear.

Taylor.

Earlier, Leslie explained—and we saw in the dramatization sense—Kelly running from him, finding one of her friends after another slaughter, and someone summoning the strength to take him on. Now the scenes play out for real, only Taylor's the heroine. Everything that he had said is coming true—a rapid-fire line of violent deaths, Dr. Halloran out for the count, and things coming down to just two more people. It's time for all Goethals' athleticism that we mainly talked about in *Phenom* and *Maguire* to be terrifyingly seen.

And, for Leslie, felt. After a fatal game of tag lands both in the barn, he's got his hands around her throat. But she just manages to grab his own curved blade and plunge it into his side.

Then, in an act that Taylor herself might have though impossible just moments before, she plants his head in an apple cider crest and twists until his skull caves, him sadly admitting that he knew this was how it would all go.

"It takes a minute to come back from yourself, to step outside the character and return to your 'real' self," Goethals says of the scene, which took just a single take. "As I was trying to calm myself down afterward, I said it was like a blind moment. The line was blurred for a moment, and felt very frightening and real. Everybody felt that there was something big going on, and it's often hard to recreate those moments."

Because, for the last few climactic moments of *Rise*, its crew felt a new co-star, one that they couldn't see or touch, but had been there all along, and was now moving from the supporting to the spotlight.

"When you're inside the world of the movie, you're doing your job, saying your lines," Goethals says, "but there's another character, which is the horror, the fear. How do you take this and bring it to a level that will resonate with people watching and get their hearts beating faster? It was almost like it wasn't me in the movie, because it was so much bigger than I had imagined."

About to receive Salem's idea of justice in late-1600s justice in *Superstition* (1982), Carole Goldman's Elondra Sharack vows she'll have dark revenge.

Carole Goldman:

Superstition

SHE'D HEARD IT all before. Generations had been there, seen this, heard that. Probably been pretty scared of it. That was, of course, the objective.

As she waited outside the door to the audition room, a large chunk of the thick wood that represented, both literally and figuratively, her potential entry to the film world, Carole Goldman listened to the same sounds, the same words, even the same *cackling* that had raged across America's entertainment radar for, at the time, almost a half-century.

The Bronx gal's big-screen debut might be a horror film. It might be as a witch. And where do American film fans typically go to at hyperspeed when such a character comes to mind?

Well, the Land of Oz, of course. The very one patrolled by a green, broom-riding villainess and her hardly merry group of soldiers, human and otherwise. For a shot at 1982's *Superstition*, Goldman's competitors followed in the pointed shoe prints that Margaret Hamilton left all over *Oz* (1939), hoping such an imitation would wow the director into the lottery-esque prize of an evil lady lead.

Not Goldman. Forget the following mess; she was going to go for a whole new trend. And why not? Why not go for innovation, rather than reminiscence? Hamilton's performance was iconic. Why mess with it?

Why not get people to marvel at something new, rather than do even the best imitation of something old?

And if it didn't work, well, she could at least hope for one hell of a first impression. Much of her work had been on New York's and Chicago's stages, then compiled a list of sitcom labor in the new lands of Los Angeles—seen by many as just as mysterious a place as the one Dorothy Gale fell into!

"Underneath my pleasant, reasonably attractive, reasonably ladylike persona," Goldman reveals, "can be a very street-tough person, and I don't get to use it. Listening to the actors in the audition room, they were doing the witch from *The Wizard of Oz*, with her high voice and laugh. I came in with a dark, long-haired wig. I put on black boots, black shirt and skirt, and looked very menacing."

It's tough to describe what she did next. From the writing sense, at least; being there would have been much more effective. Before the casting woman could even give her a cue, Goldman grabbed her straight by the sense of fear.

"Uuuhhhggghhhu. . . ." she uttered. The woman glanced at her, blood and color falling toward her waist.

"We started to read, and I kept using this, this *growl*," Goldman recalls. "It was an animal, guttural sound. I scared the crap out of her. I went home, and I found out I had the part. I enjoyed the idea that I was going to do that kind of emotional drama."

Acting out Arthur Miller's *A View From the Bridge* had won her an award back in the Windy City (scripting legend David Mamet had produced the work), and her first few years in L.A. had brought in her share of roles. Nothing, however, even close to the horror world.

"I was suddenly getting work as a sitcom actor, a comedic actor," she remembers. "I was funny, but nobody knew that in Chicago. I'm basically a dramatic actress on stage, so when I saw *Superstition*, I thought, I am gonna go full out on this, I am gonna do everything you're not able to do on a TV series. I'm very animated, and on TV, I had to be very still, because my face moves so much. Because I was auditioning for playing a witch in a horror movie, I was free to do what I want."

Combining *Amityville* with a touch of *The Crucible* (fortunately, Miller didn't seem to see it that way!), *Superstition* re-told the overdone tale of a family moving into a haunted house, unbothered by the recent wave of violent deaths happening in the vicinity. Then they find out the story behind the tragedy.

"As an actor in L.A., a part comes to you when a breakdown is sent to your agent from the casting person, and your agent submits you to the casting person," Goldman explains. "Then the casting person, or the director or producer, decides to bring you in. A breakdown describes the type of actor required, saying something like 'She should be a strong, dramatic actress of a certain age.'" Something about *Superstition*'s breakdown had convinced the actress, her agent, and the film crew that she could portray extroverted evil. Now everyone had to prove it to the viewers.

As we all figured it would turn out, there's more than just harsh reality working here. The house was the site of an occurrence that still stigmatizes American history today: a lady accused of witchcraft back in the late 1600s.

Unlike most of those that were actually charged in Salem way back when, however, this gal appears to actually be stone-cold guilty, and damned proud of it. We flash straight back to meet local temptress Elondra Sharack, shackled to a plank in a church-like dungeon, promising that she and her true father, her master from below, Satan himself, will be back to take it all out on the local priest and those that help him (*Superstition* was released as *The Witch* in some parts of the world).

It was time for Goldman to grab hold of her short screen time and slam it deep into audience memories. "There isn't a whole lot of backstory you have to prepare for," she admits, "not like a dramatic series or theatrical piece when you have to write the backstory about a character. She was going to be killed, and she was going to come back later. It was very simplistic stuff. I just had to act the hell out of it." If the fiery eternity was where Elondra was headed, she couldn't wait to go, and her furious emotion wasn't all an act her portrayer continues.

"I was tied to a plank for hours," she says. "In the process of making a film, there were a lot of shots from different directions and angles. I don't get that in my life too much. The fact that I was entrapped, in the dark, with real people threatening me, helped me feel angry, to be the angry Elondra. And once you get a feeling like that, you build on it to make it larger than it is. There was a lot of fake smoke, and old lady extras were fainting. I was like, the hell with preparation—let me get out of here alive!" Elondra wouldn't, but that just made her stronger.

Strapped to a plank and carried outside, it looks as if the witch will be burned (never actually happened in Salem), or perhaps hanged (happened far too often in Salem). Nope. She's pushed to the edge of a pond, but there's one more invocation for the priest to say.

She doesn't care to hear. Cackling, laughing in a voice far deeper than her own. Preaching that her power will overcome anyone else's omniscience. Her face starts to become misshapen, bulges raging across it, as if she's becoming a monster, or perhaps was one all along.

"I was nervous," says Goldman, her face entrapped by a rubbery cast in the scene. "I pumped up the feeling that came from where I was. Hanging very near water, tilting it back, I got really and truly frightened that I would fall into the pond."

She's dropped into the lake, still tied up, impossible to escape. But before everyone can take a collective breath, the water stars churning like a waterfall. Thunderstorms roll in at high speed, punctuated by her laughter. A church bursts into flames. Looks like Satan's just as powerful as Him.

And she's still here, in evil spirit. One priest is caught in a wine press and squashed, much like other innocents were with rocks back in Salem. The home's new occupant and her three children violently die, one daughter with a spike nailed through her head. This film's doing a hell of a lot more than necessary to show what a horror the devil and his minions can cause.

Including their victory in the end. Another priest tries to cleanse the lake that took Elondra's life, burning it with fire (*Superstition*'s been far below realistic so far, so why start now?). But as he takes a relieved step away, her hand—the mold of Goldman's—reaches out and drags him down to be her unwilling eternal roommate.

"A lot of actresses want to be ladylike and remain pretty, but I'm fine if I'm not, if the part requires it," Goldman asserts, "and I was lucky that this witch needed to be so dramatic, because I'm not afraid of screaming or showing anger. It's easy for me to access a dramatic, dark person. I can go to very tough places, and I had no problem being the darkest, most evil person I could be."

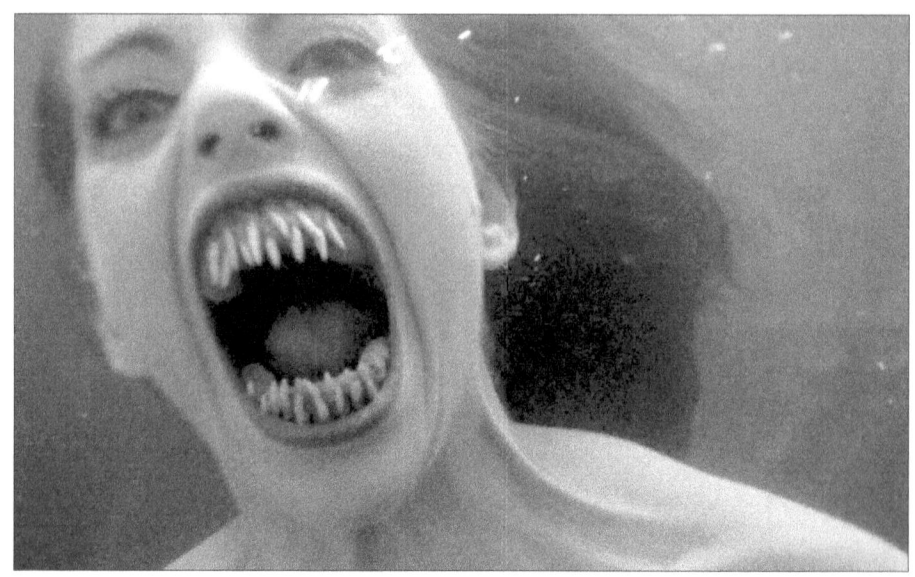

Like many lady sea creatures from history, *Dagon* (2001) main lady Uxia (Macarena Gómez) hid a black heart inside a lovely exterior.

Macarena Gómez:

Dagon

GROWING UP IN the jolly 'ol lands of Hampton Roads, one can't help but establish a connection to the sea and its inhabitants, real and otherwise. Virginia Beach and Norfolk boast at high volume of being the beach and boating capitals of the world, or at least America. At least the east coast. At least ... well, you get the idea.

So it's not surprising that up and down the watery sections of the southeastern corner of the Old Dominion, you can't help but run into creatures that (so far!) just exist in the myths of legends and fiction—although seafarers as well known as Christopher Columbus and Blackbeard reported seeing them.

Yes, we're chatting about mermaids. The unofficial mascots of Norfolk themselves, they're spread all over this neck of the woods—or waters—in drawn and sculpted form. Perhaps that's why, when mermaids grace the big or small screens, we around here might just have a stronger subliminal connection to the gals with fins.

We've certainly not lacked in choice: Daryl Hannah's work in 1984's *Splash* is legendary, and *The*

Little Mermaid (1989) has stood the test of time as technology has stepped into animation, remaining one of Disney's most popular offerings over a quarter-century after its release.

However, this is a book on fear, and, in all fairness, that's typically what we read amongst the written works on the creature-esses. Despite their typical Hollywood portrayals, mermaids are commonly known in myth-speak as evil creatures, luring unsuspecting (and hormone-driven) men to watery graves and sometimes even making meals of them—although, if one listens to Ariel's pappy King Triton, they're more scared of us than we should be of them! That's why this profile will focus on that side of mermaid lore.

How does one most effectively portray a lady of the sea? What goes into miming out a mermaid ("miming" is actually not an inappropriate term in this case—as they're underwater, fish gals can't speak either!), in terrifying fashion, while, you know, *not breathing*!

Clearly, physical expression comes straight into play. That's the first way that Macarena Gómez impressed the scouts of 2001's *Dagon*.

"I remember when I was a child I already said I wanted to be an actress," Gomez recalls. "The main reason for me to feel that way is that I was a ballerina, so I knew what (it was like) to be on stage and feel (what) the music meant to me. I had to play an amphibian, and my classical ballet preparation helped me with movements and gestures."

However, Gomez's gal doesn't show up for quite some time. It's first the story of Paul Marsh and his girlfriend Barbara vacationing in his mom's Italian homeland of Imbocca, Paul trying to comprehend his recurring nightmare of finding himself underwater aside a gorgeous woman—*with a tail and huge fangs!*

Separated from his gal in a hotel, Paul can't help but notice the shambling beings outside. Not from too much of the wine and cuisine their country is famous for—yes, these people are stuck between living and dead. Escaping to a nearby warehouse, Paul gets a bit more proof of his situation: in full *Silence of the Lambs* fashion, they're turning skin into attire.

Hoping that Barbara's still alive, Paul scrambles into an old man, who recognizes him as one of the last fellow humans. That's when we hear the title character's tale: Dagon is the local god of the sea who drenched the town in food and riches. But charity wasn't the deity's forte; you worshipped him or you died. Soon, the women of the town were given to him (we will *not* call an evil god Him!) to mate, spawning the creatures Paul was unwelcomed by—the fish-people. Now they've got Barbara, and she's about to become an unwilling mom.

Snared by Dagon's domestics, Paul and the man are taken to a barn, and the other fellow is slaughtered. But Paul escapes to a nearby house, stumbling into a dark room and finding . . . the woman of his dreams!

Her name's Uxia, and she baits Paul near. Still, we know what they say about what seems too good to be true, and this is one more demonstration: removed bedcovers reveal a frightening set of tentacles, and Paul's snapped back to fleeing fear.

"It turned to be quite tough shooting the scene in bed," Gomez recalls. "Special effects makeup artists attached tentacles to my chest as I was lying on bed and I couldn't move for eleven hours. So when I had the need to take a piss, I had to do it in a urinal. That was uncomfortable."

That adjective would be the world's strongest understatement for Barbara. Finding his way inside a hidden church hallway, Paul sees his love hanging over a pit, wearing jewelry for the ceremony, surrounded by dancing fish-men in masks made of human.

Then Uxia appears, and she's someone special, carried in by two others.

"In films, you can build the character with the help of the technical team, such as the makeup artists and costume designers," Gomez says. "You work as a team; there is much more interaction between departments with a clear objective: to make the actor feel comfortable with her character, or at least this is what I learned from my experience."

Paul goes pretty much crazy, setting some men on fire. But instead of ordering her minions to take out the outlander, Uxia stops them from doing so. She knows something they and we don't.

Then we find out—that Paul is actually the son of a fish-man. Uxia's his sister.

He makes one last grab for Barbara, but she begs him to let her go. But before he can follow her to eternity, Uxia knocks Paul into the water.

He can't even drown—gills suddenly spread through Paul's body. Finally accepting who he always was, Paul takes his new love's hand and freestyles toward the watery depth of their new home.

"I did not have to shoot any scene in the sea," Gomez remembers. "Instead I had to do it under the pool water, which was freezing. That was a very hard experience; my stuntwoman refused to do all the rehearsals because of the cold water and I had to do it myself."

Young Deke (Holter Graham) tries to figure out what the hell's going on when the machines attack in *Maximum Overdrive* (1986).

Holter Graham:

Maximum Overdrive

THE WORLD THAT Stephen King wrote about decades ago, and the one that, so far for the only time, he stepped behind the camera to show us . . . it all came true!

Machines. Technology. Our creations have become out captors. We made them—they own us!

Need proof? When was the last time we stared entranced at the TV for hours on end, forgetting that we might just have had more important things to do than watch people and plots that don't even exist? How many of us burst into hysterics if we realize we left our cell phones at home? *Would America not suffer everything but a collective psychotic break if the Internet were to vanish for a full day?!*

It's too scary to even realize. But even though it is true, it's still quite different than the author (is he a prophet? Some probably say so!) wrote down and eventually filmed.

By 1987, King had seen Brian DePalma, Rob Reiner, John Carpenter, and other household directing names bring his words to the big screen. But could any of them do it better than the author himself? (Well, hell yes, as it turned out, but King can hardly be faulted for giving it a shot).

Millions had read the tale of *Trucks*, first in the June 1973 issue of *Cavalier* magazine, and then five years later in King's first anthology *Night Shift*. *Carrie* had been the first of his works to be shown, and others had followed. Now it was time to kick things into *Maximum Overdrive* (1986), and King wanted to pull the strings of his audience from the background of directing just as he had with authoring.

But this isn't his story. It's about someone else who was taking his own new step into the movies.

"I never knew I wanted to get involved in acting," Holter Graham recalls wistfully. "I just knew who I was. 'Gregarious' was not a long enough word to describe me. With working parents, I was a latchkey kid and watched a lot of TV. I think it's something genetic, acting. Almost all kids are great at it because the big bad world hasn't forced them to separate reality and pure play. But some of us have it in the DNA and when we age out of the 'play,' we keep whatever gift it is that allows us to inhabit other lives, other stories."

Around the same time King was putting boots on the ground in front of the director's chair, one of his first stars was making her way to Graham's Baltimore homeland. A decade after almost winning an Oscar for *Carrie* in 1976, Sissy Spacek was looking for a young male co-star to show up alongside her and Kevin Kline in *Violets are Blue* (1986).

"I didn't get that part," Holter Graham remembers, "but Sissy saw something in me, and she had the casting director take a bunch of extra Polaroids, and, over the next year and a half, as she went around the country doing movies, she handed these Polaroids to anybody casting a movie that had a character my age." With her help, Graham's name became a tryout standout, coming close to acting out King's words in *Stand By Me* (1986).

He'd just missed starring next to Spacek in *Marie*, then landed just outside the time crunch in Wilmington for King's *Silver Bullet* (1985). With fate and the postal service working together, Graham's tryout tape finally landed on King's desk.

"I auditioned remotely, then they flew me down to Wilmington and I auditioned for Stephen King," Graham says. "I read a bit more with Stephen, and then he said I had the part. This time I believed it and did a handspring because I was so happy. Stephen immediately chided me and said I couldn't do dangerous stuff like that anymore because I had to get to filming in one piece." By the time *Overdrive* ended, few of its cast could come close to such a claim.

"I think acting is partly in the genes," Graham explains, "and the fact that I can memorize pretty easily and quickly reinforces that to me. That leaves me more time to just sit with a character. As I've aged, I've developed and maintained a somewhat jaundiced view of acting 'styles' and acting schools. I believe that you learn by doing. You will gain experience and insight in an acting school, but not necessarily much more than you will gain just acting—taking whatever gig you can, doing weird street theater, rehearsing monologues in the shower or while working out (I love trying to do monologues while swimming my laps), talking to yourself, just acting."

But all that was far away for his first acting role. "I just knew my lines, and found a quiet place inside me, which was sometimes a very difficult thing to do for a hyper kid," he says, "and let what made sense to me in the lines come out. Luckily, that worked, and hasn't stopped working yet."

The film starts out ominously, yet comically. We read the grave tale of this planet passing through the aura of a comet, which causes all of its mechanical inhabitants to turn against those that built them. People will suffer. Millions will die.

Then a guy walks up to an ATM. It calls him an asshole. He can't believe it.

It's King, making the same cameo he usually does in his book's films.

But things are going to go wrong—with deadly speed. A full drawbridge lifts, killing several and injuring even more. A mechanic named Duncan is blinded by a blast of diesel fuel. A line of trucks suddenly surrounds the truck stop where he works with fellow employee Bill (Emilio Estevez). One truck has the maniacal cackling face of the Green Goblin, who tormented Spiderman through decades of comic strips.

Unaware, a group of youngsters celebrate their baseball win with a few cold ones from the machine. One blasts forward, slamming into their coach. Another knocks the life from him.

Panicked, the kids scurry off. But it keeps firing and hitting with the same accuracy their fielders dream of. One, Deke, has the presence to slip on his catcher's mask for protection, but his eyes still witness a steamroller charge the field and crush one of his teammates.

He races away on his bike, but there's nowhere to go—he's barely able to outrun other vehicles, hardly able to keep his composure when seeing so many others that have suffered the machines' fatal attack. A radio broadcast tells him that this is going on across Earth.

With one option left, Deke burns off toward the drive-in and Duncan. His dad.

"There were no effects added," Graham says. "This was 1986 and the budget wasn't all that big. Every effect you saw happened when you saw it happen. We had an amazing crew of makeup artists, we had an amazing props department, we had amazing technical people—gaffers, grips, all of it—and they made movie magic. It's not like that much anymore, and I miss it."

Finally accepting his new reality, Deke makes it to the truck stop and sees the trucks going. Bill and others come out to help him into the place, but Duncan's not there.

That's because one of the trucks got him hours before. Deke can't believe it, and who the hell could?

"The crying scene was the hardest," Graham admits. "When we did it in rehearsal a month or so earlier, about my third day on set, I was so nervous and terrified that the tears just came pouring out. I felt a little humiliated bawling like that because I knew it was me and not Deke blubbering. But Emilio Estevez was really great: he put an arm around my shoulder and said 'It's OK man. It's OK, save it for the scene.' He was calm and generous and made me feel a lot better. To this day, I'm happy with my acting: the realization and outburst about my dad's fate. But when the crying part comes, I think I could have done a lot better. There was more there, and I didn't commit and fully grab it."

As day arrives, a secret, welcome, and totally illegal weapon arsenal is found in the truckstop, and the humans have one last chance. A blast of machine gun fire from a trespassing military truck takes out a few of them (mainly the bad ones!), but Deke, Bill, and others charge out through a drainpipe just before the trucks go kamikaze on the stop. Deke gets his moment of vengeance, machine-gunning a mocking fast-food menu. The Goblin truck makes one last run, but Bill blasts it to mechanical hell, and a sailboat floats everyone to safety.

What happens next? Maybe King can write that and direct it in his second try at the chair (*Trucks* was also made into a 1997 TV movie with Timothy Busfield and Brenda Bakke).

Meanwhile, Graham's moved in and out of horror, acting out fellow Baltimore native Edgar Allen Poe's work in *Two Evil Eyes* (1990), then having his mouth fatally bitten by Pollyanna MacIntosh's crazed matriarchal madwoman in *Offspring* (2009).

"Is it still French kissing if you drop dead and the woman keeps half of your lip in her mouth?" he sarcastically queries. "For (*Evil Eyes*), I had to learn enough violin technique to sell a scene . . . I had to learn the first bit of a piece by Debussy. I was instructed weekly until we shot, and I got my fingers in the right places. But the noise was so godawful that each take ended with me making a sheepish apologetic face and the rest of the cast and crew roaring with laughter."

But whether doing that, hitting full-blown campiness with his roles in a pair of John Waters films, or finding family fare with 1986's *Fly Away Home*, "I have learned the value of thought, of being a thinking individual, of thinking through and knowing your character," Graham says. "We use words. George Carlin said, 'Words are my work, they're my play, they're my passion. Words are all we have, really.' Getting to know a character, finding that hook that lets you take it into your skin, that's half natural and half intellectual. Read, read, read, anything you can get your hands on. You're preparing the ground for the seeds of character, of story. So I don't think so much about preparation as about being prepared. Think, think, think. Find something about each character that most comfortably attaches to you. It doesn't mean you are the character or that each character has to be a reflection of you. Just the opposite: each character is his or her own person, and finding even a tiny slice of them that can co-exist in you for the time it takes to play that character, is the way in, the place you return to whenever you hear someone say 'Action.'"

After all, it's among colleagues of a specific genre rather than a career objective from which an individual learner takes the most, Graham theorizes.

"Acting classes, I don't think they give you much training you couldn't get elsewhere, are places where like-minded people come together," he says. "It's important to join a community. If you're a horror fan, know that there are thousands like you: some like to act and some like to direct and some like to write and the really weird and interesting ones like to figure out how to make your head explode, freak out audiences, and not actually hurt you in the process. Find those people. Work for free, bust your ass, haul lights and wrap cable, learn every side of everything. You'll probably end up working on some labors of love that will teach you more than you can imagine. And they'll test you to see if this really is for you."

Every actor, sometimes time and time again, will be forced to ask themselves that question—and sometimes, he admits, the negative answer should be acknowledged long before it is.

"My answer tends to not win me many pals: know whether or not you are any good," Graham tells upcomers. "If you aren't good, stop. Find something to do with your life that will bring you as much joy as you can find. The high moments of acting—on stage or screen, when it comes together and you tell a story with ease and grace—are insanely wonderful. But they don't happen that often. I'm thirty years into an acting career with which I am very happy. That includes a lot of audiobooks and commercial and promo voice-over work as well as flesh and blood characters and telling stories, but on the day-to-day level my job is to be rejected. For each one you get, there can be dozens you don't. Film, TV, stage, commercials, audiobooks: the No's outnumber the Yes's almost all the time. I tell people that if there is anything else they think they can do that will make them happy, they should do it. But if you are someone like me, an addict, then go for it. I have other skills, and could probably make a life with some of them. But I can't. I'm an actor. It's like me and my wife's beloved pit/lab/mutt Lugnut saying 'I'm a dog.' There's nowhere to go with that. It's true. That's all. And all the more powerful for it."

It's curtains for *Curtains* (1983), as Patti (Lynne Griffin) readies to take out the last living obstacles in her way to an acting career.

Lynne Griffin:

Black Christmas/Curtains

IT'S ONLY FITTING that a book about horror movie preparation would include a tale of a film that touched on the topic itself.

Hoping to wow the powers that be running Hollywood, performance bombshell Samantha Sherwood (a name that probably took months to plan out in the marketing sense!) wanders into a mental institution. Not because she's overwhelmed with the soul-consuming world of box-office bombs and pessimistic critics—she just wants to find a new edge on the competition.

It's much more common today than when *Curtains* appeared in 1983, but the acting world appreciates those who can lead us through the sad, difficult, but sometimes inspiring world of mental and physical ailment, as such works tend to get quite a bit of attention and acclaim from the public.

Samantha hoped she'd be next, stepping into a ward to get ready for the title role in *Audra*, the story of a woman victimized by her mind. But while she's there, the film's director hauls a bunch of wannabe actresses to his mansion, including girl-next-door-ish standup comic Patti O'Connor, to try for the lead themselves. But doing so might have a bit too much to do with their skills off the stages—and between his sheets—so Samantha rushes in to plant her flag. . . .

But that's far from the only reason why *Curtains* found a way into this tome; its ending will stake a few new areas. Still, let's start with a film that started one actress' career and helped ignite a new subgenre of horror.

We say subgenre because, by the early 1970s, horror had been around in all sorts of aspects for decades. The classic monster films had set some trends. Alfred Hitchcock's work had made some more. Just a few years before, George Romero had set off for Pittsburgh and not left before establishing the whole "mass zombie attack" aura, which still lives healthily today.

Still, *Black Christmas* (1974) was something new. Horror fans of the times just hadn't experienced this sort of thing before. Would they accept, even appreciate the newness?

No one knew, least of all the young actress trying for a role. She just hoped they'd like *her*.

"When you're a struggling young actress," explains Lynne Griffin, "you go on auditions and you don't really know what you're going to get into when you get the job and get on the set. I had been a rather serious actress, on stage, and I wasn't really aware of the horror film genre, so it was a nice opportunity to do something very different."

For one of the first times ever, audiences watched a group of young women partying the night away alone. Viewers saw—or rather, didn't see—someone sneak up on one after another, violently killing them and leaving their bodies hidden away to find later.

While Olivia Hussey and Margot Kidder carried off the leads, Griffin became Clare, the first victim, her head violently encased in a large plastic bag, her body seen throughout the film, but never actually located by the cast (incidentally, Keir Dullea shows up as Hussey's boyfriend, and she later beats him to death, mistaking him for the killer. Wonder how all the *2001* fans of the time reacted to *that*?!).

"I wasn't completely aware that I was going to be smothered with a plastic bag, or that I would sit there for hours on end when they filmed it," Grffin recalls. "I never in a million years realized that that image, that particular death would become so iconic. It was a good thing that I was a very good swimmer and could hold my breath for a long time. Doing the takes, you could not breathe or the bag would breathe with you. There was a lot of holding my breath." The actual bad guy's never identified.

Decades later, *Black Christmas* is credited for starting the slasher flick genre, or at least helping it get bloodily going. Today, a sequel would have been made the next year (or maybe moved up on the calendar—can we imagine *Black Hanukkah*? *Black Thanksgiving*? *Black Memorial Day*?). Back then, the flick's innovation made it too new to copy, although a remake would arrive in 2006.

A few years later, Griffin stepped before *Curtains*. With Samantha Eggar in the lead as Samantha and the late great John Vernon as Jonathan Stryker, the lothario-like director, she'd be Patti, looking to go from laughter to horror.

"There was a real serious departure from the kind of work I was doing," remembers Griffin, who'd done quite a bit of Shakespeare. "I thought it was a real opportunity to play someone who does standup. I'd done nothing even remotely comedic, a very dramatic kind of actress." Her first appearance in the flick was standing up to make others laugh at a Canadian comedy club, doing a routine that Griffin had put together herself.

"In aging, I've become funnier, more peculiar or eccentric," Griffin claims, "but I was really nervous, doing standup in front of a live audience, even though I was a stage actress."

As the film gets going, two subplots kick in, one involving the actresses getting stabbed to death or decapitated, the other with Stryker taking advantage of the remaining ones' fear to seduce them. Might the two end up going hand in hand?

By the way, if anyone noticed that Stryker's listed as *Curtains'* director, that's not quite accurate. Partway into filming, director Richard Ciupka left the film over issues with producer Peter Simpson, who took over the shoot. Simpson ended up "giving" directing credit to a fictional character. These, and many other issues, are why audiences didn't see the flick until 1983.

With a few women falling prey to the knife, Stryker and another actress are caught in mattress action and gunned down. One other lady flees, only to get trapped in a warehouse and finally killed after one of the longest human hunting scenes in horror history.

Now it's just Patti and Samantha relaxing with booze, and we're just waiting for Samantha to confess to killing all that stood between her and stardom, then taking out the one person who could expose her. Remember, this early in the genre, the twist ending aspect wasn't really around much.

Looks like we're right; Samantha indeed admits that she held the gun that took out Stryker and his woman of the moment.

Patti grabs a knife. But not to defend herself. It's a trick she's been pulling all film—we just didn't know it was her.

"My scene in the end when I'm threatening Samantha with knife," Griffin explains, "those were easier to do than when I was supposed to be a cutup (don't pardon the pun!). It was easier for me to do those scenes when I was used to being called upon to cry a lot or be victimized. It was a real nice flip between those films."

That's correct—Patti has her own murderous tale to finish.

"I played a lot of people who got killed," Griffin recalls. "The twist in the character was really cool. I was always the victim, the first one to die, and it was really nice not to be the victim, that she was more of a fighter and a survivor." In a genre that's still hesitant to give women too much power in the evil, destructive sense, *Curtains* gave it to two of them. Samantha for taking out the cheating jerk and his paramour, Patti for killing . . . well, everyone else.

Ironically enough, while much of Griffin's screen time at *Christmas* had come *after* her character's passing, *Curtains* waited until the closing moments to show us that she'd been the bad girl, one of them, all along.

Now the only potential *Audra* left, Patti's finally got her shot at monologue stardom, but not before the cameras, or even the stages of her comedy club. Her only audience is the same group that Samantha played into way back at the start.

And unlike her co-star, Patti's there for all the wrong reasons . . . and she won't be heading out, probably (hopefully!) ever.

Steffie Grote:

Pawn Shop Chronicles

WHEN A FILM is tough to describe, it's usually a bad sign. When it's difficult to classify a film under a specific genre, audiences tend to get very iffy. In a world where people need everything but a two-by-four to the cerebellum to want to know more about a film, let alone get interested enough to check it out, a film that stretches out between a few different categories tends not to rack up the grosses.

That's one of the reasons why *Pawn Shop Chronicles* fell by the wayside when it arrived in 2013. There was certainly enough pitch-black humor to give it quite the comedic kick, balanced out with a degree of dramatic seriousness.

But there was also some serious torture from the inside and out. Some supernatural intervention. A bit of blood and gore. Enough that, as far as certain authors are concerned, it truly was a horror film.

But, sadly enough, the only inarguable categorization for the film, like so many in this project, ended up as "woefully underrated."

Still, the film didn't fall short for lack of star power: character acting icon Vincent D'Onofrio's title workplace forms the home-spot for an impromptu trilogy that ends up tying itself all together. The first tale has a few rednecks hilariously debating their basis for anti-Semitism. One of them's played by Paul Walker (this film, much like *Hours* the same year, only sadly shows us again what a tragic loss his death was), planning to rob the local meth man, which Norman Reedus took a short while off from battling the *Walking Dead* to portray. But it's in the second piece that we get a bit scared and even grossed out a tad.

Newly married Richard (Matt Dillon) and his wife show up at the shop, and D'Onofrio's Alton takes a break from tossing hysterical street philosophy back and forth with his friend Johnson (Chi McBride) to show him around. Then Richard spots a ring that belonged to the lady he used to love, who suddenly vanished. Forgetting his new gal, he takes the old wild goose chase straight over to a large nearby house.

That's where we'll meet the subject of this piece—but let's step back in her career time to really see how Steffie Grote helped steal a scene or three from her more established *Pawn* stars.

"I first became interested in acting in college when my grandmother thought she saw me on a TV show," Grote says, "but it was someone that just looked like me. This sparked my interest that maybe I should try it out." Classes at the University of Louisville and down in Miami followed, and a move to Kentucky put her before the frightening cameras for the first time.

"Horror and sci-fi films are one of the most popular genres to shoot when you want to break into the film industry," she says. "It was a very popular genre in the area and (these films) are usually a great deal of fun with all the costumes, blood, and special effects."

Things got rolling for her in 2009 with *American Vampire*, the tale of a young lady named Amber, looking to find her way through the brick wall that the modeling world can so often resemble.

"I was very excited to play her because she was an aspiring model/actress just like myself," Grote recalls. "I thought this would be a perfect role, for I don't have to dig very far to find the character of Amber." Soon enough, Amber realizes that her first paying gig is indeed far too good to be true—her new, experienced colleagues are indeed of the "Lady Dracula" sort.

Grote's next scarifying character was similar, but the gal's situation certainly wasn't.

Too broke to film their own horror movie—CGI and all—two guys decide to just make *American Scream King* all real. In a decision that everyone would obviously rush to, they just lock a group of aspiring performers in a room, tie them up, and start killing and filming. Sadly, chances are that such a film would end up a cult classic were someone to actually try it.

Grote was Steph, one of the first victims.

"This was an interesting project in the way the director (Joel Reisig) approached this film," she recalls. "He had actresses come in to audition without them knowing they were already cast and the audition was part of the film. Before I knew it, the audition that I just gave was the first part of the movie and I was not allowed to reshoot or try again. He wanted something true and organic. I wanted to play Steph because she was me: an aspiring model and actress and it was a great opportunity to take my improv skills into account. Everything was improv and living in the moment. Our actions, interactions and reactions made this story come to life. We had to make each moment become reality of the situation given at hand." Soon enough, the women take over and turn the tables straight around on their captors, though Steph is sadly not there to see it.

Elsewhere in 2013, Grote managed to step past the cameras of the Oscar-winning *Dallas Buyers Club*, another horror-comedy blend in *This is the End*, and—talk about another *seriously* underrated film!—*Oldboy*.

But now let's get back to the *Shop*. As Richard sneaks into the home, there's a fellow amusing himself in every sort of way. He's got a reason: the TV's showing his past bedroom conquests: himself, ahem . . . *cavorting* with *three* gorgeous women. One of them is our subject.

As the guy on the couch reaches his own self-imposed climax, Richard goes on the attack, and we see the fellow who we only knew as Johnny by name, not by face.

It's none other than Elijah Wood—and this, along with his serial killer portrayals in *Maniac* (2012) and *Sin City* (2005), make it *very* tough to equate this fellow that we watched as Frodo through nine hours of *Lord of the Rings* films, not to mention all the great stuff he did as a kid.

But Richard's not concerned with any of that. This guy took his wife, and he's going to find out how—and here's the first reason why *Shop* is in a book about horror.

He beats the hell out of Johnny, smashing him in the mouth with one very heavy instrument after another and jamming hooks and other metals through his lips and gums, to the point that the audience needs subtitles to understand his pleas for mercy. Eventually, the two make their way outside, where we find out that Johnny's far from alone.

In a building in the back, there's a stack of cages. Filled cages. And while many would label that an inhumane way to keep *animals*, Johnny's taken it even farther. Each one holds a gorgeous woman, her mind too addled to worry about clothing, Stockholm Syndrome in full force, nothing else in their lives other than to be their master's next conquest.

Yeah, some slasher flicks don't even get this graphic. Preparing to be one of Johnny's not involuntary prisoners, Grote got in shape.

"To get ready for this role I had to become skinnier and stop all grooming," she says. "I had to mentally prepare for a character. The character is an extremely mentally and physically abused individual who is practically starved, being fed mostly dog food, treated like an animal; in actuality she thinks she is being treated like a princess just like the others. Johnny has the ability to manipulate any women who show a weakness and then recondition her for his personal pet. Each girl waiting to rise to the top to be one of Jonny's favorites and embark on sexual encounters. Johnny's girl is no longer conditioned to regular society but has accepted her current situation."

Having beaten Johnny past submission—but not dead, which becomes important later—Richard releases the women. But they, much like animals who have lived in a zoo for so long, or prisoners stepping out of jail after decades in a pseudo-box, are unsure how to approach this scary new freedom, sticking together as they wander off.

Meanwhile, the third tale starts, and here comes an Elvis impersonator whose tunes have gone the way of the man he's trying to be on stage. No way is he going to avoid bombing at the town fair this evening . . . unless, of course, he gets help from elsewhere.

Elsewhere in this case meaning a creature from far farther than six feet under. Far from his usual fare, Brendan Fraser's Elvis player makes a deal with Satan to put on a rendition of "Amazing Grace" so outstanding that we half-expect his role model to make a deal with God to fly down and congratulate him.

But everyone else is certainly ready to—on the grounds beneath the stage, the three stories come together. One person after another that we've met for the past hour and a half arrive. The druggies. Richard. So many others.

And, in an impromptu procession more structured than a well-trained military group, Johnny's girls suddenly stroll in. That's right—a line of stunning women who still haven't remembered the laws about indecent (no matter how welcome!) exposure.

The men and boys gawk and cheer, and their wives and moms appear ready to beat them senseless. The newcoming women wrap themselves in an American flag, the epitome of satire.

Then, having healed up a bit, steps in Johnny himself. He works his black magic on "Elvis'" girlfriend Theresa (Ashlee Simpson). Then, like a father calling his kids in for dinner, he motions for the old girls to get right back in his truck, on the way back to slavery. They feel there's nothing to do but obey.

"The girls stuck together after being set free because they have been reconditioned to know nothing else," Grote says. "They were swaying in unison to an Elvis song. At the end of the song Johnny comes to reclaim his girls and manipulates a new girl, which gives a comedic and sick ending to the film."

She's going to keep moving forward in horror—and by this time this hits the shelves, she'll hopefully have taken a few steps into the spotlight.

"Horror is a great genre packed with excitement and fun!" she says. "There are some of the most talented people that work in this genre, from producers, directors, special effects, lighting, sound, actors, etc. They always represent their craft or characters and make themselves publically seen at many conventions and festivals worldwide by making these special appearances to support their fantastic fans! The horror genre has an enormous amount of fans. Each person is different in what they are interested in and want to become."

Even during Christmas, there's a place for fear and someone, or some*thing* to scare us, as Luke Hawker's *Krampus* taught us during the 2015 holiday season.

Luke Hawker:

Krampus

WHAT IS A surefire way to get a crazy kid to sit down and behave at a moment's notice?

The guy who writes that book will be a trillionaire in a nanosecond! But work with me here, parents.

Perhaps Christmas, instead of (or, optimistically, along with!) being a time for giving, we could turn it into the ultimate "Scared Straight" program! In the last months before that kindly old elf jumps down the chimney and drops off a mass of gifts, we warn our kids to be good, because he's always watching.

And for those kids who misbehave, well, he might not show at all. And if he does, it's coal and switches for them, right?

But being good for goodness sake isn't good enough. Instead of threatening our little delinquents with Santa not showing at all, let's go a step farther. Let's tell them about who might show up in his place.

Let's tell them about... Krampus. It's a strategy that European parents have been using for years.

Known as a friend of the devil, the K-thing is an evil-looking goat-ish creature, with huge horns and a terrifying grin stretching across his face. And for those who don't believe in Christmas goodness, they're going to pay. Santa might show up to do his job, but the Krampus knows it all, and he's right behind the elf.

To be fair, most parents mercifully call Krampus a mischief maker, rather than malicious. Like the infamous poltergeists, Krampus, despite his horrific appearance, usually isn't known to be violent; the worst he might do is steal a kid's presents, leaving a note with "Nyah nyah nyah!" or something similar written on it.

But this is horror, and horror can be all kinds of dark and terrifying. You don't believe in Christmas? You'll pay with everything. Horror has darkened Christmas before (it would be interesting to see someone go for a scary Chanukah or Kwanzaa movie!), but the Krampus is the perfect villain to introduce to put a new spin on a holiday that's known for its "goodness."

While many were out getting ready to celebrate the 2015 holidays, the Christmas bad guy got his own title chance to scare the spirit into those with the nerve to badmouth the holiday.

"Krampus's mythology is so beautifully evil and Krampus himself is such a wonderfully horrid character," explains Luke Hawker, who'd play the creature. "Like the eternal balance of good and evil, Christmas time in cinema somehow always manages to gain a positive and uplifting spin, but with Krampus the exact opposite is the case. The mythology is so elegant in its antiquity, and to perform a character that has such a rich history allows you to have confidence that its concept and presence in mythology has stood the test of time and is grounded in people's memories and subconscious." If *Krampus* worked, the whole "Scared Straight" aspect might reach out and affect all the family.

The film's start certainly was starting to look a lot like Christmas, and that was just another sad reminder. Perhaps having a flashback to Black Friday, shoppers crush each other to grab gifts they don't need, as the Engel family gathers with their in-laws to insult and annoy each other, rather than focus on what they should be appreciating.

Per usual, it's up to the kids to set an example, and young Max Engel (Emjay Anthony) blasts everyone's badness and fires his letter to Santa out the window. It's the perfect summons for Krampus, and a great starting line for Hawker, scared out of his own youthful mind by the opening of *Ghostbusters* (1984).

"The opening scene in the library still fills me with dread as a grown man!" he recalls. "With film-enthusiastic older brothers, I was constantly submitted to scenes like these much too early, which matured my imagination at an accelerated dark and terrifying rate. As I began to discover my love for performance . . . I discovered a great positive outlet for these strong harbored emotions and was easily able to bring to the surface dread and terror, and also understood the powers and pleasures that being a terrifying person or creature could give you."

He would do so through Krampus, but not for a while.

The Engels' oldest daughter, in typical teenage choirgirl mode, steps away to hang out with her boyfriend. Only we, at first, see the horned creature watching her from a roof. She hides under a truck, but there's a jack-in-the-box there, and the jack jumps out to jump her.

And if that wasn't surreal enough, a hook drops down the chimney with a gingerbread man along for the ride. A young boy grabs it for a bite, but *it* comes to life and grabs him away as the house catches on fire. Surrounded by the Krampus' minions, the family learns from the Engels' grandma (who's been here before) the story of it who punishes those that don't appreciate how good they have it during the holidays.

And it might be too late. A teddy bear beats up the aunt, a robot attacks a guy, and the jack eats a kid. Some other gingerbread men shoot someone, and even the cookies try to attack. Clearly, Krampus is determined to make these people pay.

"Krampus is much more the puppet master or overseer of his destruction and torture than the actual perpetrator," Hawker says, "making him seem all the more detached, powerful, and downright nasty! Horror is always a great way to engage with an audience, as fear and survival are such great motivations for any character, though as it is so raw the truth in the moment must be correct for the film."

A group of elves break in and abduct some others, and thumps thunder across the roof, showing that the thing in charge has arrived. As everyone but the grandmother escapes, we and she finally see him in deadly color, looking like Santa's mom had a kid with Satan.

"I really loved the reveal of Krampus at that moment, the way he seemed to pour onto the floor and rise up to stand before her," Hawker says. "I think this was where he was at his most imposing: passive and deliberate with clear intent to overpower." Getting himself to that point and staying there had fallen just short of horrifyingly difficult for the performer.

"The suit weighed more than half my body weight," he recalls wistfully, "and with the finger and leg extensions, coupled with my entire vision being through a tiny camera and mini-LCD screen, the performance started with just trying to figure out the mechanics of how to drive my new unbalanced and cumbersome body. Once I started to master the physics of seeing, walking, and turning, all very hard with a trailing pelt of red rags, bells, and chains, I could begin to add character and gestures into the performance." Even covered with extensions, molds, materials, and with no voice (Gideon Emery spoke for the character), he had to find the same way to be scary as those who'd been Jason Voorhees and Michael Myers.

"At one point I was working my usual day, making molds and such in the leg extensions in order to get my legs ready," he remembers (Hawker helped develop the prosthetics), "and felt super important! Once all the body mechanics were worked out and I knew what I was in for, I began to prepare my mind and body for a hard shoot. Becoming a non-human character can be difficult if it's just your physicality changing the way you move or breathe, but with all the added pieces on to me as Krampus, although restrictive, allowed me to feel non-human and take on a dark, removed-from-myself perspective."

The grandmother taken, Krampus sees his colleagues take some others outside. Then he hands the young boy his letter, showing just why everyone is here, doing this.

Max apologizes, wishing he could take it all back, and for the first time, Krampus might just see the error of his eyes, wiping away the boy's tear.

Nope. He and his pals drop Max's cousin into a hole to Krampus' home down below, then toss the hysterical youngster down there as well.

"This scene was by far the hardest physically for Krampus and potentially in my career," Hawker says. "Standing on the edge of the pit with nearly no sight, holding a young boy in a wire rig with arm extensions for long periods of time was excruciating . . . It was also a real challenge, as I'm sure Emjay will agree, to hold an emotional scene with a puppet. This required a lot of guess work and blind maneuvering on my part to hit the eye lines for Emjay and to make sure Krampus was seen in his best light for the camera. Seeing it in the final film made it all worth it!"

As Scrooge was lucky enough to experience, Max wakes up and realizes it was all in his head. But opening his presents shows that this isn't over, and the camera fades back to show the title guy one last time. . . .

"Many films or performances can be overplayed to highlight a character's clichéd evil nature or a relaxed cocky suavity . . . and this can very easily come off as hammy," Hawker says. "If it feels like cheap 'gore porn' on the page or in your head you're going to have a hard time changing it from that on screen . . . Every villain believes their cause is just, even if they know they're evil, and if you're playing the victim, you better like the taste of corn-syrup!"

Men like her butler can only cower in fear as the company CEO (Lindsay Hayward) roars to town in 2013's *R100*.

Lindsay Hayward:

R100

VISUALLY, THE SIMILARITIES appear to be far ahead of the contrasts. Both worlds involve performing to the extreme. Both of them are about overcoming overwhelming, even violent and dangerous odds. Both ask their audiences to forget reality once in a while. And both usually end with the heroes somehow finding their way to unthinkably difficult victory as audiences rejoice!

Yes, professional wrestling and horror/action acting might look to many to be two sides of the same coin, and moving from one to the other doesn't seem to be all that difficult.

But chances are, that belief's never been expressed by anyone who's actually had the guts to go there and try them.

"They are two very different motivations," explains one who has. "In wrestling, the goal is to kick your opponent's ass, make sure the audience has a great time, and go back to your normal life. You go through the curtain, you entertain, and you go back to your normal life.

"On set, a feature film is not like that at all. Every time, every single take, even if there are hundreds of takes, you have to continuously let yourself out into the open and then bring yourself back. Fluctuating and controlling those emotions, that tempo, understanding the script and portraying it through film, through onset performance, is the tricky part. In that part, wrestling is not like that. With acting, you have to give a bit more of yourself."

For years, Lindsay Hayward gave all kinds of herself to the sports entertainment world, spending years shocking audiences of one federation after another as Isis the Amazon (note: she was using the Isis moniker for *years* before the evil terrorist group made the name infamous).

"The reason why I got involved in wrestling because it was challenging for me as a woman," Hayward explains. "It gave me the ability to be unique. I didn't have to be the cliché of a tall person, playing basketball or volleyball, doing whatever boring thing that's expected of tall people."

That's something the California native has been facing her entire life. She hit six feet tall before she finished elementary school. Six foot eight since her teenage years began.

And ironically enough, her size and strength might have worked against her in a business built on athleticism. Guarantee you, had Hayward been a *Larry* instead of a *Lindsay*, she'd have been pushed to the moon and back in any federation in the galaxy—but being built above average can be a woman's biggest detriment in the squared circle. For someone about *thrice* the size of any other competitor (male or female), it's tough to make it if there's no one around that might have a snowball's shot at taking you out in reality. Not only that, but wrestling audiences, not known for being especially deep, still refuse to take seriously the concept of a woman legitimately outbrawling a man. Give it a break, people!

Still, Hayward had always wanted to switch from one performing profession to another someday, and it was wrestling that gave her just enough exposure. After noticing Isis gleefully (wo)manhandle another opponent—or, as was often her case, several at once!—on TV one day, a film crew member rang up her agent.

"He told me to go into the interview," Hayward recalls. "I went up to the director's floor. They took pictures of me and asked me to pose. They were like, 'Wow, she does exist!'" She was handed a script to check over—one much deeper than those found in squared circle exploits.

Reading over 2013's *R100* "was like a merry-go-round," she recalls. "It sounded a little crazy, and I didn't know if I wanted to do it. Then I thought, fuck it, why not?"

Just by stepping onto the film's set, Hayward automatically became a world record holder—her height made her the tallest actress ever to star in a film: six-footer Sigourney Weaver might have looked pretty tough kicking hell out of otherworld life forms in four *Alien* films, but she'd hardly reach Hayward's chest. It's ironic, but looks-wise, Hayward sort of resembles a taller version of *Game of Thrones* beauty Gwendolyn Christie (Hayward says she'd like to appear on *Thrones* someday), and considering Christie herself stands 6'3", that's all kinds of tough to comprehend.

With more layers than an oversized wedding cake and deeper surrealism than many American films even dare to get anywhere near, the Japanese flick tells the tale of Takafumi Katayama (Nao Ômori), balancing sales work and life as a "single" parent to his son (his wife's been comatose for quite some time).

Doesn't really sound like the roots of a horror/action flick, does it? A hard left turn will soon be taken. The protagonist joins a club called, simply enough, Bondage. For the next year, club reps in dominatrix form will show up whenever they want, and members' roles are very easy . . . to comprehend.

They may beat the hell out of you (in an erotic kind of way!), spit on you, or worse. You're just going to sit there—or whatever position they might decide to tie you into—and take it; canceling out early could be fatal.

Things go OK (well, for him) for a while. But soon, things start to spin out, although the film's constant switches from real to fantastic make it tough to really tell what's actually going on, and where. Soon enough, Bondage reps start to move in on Katayama's family. He accidentally kills a gal. Then he finds that another's into the whole cannibalism thing. Read that last sentence again, please.

Clearly, the Bondage folks have lost control. And the only one who might be able to restore it is someone we've heard snippets about all film, but never seen.

The head of the company. The person who scares the hell out of people who dominate others for a paid living.

"The main appeal to me for the character was the mystery surrounding her," Hayward recalls. "She's the CEO of a bondage corporation. Do bondage corporations even have CEOs? The whole organization is in fear of this one person. There's a buildup: who is she? For a long time during filming, it was a question I was asking myself. During the final stage of filming, I was able to render that, to fill in the gap."

Finally, she storms off a plane from Singapore, although we don't see her face just yet. It's not until the CEO storms into an employee's luxurious office (complete with swimming pool) that the momentary shocked awe that Isis so often instilled in opponents and audiences sets in, both on the screen and off. And it's not just her size that causes our pause: she tosses a human obstacle aside, then starts roaring obscenities at the top of her lungs.

In English. After American audiences have been trying to keep up with subtitles for the whole film, the CEO's the first character we can understand.

"Having to be so angry," Hayward recalls, "I just said, fuck it, I'm going to become a shark. I had to blow through the doors, push someone out of the way, and start dropping F-bombs at just the right moments. Having all that in your head was the hardest day of the shoot. After that, I was able to open myself up to so much more. It was a part of the character that I hadn't gotten into. It was a triumph in a way: you come to a hurdle and overcome it, and now you can enjoy it."

Perhaps literally trying to wash away her fury, the boss starts maniacally diving through the pool. This created a new issue for Hayward, one exclusive to the over-heighted.

"Splashing in the pool, I was very concerned," she says. "A stuntman did it, and he was like 5'5", so it looked fine, but the water was two inches above my knee at its deepest point."

Finally lowering her own temperature a few degrees, she yanks up a phone and lets Katamaya know exactly what he's in for.

"It was a little unnerving at first, because they wanted me to be bigger, meaner, screaming all the time, and that's not who I am," Hayward recalls. "The last thing I want to do is up my blood pressure. It was about lashing out, getting to this over-the-top character. It was comical, but at the same time, I really had to push myself out of my limits, to try to control the hardest thing you can control, which is anger."

By now, Hayward was sending the same effects through other parts of Tokyo as her character had on the screen, albeit unintentionally.

"When I was trying to go to the gym, I just thought the people were being very polite," she remembers. "Then they told me that there was a gang that met at a local bar, and everybody thought I was a gangster's wife, because I was tall and blonde with tattoos. Soon they started opening up to me, to be a little less fearful."

Armed with quite a few unusual weapons for a private citizen (although, again, this is a movie), Katamaya holes up in his attic. Sitting on a makeshift throne outside, the head woman sends waves of workers into battle, as if soldiers advancing on a fort at the clap of her hands.

One grenade after another takes out just about all of her foot soldiers. It's time for the CEO to take matters into her own hands.

Following in the tradition of *Clockwork Orange* (1971), the strands of Beethoven fill the air as she takes an apparently leisurely stroll toward the house. Waving the sort of cane that members of the S&M community often use for painfully pleasurable purposes, she's an impromptu conductor, hardly acknowledging the dropping blasts and bodies nearby.

"They wanted me to orchestrate to it," she recalls. "I read the script, and this was like an intense, weird thing that made no sense, mumbo-jumbo stuff, but when you actually see it on camera, it makes perfect sense."

Inside, though, it was time for Hayward to overcome an emotion that people might forget that those with her physicality even carry: fear.

"They played some music, and I started walking through the field," she remembers. "Then an explosive went off right near my foot, and blew dirt all over my face. I thought I was going to lose my hand. I had never worked with bombs or anything like that before, and it was pretty intense to be able to shoot that on the second day of shooting."

She soon drags him from the house, him struggling like a kindergartner trying to escape a hall monitor. The two make their way into a nearby barn, and we can't imagine what she's got in mind.

"When you're faced with things on set that you have to overcome, you either do or you don't," Hayward recalls. "It was good for me as a person to know that I could push myself past a certain point to get things accomplished and not hold up production. The director was able to get that out of me. I realized that I could push myself past what I thought I could do."

We don't actually know what she does. Lights flash on and off through the house as the music keeps blasting.

Then we see Katayama one more time, and he's . . . pregnant. Yeah, surrealism is very, very real in

Japanese cinema.

Watching herself on the screen, Hayward saw just one more difference between her former performing art and her new one: the criteria she'd used to judge Isis' work, compared to the CEO's.

"It was very surreal to me," she remembers. "I know I was there, but you don't ever know what you'll look like up there. It's like an alter ego of yourself. It was like all the work and all the transitions I had to make to play that character, I lived them again. It was like 'Wow, you accomplished something. You were put in a foreign country. You didn't even know their language, and you were talking through translators to the director.' It was such an honor, such a pleasure to work on something so meaningful."

Andrew Hubatsek went both female and evil to bring Stephen King's works to the screen in 1989's *Pet Semetary*.

Andrew Hubatsek:

Pet Semetary

DEATH, MAN, THAT'S something you just don't mess with. It's final, it's over, it's the end. It's never easy to handle, our own or someone else's, but once it happens, well, it's it. People have done all kinds of things to get around it, but it happens to us all, and we either accept it or suffer so much worse.

Yes, debates like this are typically confined to the horror movie community. Try to start this discussion anywhere serious or formal, and asylum representatives may come calling. But Stephen King never let the annoyances of reality stop him from becoming a household writing name, so we won't either as we analyze his work.

Let's have this tough discussion. If we could bring back a loved one, would we? Would we, if we knew early on that they wouldn't be . . . them? If we could already tell that something would be off about them, even dangerous, would we give it a shot?

Instead of debating that one amongst ourselves, let's step to the outside and look in on those who, spurred on by King's brilliance, even had the option.

Six years after the book's 1983 release, chats for a cinematized version rolled forward. Fresh off directing some trendsetting Madonna music videos, Mary Lambert was ready to ply her trade at horror—and right away, she and the rest of the *Pet Semetary* (misspelling both intentional and a story point) crew decided to take a pretty legit risk.

Rachel Creed, the story's main woman, had her own experiences with tragedy far too early. Shunned by the rest of the family and hidden away upstairs, her older sister Zelda had nothing to do and no one to turn to. When young Rachel, full of fear and brimming with all kinds of reluctance, came to feed her one day, one of too many abilities that Zelda's spinal meningitis had already stolen (along with her sanity), Zelda managed to spin her head around and choke herself to death—remember, we don't have to be realistic here.

And the saddest thing? Rachel admits that she and her family were hardly at all bereaved. It sets one hell of a tone for the rest of the tale, where Rachel and the rest of the Creeds will be battered by death.

Now Lambert had to show it. Many tried out for the role. Some were great, others not so much.

Then someone else walked in. The person had some theater experience, but little in films, nor even having read a word of *Sematary*, or any other King book. Just a hope and a dream.

"Like many actors, I was shy and trying to find a way to be in the world," explains the auditioner. "I also loved movies, and was really into Laurence Olivier's film of Shakespeare's *Richard III*. Horror fans should check out a real and funny and scary villain like the one Olivier creates in that movie." The 1955 film had Olivier in the darkly comic title role of a duke who tries to kill his own family for the English throne before being tortured by his victims' ghosts (remember what we said about leaving death alone?) and finding the fate of nearly every Shakespearean tragedy title character: violent death.

A few days after the tryout, the upcomer stepped into a New York bookstore and ran into Lambert, who'd been wowed at the vocal techniques she'd seen and heard. Zelda had had to display some extreme suffering, and the person had done a terrifyingly strong job.

"I kind of knew then, intuitively and with a rising sense of excitement," he remembers, "that I had the part."

Did you catch that? Yes, I said *he*. Lambert had decided on a fellow to play Zelda's role, hoping it would be just one more factual liberty fans would accept.

All Andrew Hubatsek was concerned with, however, was scaring. That would make the difference in the effectiveness of his role. He poured over King's words—again, few had gone to Zelda, but he could make for damn sure they wouldn't be missed or forgotten. Readers had created her voice and image in their minds; now he had to make it come true and mean something.

"I went to California to have the body cast made, which would be the skeletal makeup that would become Zelda's look," he recalls. "Knowing how she would look gave me a lot to work with. Other than that, I didn't know what to do or expect . . . I think I was just prepared to do what I did at audition with the further information I got from the book."

The title spot of *Sematary* lays behind the Creed family's new house in Maine. Rachel (Denise Crosby), her husband Louis (Dale Midkiff), and their kids arrive, Louis about to put his medical degree to work. Of course, bloody death arrives fast, his first patient being a jogger run down by a car.

And of course, supernatural-ity arrives, as both the dead man and the Creeds' neighbor tell them of the lot in the woods. It's a magic place, but not in all the right ways: burial will cause resurrection, but the new being will be evil.

Clearly, they can't leave well enough alone; the family cat gets creamed by a truck, and Louis buries it. The cat comes back wrong, but there will be much more to worry about soon.

So where does Zelda come in? Rachel informs Louis of her dark secret, and films have the luxury of visual flashback (rather than just talking about it), with Elizabeth Ureneck as the little Rachel. Her fears have a heartbreaking clash with reality: young son Gage (Miko Hughes) is hit by a truck and killed.

We can speculate on how horrible that is and we'd be right, but, after all, it's happening to people that don't exist. However, it's hard to disagree with Louis' decision to steal his son's body and rebury it in the pet graveyard—after all, a new person might be strong enough to overcome the darkness that's traumatized so many pets, right?

Wrong. But Zelda's back, tormenting her (we'll say "her" based on the character) sister's dreams, taunting her that the deaths were her fault, her voice sliding up and down the tone list.

"The way Zelda kind of springs up from a fully laying down position in one scene was an idea that I had and that I wanted to try," explains Hubatsek. "I was pretty limber then and I wanted to try something that seemed kind of unnatural, impossible, and also puppet like. I remember being proud of that."

Gage is back too, and becomes one of the youngest murderers in film history, killing the neighbor (thereby proving true the man's earlier pontification that, "Sometimes, dead is better."). Rachel comes looking for him, but Zelda's distracting her one more time.

Walking into a room, Rachel sees her sister in a corner, her back to Rachel, somehow the same age as she was decades ago.

"I've been waiting for you, Rachel!" Zelda shrieks. "And now I'm going to twist your back like mine, so you'll never get out of bed again!"

She runs for Rachel, seemingly charging straight at the audience. Many viewers probably experienced an unintentional jerking-back of the back at this point.

"Never get out of bed again!" Zelda screeches, now laughing maniacally at the top of her lungs. "Never get out of bed again! Never get out of bed again!" Her face is right up against the screen, it seems, and her laughter and voice are sending everything out of control.

Rachel collapses, desperately hoping that it's all a dream. But she sees Gage laughing, and knows that her worst nightmare is over.

Then he stabs her through the eye. By the film's end, Gage and Louis will be dead as well. Their young daughter is all that's left, and who knows what kind of therapy she'll need? King's never been known for happy endings, but this is certainly one of the saddest.

That scene, Hubatsek claims, "took place at about four or five in the morning after a full day of shooting and another full day of makeup application before that. I was tired, I had a cold, I'd been up for three days and we kept doing it over and over and over. I screamed my lungs out. That was tough."

Amy Huck remade Hollywood's finest in 2006, becoming the new nanny in *The Omen* remake.

Amy Huck:

The Omen

L<small>IKE</small> E<small>VERY</small> G<small>REAT</small> horror film, *The Omen* (1976) was jammed to capacity with moments that sent viewers' spines and blood into negative degrees.

The infamous baboon attack, and the one by the dogs. Father Brennan's impalement by his own church's spire. Jennings' decapitation by a flying sheet of glass. And, of course, the ominous grin of young Damien himself, closing out the legendary flick.

Another contender was the first shocker. As the child celebrates his (*its*?!) fifth birthday, his loving young nanny suddenly emerges from a window on the high roof. Calling out her devotion to him with a canyon-wide smile and eyes to match, the lady joyfully jumps forward, her fall and neck broken by a noose.

Three decades later, a new version of the tale arrived—not coincidentally, American audiences first saw the flick on June 6, 2006 . . . 6/6/6!

The cast certainly had changed—Liev Schreiber and Julia Stiles were the new parents of young Damien, himself now Seamus Davey-Fitzpatrick (in a wonderful inside joke, original evil kid Harvey Stephens played a paparazzi member). Holly Palance had been the nanny the first time, but not now.

"I actually hate horror films," Amy Huck admits, "and it is ironic that I am in so many violent movies. I live in Prague and the movies I am in happened to have been shot here." She teaches upcoming performers at Prague Film School in the Czech Republic.

It may not have been quite to the extent that Gus Van Zant went while directing his own personal *Psycho* in 1998, but John Moore's version followed Richard Donnor's original pretty closely. Schreiber's diplomat Robert Thorn finds out that his son passed just after birth (true, but much more tragic than he or we would eventually know), and takes another little boy, whose other mother died, as a sub.

Things go smoothly for the first few years. But as the new Damien and his friends and family celebrate, his new nanny is entranced by the sad, knowing stare of a large German Shepherd. Moments later, there's a closeup of her shoes, barely balanced on the edge of that all-too-familiar roof.

"I just tried to incorporate the director's vision and my own personality," explains Huck of being the caretaking brunette. "I did not have such a large part, so I prepared by watching the original, and then learning my lines and doing my actor homework."

Just as Palance had so many years before, Huck's gal gaily calls to her young friend. Not far from a cult member dying for her leader, she leaps grandly from the roof.

"I loved doing the suicide scene," Huck says, "as it was scary to be on top of the building and exciting to do such a big stunt scene." Her fall lasts a bit longer than the first one—we see the rope unraveling and the drop from several angles (a stuntwoman did the actual plunge). Just as in the original, it's just the first death of many ascribed to the youth—including, tragically enough, his own parents. Two sequels would lead the youngster into adulthood before Damien, now in Sam Neil adulthood, died at the end of *Omen III: The Final Conflict* (1981). *Omen IV: The Awakening* came to TV in 1991, and we're not going to talk about it.

A decade after the 2006 *remake*, it was still the only one. But never say never in horror.

"I had a very small part," Huck remembers, "but I did enjoy shooting the stunt scene. It does look really amazing in the final edit, and looks like I jumped!"

In a rarity for the horror world, John Jarrett played real-life horror in both an original and sequel with the *Wolf Creek* films.

John Jarratt:

Wolf Creek

IF IT MAKES sense to one person, that's enough.

If it can be justified in the mind of a single person, it's sufficient.

Everyone does what he or she thinks is right, from Martin Luther King down to Osama bin Laden. We're all correct in our own mental justification.

So when John Jarratt strapped in to blend horror and reality together in 2005, he realized that, while virtually everyone else would look down—assuming they could even bear to witness something so horrific at all—at his character's actions, if he could make them make sense to the guy he was playing, a big part of the toughest aspect of his job would be completed ahead of time.

"I read about serial killers and tried to understand the mindset of a psychopath," he recalls. "In the end, I think it's justification. So-called 'normal' people can kill millions of Jews if you justify it well."

We never know what's driving Mick Taylor, but he certainly does. Bad childhood? Mental illness? Boredom with hunting kangaroos? Whatever and no matter: two tales of *Wolf Creek* took us as far into such a mindset as it's safe for the sane to venture.

Early in the first *Creek* (2005), an outdoorsman (and two women) are traipsing across the western part of the land down under when, per usual for horror movie victims far from home, a car breakdown puts them on the down low. But then Mick shows up, and, also per usual, it's going to be too good to be true.

Towing them to his place, their non-savior hands out refreshments. But there's something in this water stronger than fluoride, and they're under and under his rule.

He tortures and rapes one woman. A shotgun blast doesn't put him out, or even down for long. The other woman tries to drive off, but he catches up and slices off her fingers like a master chief with carrots, then does the same to her spine, paralyzing brutality.

The first lady nearly gets away, but Mick blasts out her protecting passerby. He causes her to crash a car, then shoots her dead and burns the car, with both bodies. A video we saw back at his place showed that this stuff is nothing new for him.

The male captive was left nailed to a cross, but manages to escape. But even after his rescue, he can't describe too much of what happened, and Mick gets away, strolling off into the sunset like the hero of a western from hell, or maybe Crocodile Dundee's evil cousin.

"There's three things you need in any film: the script, the script, and the script," Jarratt says. "I loved the script. I love playing bad guys and I don't care what the genre is. Mick's an Outback bloke. I come from there and I understand those kind of people."

But what might have made it easier for Jarratt was that people had already justified Mick's actions in their own addled mentalities. Like *Texas Chainsaw Massacre* (1974), *Wolf Creek* had its own realistic basis. During the 1990s, seven backpackers were discovered dead and partially buried in the New South Wales area. Ivan Milat was given life sentences for each of the seven.

In 2001, a man and his girlfriend were traveling in the Australian Outback when a fellow flagged down their car, saying it had engine trouble.

The flagger and the man went behind the vehicle. A shot rang out. The woman ran and hid, presumably while her boyfriend's body was being disposed of. Five hours later, she was picked up by a trucker and taken to safety.

The boyfriend's body was never found. But in early December 2005 (just weeks before Americans got their first look at *Wolf Creek*), Bradley John Murdoch was convicted of his murder. That event, and others like it, showed that Mick's actions were horrific, but hardly unthinkable. So eight years later, when Jarratt brought Mick back, perhaps audiences didn't mind him becoming more of a protagonist.

"I worked on the script with (director) Greg McLean for four years," Jarratt says, "so when it was right, of course I wanted to do it. The character didn't change a bit; you just get to see more of him in the second film."

To be fair, Mick doesn't seem *all* bad as the sequel (2013) kicks off, taking out a pair of whiny corrupt cops. But when he sees a young couple camping, the monster inside comes right back out, and it's even more brutal.

Whipping out the bowie knife we've seen him wield to perfection, he performs a cranial amputation on the man. It was a scene that even Jarratt had trouble witnessing.

"I must admit, when watching back the brutal killing, I was taken aback," he recalls. "I thought, 'My God, did I just do that?'"

The woman escapes and gets picked up by a new Samaritan named Paul, but Mick blasts her brains out and chases the saver to an elderly couple's home.

That's when we truly find out how devoid of humanity this dirtbag truly is. He steals the husband's rifle, then slaughters both of them with it. If we didn't want this guy to pay before, we certainly do now.

Another capture later, Paul's tied up in Mick's dungeon, one that's been the killer's personal playground for a very long time. Showing that the Australian fascination that swept over America for a few years in the 1980s may have reached over to his British homeland, Paul wows his captor with some knowledge of the continent, only to lose a finger when he misses a question in an impromptu quiz.

Jarratt called it one of his favorite scenes in the films.

"It was like a play within the film," he recalls. "Great stuff for an actor to get his teeth into."

Paul escapes into a gaggle of Mick's old victims, but he's found once again and knocked unconscious. He's not killed, but committed to a special place, while Mick walks away into the bush at least one more time.

Still, as off as Mick seemed, as darkly crazy as he demonstrated over and over, there are things a bit less stable, says Jarratt, who also stood with Quentin Tarantino as a miner in *Django Unchained* (2012).

Like, say, giving the acting profession the what-for, or even the once-over.

"Try to audition and screen test for everything and change your middle name to tolerance and patience," he tells those considering it. "Or, go to a shrink and get talked out of such a mad move as an acting career!"

Chrissie Watkins (Susan Backlinie) started off one of the horror world's greatest sagas in 1975, becoming the title character's first meal in *Jaws*.

LEGEND ALERT

Caught in the Grip of *Jaws*

IF WE TRIED to name someone who got more mileage out of single-digit-minute screen time, Susan Backlinie would be tough to beat.

Her name might not get the bells ringing for film fans. Even her character moniker, Chrissie Watkins, may not hold a permanent spot in our memories.

But just say, "that hot babe that got eaten at the beginning of *Jaws*," and Backlinie roars to mind with the ferocity of the flick's title character!

Even before she was setting national swimming records in high school, the Washington, DC, native had been a huge fan of aquatic creatures. She'd played a mermaid in a Florida water show and done some underwater stunt work and been a pro animal trainer for some time.

In the warmest months of 1974, Backlinie headed to Martha's Vineyard to try out for a film that would add a new sense of realism to horror movies. She'd been recommended by a waterworking colleague, but the director was looking more for acting and less for stunt work.

"He wanted an actress," she recalls, "because there was a lot of acting involved, especially in conveying the terror." Still, with the possibility of physical danger far too present for their comfort, producers convinced their co-worker to let Backlinie show more acting than she'd be able to before.

After auditioning in a bikini, she arrived at the Vineyard, and came face-to-face with a visage that would become much more common to film fans for the next few decades; the filmmaker was none other than a certain fellow named Spielberg.

"He was really young and I was really nervous because he had wanted somebody from New York and they kind of forced me on him," she says. "But after I did my first scene, we got along wonderfully."

"He told me, 'After your scene, I want the audience—all of them—under the seats with the popcorn and bubblegum!'"

Her first scene, contrary to what film fans saw, was actually the only one filmed at night. It's the one where Chrissie and her boyfriend take an alcohol-induced jaunt away from a beach party and to the shoreline. The rest, the wet stuff, was actually filmed early in the morning.

Chrissie's hanging out in the relaxing waves, when a buoy chimes ominously nearby. Suddenly, we see through the eyes of the film's real star, the one that would terrify generations of film fans, and probably lowered beach populations for the time being. Some of the most menacing music ever written creeps out, and Chrissie's up against a force both unseen and unstoppable.

"I thought what could really be scary," Spielberg explains, "was to NOT see the shark in the water. We've all gone swimming, and we had the idea of this girl going swimming and the audience going with her. Having the shark come out of the water with its jaws engaged and come down on her would have been a spectacular opening for the film, but there would have been nothing primal about it. It would have been just a monster shark. This triggered our imaginations in either thinking about what was happening under the water, or blocking out was happening under the water."

With orders to make the attack "as violent as it could possibly be," Backlinie allowed her mind to venture to a place she'd never want to be.

"Oriented to the water as much as I was," she says, "I can't think of anything more terrible than getting attacked by a shark." That's why she attempted to focus the performance on evading such a battle, rather than fighting it.

"I knew floundering around, (because) starting and stopping and starting and stopping," she says, "is one thing that really draws sharks in."

But she'd have to do it alone; the shark wouldn't show up until much later in the film. Attired in a pair of jean shorts with metal attachments usually used to depict flight, she was fastened with wire to a pair of structures fifty yards apart on the beach.

"We had five or six guys on the each line, and all they did was run back and forth on the beach," she says. "It wasn't that forceful, but I could feel when my hip would start to pull the other way. I would violently throw my arms in the opposite direction. That's what gave it that real violent look." With Spielberg (who himself performed the "jerk-down" that starts the attack) and the camera crew in the water with her, and her "gear" equipped with releases, Backlinie could get out fast if anything went wrong.

"(I was) kicking to keep my body above the surface," she remembers. "When you pull like that, it has a tendency to pull you under. I put on a pair of wetsuit bottoms, which gave me a little buoyancy, and I had fins on. Steven wanted me as high out of the water as I could be, so I was fighting those cables all the time."

As Chrissie's launched up against the buoy, she pleads for help from another unseen force—but not the original scripted lines. Asked to bawl the Lord's Prayer, neither she nor anyone else around could recall the full version.

"All those guys, and we couldn't come up with it," she says. "I guess it shows we don't go to church much. I ended up screaming a different line."

Usually done for the day before noon, Backlinie checked out the flick's artificial centerpiece, getting to see the creation named Bruce—after Bruce Ramer, Spielberg's attorney—much sooner than any of her viewers. The scene where Chief Brody and a young student discover her body was the first scene filmed.

"There was all this shining metal—bronze and brass and stainless steel," she grins. "I'm a boat person and all boats have zinc plates on them (to reduce the degrading of metal by saltwater). After it had been in the water a day, they had zinc plates over it. It was a beautiful job, and it took a lot to keep that shark in shape. They had a crew going all night."

After two weeks of Vineyard mornings, she headed out. But a few months later, she was at Catalina Island in California, re-shooting the "shark-seeing" scenes because the Vineyard water was too murky (this took all of half an hour, Backlinie says).

The attack itself is rough enough, but the aftermath sends an extra chill up our spines: Chrissie's yanked under, and the waters return to their usual serene, even peaceful state. Seconds later, everything's back to normal, and a person just walking by would have no idea what had happened.

"My death is like the *Psycho* shower scene," Backlinie says. "It freaks you out. People always make the comment, 'You kept me out of the water for a very long time.'

"I always say, 'Yeah? I make myself nervous too, because when I dive, that's all I ever think about now.'" Physical acting wasn't her only job in the film; Backlinie dubbed her voice while screaming with a mouthful of water.

A year later, *Jaws* (1975) hit the screens, and filmgoers turned it into one of the biggest hits of all time. Backlinie became an overnight sensation, as *Time*, *Newsweek*, and other media outlets splashed her terrified face across their pages. The film's poster, showing the title character (his size a bit exaggerated) closing in on her, is one of the most recognizable—and often copied—in film history.

"I think it's a movie that scares people to death," she explains, "and people like to be scared when they are not going to be hurt."

Even four decades later, she (or Chrissie) is still swimming strong, although Backlinie never got much farther into the cinema mainstream. Along with a quick appearance in *The Great Muppet Caper* (1981), she went back to doing stunts and training her four-legged friends, such as a tiger used in *Apocalypse Now* (1979) and the ostriches in *Blade Runner* (1982).

"I got called in by a few really good agents, but they never picked me up," she says. "One of them just laughed at me: 'You had no dialogue (in *Jaws*).' But it didn't bother me; I wasn't one of those 'I've gotta be a star' diehards." She and Spielberg did pull off one hell of an inside joke/self-deprecation in 1979, as Backlinie reprised Chrissie in Spielberg's WWII spoof *1941*. In a near-reshoot of *Jaws'* opening, the young woman is stalked again—but this time, she's nabbed by the periscope of a Japanese submarine.

Later on, she taught people to have better underwater luck than Chrissie did, instructing divers in California. But all along, people have never stopped asking what it was like to be the first-ever victim in one of the film world's most legendarily frightening franchises.

"It's amazing that one movie has been remembered as much as it has," she says. "It's nice to have a part in a movie (with) a lasting effect on everybody."

One mistake that too many horror films make is the lack of character development of the victims. Too often, at least early on in a horror filmmaker's career, we see a person we know nothing about just hanging around alone somewhere—in the woods, on a deserted street, an empty building, wherever (typically somewhere that no one in the right mind would be!)—and then suddenly someone or something comes out of nowhere and slaughters them, often with blood and gore galore.

But that doesn't make a strong enough impact; the audience might be saying, "OK, the person got killed, and it was scary, but why should we care? For all we know, he might have been a criminal and the perpetrator might have been getting a justified revenge."

It sets the wrong tone for a horror film; right away, audiences want to know something about the people, to feel something for them, and to have it matter to us when something happens. We want to know who's good, who's bad, who's right, who's wrong. *Jaws* did that wonderfully. In several subtle ways, we got some quick lessons in the good guys and bad guy.

Check out Chrissie's flirtatious nature in the opening campfire scene, and the inhibitions that she just can't wait to toss to the wind. Look at little Alex Kinter pleading with his mother for just one last jaunt through the waves, not knowing that it will indeed be his last. And look at Mrs. Kinter's actions after her son is buried, and the way they turn the entire film around. These sorts of things helped us quickly identify with the people involved, and, if only briefly, care something about them.

As the film's crowded beach scene commences, we see a confused young man calling for his dog, disappeared into the water while joyously chasing a large stick (Pipit, the Labrador that becomes the shark's next unseen victim, was paid $250 for her short appearance, the funds donated to the Massachusetts SPCA). There's a huge group of people hanging out in the sun, working on their tanning, rafting, and backstroking skills (chances are, were the film released today, we'd probably get a subtle shot of a couple having at it underneath a blanket).

Like many Martha's Vineyard-ians (that's a great new word, isn't it?), young Jeffrey Voorhees couldn't wait to get his hands dirty and feet wet—literally here—as an extra in the film that would reach "iconomy" (we're rewriting the vocabulary here, aren't we?).

"When they filmed *Jaws*, I had just moved to the island the year before," remembers Voorhees (looks like *Friday the 13th*'s Jason wasn't the first horror icon with said last name!), "and the first thing that happens to me in Martha's Vineyard? I *die*! Eaten by a shark!"

Yep—Voorhees was Alex Kintner, the pre-teen on that infamous yellow raft that becomes fish food and triggers the film's legendary beach panic scene.

He'd just happened to stop by the set at just the right time—the $38 a day for extras was worth having to stand for hours a day in freezing water in the early New England summer (as the owner of a few speaking lines, Voorhees got a whopping $138 a day, not to mention a dressing room!).

"My friends and I were all about eleven or twelve that summer," Voorhees says. "We'd ride our bikes to the boatyard at night and try to sneak in through the back door because we knew the sharks were there. We'd usually get caught, but the guys who worked there were pretty nice and every once in a while—especially if it was after hours and they were drunk—would let us go in and take a look around. They'd show us how there was a different shark for each angle. It looked like a shark on one side and a big, mechanical engine on the other. They looked a little more real in the movie." Originally, the filmmakers had hoped to find someone who could train an actual great white shark to perform, assuming that the actors would be trusting enough to still get in the water with such an animal. That wasn't going to happen.

It's commonplace for horror films to set their tone by having gorgeous, typically little-clothed women fall victim to the main bad guys early on. But having a child get killed, particularly in uber-gory fashion, well, that's just a shattering of taboo. But then again, so was the dog's death, and most of the other things about *Jaws*.

"Once they were ready to shoot the attack, I swam out to a half raft they had placed over an underwater tank in about five feet of water," Voorhees explains. "The tank was controlled from shore (by compressed air) and looked like a giant cone filled with effects blood. The top of it was just beneath the water . . . I'd get up on this half raft, and they'd say, 'OK, when that thing goes off, it's gonna shoot the blood into the air. Go underwater and just stay under for as long as you can.'

"I said, 'This thing's gonna blow up? What the hell are you talking about?' I was a nervous kid, when it went *bam*! All this blood shot into my face!"

Eventually, the same techniques used to haul Backlinie around in the opening scene were used on Voorhees: crew members pulled him up and down as he thrashed about, not knowing what was happening.

"That's me doing the scream as the shark eats me," he says. "That was just stuntmen yanking me up and down in the water, until they finally yanked me under and gave me air underwater. They had an air tank under the water waiting for me . . . I look like I'm out pretty deep, but I was only in four feet of water." The shark that appears to snack on him was actually far from the youngster, just fins rolling around.

Mrs. Kintner (Lee Fierro) angrily mourns the tragic death of her son Alex in *Jaws* (1975).

When the attack was first filmed, blood shot out of the water like an overeager volcano, quite a bit more than a ten-year-old body (or that of any age!) would hold. As gory as the scene looks today, it was actually toned down for filming.

As the beachgoers freak and drag their unknowing children from the waves, often toppling and stepping onto each other in the process, Alex's mother revives from a heat-induced doze to wonder what's going on. As so many try to take the deep breath of relief they didn't realize they were holding, Mrs. Kintner searches for her child, hoping that he made it out . . . somehow.

Now let's learn about how a local theatrical matron became the shattered mother.

Lee Fierro had been acting since her childhood of the 1930s but had dropped out of the business, her five kids edging up on the priority list. But when *Jaws* came to the home she and her family had moved to in 1969, the acting bug started to re-sharpen its stingers.

However, when a friend met the casting crew for *Jaws*, she says, "I wasn't interested. I was busy raising my kids, teaching natural childbirth (she was a medical instructor), and building a house."

Still, she eventually went and met with Spielberg and the crew, and improvised the scene where the mother reluctantly allows her son a few more minutes on the raft.

An acting crew member "tried to persuade me to let her back in the water, but I wouldn't," Fierro says. "She tried and tried and tried, but I just wouldn't give in."

Spielberg stepped in. "Lee," he explained, "you've got to let him back in the water *eventually*, or we don't have a movie." A scene in which Mrs. Kintner goes down to the dock to see the shark that supposedly killed her son (we soon find out that it's not the actual culprit) had F-bombs dropping like an invasion.

"I said I wouldn't swear," Fierro says. "Besides, I don't think the scene is that well written. In the scene before, you've got two guys putting their cigarettes out on the shark and swearing bloody blue blazes. Then along comes Mrs. Kintner, and she's swearing too. It's not very powerful."

Even after being offered the part, she still wasn't into it. But a few days later, someone from the film called and said Fierro could do the role without four-letter utterances.

Instead, her main line became, "My boy is dead. I just wanted you to know that," to Chief Brody. It's punctuated by a good thump across his face.

As her character leaves the child's funeral, word about Chrissie's previous passing has just made its way around the island. But the chief's still reluctant to get involved.

"My character has just come from the funeral of her boy," Fierro says. "She's learned that a girl was killed a week before, and despite that, the beaches remained open. And so, filled with grief, disbelief, and righteous indignation, she goes down to the dock to confront the chief the chief of police and slaps him across the face." She had to give Roy Schieder over a dozen good whacks before Spielberg decided he'd gotten a satisfactory take. Schieder, for his part, allegedly had to see a chiropractor after his walloping.

"I had been taught how to slap, not fake slap, but how to really slap on the stage," Fierro explains. "I had been taught that in acting class—you do that with a loose arm and a very loose wrist so it doesn't hurt the person being slapped."

Apparently, both the actor and the character were hurt; the scene changes Brody's character, making him realize that Alex can't die in vain, but will have if that shark isn't caught. We get the impression that Brody might have seen being police chief as just a job up to this point, but having a personal connection to a victim gives him a new incentive altogether.

And now for the man who nearly—not quite!—stole the spotlight from the title character from the moment he roared (or screeched, as in the literal sound of nails across a chalkboard) onto the screen. The man more comfortable on the waves than Captain Ahab or Aquaman, who, if given the choice between making love to the most gorgeous woman alive or going head to scaled head with a shark would be reaching for the harpoon, who played that fellow with little screen time, but who personified the film's tenacious atmosphere.

Captain Quint was more or less a pirate without a parrot, eyepatch, or pegged leg. He'd be the one to lead the troops into battle in enemy territory, knowing that they all might die, and remembering that there's no greater honor than to give one's life for the cause.

That's the character, of course. But who would be the man behind him? Early on, no one was quite sure.

The crew had looked for Sterling Hayden, a professional fisherman and sailor between roles like that in 1964's *Dr. Strangelove*. Hayden had wanted to go for it, but tax problems had kept him out of the action. Legendary action star Lee Marvin was offered the part, but ironically enough, turned it down for a sports fishing trip. Would the third choice be a charm?

A trained Shakespearean actor, the new man had played the evil Grant alongside longtime friend

Jaws finally comes out on top in a monumental battle with Robert Shaw's Quint in the 1975 film's final death.

Sean Connery in the James Bond epic *From Russia, With Love* (1963) and scored an Oscar nomination for three weeks of work and less than fifteen minutes of screen time as the rambunctious Henry VIII in *A Man for All Seasons* (1966). Impressed with the substance he had given evil mobster Doyle Lonnegan in *The Sting* (1973), filmmakers hoped Robert Shaw could do the same with Quint.

Once again, the captain's not a hero, or even a particularly moral person—it's clear early that Quint isn't out to get the shark because he's concerned about the people on the beach: this is about getting paid first, and the secondary thrill of man-to-predator battle that the shark offers. But if Shaw could make audiences want to see Quint do his thing, well, he might have something here. Looking over Peter Benchley's book of the film, the actor saw the chance to make a relatively small character integral.

He couldn't do it alone—transforming a well-versed Englishman into a fisherman with rough skin and a rougher tongue would require work just short of Dr. Frankenstein. But just as Voorhees and Fierro had helped out as beach extras, and just as they did more times during filming than this book would ever have the time to detail, locals came to the crew's rescue.

Craig Kingsbury had done everything from throwing jabs in a boxing ring to the running of rum. He'd been shot, beaten up and down by a bull, struck by lightning a few times, and stabbed, not to mention more drunken brawls than anyone could count, or even wanted to. He'd also spent decades on the water, such as the thirty years he'd lived in Martha's Vineyard when filming commenced.

In short, he'd lived exactly the kind of life that a person making out Quint's backstory would put on semi-biographical paper. When the crew found out that a gold mine of information was literally next door, they headed out to meet him, with Shaw leading the way.

"Craig just had these very unique turns of phrase and very individual speech patterns," explains film screenwriter Carl Gottlieb. "Fifty years ago, every job in American had its own shorthand, or jargon. Sailors who worked on electric cables had their own language, as did all the fringe occupations—

carnie, traveling salesman. And Craig, having had a foot in all these different camps, just absorbed these colorful ways of speaking."

Shaw and Kingsbury hung out for quite some time through filming, with Kingsbury handing out a crash course in fisherman-speak and tales from his Vineyard time, some of which were, to coin a phrase, a bit taller than others.

"I'd tell him whatever he wanted to know about the Vineyard and the people who live here," Kingsbury said. "I used to make up a lot of stuff, tell him wild stories about incest and things, just to pull his leg. He'd laugh, and I'd tell him more. I never figured he'd believe me, but then he went and repeated it on national television." Quint was originally supposed to be chomping on tobacco, but combining it with Copenhagen, on Kingsbury's recommendation, proved to be a bit unsettling, even for the notoriously hard-drinking Shaw.

"The poor bastard," Kingsbury said, "he leaned over a chair and puked until his eyes watered. He decided Quint would bite on crackers instead."

As it turned out, Kingsbury would even grab his own moment in the film, though not in a pleasantly memorable way. Chrissie's attack at the beginning of the film has long been seen as a watershed in creating and maintaining a horrific atmosphere in films, but Kingsbury snares the film's out-of-nowhere, split-second shock moment. Early on, he's seen only in passing as Old Ben the fisherman, who has a quick chat with Matt Hooper about the craziness of those in pursuit of the shark. But later on, the two are terrifyingly reacquainted as Hooper, on a deep-sea hunt, discovers Ben's severed, partially devoured head. The scene was done in film editor Verna Fields' swimming pool.

"Dad always got a kick out of people screaming when his head popped out of the boat," recalls Kingsbury's daughter Kristen (her dad died in 2002). "He always said, 'That doesn't make sense—if the shark ate me, why would he spit my head back into the boat?'"

To get a greater feel for the ocean—though he'd get seasick during Orca scenes—Shaw hung out with a local couple hired to give technical advice and run boats on the film. Benchley also told Shaw about Frank Mundus, a shark fisherman he'd known.

As we will, right now—because without Mundus, not only Quint, but the shark's story itself may never have come about.

Months after World War II ended, Mundus approached a builder in southeastern Virginia to put together a boat that the strongest waves couldn't even rock. Put together with frames larger and thicker than usual, the *Cricket II* became a hit with fisherman across New York—including, on several occasions, Benchley.

In 1964, the ship landed a 4,500-pound great white, a battle that took over six hours. In 1986, a similar fish weighing 3,427 pounds became the largest in Earth history to be caught with rod and reel. It's one of nine records set from the *Cricket* deck.

Benchley based a huge part of his adventures into the book, the vessel called the *Orca*, and one of the main characters on Mundus, who passed in 2012.

Shaw incorporated a few characteristics of a man he'd never met into Quint.

"One of the things that great actors like Robert Shaw do," Gottlieb explains, "is build their character from one or two people, then synthesize them their own vocalization. And so Quint became a compendium of all these different people: Robert Shaw, Craig Kingsbury—a little bit of Frank Mundus."

Of course, Shaw put his own prints on the film as well. As Quint, Brody, and Matt Hooper hang out on the Orca after their first encounter with the shark—the boat was painted burgundy and black, as a rebel like Quint would never allow himself to be seen as pure enough for a white hat, let alone a full boat—the seaman reflects on the incident that kicked off his negative fascination with the scaled creatures of the sea. During his time aboard the *USS Indianapolis* in the war, the ship had a chance encounter with a torpedo, sending the men into shark-infested waters that some of them came out of disfigured, if at all.

The speech, which isn't in the novel, had gone through one rewrite after another during scriptwriting. Shaw, having knocked out several plays and novels in his time, put the finishing literal touches on the scene—and being a bit tipsy during its filming didn't hurt much either.

An outsider and damned desperate to stay one, Quint lived in a bloody shack; Shaw had a grand house and a manservant. A local crazy with a gun fired a few shots through their door early on, excusing that he thought the place was empty. But while the cast and crew might have been willing—probably prepared in advance—to deal with his imbibition habits, the locals weren't quite so welcoming.

"Everyone filming it was really nice, except for one guy, the old drunk, Robert Shaw," Voorhees says. "He ignored the island kids. They would have baseball games and cookouts for all the extras and kids on the island—all the actors would show up, except Shaw. He wanted nothing to do with 'The Island People' as he called us. As a little kid, I would go over and talk to him, 'Hi! How are you today?' He would just glare and say, 'Just go away.' He was always drunk, just a mess."

When Quint strolls into a music store and bothers a local youth in the midst of clarinet practice, Paul Goulart was there: the kid behind the instrument.

"When Robert arrived, we introduced ourselves," remembers Goulart, who got the role based fully on his percussive prowess. "Then he went to the back of the store and started singing these dirty songs that an old sea dog would sing about women and naked ladies dancing . . . I guess they were a part of his warmup and what he did to get into character. But I was just a kid and was thinking, 'Wow, I can't believe this guy's singing this stuff!'"

So perhaps the Vineyard villagers weren't exactly sympathetic when Shaw went to do his final scene. It would also be Quint's end.

Indeed, Shaw's farewell performance was Quint's demise at the hands (or, in this case, the rows of razor-sharp incisors) of the shark itself. But to be fair, Shaw wasn't in a much safer position than his character; he'd be strapped into a leather/steel corset for filming. He'd be inside the mouth of the mechanical shark, which had been malfunctioning throughout the filming process. If something went wrong, Shaw could have been dragged underwater and caught in a broken, and obscenely large and heavy, piece of machinery. There were divers underwater to save him if something went wrong, but it's likely that the comforts were very small in his mind.

Shaw, he admitted, was "scared as hell." But he made it through in two days of filming, and Quint's character would become a part of cinematic lore.

Just as a note here, the novel's ending might have worked well on paper, but comes across as incredibly anti-climactic when being imagined on screen, at least compared to the final cinematic product. First off, in the book, Quint isn't eaten, but dragged under and drowned, which would have had viewers screaming about a Captain Ahab rip-off.

Secondly, on the pages, the shark slowly passes out and dies as a culmination of all the stabbings and shootings it's taken for the entire battle. The concept of an air tank getting shoved into its mouth—the scene where Brody does so took over seventy takes—and then having Brody blast it into a fatal explosion ("*Smile, you sonofabitch!*") might seem a bit contrived, but *man*, did it work here!

Sadly and tragically, Shaw would impersonate his character not only in life, but in death. No, he didn't get eaten by a shark, but on August 28, 1978, just over three years after becoming Quint and less than a month past his fifty-first birthday, Shaw was driving through Ireland with his wife when he suddenly pulled the car to the side of the road. Clutching at his chest, he tried to walk off the pain, but collapsed, dead long before he'd be anywhere near a hospital. His alcoholism had finally caught up with him, and, just as the disease that medicine can't cure so often does, it had won the battle.

Perhaps there was indeed a small curse looming above Shaw all along: his father had been a lifelong alcoholic who'd committed suicide before the youth hit teenage years. Like his dad, Shaw had poisoned himself out of a long life. And just as Quint, he'd died painfully, but in the way he probably was fated to. Quint's early, painful death had been the culmination of the life the curmudgeonly sea captain had led, in the midst of the safest home he'd ever had. He'd lived on the sea; only fitting that he'd die there. Shaw's own life had imitated his most legendary character for the final time; he'd passed not in the way he wanted, but in the way he, as alcoholics so often push to the back of their minds, might have always known was predestined for him.

Aside from hitting the box office harder than any other film of the time, *Jaws* is credited with, if not singlehandedly, being one of the biggest factors in convincing the film world that the whole sequel thing was worth a shot, and, armed with the legendary tagline of, "Just when you thought it was safe to go back in the water. . . ." part two arrived in 1978.

But it hadn't taken so long in storyline terms; *Jaws 2* puts us back at Amity before Quint's ship can even be raised, a new shark making cuisine out of a pair of divers inspecting it. Still, the new trespasser certainly shared its predecessor's taste—don't pardon the pun!—for beautiful ladies. . . .

While her younger sister Lori Martin had gone into the performing side of acting—two years as the TV title character on *National Velvet* and then as Nancy Bowden, the young lady stalked by Robert

Jean Coulter has no idea that she and her waterskiing friend are about to become the sea's food in *Jaws 2* (1982).

Mitchum in the first *Cape Fear* (1962)—Jean Coulter tried the world of stunts, which, even decades later, is still a tough route for women.

"I wasn't a good actress, but my whole family was in the business," she recalls. "I was more athletic—I enjoyed sports and everything. I did a lot of jumping out of cars, which most girls didn't want to do. I worked a lot with horses, and did some work with cars."

After a few years of stepping in for the dangerous shots, Coulter started doing Farrah Fawcett's toughest work, standing in for the legendary bombshell on *Charlie's Angels*. When Fawcett got a big-screen shot at *Cannonball Run* (1981), Coulter was ready to follow her.

Then the producers of *Jaws 2* called. She'd managed to beat out hundreds of other upcoming gals for a small role in the 1982 flick—but, like Backlinie's, it was one everyone would recall.

"It was a part, not just stunt work," says Coulter, one of millions who'd loved the first watery battle.

Not long after the shark finishes its first meal, a lovely Amity lady plies out her waterskiing skills, her friend piloting the pulling speedboat. Sharks normally feed at night, but horror films don't play by the rules, and we see . . . something come up behind her and take her down forever.

But the woman behind the wheel doesn't, turning around to pick up her friend, wondering why her ski is all that's there.

Then she finds out what we know—the shark blasts through the side of her boat, sending her hysterically toward the other guardrail.

It was some of the toughest acting of Coulter's career.

"The shark didn't look too real, so every time I looked at him, I was laughing," she remembers. "For my crying scene, I had to turn around, knowing it wasn't real. I had a hard time with that."

Her mind far away from rationale, she hurls a gas tank at the shark, spilling some on herself. Then she grabs the only other weapon available, and it just happens to be a flare gun.

"You think about how you would feel if that was happening to you," explains Coulter, who worked with fire stunt experts to get ready for the scene, which itself took (on and off) four months to film in Pensacola and Catalina Island. "When you do stunt work, you have to program your mind anyway, so that's something you learn."

The flame scars the shark for life, but his at least continues; hers doesn't, as the boat and driver are blasted to fiery bits.

"Before you do the stunt, you just be quiet and program your mind that this is what has to happen," Coulter recalls of her mental prepping. "You program your mind and it does work: this is what I have to do; this is what's happening to me."

Ironically, five years later, Coulter would be hurt for real while stunting out some more animal-acted horror in *Cujo* (1983). Stepping in for heroine Dee Wallace, she'd be up against, and below, the film's real-life rabid canine title character.

"The dog was teased a little too much!" she remembers. "He was on top of me and digging into my chest, and he caught my nose and tore it almost all the way off."

Atum Vine (Tobias Jelinek, right) finds out he's been betrayed by Amber (Kimberly Leemans, left) near the end of *Fire City: End of Days* (2015).

Tobias Jelinek/Kimberly Leemans:

Fire City: End of Days

SOME WAY, SOMEHOW, they'd have to show the positive side of a group of folk whose very name sends an evil aura. To put some humanity in the non-human, even the anti-human. Perhaps muddle the film world's tendency to jam a warp-speed stigma onto their characters.

Quite a bit to do, and a certain lack of certainty over how. As tough as it probably seemed at the time, spending (it seemed!) a few months of time in the makeup chair for *Fire City: End of Days* (2015) was an asset, because while being cosmetically transformed into a demon, there's not much else to do but think.

Others had started the job and not even come close to finishing. In years of visual work under late legend Stan Winston, Tom Woodruff had seen it too many times. So even with more than enough to worry about in his first full-length directing job, two decades after scoring an Oscar for helping transform Meryl Streep, Goldie Hawn, and more of Hollywood's loveliest into zombie-esque undead in 1993's *Death Becomes Her*, Woodruff spread the worried word among *City* residents.

"There was never a doubt in my mind," asserts Tobias Jelinek, who'd get to experience the magic of David Elsey, one of the main reasons for *Star Wars*' own makeup Oscar. "Performance-wise, Tom helped me understand how movement reads differently when you're in a full helmet and face prosthetics. Your mode of expression is different."

Quite a bit would be different about *Fire City*, from most similar tales. First off, the demons were the main characters, if not the heroes and heroines. They're actually living here amongst us mere Earthlings, usually in pretty attractive visual format, waiting for us to invariably screw up, as it's our mistakes that give them strength. Living in an apartment building fraught with domestic and substance abuse, some of which he has to step in and assist once in a while, Jelinek's Atum Vine has found a gold mine of pain for the people and pleasure for the creatures, like his colleague Amber.

"The makeup process, from getting my life-cast done," recalls Kimberly Leemans, "to spending sometimes six or seven hours before shooting in amazingly detailed body makeup was just thrilling!" Like Vine, her Amber doesn't mind being the reason these mere mortals mess up, and she makes just about the perfect first impression upon us, seductively forcing a neighbor to sin between the sheets.

"I was literally standing butt naked in front of (the makeup crew) for some of the makeup applications," Leemans recalls, "and having someone see parts of your body that up close that you haven't even seen could seem very uncomfortable, but the detail and professionalism of this entire crew was just outstanding." That would come in even handier later on.

The demonic look isn't attractive, and it's what the *Crew* had undergone all the while in the chairs. While these beings often look just fine to their misery providers, amongst each other they see the truth, quite literally and very sadly.

"Amber embodies a lovely juxtaposition," Leemans explains. "She is so beautiful to the outside world, but can never see that, and she seems so tough and confident but is actually a very insecure, scared, and unhappy girl. I love finding parts in characters that I can relate to and also stretch myself when it doesn't feel natural." The time spent getting ready, the way everyone looked afterward, the interaction they'd undergo . . . natural wouldn't come back around for quite some time among the cast and crew. Jelinek attempted to stay that way.

"My daily preparation was meditation, something I've practiced for years," he says. "Whenever I wasn't on set, or if we were between setups, I would sit and meditate. When you are sitting in a full headpiece and your ears are raw, even bleeding, but you know it's going to be twelve hours before you can take care of it, conserving energy and keeping your attention off the discomfort is the most important thing."

Discomfort would be just as necessary to those that give his kind an inadvertent life force—the entities are there for each other, but people need to hurt for them to survive. But when Vine sees young Sara (Keely Alona) undergoing shit that shouldn't even happen in horror movies, the decency he never knew and probably hoped didn't exist comes around.

"It's a crucial shift in Atum's long life and he mysteriously develops compassion for humankind," Jelinek says. "He begins to feel and it scares the crap out of him. Suddenly the world he's known for hundreds of years, the rules of how it works and how one needs to behave in order to survive, completely changes. And that's where it becomes fun as an actor." Leemans had been stumbling across such discoveries since her time working on independent film crews in high school.

"I viscerally remember the energy and excitement of seeing all this massive equipment," she gleefully claims, "the lighting, the cameras, the overall buzz . . . and I was hooked. I needed to feel this high of creating magic as much as possible. I started to find my way in front of the camera by getting any part I could as an extra or day player. While the other extras complained of the long hours and long waits, I watched everything! I soaked it all up and didn't want our fourteen- or sixteen-hour days to end."

Something else might be ending for the demons—something larger. Ever since Vine saved Sara, the people are getting better! No more abuse, holding celebratory parties . . . are they happier? Less sinful? We can't have it! They need to suffer so demons can thrive!

Vine's never been here, and still isn't sure where to go. Amber, however, goes back to what's always worked at bringing out the self-harm in others.

To force out some "sinnery," she visits Frank and Lisa (Harry Shum Jr. and Jen Oda), who'd been on the brink of fisticuffs all too recently. Moments later, she's seductively crawling across their kitchen table, having developed a fabric phobia.

She kisses Lisa. She knocks Frank to the ground and kneels across him (Shum never had this sort of thing happen in years of playing Mike Chang on *Glee*!). Surely, such sultriness will cause a momentary lapse of monogamy, right?

Not quite. They politely, albeit uncomfortably, ask her to depart.

"Amber is letting every inch of her guard down and literally baring herself to try to get through to the humans and save herself," Leemans explains. "When you're naked, you're naked. There's no point in hiding it. It's quite empowering to be able to show your body on your own terms. It's something that I've grown more comfortable with over the years." She and Vine have a frustrated sexual encounter, getting more and more brutal along the way: much like the Klingons, who broke each other's arms during mating.

He ends up killing her, and others, saving Sara along the way. But the little girl isn't what she seems, and had some secrets all along.

"Playing scary twisted characters is one of my favorite things to do," Jelinek explains. "Worlds upon worlds exist in horror, and our fascination with the genre existed long before cinema was invented."

Sunglasses hid a dark soul inside the Father (Gene Jones) of *The Sacrament* (2013).

Gene Jones:

The Sacrament

FAMILY, PROTECTION, EVEN love.

These words can be found in any dictionary, but what they truly mean is defined by the individual. The significance depends much more on who we ask than anything anyone could ever find in a book. Labeling (often from the self-imposed top and glaring down) is much quicker than understanding, and it's always important to remember the many, *many* definitions of the words.

Is it bad? Is it wrong? Maybe, and even answering questions like that takes quite a bit of sending one's mind into territories we may never have even known existed within. But that's how the mentality expands and evolves, and how we learn more and more about our world, our society, and others.

A person without (or with, but to an unsatisfying degree) the things named above will try very hard to find them, and look in and even visit places that might once have seemed unthinkable. The lengths to which we will go to find acceptance, and even then to maintain it, might seem ludicrous to the outsiders known as the public population, but they happen.

And when they do, it doesn't always end well—and it's up to those that couldn't stop looking down to actually use an impartial eye and learn something about one more question with an immeasurable number of answers: why?

Fresh off terrifying film audiences from the director's chair of *The House of the Devil* (2009), *The Innkeepers* (2011), the similarly self-filmed *V/H/S* (2012), and others, Ti West now looked to dramatically analyze a tragedy that, even decades afterward, still shocks, saddens, and puzzles the world. As is quite often the case in the business, he stumbled upon one of the brainteaser's biggest answers in the most unsuspected of spots.

Hitting on a 2012 episode of the comedy *Louie*, West saw the title character (Louie CK) go shopping, check out a piano lesson, and see an old pal. Along the way, a pharmacist showed up for a few scenes.

Somehow or other, West looked at this man doing a short performance in the middle of a comedy, and decided he'd be right for a cornerstone in realistic horror.

It wasn't the only time the fellow had such a role as in *Louie*; the next year, he'd be at a carnival in *Oz: The Great and Powerful* (2013). It wasn't even the first—as viewers of an earlier flick, far from *Louie* or *Oz* in the genre sense, could tell.

Early on in *No Country for Old Men* (2007), an ominous-looking man strolls into a gas station, stopping off on his way to do something more important to him than the viewer will ever understand.

And perhaps he's looking for a practice swing, challenging the unsuspecting store clerk to the simplest of games: a coin flip. It's down to a 50-50 shot between everything and nothing. Quite literally, it's all the matters of life and death.

The clerk clearly wouldn't agree with this, but the scene itself was, "a case of show business working exactly the way it's supposed to," recalls his portrayer, Gene Jones. "It was the only role cast in New York (the rest was in Los Angeles)."

He and another actor headed to the tryout. A few weeks later came a callback. This time, the audience included a few very special guests named Joel and Ethan.

The Coen brothers themselves. Far from the darkly hysterical *Big Lebowski* (1998) and *Raising Arizona* (1987), their new creation was a thriller in the deep west. Cormac McCarthy had put the tale on a novel's pages years before, and now they were going to show it off.

"The only thing I knew was that it was a one-scene role," Jones recalls. "I had read the scene. The novel was available and I was offered the script, but I chose not to read either because I didn't want to invent some backstory that was not in the scene, to do some foreshadowing of something that wasn't in the scene. I just wanted to do the best scene I could do." It wouldn't be the last time he'd show that some successful performers don't use research to make things happen.

But his work worked, and he became the first to encounter the fellow we'd come to know as Anton Chirgurh, to whom human life is there for the elimination in a trek toward the almighty dollar. There's some money missing, and people far above Chirgurh have tasked him with locating it. But perhaps he hasn't convinced himself he can take so many out, and now needs a reason to do so, even if it's a person he's never seen before, whose only crime will be mis-calling a quarter.

"They called me to New Mexico about a week before the shoot to rehearse with Javier Bardem,"

Jones recalls. Adjusting to play a hitman would be tough enough for anyone, but Bardem had at least one more hurdle to jump into his role, Jones says.

The scene was the first Bardem would do in the film. Its five-minute running time would be the longest he'd done in English in his career.

"Javier Bardem was a delight," Jones recalls. "He is serious as death about acting." Considering Bardem's work as Chirgurh, that's an ironic choice of words.

The scared cashier guesses right on the flip, and Chirgurh leaves. Very quickly, we can see that he has more important things on his mind, and that getting them done is all that matters to him. People will get hurt, possibly die, but it's a job hazard he's willing to undertake to finish things off. Later on, we see just how lucky the gas man was, often starting from the same coin flip that was 180 degrees from ending his life.

But we also see that Chirgurh's a man of his word; the man guessed right and won the game, even if the prize was his life. It was enough to bring Bardem a Supporting Actor Oscar and the Coens some statues for producing, directing, and writing the film.

A few years later, Jones' agent let him know about the effect his *Louie* work had made on West.

"The things I did would not have inspired me to call (myself) up to audition for *The Sacrament*," Jones admits of the 2013 flick, "but Ti West saw this five-minute work and thought 'This guy ought to audition.'" He read over the script, his mind revisiting one of the world's darkest moments.

The term sacrament itself refers to an action showing the effects of Christianity; it's commonly associated with doing something good and right in the name of the Lord. But people have stolen, pillaged, and even killed—outward and inward—in His name as well, and back in 1978, a large group did what, in their minds, was all there was to do.

Lead by the ominous leader with an all-too-common name, an American group that proclaimed itself to be all about love and acceptance (hell, it was *called* the People's Temple) moved down to the South American state of Guyana to create a paradise far from the America they knew was too pessimistic to accept or even understand their message of love.

But it all was too good to be true . . . and the unavoidable rebellion from within and invasion from without had led to the ultimate sacrifice, though they undoubtedly saw it as a final act of sacramental unity: the mass suicide of nearly a thousand men, women, and children, all at the behest of leader Jim Jones, one of the few present not to drink the cyanide liquid that ended so many lives, instead planting a bullet through his cranium.

The tragedy will never stop being analyzed and debated, and a specific reason for it will never be located. Now West was trying to show us a new way to look over such a place with the help of the self-filmed technique that film fans keep seeing.

And Jones would be there as well (Gene, not Jim, and please don't even try to make a coincidental link between the last names—Jones has long been in the top five of most common American surnames).

"It was just a whacking good role," Jones remembers. "To me, it's always more interesting to me to play the villain than not. It was a very tight story, very succinct, one day in the life of this place. It was a terrific role."

Still, he's not seen for a large chunk of the first part of *The Sacrament*. Instead, we learn of fashion photographer Patrick, and his pals, on their way to visit the commune of Eden Parish. Patrick's sister Caroline found herself in the dark clutches of drug use, but the Parish has been a true healing spot for her and others, and it's all because of the leader.

No, not yet! The visitors first run into some fellows with large guns, ready to protect their paradise at all costs. Soon enough, it's to people who can't stop singing its praises. There's medical staff to deliver the babies that keep arriving. Men and woman of all races and creeds live, work, and play together, declaring this a better spot than anywhere in Old Glory (filming actually took place in the small Georgia town of Pooler, near Savannah), that giving up their pasts was worth it all for these presents.

Who wouldn't want to live in this spot? But this is a horror movie, and that, along with the armed guys back at the beginning, keeps audience members remembering that this is going to go the fatal way. All along, we hear a loudspeaker proclaiming the voice of the man from above.

Here's he just called Father. Preacher or paternal sense, it's what they believe.

As with *Men*, Jones prepared with the script, rather than the miles of writings done about Jim.

"My first inclination is never to do research," he says. "It's just not the way I work. If I'd known what Jim Jones ate for breakfast, where he got his drugs, and how he chose his girlfriends, it could not enrich anything in the script. There was no use bothering my head about this."

A point needs making here: the film was never advertised as being directly inspired by Jonestown, perhaps because it would have stating the blatantly obvious—was someone going to say, "Oh, gee, I thought it was about *all those other* times when a few hundred cult members committed suicide by poison!"?

Still, the fact that remains that Jim (along with David Koresh, Charles Manson, and so many others) managed to take so many seemingly nice, normal folk from all walks of society and convince them to commit the unthinkable. History has shown that, despite the positive meanings associated with terms like friendly, intelligent, and charismatic, such qualities can be the most destructive of weapons, and Jones had to find some way to show their dark sides.

"I asked myself the question: who would most people follow into the jungle?" he says. "Who would most people give up their lives, their apartments, their homes, their family, to follow into the jungle? It occurred to me, if you were in bad shape, you would follow your granddad into the jungle, and I tried to be their granddad."

Soon enough, the Father himself arrives, and, yes, he resembles Jim, complete with the ominous large dark glasses. If the eyes are the windows to the soul, Jim didn't want to chance anyone looking in and seeing darkness there.

As his followers cheer like fans of their favorite band taking the stage, the Father strolls forward, shaking every hand he can and dishing out hugs and other reassurances. Sitting down with the group, he's about to joyfully share the Eden tale. Not surprisingly, Jones called it his toughest scene, even harder than what shows up later.

"It was tough, but also thrilling," he recalls. "Tough because it was so long. It was twelve minutes in the film, but originally written, it was about seventeen minutes long. I'm not one who wants to improvise; I come in wanting to learn the script, and I memorized all seventeen minutes."

However, he had a little extra assistance, of the same sort that both Jim and the Father had enjoyed. About two hundred people showed up to play the Father's flock. Few were named. Not many had lines. Most of them wouldn't even get on camera or see their names in the credits. Still, they lit a fire that warmed Jones through a very tough performance.

"They had been there for hours," he says. "They were so good; it denigrates them to call them extras because they were so good. They inspired us all, including Ti. They started giving it to me. Usually, when you have a bunch of extras and somebody's speaking, when the (director) says so-and-so, you cheer. But they were so tuned in to what I was doing that they began to respond, sometimes in groups, sometimes individually, and always appropriately. I'd look at them not even to ask for a response, but while acting, and they would give me a response. It was the most thrilling thing I've ever done in acting. They stayed with me."

Both in and out of character; as the visitors get ready to depart, the first signs of dissension show amongst the crowd (we've gotten a few ominous messages from a mother and her child, but it's not clear just yet as to who is telling the truth). Then things quickly spin out of control: angry that someone can leave on their own, terrified that the world may learn the Eden secrets, or any of the other possibilities that a disturbed mind can create, the men with guns start killing. Back at camp, the Father now knows that someone will come looking for the visitors, and there's only one way out.

As things started to shake out of Jim's control in November 1978, a California congressman and others flew down to investigate. As the group attempted to leave, several cult members tried to go along. It was the final blow to Jonestown; shootings broke out. The congressman and others were killed. On November 18, Jim and over nine hundred of his members were dead, mostly by their own hands.

Sacrament shows us all these horrible things. And we can't stop ourselves from imagining what it was like to be there. What it must have been like to drink the poison, see others sputter away and die, and know that the same was coming to us, even if we'd suddenly changed our mind.

Perhaps even in the guiltiest of ways, we might feel a bit of sympathy for the Father, as some probably did for Jim. He'd done everything in his power to create what he saw as a perfect world, and now it was all crashing down, all the people he'd promised a better life now having lost theirs. Just as Jim did, the Father surveys his lost flock, then takes his own life as the cameras roll.

And in a rarity for the self-filmed sort, the filmers actually manage to escape, though not in totality; some of Patrick's friends are already dead, along with his sister.

We've been asking and talking about several types of questions for this entire profile: some that can't be answered, and others that have an amount thereof that rolls past possibility. Let's end this right back where we started.

As with any profession, there's another term of which the definition depends on the definer. Success is a very tough puzzle—what is it? How does one know when it's obtained? Several other questions without an answer cloaked in fact.

"Do you really want to do this?" Jones asks upcoming actors. "Are you really capable of doing this? Do you know what needs to be done? Are your standards high? Have you considered what you're up against?" Just as he didn't try to impersonate or copy Jim Jones, as with any role in his career, becoming the second coming of another won't lead one far in acting. We never really reach our potential until we approach it alone and visit somewhere else, bringing something no one else has ever truly carried.

"Some may just settle in to seeing their friends and things in plays and films and think 'Oh, I could do that,'" Jones says. "Then the poison grows in their mind and they see Brad Pitt, and they think, 'I could do that.' You *can't* do that because the reason these guys are where they are is because they're wonderful film actors. Your job is to bring a new spice to the soup. It's not to imitate Brad Pitt and fail, and you *will* fail, because Brad Pitt got there before you. What you must do is bring enough of yourself, and to do that, you must know your own way to prepare for an audition. What works best for you? You need two or three days with a script and a scene, and you'll be ready."

Ghostbusters (1984) villain Gozer (Slavitza Joven) was shocking in all kinds of ways.

Slavitza Jovan/Alice Drummond:

Ghostbusters

THEY TRULY MAKE up one of the most effective tag teams in action/comedy history. Years, even decades after seeing them the first time, audiences recognize their names, faces, even voices.

Indeed, Gozer the Gozerian and the Stay Puft Marshmallow man helped make *Ghostbusters* (1984) a smash hit that lives on, not to mention Slimer, the green ghost that we couldn't help but love to death (he was turned good when *Ghostbusters* was made into a cartoon), so let's hear from the lady that made Gozer, the Busters' eternal enemy, into a gorgeous lady with huge red eyes and the ability to blast seventh hell out of people with lightning (but there's a special surprise waiting at the end of this profile).

"I have hard time relating to being an evil god, as it is not a part of my nature," admits Slavitza Jovan. "But as they cast me to play Gozer, it must have been based on my outside looks, with my angular face, slim, tall (she's 5'8"), and such—but this look could be also used to play a Saint like Joan of Arc or someone similar to that."

A native Serbian, Jovan modeled across the globe since her youth before snaring the role of Gozer during an interview with her agent. Gozer (a fake Sumerian God) is the character that's actually controlling just about every supernatural entity the Busters face throughout the film, and it was up to Jovan to handle the buildup; when a character is discussed, but unseen, throughout a film, the payoff needs to be worth it, and she turned Gozer into one hell of an enemy, complete with huge red eyes and some eye-catching attire.

"I took it as pure fantasy," Jovan says of her transformation. "On a human level, we all have weaknesses and strengths. But the power comes from our Creator, if I can comprehend it, with my human limitations. I used a lot of my own imagination. The rest was just listening to stage directions."

Viewers don't actually hear Jovan's voice (Gozer is dubbed by Paddi Edwards, who Disney audiences would recognize as the evil eels Flotsam and Jetsam in *Little Mermaid* and the Fates in *Hercules*), but Gozer still gets in some verbal knockdowns.

"Are you a god?" she casually inquires to Ray Stantz (Dan Aykroyd).

"No," he replies, apparently showing an alarming lack of foresight.

"Then," she responds, slowly turning to the side, "DIE!"

She suddenly waxes the four Busters with rays from her hands, nearly knocking them off the side of a building.

It's left to the men to regroup, and Winston Zeddmore (Ernie Hudson), in a true "What the hell were you thinking, man?" tone, lets Ray know exactly what he should have done.

"Ray, when someone asks you if you're a god," he snarls, "you say, 'YES!'" which would have taken home "Line of the Film" honors had Bill Murray's Peter Venkman not gleefully shouted, "We came, we saw, we kicked its ASS!" after the squad's first battle with Slimer early on.

"The set was hot simply due to the fact that there were so many lights," recalls Jovan. "My costume was also very tight to my body. Occasionally, when I was around, (her co-stars) would tease me as they passed by. They would say (things like) 'What a dangerous woman.'"

During the three weeks she spent shooting Gozer, Jovan remembers, "I would have to stretch my imagination into some other dimension. I would have to do some of the stunts myself, being high up on the stairs (Gozer had to do some pretty impressive acrobats to avoid the Ghostbusters' shootings). I had to be lifted up in the air, so of course I was a bit uncomfortable and scared."

Those infamous all-dark, no-pupil eyes of Gozer's? They created some of the toughest tasks for shooting for Jovan.

Her huge contact lenses, she says, were, "Very uncomfortable. I could only wear the contact lenses for twenty minutes at a time. The doctor was there to give a rest to my eyes. I had to take 45-minute breaks. The hair and make-up took a long time to do. It was very uncomfortable and sticky." She often had to rise before sunrise and undergo the makeup procedure before sputtering all the way to wakefulness, she says.

So even though Jovan acted sporadically after *Ghostbusters* (she did appear as a deranged nurse in 1999's *House on Haunted Hill*), she'd always have the experience of showing up in one of the film world's biggest blockbusters.

"As long as I had my hair short, I would get recognized by people on the street and the paparazzi," she says. "It was nice to be spoiled and work on a high budget film where everything is organized."

Long before we meet Gozer or any other supernaturals, we see their first victim, and before the credits even roll.

Alice Drummond's librarian becomes the spirit's first victim in *Ghostbusters* (1984).

The same librarian we see in just about, well, every movie ever made, a small old lady with layers of thick clothing and no wedding ring, makes her way around the literary land, one that seems more and more foreign to today's tech-obsessed society.

Down in the basement, weird things start happening. Books float around, drawers empty—they're called *card catalogues*, kids! That's what people used to look things up before everything could be Googled!

She freaks, tearing through the library, its thin halls looking more and more ominous. Then she reaches an open spot, but something else is there first. Still, she's the only one to see it, although we hear its roar and feel its blast as her hair is blown every possible way as she screams into catatonia.

"That was the opening moment of the entire film: me and my big mouth!" remembers Alice Drummond. "I loved the whole movie and the part was just so goofy and funny. I particularly loved playing this meek little librarian who screamed bloody murder in fear."

Unlike Jovan, Drummond's career had already been going strong for decades and continued to do so.

"I was in a play in high school and everyone laughed, loved, and applauded everything I did," she recalls. "I knew then that I wanted to be an actress, and besides, there was nothing else I could do!" After honing her skills a bit more at Brown University, she ended up doing over a hundred.

There was a mental patient in *Awakenings* (1990), a kindly old lady who finds her hometown invaded by some foreign-looking creatures in *To Wong Foo* (1995), and a kindly old lady (well, almost) who saw her son's football career, and soon, him as well, vanish after a blown field goal attempt in *Ace Ventura: Pet Detective* (1994)

"Dan Marino should die of gonorrhea and rot in hell forever!" she explains to Jim Carrey's title character. When a tiny grandmother-type says that, you don't forget it.

"Every time I get a part, I read it and say, 'That would be such fun to do,'" she says. "I have no special 'preparation:' you just become the part! I oftentimes see the visual image of the character, and that makes it easy to 'become' the part!"

So much cuter than Godzilla! The Stay Puft Marshmallow man hits New York in *Ghostbusters* (1984)

Still, the spiritual comedy opener is still the role she'll be forever recalled for, and so will what the lady, herself named Alice, saw.

"I don't remember seeing any legs," she gasps to the title characters, "but it definitely had arms, because it reached for me!" Clearly, it was the green guy with a weakness for thick liquidity and taste for hot dogs.

"I knew I could play it and it certainly was thrilling to see the whole movie with those wonderful special effects," Drummond recalls. "You never know what it is like, just filming it and saying the words, until you see the final cut."

And now, for that surprise.

How do you profile a fellow whose only lines were roars, let alone a guy who got painfully melted into white goo in the end?

That's where a good interviewer comes in. Get ready to hear from the man himself, the legend.

Finally, the Stay Puft Marshmallow Man speaks!

"I have heard the movie described as a great joke, perfectly told," remembers William Bryan. "And I was being offered the chance to play the punch-line."

He'd just finished doing costume work on David Lynch's 1984 bomb *Dune*, and the Virginia native got a slightly different script.

"I thought it was the funniest thing I'd read in a long time," he remembers. "When I was told that Bill Murray and Dan Ackroyd were involved, it heightened my interest." Now he'd get to wear his own costume.

"The Marshmallow Man was, to me, a sweet confection, made of equal parts: Godzilla, a Macy's Thanksgiving Day parade balloon, and smiling sugar," he remembers. "What's not appealing about that?" He'd had a hell of a job creating attire for those traveling the galaxy for *Dune* warfare, but this was something else entirely. Something that could only be found in the minds of both Ackroyd and the man he played. After banging out the script with the help of co-star Ramis, Ackroyd's own Ray Stanz can't resist Gozer's temptation, admitting that, "It just popped in there!"

What? What just popped in there?

It would take Bryan some time to find out.

"The first steps in preparing for the role included building the suit, which entailed figuring out how to make it lightweight, comfortable, wrinkle-free, and convincing," he remembers, (along with) finding the proper speed to move, to give the impression of massive scale, (and) determining how to achieve the effect of burning marshmallow without dying." With the help of a specialist in fire-stunting, he became the makeshift marshmallow man, finding his inspiration in the memories of seeing parade balloons.

"To get the speed right, I would walk and chant 'Boom! Boom! Boom!' at varying rates until the director shouted, 'That's it!'" explains Bryan. "I also gave my walk a 'double bounce,' like that used in character animation, so it felt as if the great weight of gelatinous material was reacting properly to the impact of each step. My task was basically to carry the character and not to distract from its smooth perfection."

Like his city-crushing counterparts Godzilla and King Kong, the marshmallow man didn't seem to mean any malice, at least at first—his permanent wide smile belied that he was just a stranger in a strange and strangely small land.

Until the Busters blast him, and then it's on.

"The moment when I had to look up at the Ghostbusters on the rooftop, I had to lean way back because the head couldn't turn that way," says Bryan. "I actually sat on someone's back to get the proper position. We also built a double-wide puppet with oversized hands for forced perspective, for the scene where Stay Puft is climbing up towards the camera as a fireball whooshes up."

Yes, yes, of course he'd melted, and it's hard not to feel a strange sense of sadness. Watching it amongst a full audience who had no idea how close they were to someone who'd created Stay Puft himself, Bryan felt history.

"The entire audience had obviously seen it several times by then, and they sang along with the opening music and quoted their favorite lines," he remembers. "I was and still am proud to have been so intimately involved with something that had become a cultural phenomenon."

A murderer gets a fatal taste of his ancestry in *Creepshow 2* (1987).

Dan Kamin:

Creepshow 2

EVEN IN FILMS based on comic books, there's still a strong need for credibility. Part of the challenge of putting together a horror film is knowing where to look for actors that can help make nightmarish visions seem all too real.

As luck would have it, back in the early 1980s, a crew and a fellow working toward a similar goal would just happen to run into one another. Let's meet the man first.

He'd been a horror fan since he'd been a film fan, but seeing Tony Curtis portray the world's most well-known magician in 1953's *Houdini* had launched Dan Kamin towards his own career as a young magician. A few decades before that, however, another performing legend had laid the groundwork that Kamin would follow all the way to a lifelong career.

Considered by many to be the finest work of Charlie Chaplin's career, *The Gold Rush* had the acting icon trapped in a snowed-in cabin, with only his shoes to feast upon and a companion that hallucinates him straight into a living, breathing piece of poultry. Back in 1925, Chaplin didn't have sound to work with; then again, neither did any other performer in America, as talkies weren't around of yet. But Kamin, in the midst of his college years, looked through the door to Chaplin's cabin and saw his own newfound future.

"I abandoned my studies of industrial design to become a mime," he recalls. "This might be seen as an unfortunate career choice, but imagine the havoc that might have been unleashed upon the world had I been inspired by *Not of This Earth*, or the goldfish-bowl-wearing gorilla of (1953's) *The Robot Monster*!" 1957's *Earth* had Paul Birch playing an alien whose mere stare could burn out the eyes and brains of earthlings.

Channeling the spirit of everyone from Chaplin to Marcel Marceau and all silents in between (including comic trendsetters Sid Caesar and Red Skelton), Kamin performed across the nation and eventually the world, before theater audiences, college students, anyone who could appreciate the creation of laughter by a muted man.

A few years before, arguably the two greatest minds in horror (although neither might have reached his peak by then) had worked together to terrify holy hell in and out of viewers; having George Romero behind the camera and Stephen King holding the screenplay pen is a horror dream (or welcome nightmare) team, and 1982's film audiences had gotten the most pleasantly terrifying of gifts with *Creepshow*. Five years later, Romero's cinematographer Mike Gornick was leading up a squad to recapture the terror, and a certain native of Pittsburgh (the same city that Romero had commandeered decades before to landmark cinematic fear with 1968's *Night of the Living Dead*) found himself in a tough situation.

With today's CGI effects not even a pipe dream, and animation carrying the danger of looking too cheesy, Gornick had a tough request to make of his performers. Fortunately, someone who'd gotten a good grip on acting without sound or much facial expression would be a good choice. With word of Kamin's mime work spreading through Pittsburgh, Gornick gave him a ring (perhaps wondering whether the silent performer would even answer the phone!).

"Basically, he wanted someone who could move well and was skinny," Kamin recalls, "so that the Indian costume could be built around him." Those who've seen *Creepshow 2* (1987), or even the first part of it, know where this one's going, but not everyone may be aware of what was behind the wooden man who welcomes the chance to roar to war, even for the saddest of reasons.

Like its predecessor, the film brings the oft-disgusting world of comic books to life, so reality doesn't have to be a cast member. Much like *Halloween II* (1981), the next *Creep*er starts shortly after its elder, and a cartoon named Bobby, admittedly a bit young for this sort of art, can't wait to check out the latest edition.

It's the tale of Old Chief Wood'nhead (that's the correct spelling—no one has any right to expect grammatical correctness in comics), the night and day watchman and gatekeeper for his owners, themselves sadly accepting that their ominously titled mining town of Dead River is on its last legs, and that their general store will go down with it. The Indian warrior statue outside the store stands vigilant but frozen, a poignant reminder of the dignity and power of a vanquished race. The Indian, like the town, has become obsolete.

Still, along the way, we get the feeling that the humans here know something we don't. An old Native American bids a humorous farewell to the statue, and we see its subtle nod. The man notices, but doesn't really react, indicating he might have been here before.

"The idea of an statue coming to life had great appeal to me," Kamin recalls, "since I had spent years learning to control my body for the purpose of doing convincing mime illusions, which are, of course, special effects created solely through movement. Playing an inanimate thing that comes to life was right up my alley, and it was fun to become the golem-like creature."

Making the statue walk like a non-man would be tough enough, but Kamin had a difficult journey before the chief took a single step.

"The hardest part was the costume itself," he says. "Making it required a grueling day, during which the special effects crew made a plaster cast of my entire body and head . . . Working with the finished costume also presented special challenges. Putting it on was like getting into a giant condom."

Long before he'd be called to "Action!" the crew had transformed Kamin into chief mode.

"I was in it for about fifteen hours that day," he painfully recalls, "and when we pulled it off I had huge blisters running up one of my arms where the seam had been glued. Following my midnight visit to the E.R., I was no longer made to wait for hours in the costume."

As the humans outside the chief started acting out the real-life horror we'll talk about shortly, Kamin's work was even scarier, even if all he had to do was stand still.

"There were motors in the head to operate the eyebrows, eyelids and mouth, and I could barely see through the eyes," he says. "And because the costume was sealed tight I had to have air pumped in from an aqualung. The air made a whooshing sound, so I was effectively working blind and deaf. I wore an earpiece so that the director could speak to me through a remote microphone. The sensory deprivation made my opening scenes in front of the general store a bit disorienting. I had to stand immobile on top of a tree stump, which was itself sitting on the edge of a porch, putting me about four feet above the ground. It was pretty frightening."

But it all would be very, VERY appropriate soon enough—Kamin would get plenty of chances to use the chief to take the cap off his pent-up emotion.

Three scumbags break into the store, robbing and needlessly killing the elderly couple, then have the nerve to blast the chief himself. Off the set, Kamin got some extra help from another horror household name, as special effects legend Tom Savini, his own star still rising back then, finished out the chief for his main event.

"It was quite nerve wracking to be blasted by a shotgun," Kamin says. "I knew the gun wouldn't have live ammunition, of course, but Tom Savini had put explosive squibs in the costume, and a plate glass window behind me was set to shatter at the same moment. I know Tom Savini, and he's a madman. A very nice madman, but a madman nonetheless. So I was relieved when that shot was completed with my real body—which is, after all, the tormented inner soul of that Indian—intact."

Indeed, the Wooden man has had just about enough of this standing still shit; adorned in the face paint his ancestors wore to battle, he's ready for another fight, pulling free of the tree stump and off to the hunt.

One thief is kicking back in his living room, only to find himself suddenly punctured by a group of arrows. Another gets caught in his garage, the shadow of the chief's towering figure planting a tomahawk through his cerebrum.

"Over the years, I had learned to use the parts of my body the way a puppeteer uses puppets," Kamin says. "My hand becomes a paintbrush in one of my mime pieces, for example, and I become a marionette in another. So turning into a revenge-crazed wooden Indian was a snap. And after my arm blistered up I had no trouble working myself into a homicidal rage."

As is usually the case, the group's leader, a nephew of the Native American that saluted the chief early on, goes down the toughest. Desperately firing off the same weapon that killed the chief's owners, he can't believe there's no effect. Like the coward he always was, he attempts to flee through a window, but the chief's strength is as superhuman as his pain threshold; he punches through a wall to drag the guy out, then engages in one of his people's oldest traditions: the scalping.

Unlike the sad ending that came to reality for generations of real-life Native Americans hundreds of years ago, not to mention the shocking climaxes of *Creepshow*'s last few features, the chief's story has as happy an ending as a horror film can, as the last shot shows him triumphantly back at the store, displaying the scalped prize.

There alone would be one of the main reasons the film roared into eventual cult classic status, and it was back to the miming stages for Kamin. But his work would be seen again on the big screen, in some capacity.

He'd written a book on Chaplin a few years before, and it made quite the supreme impression on someone special; getting ready to play the comic in 1992's *Chaplin*, Robert Downey Jr. flew to Pittsburgh to work with Kamin, a crash course in physical comedy that would carry the two back to Hollywood, as Kamin created the film's comedy scenes.

It also carried Downey Jr. all the way to an Oscar nomination. The next year, Kamin did similar work with another upcoming superstar, creating Johnny Depp's physical comedy bits in *Benny and Joon*.

Still, he'll always be quite the horror fan, and not just because Kamin trained an actress to be an evil relative of E.T. in Tim Burton's *Mars Attacks!* (1996) His final piece of advice for those on the way up or even at the top of horror is something that Bobby, the chief's first and biggest fan, would probably love to hear and follow.

"Follow your dreams," Kamin ominously recommends. "Especially your nightmares!"

In the second part of the trilogy, a group of college folk brought some words that King had published in 1985 in his *Skeleton Crew* anthology. Drably titled "The Raft," this story let us know that there's things in the water more dangerous than great white sharks and lake (or Loch) monsters.

Acting, remembers Page Adler, "is something I started doing when I was about eight. I always enjoyed the adventure of what each role brought and the different people you got to inhabit. You audition for all sorts of parts, but there's not many that are more adventurous than horror. You have to suspend reality and/or make the horror film the new reality."

A big fan of the first *Creepshow* and an even bigger one of King himself, Adler turned herself to Rachel, part of a foursome of college kids who roar out to a deserted lake to have one last fling of fun

Rachel (Page Adler) desperately reaches for help as she becomes a sea blob's first victim in *Creepshow 2* (1987).

before the terrors of fall quarter. Out in the lands of Prescott, Arizona, Adler and her co-stars got ready to get wet . . . for the last time.

Rachel's boyfriend Randy (Daniel Beer) and his friend Deke are first to reach the huge title prop in the midst of the water, but Randy notices a huge black form ominously making its way toward them. Deke's girl LaVerne and Rachel just barely make it, and everyone relaxes with a little inhaled relaxation.

But Rachel's a bit entranced by the watery mass, and reaches down to see what it might be. . . .

"Most of the preparation for that part was going in and working with the special effects people," Adler says. "What always gets me in scary movies is that if you feel that it's real, that it could really happen to you or someone else, that makes it more frightening. My goal for that character was to make people feel that it could happen to you, to your neighbor, to your best friend."

As Rachel's hand breezes through the water, she's grabbed back. The blob, now like black quicksand, slowly yanks her down into it, overtaking her so slowly and painfully. The hysterical beauty cries out for help, but it's too late: her skin, and ultimately her life, are ripped away.

Ironically, Adler wasn't the first actress in her family to literally swim across the acting world—she's the younger sister of Daryl Hannah, who three years before had become a lovely mermaid in *Splash*.

"It was as shocking to Rachel as it would be to you if you found your way into a horror film," Adler says. "It was the first time I'd ever done the prosthetics, where they made a cast of the top half of my body. Scuba divers were there, but it was pretty safe."

Well, maybe not always. King's words tell of the times of October, far from ideal swimming

Daniel Beer's Randy can't escape the lake creature in 1987's *Creepshow 2*.

weather. Perhaps the crew might have tried a bit too hard to make things realistic, Beer remembers.

"I got hypothermia," Beer remembers of his film debut. "It was brutal; I thought I was going to die. I got a permanent hypothermia injury—I still get cold very quickly in the water. They poured water on us, and it was so hard to film on the raft, trying not to shake."

The thing, whose origins or motives are never even remotely revealed, yanks Deke and LaVerne straight off the raft, a larger meal that even Jaws ever enjoyed. But here's where things change a bit: in the writing, Randy allows the blob to hypnotize him, giving the impression he probably sacrificed himself to it, perhaps even a paragraph after the story ends. The film, though, has him taking advantage of LaVerne's consumption by freestyling his way back to shore.

The thing, apparently in the midst of a bulimic-type eating binge or something, can't let its last prey escape, pursuing him all the way; Randy, in true horror genius form, keeps glancing backward instead of hauling ass to safety, but finally makes it. But again, as those in horror tend to do, he stupidly stands there and crows at it, rather than beating feet to safety.

And he pays: the thing rises out of the water above him, and he's gone.

"That was tough," Beer says of the final scene. "We had to time it, because (the creature) was controlled all on the pulley system."

In 1999, Adler, Paul Newman, and others founded The Painted Turtle, a California summer camp for kids with serious medical conditions. As luck would have it, the camp itself is located right near Lake Elizabeth, on the San Andreas Fault.

Tom Wright's hitchhiker is out for revenge in the closing moments of *Creepshow 2* (1987).

"I'm scared of scary movies, but like them at the same time," Adler says. "I'm slightly terrified. It's a lot of fun to do something that's different and dramatic."

Even now, it's far too easy for so many to gloss over just how innovative a few of Tom Wright's roles in horror truly were. Not because he did a great job playing a member of the undead community, as many had done that. Simply because, while it took a bit of mental digging to realize this, his roles actually put those who had stalked and slaughtered and caused all kinds of terror into the heroic seat. Wright's characters weren't far from those we'd seen in legions of zombie films, but their motives certainly were. In his cases, the people, the dastardly *humans* he staggered down, well, they actually deserved it. His zombies probably didn't think of this, the undead aren't known for scholastic mentality, but justified was a word we could apply.

Unlike Beer and Adler, he'd been in front of cameras for a decade.

"I was a stuntman for ten years," recalls Wright, who'd done the work in *Splash*, *Sid and Nancy*, and other flicks beforehand. "When they heard that I was a stuntman and an actor, that's how I got the role." One of his first *acting* credits was the title character of *Creepshow 2*'s final tale, "The Hitchhiker."

On her way home from a forbidden rendezvous, Annie the Adulteress (Lois Chiles, far from the brave Holly Goodhead that had bagged James Bond in *Moonraker* of 1979) hauls down a dark road, too busy to notice Wright's man on the side, just looking for a ride. Until it's too late: he's little competition for her Mercedes, fatally crushed by its bumper.

But who cares, right? After all, she's a rich woman of importance with a secret that could destroy everything she's working so hard to steal, and he's . . . just some guy. Convincing herself that she's too important to have this blemish her lifestyle, she speeds off to safety.

Not happening.

He appears outside her window. He jumps atop her car. She drives for miles in high-speed terror, but he always shows up next to her, terrifyingly quipping, "Thanks for the ride, lady!" She smashes him into trees and drives over him, even shoots him a few times, but he can't or won't go away for good.

"I did all my own stunts," Wright recalls. "On top of the car, in the gravel pit, all that stuff. This is when I was younger, so it was much easier. Filming in Bangor, Maine (King's homeland), you have to be ready."

Ironically enough, after withstanding a night's worth of abuse from Annie and her car, one that pushed Wright through *five* stages of makeup for a single job, he didn't get to personally exact the character's vengeance. As Annie finally makes it home, the fellow appears from under the car one last time, one fatal time for her . . . but this time, it was a dummy.

Two years later, Wright did some stunt work for Spike Lee's legendary *Do the Right Thing*. When Lee produced the black-themed horror flick *Tales from the Hood* in 1995, Wright stepped back before the camera.

Like the *Creepshow* films, *Tales* was an anthology, the wraparound being a group of young men harassing a funeral home owner for drugs and cash. Along the way, he regales them with stories of some recent "additions" to the home, the first a supernaturally horrifying twist on the too-common trend of police brutality.

Wright is a city councilman, crusading against those who shame the badge. But it's the very ones he's fighting that take his life, beating him half to death after a traffic stop, then finishing the job with a shot of heroin that ends his life and kills his legacy.

But a year later, he comes back to do karma's deeds. He bursts from his grave and mutilates one cop, then yanks the head off another. Finally, the former fellow kills the last bad cop with the same needles that were used on him.

The *Tales* crew, Wright remembers, "had seen *Creepshow 2*, and wanted me to do it. I said sure. You don't prepare any different for a horror film than for a regular film. It's all about characters and reacting to situations. What was fun about this role was that I was sort of a revenge zombie. I go and track down the men that killed me."

Dr. Hysteria (Andrew Kavadas) and the rest of his Cabinet of Horrors searches for new members in 2015's *Monsterville*.

Andrew Kavadas:

Monsterville: The Cabinet of Souls

HORROR IS THE name of a film genre, but it's also a pretty relative term. What scares you, and why? Why do so many people find so many different things so frightening? You put ten people in a room and do a huge survey, and chances are, all of them will have a different opinion as to exactly what constitutes a fear-generating work.

It's pretty wide, and it certainly doesn't single out any group. However, the same things that scare us as adults probably scared us as kids, just probably not in as graphic a manner. That's why this piece is here.

Hundreds of millions of adults (such numbers seem accurate when you're young!) have been creeped out by the words of Stephen King and so many others like him. But youths have had their own literary terrors for generations, and it came in the words of a man named Stine. Not the guy with "Franken" as a surname (Ha!), but the one initialed R.L.

Ever since Stine first led his readers down *Fear Street* in 1989, millions of youths around the world have hidden his stories inside large textbooks during boring lectures, loaned and traded with their friends, and maybe even written a book report or two. His work about halfway between Hardy Boys/Nancy Drew stuff and King's works on a PG (well, maybe PG-13) scale, horror was an iffy world for youth adult literature until Stine explored it.

A few years later, he stepped down the age roster a bit farther, giving the single-digit-agers something to read and fear with *Goosebumps*. From 1995 to 1998, the series hit the small screen, right up next to Nickelodeon's trademark *Are You Afraid of the Dark?* In hindsight, it's surprising that Stine's work didn't make it to theaters until Jack Black took all kinds of fantastic liberties with the author and his tales in 2015's *Goosebumps*.

By the time Stine made Fear Street as nightmarish as Wes Craven did Elm Street, Andrew Kavadas might have already aged out of Stine's literary interest area. But even after decades on the screen, Kavadas still finds his first bit of performance inspiration in another area of writing.

"Read, read, read, read!" he advises up-and-comers. "When you read a well-constructed character in a well-written piece, you always gain tools for your arsenal as an actor. You also just naturally build characters 'off the page' in your imagination. You visualize and create and kind of 'play' all the characters when you read. You have your 'versions' of each character as you read. You 'see' them your way. Typically in a screenplay, the writer gives you the facts and the bones. You find the nuances that flesh it out and bring them to life. Use your imagination. Don't be afraid to follow your instincts!"

Kavadas's own intuition took him to the theater of his high school.

"As soon as I stepped on stage, my very first rehearsal, I just felt at home," he recalls. "Even though I was playing a character, it just seemed perfectly natural, a place to employ my whole self . . . That experience actually gave me the confidence to crash a professional stage audition, talk the artistic director into seeing me, and bagging the job."

Checking over his résumé, baggery doesn't appear to be much of a problem. But there's a difference between an outsider seeing a list of jobs, thinking that a few roles a year might look pretty impressive, and the performers themselves, whose jobs often add up to a few small paychecks every few months. Cartoon voice work, video games, TV shows, and small-screen films even all added together don't always combine to bring in financial stability, let alone success.

"Naturally you need a certain hunger for the spotlight to enter into this field," he says. "But remaining open and vulnerable, essential for good work, doesn't jive with an inflated sense of self. Swagger is over compensation. Confidence is calm. And you will face rejection—a lot, no matter how 'spot-on' your audition may have been. Excellence is the minimum standard. Your work as an actor should be 'cast-able' at any audition you attend. Of course you are all charismatic, talented, and beautiful, but never forget as an actor you are an assistant storyteller. You serve humanity, and you are a student of the same for life."

Some performers are happy getting into one vein and staying there, especially quite a few in the horror genre. Kavadas, quite simply, wasn't.

As the new millennium moved toward its second decade, "I chose to refuse all of the darker auditions," he explains. "I am not a violent person, and committing horrible criminal acts, even make-believe ones, was getting to me." One day, he heard about *The Haunting Hour*, a new TV series based on Stine's work.

Too old to get hold of Stine's books and hoping to get away from the horror world, Kavadas came *this close* to saying no.

"I am so glad I attended that audition," he admits. "I love a good morality piece that doesn't ever play as a morality piece. I believe that to be an essential quality in elevating the horror genre beyond sensationalism." He showed up on one episode in 2010, another the next year.

"Because of the young audience for Stine's work," Kavadas says, "as an actor, you need to rely on psychology in order to, you know, *terrorize* them. Blood and gore and other more 'adult' terror tropes are off the menu and there was room for more than a little humor, something I strive to infuse into any character I audition for."

Four years later, he'd get to do so on a larger scale. In September 2015, just a month before Black's *Goosebumps* hit the big screen, home audiences saw *Monsterville: The Cabinet of Souls* (Stine was a producer).

In typical Everytown, U.S.A., a group of ordinary, friendly high school students hope to spend their Halloween munching on candy and finding fall love. Then, right in the middle of festival warmups, steps forth a tall, sinister man, complete with requisite goatee and dark clothes, here to entrance everyone to his new haunted attraction. And, hey, he's a doctor, with a lovely daughter by his side, so he's *got* to be safe, right? Never mention the surname.

"Dr. Hysteria is intelligent, charming, funny, so very accommodating—and just plain dangerous!" Kavadas analyzes. "I saw him as the human ego: the 'Id,' perhaps. All the lies he tells you are the ones you already are telling yourself. He will flatter you, he will sympathize with poor, misunderstood you, he will tell you what rewards you really deserve, without commitment and/or effort on your part . . . and eventually, like the ego unchecked, he will consume you!" Such a role, however, is attractive for many reasons, reasons that, as Kavadas seems to feel, go far past a paycheck. So a bit of background of acting out Stine's work wasn't going to be enough to hand him the role right off.

"We went through multiple auditions, featuring many excellent actors, all more than capable of delivering a great job," he recalls. "Fingers crossed, I got the call!" Now full of incentive, he studied the underrated *Something Wicked This Way Comes*, the 1983 flick put together by the unlikely team of Disney and Ray Bradbury. Jonathan Pryce played Mr. Dark (talk about an ominous title!), owner of a mysterious carnival that comes to a small Illinois town, looking to kidnap some naïve, innocent souls.

Monsterville paid a bit of homage to *Something*, but Kavadas avoided much of Pryce's work, looking for the authenticity he considers another career trademark.

"I actually based Dr. Hysteria's outward persona and show-biz bravado/midway barker elements on a cheesy hypnotist who used to tour through my little hometown with a tired illusionist/mind-reader act when I was a kid," he recalls. "He had an aggressive stare as if he was looking right into your most private thoughts. He dressed in velvet and frills, he had the beard and the grooming and the ringleader's command and charisma, and he did most of it with his voice. He used his voice as a powerful tool to seduce his audience into looking the wrong way so he could manifest his illusions."

Nothing seems too far out of the unusual—well, as haunted houses go!— at first, as the film's main men and women make their way through. But when Beth (Dove Cameron) gets separated from the friends, Hysteria's employees appear to be a bit much in character, staying in zombified or vampiric persona in the background. And when Hysteria manages to get a few of his visitors alone, visions of their dreams moving to reality put them squarely under his ownership, moving toward façade-ship in his house.

"Of course, you are always geared and focused to do your very best," Kavadas says. "I was performing with a group of wonderfully talented actors, and you are always a little nervous, in a good way, to give your very best work and be part of a solid team. It really was a joy working with this cast and director. I can honestly say I looked forward to each and every scene."

As he and the rest of the cast had fewer and fewer scenes to work through, Beth's the only free one left, trapped between Kavadas' self-made Utopia and her old life, up against the doctor and his ever-growing minion squad. But just as the stuff has put down and sometimes all the way away one fanged eternal one after another throughout horror history, a bottle of her own personal holy water (Google can teach us everything, can't it?) douses them into distraction—not death, as this is still sort of a kids' flick!—long enough for the good guys and girls to escape.

"I am one of those actors who keeps finding what I could have or should have done better, once I see myself in the film," Kavadas admits. "Not that I felt anything was outright bad; it is just a professional hazard . . . Of course, it is always fun to watch when the special effects are in place, especially when you yourself don't really know the little tricks that made it come together even though you were there shooting it. I really had fun watching this movie with my family and friends."

On just a few days' rehearsal, Daisy Keeping was sent to become Jenny and search the Italian *Neverlake* (2013).

Daisy Keeping:

Neverlake

BASICALLY, DAISY KEEPING would be hiding a secret from herself.

The young actress decided to live not *as* her character, but next to her. Her portrayal object wouldn't know what would happen in the story, but the performer would. Still, the two would be making their way through the tale together, one not knowing what would occur, the other just not revealing it.

"I decided quite quickly that the main thing I wanted was to keep Jenny uncomplicated and open, to see clearly how she is affected by all the strange goings on," Keeping explains. "I didn't want her to be clouded by complex character choices." No need to—coming up with a heavily developed burden might have detracted not only from *Neverlake*'s (2013) storyline, but from Keeping's work, certainly something to avoid for one of the first leads of her acting career. The scarifying story would give her plenty to work with as it progressed; better to start off with very little, and let herself, or at least Jenny, try to keep from being totally overtaken.

"Occasionally an audition or role comes along that you have a gut feeling about," she recalls, "almost a faith, that, given the chance, you know you are right for the part, that you could play this part convincingly. That's how I felt about Jenny. I also loved how different and poetic the story was and just how much of a journey Jenny goes through from the beginning to the end."

Along with the film, the young lady arrives in the Italian countryside for a summer with her single dad and his new girlfriend (Keeping, shoved into acting action just days after getting the role, called the Tuscany filming spot one of the more attractive offerings of the job!). It's a favorite hangout of Mary and Percy Bysshe Shelley, perfect for the young literary fan, herself the film narrator.

But long before Shelley or anyone else of the time happened by, the ancient Etruscans used a local lake as their personal River Styx, paying it in statuettes for its healing powers and making it a haven for archeologists and treasure hunters of the 1800s, who fished out hundreds of pieces to keep or sell. Today, some hang out next to the *Mona Lisa* in the Louvre.

And, as a strange group of children lets Jenny know, there's still a few left, only her dad's keeping them. One youngster is missing her limbs, another her eyes. Still others are scarred across and about the torso. Getting the jewels back is a shot at redemption for the kids, themselves left to rot in an ominous-looking house near Jenny's place.

"Jenny is a fair few years younger than me," says Keeping, in her 20s as she played a high-schooler. "This is something I kept working on, bringing to my physicality. Also, finding those youthful emotions really was my main tool in keeping her open, which is what I really wanted for Jenny."

As filming stretched out over a month, she and Jenny made their way through the Italian surroundings and the supernatural. Jenny became something not unlike a maternal source for the local kids, reading them her favorite works of rhyme and reason.

"I re-read the script a lot to get every last bit of information about Jenny out of it," Keeping says. "I like to know all the facts so I can get on set every day, sure of the fundamentals of a character, allowing me to feel confident to work off what the other actors bring."

But her stability didn't make its way inside; dreams of being forced underwater and mutilated kept waking her up at night. Soon she found herself in a hospital, her doctor father assuring her it's going to be all right.

"It's amazing to see what can be achieved in post-production," Keeping remarks. "It is pretty difficult to imagine what the end result will look like when all you have to work with is a few well-placed dots on your body, but you have to act like a chunk of your torso is missing!"

That was when it came time for dreams and realism to meet for the young girl. Jenny finds one more victim in a bed, one suffering worse than any other she's met before. It's her sister, and she's slowly turning to stone, her only hope some organ and limb donations, voluntary or otherwise. Jenny's next in line, as her hospital visit was much more graphic (and important to the father that's using her as a human supermarket) than anyone would say.

And she's not the first. All the kids she's met have been her late siblings. The body parts they lost were given to this girl before they passed. It's why her mom's been gone for so long; dad's been breeding them from her, only to take what he needs and leave her bedridden and mentally wracked.

But this is a horror movie, and that means that Jenny's got one last chance to save them and herself, even if it means the death of her dad and half-sister. It's about heading back down to the lake and through its dark depths, finding the statuettes that represent the lives stolen away.

Her dad in watery pursuit, Jenny makes it there. But she's got an ally that's much lovelier on the inside than out: there's a beast at the bottom of the lake (we've seen bits and pieces of it in Jenny's dreams), who yanks her father down for too long as his daughter returns the icons to dry land—and doesn't have to drown herself in the bargain!

"We spent a weekend filming the underwater scenes, which at first I was really excited about," Keeping remembers, "but it soon became clear just how difficult the weekend would be. I love to swim and be in the water, but hours of sinking, swimming, and diving really takes its toll and I was completely exhausted by the end of the two days."

She makes it out and back to her mom, her siblings fading away as her half-sister dies, much more painfully and plasma-filled than we expect, suffering much worse than their dad did. Now we can only hope that Jenny might be OK too.

Keeping probably will be.

"I'm not sure most actors or actresses ever stop looking for their big break!" she asserts. "There are definitely still lots of things I would like to achieve in my career, but I am proud of my successes so far, big and small. It is a tough industry, so you have to be kind to yourself."

Showing once and for all that evil spirits have no loyalty, the demon Tak leaves involuntary carrier Ellie Carver's body for a vulture in *Desperation* (2006).

Sylva Kelegian:

Desperation

PIPER LAURIE HAD done it, and nearly won an Oscar. Dee Wallace had done it (albeit it all kinds of different ways!) and, many felt, should have gotten an Academy shot.

Yes, playing a mom in a Stephen King-based flick had paid off in the past, so of course Sylva Kelegian gave it a shot, and got to balance out the tough maternal-ism Wallace used in *Cujo* (1983) with the . . . well, absolute *wackjob-ishness* Laurie gave Carrie White's mama.

"She was a fierce mother with a lot of emotion," Kelegian recalls of *Desperation*'s Ellie Carver in the 2006 film. Ellie's emotion and fierceness, however, wouldn't always go in the right directions. . . .

Ten years after King's book hit the shelves, *Desperation* followed in the tale of *The Stand* (1994), *Tommyknockers* (1993), and many others in bringing his words to the small screen. Oh, and if Ellie's name sounds familiar, it's because she was also a character in *The Regulators*, which came out at about the same time and was written by some guy named Richard Bachman, whose words *somehow* bore more than a passing resemblance to King's!

"I was never a Stephen King fan, as I don't like scary stories, but of course I read the book before we started filming," remembers Kelegian, who played a nurse in 2004's Best Picture-winning *Crash*. "I am not a horror film fan and never will be. I get scared easily. The last horror film I saw was *The Exorcist* when I was thirteen."

Much like happened to poor Regan MacNeil in that legendary flick, *Desperation* yanks possessions straight into the storyline, this time in the form of an evil being called Tak (probably because it's easy to repeat fast, as its "prisoners" often do). Before the film begins, the creature's already grabbed hold of Collie Entragian (Ron Perlman), the sheriff of the title town. We also don't see it, but Tak's enticed Entragian to slaughter just about everyone there, and imprison the Carver family, making their young daughter one of his victims. Killing Peter Jackson (obviously *not* the director!) and tossing his wife Mary (Annabeth Gish) into the cell with the Carvers, Entragian (or "Entragian") goes looking for Tak's newest impromptu owner.

That's one of the biggest differences between Tak and your typical every film demonic possessor; it makes its victims larger, superhumanaly strong, only out to take human life, but it doesn't last. The possessed bodies fall apart quickly after doing its bloody work, forcing it to go off and find someone else to steal.

And Ellie becomes its next victim.

Filming in an Arizona town not unlike the Nevada land where the story takes place (filming happened in 2004, two years before release), Kelegian found herself behind bars, calling the jail scene one of her favorite parts of filming. Sacrificing herself to keep Entragian from taking her boy, Ellie's stolen to become Tak's newest carrier.

"I always prep the same way," she explains (Kelegian played a protective mom in 2002's *Spiderman*). "I put myself in the mind and emotion of the character, stay in the moment, and let it carry me where it will." It ended up carrying Ellie to places that King has always specialized in helping his readers visualize.

Getting ready for Ellie's return, Kelegian found a new way to blend her character with Tak. Being possessed would indeed make Ellie into a larger, tougher version of herself, but, as had happened with Collie, it would cause her skin—and later things larger than that—to break out and break away.

"I spent almost an hour in the makeup chair putting on the prosthetic face," she remembers. "Once the freaky lenses were put in my eyes, I looked in the mirror and knew who I had to become, and the fact that they were so uncomfortable made it easy for me to turn into the angry monster woman." She'd stepped into the role (and the chair) nurturing and protective, and come out the very thing she'd been protecting her family from!

Ellie's family has escaped and seen more and more of Tak's actions. But soon enough, the she-Tak has them trapped in a theater, forcing in a mountain lion to massacre one of their companions. Mary's kidnapped and carried off, but manages to escape in a car, ripping off Ellie's arm in real *Living Dead* tribute action, forcing the demon to leave her body—now all the way dead—and whisk itself into a passerby vulture. Eventually, Tak's plans get shoved off track until it's trapped in a mine and blasted back to the Hell that created it.

"The toughest thing for me was running down the hill with all those rocks at night, so they had the stunt double do it," Kelegian remembers. "The makeup helped a lot with the possessed side: once I looked in the mirror and saw those eyes staring back at me, it was pretty easy to turn into someone/something else."

Bughuul (Nick King) sends a new protégé into action in *Sinister 2* (2015).

Nick King:
Sinister 2

It doesn't always take too much to win a spot in the collective hearts, minds, and admiration of the horror film world.

For one of its newest, it took just one film, of which his character was certainly important, but not very visual. His creation didn't do much, just stoically lived up to the film's title, at least until the end.

Still, whatever Nick King and the rest of the *Sinister* crew put together for the 2012 hit flick, it was enoug —enough for King, and the thing (can't really call it a man or even a person) he played to become the newest recipient of everything right that horror fans represent and respect.

"It's going crazy," King says of being the newest face of horror, even if we couldn't actually see his face in the role. "It's fun. It gives me a chance to go to all the conventions and talk to the fans about the movie. It's a blessing. It's gotten so big across the world that it's amazing. I have people literally around the world messaging me on Facebook and Twitter, saying 'Great job!' and asking questions and stuff like that."

As with his character, few films have lived farther up to and past their names like *Sinister*, the tale of the demonic Bughuul and the youths that become its murderous army, violently and stoically slaughtering their loved ones in manners that would terrify even the world's worst serial killers, all at his mental whim. King was the entity itself, a grim reaper-esque creature strolling through the aftermath of his minions' work, proudly welcoming them into a fraternity from hell (a tale *heavily* detailed and dissected in my first book, 2014's *Welcome to Our Nightmares*, available online, and maybe even at a few garage sales, everywhere!).

In the film's closing moments, Bughuul itself leaped straight into the screen, not quite subtly letting us know it'd be back. Three years later, it, and King, made it.

"They told me they were happy with the way I did everything," he recalls. "That was my reason for wanting to do it again: the sheer fun of making the first film."

Still hurting from the loss of his friend Ellison Oswalt and the rest of his family, James Ransone's Deputy So and So (yes, that's really his name—remember that *Get Smart* went a full series and then a 2008 movie without ever telling us Agent 99's actual moniker), chasing an evil he can only imagine across the country.

Shannyn Sossamon's Courtney and her twin sons Dylan and Zach (Dartanian and Robert Daniel Sloan) are fighting just as tough a battle, desperately trying to stay a step ahead of Courtney's abusive, and very rich, ex-husband. Soon, they all turn up at an abandoned house, the type that a bogeyman like Bughuul would thrive to overtake.

"I kind of went back to my roots from the first one," King recalls of his prep work. "I went into makeup, doing all this stuff, talking to the director, Ciarán Foy. I isolated myself to think about how they wanted it done, making it realistic and scary at the same time. I got myself into a dark state of mind."

Bughuul's young ruffian group had already shoved Zach straight into such a mentality, cornering him in the basement to show him their proudest accomplishments. One had gifted a family of alligators with a full-course family cuisine; others had incapacitated their families into electrocution or being frozen to death.

And the last one depicts one of Zach's "friends" alongside his family, them tied up on the floor of a small church. The kid places several rats on their midsections, then a metal pot over the rodents.

Then, with Bughuul watching (we just know that there's serious glee running through the creature!), some scalding coals are laid across the pots. Trapped inside, the heat rising around them, there's only one way for the rats to go: down through the flesh and out the side. King called it one of his toughest scenes to film.

"That scene took a few takes," he recalls. "(Foy) told me where he wanted my hands, and how he wanted my fingers to look when I lift my hands and the rats come out."

Perhaps this was the sort of thing that had enticed Ellison's daughter Ashley in the closing moments of the first film, bloodily disemboweling her family to win a spot on Bughuul's crew. It's starting to work here, as Zach's getting abusive with his voice and fists, using both his dad's and Bughuul's teachings.

"Working with just body gestures, it's difficult to have a certain persona," King explains. "The director told me what he wanted, and I kind of went up for that. It's a little more difficult when you don't have lines or facial expressions. It's pretty much body and hand gestures. I just ran with that."

Courtney's ex arrives and takes everyone back "home," but Zach's still got a job to do, and it begins in true *Children of the Corn* fashion: in the ominous midst of a dark cornfield, he films everyone tied up to crosses, then lights them on fire. His dad's the first to go, evil becoming the victim of itself.

So and So shows up to save everyone, burning the film and herding the rest of the family inside a house. Zach looks desperately for help from his friends, but it's too late; Bughuul's punishment for treason, even unintentional, is more brutal than anything in the Armed Forces, as a simple touch combusts the youngster to ash.

"The kids were awesome, very talented," King recalls. "I came around the corner in full makeup, and everyone on the set got freaked out. Some of them didn't even know what I looked like. It was funny, walking around and seeing everybody jump."

Angela (Amelia Kinkade) got some serious personal pleasure from possession in the *Night of the Demons* films.

Amelia Kinkade:
Night of the Demons series

IF ONLY GUYS like Michael Myers and Jason Voorhees had decided to go straight!

Protecting the world from humanity's darkest spots? They'd have it made! They've been shot, stabbed, dismembered, drowned, all kinds of stuff, and they kept coming back for more and more sequels. These are exactly the type that would be the greatest weapons the cops ever saw. Sending an indestructible force into battle against those that had deserved it? They could have been worldwide heroes.

If they'd gone to the side of law and order, crimes rates would be in the negatives. You think any mob boss, serial killer, scam artist, or anyone else would have the sack to square off with *those guys*? Seriously, take a hardened public enemy, put him in a room with them, and broadcast what happens to him around the globe—people would pay millions, we'd get personal redemption, and it would have scared any criminals so straight they'd never so much as jaywalk!

Sure, we'd have missed out on some of the greatest horror escapades in film history, but more people would be safe, right? I know, we're talking about saving fictional characters here, and debating career choices of monsters, but since when is legitimacy relevant to conversations about horror? It's not that different from debating who'd win a fight between Superman and Spiderman, right? (By the way, Supes would destroy Spidey; as smart as Peter Parker is, he couldn't find kryptonite fast enough to mount an offense. Let's go ahead and end that debate for good. . . .)

Yes, the rules governing good and evil in horror are written by the fans that analyze them. While many have, for all kinds of good reasons, labeled her legendary character the villain, the evil succubus of the *Night of the Demons* films, Amelia Kinkade can't get over the amount of people that, for the same reasons that we cheer for Jason, Michael, and others, still see her, and her Angela, as admirable.

"I'm so blown away, grateful and humbled by the impression Angela has made on an entirely new generation of fans," Kinkade recalls, "and I can only assume that this Kali-type energy, this underdog-gone-destroyer-Goddess, is needed in today's world. The stories I hear from my fans . . . are so heart-breakingly beautiful and touching—about how Angela 'protected' them as a child. I had no idea of the healing powers of movie villains."

Like many ladies of action and horror, Kinkade's first steps toward the acting world were of pirouettes and tour jetes.

"I'd sweated ten to twelve hours a day, six days a week, training as a ballerina and Graham modern dancer," she recalls, "so it was a combination of skill, preparedness, and the ability to trust God and take outlandish risks."

A quick chat with her aunt, Rue McClanahan of *Golden Girls* fame, convinced Kinkade to hitchhike from her Oklahoma hometown all the way to Los Angeles to broaden her performance horizons. Still, it was the musical motion arts that put her before the cameras for the first time.

"I'd spend the previous six months absolutely miserable in college in Oklahoma and my refuge was the rockabilly band The Stray Cats," she remembers. "I'd danced to the Stray Cats album every night in the mirror back in miserable Oklahoma, pretending I was the lead girl in their next rock video. That was a form of fantasy and prayer I engaged in every night of my life. Somehow, God made that a reality." Up against dozens of women with more experience and name recognition, she grabbed a role in the Cats' video "Sexy and 17."

"The experience is an example of what can happen when we focus the powers of the mind, and learn how to concentrate, trust in the goodness in this world, and let miracles happen to us," Kinkade says. "I'd worked *hard* as a dancer—make no mistake. There was no 'luck' involved in this." Then it came time to bring her aunt's hopes to reality. Having never even seen a horror flick to that point, Kinkade had a shot at being the dark lead in a new series.

"*Night of the Demons* gave me an opportunity to actually *be* the villain, so how could I resist the chance to play the character with all the power?" she rhetorically wonders of the 1988 film. "Perhaps it was the complete void of the horror genre in my life that gave me the artistic freedom to not do anything that had ever been done before, because I could not mimic another movie 'monster' because I had simply never seen one." Fortunately, her dancing past and cosmetic present would team up to get her as ready as anyone could be for such a role.

Up alongside legendary horror titaness Linnea Quigley, Kinkade's Angela and the rest of her friends kick back and forth at a Halloween party in a former funeral home, one rumored to be haunted by the spirits of its former owners and the man who murdered them.

An impromptu séance brings one of hell's residents to the event, but no one believes it from Angela. Bad idea.

The demonic entity takes hold of her, and, as it usually does in the movies, transforms Angela straight into seductress, her long dance routine attracting the men like flies to a web. "The dance scene in the first film was the only thing I rehearsed before we filmed it," Kinkade recalls, "and I prepared for it by choreographing some wild thrashing around my living room in my little apartment in Hollywood. The second they turned on that music and let me go wild in that dance was like a thousand Christmas mornings! The spirit that roared out of me was simply organic, and I think it was spurred on by the frustration I was feeling as a trained modern dancer in a very shallow dance scene in Los Angeles, and my body wanted to absolutely let loose and go wild."

But not in the way the men hoped: she chomps off one's wandering tongue, then helps trap all the unaffiliated in a vault as her transformation hits at high speed. Still, it certainly hadn't seemed so leading up to filming, and that had helped Kinkade find Angela's madness as well.

"While sitting in special effects makeup for six hours at a time, which is very uncomfortable and unsettling," she recalls, "then performing in grueling all-night shoots, one slowly becomes the creature one sees in the mirror. I didn't need any special mental preparation. The makeup is so agonizing and the all-night filming hours were so long, the invention of Angela became 'method' acting. Angela was just a true expression of exactly what she represents: the little nerdy, wallflower, underdog getting revenge on arrogant classmates who had done her wrong."

As the night goes on, more and more partiers die. But the demons find a sad commonality with those of the blood-sucking, fanged trade: getting caught outside at sunrise changes them to dust.

Eight years later (six in storyline times), Angela's next chapter was written, and began with her giving the Michael Myers treatment to some Bible-thumpers unlucky enough to wander into her abode. Her parents had offed themselves, leaving her little sister alone—until October 31 arrives, as she's yanked back to Angela's place for another party.

Once again, Angela debuts with an act of tabletop seductive gyration. Some die, and others are possessed. One woman's breasts suddenly morph into hands that reach out and choke a guy dead, and a more hysterically creative murder in horror history would be tough to locate.

In a film with a lady as the strongest evil, it's only fitting that a heroine would be leading the good guys, and a nun, seemingly black-belted in the martial arts of faith, resourcefully fights off the demons with a rosary in nunchuck mode and a water pistol equipped with holy water.

But horror movie villainesses always come back for one last scare, and Angela follows tradition, suddenly morphed into a Lamia, a snake-like creature with an appetite for youth. Her kind first showed up in Greek mythology, when goddess queen Hera, ticked about Lamia's dalliance with her hubby Zeus, turned the mistress into the same sort of creature that's been doing Satan's work since tempting Adam and Eve with the apple.

The time she'd spent becoming Angela the first time would seem like a luxury for these scenes, but Kinkade welcomed the same type of preparation that had worked so well before.

"I spent *twenty-seven* hours in makeup, strapped in a trench, glued to a teeter-totter," she remembers reluctantly. "It was a world's record in Hollywood for the longest any actor has performed in agonizing special effects makeup. By the end of the shoot, I felt like I didn't even need the makeup anymore: I was ready to kill everybody in sight!"

She didn't get the chance; Angela—or rather, her tail—knocks back a few folk, but someone kicks a hole in the wall, and the trespassing sunlight gorily explodes her before and all over everyone.

"I was channeling some big mojo in the possession scenes," Kinkade recalls, "and I'm proud that when I turn into a wild animal the world seems to like it!"

Part three arrived a few years later, with a bunch of teens on the run from the law ending up at Angela's house. Once again, her dance moves grab the men by the minds and libidos, and, once again, the same pitfalls that have taken down so many of Dracula's friends snare her as well, as Angela disintegrates trying to cross running water.

"*Night of the Demons* part two and three were written specifically for me, so there was no way I could say no," Kinkade explains. "If someone came along with a script and said, 'I wrote this movie for you. Would you like to star in it?' would it ever occur to you to say no?" A 2009 *Demons* remake put Shannon Elizabeth into Angela's role.

As it turned out, the prep work Kinkade did for both dance and horror helped her get ready for a different role, one that she seems quite a bit more proud of than becoming Angela.

"My only thought of acting was a dream that I could somehow help the animals on this planet," she says, "and I knew that if I became a movie star, it would give me the clout to start my own charity, which I have done." In 2015, she launched Amelia's Ark Angel Society.

"I go into schools in rural communities in the African bush to teach children about wildlife conservation," Kinkade explains. She hopes to get fellow terrifying performers' help to protect a community that can't defend itself (and if animals do fight back against people, they're usually vilified). The organization aids species dying off far too quickly around the planet, such as elephants, tigers, and sharks.

"It's the best use of my acting and dancing training that I could imagine," says Kinkade, who's also written several books on animal communication. "I can join forces with other horror movie stars to defend animals and make sure that the horrors we portray stay on the screen. My horror movies were make-believe, but what many animals endure on this earth every day are true horrors, and I want to use my celebrity status to try to make that stop."

Death comes from above for Tim (James Kirk) in *Final Destination 2* (2002).

James Kirk/Haley, Webb/Ellen Wroe:

Final Destination

SOME PEOPLE IN Hollywood just couldn't *wait* to die!

Wow, that sounded horrible, didn't it? Even appealing to the most deep-midnight blackest side of humor, it would be tough to get anyone to so much as crack a grin with that sort of statement! Looks like a humorist career isn't in the pages for *this* author!

OK, let's see if we can start this another way. A large group of upcoming performers really, *really* wanted to be a part of one of the horror world's hottest sagas! It just happened to include an enemy that, even if one were to take a 10,000-film series, would always win the battle.

It's called death itself. Sometimes it's quick and easy, sometimes agonizingly painful, sometimes peaceful, sometimes violent and terrorizing (like here!), but it comes for us all. Whether we believe in predetermined fate or individual destiny, it's going to get us, one time or another.

The *Final Destination* series takes us in the fate direction. We're supposed to go one way, and if we don't, there's death to pay. That grim reaper fellow might have been willing to let us go fast and out of nowhere—merciful for us, hellish for our loved ones—but if we thwart his (its, whatever the hell you believe) plans, and he decides to take it out on us, there's nothing we can do—even if, as some throughout the series have tried, we try to do its job for us. Death will get us one way or the other, and if we don't go when *it* wants, well, we'll go so much worse later on.

Perhaps in need of something earth-shattering and attention-snaring to remind everyone of exactly who's running the show, Death stepped in to make things happen as the first *Final* started out in 2000, ready to detonate a plane and blast everyone straight to afterlife.

It mostly happens. The plane blows and everyone aboard feels their collective bucket kicked. But not everyone Death was hoping for: one fellow dreamt the blast ahead of time, and he and some others escaped.

But almost isn't good enough for Death. These people, these *cheaters*, outreached him, and now they're going to pay dearly, in all kinds of ways. One girl is hit by a bus. Another falls in the bathroom and gets inadvertently lynched by a rope. A woman's house explodes, and somebody else gets squashed by a falling sign.

And no reason to stop there—death can get us any way it wants, and one film could never be enough.

"The great thing about horror is that there is rarely something that can give you that sense of unpredictability," explains James Kirk. "That is what I believe is the beauty of horror: not letting you know what to expect and the greatest fear is the unknown."

Along with millions of others, he'd felt that sort of thing all the way through the first flick, right around the same time the youngster's career was starting to take off, mainly through TV work. Two years later, tryouts for the second *Final* arrived, and his first step was reviewing the past flick.

"I feel this is very important in preparation for any role," Kirk says, "to watch any movie that is in the series, look up directors and their past work to see their style and how they approach each film they had made, and to just see if you can find out everything you possibility can about the project."

The sequel started out much as the first one had, albeit in a different setting. A college gal on the way to spring break Utopia in the form of Daytona Beach mentally witnesses a car pileup in front of her. Stalling her car on a ramp saves her life, but some of her friends get taken out by a truck.

Still, others were supposed to die, saved by her intentional traffic jam. One was a young widow named Nora and her son Tim. He would be Kirk's newest exploration.

"When a movie of that size comes around," he explains, "it makes it even more exciting and pushes you even more to do your best to be a part of it." Three weeks of filming were spent on the opening sequence, he continues.

Sadly, both Tim and his mom would quickly join the father, feeling Death's revenge early on.

"The toughest part for me of the whole experience was actually during pre-production," he says. "Before filming, the special effects team needed to take a mold of my body to make a 'dummy' for Tim's death scene. I remember the night before finding it hard to sleep wondering what the next day would ensue. Much to my delight, the next day was even more exciting than I could imagine."

With him forced to stand still for a period that was certainly nowhere near as long as it must have seemed, the teen's entire body was covered with plastic mold, one limb at a time. Then came the head, crafted into an expression of shock and terror.

That's because a trip to the dentist—still a nightmare for many of any age—becomes even worse for the youngster. Stepping outside with his mom, Tim gleefully charges into an unsuspecting group of pigeons, ready to give them his own kind of horror. But a startled construction worker's shoved into a control belt, dropping a plane of glass slam across Tim's head and flattening it as his shattered mom can only watch. Soon after, she finds the rest of her body as broken as her heart, as an elevator removes her own head.

"Plaster was poured all over my head, and two straws coming from my nose was my only sense of air!" Kirk says. "I couldn't wait to see the final project, and this brings me to my favorite part of the experience: getting to watch myself get crushed. It's not something that gets to happen every day—walking around and seeing what you look like when you stand right beside yourself . . . the special effects of the death cemented my pride in being a part of this film."

2006 brought the third edition, with Death getting revenge on those who had the audacity to escape his pre-planned roller coaster crash. Three years later, *The Final Destination* arrived for the second time.

That's right—that's what it was called, not Part 4 or IV or anything else. Perhaps the people behind the saga intended it to end.

Still, it wasn't the last *Final*. Just as the Star Trek crew went back out on the Enterprise after *The Final Frontier* and Jason Voorhees came back after *The Final Chapter*, the *Final* series continued to a fifth edition in 2011.

The fourth shot bringing in more green than any of its predecessors probably had something to do with the decision as well. Now let's meet one of the reasons for this.

"'I am not a huge fan of horror films, as I admittedly get too freaked out," admits Haley Webb, "but I have a great appreciation for the genre. There is such a rawness of emotion with horror films that I find intriguing, but it's that emotion mixed with, well, the fear factor that make it hard for me to watch with any consistency."

The aforementioned C-word came straight into play in the fourth flick—*once again*, soothsaying abilities help a college kid avoid a disaster, this time from the stands of an auto race. *Yet again*, people start dying in really weird ways: a lawnmower blasts a pebble straight through a lady's eye and ends up in her brain, a propane blast obliterates a guy, and another fellow finds his vitals sucked out by an overeager pool drain.

"I was a fan of the first few *Final Destination* films because I found the premise so clever," Webb says. "It was thrilling without being slasher-scary, so it was something I really got into. It was a bit of an honor to be a part of such a cool franchise."

Main man Nick (Bobby O'Campo) and his girlfriend Lori (Shantel VanSanten) try to convince everyone that the eternal seeker is after them and highly pissed, but, in another (far too) common theme for the series, most just don't believe.

Like, for example, Lori's galpal Janet, who Webb tried to catch.

"There's something about not getting a lot of character breakdown when I receive an audition that excites me," she says. "Perhaps because I feel it leaves me open to create whatever I want, and that's exactly what happened when I received the audition for Janet. All it said was 'early 20s, female, Lori's best friend' and I found that to be a delicious challenge, so it was extremely fun for me to go into

She got out of this predicament, but Haley Webb's Janet later became one of the last victims of *The Final Destination* (2009).

the casting room prepared to do whatever the hell I wanted and I did."

Checking over what little of the script she was given gave Webb a bit more about the girl.

"It was clear that Janet was the sort of uptight, proper, sorority-type girl who probably planned all of the parties, socials, etc. for her friends, had everything in place and her entire life planned," she remembers. "I hadn't quite played a character like this before, so I relished the opportunity. It was appealing to me to play someone with this personality type, because while I could see certain similarities, as a whole she's quite different than who I naturally am. I figured that the more uptight she was, the more satisfying it would be for the audience to see her squirm."

With just a week between snaring the role and acting upon it, Webb rolled down to the Big Easy for a difficult work, one that kept rolling for her after the cameras started doing so.

"I worked every day that week and every day I was actually in New Orleans shooting," Webb recalls. "I was 'that kid' who didn't go out at night and just stayed in my apartment surrounded by books, films, and music that inspired me." She gave Janet a backstory by listening to the sorts of music her character would enjoy, and even personified her in public far from the set.

"I would be extremely picky with food orders, always use a tissue to open public bathroom doors, and be bossy with really inane things," Webb says. "I got a lot of exasperated sighs and eyebrow raises from people, so that let me know I was on the right track."

Right around then, she was lucky enough to find a special source of inspiration and realistic fear right down the street: *There Will Be Blood* (2007), undoubtedly one of the most intimidating flicks of the millennium, was playing nearby, and Webb kept checking out the role that brought an unusually villainous Daniel Day-Lewis his second acting Oscar.

"I'm not as uptight or fearful as Janet, but I have my own things in life that I could hook into and exploit in order for me to make those colors as vivid as possible when I played her. I always feel like I can go even deeper into my work and make it more specific. I spend hours and hours working toward that and this was no exception. I also felt that the more convincing I could be as Janet, the more the audience could relish in the experience of her near-death experiences."

While we see her friend losing his fight with the pool, Janet's suddenly caught inside a car wash. Her wheels jammed into the grates, her sunroof opens from above, just conveniently enough placed so a broken pipe above can stream a heavy rush of water through it. She may be electrocuted somehow, or even drown. Or Death might be just about to coldly send her straight into a rotating brush to grind the skin right off her skull.

Lori saves her just in time, but that just makes Death want Janet more. At the movies, a fire erupts behind the screen, and an explosion sends debris straight through Janet.

Except it doesn't. Her death was as much a vision as the mirage Nick had back at the start.

"How does someone that tense act after they feel they've conquered the entity of death?" Webb asks, in a question her performance answered. "It was a joy to examine and fulfill both sides of her. To still be orderly, but loosened up. To still be cautious, but not fearful. When that happens to someone like that, they're still who they are, but they've been altered, and I absolutely love stories like that."

Sadly, Janet's final alteration would be the last of her life, and this one was real. As she, Lori, and Nick celebrate their new gifts of existence inside a café, a truck suddenly crashes the event in every sense of the word. Automobile vs. human battles don't tend to go well for the living, and this one's another tragic example—the last we see of the three is an X-ray image (the film was the first of the series to be in 3D) and the lethal injuries they suffered.

"With a heightened storyline like *The Final Destination*," Webb says, "the dialogue can tend toward the expository, which at times can be difficult to justify emotionally. The physical scenes I did didn't seem as difficult to do as some of the more 'What do we do next?' scenes. As the actor, you're worried you may not be doing enough, but you have to trust that the limbo you feel is the limbo the character feels. That was a fun challenge. Saying lines like 'That's weird. . . .' when you, as the actor, know what's going on but as the character you are ignorant to, was another fun challenge."

Part Five of 2011 brought a group of similar young adults away from a bridge collapse, only to have Death chase them all to New York City. Soon after, Peter (Miles Fisher) tries to take his mind off the tragedy, watching his gal pal Candice (Ellen Wroe) sharpen her balance beam skills.

But we see what they, and everyone else in the room, just *happen* to miss: an ominous screw, pointing skyward, sitting at the end of the beam.

Candice misses it, and steps away. Maybe the crew was playing games with us.

With Candice swinging back and forth on the uneven bars, a teammate takes the beam. But that screw's still there.

Anyone familiar with the series had seen the crew take all kinds of ironic liberties with death, but

Death angrily went full throttle on Candice (Ellen Wroe) in *Final Destination 5* (2011).

this one is tough to beat. The lady steps on the screw, flying off balance, knocking into a container of chalk that gymnasts use for their grip.

A huge fan blasts a cloud of the substance square into Candice's face, just as she's swinging in. Losing her grip, she flips skyward and lands wrong.

Very wrong. She's folded slam in half. Her friends, her teammates, Peter . . . everyone's shocked and sickened.

And so were audiences—including Wroe herself.

"Everyone had warned me how gruesome my gymnastics death turned out," she remembers, "so I thought I was prepared, but nothing can prepare you for seeing yourself split in half on the big screen. It's surreal, disgusting, yet awesome and, for whatever reason, hilarious." Candice had given the young actress a chance to rediscover a different kind of performance passion.

"I had been a competitive gymnast for thirteen years and jumped at the opportunity to get back into training," Wroe recalls. "Gymnastics was a huge part of my childhood, one that shaped me immensely. The chance to re-live my gymnastics years was a dream come true."

For months during filming, Wroe went from being Candice on the set to being her in the gym. Helped along by the stunt crew and Brittany Rogers, who'd done gymnastics for Canada at the 2012 London Olympics, Wroe dug out her gymnastics roots.

"With their help, I was able to re-learn a majority of my uneven bar and beam skills," she says. "I was training in the evenings after we wrapped filming, and on weekends."

If the bridge horror didn't do enough to Peter's psyche, this is the knockout punch: he ends up going nuts and taking some friends hostage in a restaurant, forcing another friend to kill him. But things go all the way around; as two other top characters board a plane, we in the audience get another very weird feeling.

Yep—it's the same one that blew apart the first film around back in 2000. It happens again, only this time taking out the main character back on the ground. It so occurs that he's standing in the precise spot that some lost landing gear is reserving!

As of 2016, that's all from the series. For now.

"The *Final Destination* films bring a rare new sense of horror to the screen," Kirk explains. "Instead of your classic 'murderer holding a machete,' the 'murderer' is Death, a killer we see in our everyday lives. The thought of death creeping up on us as it does from birth is a story everyone can relate to. This is what makes the franchise so successful: the humanization of death taking his victims one by one."

You know, in hindsight, maybe that comment back at the beginning wasn't so out of line after all. Because the *Final Destination* series takes death and makes it into a demonic Rube Goldberg machine creation, kicking a series of events into motion that end up with someone or many someones going the wrong way in the most painful of ways. And the unexpectedly bizarre nature in which they do does indeed call up a certain aspect of humor. Dark and sad, yes, but sometimes, even at the worst of times, we can't help but crack up a bit. Once in a while at films like this, there's really nothing else we can do.

Just like when Death wants us home.

Heather Langenkamp battled Freddy Krueger through three rounds of bloody *Nightmare on Elm Street* action.

Heather Langenkamp:

Nightmare on Elm Street

EVEN IN THE same series, even playing the same character (or more than one within a film), Heather Langenkamp's work changed throughout the *Nightmare on Elm Street* saga.

A victim. A counselor. A mother. A true savior, of her friends, her students, her family, and, always last on the priority list, herself, in her battles with a monster who attacks from the one place in which we can never control or defend ourselves: our dreams.

In a decade's worth of three films, Langenkamp and the Nancy Thompson she portrayed did far more than the typical heroine fare of watching friend after friend violently die at the hands of supernatural evil, only to *happen* to find some way to vanquish it and limp off into a painfully optimistic future, nearly alone but newly self-confident, as if killing someone is normally a motivationally inspirational experience.

That's just one of the many things that turned *Nightmare* into its own icon in American history, far more than the reasons it's spawned six sequels and, as of 2016, one remake. Freddy Krueger is known and feared (and, yes, even cheered at times) for reasons far past anything he did on the screen, but he needed someone to bounce off of, and get destroyed by, to elevate to that kind of stardom. Three times, it's been Langenkamp.

"There are very few horror movies where it pits two people against each other," she says. "Usually, it's a monster against whoever is in his way or in his path. In this, he has a target, and you are it. There are very few movies like that."

That was shown in 1994, when the series stepped away from the same fare it had tried for its first six films. Rather than crossing the line from supernatural horror to reality, *New Nightmare* chose to dance all over it, and Langenkamp led the crew along for the ride.

But since that was the end—again, as of 2016!—of Langenkamp's *Nightmare* battles, let's make it the finale of this profile as well.

Back in 1984, the young woman was tossing journalism and acting back and forth as her career choices. She'd appeared in a scene from *The Outsiders* (1983) that didn't make the final cut, then showed up at the top of the cast of the drama *Nickel Mountain* (1984), playing a young mom torn between men.

Meanwhile, a fellow named Wes Craven, himself looking to plant a Hollywood foothold, had patchworked together a tale of an evil killer that death couldn't even stop, venturing back through dreams for revenge, vengeance against the children of those that had killed him. On the good side, Craven had created a young beauty named Nancy Thompson, one based on his own daughter.

Langenkamp ended up being perfect in more ways than a few.

One common trait among those that end up coming out on top in horror films is that there's usually nothing particularly special about them early on in the films. Those with a standout personality are usually the first to be slaughtered, with her left to pick up the pieces and add them to herself to get stronger as the film moves on.

That's certainly Nancy; it's easy for us to imagine her as a common face in school organizations, maybe the student council or Key Club, in between field hockey games—not the captain or president, but perhaps the second-in-command. Not bland by any stretch, certainly very likeable, but not really a leader by nature.

"I didn't realize it at the time," recalls Langenkamp, whose then-boyfriend wrote the ominous rhyme we'd hear throughout the series ("One, two, Freddy's coming for you. . . ."), "but that part was very rare. People weren't writing a lot of characters like (Nancy). She was written as an average teenager, not that sexy. There was nothing clichéd about her. She had a lot of integrity. Every relationship she had was very real." Including the one with her boyfriend, a certain fellow with a James Dean-type edge named Glen Lantz; Langenkamp would give Johnny Depp his first onscreen kiss, before Glen's violent death at Freddy's hands becomes her final push into war.

Like most horror heroines of the genre, Nancy personified a sort of independence, a type of womanhood that showed her as not needing—though perhaps wanting, once in a while—the safety of a relationship. Another typical horror gal trait is to get up and go if only her life is in danger, but be-

It's one of the most legendary images in horror history: Freddy won't even give his lady victims some bathtub privacy in the first *Nightmare on Elm Street* (1984).

ing always ready to rush in and fight for someone else, even in the strange and frightening world of dreams. As her friends start to violently die, Nancy, perhaps picking up and exceeding the law enforcement instinct of her policeman dad Donald (John Saxon), realizes that there's something subconscious at work here.

But just as she starts to realize the final method to Freddy's dark magic, Nancy nearly becomes her own victim. When sleep might be fatal, a warm bathtub is probably at the top of the list of places to avoid, and Freddy nearly makes it her last.

As Nancy dozes off in the midst of self-cleansing, a sinister glove reaches up between her legs, her mom's loud blithering outside the only thing that wakes and saves her.

"It was almost like a two-story box, with a bath at head level, and a chamber below that, (a crew member) was going to be in in scuba gear," Langenkamp recalls of the scene, which took a full day to put together. "The whole time I was kind of freaking out, because it didn't look like it would really pan out."

Gotta mention something here: despite becoming the face of a horror franchise in one of the most ominous debuts in film history, Freddy actually gets less than seven minutes total screen time. Tough to believe, isn't it? But Nancy appears to take him all the way out, and the whole thing looks like it might have been a dream after all (*The Wizard of Oz*'s evil twin, eh?). But as Nancy and her friends start to drive off to school with her mom cheerfully waving goodbye from the porch, something very strange happens.

The windows go up. All the doors suddenly lock at once. The car starts to pull off on its own.

Nancy realizes it, crying out for her mom. But it's too late for everyone: as Nancy's carted away, an arm reaches through the window on the door to the Thompson home, yanking through the screaming mother. This isn't over at all.

In the audience, Langenkamp herself didn't know what to expect.

"(Craven) really wanted it to be clear that Freddy was coming back," she says. "In one ending, the car turned red and green (like his shirt), and we don't even know. In another, Freddy was driving the car."

But things worked out; after costing less than $2 million, the film brought in over $26 million at the box office. Craven, Langenkamp, and Robert Englund weren't quite household names—yet—but their careers had found meteor-esque life. Even President Reagan, whose own acting career never got *near* the blood and guts genre, mentioned the film in a speech just after his reelection.

Nancy stepped out of the *Nightmare* spotlight in 1985 for *Freddy's Revenge* as, in a deviation from the norm in horror, a male became the monster's main target; ironically, Langenkamp would star alongside Mark Patton, who played Freddy's new prey Jesse in *Revenge*, in a 1986 TV after-school special. Part II didn't work as well, but Nancy was still around, and the next year, she came back in a new form for *Dream Warriors*.

Freddy was still after her, but smart enough to know he couldn't do it alone. Just out of school and studying to be a mental health worker, Nancy's trying to help lead a troop of youths from a troubled past to a solid future. But capitalizing on the vulnerability of those that have already been victims, Freddy goes straight at them, stealing their own secret powers to use against her.

It was a new burden for both Nancy and Langenkamp. Just as Nancy certainly had in "reel life," her portrayer studied up on the effects of dreams. She spent time at hospitals, examining the relationships between patients, doctors, and nurses. She worked at a group home, meeting several of those who'd lived the same sort of lives as Nancy's charges.

"As a teenager (in the first film), that was just me being real," Langenkamp says. "I could be as natural as I could. Being the counselor, the young doctor-to-be, I had to be a lot more reserved emotionally."

Rather than go straight at the one who's whaled him before, Freddy does his bloody work on one youth after another, stealing their souls to add to his own fortitude.

And, heartbreakingly, it works, for a while; still in protective mode, Nancy sacrifices herself to help a target escape. Freddy's eventually destroyed again, but that's not a happy ending, as Nancy's funeral is one of the last scenes.

"I loved it!" Langenkamp proudly proclaims of Nancy's death. "In terms of storytelling, it needed to happen: somebody sacrifices themselves to Freddy to make them less powerful. When someone dies, it makes you appreciate them that much more. Nancy became much more of an important character after she died."

Hey, if dying over and over again couldn't stop Freddy, what makes us think that one simple termination could take Nancy out? No way! Seven years and three *Freddy* chapters later, Craven and Langenkamp got back together (though she'd had a brief role in his 1989 scarer *Shocker*) in a task Craven had wanted to try for quite some time.

New Nightmare would be a whole new challenge for everyone. Not only because it was a risk bringing the same character back for a seventh film, especially after "officially" proclaiming him deceased in *Freddy's Dead* back in 1991. Also because the film attempted to blend fantasy with reality, to discuss *Nightmare* from both the inside and outside, something that only the series' longtime main fans would truly grasp.

In the *New* world, away from acting for the time being, Langenkamp's doing the much tougher job of motherhood, but her phone's ringing off the hook with the voice of someone she thought was a character villain, interrupting her nightmare-filled slumber.

She's trying to live her new life, but the old world keeps coming back, as Englund himself shows up as Freddy to shock her on a talk show, aided by an audience of high-class adoring fans. The two even have some comical banter afterward after getting together on film—"Just because it's a love story doesn't mean it can't have a decapitation or two!" he quips—and we're not sure if this isn't everyone's personal inside joke (in a nice sort of irony, Englund had married a lady named Nancy in 1988).

Until things turn tragic: Langenkamp's husband falls asleep at the wheel and dies in a wreck, and her son, in all his grief, starts to go through tornado-type seizures, punctuated with certain rhymes we've only heard in scary make-believe before.

After vowing to stay out of the *Nightmare* world, at least for the time being, the desperate woman now asks her former director for help. Rather than following in Alfred Hitchcock's footsteps of doing walk-bys in his films, Craven took a sizable role as himself, explaining that his own creation had been the artistic prison from which Freddy couldn't escape into reality. Killing him on the screen, however, had given him the ability to live in the real world, and he's here now.

With all this in mind, it would have been very easy for *Nightmare* to generate into slapstick silliness, an inadvertent act of self-deprecation. Going this far with the blend of realism and fiction is taking a huge chance that enough fans will be faithful enough to follow the path, and *Nightmare* could have gone in the whole wrong direction with a single misplaced step.

Fortunately, there's enough fear not to go that far, even with the insiders. Nancy snarls, "Screw your pass!" at a nosy nurse, much like she did to the hall monitor in the opener. Saxon shows up and starts strangely calling her Nancy. She picks up the phone, and a tongue bursts from it, just like in the first film. With Dylan apparently safe in a hospital bed, Freddy shows up and massacres the boy's babysitter, bloodily dragging her around like Tina Gray's legendary series-opening death.

For his last few films, Freddy had developed (not evolved!) a personality that made him scary, but also sort of cool, with one-liners and sarcasm. But that hadn't happened back in the first film, and it sure as hell didn't happen here: this guy was pure malevolence, pure violence, pure suffering of others, there to hurt and be proud of the pain he caused. Remember, he's not Freddy the fictional bogeyman here; he's the absolute personification of evil, with a new outfit and appearance and without the first good goddamn as to what anyone thinks of him.

And for the first time, Langenkamp will have to use the same techniques she taught herself as Nancy to win one more battle. In order for everyone to bring things full circle, a line needs to get crossed.

With Dylan kidnapped, his mom drops a handful of pills to go full-force into the dream world. Ironically, she's back in the same sort of steamy basement-type furnace spot in which Nancy and Freddy first fought decades ago.

Being a mom by this point in real life helped Langenkamp empower herself with the same sort of maternal protection she shows on the screen.

"Nancy being a mom was an important evolution of the character because you've seen her in the parts of being a woman," Langenkamp says. "It was such a unique experience to play a mom after so many people had seen Nancy as a young teenager falling in love. It made the stakes a lot higher."

Freddy obscenely wraps his tongue around her head, a scene Langenkamp called one of her toughest to film. But Dylan saves his mom, and the two become a modified Hansel and Gretel, shoving him to a fiery death in a stove as they roar back to reality.

Will it be Langenkamp's final face-to-face with Freddy? After 2003's *Freddy vs. Jason*, and the 2010 remake of the original, it's tough to imagine Nancy's return. Langenkamp's moved to a different aspect of horror cinema, working on the prosthetics/makeup crews of *Dawn of the Dead* (2004) and 2012's *The Cabin in the Woods* (she also did the same work on 2005's *Cinderella Man* and then *Evan Almighty* two years later). After doing some cosmetic work for the crew of *Star Trek: Into Darkness* (2013), she was rewarded with a cameo as the lovable green security guard Moto, a job that required more time in the makeup chair than Englund *ever* spent during his Freddy exploits!

But as we as horror fans have learned to take very well for granted, only time can tell. Now let's meet some of the most underrated fellows from the *Nightmare* series....

New *Nightmare on Elm Street* heroine Alice Johnson (Lisa Wilcox) had had her friends with her in her first battle with Freddy in 1988's *Dream Master*. But for *Dream Child* the next year, her role suddenly switched to protector, as Nancy's would later, before and after she realized that the burned-face man was back in dreamtown.

After her boyfriend Dan's death, Alice found herself tormented by the same visions that drove her to cling to the edge once before. Now, however, she had an inadvertent partner along the way—someone with whom her relationship got closer than she ever dreamed (in every sense of the word) possible.

"I guess I was a pretty evil-looking kid!" laughed Whit Hertford, who played Jacob, the young boy who Alice keeps finding in her subconscious.

But as horrifying as he was in the film, Hertford got a taste of his own medicine early on set, coming closer to Freddy Krueger than any dreamer would ever desire.

"People ask all the time if I was scared while I was on the set, but I was never really scared except for the first time that I meant Robert Englund," he remembered. Actually, he didn't meet Englund himself—he came face-to-face and claw-to-hand with the fellow Englund's made legendary.

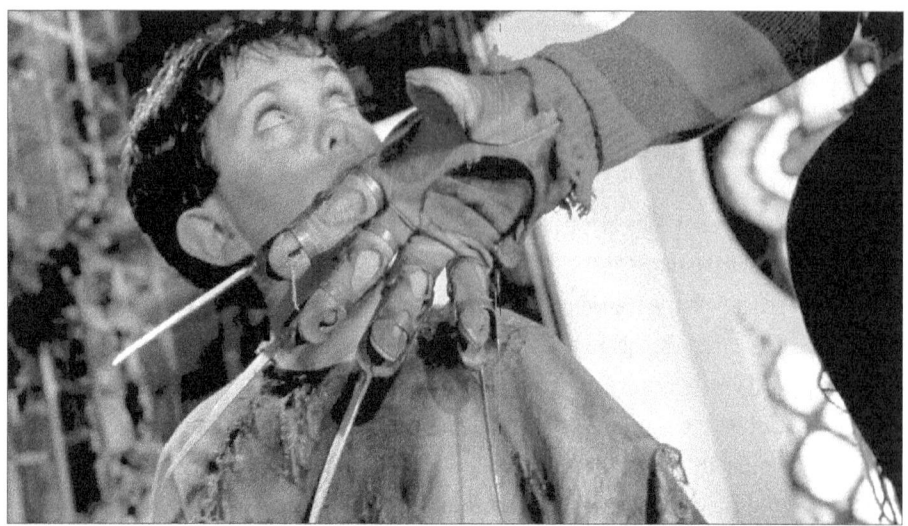

After getting whomped by young women in the first few *Nightmare on Elm Street* films, Freddy Krueger met his downfall at the hands of a young Whit Hertford in The Dream Child of 1989.

As Hertford headed in, he watched Krueger force-feeding Alice's friend Greta (Erika Anderson)—until her head nearly explodes, then leaving her to die.

Common everyday occurrence, right?

"I remember all the smells from the smoke machines and the plaster being made for all the plaster cases," Hertford says. "(Director Stephen Hopkins) motioned to Robert, and asked him to come over. He came right over, and he was really nice, but it was a strange moment! It was one of a lot of small memories I have from that film that I'll never forget, but that was my first introduction to it all."

Well, perhaps it wasn't QUITE his introduction; Hertford had scored a small role in *Poltergeist II* a few years before. It certainly wasn't his introduction to acting in general; his groundwork came from home, where he'd learned from a father who taught theater and a mother who spent her own share of time on the stage.

Tragically, the younger had lost his own father just before filming began.

"It was really great to get to work and forget about (the death)," he says, "and just be in a real state of imagination."

Even before Hertford had the role, his family experience was paying off; the film's original screenplay had ten-year-old Jacob shouting, "Fuck you, Krueger!" during the climactic battle. In auditions, Hertford's mother changed things around.

While he was auditioning, Hertford remembers, "There were those lines, and my mom didn't want me (cussing). You wonder that if you're putting your kid in acting, why is cussing a big deal? But the wisdom in it is that it improved the writing, because you can still have this demented, corrupted, and strange character without going to the Nth degree. A ten-year-old kid having to say 'Fuck you' in a horror film is a cliché, and it diminishes from some of the unspoken things, when people say things instead of showing things through action and movement."

Still, Hertford didn't use those tools much throughout his role; his ghastly chalk-skinned appearance and wide, resigned eyes let the audience know that he was always a step ahead of both them and Alice—and he didn't like what his mind saw. Much of the role consisted of him standing nearly still in Alice's dark dream world, his mind elsewhere, slowly allowing Alice to break through to him and away from "my friend with the funny hand."

Of course, audiences had to pay close attention to notice one of the tougher parts of Hertford's performance.

"Jacob's wardrobe gets dirtier and dirtier, but his wardrobe is really just a hospital gown and a pair of underwear," he says. "Depending on what scene in the movie we were shooting, I would be wearing matching dirty underwear and a hospital gown. It was weird, putting on underwear that's been dyed and covered with grays and browns. It was actually clean, but I was freaked out by having to put on dirty, soiled underwear. I never had to do that for any other role."

Fortunately, his parents weren't the only ones available to get him through it.

"Kids can be hard to direct, and I'm sure I was just like other kid actors with no attention span and not the most exquisite approaches to acting," Hertford says. "But (Hopkins) let me play. He asked 'What do you think?' No one had ever done that. Kids don't usually get that kind of respect. When you're that age, you're cast as a son, a younger brother, or really a kid. I was playing myself. I was playing through the character, with things going on and a heightened reality."

Eventually, Alice learned that Jacob was the son she so desperately wanted to save, and Jacob realized that Freddy wasn't his friend after all.

As Alice and Freddy went to war one last time, a new face appeared on the scene—it was Freddy's mom Amanda herself. She let Jacob know that if he doesn't do something, he'll never exist. It was time for Hertford to show the skills been practicing since the day he auditioned.

Turning away from the camera for a moment, Jacob let the audience know whose side he was on. Then he twisted back around, and showed the same side that Alice was trying to destroy.

"School's out, Krueger!" declared Jacob, firing out the line the filmmakers had used to stop him from cursing. His face imprinted with a small dose of Krueger's trademark burns, Jacob blasted from his mouth the souls of those that Krueger had stolen, spiraling forth like a psychotic tornado and tearing Krueger apart once and for all (at least, until *Freddy's Dead*).

"That was a longer process, because of all the special effects," he remembers of the climax. "They made a plaster mold of my face. It took two days, an hour and a half a day. They poured plaster over my head and up my nostrils. There were times when I thought I was going to die, but they knew what they were doing."

Even after filming wrapped, Hertford had more to learn.

"The first screening was a cast-and-crew premiere," he says. "I remember being quite scared during that movie."

For the first time, he got to meet Englund in regular mode. He went to screenings in a cemetery and chapel. He got to meet Freddy's denizens.

"There were a lot of fans!" said Hertford, who still has the skateboard that Hopkins gave him after the cameras cut off. "*Nightmare* fans kind of freaked me out, because they're so devoted. I saw a lot of Freddy sweaters."

By the sixth go-round of the man named Krueger, we in the seats knew quite a bit of *why* everyone was so ticked at the guy, and why he was pissed right back.

He'd hurt their kids. They'd killed him. Sounds pretty justifiable, right?

But the *who* (and, to an extent, another *why*) weren't clear—until, of course, right before it was time for Freddy to die!

Who had he been before? What had his life been like before the inch-deep facial scars and the gloved hand? And why in holy hell had he done the things he had? What pisses off a person so much that they cause so much pain to others, even those they'd never ever met before?

Well, those questions get asked all the time every time we hear about random acts of violence in society. In 1991's *Freddy's Dead*, we got a few explanations about his past, much deeper than his disgusting conception story of *Dream Child*.

As Freddy's next round of victims starts to add up in number, one fellow who thinks he has something to hide and a lady who doesn't know she does head to his old stomping grounds of Springfield—clearly one far different than the Simpsons' hometown! An orphanage and school full of creatures that show that Freddy might have been one of the *saner* town alumni tell his story, and we see it.

Just as is so often the case with criminals real and cinematically created, the seeds for trouble were sown in a classroom full of little brats who don't realize how deep their harm can go.

As those his then-age shouldn't be, Chason Schirmer wasn't aware of the *Elm Street* phenomenon way back then—not exactly the sort of thing grade-schoolers should be checking out.

"The only exposure I'd had was years prior to that," he recalls. "A kid brought a deck of horror movie playing cards, and one had a picture of Freddy on it. I had a recurring nightmare throughout most of my childhood that I was getting chased around by this monster Freddy."

Still, looking for a way through the door to acting, his folks carried him to a shot at the "last" *Nightmare*.

"It was totally random," he says. "I just showed up for a random call. I was pretty much doing acting work on the side: in my parents' view, to get college money, and in my view, to get out of school."

But after he got picked to be the youth Freddy, the two would coincide. For a brief moment, we saw Freddy's disturbed world, from within and out. During a normal day of schooling, he stoically removed the class hamster from its cage.

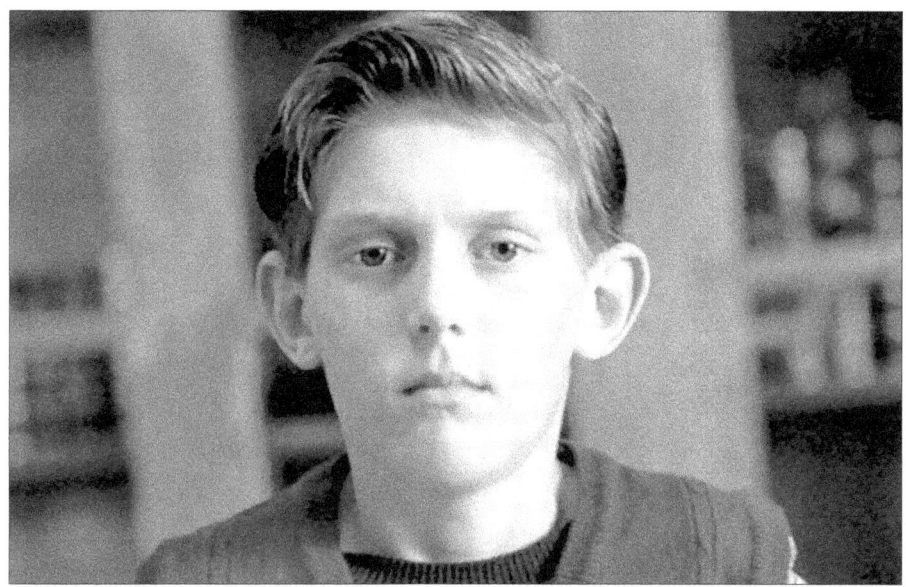

It took six films, but horror fans finally got a look at Freddy Krueger's childhood in the persona of Chason Schirmer in *Freddy's Dead* (1991).

Then he flattened it, looking as emotional as he would moving a stack of books.

The crew told him, "In front of a bunch of kids, hey, you're going to come up here and smash this hamster, but not really!" Schirmer recalls. "Coincidentally enough, in school, I generally was the picked-on kid, so it was really, really easy to slide myself into the oddball, just by remembering school. I thought about what it had been like in school, getting picked on. You wonder what you could do, if you'd strike back. It's not really anger, just a need to put everyone where you are, so they understand what you do."

As his classmates crowd around, filling the air with taunting chants, we see the first sign of pain and emotional run through the child's eyes.

"I was like, 'Oh crap, I'm back in my regular class, getting picked on again.' But it made it easy, because it was all right there; I wasn't imagining the kids doing it."

Early on in *Freddy's Dead* casting, Tobe Sexton had had the lead role in mind. Fresh off a small role in the 1989 slasher *Offerings*, he'd gone for John Doe, the guy who *thinks* he and the Gloved One have a genetic connection.

"They were looking for more of a Johnny Depp-type," he recalls (Shon Greenblatt ended up with the role, with Depp in a hilarious "This is your brain on drugs" commercial cameo spoof). "They told me I had done a really great job, but wasn't what they were looking for." A month later, however, he'd gotten a call and a new chance along with it.

Well into his downward mental descent by the midst of his second decade, the abuse Freddy had tasted in his youth hadn't changed at his foster home . . . but his response to it certainly had. While

By his teen years, Freddy Krueger (Tobe Sexton) was straddling the line between pleasure and pain, or so we learned in 1991's *Freddy's Dead*.

many of us shy from pain and cringe at its first arrival, this fellow was making it his own weapon to return outward, starting with the provider.

Getting ready for a shot at the pre-incinerated Freddy, Sexton checked out the character's previous ventures. Then he got ready to head in to try out.

"A friend of mine happened to have made a Freddy Krueger glove for himself, of copper and steak knives," he recalls. "It was actually pretty sharp, looked like a pretty lethal weapon. Right then, I ended up having a lot more respect for the design elements and what actually was Freddy's favorite weapon."

He borrowed the creation and visited the crew. In the midst of his tryout, he yanked the glove out of a bag. Perhaps, for one moment, they might have thought that Freddy's arrival into reality was occurring a few years ahead of *New Nightmare*.

"They looked at it, and realized it was a real weapon," he says. "It gave me something to work with. Horror fans know where Freddy puts his glove on, he's Freddy Krueger. When he loses his glove, it takes away his power." Another call brought the good news, and he was back to checking out Freddy's past.

"I worked on the mythology of Freddy, his dealings with the dream demons and the 3D section," Sexton recalls. "He was the son of a hundred maniacs who tortured his victims. How do I go about making this guy real, making his psychology real? I created my own mythology and psychology for him."

On the other end was a fellow who'd been jolting and occasionally terrifying entertainment audiences of a different sort for decades; after becoming a household name (albeit an unusual one for a male!) in shock rock music, Alice Cooper became Freddy's abusive stepdaddy—remember that his actual dad was probably that inmate that Robert Englund played in *Dream Child*, the one that raped Amanda.

"I had all of Alice's albums," Sexton recalls. "It was interesting to find out his real name (Vincent Furnier). It helped with the demystification of the Hollywood process. I used this to ground myself in the world as Freddy, having Alice be there. I learned what was going on with iconic figures."

Including, as it fortunately turned out, the man behind the older Krueger himself.

"I got to work with Robert a lot," Sexton recalls. "I worked on how to develop Freddy's voice. I learned the techniques of breathing and projection, making my voice different ways. It was very interesting to see how he could do Freddy's voice, and I worked with him to match him from when Freddy was younger."

He looked over Freddy's movements, like the slumping right arm that Englund often utilized.

"I was able to emulate a bit of his character, but also make it my own," Sexton says. "I was able to do a good homage to what Robert had created: true to the character, true to the moment. It was really, really important to me, because I didn't want to spoil it for the audience."

That's where, for one of the first times, Schirmer found himself.

"I really didn't find out until later how big of a cult *Nightmare* really had," he recalls. "It was a neat feeling of being a part of something big for all of my horror friends' lives."

When it came out in 1972 and again when it returned with a different cast in 2009, *Last House on the Left* showed us all that horror can be all too realistic, terrifyingly possible.

The First and Second *Last*

As the 1970s began, America had quite a bit to be royally pissed off about.

Blacks were fighting so hard through the civil rights movement they'd started the decade before, and many just refused to get the hell out of their way and accept that equality was inevitable.

Even in the worst of ways. Four innocent little girls were killed in a Birmingham church bombing. Martin Luther King, who'd done his best to stop his friends from resorting to violence, had himself become a victim of it, and Medger Evers and far too many others had gone the same way.

Women were tired too. Tired of being confined to the kitchen. Ready to go out and become their own people, rather than some guy's wife and some kid's mom. It had taken them over a century after America began to even get the right to vote, and many were still trying to even keep that from them. Inspired by those who'd fought to make people look past their skin tone, women wanted gender to stop being a factor, but their coup wouldn't be without pain and suffering either.

Fear often leads to anger, and we had plenty of both to go around. Richard Speck slaughtered eight nursing students in the summer of 1966; less than a month later, Charles Whitman sent a new wave of terror through America with a rifle from a Texas tower. At the whims of a Rasputin-type leader named Manson, a cult had brutally slaughtered five people in California, one a pregnant actress who had her fetus ripped from her body—and those are just their killings that we know of.

But perhaps most of all, most infuriatingly heartbreaking of all, was the pain suffered by mothers and fathers, sons and daughters, husbands and wives across the country. People who could only helplessly watch on TV and read in the papers about a war going on in a land few had even known of until their nation had been involved in it about a decade before.

The battle cries of patriotism had been proudly called in the first years of the Vietnam War, but as its goal become pitch-black murky, as more and more who had, voluntarily or otherwise, headed over to fight, began to come back without their lives, or never at all, forgotten by the government that had sent them, we had no peace to find.

The problems of two wannabe filmmakers wouldn't add up to jack in the midst of all the pain, the suffering, the death. But the story they would tell would become sadly relevant, even realistic, and repeatedly so. They'd put together a tale that would, to a fully relatable degree, show what we do when rationale goes out the window, when we have all the right reasons for doing harm, why anger is everyone's worst enemy and strongest weapon.

We'll see them in a second. First, let's examine the sad similarity as to why, four decades later, our situation isn't very different. Today we're still angry, still for some of the same reasons.

We were furious when thousands of innocents suddenly lost their lives on 9/11, and felt it all exacerbate during the near-decade it took to catch the piece of shit who masterminded it all. We could only watch as evil gunmen slaughtered many who'd done nothing wrong in Colorado, Connecticut, Virginia Tech, and other places. We steamed as O.J. Simpson and Casey Anthony committed horrible crimes, then gleefully laughed in our faces as our system let them walk away. We got a little satiated watching Jerry Sandusky get put where he belonged, but still felt enraged at his getting away with everything for years, and toward those that looked the other way when he did.

And even today, more spouses are becoming young widows and widowers. More children lose their parents. More parents lose their children. Thousands keep coming home in boxes from senseless, needless, directionless wars in Iraq and Afghanistan, and we're left to console each other with shit like, "Hey, at least s/he died a hero!" After a while, that saying doesn't seem very effective.

We see and feel pain that never seems to stop, and we can't do a damn thing about it. We can't reach out and stop mass murder. We can't snap our fingers and bring our loved ones back to us. We can't replace law with justice. There's no medication for this suffering. Pain and hopelessness all too often go together, and they've been back and forth across this country for years.

So maybe it's appropriate that two people who'd first dared to step where few had tried before in the film world got a new chance to sit behind the scenes, to pull their strings of the actors and audiences.

Anger has always caused pain, both inner and outer, but sometimes it's the right emotion to give control for a little while. That's a rule that was true when *Last House on the Left* arrived in 1972, just as it's true today.

It's why the second version, arriving in 2009, wasn't so much a remake as a revisiting of a time and mindset that we've been through before. Same story (well, almost), same pain, same death, same dark satisfaction at the end, along with some secret self-assurance that we could do the same thing to the scumbags that did that shit to our children.

Directing the 1971 drama *Together*, Sean Cunningham ran into a fellow named Wes Craven behind the producing scenes. The next year, the two would switch positions.

Craven's screenplay, banged out in three days, took from the Swedish film *The Virgin Spring* from a decade before, in which Max von Sydow played a father who trapped and killed three people who'd murdered his daughter. Craven also harnessed the rage, the fear, the uncertainty that kept giving Americans a reason to live on edge, a feeling they had no reason to believe would ever leave.

With Cunningham now producing, the pair cast and shot the film, and sent it toward theaters. Even then, they couldn't figure out a title, going through *Night of Vengeance* (superficial), *Sex Crime of the Century* (defines redundancy), and *Krug and Company* (?!). Then one day at a test screening, an ad guy came up to Cunningham and asked that the flick get called *Last House on the Left*.

"I asked him, 'What the hell has that title got to do with anything in the movie?'" Cunningham says, "to which he answered, 'I don't know, I just like it.'"

It worked; throngs of fans arrived and were handed vomit bags at the theater. Film taglines warned viewers "To Avoid Fainting, Keep Repeating: It's Only a Movie" (although viewers in Australia and much of the UK never got the chance to, as the film was banned in those necks of the woods for far too long). Craven and Cunningham even used it as springboards for their own cinematic inspirations, becoming the driving forces behind the iconic *Nightmare on Elm Street* and *Friday the 13th* franchises.

Decades later, as a new wave of helplessness and frustrated fury rolled through Old Glory, a shot at a remake would come along, and a new round of people had to get ready to dish out the suffering, both committing and feeling. Craven and Cunningham would be back behind the cameras, producing while Dennis Iliadis snared the director's chair.

"It doesn't look away from a very ugly truth," Craven explains. "It does not cut, does not fade to black, it just stays until the act plays out, and then you see all the aftereffects, unblinking. Many people depend on films to blink at a certain point. *Last House on the Left* does not blink."

Then and now, two guys had to get ready to be the leader of the pack, the group of bad guys that captures two women, push them through some of the worst pain that someone can undergo, then appear to be in the clear until a victim's parents inadvertently get hold of them and find it from within to dish out some of their own medicine (literally, as the father in question is a doctor!).

One way or another, David Hess and Garret Dillahunt would become David Krug, the rapist, the killer, the bad boy with a taste for beautiful women, leading his son into the worst example setting in the world.

At the outset of the 1970s, Hess had some experience in the entertainment world, but more in a different sense: music was his game. Then one day, he got a phone call from his girlfriend's brother. A budding actor himself, the brother had gotten a shot at the main antagonist in Craven and Cunningham's new film. He'd decided to try for a smaller role, but he knew just the man to get bad.

One problem: Hess was a bit too shrimpish. Krug was a sparkplug of a man—clearly hitting the gym hard in the prison he'd just escaped from—and Hess couldn't look the part without help.

It came in an inadvertent wardrobe switch. Hess found himself suddenly swimming in bulky sweaters, on one of the hottest days of the year. Stepping out of a car and onto the sidewalk, Hess didn't know what was going on: nothing about the film, his character, or anything else. He spied the filmmaking office up ahead, and stormed forward like a Category Five tornado.

"By this time I'm livid," Hess recalled. "We've been stopping and starting in traffic, it's hot, I'm caked with sweat underneath all these sweaters. I'd just come back from a workout, this is not my idea of fun."

He roared upstairs and barreled toward the first office he saw.

"*Listen, I'm here for a fuckin' audition, now who the fuck do I gotta see?!*" Hess blared. "I mean, I'm swearing like a madman. Wes and Sean came out of an office with their eyes as wide as saucers. They think I'm gonna kill 'em!" A first impression was all they'd need; about fifteen minutes later, Hess had snared the role, and he'd end up contributing to the soundtrack as well.

"My style of acting is to go over the edge during rehearsal," he said, "to push it as far as I can possibly push it, just to see how far I can go. And then I set my parameters. Once I draw that box, once I have those boundaries, then I'm free to do whatever I want within my character."

By the way, that brother that pushed him in the ultimate direction? His name was Marty Kove, who played a bumbling deputy in the film and later darkened the spotlight as the evil sensai Kreese in the *Karate Kid* movies.

By the time it came around to the second version, the filmmakers had the time, money, and credibility to be a little more picky with their casting. It would take more than just a banshee screech to snare the lead.

Fortunately, Dillahunt had quite a bit to offer; namely, the most valuable asset of experience. He'd been a Terminator on TV in *The Sarah Conner Chronicles* (2008). He'd played Wendell the helpful deputy in 2007's Best Picture victor *No Country for Old Men*.

"I thought that's what we were supposed to do as actors," explains Dillahunt, who, ironically enough, would be Jesus in the short-lived 2013 show *Book of Daniel*. "One day you are the king and the next you are the beggar. I feel a sense of accomplishment if I can pull off a character that is very far from me or from the last character I played." Fortunately, Krug would fit those specifications to a K.

So yes, Dillahunt had down the tools to morph into another. But he'd never had to make this kind of change. Flipping through the literary offerings of his new Kindle, he found a book by a former member of the FBI.

He learned a bit about putting new people at ease with an agenda still to hide; the man had used such methods to coax a confession out of unwilling and unwitting criminals. Krug would use them to charm his way into the calmness of his victims.

Dillahunt also went over the tale of serial killer Andrew Cunanan, whose murder of fashion icon Gianni Versace launched a nationwide manhunt in the summer of 1997. Cunanan's murder of Versace pushed him into the national spotlight, but it wasn't his only or even first theft of life—at least five murders are credited to the cretin, found dead by his own hand just over a week after the Versace murder.

Cunanan, Dillahunt says, was "nothing like Krug, but there was one killing he had done that I had forgotten about or never heard about on his cross-country trip where he really just brutalized this older man in his home. They were remarking on it because the brutality was strange." Cunanan had duct-taped the man helpless, beat and stabbed him, then slit his throat before running him over with a car.

"He would not stop with the strange," Dillahunt says. "They surmised that he reminded him of his own father. He personalizes everything so much that this boundless rage would come out, and that what I wanted for Krug. I thought he was a rage-o-holic."

Still, anyone gets angry once in a while; then and now, Americans have all sorts of reasons for rage. But to rape, to kill, to torture as Krug so often gleefully does, well, that's more than just a high state of pissivity.

"This is evil," Dillahunt says. "Evil has come to your door, and what are you going to do? There's no explanation for it, it makes no sense, it's something outside your realm of understanding, but it's here, so what do you do? And there are all sorts of parallels to that going on in the world today, however you define evil."

The first Krug's second in command had had her own experience in this sort of thing—acting-wise, at least; Jeramie Rain was playing Manson slave Susan Atkins in an off-Broadway play even as filming began. Like Hess, it wouldn't take much time for her to earn the role, playing Krug's lady Sadie.

"There was no preparation for any of this," Rain recalls, "I read a couple of scenes, and when they weren't looking, I looked through and saw a couple other scenes, and it said that I cut some woman's breast off and ate it. I said I couldn't do it. They said they weren't going to use any of those things." Still, Sadie would end up helping out in rape and murder, her evil cackles echoing through the scenery as filming went on.

In her own shot at the role, Riki Lindhome got to go all out, even further. While the first film begins with the young women traipsing toward a concert, in search of some smoked relaxants along the way, 2009's version kicks off with Sadie helping Krug escape from the law, putting a bullet through a cop's head in the bargain. Not just that, but just after the murderous group arrives at the hotel in which the yet-unknowing captors' nightmare will begin, Sadie's casually topless in front of total strangers. There's something both awing and terrifying about such cavalier-ness.

It wouldn't be the first time Lindhome tried to get under the skin of audiences; her biggest role yet had been as boxing champ Maggie Fitzgerald's greedy little sister in *Million Dollar Baby* (2004). But to kill, to watch rape, and to hardly show much emotion along the way, that was something fresh.

Fortunately, Lindhome was surrounded by newness; her naturally light hair was dyed as pitch black as Sadie's heart, she was alongside many performers she'd never worked with before, and everyone was in a whole new world, as the flick was shot in South Africa.

"I didn't know anyone; it was a new time zone," she says. Filming the attacks, "was pretty intense. Those weren't fun days. I would just go back into this tent in between shots and try not to think about it because I believe Sadie doesn't care.

"It's always the men behind the masks," continues Lindhome. "That's the reason I loved this part. I don't remember the last time the woman was right there with the men. Sadie is equally as bad as them; she might even be worse as soullessness goes. They don't tone her down at all. She's not wimpy or subservient. She's as brutal as everyone else." Just as Manson's family was willing to die for him, Sadie appeared to see Krug as something far beyond the levels of mortality.

"When I first read the script, I thought (Sadie) was simply sadistic," she remembers. "But once I realized she was doing all these things also because of love, my view changed. I think she's just an incredibly bored person who loves sex, drugs, and adrenaline. (The men) give her that. Everything she wants is with them, but there are moments I believe that she wouldn't have taken things as far if it wasn't for them."

Much is made of the scenes (which were improvised) right after the shooting of one of the victims in a lake, when the killers glance around at each other, even shedding a tear here and there (this is in both films). Some feel that it's some actual remorse inside a monster, that even a tiny heart lives somewhere in their darkness.

Sadistic pessimist I can be, I have a different view. I feel it's not that they're sorry for the lives they've stolen, but because it was a tough but necessary part of the job. Think of a soldier forced by her commanding officer to fire on civilians. Think of a vet putting a beloved family pet to sleep. Think of a personally pro-life doctor performing an abortion. Think of medical personnel in the midst of a hysterical family, helplessly watching a loved one slip away, unable to accept that the DNR order they signed forces everyone to do nothing. It's a part of your work you hate, but you knew going in that it might happen, so you don't get to get too worked up when it does. Not actual repentance, only a final realization of the difference between possibility and reality and getting shoved across the line between the two.

Still, that scene is as close as we the audience get to seeing something behind the monsters these people are, and seemingly always were. It would have been so easy to include a short scene of a private chat between Krug and another character. It would have taken all of two minutes to write, film, and add a viewing of him or them growling about child abuse, parental abandonment or loss, or anything else that we so often see in the pasts of horror movie villains.

But it doesn't happen, and that's probably intentional. Because people who do this sort of thing don't have a reason or explanation. There's no justification behind a person who does this, and we don't need one. There wasn't for the mass murders decades ago, or today. We don't need or want to know why. We just want some comeuppance to get shown fast.

It added something else to the performers' work, one more burden for them to pick up and carry.

"I thought my character was creepy for no apparent reason, which chilled me to the core," Lindhome says. "I feel they don't really justify why the three of us do what we do, and I love that. In every other horror movie, it's 'Oh, he has a mean mom.' In this, it doesn't matter why, they just did it!"

And now for the women to whom everything was done. Let's finally meet some of the victims, those who had to act out things that have happened to far too many people in real life.

In the original, they were Sandra Cassel and Lucy Grantham, acting out Mari Collingwood and her friend Phyllis. Nearly forty years later, the actresses would change to Sara Paxton and Martha MacIssac, and Phyllis' name would be the more modernized Paige. Mari's parents would switch monikers too, and not everyone would meet the same fate as before.

"When you talk about breaking ground," says Grantham, "you talk about Picasso or about certain musicians who led the way, who broke with tradition and began a new form of the arts. I put *Last House* in the same category . . . by today's standards, it's not that scary, because these kids have seen so much . . . But when you put *Last House* in its correct time frame, it's remarkable, it's gutsy, and it has a wonderful combination of humor and horror." Her Phyllis would be forced to urinate on herself, made to have sex with her friend (not retained in the second version), and be assaulted by Sadie.

"It was very scary for me to do the chase scenes, because my part was much more physical than

I'd realized," she says "There was a lot of running downhill on very precipitous slopes, where there were a lot of branches coming out of the ground, things you could trip on . . . (it took) a lot of rehearsing to work up my courage so that I could run in a way that was realistic." MacIssac also called the pursuit scenes some of the hardest to act out.

While Hess admitted that the scene where Phyllis is disemboweled and dismembered by the group gave him a bad case of the dry heavings, Grantham called it one of her favorites.

"I loved it," she says. "A scene like that really allows you to go all out as an actress . . . you can emote to the skies!" Just as Sissy Spacek would be legendarily drenched a few years later in *Carrie* (1976), Grantham found herself soaked in Karo syrup, the propping everyman's blood of the 1970s.

Paxton's trendsetting counterpart Cassel acted just a few more times, never in the mainstream, after *Last House*. Gearing up to become the second Mari Collingwood, Paxton, already with a decade of experience and more roles than Cassel ever had, thought about what she wanted to *not* do.

"When I see something that's a remake, I get all pissed off," she admits, "especially if it's one of my favorite movies. But I think we tried so hard to keep other people in mind while we were filming this movie." That's part of the reason she decided not to check out Cassel's work before retaking the role.

"I didn't want to have any kind of preconceived notions of the character or the film or anything," Paxton says, "because we are not trying to copy the movie . . . remake page by page. We're just trying to breathe new life into this story."

Still, some of her old techniques would come in handy; the first time we meet Mari, she's freestyling through a pool, both a foreshadowing to her fate and a flashback to Paxton's performance as a mermaid in *Aquamarine* (2006). But both she and Mari would end up far from there, a ways out even from Bikini Bottom, where Paxton had hung out doing voice work on *Spongebob Squarepants*!

Like Lindhome, the continental separation of filming in a separate nation had an effect on Paxton. "We were in a real forest with real live animals and bugs and rocks and everything around us," she says, "And that really gets you into the mode immediately. It was so emotionally challenging, because that whole morning I was so nervous coming to set at six o'clock in the morning. I kept running over to the trashcan. I thought I was going to vomit every five seconds. I couldn't get it under control. And then it kind of went away and we had a talk for ourselves before we began the day, and it really helped a lot."

There's no surefire way to prepare to act like one is being raped, to imagine what it would be like to watch one of our friends get slowly tortured to death. Paxton had to take her mind and body where it hadn't been before, and not just concerning her acting career.

"I wanted a challenge and I got a challenge," she says. "It was the most challenging thing I've ever done—mentally, emotionally and physically—in my entire life. We seriously all got beat up every day . . . Everything is really real . . . It makes it a lot easier when you're working with people that you feel safe with." Ironically, she'd been alongside Dillahunt in another type of remake, a TV pilot that didn't get the *Mr. Ed* show back off the ground.

Now, for both Cassel and Paxton, came one of the toughest scenes to do and for us to watch. After being raped and finding out her friend is dead, Mari makes her way into a pond. Cassel made it a slow walk to a death she knew was unavoidable, even welcome. Paxton turned it into an attempted escape, firing through the waves once again.

Both women were shot. Cassel's Mari floated to the surface, slipping away quickly. Paxton's character sank, blood slowly billowing from her. But unlike her predecessor, she had just a little left.

If acting out the violent scenes had challenged her as a person, becoming Mari afterward gave Paxton an extra new burden as a performer. Near death, Mari had to stay at least semi-conscious, unable to speak or barely move, but still sort of responsive. Paxton had gotten to go all-out aggressive in the violent scenes; now it was time to turn to uber-subtlety.

"It was pretty tough—wanting to say something and having to use just your face and be scared," she says. "I like to challenge myself."

As fate, or probably karma in this case, would have it, the killers wind up taking refuge from a storm at the home of Mari's parents, although neither group knows who the other is just yet. Just as before, let's go over these separately.

In the original, Mari dies of the gunshot. Her mom Estelle figures it out when she sees her daughter's necklace hanging from the neck of one of the killers, then hears them talk about it. Estelle and her husband John (Cynthia Carr and Richard Towers) find Mari's body just ashore, and take her inside as she breathes her last.

What could a person do here? How could anyone have the first idea? The parents aren't naturally violent, at least there's no indication thereof. But to watch your beautiful daughter violently die, and have a chance to dish out your own justice, to not have to worry about expensive trials, incompetent judges, lying lawyers, and juries without a heart or a damned clue (remember O.J. and Casey)? That's a temptation just too big for them to resist. They're going to fight fire with fire, and it's a match flame against an inferno.

Estelle orally castrates one villain. John rips off Krug's head with a chainsaw (Hess called filming the scene one of the toughest of his life). Sadie puts up the toughest fight, but Estelle gets the drop on her in the pool, using Sadie's own knife to dissect her esophagus.

With a whole new fight to fight now, one probably much more difficult, the couple consoles each other, not ready to accept that their child won't be coming home.

Now let's get to the new version. Unlike before, Mari's parents (now *Emma* and John, with Monica Potter and Tony Goldwyn becoming them) have already lost a child: their son died before the story began.

When the killers get here, John the doctor even fixes one of their broken noses. But when the new Mari arrives, she's alive, and some emergency makeshift surgery from John keeps her that way. Then Emma sees her daughter's necklace on one of the group and realizes who they're dealing with here.

The new tag team's methods are different, but no less effective.

They beat one creep nearly to death, finishing him off by jamming his hand into a garbage disposal, flipping the switch, and putting a hammer through his brainstem. Emma blasts a bullet through Sadie's eye, then helps her husband knock Krug out. Soon after, they ride off in a boat, with Mari beaten, but still alive.

But it's not over for Krug: having gone to the opposite of the Hippocratic Oath, John uses his medical methods to paralyze him. Then, perhaps bending the rules of realism, he jams Krug's head into a microwave, and tries to fight off a smile as the cranium blows like a nightmarish balloon.

You know, it's ironic, but Potter and Goldwyn actually show more sadism as the good guys than they did as villains. Playing the mastermind behind a kidnapping in 2001's *Along Came a Spider*, Potter killed a man and nearly the child she'd help steal, but nowhere near the brutality Emma utilized. Goldwyn had arranged the murder of his friend Sam (Patrick Swayze) in the iconic *Ghost* (1990), but his John took the lives himself.

What else is worth considering here is what might happen next in the storyline, the part we never see. A luxury that performers and audiences have is that the story ends with the credits; performers go off for their next role, viewers can just worry about what they saw, not what happened afterward. For many, looking into a fully imagined future isn't worth the effort. But if we came back and visited the Collingwoods in five or ten years, what might have happened?

Would the parents from the first film still be together, or break up, as couples who lose children have a sad tendency to do? In the new group, would Mari ever make it even remotely close to back, physically or mentally? Would her swimming career have continued? Would her father be able to return to his medical practice, knowing that there's a chance he might have to help heal someone who'd done deeds like Krug? Would Krug's son be able to emerge from his father's darkness, or still get yanked back down into the criminal lifestyle?

"What happens to everyone?" Paxton hypothesizes. "I really don't know. I don't think they'll ever be coming back to the last house on the left. That's for sure. I don't think they'll ever go there for a family vacation ever again. They'll probably just stay inside their home and lock their doors for the rest of their life and be traumatized and crawl into a ball on the floor and cry."

So what was it like for everyone afterward, either a few decades or a few years? What was it like to watch oneself on the screen, to examine its legacy and assess the magnitude of the first film's impact on film culture and the second one's kick at the can?

"I'm not afraid of every shadow," Paxton says. "I'm not afraid of every person; you still have to go on living life. But I definitely think that some people get caught up in this dream world where everything is perfect. And they refuse to acknowledge what's going on around them and what is really happening in the real world. And I think that this movie is very powerful, because you really leave affected. I was in the movie and I knew these people and I still left feeling shaken up."

Rain, who spent her paycheck for the first film on a new family dog, says her parents didn't talk to her for a year after seeing her as Sadie. After just one more go-round in front of the camera, she went into writing and producing, eventually marrying and divorcing Oscar-winner Richard Dreyfuss. Hess, whose music was heard on the soundtrack for Eli Roth's 2002 thriller *Cabin Fever*, mentioned that people crossed the street to avoid him when it came out.

Grantham went back to school and got a PhD. "The good part about *Last House on the Left* was that it gave me a sense of fulfillment, because I had been involved in a project that was a major success," she says. "I didn't (quit acting) with this feeling of 'coulda, woulda, shoulda, maybe, can I.' I never felt that those years acting were lost or wasted . . . I learned so much from *Last House*, and I felt that I did what I set out to do. A lot of kids who go into the field never even get to feel that."

Hess worked under Craven a decade later in 1982's *Swamp Thing*.

"I've always felt that *Last House* was an *other*-drive movie; it wasn't an Earth-driven movie," he said. "It was created by some other kind of force, because all of us have gone on to do many other things, but none of us have ever made anything that had the initial impact of *Last House* . . . it was like we were tools of something else!"

Two years after watching Dillahunt try out the role he'd set the trend for (Hess claimed he didn't like the remake), Hess passed of a sudden heart attack.

"We're constantly during our lifetimes trying to cleanse ourselves of those things that are aberrational to us," he said shortly beforehand. "And what do you do if you sit across from an analyst? You open up and you dig as deep as you possibly can into that unknown territory that you don't want to know about . . . and try to bring it up and look at it and understand why it is that you do these things. If you're able to act them out in locations and in scenes where it's protected because you're making a film . . . you're not doing it in real life even though it looks real . . . well, there's very much of a cleansing process."

Ramon Llao:

The Green Inferno

IT'S A PRETTY good place for an actor to be. Someone has enough faith in you to just call you up one day and offer you a job, and you have the confidence in them to just say yes. The plot, the location, your character, none of that's important just yet. There's just trust. If it's all you need, you're doing well in the business.

Sobras International Pictures and Eli Roth had their hands and minds all over the next big Hollywood horror hit, and they knew who to call.

"Because of the friendly relation we have," Ramon Lloa explains of Sobras, "most of the time when they offer me a part, I just take it, not really knowing what it is about."

Here's another admirable spot for a performer—hearing about a role already signed for, and hardly reacting at all. Learning what he'd be doing and who he'd play in

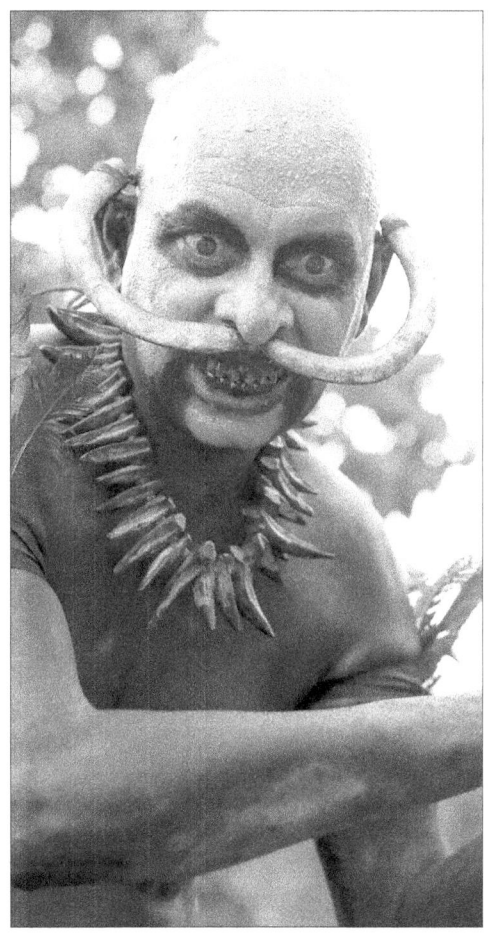

Ramon Llao's head headhunter set the *Green Inferno* in 2015.

The Green Inferno (2015), Lloa . . . just did it. Sobras and Roth had relied on him to pull off the character, and he just showed up to keep his word. If a performer can be so restrained getting ready for his *Inferno* man, it shows that his act has long since been gotten together.

"It took me the time until the makeup was ready," Llao explains. "I got the part just by lifting the phone and saying 'Yes, I take it.'" In a character in a film that, like much of Roth's work, has the subtlety of a tsunami, it's tough to believe how stoic everyone sounds.

Down in the Amazon, both in storyline and reality, a group of upbeat Americans is on the way home. They just stopped the destructive, uncaring corporate loggers from destroying a village of the helpless, victimized locals, and it's time to head back to Old Glory and feel the admiration!

Then the plane crashes. Some die then, some soon after. Blow-darted into submission, the group's headed to a tribal site and jammed inside cages made of bamboo.

One visitor, the largest one, is given a quick drink by the natives. Maybe they're actually OK. Maybe their first attack was impulsive self-defense, and now they're going to help.

Wishful thinking that a genie wouldn't grant. He's slowly decapitated, dismembered, and chowed upon—eyes first.

And the saddest part (well, in a relative sense)? The visitors realize that these are the very people they came so far to protect. Now they're becoming their cuisine, with Llao's general leading the way.

He'd had quite a bit of time to get mentally ready in the makeup chair, with his whole head painted yellow, his teeth deteriorated into a dentist's nightmare, and some headgear made from bones jammed through his face, and that's just from the neck up!

"There wasn't any special preparation," Llao claims. "It was just, get to the Amazon and follow the director's orders. I think this is a character that exists in the jungle and was born there." As more are taken apart, one person shoves some pot inside a deceased friend.

It works, and it doesn't. Eating her, and it, makes them sick, allowing some to escape. But when the cannibals have the munchies, well, it's not a pretty sight to those still around. Llao called it one of his favorite scenes.

Escaping the tribe and a nearby jaguar, main woman Justine (Lorenza Izzo) finds herself saved by the loggers we saw before, and their guns take Llao's man out, along with his family and friends, as their makeshift town burns. There's really no one to root for. Making it back home, she hides the story from everyone.

Filming took place in 2013, but it was another two years before viewers got to see it. During the in-between, Izzo and Roth married.

You know, maybe that was an overstatement back at the start of this profile. Perhaps Llao's impassiveness at the role was more appropriate than we established. Eating one's guests is probably unthinkable to much of the world (much?!), but for these people it wasn't just common, but necessary. A part of their lives. Murder, dismemberment, cannibalism—dirty words and deeds in much of the world, but all in a day's existence for them. They're not too worked up about it, so perhaps Llao shouldn't have been either.

Still, he did find a bit of himself in the character, or perhaps a part he wished was there.

"The character and myself are not very alike," he grudgingly admits, "but on many occasions, I have wanted to kill and chop some assholes like he does. The only difference is that he does it, and I don't."

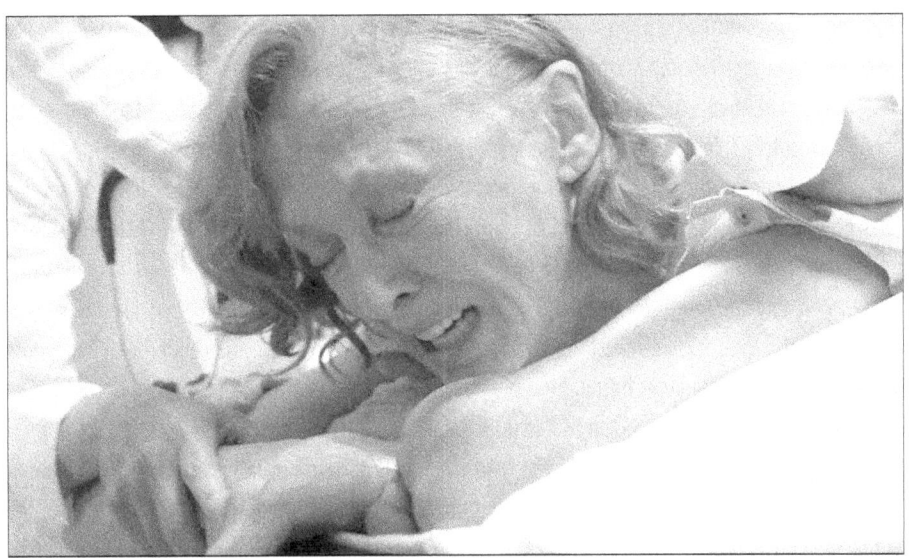

As sad as Alzheimer's can be upon its innocent victims, Deborah Logan (Jill Larson) found herself the prey of demonic possession as well in 2014's *The Taking of Deborah Logan*.

Jill Larson:

The Taking of Deborah Logan

HAVING A KINDLY old lady turn out to be the main villain in a violent, gory horror film is hardly new. Betsy Palmer (who sadly passed away just before this book went to publication) blazed the trail as Jason's mommy in the original *Friday the 13th* decades ago, and, just to name another in a lengthening list, Lorna Raver terrified holy hell out of us in 2009's *Drag Me to Hell* (and, considering how hard I hit both of those portrayals in my literary debut *Welcome to our Nightmares*—published in November 2014—no one has *any* right to be anything but a scholar on them by now!).

Still, that's not really a positive for an actress looking for such a role—the more popular a film and part are expected to be, the more competition one can anticipate at tryouts. A welcome problem for a casting crew, but a higher hurdle for an actress.

Would it be enough? Would a few standout entries on Jill Larson's acting résumé convince enough people that she was right for what could be the first headlining film role of her decades-long career?

Or did she actually want it to? The title role in *The Taking of Deborah Logan* (2014) is of the focal point of a study on (it appears!) Alzheimer's disease, slowly raking away her body and mind. Larson had been one of the millions who every year can only stand helplessly by while a loved one slips away from the horrible, incurable disease—after losing her own mom to the heartless, merciless villain not long before, playing Deborah might just too quickly yank away the line between fact and fiction for her.

As is almost always the case for performers at any stage, the questions outnumbered the answers by about a millionfold. Thinking it all over, Larson looked back to her first big steps in front of American audiences.

They'd been on the small screen; her soap debut was in 1986 on *As the World Turns*. Two years later, however, she'd all but exploded (in an ironic choice of words!) as *One Life to Live*'s Ursula Blackwell, whose love for bombs would have been a lifelong marriage if the destructive tools were human.

"I was only supposed to (play Ursula) for eight days," Larson remembers. "They liked what was happening with the character, and the writers started writing more for her, and I ended up having more storylines, with the character becoming more dastardly and villainous with each day." Ursula would stay there for about all of 1988, bombs and guns galore, before leaving.

"It was great fun, but my mother was glad when that part was over because she worried about fans," Larson says. "I did have people yelling out of cars at me and things like that. That's part of the quote-unquote 'fun' of it, but all you have to have is one or two people who actually are a little unbalanced. That's when it can become problematic."

Then yet another daily show had come calling: *All My Children*. From 1981 to 1983, Dorothy Lyman had been Opal, around long enough to forcefully shove her daughter Jenny into the modeling world. In the midst of a city council run, Opal had run into James Mitchell's legendary Palmer Courtland, who'd set the standard for male soap opera acting over his decades on *Children*.

Then Opal's boyfriend flipped for Jenny, sending him out of her life and her into the arms of another and out of Pine Valley and off the show. Years later, Larson got a shot at reviving her.

"The people at ABC saw my work on *One Life to Live*, and it seemed like I would be a good Opal," Larson recalls. "It was very hard for me, because I had never seen Dorothy on the show, I'm embarrassed and ashamed to say. I asked the producers if I could see some tapes. They told me no, to bring what I wanted to the character."

It was enough: for over two decades, she'd turn Opal into a show fixture. She and Palmer married and had a son before things fell apart for the two. She became close with Erica Kane, the role that Susan Lucci rolled to the Emmys eighteen times before finally winning in 1999—Larson herself was nominated for a pair of Emmys along the way. Then Palmer passed away in April 2010 (the actor himself had died the January before), and Opal carried on until the show ended in September 2013.

"A lot of it has to do with the writing and what they write for you," Larson says of Opal's success, "and sometimes you get lucky, and sometimes you have long periods of not doing much."

OK, let's get to the movies. In 2009, Larson had unsuccessfully tried out for a commercial that none other than legendary film man Martin Scorsese was putting together.

"It was some kind of a period thing that took place in the '40s," she remembers. "I was playing a librarian or a museum curator, wearing a little sweater set with some pearls. I never thought another thing of it."

A few months later, her agent called with a film offer. "He said it was a very small part and I wouldn't even speak, but it was with Scorsese and di Caprio," she says. "I was speechless. Why would I *not* want to do it?"

She checked over the script that would soon become 2010's *Shutter Island*.

"The first time I read it, I was so engaged, I got all the way to the end and said, 'Where's my part?'" Larson says. "Then it dawned on me as I read it again: I was a weathered, toothless, balding old hag, a scar on her neck that looks like dried licorice. When I read the role, I thought, why me? Do I look like an old toothless hag?"

Up in Massachusetts, Larson spent some time in the makeup chair, her hair covered and teeth enlarged. Then she strolled around the abandoned institution that would become the filming grounds.

"I had lots of time to soak up the environment of a character like that," she says. Indeed, her character wouldn't have a line, or even a name. Still, it was the first impression that many received of *Island*.

Di Caprio's Teddy Daniels and his fellow U.S. Marshal cautiously stride across the grounds of the title island's Ashecliffe Hospital, there to search out a missing patient. As they walk up to the doors, an old woman gazes at them with wide eyes that clearly aren't seeing much. But they, and we, can't look away, even in slow motion. She was Larson.

"I realized that that shot was very important," she recalls. "It tells the audience the world they're entering into. It was an important shot, even if it wasn't a major role. We did it many, many times." It would end up kicking off several trailers for the film.

"When you're in something, you don't have the experience of seeing it for the dramatic impact that it is intended because you've already been on the inside," Larson says. "It was positioned and used in such a way that it had far more tension than I ever imagined."

Finally, *The Taking* arrived. It's the tale of a Virginia matron who reluctantly agrees to be the subject of a new documentary about Alzheimer's. Larson didn't know if she could or should become her.

"When I read it, I thought it was way too creepy," she says, "and there was a chance that it would end up looking really corny and stupid."

She asked for some time to consider. That's when her feelings as a person and a performer started to run together.

"I started thinking about it being an Alzheimer's piece," Larson says. "My mother died of Alzheimer's, and it started to have more meaning for me as an actress." Adam Robitel, behind both the script and camera, had based the storyline on seeing his own grandma slip away.

"I felt that if that was the genesis of the role," Larson says, "it was going to be treated with kindness and I had a little more trust about putting myself in the hands of a stranger. That was my first time playing a lead in a film. Where I am in my career, at my age, in my gender, there was a good chance that this would be my only chance. Most roles that I do are one- or two-scene roles that I pop in and have a specific purpose. This was a glowing opportunity for me as an actress and as a person, because it was scary." Scary not just because Alzheimer's can become its own terrifying and mysterious world, but because it turned out not to be the only thing afflicting Logan.

But we don't know that just yet, as Logan's mood swings and steps back to her own past are ascribed to her "condition."

"I spent a lot of time thinking about my mother and other people I had met that had Alzheimer's," Larson says, "people who were far more advanced than my mother, who, thank God, passed before her Alzheimer's got so bad that she couldn't speak or recognize anyone. I looked at videos of people who had advanced Alzheimer's." She checked over the 2007 novel *Still Alice*, neuroscientist Lisa Genova's masterwork about a young Harvard professor who suddenly finds herself afflicted with the disease (Julianne Moore won an Oscar for bringing the role to the screen in 2014).

"The early stuff, when I was just beginning to lose my memory were very hard for me to do," Larson says, "because I was playing my mother and reenacting what I saw her go through. What person over fifty doesn't just live in some form of terror about ending up alone with Alzheimer's, and what a terrible final chapter that would be? It was something that rings very, very true to me. It was painful. It was just hard. I would come home every night and cry."

But, again, Logan's condition isn't only Alzheimer's. There's another problem, one not even medical. She's being possessed not only by one of the real world's worst nightmares, but by something else: the spirit of a local doctor who vanished after killing four young girls.

As it turns out, his disappearance was Logan's doing, but now he's tormenting her from within, and looking to continue his murderous ways, using her to kidnap one more victim. It's a young girl with cancer, and Logan takes the victim to the doctor's old hangout, surrounding by the slithering kind as she tries to steal the girl's life.

"I could manage the snakes and digging around mud with it being ten degrees out," Larson says, "but the fake blood in my mouth really creeped me out! I was bringing my mother back; I miss her and love her, and I was acting my greatest fears. Living alone for years, not being able to speak, not knowing anyone, it's a hideous demise."

Like Palmer, Raver, and others before her, Larson realized the world of horror at the age when most performers are thinking about pressing down on the career brake pedal.

"Some of it was like when I was just starting out in daytime," she says, "and there was this whole other world opening up to me. I never knew that there was this massive audience of really passionate fans for this genre of horror, that there is a formula. It's also fun because that is beyond the realm of my own personality. That's the fun of acting: that you get to live out something you know you would never do in real life."

Joan McCall:

Devil Times Five/Grizzly

WHO WAS SHE? Whom did she hope to become? What did she like to read? For whom would she be likely to cast a vote? Did other enjoy her company, or were they just being nice to her face?

Yes, by the time she steps into a role, Joan McCall is several times more familiar with her character than those on the outside audience will ever be, long after the credits roll. If it means comedy, if it means drama, or if it means getting ready to square off with demonic kids or psychotic bears.

"No observer will know the lengths to which I have gone to develop my character," McCall explains, "but they will see that I am an honest-to-goodness alive person and I have done my best to live the part and serve the story. That satisfied me . . . and still does." It's a technique she began during her early days of stage acting, and kept up in the transition to the screen. As it has for so many others, the trip started in horror.

"I don't think any serious actor wants to play roles in horror movies," she says, "unless it's a big budget, made from a bestselling book, and beginning actors don't usually get those roles. An actor would love to have more control over the parts they play, but when he or she is starting out, she takes what she can get."

She was certainly "gotten" for all the worst reasons in her screen debut of 1974's *Devil Times Five*. Her Julie was hanging out with her pals (including Sorrell Booke, who *Dukes of Hazzard* fans will forever remember as the scheming Boss Hogge) at a winter vacation home when a group of kids wander up, claiming they're the only survivors of a car crash. But this is horror, so things will of course end up very far from what they seemed.

McCall started quizzing her way through the person she'd portray. Was Julie the popular sort around the neighborhood? What kind of work did she do? Any phobias or traumas in her past?

"I thought about and created her relationships with her father and her sexy, jealous stepmother and I wrote about them," McCall recalls. "I was a serious actor, had been on Broadway . . . so I did my preparation. But making films is exhausting and boring. I sat around all day waiting for my scenes to be filmed. Most of the time, my scenes would be shot at the end of the day. My hair and make-up would be done first thing in the morning, then I'd have to sit around all day, getting stale and then I would almost not care any more. Acting in films was nothing like acting on Broadway! Broadway was a lot more fun . . . especially for the actor."

As her friends start to violently die, Julie and the rest can't bring themselves to believe that a few youths could or would do this sort of thing. But just as they finally figure it out, or at least, accept it, it's too late for Julie, one of the final victims.

"The scene where I was killed was saved until almost the last day to film," she says. "I guess they worried about my getting injured, and as a matter of fact, my neck did get cut with the retractable knife. I was a nervous wreck preparing for that scene, because I knew the special effects people were concerned about the 'knife.' It rubbed off."

Two years later, she'd be in the midst of a war with nature, more realistic than the Devil and probably even more dangerous. Less than a year before, millions had been traumatized by the tale of the greatest great white shark in film history and the havoc it wreaked on the poor unsuspecting island of Amity. *Grizzly*'s premises might have even been scarier: a shark can only get us if we wander into its watery lair, but this title character can find us anywhere it's strong enough to invade.

Like the shark's flick, *Grizzly* (1976) opened with the violent death of a pretty girl at the hands and claws of something we couldn't see. Then another gal was slaughtered the same way. Looks like the producers wanted to let everyone know just who'd taken the crown of king of the destructive animals.

Looking for the ladies, the ranger Mike Kelly (Christopher George) and his lady companion Allison happen on the unlucky find. McCall had led Allison through a new backstory interrogation.

Would she sacrifice herself for the right reasons? What might married life hold for her? How had gone her upbringing? These questions and so many more helped her gear up for the supporting role to Teddy, the Washington native and title character (a year later came the birth of fellow Kodiak bear Bart, who'd stride before the cameras in 1994's *Legends of the Fall*, 1997's *The Edge*, and, ironically enough . . . 1988's *The Bear*!).

"I thought about who Allison was, how she felt about living out in the wild, how living there had inspired her to photograph nature, etc. and how that had developed into a career," McCall says. "Falling in love with a ranger wasn't part of the plan, but she did anyway."

Like his finned colleague, *Grizzly*'s furry friend found himself blown to bits. Alone and face-to-face with the critter, Kelly blasts it away with a bazooka. It would be one of McCall's final hurrahs before a camera.

"I hoped (*Grizzly*) would lead to better roles" she recalls, "but I became discouraged over the lack of well-written roles for a beginning actress and I began to write the roles I would have liked to play. I wrote a screenplay—that led to my becoming a professional writer and that's how I make my living currently." She's churned out over two hundred filmed works of words, including tons of soap operas and *Heart Like a Wheel*, the biopic of lady auto racing pioneer Shirley Muldowney. McCall also helped bang out *Grizzly II*, which would have had Teddy's counterpart crashing a concert. With Charlie Sheen, George Clooney, and Louise Fletcher there to act, the 1985 film fell apart partly through filming because of financial problems.

Still, even when she's in the transcription aspect of acting, McCall still approaches her characters the same way. Once again, those who see her writings being performed will never know as much of whom they're watching as their literary creator.

"When I'm writing, I develop my literary characters asking the same questions," she says. "When I've answered these questions, I know my character in and out and I allow them to become flesh and blood."

Young Robin (Jennifer McKinney) is nearly overtaken by the evil entities of 1980's *Death Ship*.

Jennifer McKinney:

Death Ship

THIS PIECE JUST became very, very tough to write.

A few days ago, Jennifer McKinney and I had a wonderful conversation about her work in the underrated *Death Ship* of 1980. She played a young girl, forced, along with her family and some others into a battle in the midst of the sea, one of the world's most ominous places, one that's provided horror crews and fans with all kinds of options to tell their stories for decades, and will never stop doing so.

Then, as I sat down to pay transcribed tribute to the film on Leap Year Day of 2016, CNN dropped some horrible news before my eyes.

George Kennedy, who'd stepped away from the action and drama that had won him an Oscar for *Cool Hand Luke* in 1967, and would soon be hysterical as the straight man to Leslie Nielsen's Frank Drebin in the *Naked Gun* tomes, had gone supernaturally evil to pilot the title object in *Death Ship*. Possessed by the spirits of sin that had committed acts far worse than anything we'll ever see in horror, Kennedy's Captain Ashland had gone from curmudgeonly to murderous, trying to help the ship live down to its name.

Now Kennedy was gone forever. And unlike in *Ship*, this passing would break our hearts.

"He was such a nice man," McKinney recalls. "He was just so kind and helpful." That's probably a pretty common opinion of Kennedy as a whole; one doesn't sustain an acting career for decades without such an attitude. As a character, however, Ashland would be *far* from that mindset, but one step at a time here.

Time and again and probably some more later, McKinney's mom opened her little girl's school reports to read the same message. Intellect was there in abundance, but not Jennifer's top priority.

"The report cards were always saying 'Jennifer could do better if she would just listen and just pay attention, instead of performing for everyone!'" the now-adult remembers. Ironically, one of those very teachers happened to be pals with a casting agency employee in everyone's Toronto homeland.

"She asked my mother and me if I would be interested in doing it," McKinney remembers. "I loved it. I was ready to perform for anybody." She did a few commercials and some other work.

Then it suddenly came time to board the ship. Doing so would almost automatically kickstart McKinney's preparation methods.

None of that soundstage stuff here—she was herded down to Alabama to act out the tale on an actual old warship, just off the coast of Dauphin Island.

"Every morning, they would take us by speedboat out to the old ship in the Gulf," she says. "I remember every morning, being on the speedboat, with dolphins jumping everywhere. It was a wonderful experience." Her young Robin would have the luxury of being able to torment a younger sibling, as McKinney did herself (though it can be a downfall at times, as the firstborns in a family tend to get blamed for everything).

So a certain degree of preparation was handed to her. But no life experience could get her all the way ready for what happened to Robin, the rest of the Marshall family, and so many others aboard the not-so-tiny ship.

As Robin and little bro Ben embark on an impromptu expedition (McKinney called exploring the old ship one of her other prep highlights), a full party's in swing in the ballroom, although Kennedy's Ashland, in one of his last cruises before retirement, can't get away fast enough to attend it.

That's because he and the rest of the crew notice a huge black freighter steaming right at them. There's no way to communicate, no chance to get out of the way, nothing.

The ship smashes them straight on, and everything goes black. Clearly, the tidal wave that took out *Poseidon* back in 1972 has nothing on the supernatural!

The next morning, the Marshalls, Ashland, and too few other survivors float on a lifeboat, unsure where they are or where they're going. But a freighter just happens to float by with its ladder down, and they don't notice that it's the one that put them in the waves to begin with.

An injured Ashland gets carried on board. The ladder almost collapses, but it was certainly an accident. Then, before Robin's terrified eyes, a crane cable's suddenly equipped with terrifying powers of reason, snaring a guy by the leg and lifting him ominously up and down before dropping him forever into the waves.

Spooked, Robin and Ben return to their exploratory ways. McKinney had already had some practice here. "In one room, I opened a drawer, and I didn't realize it was a prop room," she remembers. "There were gold teeth, fake teeth, dentures, all kinds of instruments to torture people. I was fascinated. I didn't know they were props. The whole experience was amazing."

Far from Robin and the others, Ashland appears comatose. Then his eyes pop open—*explode* might be a more accurate term—and he's clearly not who he was just moments ago. But he's not the only one afflicted....

Robin's mom stumbles onto a projector that turns on a bit too easily, showing a rhythmic musical as a welcome distraction. But, perhaps with her own secret sixth sense, Robin happens to glance at another woman, the lady's face suddenly twisting into all sorts of diabolical transformations.

The kids freak out and flee, and the lady staggers into Ashland's room, where he crushes the life from her disfigured throat.

"I remember having to do that over and over," McKinney says of the scene. "I'd seen them put on her makeup, so I couldn't get this terror. The fun, the happy, the bratty, the scared, you feel that every day. You can draw on it. But not a lot of people at eleven have experienced pure terror."

While Ashland goes all the way to another side, and persona in the bargain, Robin's dad Trevor (Richard Crenna) finds that this boat's horror comes from a place worse than anything we'll ever see in horror. There's Nazi memorabilia and a film of Hitler they can't turn off. Those teeth that McKinney found represented the real-life practice of Nazis stealing anything they could find from their victims.

And who are still here themselves. Ashland dumps a man into a net of bodies, then drowns him. A whining noise roars from the electronics, nearly driving Trevor over the edge—although Crenna would face much tougher opposition during three rounds as Col. Sam Trautman in the *Rambo* films!

By now, McKinney could feel the film's fearing nature creeping through her, along with the sea breeze.

"At the time, I had a concept of the fact that it was scary," she says. "I remember going over the whole script, with my mother asking me 'If this happened to you, would you be sad? Would you be happy? Would you be scared?' I knew bits and pieces about the Nazis, that they tortured people, but not about the Holocaust."

She steps into the control room, with strange sounds emanating from the radios. One appears to be singing, another speaking, but in a language far from any she's heard before. Ashland grabs her and her brother, but Trevor arrives before anything happens. The ship's lifeboats fall and float away, with no one anywhere around them. Trevor braves his way through a freezer full of those who didn't make it, to find some life jackets and rafts. By now, McKinney didn't need to act much of Robin's horror.

"Once you're on the ship, in your uniform, covered in dirt, doing the scene, that's when I really felt it," she says. "When everyone around you is in character, it just happens. Being in the moment was natural, on a big ship that's groaning and moaning, with people getting seasick, the whole experience. All of that helped me feel everything I was going through."

The kids are tossed overboard to the raft below (a shot that a reluctant McKinney had to hand over to a stunt double!), and the parents follow.

"I begged them (to let her do the stunt)," she remembers. "Production said if anything happened to me jumping from such a height, it would delay the movie. The insurance company for the movie said no, and then with the constant blood in the water from people shark fishing . . . well, they wouldn't let me!"

Back on board, Ashland's all the way gone, shooting at the ship to make it obey his will. But evil has no loyalty, and he's shoved into the steer gears and dismembered all the way to a slow death.

A chopper swoops down and saves the Marshalls . . . but this may not be a happy ending, even for them. Because we see the ship, which has already proven it can do its job unmanned, barreling in on another unsuspecting water machine.

"I have a pretty good suspension of disbelief," McKinney reveals of watching the flick. "Reliving all of that was great, and the music and everything just heightened it. I don't like seeing myself act, because you want to critique yourself. You don't want to see any flaws in yourself, saying 'I should have done this.'"

But she's glad she did, largely because of Kennedy.

"Kennedy was a very, very big man, and quite intimidating to see and be near, especially for an eleven-year-old!" she remembers. "But then he would smile, his face lighting up, and you were immediately put at ease. He never complained and was always giving of advice, mentoring in a way that didn't make it feel like he was talking down to you. As a child actor, that was reassuring, and I actually listened much more closely than if he had lectured me!"

Pam (Teri McMinn) became the first lady to experience Leatherface's torture in *Texas Chain Saw Massacre* (1974).

Teri McMinn:

Texas Chain Saw Massacre

AS DO MANY who utilize this kind of exercise practice, Teri McMinn spent her bike ride far deep in thought. With every peddle, the budding performer focused on the task before her, the next step in the acting career she'd been dreaming of pursuing since her early days in Houston.

For the role she'd looked to, there had been nothing to do, nothing to read, nothing to research, nothing to study. Nothing to learn from. All there was was imagination, and even that would be tough to come by in this situation, one of taking the near-impossible and wondering what we'd do, how we'd think if we could at all, how we'd act if we were forced into this situation, one that, way back then, didn't even happen in the scariest of movies.

Stepping before a camera, at least a taping one, would itself be new; McMinn had rung up quite a résumé from theater stages of the area, and done some modeling as well, but this was her first shot at the films. Not only that, but she'd have to outdo the hundreds of other ladies from the area who wanted the role just as badly, and had already plied their trade before the film crew.

And assuming she even did succeed, even if she managed to shine her star above all the others, well, that might be the easy part. This was horror. Independent horror. Slasher horror. Many genres the American film audiences hadn't gotten the chance to explore. So even if McMinn, and everyone else involved with *Texas Chain Saw Massacre* (1974), did their job past the highest of expectations, it might end up a waste of time and money. They could only hope that the film would even be finished, let alone make it to theaters.

But, hey, that's where every great horror series starts—the same year, *The Exorcist* had sent spiritual shockwaves straight through America, far beyond the cinema. And sometimes, the people with the wherewithal to undertake the task end up pushing it up through the ionosphere of the genre. McMinn and the rest of the crew were hoping for just a smidge of that exposure.

"At that time it was a scab film, a non-union film," McMinn recalls. "The independent film world wasn't popular, but looked down upon. It was just a step above doing soft-core porn. There was *The Blob* (1958), they had some Vincent Price films, but hardcore horror wasn't really a thing."

It certainly hadn't been on her mind much, even as an actress. McMinn had performed on stages across Dallas and Austin's University of Texas, then at the nearby St. Edward's University. The film crew had seen a shot of her in a newspaper, and decided to take one with McMinn. They'd found lead Marilyn Burns at the University of Texas, had picked Gunnar Hansen to be the lead villain, and now were searching for the flick's main supporting gal.

McMinn hadn't exactly been wowed.

"I wasn't very attracted to it," she admits. "I had trained for years in theater, and I was looking to do something more legitimate than hanging on a meathook. It was just an old thing to be asked to do."

But she'd changed her mind, and been good enough to be asked back for a second tryout. Clad in the very short shorts she'd be asked to wear, McMinn finally arrived and parked her bike at the apartment for her audition, just as good a place as any for an inexperienced group with little green to fold.

She read for the part. She got the part. Then McMinn found she'd have to act out the whole thing a few days from then.

She and Bill Vail, playing Pam's boyfriend Kirk, sat down to sort their characters out.

"We did all of our preparation," McMinn remembers. "We had to sit around a lot. I'd been training in stage for years, forming characters, and you get used to doing it."

Burns' Sally Hardesty leads a group of friends deep into the heart of Texas to visit Sally's grandpa's grave, and Kirk and Pam leave everyone behind to go for a swim. The hole's dry (McMinn refused to film a nude swim scene), but they see a house nearby, and Kirk boldly strolls up, hoping that someone there might have some fuel.

We know where this is going. But for too many times during filming, the cast and crew didn't, not always.

"We started shooting," McMinn recalls, "and within ten days, we ran out of money. They gave us contracts that promised deferred money that we'd get on the profit." For about a month, the cast wasn't paid. But even working on faith, they still had a job to do.

Kirk steps into the house, and, in one of the most famous moments in film history, Hansen's Leatherface happens upon him, helped by a slow, ominous full-body shot, and bashes his head in with a hammer, quickly removing the body from the scene. He's probably been here before.

Now came some of the toughest parts of McMinn's duties.

Pam goes looking for her man, but she finds a something different. Not just worse—not even thinkable.

A house dirtied with caged, wild animals. Various pieces of things that used to make up a skeleton. A place that, up until that point, didn't even exist much in horror movies.

Then the "human" that's the living personification of it all, who grabs her and drags her into another room, where the body that once held Kirk's spirit is laying.

"The shots of me fighting Leatherface took all day," she says. "I lost my voice from screaming. You fight a 350-pound man for your life, to make it look real, that's tough." It took about a full day to film that scene. The ones we most remember about Pam, well, they were actually a bit faster.

Leatherface yanks his lovely prey across the room, where a hook built to hold hundreds of slabbed pounds of meat ominously hang. Pam will be one of its easier tasks, but unlike the cows that used to be what it usually holds, she's alive. And even after the Leatherman plants her on one, the gutsy gal stays that way.

Director Tobe Hooper "asked me what I thought," McMinn recalls. "I thought that if she hadn't been hung in a strategic part, like in her spine, she would probably try to get off the hook." That just took about three hours.

We think Pam's dead. We sort of hope so; at this point, it would be a merciful passing. But she's not so lucky. Sally's other friend soon goes looking, and he happens upon her, still alive!

In a freezer. Leatherface takes him out, then shoves Pam back in. This time, she won't escape. As would become the norm for these sorts of films—like *Halloween*, *Friday the 13th*, *Nightmare on Elm Street*, and so many others that hadn't even been thought of—it boils down to Sally as a lone female, somehow managing to outwit the family and escape.

Of course, there's always the possibility that Pam makes it through. We don't actually see her dead, and this is, after all, horror, where people's powers of self-healing tend to reach far past realism. Still, the sequels went in all new directions, with Leatherface and his family becoming the centers, rather than those who came to see them. After all, who in hell would go back there after getting chased away and nearly killed?!

"For every angle you see, we did four hundred takes," McMinn estimates (perhaps Hooper was channeling the techniques of legendary film perfectionist Stanley Kubrick!). "At that time, it wasn't digital, so you weren't sure what you had all on film. You just believe what's going on, and you know if somebody's trying to grab you and take you, you just have to believe it. You suspend your reality and you just do it."

It's difficult to swallow in hindsight, but *Massacre* nearly scored a PG rating, perhaps because, like *Psycho* (1960), the majority of the violence isn't that graphic (*Jaws*, which came out shortly thereafter and is arguably just as rough, was rated PG). Kirk's death is done in a faraway shot, and Pam's hanging is seen from behind Leatherface—we don't actually see the hook piercing her. Other deaths, and Sally's torture at the hands of the whole family, ended up pushing it to the R-rating levels.

"At the time we did it, (blood) wasn't allowed," McMinn says. "The first one is known because you don't see any violence, any real blood." Kirk's death was a bit more graphic in the 2003 remake, with Eric Balfour now in the role named Kemper. Pam's slaughter wasn't in that flick, but tribute came in 2013's *Texas Chainsaw 3D*, in which Tania Raymonde's Nikki ends up jammed into a freezer with a bullet in her head.

Those films, and the other sequels and remakes, represent just a small section of the impact *Texas Chain Saw Massacre* ended up making, and not just because of its smashing of the box office at the time. The slasher genre it helped ignite became its own subculture of horror, and the films and filmmakers it influenced would fill up a full chapter of books like this one. It's been called a landmark, not just for horror films or independent ones, but American movies in general. Hansen's creation, and those who followed him in doing so, have landed Leatherface right alongside Freddy, Jason, and Michael Myers as household visages for frightened fans.

Still, not everyone got a chance to step into Leatherface's world. Many fans across Europe didn't see the film until at least the 1980s. It wasn't allowed across the United Kingdom for a quarter century. Germany didn't release it until 2011. Even McMinn wasn't thrilled with the product, at least with her part in it, right away. More print modeling, theater, and the occasional commercial peppered her résumé for the next few decades.

Then, about thirty years after becoming Pam, she stepped into the convention world, meeting those she'd helped to terrify. And, as has been with so many other performers of the genre, she got a new sense of *Massacre*'s true impact, and of her own.

"That's when I really understood how much the character was loved, how many people enjoyed her," McMinn remembers. "Now I get it! I like my death scenes, from walking out of the house to being hung on the meathook to popping out of the freezer!"

Note: On November 7, 2015, horror legend Gunnar Hansen passed away. The *Massacre* series, and the horror film world itself, would not be near the heights it is if not for him.

Rachel Miner

It's all out there.

They're all out there.

Out there to talk to. Out there to spend time with. Out there to learn from.

Perhaps my writing colleague (not the *slightest* bit of self-serving hyperbole there!) Shakespeare had it right when he mentioned that all the world truly is a stage and its inhabitants the players. The storylines we can learn from people who've been to places and seen things we haven't, who know what we don't. It's not a question of education or even intellect, simply experience. Experience at the whole living life practice. Looking back into our pasts and telling stories strong enough to rivet our listeners as effectively as any stage or screen performers.

It's people like that that have started Rachel Miner on one acting path after another. They are

From victim to villainess, from realistic to supernatural and all the way back, Rachel Miner keeps finding new marks to make in horror.

the ones that have helped her get ready for so many of the characters she's become before the audience's eyes. Not celebrities, not fellow performing colleagues—just the people that we far too often walk by every day, not enough of us realizing that they may have something special to teach us.

This, of course, isn't to downplay the value of acting coaches, fellow performers, instructors, and all others with a strong background in performing itself; Miner has benefitted from them as much as any in the field. It's just that, once in a while, she's found a bit of unusual guidance, some inspiration in the unlikeliest of spots.

"A lot of the preparation for any of these roles happens in my down time," Miner explains. "In life, I'm always trying to better understand human beings and thinking conditionally. I read a lot. I love to talk to people, love to talk to strangers, ask questions and find out about things in their world and what their life is like.

"Empathy is a huge factor. Once you have that storage, those thoughts and knowledge, when it comes to playing a character, I don't even register what I'm drawing on specifically. It's not a very thought-out, analytical process, but from all that life experience, I try to be a real human being going through those scenes." Even in the most unrealistic of situations, as we will learn. . . .

Miner's entry into the acting business was hardly a surprise; it's a family tradition. Her grandfather Worthington was one of the first noted names in the early days of television production and directing, mainly behind the camera, and her grandmother was actress Frances Fuller. Her dad Peter won two Emmys during his directing of decades of *One Life to Live* episodes, and he and Miner's mom Diane are longtime acting instructors.

Still, that doesn't mean she was pushed, or even encouraged in the direction.

"Becoming an actress," Miner recalls, "was more realistic, just like any job you see your family doing, but if anything, my parents we wary of me going into the acting industry, because they knew how difficult it would be. They gave me to the lowdown about how much work it would be, but once I chose it, I was ready for the disappointment, or the potential disappointment. It encouraged me to go to an acting teacher first and do the work and see how that worked out. I loved it."

Things didn't take long to start paying out for the third-generation star; her first audition won her a title role in 1990's *Alice*, with a fellow named Woody Allen behind the camera. Note: I said "a" title role, rather than "the" role, for a reason—while Mia Farrow carried the majority of being *Alice*, Miner got things started, playing the pre-teen version of a lady who ends up using invisibility to find out her effects on others (Kristy Graves played the young adult version of the person).

Miner checked out some of Allen and Farrow's earlier work. Still, the techniques we discussed earlier, the ones of simply going out and experiencing, started to come into play for her.

"A lot is about relaxing and trying to be another person," Miner says. "I focused on who Alice was and tried to capture that essence. Most of it was trying to not be nervous and be comfortable. Acting is about divorcing yourself from any sense of ego and becoming other people, and this goes along with that. I've always been curious of people, and I liked meeting people from all walks of life and trying to emphasize with their thoughts. Acting was a way to nourish the imagination as well."

Sharing character credit would become a tradition in Miner's career; just after finishing up as the youngest Alice, she stepped to the small screen. Anna Tendler had begun the role of young Michelle Bauer on *Guiding Light*, but the character, too small to play much of a role in soap opera storylines (Kimberly McCullough's near-lifelong run as Robin Scorpio on *General Hospital* was the extreme exception to that rule), had been off the series since 1987.

Until, of course, Miner brought her back in early 1989. In keeping with common soap opera tradition, the character had aged about twice as fast as in real time.

"I wanted to be in a soap opera because my father had directed them," says Miner, whose dad also handled a few episodes of *All My Children*. "It was just a matter of luck of the draw that that was what I happened to get. I like to challenge the myth that acting careers are by decision only, rather than luck and going out and doing the work of auditioning."

She'd spend the next six years growing up with Michelle's father and stepfather, making friends across Springfield, the town in the Midwestern nowhere lands (looks like *The Simpsons* weren't the only TV family to hang out there!). Eventually, though, Miner had to make a tough choice.

"Doing the same show for a while, the cast becomes like your family," she says. "I wanted to continue that. There was a decision when I hit high school when I had to decide if I was going to keep acting or go to a more rigorous school. I decided to stay: motivated a lot by the people I was around every day, I wanted to continue that and live a life I knew."

Sadly, Michelle's dad had an affair, and her stepmom died in a car wreck. The family would eventually mend fences, but the father's new love was killed in 1995, the same year Miner snared an Emmy nomination for her role.

In the summer of 1995, Michelle went to Europe. When she returned that winter, she'd transformed from Miner into Rebecca Budig.

Miner's first big step into horror was painfully realistic, simply because it was a true story, hardly even a dramatization. In 1993, Bobby Kent was brutally murdered by seven of his friends, including one he'd (allegedly) impregnated, who claimed he'd been physically and sexually abusive to them, some for years.

In the cinematic version of *Bully* (2001), Nick Stahl, far from his heroic turn in *Terminator 3* of two years later, was Bobby, with Miner as Lisa Connelly, terrified she's pregnant from Bobby's rape, one of several he's committed.

"I was scared of it on some level, because (Lisa) was such a dark character," Miner remembers. "I knew I was getting into sex and nudity and all these areas I was nervous about, and also nervous about portraying that character who was troubled. I didn't want her to come off as something admirable or cool. I had a lot of trepidation about it. But it was a very fulfilling experience, and what I loved the most about acting, which is trying to understand people that you might not understand off the bat. When we enter the mindset that allows that, we find acceptance and understanding of them."

Down in Florida a few weeks before filming kicked off, Miner acquainted herself with the area, both human and geographical. She read up on the case time and time again.

"One of the most helpful things," she says, "was getting to know the place where (the actual event) happened and feeling the temperature and how it affected me physically, and the reactions of the community to where it had been. With acting, there is an infinite number of calculations that are done, but I think they're done on a subliminal level. You're comparing yourself to people who've seen, circumstances you've been in, feelings you felt, and all these things."

After Bobby abuses her friends, including another rape, Lisa comes up with the idea to send him to a permanent end. Eventually, it happens in full-blown violence, but, typical teenagers, no one can keep their mouths shut, and eventually everyone's arrested, with Lisa getting life in jail (the real Connelly, who didn't actually take part in the killing, was released in early 2004, having given birth to a daughter in prison).

Miner found herself on the other end of painful aggression in *Penny Dreadful* (2006), playing the title role of a traumatized young woman, kidnapped by a hitchhiker and tortured for hours before escaping.

"For me, accessing fear and pain is not that difficult to do," Miner says. "It's something that's so prevalent throughout society, so universal, the way people go, that I've seen it so often and experiences I've felt so often that you draw on that, and when we get the specifics, it's a natural human response that is pretty easy to access. It's not an intellectual leap to imagine if someone were in a scenario, doing those things to you, that you would react that way."

After another round of real-life horror the same year with *The Black Dahlia*, Miner unleashed an evil entity in 2007's *The Cult*, and found herself in the midst of *Tooth and Nail*'s post-apocalyptic brawl between cannibals and "normal" survivors.

Acting is "a very quick process," she says, "because so much is relying on the work you do ahead of time: not for a specific project, but what you've done in your life. So much of acting is about being comfortable and staying in that character's head space despite crazy circumstances, especially in a horror shoot. There are so many factors that could distract you in terms of the shooting scenario. Often you'll be up for twelve hours, and at the last minute, you've got three seconds to get a shot in, and it's very technical. A lot of it is about imagination, being able to sustain in that moment, a reality that is nothing like the reality around you."

Right around that time, she was right back on television, the third performer to be taken over by the Meg Masters demon in *Supernatural* (2009). Daughter of demon king Azazel, who killed the mother of the protagonist Winchester brothers Sam and Dean, Meg continued her daddy's work, with Nicki Aycox playing her in the series' first season.

Meg got sent to hell at the end of season one, but escaped in a stronger form and snuck inside Sam (Jared Padalecki) in the second go-round. Still, the good guys managed to force her out of him, and it looked like Meg was through.

Until Season Five, however, which began with the aptly titled episode "Sympathy for the Devil." Meg (now Miner) and Lucifer called the grim reaper to play, and Meg used a pack of satanic dogs to take out some of the Winchesters' friends. But evil can't co-exist in harmony, and demon Crowley took over when Lucifer got sent home, sending Meg away in fear he'd take her out too.

"That was a great experience," she remembers. "I really liked what they did with the humor and intelligence. I had no idea that they were going to keep bringing me back. Meg had been alive for hundreds and hundreds of years: imagine what it is to do that. It was so much of what I'd drawn on the spiritual level, reality that you don't come across in your daily business."

Over the next two seasons, Meg turned to the Winchesters for help. In Season Eight, she embodied the episode titled "Goodbye Stranger" by giving her life to help them get away from Crowley.

Before her time as Meg came to an end, however, Miner learned she'd be facing a new battle off the screen, one that she wouldn't be able to leave behind as easily as a cinematic enemy. But she kept it quiet for a few years, and so, for the time being, we will as well.

Just as she had as Meg's vehicle, Miner became the bad girl in 2012's *In Your Skin*. As the Hughes family (led by Selma Blair's Mary) moves in, mourning the death of their daughter, Miner is Jane Sakowski, a member of the neighbors. Soon enough, the newbies realize that there's something off about this group. The Sakowski son terrorizes their own child. The Hughes' dog is killed. Mary's brother-in-law is shot dead.

Eventually, things wind up in a hostage situation, and the Sakowskis simply admit that they just wanted the Hughes' Utopian lifestyle, and that Jane and (we find out!) her little brother were kidnapped by a guy who felt he was doing right. But Mary's husband takes him out, and the Sakowskis are snared by the law.

"Even though she's, quote-unquote, a 'bad guy,'" Miner says of Jane, "so much of her is her innocence. She was taken at a very young age and very malleable. I don't think she had a lot of malicious intent, but was more about open curiosity than manipulative. She had very little responsibility for her actions. But so much about that character was about being open and in the moment. She was almost enamored with Selma Blair's character. It was mimicry; I had to watch and admire her and do my best for that."

Still, it's never been too hard for her to find a place to do so; all one needs is not so much a place to look, but the willingness to keep looking if nothing's found right away. In our past, in our surroundings, wherever.

"Probably why I end up playing these characters in a lot of unrealistic sort of situations," Miner says, "playing demons or murderers or all those other things that I've done, is that it's not a huge mental strain to match up with that type of reality. The mental games I play in life that allows that."

But her biggest fight, at least on the personal level, well, we could only wish it was a game. In 2013, Miner announced she'd been living with multiple sclerosis for the past three years.

"I didn't tell anyone for a while, because it's not in my natural inclination to draw attention to something like that," she explains. "I didn't know how to make it a light, interesting topic. More and more, it became a factor, and I don't like being dishonest, so it became something I addressed."

For those afflicted with one of the medical world's biggest puzzlers, no one in any profession has the greatest of certainties what will happen in their futures, personal or professional.

"There's no two cases that are the same, no real prognosis," Miner says. "On a daily basis, it's an exercise of living in the moment, because I don't know how things are going to go on different days. I try not to let it affect me on a mental level, but it definitely affects me on a physical level. I've had to readjust and strategize my life based on the logistics of it."

It almost seems sad to try to end this profile on an upbeat note. When things like this happen to the last people who'd ever deserve it, it makes you, sometimes painfully, remember that the people that work so hard at entertaining us, even if they're scaring the hell out of us, the ones that go so far to convince us that they're actually other people, that away from the cameras, they're just as real as any of us.

Real issues. Real concerns. And, all too often, real problems.

But that wouldn't work either. Because no one wants to have their negativities, even ones far beyond their control, to be the first thing that comes to anyone's mind when thinking of them. No one wants their most prevalent place in the minds of others to be sad and depressing.

So the next time (probably many) we see Miner on screens big and small, let's take a moment to remember that, for her and so many others with MS and situations just like it, it's still a reminder to hope that someday, someone will find a way to make these things go away.

"Whatever you're doing in acting, the number one thing to work on is just being yourself, being comfortable, being you," she remarks. "That unique view of the world that you bring to the table is what gives you value. Being a copy of someone else will lessen your impact. There are hundreds and hundreds of copies out there, but there's only one person who can bring what you bring to the table."

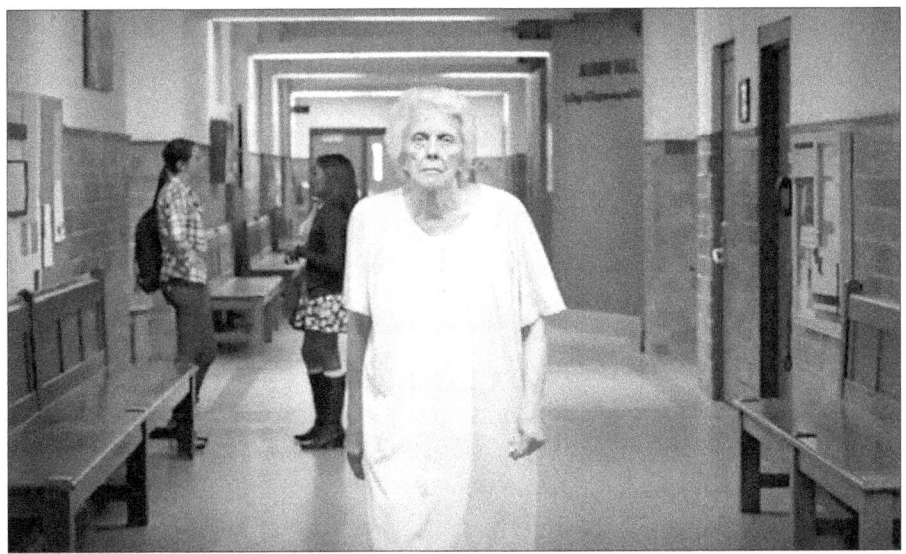

Death has taken many forms throughout legions of film, and hid inside Ingrid Mortimer and *It Follows* (2014).

Ingrid Mortimer/Bailey Spry:

It Follows

WE'VE ALL HAD that dream a time or twenty.

Not the one where you think you're awake, only everything's pitch black and you can't move. There's a dump truck on your chest, and usually eerie cackling cascading down on you.

No, not that one. The one where, no matter where you go or what you do, *something* is following you.

Maybe a zombie. Perhaps someone you, in reality, *want* to leave you alone, like an ex or something. Maybe even a giggling gremlin wearing a straw hat, riding a bike with training wheels. Maybe that last one was just me....

You fly to another country, it's there. You go into outer space, or out into the ocean, it's behind you. You lock yourself inside a closet or some other dark room, it finds a way inside.

Yes, we've all been there in our nightmares. And, since horror specializes in gleefully bringing our bad dreams to life, the story made it to screens in 2014.

Some accused *It Follows* of having a misleading title. Sure, the title pronoun certain strolled after the prey, in the same stalking techniques that Jason Voorhees used to walk down many in his exploits. But what, or who, was this *It*? Like the persona-shifting title character of one of Stephen King's greatest works, the answer would end up both clear and murky.

Annie (Bailey Spry) became "Its" first victim in 2014's *It Follows*.

Smarter than the average horror villain, the creature, the thing, the *entity* (a word that just *sounds* dark when you say it!) changed shape throughout. Hard at work in the art of following, it became a woman who looked like she'd just gone ten rounds in a UFC competition, a guy who'd apparently gotten tired of and ticked off at his eyes, and a gorgeous lady who'd forgotten her clothes (yes, the whole "WAY too good to be true" carrot is one that horror *loves* to dangle in our faces).

They followed. Wherever their targets went, however they tried to escape, something always followed. Moving slowly and steadily, not speaking, only staring, blasting an ominous glare straight at us and only us, sure to drop one's blood temperature double digits of degrees. Done right, these skills can turn just about anyone into a frightener.

Even, as we all shook while discovering, a great-grandmother.

"I had never seen a horror movie in my life," admits Ingrid Mortimer, "but it was a very interesting picture, to me. What I liked about *It Follows* was the series of the story, the people in it. I had the feeling that this was going to be more than just a horror movie with a lot of scary things in it."

In just the second role of Mortimer's career (she'd spent decades selling real estate in Michigan, where filming took place), she'd be one such . . . *thing*. One piece of weaponry, there to punish someone who'd committed an act that all too often results in horror flick victimization.

Right off the credits, we see *Its* first work. Young Annie stumbles from her home, terrified by something only she can see. She drives off to the beach, calling her dad, apologizing for something, trying to make some amends that might heal her karma.

"I always wanted to be a part of a horror film," says Bailey Spry, portrayer of Annie. "I liked that she opened up the film, and had a mystery about her. In my process as an actress, I memorize the lines emotionlessly. I just get them in my head and my body. I approach it very much in practice, I guess. I want to make sure I can vocalize it, and then I almost improvise the emotion in that way. I just try to find something I may not have had before, so that when I get in front of the camera, I just want to look natural as possible." The conversation with her dad, while tough, was far from the most natural part of her work.

"When I was on the phone, I just pretended that I was talking to my dad," she remembers. "That would have been incredibly difficult for me, because I actually have a good relationship with my dad. I had to pretend I had this weird relationship."

Annie makes it to the sand, but something has obviously put the film's title to work. We can't see it just yet, but we'll see its work soon. The next day, she's been taken apart, literally. Beaten severely, limbs broken, some all the way off. Whatever got her, it was brutal, even for a horror movie.

"I was just as shocked as everyone else in the audience when I saw myself dead," Spry recalls. "What is it that kills her? Why did she die? Why did she have that conversation with her dad? It was an interesting process to wear a prosthetic leg."

Now what? After that kind of impression, where the hell do we go? Well, we soon see Jay (Maika Monroe) chilling with her boyfriend, who keeps talking about this bombshell following him that she can't see. But, in typical man of that age (and, yes, *many* other ages!) style, he appears to be just sweet-talking her into the sack.

Still, once that's done, she finds out the whole story. The woman was there, in a certain sense. She the representative of a curse, one that follows an individual after he (in this case, the boyfriend) has sex with someone else. It pursues that person until catching and slaughtering them, at which point it goes after the last person who had it (apparently, he and Annie had recently gotten down) until he or she gives it away—only between the sheets.

Basically, the only way to get rid of it is to have sex with someone you'd wouldn't mind suffering a horrible death. If *Contracted*, the 2013 flick about a woman who has a one-night stand, then slowly deteriorates into a zombie, wasn't the greatest abstinence argument in horror film history, *It Follows* probably was!

But it's time for school. Heading to class, Jay looks up. She sees something. Someone. Someone that seems far out of place in this world.

At the University of Detroit, her own alma mater, Mortimer got ready for her next role.

"I observed, rather than ask questions," recalls the newbie performer, who did the whole job in a few hours. "I listened. I watched different scenes that other people were doing. I wanted to do it as well as I could, giving it the very best of me."

Clad in a hospital gown, her lady somberly marched toward Jay, the look on her face silently screaming that Jay's about to undergo the same treatment Annie felt. Not for any malice on her part. This is just what the bad guys do in horror movies.

"I did not feel awkward," Mortimer says. "They asked me to walk a certain way, to put my shoulder in a certain position. It wasn't like a dream, but it was like something was happening to me that I had never experienced in my life, and I realized that I liked it very much."

As the story goes on, more and more people ("people") follow Jay and her friends (like Mortimer, many entity portrayers were recruited from around the Motor City). It becomes a huge guy. It's a naked guy. She desperately has sex with a pal, but the thing becomes his own mom to take him and get right back on Jay's trail. It even morphs into her dad.

Finally, they take it out. Or appear to. Just before the credits roll towards us, something else looks like it's still rolling toward Jay. . . .

"That was a touch of what life is, what life can be, what life would be, whatever life brings to someone," Mortimer explains, "when you're feeling and working with your thoughts as human beings, and I used what I had at the moment as well as I could. I knew if it was going to be successful, I had to believe what I was doing at the moment. It had to be as real as I could make it, if I was going to make it in that world."

David (David Naughton) was turned, or bitten, into personifying the title creature of 1981's *An American Werewolf in London*.

David Naughton:

An American Werewolf in London

TO HEAR HIM tell it, horror would be the last thing you'd expect for David Naughton to be discussing.

"I always approached the character in the classic sense," Naughton recalls of his legendary terrifying turn. "Does the hero have a tragic flaw? I saw it as something like a terminal illness. He had something that he was not going to accept, in total denial about what was wrong with him."

Sounds more like a dramedy, doesn't it? The new hit on Lifetime, a story of a lost soul of a man, knowing he has little time left, only to suddenly find love in the most unexpected of places, inspiring her and all those around him before reality reaches out and tearfully steals him away from his loved ones as the music swells!

Not quite. Hot off throwing fastball pitches for Dr. Pepper and the eventual cult classic *Midnight Madness* (1980), Naughton was into something all kinds of new. But the onrushing territory was even less explored for the fellow behind the camera.

In just a few years, John Landis had turned out a pair of flicks that will live forever in cinematic comedy. *Animal House* (1978) and *The Blues Brothers* (1980) had launched him into the starry stratosphere like few other directors can even claim today. Still, film audiences aren't always so appreciative of diversity, and the director nervously brought out the screenplay he'd banged out just after hitting the legal drinking age.

One line of the *An American Werewolf in London* (1981) screen tome would elevate the film, in at least one respect, to the classic level. It would be up to Naughton and a make-upper (great term! Maybe it'll catch on!) named Rick Baker to show Landis' words. Baker had helped out with the cosmetic side of *King Kong* (1976), *Star Wars* (1977), and other flicks, but this would be, ahem, *far* from them.

"It was about the work," Naughton remembers. "It's a very real approach to a situation that is very surreal." We can only wish that adjectives stronger than surreal could be found somewhere in the English language to describe this experience.

Naughton's David and Griffin Dunne's Jack Goodman find themselves traipsing through the greatest of Britain one night when a wolf on steroids, rage and all, tries to make them lunch. Jack doesn't make it, but David does . . . kind of.

During nearly a month in the hospital, David seems to be other than himself. That's punctuated with a sledgehammer when a nurse slams in, only to gaze into his huge, strangely colored eyes and teeth the size of a saber tooth tiger's. Naughton called the scene, requiring him to wear huge contacts actually made of glass that kept him from seeing, one of the toughest to put together.

Still, he's released, and living with a lovely nurse just looking for her own wild side. But Jack's back, at least in spirit: deteriorating a high speed, he pleads with his pal to sacrifice himself, ending the wolfing curse and saving lives.

"Getting the part was very unorthodox," Naughton recalls. "Getting a part, you normally have to jump through some hoops, but on that particular film, John was THE GUY. It was his baby; he was raising the money. He and I had a conversation, very informal, that led to him calling me up and saying, 'Hey, do you want to be a werewolf?'"

David's not convinced—at least, until the full moon rises. One transformation later (which happened far outside of real time, as you'll read shortly), he's on human patrol, piling up victims faster than Jack the Ripper ever did on those very streets, and waking up naked in a zoo: physical fitness was a large part of Naughton's prep work for the role!

Now realizing the sad truth of Jack's words, David can't stop himself from switching over and stealing a few more lives. But when he's cornered by cops with guns—hopefully with silver bullets inside—the nurse's desperate declarations of love aren't enough, as he lunges forward to finish off the "suicide by cop" practice.

"He was getting information from his dead friend, information that he was not willing to accept," Naughton remembers. "The tragedy of it is that he can't overcome it. I looked at it as a guy with a tragic flaw."

You know, in hindsight, maybe David's plight wasn't too different from some tear-yanking romance after all. He was the innocent victim of infection. He *did* find love in all the unexpected places. And he did pass away in as inspirational a manner as a werewolf can, sacrificing himself to save others.

Now, of course, came the hard part. Those human-to-lycanthrope conversions would take some private time, and now that everything else was done, Naughton and Baker turned the makeup room into a secondary residence.

Landis had the whole thing down in just one script line: "He turns into a werewolf." Far more easily written than done.

"It was just me and Rick and his crew for six days, ten hours of makeup," Naughton says. "We would shoot for about an hour, and it took an hour to get it off." All this for less than two minutes of screen time in the finished project!

The next year, the film became the first-ever victor in the outstanding makeup Academy Award race. Two years later, a music man named Michael Jackson brought Landis, Baker, and others from the *Werewolf* crew to do similar work on him for the iconic *Thriller* video. Three decades later, Baker would win another Oscar for 2010's *The Wolfman*.

Werewolf's influence continues to shine. A 1997 Tom Everett Scott remake moved the scenario to Paris. In 2009, Naughton guested on an episode of *Psyche* that spoofed the film.

"It's a juicy, meaty role," Naughton exclaims, "if you'll pardon the pun. Is it horror, comedy, what's going on here? It's gone from a pretty successful film, to a cult classic, to a something everybody should have in their DVD collection of horror films. Its story really holds up."

As the whole story (i.e., the one that Stephen King wrote, nothing sanitized) of *Children of the Corn* was finally told in 2009, Daniel Newman (back row, taller) became Malachai.

Daniel Newman:
Children of the Corn

IT WAS TIME to get real.

Even in a dark tale of the evil supernatural, the truth needed telling.

The whole truth. The gory truth. The Stephen King truth.

For a quarter century, horror audiences had been seeing one take after another on one of King's first novellas. Sequels, remakes, whatever—half a dozen versions of *Children of the Corn* had been done, yanking the story all over the country and so far out of reality that it was tough at times to really keep caring much. But all of them ended about the same: just as the heartless young'uns seem to get too strong, someone shows up to save everyone, and, addled by a heroic death or so, the good guys and girls manage to escape while the baddies die, usually with explosive assistance.

But that wasn't the way King's story had ended when it was published in 1977 and put into his *Night Shift* collection the next year. By 2009, after the story'd been modified out of sense, someone decided that honesty, brutal though it would be, might be the best policy.

That chap deserves his props: it was Donald Borchers who had the guts to script-write, produce, and direct the "new" version. It started out about the same—a small town in Nebraska is drying too far out for its faithful corn to grow. Voice of reason comes in the form of young Isaac, far from his introverted Biblical namesake, who preaches the kids into bloody rebellion and genocide of local adults.

First off, unlike the 1984 original, Isaac was actually played by a kid this time around, with elementary schooler Preston Bailey running the show (first Isaac John Franklin had been in his 20s at the time of filming). As with the first film, bickering newlyweds Burt and Vicki stumble into town—except now, they're an interracial couple (David Anders and Kandyse McClure), something '80s filmmakers would never have had the brass to try.

And they're still prey, just like everyone else (above drinking age) who's been by since Isaac ran the show; the little leader and his main henchman now have some new outlanders to hunt down and out. Where Courtney Gains had been Isaac's both-hand man Malachai way back when, it was Daniel Newman's turn now.

"With my life in the Deep South, Bible Belt country, I knew people growing up that were almost straight out of *Children of the Corn*," remembers the Atlanta native, "and no judgments: I realize we're all limited to our own life experiences, and we all try to conquer our own elements and struggles the best we can to survive. We're all limited to what we've learned to believe, and we all make our efforts at survival based on those beliefs: our ability to produce, and nurture, and take care of our basic needs."

Sadly, he'd needed all of those and so much more all too recently.

Shortly into 2009, fresh off a small role next to Heath Ledger's farewell performance in *The Imaginarium of Doctor Parnassus*, Newman was in the worst place at the worst time at a Hollywood intersection.

"A drunk driver ran the red light at fifty miles per hour and drove into me, crushing most of the major bones on my right side and skull, jaw, and brain," Newman says. Doctors gave him less than a one-in-four chance to live, and even if he were to win over the odds, few thought he'd ever walk, talk, or communicate to any legitimate degree.

They didn't know who they were chatting about.

"After being brought back to life and (being in a) coma," he proudly proclaims, "and months of incredible surgeries . . . they put me back together, followed by years of physical therapy and recovery, to the point I'm almost as good as new, now with only a few tiny, unnoticeable scars. It's a miracle." A scene early in *Corn* where Burt and Vicky run over a small boy was probably tough for Newman to watch.

Hey, let's get back to his prep work. Newman had seen an only slightly less malicious form of the *Corn* kids back home.

"I was bullied a lot as a kid, and I saw that people in my small town worshiped performers," he recalls. "So as a child, I decided that's what I wanted to be. Then I discovered the visceral world of the enigma machine, metaphorically; acting and imagination and the transformation that acting afforded its participants. I got so addicted to being able to have that freedom, to live my life fully, beyond any limitations of my circumstances. Acting nurtured and fed my aspirations and gave me the awareness that anything's possible if only we create what we dream." He wouldn't just do so in acting; Newman pinballed around the worlds of rock music and modeling across New York.

"I really feel being a musician compares to acting," he says, "the same as performing any character in one language would be to perform it in another. The two just go hand in hand. It's all the same, uses the same tools: performing, discipline, focus, rehearsal, working under estranged circumstances, working with a multitude of variables and people, giving expression of yourself and your experience to others. Both have drawn from the other and built upon one another." He and the rest of the crew tried to build on one of King's first tales while not taking *too* much from the franchise's previous cinematic works.

"There's a reason Stephen King has an empire," Newman explains. "He writes of the human struggle. No matter whether you care for horror and drama, or his own brand of comedy, everyone can relate to his parables."

He took everything from his past, the study and training he'd done on both coasts, and as much as he could invent into the present to relate to Malachai.

"I literally drove my car around L.A. in the summer *blazing hot heat*," Newman sighs, "with all my windows up and no air, so I would be drenched with sweat like out in a cornfield. I took ketchup packs from a local fast food restaurant and kneaded ketchup into my long, dirty hair and mixed it with the hot sweat and let it dry as blood, as well as on my hands, arms, and some sparsely on my face. I thought to scratch dirt into my nails and applied it naturally to the rest of me. So I walked into the casting building looking like a farm boy: a very *distant* farm boy."

That worked for him, but not for Burt or Vicki. His wife already dead, Burt's lost in the cornfield, which itself is closing in on him. He got away from the kids, but not from the "He Who Walks Behind the Rows" character we've heard about in just about every franchise flick.

It's a giant creature that personifies monster to the extreme, and Burt's done.

But the movie's not. Isaac sadly lets his flock know that the Rows Man is upset, and now anyone above eighteen must give him their lives. Malachai sadly walks toward his Savior for the last time, and, as he leaves a pregnant gal behind, it's hard not to feel a bit of sympathy for him. That's how King wrote it the first time.

"Regardless of how a film turns out," Newman says, "every actor, and crew member for that matter, has a relationship during the filming process with the work that may or may not relate in any way to the way the film actually turns out in the end after all the editing and choices of the director, studio, etc. So there's only so much you can do before you just have to let go and realize you're a part of someone else's vision and your character and performance are going to be shot and edited however they feel like it. I really love being a part of a cult classic series."

Hey, before we head out, let's hear from someone special that those in the horror know might not have heard from. These books are all about paying tribute to the underrated, and someone from the first trip through the *Corn* has never gotten enough credit.

Like Franklin, Julie Maddalena was a bit older than the lady she'd portray next to him. Like Newman, her entertainment career has been filled with much more than acting. She'd been doing voice work for a while, up with improv, theater, dance, and more.

The last Child of the Corn, Julie Maddalena stalked the good guys in the 1984 original.

But her film debut would be quite different, and not just because it was horror.

"It's one of those moments as an actress when you think, 'Are you sure you want to do this?'" she remembers. "I was playing against type. I was more of a Gidget-type personality, not a midnight, knife-wielding, psychopathic, pregnant, ritual actor. It was challenging to find her and keep her."

Franklin's Isaac had already done so, her Rachel becoming one of his most faithful followers.

"She was a firm believer in what Isaac was doing," Maddalena describes of her role model. "She was a teenager, but a teenager with conviction. Just tapping into that dark place, that sad place, finding those elements within me that I could relate to, to add those layers to her, I had to set myself aside and think about what she had done already and what she was about to do and keep her whole story in the forefront of my mind the whole time, so whatever scene I was doing had the whole picture to show me." That was something else she'd have to put together alone; Rachel wasn't even in King's words. But leaving behind Maddalena's actual Leader to hear her new one speak His words would be just as difficult.

"The scene in the church was very intense, particularly because I happen to be a Christian," she says. "I had to compartmentalize myself and say, 'I don't believe this, but my character believes this.' I remember sitting up in the balcony of the church and having to pray to myself and concentrate on the kind of place that (Rachel) would be in to go through that ritual."

As Peter Horton's Burt and Linda Hamilton's Vicky, along with some young kids they saved, make their way back to their car after escaping from the original *Children* (1984), we just know that there's one more scare to feel. Again, this also wasn't found in King's book, as this sort of thing tends to work better when we can see it.

"The ending was written while we were there," Maddalena remembers. "They kept telling me, 'We have a surprise for you!'"

As Burt steps into the car, Rachel pops up, scythe blade in hand, to finish the job her friends couldn't. But Vicki manages to introduce her head to the car door, putting Rachel down long enough to leave.

"I loved the scene at the end," Maddalena says. "I'm not a physical person, so it was a blast to do that. I loved the challenge, loved the extra bit of action for (Rachel), loved the element of surprise. It was fun to be a part of that."

As Ellie, Stacey Nelkin played both a victim and tool of the Shamrock Toy Company in *Halloween III: Season of the Witch*. Looked down upon by the horror community after its 1982 release, the film has established a cult classic foothold over the past few years.

Stacey Nelkin:

Halloween III: Season of the Witch

LOYALTY AND RESPECT are undoubtedly two of the *luckiest* words in the English language.

Why? Simply because there's a positive connotation immediately attached to them every time they're used. Just inserting the words somewhere in a sentence raises its tone a few enthusiastic and perhaps sentimental points.

However, there can also be a dark side to these nouns, at least in the way they're demonstrated. While the horror community has always been there for each other, sometimes we are forced to take sides in a debate, and someone always gets hurt.

That's something that Stacey Nelkin has felt and heard ever since she and the rest of the cast and crew of *Season of the Witch* took the *Halloween* saga in a new direction (i.e., away from Michael Myers and the Strode family) back in 1982. With the horror family's tremendous loyalty has always come a resistance to change, partly why the third *Halloween*, for far too long, got a bad public rap. Respect for Michael and Laurie kept away more fans than had come to see them beforehand (to be fair, the film still made $14 million on a budget of less than $3 million, hardly a bust), forcing the series back Michael's way when part four arrived in 1988.

A common convention connoisseur, Nelkin has heard from more than a few horror fans their tales of enjoying the flick. It's just that she usually has to lean close to pick up the whispered confessions.

"People don't always want to admit they like it," Nelkin admits, "because they feel like they're betraying Michael Myers and the other films."

Though she, like so many others of the time, found herself traumatized and nearly turned all the way away from horror films upon viewing of *The Exorcist* (1973), Nelkin's acting beginnings came as a way of escaping from a very different, far too common, and tragically realistic type of terror.

"I had been acting since I was in third grade," she recalls. "I came from a very dysfunctional, broken home. Acting was out of fantasy about being loved, about having a father, that kind of thing. I had a lot of rescue fantasies."

Her first agent came to a play when she was fourteen. A few jobs followed—she almost got a role in *Jaws 2* (1978). While she was in high school, Nelkin met a fellow named Woody Allen, putting together *Annie Hall* (1977).

Her *Hall* scenes wouldn't make the final cut, but the two would date for about two years, and Nelkin nearly landed the lead in his *Manhattan* (1979). She says things ended for the pair on her nineteenth birthday, but Nelkin later worked for the director in *Bullets over Broadway* (1994).

A few years later, a friend of Nelkin's then-fiancé was helping put together what everyone hoped would be a new tradition in the *Halloween* saga. Rather than the same tale of the same killer and killings again and again, *Season of the Witch* might become an annual event, telling a new story every October 31.

The friend really wanted to be the makeup man for the film. Problem was, he had no one upon whom to ply his trade: the film's lead lady role hadn't been cast, and it wouldn't be Jamie Lee Curtis the actress or even Laurie Strode the character this time around.

Witch would be the tale of Dr. Dan Challis, a recent divorcee who can't figure out why everyone's so excited about these Silver Shamrock masks that they can't wait to wear next week for Halloween. A guy carrying one arrives at the hospital, gasping out that the masks will be the death of all, but Dan puts him under, hoping sleep will heal his psychosis.

Then another fellow arrives, rips the guy's head apart, and blows himself up in his car. Some problems you can't learn about in medical school.

The dead man's drop-dead gorgeous daughter arrives, and her name's Ellie. But who would play her? Crew members vigorously asked Nelkin.

"I got the script, and it was a really fun audition," Nelkin remembers. "The song was ringing in my ears."

With less than two weeks before filming began, everyone rushed to action. Plaster molds were made of her arms and face for a scene that will be discussed shortly. Nelkin rushed out to watch Curtis do her thing in the first two films.

Alongside Tom Atkins as Dan (and *Halloween* alumnus Dick Warlock in a small role), Nelkin's Ellie learns of her dad's toy company, one of the top local sellers of Shamrock masks. As Halloween draws near, the Shamrock Company promises a *huge* giveaway in a commercial during a showing of *Halloween* on the big night—but viewers must wear their masks to be eligible.

The pair drive off to visit the Shamrock factory, but it's in the middle of a near ghost town, though they do meet a company salesman and his family. Another woman is suddenly struck by lightning and dies, and everyone strangely ignores Dan's doctorate.

They make it to the factory and even meet the owner. Then Ellie sees her dad's car and rushes it. Suddenly, men who resemble the one that killed her dad take her away. Another attacks Dan, and a roundhouse exposes wire and oil from within the thing.

It wasn't a man at all. Just a machine made by the factory. Two more grab Dan, and he's down for the night, Ellie nowhere to be found.

Once again, Nelkin had had little time to get herself into Ellie manner. During filming, she turned to the ominous world of true crime to find it.

"I was reading *In Cold Blood* to get myself into a dark, scary, creepy mode," she explains. "As an actress, you find different ways to feel out who that character is. The book put me on the edge of my seat, and that's where Ellie was for the entire film." Over two decades later, Phillip Seymour Hoffman would win an Oscar for playing *Blood* author Truman Capote.

The factory owner shows Dan a monitor depicting the confined Ellie. Then we see the salesman and his family in another room. The commercial that's coming on later that night is tried out, and the son is dressed for the occasion.

The youngster suddenly grabs his head and collapses. A small rock had secretly blasted through his underdeveloped skull. Tons of snakes and bugs suddenly swarm from the mask and take out the parents. Everyone's dead in seconds. It's all part of the factory owner's continuance of a long Celtic sacrificial tradition.

Dan manages to escape and save Ellie. He even rigs the factory to catch all the "workers" in their own trap, causing the masks to blast them all, destroy the owner, and burn the place down. But as Dan and Ellie drive away, the commercial's still set to air.

For someone who's been through what she's seen, Ellie's remarkably composed. She doesn't cry or even speak. Then she looks deeply at Dan.

And attacks him. It's not her. It's not the Ellie we've cheered for over the rest of the film. She's the same sort of robot clone that killed Ellie's dad; the original died back at the factory.

Dan crashes the car, and one of Ellie's arms is torn off. He's forced to remove her head with the help of a tire iron.

"The most bizarre moment was after my head gets cut off and my head is a few feet from my body," Nelkin says. "They had my stand-in do the shot, and she was of a similar size and body type to me, wearing the exact same outfit."

To play Ellie's decapitated form, Nelkin stepped under a platform and poked her head through a hole, surrounded by fake dirt and grass.

"My stand-in was a few feet away, her head covered, wearing the same clothes," Nelkin says. "It was a very bizarre experience. There I was, looking at my body."

Back to town with seconds to spare, Dan begs a TV technician over the phone to stop the commercial. As two children run by to see it, the ad disappears from two stations. But a third one continues to show it, and the trigger's about to be pulled as Dan loses his shit entirely. . . .

And we'd never see the effect. Badmouthed by critics and fans alike, the *Halloween* men and women brought back the evil being in the William Shatner mask in 1988, now chasing his niece Jamie around for the appropriately monikered *The Return of Michael Myers*.

Eventually, though, more fans gave *Witch* a chance than had wanted to admit it out loud. Michael's been back time and time again since then, but it didn't take *that* long for Nelkin's outing to reach cult-classic status and get the respect it was due. More and more fans at conventions let her and the rest of the crew know it, and some of them aren't afraid to *say* so, not just mutter.

"It's amazing the kind of following it has found, thirty years later," she says. "I thought about my job in the story that we were telling. I think it's a little more intelligent than the other films; it's more sci-fi, not just a slasher-scary film."

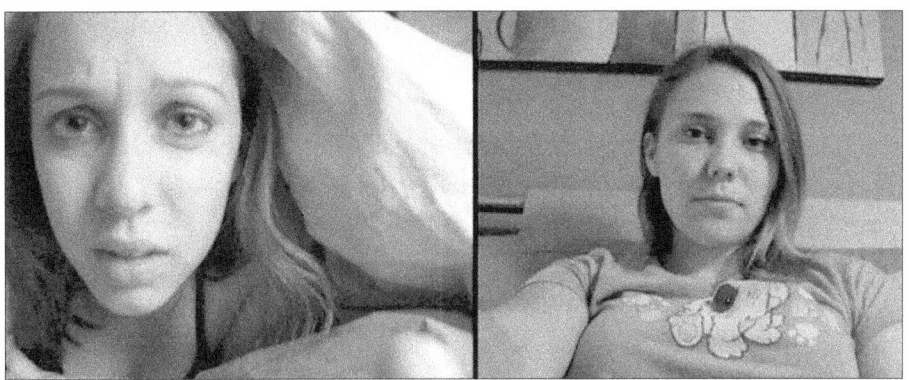

Megan (left, Rachel Quinn) and Amy (right, Amber Perkins) each became victims of an online predator in 2011's *Megan is Missing*.

Amber Perkins/Rachel Quinn:

Megan is Missing

IT CAN'T HAPPEN to us. Our children are safe. People like *him* don't live around here.

Those are the viewpoints of far too many parents and children today.

More and more frequently, we turn on the news, open the paper, and peruse the Internet to find heartbreaking stories of those who suffered the most and deserved it the least. Dark tales of youths who fell victim to sadists, dirtbags who lured them away to helplessness, only to torture and usually slaughter those too young, too weak, too afraid to fight back. Perpetrators caught far too late to save the lives they heartlessly and needlessly stole.

The horrors themselves are nothing new, but there's a new way to do it.

Usually, these people—almost always men—are caught before anything happens. Arrests for sending and possessing obscene material are much more common than those caught acting out their nightmarish fantasies.

Still, they do happen. Abductions, sex crimes . . . murder. These things occur. But always and only, we've convinced ourselves, to others.

"In cold darkness, we are reminded that evil exists, yet we dread it and are loath to acknowledge it. We excuse it and deny it, yet it denies us not. We pity its victims, yet offer no solutions for its cause."

Next time you think of that, remember a youngster named Adam Walsh, stolen from a busy Florida mall in July 1981, his severed head found three weeks later over a hundred miles away, a murder that all but forced a multitude of child-protection laws into place.

Back in March 1991, Hampton Roads was terrified and ultimately heartbroken when two young boys disappeared in Virginia Beach, their murdered bodies found a day later. The next year, local teen Shawn Novak was convicted of the murders when the jury rejected an insanity defense (he sadly didn't get the death penalty, his attorneys ludicrously arguing that a goddamned *child killer* was *too young for execution*!).

Remember Amber Hagerman, the nine-year-old Texas girl whose still-unsolved 1996 abduction and murder are the reasons that Amber Alerts let us know when a child has been taken, or Megan Kanka, whose rape and murder in 1994 New Jersey led to "Megan's Law," letting us know when perverts move in nearby.

And think of a young girl named Polly Klaas, the California pre-teen whose 1993 kidnapping and murder shoved this matter straight into the eye of a public who still doesn't take it seriously enough. Still in its public infancy, the Internet was used for the first time to spread word and appeals for help across the globe, with billions of images of Polly sent across Earth.

If it doesn't happen to us, we typically don't act on it much, if at all. So while films like 2011's *Megan is Missing* certainly scare and sadden us, if they can push us to take just a few steps to prevent this sort of thing, it might make all the differences between life and too many deaths.

The Internet is unavoidable, and it's usually a very beneficial object. But in the course of a single film, we see too close up the stories of its potential dangers. In the news every day, there's stories of those who fell victim to those using it for the most despicable of reasons.

And like so many films like *Megan is Missing* (2011), it's scariest because it's true. Not just because it's realistic; the story itself is based on fact. Writing the film, Michael Goi based it around seven real cases: everything we see and hear directly happened, and we'll find out some even sadder information about that in a while. For now, let's meet the pair that acted out the horror that more and more find in reality.

"I was a little iffy on it, because we got an excerpt on what it was about, but nothing really major," Amber Perkins remembers of her first audition. "At first, I just wanted to do something I loved, and I didn't really know what the story was about. When I found out, it was so much more than that. I needed to do it because of the story."

Elsewhere, another up-and-comer strolled into her own tryout.

"They had sent the sides for us to prepare for, and I came in ready to go," recalls Rachel Quinn. "Then I found out they'd sent the wrong sides, and it was a completely different scene."

She and the rest of the auditioners pored over their new task.

"It was pretty on the spot, which was nice for me, because I think that helps," Quinn says. "Megan the character is so naïve and unsuspecting, and it helped with the character and how I prepared for the role. At least for the audition, I was just falling into the scene."

With Quinn going for the title character, Perkins hoped to be Megan's friend Amy, the unsuspecting introvert that balances out Megan's social butterfly aura. But even before that, this was about more than a role for her.

"I have two nieces and a nephew that were taken by the dad a long, long time ago," she recalls (her family members were eventually found unharmed). "I have twenty nieces and nephews, and I could never imagine if something like that ever happened to them. This is a story that needs to be out there. You see this on TV all the time, like on *To Catch a Predator*, and you don't really get to see what really happens, with all this freedom on the Internet."

Still, there was the matter of snaring the role, and Perkins had some outside influence there as well.

"Some of my family members and friends who act gave me tips, advice, things like that," she says. "I had no idea what the story was going to be about, so I couldn't put so much thought into it." Her own tryout was about Amy chatting online with a fellow named Josh, with no idea of what he's planning and what he's done.

"To me, it would be terrifying if a guy was on the other side of the screen, saying all these kinds of things to you and you can't even see him or know what he looks like," she says. "That kind of kicked in when I had to audition with that scene. It was nerve wracking."

But it worked—over the next month, she and Quinn got rolling toward their characters. Quinn perused the script; Perkins thought Amy out.

"I absolutely could see the point of why (we) were making the movie," Quinn says. "Hearing the stories it was based off of was completely devastating. From there, I can really dive into character development."

As many do while getting ready to perform, Perkins peered back to her past.

"I feel that Amy and I had a lot in common, and I'm not sure if that's because I tried to find what was in common or if it was just there already," she says. "We both are the shyer ones, not the popular one, the one who likes to watch documentaries. I was drawn into Amy because I could understand her and what she was going through."

Early on in the film, we learn—mainly through our friends the online cameras—of Megan's proclivity for the party gal lifestyle and Amy's aversion to it.

"Drinking, smoking, talking about all that stuff, it was new," Perkins recalls. "I have a lot of nieces and nephews, and I'd watch them, take them places, see how they interacted with each other."

Quinn didn't need as much help; as Megan meets the new guy Josh on the 'Net and finds herself drawn to his looks (ominously just in photo form, not live) and knowledge of surfing, there wasn't much here too difficult. Not yet.

"It was actually really fun," she says. "That was what Megan was doing: living life, going out with her friends. It was easier than when she goes missing, easier to deal with mentally and emotionally."

Indeed, as we've known since the title, something's going to happen. Something tragic. And as Megan agrees to meet her new pal for the first time, we can see it coming, if only because she does so behind a building.

She's never seen alive again.

Amy's sure that something's gone horrific, but too many around her keep believing that Megan left on her own.

Until a newscast shows Megan behind the building, being grabbed and led away by a guy who looked nothing like the Josh she thought she saw. Amy finds Josh online and goes at him harder than she's ever hit anything before, then to the cops.

Eventually, she and her trusty camera make their way to the girls' hangouts. The diner. The park. Under a nearby bridge.

Still, nothing happens for weeks. Then, in an act of brazenness or utter stupidity, Josh posts some photos of Megan on the net—on a page for fetishists who rely on erotic humiliation to get their hormonal motors running. But its webmaster has a heart, contacting the cops.

Remember, all of this stuff happened before Megan's dramatic story was told. It occurred in reality. Getting ready for filming, Goi went over his photographic "inspirations" with Quinn.

"Michael showed me pics off some web site a couple of days before," Quinn says. "They were of a girl who'd been kidnapped and tortured. He didn't want to shock me on that. That was almost as hard as doing the scene, if not more so. It was so horrible."

The photos' first standouts are Megan's eyes, plate-sized wide and seeing wild. She's locked inside a table, her mouth tied open, her head backward. Hands, feet, knees all bondaged and bloodied.

"When I was put into the board and face thing, I didn't even have to think about anything," Quinn says. "It was so uncomfortable and felt so horrible. My knees hurt from being in this thing, and I was immediately put on edge. I was scared of the position I was in. But I didn't want to stop filming; I wanted to be in that mindset."

With even her own hope just about gone, Amy steps back under the bridge, all of it on camera. Then a hand reaches in behind her . . . and the scene ends.

"That day, we had done of bunch of other scenes," Perkins says (after waiting over a month to start the movie, the crew burned through filming in just over a week). "At the last minute, they decided to do it. My mom was next to me, driving there as I studied my lines."

We see newscasts telling the story, friends and family searching for the girls. Finally, Amy's lost camera is located—probably just as anxious to show off his work as he did with Megan's photos, Josh didn't make it tough to find. These last few minutes are going to be tough for us all.

Her lost footage starts with Amy, stripped and dirtied, chained to a wall in a cell, looking like a basement or underground (it was actually filmed in an abandoned church). Gleefully recording her pleadings for release, Josh beats and rapes her again and again.

Getting ready for the scene, "I had talked to a couple of people who were physically assaulted themselves," Perkins says. "Not in this manner, not kidnapped, but assaulted. I wanted to understand as much about this as I could about what it was like to go through this."

Yanking her over to a nearby barrel, Josh promises to use it to transport her home. Then he opens it up. It's Megan—long past the same suffering Amy's going through now.

"I'd never had prosthetics or contacts," Quinn says of the scene. "I actually couldn't see, a totally new experience. I was walking around set, not able to see. It gave me a completely new appreciation for sight."

Josh shoves Amy in the barrel and seals it for good.

"I tried my best not to think about (the scene), but it was always in my mind," Perkins says. "I didn't want to psyche myself out. It made me realize that I was in character. You try to not remember everything that's going on. You try not to think, and I felt like that was my character. Leading up to it was a lot on me mentally that day. I didn't eat a lot that day. I was really stressed out, more so mentally than physically. I didn't talk to many people that day. It's really hard to get past, when you're sitting there, and you know that this stuff is happening to children, to little kids."

Indeed: remember earlier when we discussed the realistic basis of *Megan is Missing*? Here's perhaps the saddest fact of the background: what we see Amy going through indeed happened in real life.

To an elementary school student.

Hope now gone for all, Josh methodically digs a large grave, unaffected by Amy's screams (prerecorded, Perkins says). Tipping in the barrel and filling in the hole, we see him walking away again, knowing that Amy's desperate pleas for anyone at all to help will never be heard, and that she and Megan won't be the last.

"It's really a cry for help," Quinn says of the film, "and a cry for people to be more involved with their kids, with their friends, doing things they may not know about or are dangerous. The first time I saw it, I was dreading the last twenty minutes of the film."

> "Megan is Missing demonstrates the varied and creative ways that children use communication technology, and how they make themselves vulnerable to victimization by doing so. That they are able to access the Internet, chat rooms, and social networking sites while walking down the street or sitting in a classroom should serve as a wakeup call for parents everywhere . . . Megan is Missing reminds us that evil is the face on the other side of the mirror and it mocks us and makes us turn away in fear."
> —Marc Klaas, father of Polly herself

Soon after their loss, the Klaas family established the Polly Klaas Foundation and Klaas Kids in her honor, offering help to law enforcement across America to find missing kids. The Foundation gives parents tips on what to do if a child turns up missing. It's assisted in finding thousands of missing kids. Klass Kids helps form programs for at-risk youth, and works on passing stronger laws against violent criminals.

One day not long after filming, Perkins lunched with Klaas and his family.

"Knowing the passion that he has for this made me feel like a failure almost, because he has done so much for so many and is continuing to because of what happened," she recalls. "We talked about what happened. They gave me a pin they were wearing that had Polly's picture on it, and I still have it. It really meant a lot to me, because I know she meant a lot to them."

That's how important it is to take a film like *Megan is Missing* and react to it, and not stop reacting until we've gotten something done. Taken a step to protect our kids, and ourselves, from people like Josh, who are much more common than we think.

It takes a lot of guts to turn a personal tragedy into gain for others, and we've seen it over past few decades. The Walsh family, the Klaas family, and others have taken an immeasurable loss and done what they could take help others *not* share their pain. But we have to take on some responsibility for ourselves and our younger population, and as beneficial as the Internet can be, it's given us a whole new set of potential troubles to take care of.

So what can we do? Here's just a few of many steps for social networkers young and old.

Do NOT make "friends" with people you don't know personally! Remember that others can look at someone's profile and see your "friends," then text you with something like "Hey, I know your friends Jane and John! Let's be friends!" If you don't know them in person, they're not worth knowing electronically.

NEVER give out personal information online. That's on the networks, by e-mail, whatever. Address, phone numbers, places you hang, where you're going, where you are. If people don't know you well enough to have you tell them that face-to-face, don't give it to them voluntarily. Remember that all a "friend" has to do is "Like" or comment on your saying, and everything's open to their friends as well. This information can go viral at high speed.

By the same token, never call or e-mail anyone who sends you their personal contact information. If you e-mail them, they have your address. If you call them, they probably have your number, what with cell phones and caller ID everywhere. Don't assume that they're just being social.

1. NEVER give out photos online. Once it's there, it's all but impossible to take off. It takes all of two seconds for someone to click on your photo and save it to their own computer, where they can (illegally, but what difference does that make?) do what they want with it.

2. NEVER meet anyone you only know from online. Voice synthesizers, false photos, and biographical lies are just a few tools predators use. It's never going to be worth it.

Hey, parents!

1. Keep your computer in a main room—if your kid can get alone with it behind a locked door, it's too private.

2. Do what you can to block features that not everyone should see. There are several

programs that can do this. If you'd like to visit some adult-only sites on your own, get your own damned computer.

3. If your child shows you a threatening, or even unusual message, report it right then and there. It might be a smartass kid playing a prank, or something worse, but better safe than sorry here.

4. If your child makes a new "friend," check over the acquaintance's profile online. Also, when (please don't do "if") you check into your child's profile, don't barge in: it makes you look invasive and puts them on the defensive, removing the importance of the issue at hand. Say something like, "Tomorrow, you and I are going over your profile together." Yes, they'll clean it up, but it also shows you have a sense of trust in them.

Norman Bates' (Anthony Perkins) blood-chilling smile straight at the audience gave *Psycho*'s (1960) audience just one more scene no one would ever forget.

LEGEND SPOTLIGHT:

Anthony Perkins/Janet Leigh: *Psycho*

PSYCHO IS THE story of a boy and his mother. It's the tale of how one of the cinematic world's greatest filmmakers put together a work that would inspire colleagues in all aspects of the acting world for the rest of history. It's a horror movie in the most frightening manner—one that could not only truly occur, but whose "villain" has more of a personality than any of his genre colleagues truly get, which gives us a glimpse into the dark side of the human spirit that many of us like to deny.

Sadly, it's also the tale of a young actor who was never truly able to escape from the typecasting that plagued him for the rest of his life—and, as no one knew until it was too late, a (supposed) trip back to a childhood that was an even larger burden.

Like many other horror films of all generations, *Psycho* (1960) took at least part of its inspiration from the story of Ed Gein, the Midwestern serial killer/necrophiliac/waste of human life. Alfred Hitchcock, long since established as one of the finest at his trade in Hollywood, got his own inspiration from the small novel *Psycho* by Robert Bloch, a scriptwriter for Hitchcock's television show.

In particular, there was a certain scene where an attractive young woman steps into a shower. Seconds later, she's brutally slaughtered by a knife-wielding human monster.

Hitchcock, so willing to do the film that he offered to finance it with his own money and temporarily waive his salary, picked budding star Anthony Perkins to be Norman Bates, the shower stabber with so much more than meets the eye.

Factoid: It was once common practice for theater employees to check their seats after horror flicks to comically ascertain how many viewers had inadvertently relieved themselves during the flick.

"The aim is," Hitchcock explained with tongue firmly in cheek, "there's not a dry seat in the house."

For Bates' famous victim, Hitchcock also quickly signed up Janet Leigh, who got ready for only the second film of her career by reading Bloch's book. Like Perkins, she'd forever be linked with the person she was about to become.

"I didn't need to ask why my motivation was," Leigh recalled. "It was passion. That's a pretty good motivation . . . (Hitchcock) made me so aware of the power of imagination. I always took it for granted. There had to be something that the audience has to imagine in a characterization, and they'll never forget what *they* put in."

Naturally a bit oversensitive as a person and actor, Perkins had wowed Hitchcock, and many others, with his display of mental disturbance in the recent *Fear Strikes Out* (1957). That, combined with Perkins' naturally attractive yet distant expression, and his Oscar nomination for *Friendly Persuasion* the year before, convinced the director that he was right to be Norman.

"I was a little worried about playing a homicidal transvestite," Perkins said. "It seemed to me that there was some risk to my career in taking on a part like that." How in hell does one even predict such a career effect?

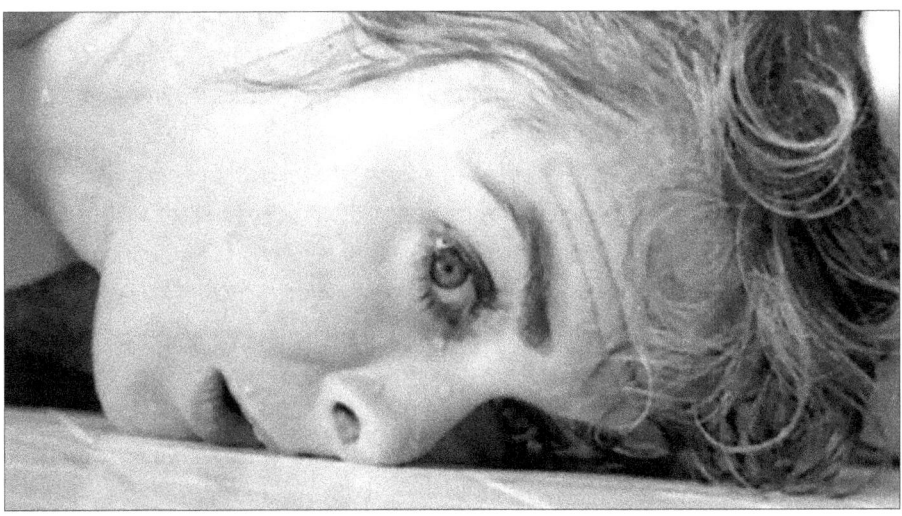

The shock of death across Janet Leigh's face was the only appropriate aftermath of *Psycho*'s (1960) legendary shower scene.

Perkins, whose desire to work with Hitchcock enticed him to sign on without even reading the script, got ready by developing some of the subtle qualities that Norman would display throughout the script, a blend of child-type innocence and psychosis that keeps the audience from ever really seeing him as the villain. He came up with the idea to have his character chew candy corn throughout *Psycho*, and worked out a big part of the script, unconfirmed as his "We all go a little mad sometimes" monologue to Leigh. He even saw a psychiatrist every morning before filming, though his exact reasons are unclear.

"(Norman) would not plot malice against anyone," Perkins says. "He has no evil or negative intentions. He has no malice of any kind."

The lifelong shyness that Perkins felt around women—to the extent that stuntwomen Margo Epper and Ann Dore were the stand-in killers in the shower scene—is evident in his work, although, again, he may have had some all-too-wrong reasons for feeling this way.

Like Perkins, Leigh—who worked for less than half of the film's forty-five-working day shoot—used subtlety at high volume in her work. Throughout the driving scenes that make up a good chunk of the movie, we see that there's much more going on inside her head than the spoken word can ever express. Hitchcock worked Leigh through the scenes by feeding her voiceovers of the characters she was running from.

Despite having stolen a ton of money from her chauvinistic jerkweed of a boss, we know that Marion Crane has a decent heart and an innocent soul, and that she's going to make amends. Stealing the green wasn't a malicious crime, just a glorified childish prank.

"She was basically a compassionate, honest woman, not a thief," Leigh said. "So her momentous, out-of-character decision to commit the robbery showed her passion and terrible frustration."

Crane, Leigh felt, was "an unspectacular, simple, frustrated person, getting older, seeing herself become an old maid, afraid (her lover) would go off, never having enough money."

With his legendary sense of humor and childish prankster-ism on full display, Hitchcock helped both Leigh and himself prepare during filming; once in a while, Leigh would take a break from filming, only to discover her trailer occupied by an uninvited lunch guest: Mother Bates' corpse.

"The horror in my scream registered on his Richter scale," said Leigh, who enjoyed a stellar career until her death in 2004. "Some hair-raising screams emanated from behind my door when I walked in on these hideous, shriveled monstrosities. I puzzle over whether this was just a gag or an effort to keep me on edge, thus in (Marion's) jittery state of mind." Rita Riggs, a costumer on the flick, said that dressing the corpse had such an effect on her that she did so standing in back of it.

And now, for the infamous shower scene, the one that destroyed just about every taboo Hollywood was clinging to at the time—starting before the first drop of water falls. It seems totally unreal decades later that the scene of a flushing toilet, the first of its kind in Hollywood history, would have ticked critics off more than a nude lady getting knifed to death. But enough about that—this film took the unprecedented step of having the heroine suddenly (and violently) die, and flipping the film around 180 degrees, a plot twist that no maze-maker could ever duplicate.

As Marion freshens up before bed, the film's real object truly comes to light in the darkness. As the unsuspecting lady washes off, we see a shadowy figure slowly inching up to the shower curtain.

"The shower was a baptism," Leigh said, "a taking away of the torment of her mind. Marion became a virgin again. (Hitchcock) wanted the audience to feel her peacefulness, her kind of rebirth, so that the moment of intrusion is even more shocking and tragic."

Then the curtain is torn open. She screams. The sounds begin to emit. A huge knife slams up and down as the film shifts into a machine-gun myriad of shots. We don't see the killer's face—is it Norman? His evil mother? The boss that Marion betrayed, who somehow followed her?—which makes things even more horrific. She tries to fight, but it's too late, and Marion is left the victim of an attack that shifts the film like the earth's plates during a quake.

First, let's clear up some old rumors. One: Leigh was never nude during filming, nor did Hitchcock ever ask her to do it that way (body double Marli Renfro handled the unclothed scenes). Second, Hitchcock, and *no one else*, directed the scene (stories have arisen that he was ill, felt that he couldn't do it justice, got temporarily kidnapped by aliens, whatever, and temporarily handed the reins to someone else). Oh, and unlike what a film we'll discuss in a moment told us, he didn't terrify Leigh into realism by playing the stabbing role out of nowhere.

"I was in that shower for seven days," Leigh asserts, "and believe you me, Hitchcock was right next to his camera for every one of those seventy-odd shots." The part took more time than any one shot in the film.

Though it lasts less than a minute, the scene is still more terrifying than most shots put out even decades later. It's not just the "soundtrack," though the violin-created shrieks, combined with Marion's own, are horrifying (watch it on mute sometime; like the climactic scenes in *Jaws*, it loses something without the sound). The shots, though considered obscene for the day and time, aren't especially graphic; we never see Marion's private areas, only briefly see the knife contacting her body, and there's not a huge amount of blood.

Speaking of which, the blood was chocolate syrup, which maintained its consistency in the shower scenes far better than fake blood or ketchup, both of which were attempted—Hitchcock said that, had regular movie blood worked, he might have made the movie in color.

It's the entire setting that really gives the atmosphere a high level of ominous-ness. Marion, bothered by her inner feelings at committing a theft, was planning to do right; she appears to see the shower as a kind of baptism, the first step of a cleansing that will continue when she takes the expected trip tomorrow.

Also, there's the setup: nudity, even pseudo-nudity, brings with it a sense of vulnerability, and being in a small, confined setting could cause tension even in one not suffering from claustrophobia. Showering is a situation that we all find ourselves in at least once or twice a day; *Psycho* probably traumatized many away from the standing bath, at least for a little while.

Including its star.

"It's true that I don't take showers," admitted Leigh, who said she screamed when watching herself get killed on screen. "If there is no other way to bathe, then I make sure all of the doors and windows in the house are locked, and I leave the bathroom door open and the shower curtain and stall door open, so I have a perfect, clear view. I face the door, no matter where the showerhead is. The room gets very wet."

Critics were mostly nice, and *Psycho* became the then-highest-grossing black and white picture of all time. However, when Oscars were handed out, Perkins was left in the cold, while Leigh would lose the Best Supporting Actress honor to *Elmer Gantry*'s Shirley Jones. Hitchcock watched Billy Wilder—who'd previously beaten him in 1945, with *Lost Weekend* to Hitchcock's *Spellbound*—take home the Best Director and Best Picture award for *The Apartment*. All in all, Hitchcock would go eight Oscar nominations without winning, and fans today still nearly come to blows over the Best Director Never To Win an Oscar honor, with Hitchcock, Stanley Kubrick (who won an Oscar for visual effects with *2001*, but not for directing), and, as of the 2016 awards, Spike Lee all in the forefront.

In the years following *Psycho*, Perkins wisely learned to mock his own acting persona: as Norman, he gave tips on how to run a motel while hosting *Saturday Night Live*, and often pranked visitors to his Cape Cod estate by leaping out to scare them, dressed as Mother Bates and carrying a knife.

Still, there were parts of Norman that afflicted Perkins in a way he could never prepare for, on the voluntary scale. Just like Norman, as he sadly explains to Marion early on, Perkins had lost his father at an early age (Osgood Perkins, himself a performer, passed when his son was five; Anthony would name his son after his dad).

As Norman did, Perkins struggled with his sexuality: during Bates' peeping-tom act on Marion, we get the feeling that this man has never gotten within an area code of first base with a lady, and had no clue how to get there. Perkins, on the other hand, tried to "overcome" his homosexuality by using therapy and hiding behind a farcical marriage and parenthood—he'd have two sons with wife Berry Berenson.

But what went on in Perkins' childhood, he claimed to a magazine interviewer in 1983, were far beyond anything a scary movie could inspire. In a *People* article that displayed him on its cover standing arrogantly in front of the Bates home with the mother's ominous shadow in the background, Perkins handed out some revelations about his childhood that would have shocked Gein himself.

His mother, Janet, had been a "strong-willed, dominant" woman. "Whenever my father came home, I was jealous. I loved him, but I wanted him to be dead, so I could have her all to myself."

Chances are, quotes like that would have already had the gossip tongues on fast forward. It was what came next, however, that drew a dark parallel between Perkins himself and the character with whom he would forever be associated.

"(Janet) was constantly touching me and caressing me," Perkins claimed. "Not realizing what effect she was having, she would touch me all over, even stroking the inside of my thighs up to my crotch." Perkins also claimed that he'd repressed the memories until just before his mother's 1979 death.

The shockwaves hit at high speed and volume. Many of Perkins' friends were outraged. Some said he'd made up lies for publicity; others, while not calling his claims untrue, raged at the married father of two children, opening them up for a Pandora's box of horrific exposure.

Whatever his reasons for airing the dirtiest of laundry, Perkins finally tried to take a stronger advantage of his relationship with Norman, making three sequels (one was for television) from 1983 to 1990. The sequels—one of which starred Osgood as the younger, flashbacked version of his daddy—explored the lives of Norman and his mother before and after the Crane murder. They also made many people glad that Hitchcock wasn't around to see his work get soiled.

Gus Van Sant had ironically met with Perkins a few months before the actor's death to try to convince him to appear—as a drag queen!—in Van Sant's production of *Even Cowgirls Get the Blues* (1993), and Perkins probably would have done so had it not been for his illness: AIDS took him in September 1992. In 1998, Van Sant put out his own version of *Psycho*, a near-identical reshoot with Vince Vaughn and Anne Heche playing Norman and Marion.

It didn't work, and it taught some lessons to filmmakers across the world. First of all, classics shouldn't be remade, because it's a burden that can't be met and shouldn't be tried. Second of all, it's up to them—the directors, the performers, and the rest of the entertainment community—to make their own classics. Fifty or sixty years from now, the films coming out today may just be seen as classics by the film world of the future, but we can't know that now. Originality is what sells, and, as the new *Psycho* showed us, a new version of an archetype might recapture the physical and verbal effects of its predecessor, but the magic is gone.

"I think the reason that *Psycho* has endured is because of the restrictions that were put on us," Leigh explained. "Mr. Hitchcock had to come up with a suspense story without showing what today is normal, and he allowed the audience to create what they thought they saw, and when the audience becomes a part of the creative process, they're not going to forget that."

Finally, let's go back to one last look at the relationship between Perkins and Bates, one of the most estranged in movie history.

"I asked Dad once," Osgood said, "'If you could go back to 1959 and either take or not take the role in *Psycho*, knowing that taking it would mean you would be typecast for the rest of your life, what would you do?'"

His father hesitated for about a day. Then he came back in the assertive affirmative.

"I think it was because he understood about the integrity of the part, and not the integrity of one's career as a whole," said the younger Perkins. "He was more interested in doing right by one part than in doing right by one's entire career. Instead of spreading himself thin over a bunch of movies, he would rather have made an impact in one picture, which he did."

Over half a century after Leigh stepped into the shower for the last time, another actress followed her down the path. Not Anne Heche, who played Marion in the 1998 *Psycho* remake; this is something else entirely.

Scarlett Johansson played Janet Leigh as *Hitchcock* (2012) turned into a film within a film, the infamous shower stabbing scene moving from fantasy to reality.

In the midst of creating *Psycho*, Hitchcock's life away from the camera was much more realistically difficult: his career had hit a snag, and audiences at the time weren't exactly known for gravitating towards the frightening genre.

Even beyond that, though, his marriage appeared to be going the same wrong way as his career. How rough it actually was will probably never be known, but 2012's *Hitchcock* told the tale of the director's struggle to balance his professional life with his personal one, as Hitchcock (Anthony Hopkins, nearly unrecognizable in an Oscar-nominated makeup job) finds himself troubled by his wife Alma Reville's (fellow Oscar winner Helen Mirren) work collaboration with another screenwriter. Not that Hitch's hands are squeaky clean either: Alma's ticked at his closeness to Leigh (Scarlett Johansson), whose marriage to Tony Curtis was also heading down the wrong road at the time, ending in 1962.

Leigh's own children are only mentioned briefly in the flick (they were in single-digit age at the time it takes place), but anyone who cared enough to check it out knew the punchline to that inside joke, which you'll get in a minute.

"For me it was about capturing (Leigh's) essence," Johansson says. "I didn't really try to mimic her, we're very different, but it was the process of being able to meet her through people that knew her, through her biographies, her work. It was a pleasure: she was beloved on-screen and off, she was a wonderful actress. It was nice to be able to have a character like that to invoke that every day."

It wasn't Johansson's first foray into portraying a real person; she'd been Anne Boleyn's sister Mary in *The Other Boleyn* girl a few years before. To really reach Leigh, though, Johansson knew a source that could take her farther into the character than just about anything or anyone else.

"I just think, more than anything, it must be very strange to have somebody play your mother—and especially someone as beloved and celebrated as Janet," Johansson says.

Indeed—the then-youth we mentioned earlier was none other than longtime household acting name Jamie Lee Curtis, who gave her mom a run for the "Scream Queen" money with her own work in the *Halloween* movies (she'd made two of them, as well as 1980's terrifying *Prom Night*, before Johansson was even born), and some other scarers as well.

"Jamie was lovely," Johansson recalls. "She sent beautiful photographs and gave me some wonderful stories."

As Leigh and the wide-eyed, uncomfortable Anthony Perkins (James D'Arcy) get to know their characters and each other, Hitchcock's issues with his wife start finding their way into his work. As everyone gears up to do *Psycho*'s most infamous scene, the man called Hitch feels his frustrations towards women in general starting to boil over. Leigh doesn't quite give Marion Crane enough emotion for his liking—at least, in that exact moment—and he's going to force it through her.

In the midst of filming, Hitchcock grabs the prop blade, and starts pounding up and down himself. It's as if he's suddenly stabbing away not only at the wife he's pissed at, but every jezebel who broke his heart, every jerk who's been screwing with him lately, and that he's within nano-inches of snaring the ultimate payback (from a messenger it will be, but few in his position worry much about ethics).

Leigh's terrified, and Johansson says that this wasn't a total act.

"You have got to be brave, get into the shower, and face Anthony Hopkins as Hitchcock jabbing you in the face with a twelve-inch kitchen knife," she says. "Maybe I watched *Silence of the Lambs* (1991) too many times when I was a kid. Maybe I was having some flashbacks. So I didn't need too much preparation for the scene."

Still, unlike Leigh's weeklong fatal bath, Johansson got to pop in and out of the tub, still channeling Leigh's spirit in the meantime.

"We only had the luxury to shoot the scene for a day, and everybody was feeling very nervous because it involved water and nobody wants the actor to get wet," she says. "They were concerned with modesty and all these things—but I don't care about any of that stuff and Janet Leigh never did either."

Knowing that the *Hitchcock* shower scene was a figment of cinematic creative dramatization (i.e., in real life, Hitch didn't actually grab the knife and act it out) downplays its meaning quite a bit, but it's still awfully strong. And, again, Perkins not being there was indeed true. Instead, someone else had to become Epper for a few days.

"You had to be at least six feet tall to read for it, so I just made the cut," remember Melinda Chilton. "There were no lines at the time. When we improvised the audition, it was pretty much silent, which was tricky, because actors like to talk."

Not only that, but Chilton's tryout assignment was to display acting intended to be subpar! Hitchcock hadn't approved of Epper's performance the first time around, so Chilton tried to do things the wrong way at the start.

"Apparently, he didn't like the way she was doing the stabbing," Chilton says. "He wanted it to be

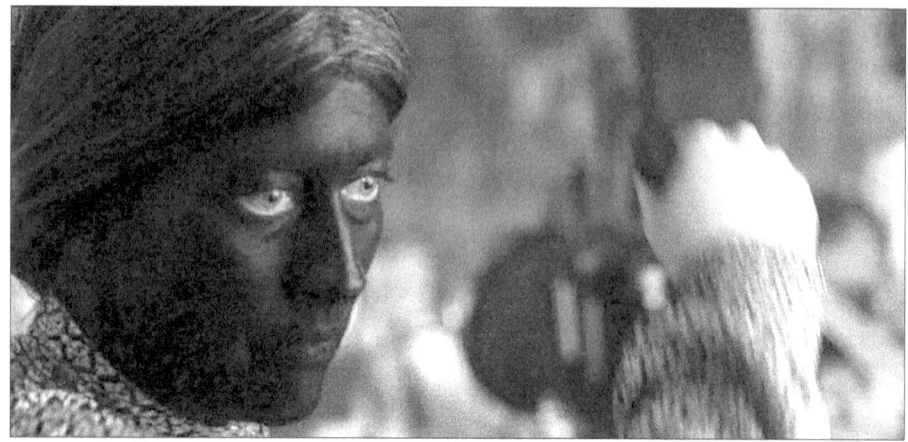

Stuntwoman Margo Epper, who acted out the stabber in *Psycho*, was played by Melinda Chilton in *Hitchcock* (2012).

more forceful. So on the audition, I had to show bad stabbing and then good stabbing."

Once she had the role, however, Chilton had to find her way inside a real person, and she didn't have the resources that Johansson had enjoyed.

"I really researched Margo," she recalls. "I tried to find her, and wasn't able to. I talked to people who knew her family to see what kind of family she came from, what she was like on the set."

Doubling had been a family tradition for Epper, whose father John had done the job for names like Errol Flynn and Gary Cooper.

Like Chilton, Epper's stature gave her some extra presence on the scene. Strapping for her profession, Epper had played a wrestler on an episode of *The Beverly Hillbillies* (1963). A former bull rider, Chilton could relate.

"That showed me something about her physically," she says. "There's definitely no fear. If you have fear, you just acknowledge it and do it anyway. I saw her as someone who surely could pull her own. It's interesting playing a real person, because you get all the facts and then fill in the blanks and make it your own, so you're not acting out that person, but showing your idea of her essence."

As she embodied a stunt family from the past, Chilton got some help from one of the present. Working with a huge knife, even with one scene, required supervision from a stunt coordinator; for this film, it was Eric Norris, son of a legendary martial artist named Chuck.

"Holding a knife looks threatening . . . period," Chilton says. "Eric helped me come up with both strong and clumsy movements with that famous knife. It was a bit of a challenge. So, to watch Eric Norris come up with a 'less threatening,' more clumsy way to hold a big knife was interesting and fun. I think Eric came up with some great moves for me, moves that were both strong and creepy and moves that were a bit weak and would definitely cause Hitchcock to stop the scene."

A few days before filming, Chilton arrived for her cosmetic transformation.

"They were very, very specific about every little detail for the dress," she says of the crew. "They checked over the dress to see where it would sit on me as it had on Margo, what I had on under it, everything."

Then a crew member came in and explained something a bit extra and quite unusual. Hitchcock's crew hadn't had the luxuries of special effects that directors enjoy today, and a new step would have to be taken to repeat his technique of concealing the killer's identity.

For the ominous shot from within the shower, we see the silhouetted figure step through the door and up towards the curtain. Dark attire would cover up the person's identity to an extent, but the face would still show, and a mask wouldn't work here.

"Margo was blending in with the curtain too much," Chilton says, "so they painted her face black, to really help create that silhouette. They must have asked me ten times if I was going to be OK with that."

Of course she was, and even got a bit of unexpected assistance in that department. While Hitchcock hadn't been known for his amicability on the set, his portrayer certainly was, as Chilton happily learned.

"Anthony Hopkins, besides my own father, was the most gracious man I had ever met," she says. "He came on the set, said hello to everyone, every crew member, and learned everyone's names."

During a break in filming, Chilton stood in full makeup, clearly a job the crew didn't want to be forced to redo. Hopkins asked if she'd like to sip some tea.

"There I was in blackface, and we talked about acting, life, serial killers, everything," she remembers. "I told him that no movie had creeped me out more than *Silence of the Lambs*."

And she had a special reason: Chilton's last name is the same as Dr. Lecter's nemesis in the film, the head of his asylum, the fellow we see the doctor pursuing as the credits roll.

Hopkins smiled. Then he stepped out of Hitchcock for a moment.

"He turned his head towards me, and you could see him go into Hannibal," Chilton says. "Then he looked at me and said 'Dr. Chilton, I believe I had you for lunch.' It was the greatest moment!"

Back on the set, Chilton kept checking out Epper's work in the shower scene.

"It was very exciting," she says. "I had chills. I didn't realize what a creepy, creepy performance that was."

Then it came time to act things out. On a huge soundstage, created to resemble the sort used back during Hitchcock's work, Hopkins, Leigh, Chilton, and the rest put together the scene that shoved *Psycho* into legend.

"To be able to recreate that infamous, amazing scene in cinema history was a thrill," Chilton says. "When I'm ninety years old in a rocking chair (perhaps she's thinking of Ms. Bates there!), I'll be thinking of that day."

Per usual, Beverly Marsh (Emily Perkins) had to show the boys how to get tough during *It* (1991).

Emily Perkins:

It/Ginger Snaps

THE REASONS WHY Emily Perkins stepped into acting itself ended up being pretty ironic. The role that started her off there was just as much so.

As an elementary school student, recalls the Vancouver native, "I thought acting would be a way to escape death—to have many lives instead of just one." In a sardonic kind of way, it's strange that she'd end up spending so much time as an actress escaping death—albeit in a much more cinematic fashion.

Still, in a much sadder way, one of her first big roles had its own share of dark irony as well.

The first ten minutes of 1990's *It* are scarier than several full-length films, including those rated R in theaters, beyond this TV miniseries. A child is violently murdered, and this sort of thing just keeps happening in the sad town of Derry. One local fellow has seen this sort of thing before, far more up close and gorily personal. It's the thing that took out some of his friends and nearly him so long ago, though it probably seems like yesterday right now. He's the only one left around—but *It* has been defeated before, and it can happen again, if the right people show.

Flashing back, we see how the group came together, and why they joined to take out the evil that had slaughtered so many of their friends—and, in the final straw, one boy's little brother.

And in the persona of Beverley Marsh herself, a sad sort of irony—that the monster that can strike anytime, anywhere, in reality or our imaginations, isn't the toughest thing for the young woman.

The neighborhood delinquents ready to try out their masculinity on her, with or without consent. Growing up without a mother, stuck with a father who abuses her when he can pull his head out of a beer bottle.

Still, it's what makes the story's most prominent female perhaps its strongest character of all, and it's what brought Perkins into Beverley's horrifying world.

"I really admired Beverley's resilience," she says. "She was a girl with a very difficult home life, but she takes action to kill a monster that is terrorizing her town. I liked the psychological element of the story—the idea that through friendship we can find the courage to destroy our demons."

Other King stories have explored that very theory before—1986's *Stand by Me* comes to mind at high speed—but *It* arguably does so more effectively than others. The kids' battle with the title character isn't all we see of them; there's the camaraderie of the innocence and fun that should fill every childhood, and we see them be there for each other just because kids seem to know what's right better than adults once in a while.

"Horror films are most successful when we actually care about the characters," Perkins says. "Horror films should focus on developing three-dimensional characters we can relate to. Too often, the thrills feel cheap because of poor characterization."

Decades away from the electronics and other objects that keep too many of today's kids square on the couch, slowly expanding in size along the way, *It's* kids explore, ride bicycles, all the things that make childhood the best times of our lives. And it wasn't all an act, Perkins recalls.

"I remember there being some rehearsal time and bonding activities for us kids, like going to movies," says the actress, who read up on Beverley's actions in King's book along the way. "It was a lot of fun."

With their main woman as the group's slingshot champ, the kids manage to catch It itself—in Pennywise's clown form of Tim Curry's legendary performance—in the dark corners of the sewer, where Bev blasts a hole in Its head and send it careening down a pipe. But just in case it's not all the way gone, they make a solemn vow to fight again if the need arises.

Back in the current, we see the new adult Bev. Like many of her old pals, she's doing pretty well financially, a maven of fashion design. But also like many of them, her personal life has gone the other way: no children (none of them have any yet), and, like most girls who grew up in Bev's sort of settings, married to a guy who does the same stuff as her dad.

But her friend's call to get back home instills a strength in Bev—now in gorgeous Annette O'Toole mode—she hasn't felt for years, knocking back her gutless opponent and letting him know that murder's the next step if he ever tries anything again. She's back to Derry and back to battle.

To be fair, the book's depiction is *much* more graphic, and darkly satisfying—the novel-esque Bev methodically beats the holy shit out of her wife-beating dirtbag husband, culminating in a belt-whipping to the genitalia that probably made quite a few of King's readers (mostly the female ones!) drop the book and run around the room, cheering their new literary hero! Not just that, but the husband disappears from the film right after Bev escapes—in the book, he chases her all the way to Derry, where he comes face-to-face with the title character and gets the ultimate in just desserts! Oh well, making a film out of 1000-plus-page book, one must give up a little. . . .

After a few years away from the screen, Perkins came back to supernatural horror. This time, family was the key. In 2000's so-aptly titled *Ginger Snaps*, Perkins was Brigitte Fitzgerald, sister to Katharine Isabelle's title character, with whom she shares both a fascination with death and a pact that they'll arrive in eternity together. But events far beyond their control, and reality, will force their words to be broken.

One night, the sisters are attacked by a crazed furry creature too large and mean to be a housepet. Ginger's hurt, but her wounds heal at superhuman speed. Then hair and a tail sprout from her, and her sexual appetite grows through the roof. In the know, Brigitte desperately tries to save her, only to end up infecting herself.

But not even that works—with her sister now in full lycanthrope mode and stalking her through the family home, Brigitte accidentally stabs her, watching Ginger die as the credits start to roll.

"The feminist aspect of the script attracted me," Perkins says. "I loved that the film makes visible the fact that the meanings of the female body are socially constructed ones, and that female sexuality is constructed often times as monstrous. I drew on my own feelings during adolescence to prepare for the role, feelings of being isolated and resentful of my body."

Four years later, she and Brigitte would take the story even farther (Perkins won a 2003 Leo Award—the Canadian Emmys—for her role in the TV crime drama *Da Vinci's Inquest*). In *Ginger Snaps II: Unleashed* (2004), Brigitte finds herself stalked by a werewolf, then trapped in a rehab clinic. Slowly, her infection from the first film starts to take effect, taunting from her phantom sister not exactly helping. Soon she and a friend manage to escape, but the friend won't give Brigitte the mercy killing she begs for, instead trapping her in a basement and starting a comic book about the matter, preparing to use Brigitte as her personal weapon.

The same year, the sisters went back in time in *Ginger Snaps Back: The Beginning*, which told the tale of their werewolf beginnings, starting in a fort in the Canadian wilderness. Under attack from the wolves, Ginger is bitten. But the two manage to escape, only to mingle their blood together to infect them both.

"The special effects were great," Perkins says, "but these are really films about coming of age—they are character dramas, and, for me, the special effects were secondary: a projection of the psychological reality of the characters."

Few people, male or female, have made as many contributions to horror as Linnea Quigley (right). Hundreds of roles, decades of film, Quigley personifies what a scream queen should be.

Linnea Quigley

ENOUGH BLOGS TO crash the Internet.

More books than the world's biggest library could hold.

Every compliment in the English language, and a few we'd take the time to invent.

All of them combined wouldn't come within six area codes of accessing the effect that this lady's had on the horror genre.

She's done it all, done it all again, and gone out and done some more. The thanks and a tribute, it may never be enough—but we're certainly going to try.

"I believe horror people are the best," Linnea Quigley asserts. "The horror conventions are great to meet fans, filmmakers, directors, producers, etc. Going from ingénue to mother to grandma, it's all been so much fun. I'm still always nervous every time I get in front of a camera and public. That hasn't left." Fortunately for generations of horror fans, she hasn't either, ever since stepping before the cameras about 150 films ago.

The Iowa native arrived in Los Angeles a few decades ago, hoping to parlay a modeling career into acting. "The advice I would give actors is to start wherever you can," she says, "extra work, modeling, whatever gets you used to learning and getting your name out there. Take acting classes and know your strong points. For horror, watch the old and new films, and get into the horror world conventions and the like. I'd say a lot of the success in this industry is sheer luck." Commonplace for the movie profession, that didn't come easily or immediately to Quigley, stepping into the slasher flicks with 1981's *Graduation Day*, then helping do to Christmas what Michael Myers did to Halloween in *Silent Night, Deadly Night* three years later.

Years before, Linda Blair had stamped her own name into horror legend in *The Exorcist*. *Savage Streets* (1984) put her all the way on the offensive, her local tough Brenda taking a step for female equality in the areas of street fisticuffs.

At least, that was Brenda's public image; at home, she was the uncommonly caring big sister, her sibling Heather victimized by deafness. But when Heather becomes the prey of a group of scumbag rapists (and another friend of Brenda's is murdered), there's no quarter or mercy given—Brenda's a stronger force than that demon that tortured her poor Regan McNeil.

Oh, and Heather? That was Quigley, still in fan mode herself.

"When I learned Linda Blair was in it, playing my sister, wow!" she remembers. "Then also having to be deaf, not breaking character, was probably the most I've felt I was on my own." If Quigley had placed a dot on the horror landmark map, her role the next year, still considered by many to be her career highlight, turned her into an icon.

Chilling out in a cemetery—yeah, *nothing* bad *ever* happens there in horror films!—a group of young rebels without a cause or clue just kick back and wonder what life and death are ever going to throw at them.

Apparently she's not aware that she's in a flick called *Return of the Living Dead*, or maybe she is and simply doesn't give a damn. In any case, these deep discussions about death are causing some familiar and certainly welcome feelings inside redheaded and fully (perhaps overfully) made up punk-ette Trash. Lustily dreaming of one day becoming cannibal fodder, the young babe does everything she can to entice others to approach: namely, dancing on the graves as her clothes slowly disappear.

"Who *wouldn't* want to play a punk living the life of the dark side," Quigley queries, "and just being so in control she would dance on tombstones?" By now, acting and modeling weren't her only performance ventures; Quigley'd formed and lead some other ladies in the band The Skirts earlier in the decade (she'd later write a few books on the aspects of entertainment).

"That may have helped," she remembers of singing, "but as one famous actor said, 'Just act.' (Many have made such a statement). I don't really prepare; I expect to learn my lines and let it come out. Memorizing is my hardest part." Even harder, it appears, than Trash's wish coming true, as she becomes a zombie meal.

After backing up one horror champ in *Streets*, Quigley worked alongside another in *Hollywood Chainsaw Hookers* (1988), with the former Leatherface himself, Gunnar Hansen, leading the cult of title characters. The same year, she helped get revenge on Freddy Krueger, playing a stolen soul who popped from his body in the closing moments of *The Dream Master*.

Another of Quigley's most memorable roles was one she'd nearly skipped on purpose.

"For *Night of the Demons* (1988), I almost didn't audition," she admits, "but my manager kept calling me saying that they really wanted to see me. I didn't want the rejection. I walked in and they said, 'You've got the role. Surprise!'" Trash's sex appeal had seduced a genre; Quigley gave *Demons'* Suzanne perhaps the decade's most memorable debut.

As lovely as her face is, it wasn't the first thing we saw. As her friend Amelia (Amelia Kinkade, the project's future villainess) secretly helps herself to a convenience store's (unknowingly!) free goodies, the clerks can't take their eyes off the scantily clad backside that Suzanne just *happens* to be showing off. How long the hormonal claws of puberty clutch on to some!

The group finally gets to a private party, but decides to invite some other guests back with the act of the séance. Proving that humans aren't the only ones with fine taste in ladies, a demon first takes control of Suzanne, turning her into its monstrous, murderous tool before snaring Angela.

"The special effects were torturous, even more so than *Living Dead*," Quigley remembers. "Some took eleven hours. Another obstacle for me was working in high heels! I still can't, and really wish I could." Decades after the first *Demons*, Quigley cameoed as a ballerina in its 2009 remake.

Her roles and films have varied in size and success, but neither has stopped. Usually a few times a year, Quigley's name has appeared in one set of credits after another, almost always in horror—including a few still scheduled for release when this book went to press in early 2016.

"Rock 'n' roll and horror go together, so it spans out to a lot of genres," Quigley says. "I've learned from bad movies and good movies; there is always something to learn." Tribute isn't always appreciated in horror—except, of course, for books like this and their readers!—but a special kind came for three of the genre's top-ever women in 2014 with *3 Scream Queens*.

Early in their careers, Quigley, Brinke Stephens, and Michelle Bauer had battled a Muppet-like evil imp in *Sorority Babes in the Slimeball Bowl-a-Rama* (1988). *Scream Queens* had the three playing characters similar to themselves, invited to a private screening of the type of film that they, in and out of character, helped to elevate to its own special section of horror. Per usual, things cross the line from fun to bloody realism....

"That was really fun," Quigley recalls. "I played a character who was a diva scream queen. All three of us working together . . . after so many years kind of made me sentimental . . . melancholy."

Sadly, and unfairly, it wasn't the first or last time horror work has instilled such a feeling in perhaps horror's top lady. She's been called "The Queen of the B's" for her work in what too many consider B-movies, such a self-righteous label by those who criticize others for doing what they won't, or can't. A-, B-, C-, all the way down to T-rated films, everyone from the cast to crew too often start with little or nothing and work harder than many to put something strong together, often getting just as little appreciation or remuneration in the process. Performers like her and the films they put out are too often looked down upon simply because they don't always get the type of exposure and publicity that the big studio ones can, regardless of the possibility—usually reality—that the smaller films might actually have the edge in quality!

"It always makes me upset when people make horror movies sound 'low class,'" Quigley says. "I used to get 'You do *those* types of movies.' Being in a book after so many years is still a surprise, a nice one. Going from a shy girl to dancing naked on tombstones is quite a stretch. I'm proud of that."

It is. And it's more than far too many will ever do, or have the guts to try. But when Quigley, and so many of her colleagues, venture out to those conventions we heard of earlier, or look over one of the web sites or books we talked about way back in the introduction, here's hoping they'll never forget that they *are* appreciated. They'll continue to be cheered for. And, although we could have written this about her a few dozen films ago, people like her will *never* be forgotten.

Assuming, of course, that the whole demon-possession, zombie-cuisine, psycho-slasher things don't follow her into reality or anything!

Grabbing hold of his shot at a legend that's inspired countless horror films and Hollywood costumes, Duncan Regehr became Dracula in *The Monster Squad* (1987).

Duncan Regehr/Andre Gower:

The Monster Squad

IT HAD BEEN nearly a century since the story of *Dracula* first found its way to paper, from the pen and brain of Bram Stoker. It had been over half a century since the story of the fanged count had first explored the worlds of theater and cinema. But for his turn to follow in the footsteps laid by Max Shreck, Bela Lugosi, Christopher Lee, and so many others, Duncan Regehr gave the count a new medium to terrify—the same one that would eventually win the Canada native acclaim around the globe.

Not the boxing skills that nearly won him a spot on North America's northernmost nation's Olympic team, although that would certainly help him cut quite the intimidating figure in the villainous roles that soon peppered his résumé.

The expression of the arts. While Regehr certainly had enough past role models to look to for the vamp's resemblance, finding a new image in his mind and pulling it out with paints and pastels would truly set the stage for the role, and not the kind of stages he'd performed from for so long before *The Monster Squad* came about in 1987.

"I prepared for the role in the same way that I approached many of the more iconic characters I've played," recalls Regehr, "by drawing and painting ideas on paper. As an artist, I often find that rendering a physical vision helps to define the distinct nature of the individual . . . From an early age, I knew that my vocation in life would involve three areas of expression: painting, writing and acting." That would continue to kick into high gear for the next few decades, as his artistic works have filled up several published books and won him an honorary doctorate from Canada's University of Victoria, as well as a Royal Canadian Academy of Art lifetime award.

Andre Gower's Sean and the rest of the Monster Squad celebrate their
accomplishments as the 1987 film reaches the closing credits.

Still, this was about making a new mark in a well-traveled area of horror. The *Squad* title characters were the typical bunch of '80s film rugrats, just *happening* to stumble into a blending of reality and fantasy that makes their monstrous film interests more real than they could have ever expected or wanted.

And, of course, every such group needs a true and fearless (or so he claimed!) leader.

"I'd read for the role of Rudy," recalls Andre Gower. "He was the badass. He smokes, dressed cool, had the cool hair, chased the girls, he was cool." He made it all the way to the screen tests, the Rudy finals, before getting the fateful phone call.

"They said I had the movie, but wanted me to play the lead of Sean," Gower recalls. "I was a bit miffed, but Ryan Lambert pulled off Rudy probably better than I would." Sean, Rudy, and the others got ready for a battle, gleefully leaving Sean's little sister Phoebe (Ashley Bank) behind. After all, at that age, boys just *know* that *a girl* can't possibly be strong enough to take on the baddies!

Once a century, nightmares have a chance to make their way to reality, and the characters that the Squad saw, and probably rooted for, on the screens will show up and snatch an amulet that gives them control of the world.

Of course, this occurrence will be occurring in just a few days. And, of course, the jewel involved is in a nearby house, where the youngsters just happen to snatch it before the monsters do.

And what a murderous murderers' row of bad guys it is. There's the mummy. The creature from the darkly colored waters. A guy who goes lycanthrope every time the moon reaches its largest mass. And Frankenstein's monster is here as well, although his loyalties aren't quite certain.

And who is at the lead? Why, the count himself! He is, after all, the only one who can speak, so to have someone else running the show would be a bit awkward. Liam Neeson had almost grabbed the role, then Regehr stepped into the first, and so far only, horror flick of his career.

"I've had the good fortune to play many iconic heroes and villains," Regehr says, "among them, Dracula in *Monster Squad*, Prince Blackpool in *Wizards and Warriors (1983)*, Charles in 1985's *V (Robert Englund was on that show as well)*, Lydon in *The Last Days of Pompei (1994)*. It's interesting to note that all of those characters were dressed in black."

Clearly, he had experience at the profession, if not the genre. The same couldn't be said for Gower and his Squad colleagues.

"A lot of people put in a lot of effort in the process," he explains, "but it's a little more different when you're a kid, because you don't know what you don't know, if that makes sense." He, director Fred Dekker, and the rest of the youths did what they could to make their new world as normal as possible, monsters notwithstanding.

"(Dekker) did good job of making sure all of us got together at certain time," Gower remembers. "It was important for all of us to gel as friends and not just as co-workers. When you get a bunch of thirteen-, fourteen-year-old kids on the set together, some kinds of natural processes and hierarchies take place. You put them in an environment that will enable naturally and organically to happen what you want to see, and then you make little tweaks as you go along."

Fortunately, he didn't have to make many to cross over into Sean.

"He was in a leader position, a real out-of-the-box thinker," Gower says of his role model. "You can't put too much into stuff like that when you're working with a bunch of kids, because it'll just get confusing, and kids will stumble over and try to do too much. (Dekker) wondered what it would be like if the Little Rascals fought the classic monsters. It was an innovative mashup that came across."

With the count and his friends on the hunt for things even more important than the vamp's life-giving plasma, Frankenstein's creation meets young Phoebe and starts helping them. But this Dracula has some weaponry that wasn't available to Shreck's and Lugosi's characters, blasting the squad clubhouse and some cop cars away with dynamite. To be fair, Regehr also had more outside help than their crew did: at the *Squad* special effects helm was Stan Winston, who'd win an Oscar that year for *Aliens*, the first of his four career statuettes.

Sean's gang manages to dispose of the fanged fellow's followers pretty easily—hilariously planting one of the Mummy's bandages to a tree and unraveling him is one technique. But even battling the worst horror ever saw and coming out on top wasn't always fun, games, and ego feeding, Gower explains.

"A lot of people think sets are really fun, and they can be in a good environment," he says, "but you have to be professional, you have to know what you're doing, be on time, on spot, be able to switch gears and understand what scene you're doing, because hardly any films shoot in sequence. That's tough for kids, and a lot of the time, it's tough for adults."

Vampire fiction has evolved since Stoker's time; the blood consumers aren't always the villains.

But even today, they're certainly not known for their caring ways, and Dracula, after all, was always supposed to be the bad guy. The end of Francis Ford Coppola's version in the 1990s might be considered the turning point towards possible undead decency, but not in *Squad* land. His crew might be all gone, but Regehr's guy couldn't be bothered; he was still here, the amulet was all the way up for grabs, and if it meant running roughshod through a group of police officers like pesky flies to snare it, it was worth it.

"There were some interesting challenges offered with the role of Dracula," Regehr explains, "to play him differently than he had been portrayed in the past by so many others. I tried to infuse the character with the right balance of malice and humor. I felt that he had to be extremely dangerous—lethal without mercy, and yet 'camp' in his commentary, enough to take the edge off his dire actions. In that way, he could be less of a monster in the bestial sense, rather more psychotic, more human or sociopathic in the drive to achieve his goals."

There would be nothing even remotely campy about the film's roughest saying, and we're not talking about Phoebe labeling her bro and her friends "chicken shit!" when Frankenstein's monster arrives—they flee in terror on his arrival, while she stood calmly still, showing who truly had the guts there.

As the young girl tries to read—in German!—a chant that will send these SOBs right back where they came from, Dracula steps forward, stroking her face almost paternally.

Then he lifts her up by the throat.

"Give me the amulet," he demands, "you *bitch*!" His fangs and eyes glow, and Bank's screams aren't an act.

"At the time of filming, it was a risky thing to say," remarks Regehr, "particularly when spoken with extreme venom to a six-year-old girl. It seems to have stood the test of time."

Her chant finished, a portal opens, ready to pull away the villains. The doctor's creation saves his young friend, planting the vampire on a fence post. But only a wooden stake can kill this kind, and Dracula's going to take Sean out with him.

"Our darker human side can be so malevolent, complex, terrifying." Regehr says. "I felt that by incorporating those darker aspects, I could elevate Dracula beyond the ideal of basic 'monster.'"

But who should arrive? Why, who else but vampire fighting champ Abraham Van Helsing, of course. Who else could it have been? He yanks the Count out of the modern world and straight into the gateway where he belongs. Sadly, Phoebe's friend is sucked away as well.

"There were five or six gigantic airplane engine fans, and we had three or four of those rolling at a time," Gower says of creating the galaxy gateway. "There were crew members throwing dry leaves and Styrofoam bricks. We did that for a few days, getting beaned by fake rocks and real twigs."

As they have all film, and usually for this type of flick, the adults just *happen* to show up right after they're needed, a military troupe with enough weaponry for D-Day: Part Two suddenly appearing on the scene when the enemies are already vanquished. Sean and his friends, now filled to the eyebrows with typical young boy bravado and testosterone to match, let them know just who those monsters were dealing with.

"We're the Monster Squad," he proudly and near-emotionlessly boasts to a disbelieving soldier. Getting ready for the film's final line, Gower had found some extra help from a legendary source.

"(Dekker) and I are both Clint Eastwood fans," he says. "I had done that line a couple of time, and I might have overplayed it. In the spaghetti westerns and the *Dirty Harry* movies, Clint is very powerful, yet understated. He really says a lot of cutting lines, but he says them to the side. (Dekker) told me to do it like Clint would do it. I tried to do it a little more subtle." After virtually all of the flick was spent on the opposite side of the spectrum from that adjective, maybe it's fitting to have it apply to the end.

"You have to appreciate the fact that not many people get to do that," he says of horror hero stardom. "When you look at the microcosm of Hollywood and entertainment, there seems to be a ton of actors out there, but your compare it to the population of a country, it's a very small number. You're part of a very, very small percentage of people."

Tristan Risk:

American Mary

WE'RE ALL USED to hearing it. Some of us may even be guilty of saying it.

"Man, I could be a better actor than *him*!"

"I should try to write a screenplay—or a book."

"That's it, I'm getting some headshots and an audition... next week... maybe...."

Yeah, words, words, words. But what miniscule percentages of them actually translate into action?

The simple answer is, well, not nearly enough. Probably in the single-digit percentile. Too many people jump up on their high horse, then just let it buck them right off. We all have a shot at success, even stardom, but far too many of us are afraid to take it.

And some of those with enough guts to do so just can't understand why.

Tristan Risk combined horror and animation by personifying Betty Boop in 2012's *American Mary*.

"We live in a time when, with this technology, we have the ability to go out and tell our stories," muses Tristan Risk, who's been living up to her last name for decades. "Reach out to others and create and collaborate. Get on social media, meet like-minded people, get together, and just DO it."

"It" for the Vancouver native, as far as entertainment went, started out on burlesque dance stages around the globe, and, as of 2016, it's still there, to an extent. But she always hoped it would go elsewhere at some point.

"I've always been interested to flirt with the screen," Risk recalls. "I think after being a live performer for most of my life, I was ready to try a different kind of medium. It always fascinated me and there was just a dimension that is created for film versus what you are able to achieve live."

After so much high kicking on the stages, one might expect someone with Risk's experiences to try out for the musical genre. They'd be mistaken.

"In terms of what attracted me to horror, I've always been a huge fan," she says. "Growing up, I was a voracious reader, and I loved reading Stephen King, Anne Rice, Bram Stoker, Mary Shelley, you name it. I've always preferred the dark and the fantastic, so being given the chance to not only participate in these genres but to help evoke what I hope is the same feelings I had reading these books and watching these films is amazing. I think so often that it's the stories of what makes us human goes back to primal emotions—fear, love, anger, sadness—that we are able to weave more elaborate trappings with the genre around them."

Risk certainly got to hit the primitive feelings hard in one of her first starring roles, along with the rest of 2012's *American Mary*. Katharine Isabelle scored the title role as a surgeon in training who turns to the gentleman's club stages for a little tuition help.

At first, Risk had expected to do all her work behind the cameras; Jen and Sylvia Soska, two more trying to break through the glass ceiling that horror directing still places over women, had asked her to coordinate *Mary*'s dance moves.

Then they realized that she'd be perfect to become one of Mary's club-dancing colleagues.

"I got the opportunity to audition as Beatress," Risk recalls, "and, having read the script, I naturally jumped on the chance! She was such an interesting and unique character and such a contrast to Mary." Beatress Johnson, whose standout nature began with the unusual spelling of her moniker, had grabbed hold of America's fixation on the past when it came to entertainment, and used it all the way to her successful advantage.

She's already been under the knife that Mary herself hoped to wield someday: to become the legendary diva Betty Boop.

"(Beatress) really jumped out at me and I could hear her voice just looking at the dialogue on the page," Risk says. "She fascinated me and it gave me the chance to play a character that was a caricature without being too much of a cartoon."

Naturally, Risk got ready by checking out some of her role model's animated romps. Tunes from the legendary musical *Little Shop of Horrors* helped her find Beatress' mindset, and Madonna's tune "Who's That Girl" helped get her into seductive rave mode.

"Being a dancer, I tend to 'talk' with my body," she explains, "so working out little nuances of movement with the speech was really fun for me. Beatress was just as much about body language as she was about dialogue. I'd go round to the Soskas' house and show them my ideas, and they would give me feedback. It was very helpful and cut down on having to workshop things too much on the day, given our tight shooting schedule."

Beatress gets Mary to surgically transform her friend into a living doll (i.e., sexual parts removed), just as Mary makes it to a residency. Once there, however, she's raped by a former teacher, and her medical brilliance becomes a weapon, doing shit to him that would scare Dr. Frankenstein.

As word spreads, more and more are willing to lay down for Mary's work, including the Soska twins themselves, who cameo long enough to have their arms exchanged. But things slip out of everyone's control, and Beatress winds up dead, killed by an angry husband of one of Mary's patients. Then he attacks Mary, who only lives long enough to take him out before she slips away, her attempted self-surgery falling short.

"The only thing I wanted was a specific tone for was Beatress' death scene," Risk says. "I didn't want to over- or under-do it . . . It was also quite cold when we were shooting, so they were concerned I wasn't spending too much time on the floor, mostly naked and covered in blood. There wasn't a great deal of extra effects added to the film, since everything was practical."

In a slasher flick like *Mary*, no one's expected to really take things *that* seriously. The blood, the guts, the characters, it's all more there for the darkly pleasurable sort of enjoyment. But while Risk's next role was just as violent, just as horrific in that sense, she and everyone else had a duty to put humor all the way outside—because this one wasn't just realistic; it became its own black cornerstone in the saddest and scariest annals of American history.

2014's *House of Manson* took its turn, as several others have in both film and literature, at telling the terrifying tale of the cult whose crimes were worse than many horror films (even scarier is the near-certainty that Charlie's group probably did a hell of a lot more than anyone was ever convicted of).

Sharon Tate is usually the first name that comes to mind when we think of the Manson murders because of her budding acting career. But six other people were killed on those horrifying nights of August 1969, and Risk became Abigail Folger (Suzi Lorraine played Tate, with Ryan Kiser as Manson, the type of fellow for whom the death penalty was created).

Folger, like the other victims, often gets reduced to a mere name (compared to Tate) when discussing the crime. Risk showed us all truly who she'd been and wanted to be.

"I researched as much as I could about her and tried to learn more about her history and background," remembers the actress. "She proved to be a very interesting woman." Folger had been a volunteer for Robert F. Kennedy's campaign, and worked for free in Los Angeles' welfare system. She'd worked with inner-city kids, and helped raise funds for a San Francisco clinic that treated members of the very cult that would steal her life.

"It was actually really heartbreaking to get to know this fascinating woman better," Risk says, "only to know what fate ultimately befell her simply for being in the wrong place at the wrong time." Folger, just two days from her twenty-sixth birthday, died on August 9, along with her lover Wojceich Frykowski, Tate, Tate's friend Jay Sebring (her husband, director Roman Polanski, happened to be away at the time), and Steven Parent, a friend of the property caretaker, killed only because he happened to be driving by as the killers arrived. The next night, the killers went elsewhere in the neighborhood and found the home of Leno and Rosemary LaBianca, where two more innocent victims were heartlessly slaughtered; sadly, trial testimony from a gas station attendant brought out that a frightened Rosemary had discussed the Tate murders with him as she read the story in a local newspaper.

Suspicions will never stop as to why Manson manipulated his slaves to commit the act: some say he blamed the former owner of Tate's home for interfering with his musical career, while others say he hoped to trigger a race war. In his twisted mind, the blacks would be strong enough to win, but not smart enough to run the world, at which point he and his cult would re-appear and lead them to glory.

"Playing a person who still has extended family, who passed away in such tragic circumstances," Risk says, "I wanted to be mindful of how any of them would react to seeing the film, if they cared to. This wasn't a cartoon, and I didn't want to glorify anything that the Manson family members did. I wanted to show that this was a human being."

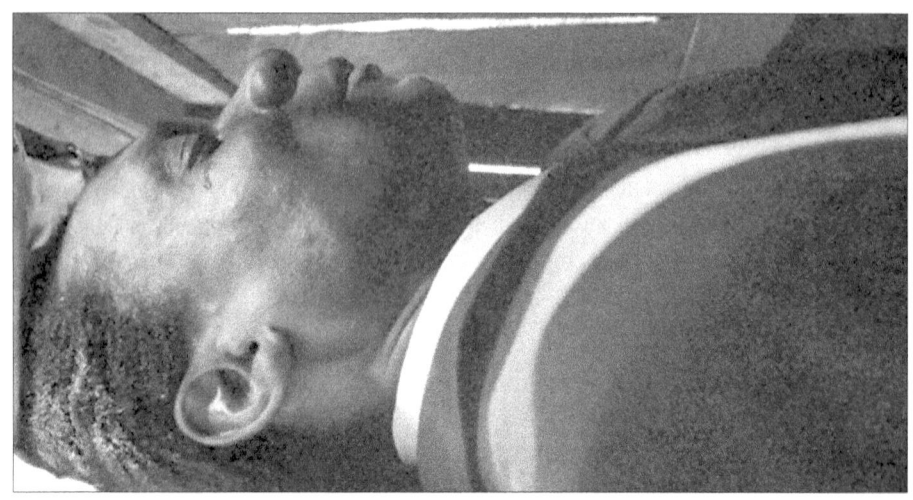

It seemed that Christophe (Conrad Roberts) was dead at the start of
The Serpent and the Rainbow (1988), but it only seemed that way.

Conrad Roberts:

The Serpent and the Rainbow

IT COULDN'T POSSIBLY be a true story.

We saw zombies, potions being drank, resurrection, living skeletons . . . so much. More than enough to scare the hell out of us. *The Serpent and the Rainbow* would undoubtedly be one of 1988's most effective horror films, but such a tale could only emerge from the darkest caverns of the creative human mind. Certainly not from reality, right?

That's what the American public figured when the film previews first started appearing on TV in early 1988. Wes Craven had done some legendary work with realistic horror in *Last House on the Left* back in 1972. His *Nightmare on Elm Street* (1984) had taken some liberties—to say not even the least!—with a true story (a point that wouldn't really become public knowledge until the Internet was around to blow it up), but this was *way* out of possibility. Zombie flicks wouldn't become commonplace for another quarter century, so, George Romero notwithstanding, this was pretty new, and certainly impossible.

Well, wasn't it?

Two men had shown and told us otherwise. One had been through living proof of how blurry the line between life and death could be. The other had written about him.

Craven was out to bring their stories to the cinema, and he'd need some help on the other side of the camera. One who would help there had already lived through horror of the worst kind—not just that which was possible, but had already occurred.

"I ate turtle and turtle eggs, and lived in forty acres of rainforest for sixteen years before I came to America," he remembers. "I pursued knowledge as people pursue money. I read all over Europe. Books changed my life. I became an artist. My motivation is my love for the human race, which should never be partitioned. We all laugh, we all sing, we all grieve, we all love."

Still, some of us have different ways of showing these emotions. Faith and education teaming up to help him along, Conrad Roberts had made it to the Big Apple and become an obstetrician, even delivering his own son. So when so many saw his TV acting debut in 1968 in *The Doctors*, acting out Edward Stark wasn't all an act, but a bit of an inside joke as well.

But enough with the light nature here. It's time to get serious. Somewhere along the way, certain people had become upset with him. People who will do whatever it takes to grab the oft-irresistible illusion of power.

"They tried to kill me in New York," he recalls. "They thought I would become prime minister of the Antigua government. They destroyed my life, my business." He'd started on the West Indies island, and certain folk didn't want him back.

"They threw me off of a building from four stories high," he remembers. "I remembered the thirty-seventh Psalm: don't go headlong." The saying tells the story of a man who will be saved by the Lord if he believes deeply enough, that the Lord will hold a man's hand if he is thrown.

"I fell on my foot," Roberts recalls. "I prayed to the Lord and the Lord saved me. They thought I would never walk again. Now I can dance, sing, do all my karate movements better than I could before." It's horrible that he even had this type of memory to use for prep work for *Serpent*, and it wouldn't be the only aspect thereof.

Voodoo calls the rainbow a spirit of heaven and a serpent one of Earth—clearly taking a more optimistic view of the slithering type than the Bible did. Wade Davis' 1985 book explored the relationship between the two.

The ethnobotanist (one who studied the relationship between plants and humans) had journeyed to Haiti throughout the '70s and '80s, studying voodoo and its effects. A decade after Romero had shocked the horror world with *Night of the Living Dead* (1968), Davis found fact in what we all thought was fiction.

He learned of certain powders used in voodoo, said (stereotyped might be a better word) to caused mind and behavior control. Even to bring back the deceased. He learned of one Clairvius Narcisse.

Narcisse had been pronounced dead, supposedly through ingesting tetrodotoxin, a toxin found in puffer fish. He'd even been buried.

But that wasn't the end. Some voodoo practitioners had dug him up and given him some of their "medicines." He'd been revived, but not the same. He'd spent years under their control, forced to work on a plantation. Then one day, Narcisse had recovered and come home.

How much truth lives in this story? We'll never know. But it certainly made one hell of a basis for horror. Davis' book was just one of many Roberts checked out to get ready for the role. He read *Tell My Horse*, Zora Neale Hurton's 1938 report on voodoo props, one of the first non-fiction works on the subject. He saw *Divine Horsemen: The Living Gods of Haiti*, a documentary compiling several years on the subject.

"I became adept at the subject," Roberts remembers. "It takes knowledge to be an actor. It takes great universal concern to be an actor."

One scene into the film, his character, the name switched to Christophe, is already dead, passing away in a Haiti missionary clinic (filming took place partly there, partly in the Dominican Republic, and a bit in Boston). Shortly after, he's lowered into the ground.

Then his eyes open, and a tear leaks out. An involuntary reflex that took longer than usual? Probably not.

"Going into the coffin was quite real to me," Roberts remembers. "My best friend was an undertaker, and he was very serious about that. When my aunt died, we rode in the hearse with her, and my father drove her."

Davis becomes the focal point for a while, only now he's named Dennis Alan in Bill Pullman's body. He's been asked by some pharmaceutical fellows to go back to Haiti and collect the drug, hoping it could revolutionize the anesthesiologists' industry. But the voodoo-ians, never the extroverted type, will do just about anything to keep it secret, including torturing him. Christophe is back as well, explaining his newfound zest to live in the cemetery.

With it becoming more and more difficult for him, and us, to tell the difference between dreams and reality, Alan escapes, only to have the priests' possessions follow him across the ocean and into the minds of his friends. Back in Haiti, someone sprays him with the powder and buries him, adding insult to injury by placing a huge tarantula on his face!

But Christophe, remembering his own sad experience here, saves Alan from the fate he himself had escaped—and not just as a performer. We hear in the film that the drug is much more effective through the system than the nose, and Roberts had been through this as well.

"The mafia put drugs in my food and drink," he remembers, "and it caused me to hallucinate. I ate the Aloe Vera plant, which can eradicate poison." He'd gotten away, and Alan does as well.

As of April 2016, Narcisse, who died in 1994, is the only case in history with anything close to scientific proof that zombies can exist. The community of study has dismissed the concept for any kind of reason. But several similar cases have been reported (by the media, at least), and not all of them can be chalked up to nature or imagination. These things may have happened. They still may come true, in America and around the world. After all, it certainly can't be *disproven*!

Today, with enough spins on Romero's work to make zombie films their own subgenre rank, and with *The Walking Dead* becoming a new landmark in American culture that goes far past its TV ratings, seeing the undead is commonplace. So the next time we sit down to check one out, let's remember that it's not possible at all. These things can *never* come true.

Or . . . can they?

Debbie Rochon has seduced, terrified, and even made us cheer
a time or several throughout hundreds of horror films.

Debbie Rochon

IT'S A WILD and crazy ride that can go anywhere and do anything, take us anywhere and let us hang out and maybe never bring us back, and we might not want to come back anyway. Sometimes, especially in horror, the line between those who perform and those who watch can get stretched out and destroyed. Going to places of which so few minds can even conceive, it's a hell of a journey, or some might say, escape.

It's been said by enough people that brilliance can't come to light without a bit of madness holding its hand, or some form thereof. What are we saying?

"Work as much as you can and mix it up," our subject tells up-and-comers. "Try the biggest variety of roles you can, regardless of the amount of lines! Practice. Take classes, and remember this is a lifelong journey, not a shortcut to any sort of stardom. That's my opinion. You have to be in it for the long haul, a lifer. Realize you could get acclaim quickly or it could come in twenty-plus years (it didn't take that long for her!), and you have to be OK with that. Your work quality should be your biggest concern."

That's pretty sage, but not exactly specific, is it? We could hear that quote from many performers who have shined in any specific genre, not just horror. Nothing compartmentalized, not just yet.

But to really assess the impact of the work that she and so many others have done so much of, one must look not just beneath the surface: not just think outside the box, but step forward into a world that many refuse to even acknowledge, and those that do are far too often too scared to enter.

You go to these places, and then you find other ways to go there again. It's not a form of reality, and that's fortunate as hell, but it's a life for some, particularly some in the acting profession.

You do it, and you do everything else because you enjoy it. It's not *work* that way. Not easy by any stretch, but certainly worth it in the end if you, the crew, and the audiences that keep coming to see you will look at it and testify, even all the way under oath, that it was more than worth it for us all.

And if you get to step far away from your world, far away from any reality, well . . . that's as great a career as any for those willing to go into it full force, isn't it? The devotion to the craft of horror performing and the loyalty of those who make it as real as it could ever be, it can be a ride that can't end—and damned well shouldn't.

For Debbie Rochon, a few of her colleagues, and people like us that keep watching, it hasn't. It's why, after hundreds of her fear-forcing flicks, people keep watching. Why this book is only the next in a long line of literary profiles about her. Why the horror community, as it so often does, has taken care of one of its special own with one honor after another.

And, in particular here, why it was so damned hard to decide which roles of hers to summarize. Before we even reach that point, however, let's look back at when horror for the young lady was far too real.

As in, being taken from her birth parents before she'd even finished elementary school. Tossed from one foster home to another like a gift that people pass back and forth at a family Christmas game of Pollyanna. Homelessness on the cold streets of Canada in her teenage years, punctuated by a near-fatal robbery and attack that left her forever physically scarred.

Ironically enough, though, it was a fellow homeless person that alerted her to the career that would change Rochon's life forever. One day, she heard of an open casting call for a film far from horror.

Seven years after helping make the legendary *Rocky Horror Picture Show* of 1975, Lou Adler was directing the slightly more realistic *Ladies and Gentlemen, the Fabulous Stains*, the story of a group of young girls who blast across the punk rock stages, only to flare out just as quickly. For three months, Rochon was an extra behind main women Laura Dern and Diane Lane.

"I found it rewarding and exciting," she says. "From that moment on I studied and worked towards becoming an actor. The fact that I ended up in the horror genre was a combination of circumstance and love of the genre." Ironically enough, she'd walk by the cameras of the childish tale *The Best Christmas Pageant Ever* (1983) before heading to the Big Apple to do some serious scaring.

"Working with a number of NYC horror or cult movie directors just put me in casting situations where I made more and more horror movies," Rochon recalls, "even while I was acting on stage with various theater companies. Once I started going to horror conventions in 1992 to promote the films, then I became even more involved with the genre and really never left it." Right around that point, she got involved with the infamously cultish studio Troma Entertainment, doing shorts, skits, and TV shows, with Lloyd Kaufman—a name that's household to everyone with any business calling themselves a horror fan—in head honcho mode. In 1996, Rochon, Kaufman, and the rest of the Troma team put together *Tromeo and Juliet*, a version of the legendary tragedy that undoubtedly made Shakespeare himself glance down from heaven and say, "Wow, I wish I'd made *my* story like that!"

Indeed, *Tromeo* is perhaps the most faithful re-rendition of the tragic work. OK, so Tromeo's family was surnamed Que, rather than Montague. And yes, perhaps Juliet's soporific, which only "comatosed" her in the original, turns her into a deformed cow. Oh, and Tromeo and Juliet end up not just alive and married, but raising a family in New Jersey.

Aside from all that, however, it's about scene for scene the same as what English audiences first saw in the Globe Theater.

One more difference? Well, maybe. Rather than the commonplace matronly maternal nurse to watch over her, Jane Jensen's Juliet finds herself *very* well taken care of by the Capulet domestic Ness, in all *kinds* of ways.

"Once they offered me the role of Ness, I realized from the script that she would be remembered for the lesbian scene, no doubt," Rochon says, "but what I saw was an emotionally tormented character that gave up the love of her life—Juliet—so that (Juliet) could be happy, not Ness. So I really spent my time connecting to her selflessness and feeling of being marginalized, knowing that Ness could never give Juliet what she really wanted—a traditional family—in the Troma sense of things. I worked on what it would feel like to love somebody so much that you would actually encourage the person you love to be with another for their happiness."

A true model of devotion, Rochon even . . . *got her own real-life naval piercing to become Ness!* But she'd only go so far, until the cameras were actually rolling. In the midst of rehearsing, director James Gunn handed out a special request to his top two protagonistas, asking that they "practice act" in the altogether. Rochon was forced to decline.

"I went into the lesbian sex scene with just a 'go for it' attitude and Jane Jensen was so easy to work with that made it very easy to genuinely get into it," she says. "I think because we played that scene so sincerely that people responded to it. It wasn't just because it was a lesbian sex scene, which would get attention regardless, but because we played it real, it helped a lot." A decade later, she'd show up in Troma's *Poultrygeist: Night of the Chicken Dead* (2006), just long enough to get waxed with a beer.

Since the mid-'90s, it's been one flick after another for Rochon, and sometimes several at the same time, usually in the fearing features.

"I love the roles, some more than others, that horror provides actresses," she explains. "There is a much larger range of characters in independent films than there are anywhere else, and that was very attractive to me as an actress." From realistic to impossible and oftentimes in the lost lands in between, Rochon's been at every corner of the horror globe. *American Nightmare* (2002) might not have had the most original of titles, but it put a whole new spin on a sad story told often.

A name commonplace to the true crime educated, Jane Toppan was probably the first American female serial killer (believe me, Aileen Wuornos had *nothing* on this thing!). After becoming a nurse in the 1880s, Toppan poisoned one patient after another, at several hospitals and in private practice, then killed her foster sister, landlords, a family of four, and, she claimed, over thirty people. Guess now we know who Stephen King might have had in mind when he was putting together Annie Wilkes' backstory!

Rochon carried Toppan's forename and nursehood career in *Nightmare*, but the tale was updated to modernity, as she stalked two Halloweens' worth of teenagers to their untimely demises with as many means as *Saw*'s Jigsaw.

First off came learning more and more about her terrifying namesake. "(I was) researching her and understanding that she was a very disturbed and neglected, broken person, and tweaked it to modern times," Rochon says. "I think the key to that character was the rage. Rage of discrimination, rage of her circumstances, and rage towards people who had much more given to them in life. So the core to that character was her anger at society, mixed with insanity."

Confident she had Toppan's murderous ways in hand and mind, Rochon headed to Texas to follow in Leatherface's gory massacring techniques.

"One thing that was very important to me was that she was completely believable," she says. "There was no way she could physically overpower the men like some serial killers do in movies, so not only did I work on her craziness, but also made sure each kill was possible."

Toppan herself, in both fiction and reality, showed it was—and we've seen others give the same sort of sad proof from the leadership of cults, factions that people, often scared with no direction home, join to find some semblance of stability, the same reason so many youngsters end up in gangs. To lead the way through the same sort of group, Rochon launched into all kinds of cult-based research for *Exhumed* (2011). It's the tale of a cluster of people with little in common, but apparently suffering from a collective case of agoraphobia that keeps them in their home. And that's just the way their leader likes it.

Just as Toppan's gender made her the exception to the serial killer rule, we haven't really had a sole cult-heading queen. Perhaps that's why Rochon's character in *Exhumed* isn't named— except for The Governess.

"It's not what is said but often what is not said that is driving the scenes," Rochon says. "As an actor, this is heaven because you really get to use your training and fill in all the silent moments the character has." She blended Joan Crawford's (alleged) abusive elements of motherhood with the atmosphere of *Spider Baby*. A 1964 pitch-black comedy horror flick, *Baby* put Lon Cheney Jr. in charge of a family of orphans (Sid Haig, still rolling strong through horror today, was one) suffering from Merrye Syndrome, which, in kind of the demonic side of *The Curious Case of Benjamin Button* (2008), causes regression inside and out once the pearly gates of puberty are reached.

Acting in black and white for one of the few times of her career, Rochon used the depressing atmosphere to the Governess' advantage.

"The Governess was a control freak that was very much out of control and was doing her deadly deeds out of a deep fear," she says, "as opposed to, say, killing just for fun. So of course I needed to have some deep chinks in her armor that could be exposed by the end of the movie. If you are to play any sort of killer realistically, you need to know their weaknesses not just their strengths. That is a big mistake you see being made in movies quite often."

With fewer and fewer exceptions finding their way around the rule, horror performers don't get near the mainstream credit as their counterparts, as far as awards go. So they're left to make up their own—and while the Phantom of the Movies' Videoscope award for Best Psychette statuette that Rochon won for being Toppan doesn't quite carry Oscar name value, it means more than enough to the right people, just as much as being voted the Scream Queen of the 1990s by *Draculina Magazine*'s readers, or finding a spot in the B-Movie Acting Hall of Fame in 2004.

Not to mention scoring the Best Actress honor at 2010's Eerie Horror Film Festival for *Slime City Massacre*.

Remember the opening bilge about horror acting allowing us to visit places that many don't even want to imagine? Here's a great example, perhaps part of the reason that so many appreciated Rochon's (and her co-stars') work in *Massacre*.

Searching for food in bomb-torn New York City, Rochon's Alice is part of a group that stumbles upon a new kind of frozen yogurt. Feasting upon it, however, turns Alice and her friends into creatures of slime, out for murder. But they're not the full bad guys here; there's a group of hitmen looking to take out both the turned and the human, and a three-way world war is the only plausible conclusion!

"I decided (Alice) was just a ruthless, typical junkie deep down and would do anything and sell out anybody just to get a fix of her new addiction," Rochon says. "So I really worked on her being untrusting, conniving and yet a fun partier much like typical street H-heads are."

Did you think we were done defining the terms of outlandish here? Silly reader! Two years before, Rochon had found herself undertaken by a devilish force drilled from the ground of her family's well in *Colour From the Dark*, adapting the legendarily evil writing "The Colour Out of Space" by H.P. Lovecraft. Rochon's afflicted Lucia suddenly mocks priests and burns down crucifixes with her eyes, and appears ready to bone-jump just about anything that walks by.

"Material like Lovecraft is always going to be full of symbolism," Rochon says. "It was actually harder to play the 'before' scenes, because I had to work on what it meant to be a simple, hardworking farmer's wife, which I knew nothing about. But if this was going to be believable, it was vital that I really played her sincerely and as realistic as possible which I did. So when she slowly slipped into being possessed by 'The Colour,' it became a different set of acting skills. To be possessed and not come off silly or hammy about it takes restraint. So I really worked on internal disconnect with the world and let the written word do its work."

It would be only fair to at least mention Rochon's non-horror work, and, yeah, we *could* talk about her portrayal of Eleanor of Aquitaine in 2015's *Richard the Lionhart: Rebellion*. But it would be *so* much more fun to discuss *Nowhere Man* (2005). Not just because of the film's balls-out (you'll see how painfully literal that term can be!) atmosphere, but because it reunited Rochon and Kaufman.

Conrad (Michael Rodrick) and Rochon's Jennifer are about to have the Hollywood wedding and fairytale marriage. They'll be living the dream life together, and, if Blue Oyster Cult was right about Romeo and Juliet, even maybe together in eternity.

Then comes a monkey wrench. Actually, it's more like an A-bomb strapped to an H-bomb with dynamite glued to the side.

Conrad happens upon a videotape of his wife's former life. She was long ago an adult film star, and he never knew. He's thirty-seven feet off his rocker.

Up to now, we have quite the sympathy for this character. Who wouldn't flip over and out upon finding out his fiancée used to mattress mambo on camera? But it's what Conrad does to her next that put us squarely on Jenn's side. Namely, every single kind of abuse.

"She is so repentant for this past mistake and begs for forgiveness in every way possible," Rochon says, "but he will have none of it."

Impersonating Lorena Bobbitt, whose genital mutilation of her husband made her a villain to men and a feminism hero, Jennifer goes downstairs with a knife and runs off into the night. But unlike Lorena, who had the common decency to toss her contraband out into the open in time for it to be found and reattached, Jennifer's a bit more vengeful. She has what every man lives for and too often thinks with, and she's not giving it back without a fight. Not just that, but her old porn pals are on her side, no doubt many of them having suffered similarly in the past. Desperately trying to hide his terror under fury, Conrad stumbles off into her old world and his new one. While the situation itself might be the epitome of horror for men, *Nowhere* was more about straddling the line between drama and midnight-black comedy.

"What an emotional ride this movie was to make," Rochon says. "Between shooting the rape scene and the fake porno scenes, and then all the highly emotional stuff in between, this took everything out of me. In a good way, in a way that is very satisfying as an actor. It was difficult to go to such deep emotional places, especially when he is abusing Jennifer, but I had to completely let go and let it all happen emotionally. If I had any resistance to being so vulnerable, I would not have been able to play the scenes."

But even after decades of attempts and hundreds of films, Rochon still cautions those looking to follow in her bloody footsteps. Acting's certainly not for everyone as a full profession, and horror performing, she expresses, is probably for even fewer.

"If actors are looking for a big break in mainstream work," she admits, "they should not do too much independent horror work. I am a huge fan of these films, so it may sound strange to say that. But in today's age, folks love to post compromising or naked pics of actors all over the Internet and a big company like Disney, for example, can't be associated with that. If you are not looking to work with Disney or its ilk and love horror as I do, then the best advice I can give is be choosey about what material you accept. It doesn't have to be a big or medium budget film, but the material is everything."

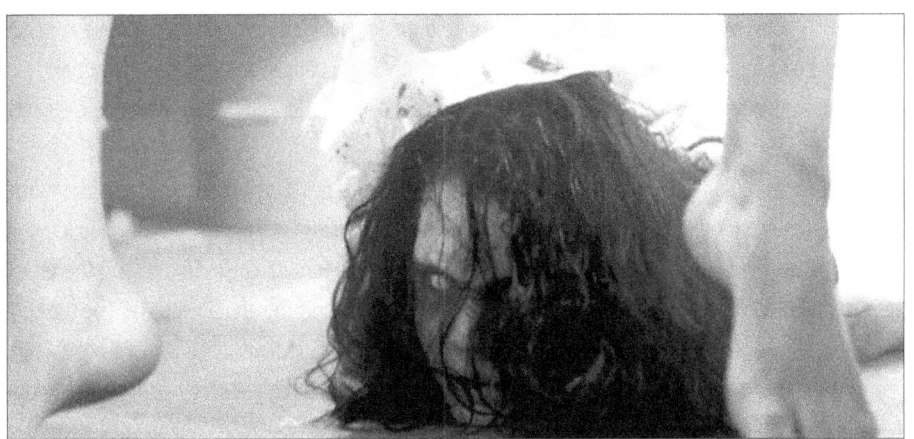

The devil contorted Rachele Brooke Smith into all kinds of shapes during 2013's *The Cloth*.

Perla Rodriguez/Rachele Brooke Smith:

The Cloth

EVEN WHEN DEALING with one of history's eternal mysteries, we can't be too careful.

Portraying a human possession of evil hadn't actually invited the Dark King (or Queen, or Knights, or whoever) into the bodies of those doing the performing, but let's remember that many of them, from *The Exorcist* (1973) to *The Exorcism of Emily Rose* (2005), had found their beginning basis in fact.

Preparing to take her place in one of the longer lines in Hollywood horror, Perla Rodriguez did everything in her praying power to ensure that what went before the cameras stayed there.

"I was terrified because of the dialogue," Rodriguez says of *The Cloth* (2013). "I'd say my prayers before I rehearsed my lines. I didn't really want to invoke something evil into my home, or myself. It's really a serious matter that really shouldn't be tampered with. I never took it as a joke."

But she didn't always feel that way about her artistic career. Right around kindergarten age, a family member inquired as to the youngster's career plans.

"I quietly responded 'I want to be a cartoon drawer,' with a giant smile from ear to ear," Rodriguez remembers. "My aunt responded, and my cousins giggled, 'A cartoon drawer? That's not a real job.' I understand what she meant, but I didn't care. The reality of that moment was that I enjoyed the stories and I wanted to make them."

With the help of a new CD, she soon was hard at work.

"One day I found a tool where you could put pictures together, add music, and your own words," she says. "I edited my first video then. At twelve, I did my first local commercial, but when the editor opened his editing room to show me where he worked, my heart skipped a beat. I saw my future."

As technology started to shift into overdrive across North American culture over the next few years, Rodriguez's passion went at about the same speed.

"At fourteen, I made movies, which are still in mini-VHS tapes. I would also compose the music and have it play back while recording. At fifteen, my parents bought me a webcam that had a green screen option. The way it worked was to have it record the motionless environment, and the green screen would fade in. Then you'd step into it, and since you're the only moving object, you'd be the only thing that wasn't green. I drew worlds and recorded myself dancing in them along with my best friend.

"At sixteen, they bought me my own mini-VHS camera, and I bought an interface where you can transfer the footage into the computer and edit with Windows Movie Maker. The fun was never ending."

She'd soon find a home on *YouTube*, putting together a parody video for a contest that won her a meeting with international tune sensation Shakira. Clearly, acting in front of bigger screens and better cameras was only Rodriguez's next natural step.

"It's safe to say that I initially became an actress for myself," she explains. "I have always been a quiet and soft-spoken girl, but the idea of performing was a magical rush. What it all comes down to is telling a story, through music, through dance, through words."

But when *The Cloth* yarn began to spin in 2012, Rodriguez was there to work off screen, producing behind the filming. Still, when the main woman didn't show, she was thrown into battle, from within and out.

She'd become Laurel, the film's object of affection for both the living and undead. Young Jason (Kyler Williett), a man angry at God for the tragic and violent theft of his family, gets pulled into the title organization, a Roman Catholic Church team with tabs on the ever-increasing number of dark minions spreading across the land. Laurel is their main woman, as even head fellow Father Tollman (Eric Roberts) is a secret bad guy.

"I read the sides they offered in the audition and gave the character the best piece of me to bring her to life," Rodriguez states of the character, who she finally won after a couple of quick callbacks.

"Give it all you have in the audition," she tells upcomers, "because they want to see if you can be a real person in a real situation. After that, have fun; it's all fake. Be a go-getter, don't be afraid to get messy. I don't think I became Laurel, I think I already was a lot like her, conservative-wise."

Her new form spent quite a bit of time checking over the Book of Sage, a Muslim writing about a man finding his totality in Islam.

"I chose to accept the idea that there are fallen angels roaming the world waiting for a chance to be a part of it again," Rodriguez says. "Again, I never took any of this a joke, and respected its boundaries. I did however do more research on the Catholic faith, prayers, saints, and demons." It was the last entry on the list that would be Laurel's true finale.

After flirting their way towards love through the first part of the film, Laurel, Jason, and the rest of the Cloth have battled one group of demons after another, helped along at times by an arrow-blasting crucifix that causes the afflicted to explode on contact. But it's just about over now, as Jason and a teammate go searching through some broken-down wreckage, looking for one's girl friend and another's girlfriend.

Then she's there, but nearly comatose, and we've seen enough possession films to know exactly what's being foreshadowed here. And we're right. Her eyes open, wider than any human should. She springs up, arms rocketing toward the sky. We can't tell if she's forcing power from her body, or welcoming the near feelings of ecstasy it brings. Laurel is the last chance Beelzebub has to destroy humanity—well, in this film—and perhaps taking control of one of its strongest weapons will empower him.

It certainly appears so; Laurel's superhuman telekinesis blasts the ceiling down and her former friends across the room. A last group of minions comes to attack, and Jason and the other fellow are just able to hold them off.

With his and her chances running out, Jason finally turns back to the faith he'd tried to leave behind, planting a cross on her forehead and spitting out more Latin. Just as he had a few decades before in *The Exorcist*, the demon tries to leave an innocent young woman for a priest nearby, but Jason takes care of that as well, and he and Laurel are finally free (again, unless there's a sequel).

Once again, she and Laurel appear to be following the same set of rules and Rodriguez continues to roll toward music stardom.

"Always work very hard, and surround yourself with the right people," she says of the trek. "The right people are the ones that will not let you fall when you are feeling down—they are the ones that will remind you about what you stand for. I was blessed to be surrounded with parents and family that always supported my silly ideas. Respect everyone, and be as helpful as you can. A movie is collaborative art where everyone works hard, where everyone works together."

The physical assistance was on in all *kinds* of abundance, and not for enhancement purposes for this role. The rehearsal was tough, and had been through and through. All that was left for her was a simple step towards stardom.

Literally, that's all Rachele Brooke Smith needed.

"After spending hours in special effects, make-up, hair, wardrobe," recalls the young actress, "I put a book on the floor and physically and symbolically stepped into the character of Julia." A technique she'd picked up in acting training, it gave her the final answer to a question so many before her have pondered in film history: how can I show others what a demonic possession *looks* like?

Well, her way was pretty straightforward . . . actually, let's not hit that just yet. Quite a bit more to build up to this.

As anyone who saw *The Cloth* can attest, Smith's role filled her with physicality up to her forehead. But that was nothing new—gymnastics were her childhood jumping-off point in this regard.

However, after an injury put her on the sidelines as her teenage years got going, the youngster saw her future on the big screen. The story of a group of hopefuls looking to make it in one of the toughest areas in entertainment history, *Center Stage* (2000) concluded with a few teens (including Zoë Saldana, years away from *Avatar*) hitting the nationwide platforms of ballet.

In the seats, a certain middle-schooler knew she'd found a new goal, though hardly a surefire way of reaching it.

"I had this overwhelming experience where I sat in the theater after everyone had left," Smith recalls, "and I just cried and committed to myself that I was going to do that with my life: I was going to be that girl up on that screen that inspired me so much! I know then and there I wanted to act, dance, sing, and inspire the world!"

How many have started out in acting with such a mindset? Plenty. But considering how many follow through, the digits drop at high speed. Fortunately, Smith was one that stuck fast.

Along with the gymnastics, she rolled through all kinds of dance style. She stepped from performing to music to actually making it. Many see activities like skiing, surfing, and rock climbing as recreational; she used them as part of the potential job.

"I want to be ready for anything and everything that a role might call for," she says. "The more skills sets you have, the more opportunities you will have for roles, and the more full your life will be."

Nearly a decade after seeing others take *Center Stage*, she led out its 2008 sequel *Turn it Up*, playing a dancer who starts things out seeing her dreams for induction into America's top ballet studio dashed, only to make it to Broadway just before the closing credits.

"If I would not have had a dance background, I could have never landed my first lead role in a film, or any other dance-related role," she guesses. "*Center Stage* also called for me to do everything from point to breakdancing, and most dancers are only trained in one or another specific type of dance, so being one of the most versatile dancer/actresses helped my chances of booking the role dramatically."

And several others in the same vein: she made dancing music alongside Cher and Christina Aguilera in *Burlesque* (2010), a group of rodents in *Alvin and the Chipmunks 2* (2009), and Robert Downey Jr. in *Iron Man 2* (2010), not to mention buffing up to help Lea Michelle's Rachel Berry act out a Britney Spears fantasy on *Glee* (2009).

Still, *The Cloth* would provide a new challenge for the non-horror fan. Such films "usually freak me out too much and I suffer from horrible nightmares," Smith admits. "However, oddly enough, they are really fun to act in."

Her Julia was the first gal *The Cloth* fans would see. In flashbacks to the landmark *Exorcist*, a veteran priest (Danny Trejo, FAR from Max von Sydow), stumbles about, searching for a way to extricate the dark forces from the young woman on a nearby bed, her lovely features slowly giving way to possession, her voice deepening to near Vincent Price levels.

"I watched some other great performances from actresses that played similar roles and really tried to tap into my inner 'demons,'" Smith says of the question we pondered back at the beginning. "I think we all have things as people we would never do or say, but on some level would absolutely love to experience what it would feel like if we did. And in playing Julia I got to do exactly that."

As another, younger priest roars in to help his mentor, Smith started twisting Julia into contortionist shapes audiences hadn't seen since Bonnie Morgan's scene-stealing work in 2011's *Devil Inside* (much tougher than the book-step she'd taken to reach character to begin with!). Overcome by the possessor's evil, the older priest falls, much like Sydow's Father Merrin. Fortunately, his protégé has a secret weapon—a supergun disguised as a cross, which he uses to blast Julia to bits.

"The magic of moviemaking is such a passion of mine and I think will always fascinate me!" Smith says. "I have such admiration for people that do special effects. It is such an amazing skill and talent that I think is somewhat underappreciated, especially due to how much time and energy it takes to make it look good!"

Tara the Terrifying Wolf Girl (Victoria Sanchez) in 2001's *Wolf Girl* often felt the very emotion she instilled in so many audiences.

Victoria Sanchez:

Wolf Girl

THE TIMING OF this next piece was the key to starting it; if I'd tried to write this a year ago, like as part of my first book, it probably wouldn't have worked.

Having just finished watching the fourth season of *American Horror Story* (2014-5), I, along with millions of other lucky horror TV fans, got a taste of how the others live during the "Freak Show" atmosphere that told the Season Four *Story*. It's not as common today as it once was, but people labeled "freaks" by society—almost always stuck in afflictions over which they have not the slightest control—are still found by carnival goers willing to search hard enough.

People pay to see them, and audiences may not be necessarily disrespectful, often gazing in wonder, even admiration, of the performers. Still, what would we do if we encountered one in public life? The thought of actually befriending one, getting to know them, standing next to them in everyday society, is just about impossible to consider.

Story gave us an inside look at such a show from within, showing us the sad, ignorant world in which the "freaks" live, often left with nothing but each other for comfort and friendship. It's the only world that the title character in 2001's *Wolf Girl* had ever known, and, to become her, Victoria Sanchez had to find her own way inside.

She started off by looking beneath the features that had made Tara the main attraction of her circus—issues that ravage many people, particularly young women, who have never been near a freak show.

"What appealed to me the most about playing Tara and *Wolf Girl*," Sanchez remembers, "was that I felt a deep and strong affiliation to her and the story, an unexplainable understanding of someone feeling completely lost in their own skin. Uncomfortable, confused, unloved, that typical teenager feeling of not fitting in. There was also the fact that I had always been fascinated by oddities, and the truly unique people of this world."

But there was still the manner of bringing in the gal's involuntarily animalistic side. For a few months, Sanchez roared (pun *completely* intended!) through the worlds of her favorite animals, two- or four-legged.

"I have always loved wolves: their acute sensitivity, their loyalty, and their loneliness," she says. "I also trained with professional circus performers to learn how to act and move like a wolf. I researched everything I could about oddities, hypertricosis, wolves, and travelling road shows."

That H-word she just mentioned? It's also called Ambras syndrome, and, too often, simply titled werewolf syndrome. It causes abnormal hair to grow all over the body. Some sufferer only find various areas of their body afflicted; others, like Tara, are coated all over.

Sanchez even chatted with a teenager girl with the condition, living in the same traveling road show life that Tara had been all but forced into.

"She was from South America, and was seventeen years old at the time," she recalls. "Lilly was grateful that I reached out to her and that I was trying to get information on what it was really like to be part of a road show."

But with a shot at normalcy that few of her colleagues are even given, Tara finds a new friend whose scientist mom is hard at work on a drug that will make her hair fall out—few women would even conceive of that, but, then again, as seriously as ladies take their haircare, few of them are in her position!

"I almost lost my sanity working twenty hours a day in extremely uncomfortable prosthetic makeup (hair!)," says Sanchez, who sometimes spent nine hours in makeup alone, "and the pictures of me as a hairy woman probably freaked out every producer who ever thought of casting me in anything at all. But I have absolutely no regrets about playing Tara the Terrifying Wolf Girl. I would do it all over again, if I had to."

Searching desperately to break into the "real" world—people who live in freak shows would probably be unpleasantly surprised at how confusing and terrifying this place can be!—Tara secretly starts taking the drug. But there's a reason it's not on the open market: the meds cause her mind to resemble the character that audiences see from the outside, and soon things spin violently out of control.

Soon enough, Sanchez and the rest of the *Wolf* crew could identify: filming in Romania's freezing cold Shagov forests, everyone clung desperately to humanity.

"I would have to stand up in a jumping jack pose for hours on end," Sanchez says. "The water was well below zero and I had to act like it was warm . . . The makeup was glued on, and almost impossible to remove without feeling like a mosquito bait tape. My legs would literally stick together, and I had to almost rip my skin off to unglue myself. I highly doubt any other actress would have come out of that shoot with any sanity left. I was surprised that I did."

Enough so that, the same year, she played the bad girl on a much smaller, family friendly scale. A decade after the first two *Neverending Story* films had hit the big screen, the fantastic tale of Fantasia made it to the small ones in *Tales from the Neverending Story* (2011). Sanchez became Xayide, the sorceress with an outside as gorgeous as her heart is black. Apparently having recovered from the explosion that took her out at the end of *Neverending Story II* (1990), Xayide was now the sister of Audrey Gardiner's Childlike Empress, trying to steal Fantasia from her banished home of Dark City (Mark Rendall became the new portrayer of main *Story* man Bastian).

Despite being a huge fan of the first *Neverending Story* flick ("I mean, who isn't?" Sanchez rhetorically ponders) back in 1994, she hadn't seen Clarissa Burt play Xayide in Part II, and unlike with Tara, she stayed away from the books and interviews this time around.

"I brought my own interpretation of the character, and decided to base (Xayide) loosely on Gloria Swanson's role in *Sunset Boulevard* (1950)," Sanchez explains. "I felt she had to be animated, dramatic, big. I loved my costumes, hair, and makeup, and, most of all, riding my big black horse. She had to put on a mask to hide what remained of her scarred heart. Xayide once was a good person, but she got hurt, emotionally hurt. She was always cast aside by her parents, who clearly favored her little sister over her, to whom they handed over Fantasia. Xayide was forced to create an imaginary world of her own, in which she lost herself, and created her own empire."

In 2004, Sanchez got a chance to hand out an updated version of the horrors of true crime. As a detective searches for his missing wife in the first minutes of *Eternal* (2004), he stumbles upon a rich lady named Elizabeth Kane and her maid Irina. Falling under the looks and aura that Kane exudes, he misses the local body count that keeps rising, the secrets from her past that he desperately wants to ignore, and her connection to one of the world's most prolific serial slaughterers—the Countess Elizabeth Bathory herself.

With Caroline Neron in the protagonist(ess) role, Sanchez was Irinia, acting out the film that her brother Fererico had written and helped direct.

Bathory killed hundreds of virgin girls to bathe in their blood, which she believed would keep her young. Researching her, Sanchez found that those methods might just have been more effective than anyone ever wanted to admit.

"Apparently even at the age of fifty-two, when she died, she looked surprisingly youthful," she says. "To know that a woman like that lived in this world in the 1600s, and got away with doing what she did, was incredible to me. The way I chose to play Irina was feeding on that fascination. If a girl like Irina did what she did, it was obviously due to a mental illness, a deep fear, and an obsession of some kind."

Just as with almost every career, knowing what to avoid can be just as helpful as trying something new, especially in acting. Sanchez has seen things from both sides.

"In the case of a young actress, I would say never to play a hairy girl!" she laughs. "I say to keep in shape both physically and mentally, because it's a strenuous job in every sense. And my biggest piece of advice would probably be, if you are not passionate for the art, you are wasting your time. But if you truly love acting, and if you can handle the instability of the film business, don't be afraid to take risks, don't be afraid of failure and rejection, don't worry about the competition . . . just dive into it to the fullest, and don't forget to have fun!"

Writing, directing, producing, acting in and out—for 2013's *The Devil's Rook*, it's easier to count the things James Sizemore *didn't* do.

James Sizemore:

The Demon's Rook

YOU EXPECT TO get scared in a horror film. You hope for it. You want it. A horror film that *doesn't* scare you? Its job's not done! We should just give up and go watch PBS or something.

But there's another aspect of the genre of which we shouldn't be afraid. We can't be afraid. Because this is our chance to show that we can do this, that we're skilled enough to become a part of horror.

That's where taking a risk comes in, and it comes hard! Taking a shot. Looking at the gap between what we have and what we want, and bridging it ourselves, rather than sitting around and hoping some other creative construction engineer walks by.

Why let someone else get your credit? Grab it yourselves, and hope it becomes worth something, more than enough to step through a door you had the guts to open!

Join the group of those who tried to chart their own course in a world that doesn't always respect creativity—every writer, painter, sculptor, filmmaker, everyone who ever dared to cross the line between real and hope. And people like James Sizemore have done it in more than one way.

"For years, I told my stories through paintings," he remembers, "but after working as an actor and key makeup effects artist for a haunted house, I realized I had the potential to move my stories to the screen. Every night working in the haunted house, I'd make up all these monsters, and then once I was done, I'd dress myself up as a crazy person and join in on the scaring." Like many who've worked in that area, Sizemore's cosmetic experience pushed him to dream of moving to the next level. Not just helping others look good (actually, making them look satisfyingly terrifying!) and putting on a seconds-long performance, but moving up and out in entertainment—up to the movies, and out to a full-length flick.

Unlike most, though, Sizemore didn't stop at only *hoping* and *wishing* these things would occur.

"Even when I was a child, my friends and I would make little shorts on my parents' VHS camcorder," he remembers. "I wasn't allowed to watch horror movies as a kid, which made my fascination for them even stronger. The adrenaline rush alone from being scared shitless is what really hooked me."

Could he send it through someone else? Rhetorical question; many of us *can*. Whether he would try, however, was a question that all too commonly gets the wrong answers. Our own creativity, or, to be more blunt, our *fucking guts*, sometimes just have to be our biggest weapon. That's a lesson that many have taken upon themselves to learn, in almost every aspect of performing, not just horror. There's never anything wrong with asking for help to make it in the film world, but sometimes, well, you just have to reach out and hope to hit gold.

And Sizemore struck out in more places than Medusa's hairstyle. He wrote a screenplay, headed up the special effects, directed, filmed, and produced something weirdly titled *The Demon's Rook*—apparently, entities play Bobby Fischer's game too. If cloning were in full force yet, he'd have probably played the entire cast!

Well, maybe not—all the makeup and prosthetics in Hollywood couldn't have turned him into the flick's first protagonist. Kids being what they are and what they imagine, young Roscoe's visited at night by the demonic Dimwos, complete with the ominous horns and beard that's never truly "out" in underworld fashion.

But Roscoe doesn't jump under the covers or call for Mommy; this thing's actually the closest figure to a father he has. Soon he decides that the backyard portal's a preferable living spot than his home, and leaves what little he has behind.

Things go OK for a few decades. But eventually, much like Anakin Skywalker did, Roscoe realizes that he can't express something beautiful in his status.

Love. Not for Anakin's Padme, but for a little lady named Eva he grew up with. Like the kid who'd be Vader, Roscoe rebels against his mentor and runs off—or rather, up!—into a world he couldn't even remotely comprehend, on the hunt for his old and slightly younger flame.

Now Sizemore could add the rank of flick protagonist to his résumé, although a debuting Emmett Eckert had played the character's youth form.

"Emmett was a natural," Sizemore says. "He was a quick learner and fun to work with. He seemed to get the most excited when we brought out the demons." Sizemore had more of his share of the burden to lug around.

"Acting was the most challenging for me," he explains. "I don't really consider myself an actor, but

I couldn't find anyone else that would be willing to grow his beard and hair out and shoot with me on the weekends without pay for two and a half years. So I just had to do it."

Like he didn't already have enough. For over two years, usually for only two days a week, the remaining time usually deemed for rest, Sizemore and a tiny group of helpers told the story of Roscoe, the man he becomes, the girl he loves, the demons he brings with him, and the war he starts.

Yep—while Roscoe's trying to win back his youthful love Eva, three darkhearts from below followed him up, and they're ready to slaughter. That's just what zombies and monsters do.

One's an indestructible brawler, who shows his fatality-causing skills to several unsuspectings. The other, the only lady, mind-screws others into doing the serial murderous deeds that can't get her clawed hands dirty.

And another has the possessing power to . . . get gorgeous women to suddenly feel the urge to bare it all and worship him! OK, so there might be some upsides to the whole non-human thing.

"We did the movie one hundred percent practical," Sizemore exclaims, "which was so great, because I could see the special effects occurring as we filmed the scene. We knew right then and there if it was going to look good or bad. Making films practical is just so much more fun. The actors get to respond to actual monsters, as opposed to a flying tennis ball on a green screen." On an even bigger upside for him, the lady who played Roscoe's rock became Mrs. Ashleigh Jo Sizemore during filming.

"I did more than most people realize for preparation," he continues. "Since my character was supposed to have lived in a cave for the past fifteen years or so, I kept myself out of the sun as much as possible so that I'd be pale and look more the part. To add to the effect, I also maintained long hair and a huge beard for those two and a half years of filming on the weekends." He and Eva manage to knock back some of the bad guys, but, back to the *Star Wars* analogy, they don't have a happily ever after ending either. . . .

With the cameras rolling for so long, we might expect a ten-hour miniseries or something. But this is a monster movie, and the typical such audience attention span isn't quite so long. That's just the way it works when a group of people, all so new to the business, get together and try to make a difference on their own.

"I had no assistant director and a very small crew, so we all had to wear a ton of hats," Sizemore asserts. "I basically just had to bounce in and out of my character while filming. It was tough. I probably wouldn't choose to act a leading role again. But making your first feature is a huge learning experience, especially for someone like me who didn't go to film school or anything." With a goal out of sight, one that nearly everyone involved at one time or another thought unobtainable, the *Rook* crew demonstrated a tactic shared by everyone who's even sniffed success in the acting field—an inability to just give the hell up and go home.

But the end result became a lesson: a pitch-black terrifying film was a shining example to those who haven't quite worked up enough reasons in or out to try. It made it. They made it. In 2013, *Rook* slipped into distribution, to one festival after another, enough to take home some strong critical reviews in the bargain. Because one of the best offerings of the film world is the respect that those on the inside, as well as the audience, have for the sort of fortitude that the crew showed. You work your ass off and back on until the finish line is crossed, and people will be there to greet you—and they'll respect that you did what you could with whatever little you had. Experience, money, education—these things aren't always what makes a mark in horror cinema.

"Don't be afraid to get bloody, and throw your passion into it a hundred percent," Sizemore tells those who are where he and the *Rook* group began. "Even if you're not that good at acting, at least it'll look like you're having fun. Just taking a shower at the end of the day in order to wash off all the blood was a fun experience. You had to get down and dirty, and we all loved that."

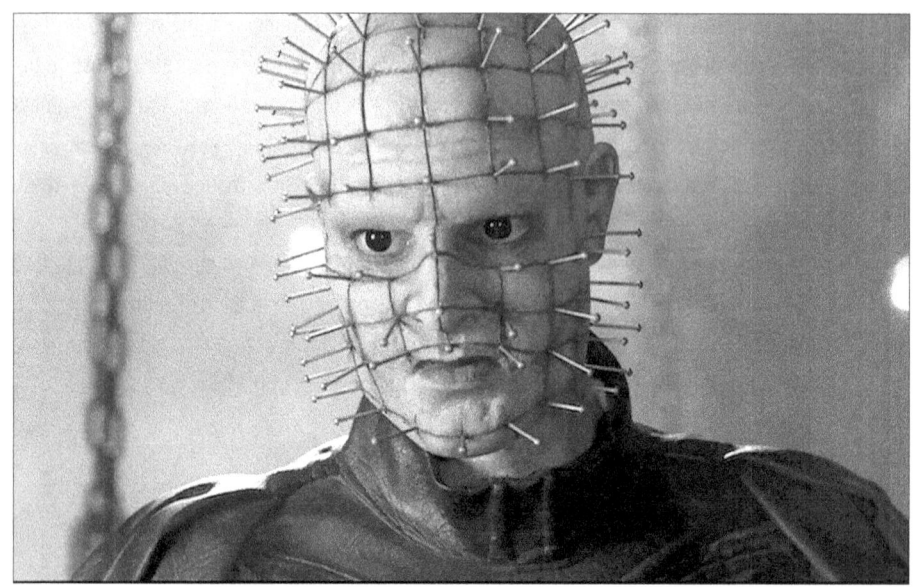

Doug Bradley may have established the Pinhead tradition in the *Hellraiser* series, but Stephan Smith Collins carried it on in *Revelations* of 2011.

Stephan Smith Collins:

Hellraiser: Revelations

Ever wonder what it's like for the second-stringers of the sports world? Imagine backing up the greatest athletes the world has ever seen. Think about what it must have been like for the men who watched Michael Jordan, Wayne Gretzky, Joe Montana, and so many others play out their careers from the closest seats in the house, even if it meant sitting on the bench.

And now, consider the scariest, and yet still most exciting moment for a second-in-command in the sports world: the times when those fellows decided to call it quits. Seeing them take the farewell tour—and knowing, in the back of our minds, that we'd have to follow in their footsteps, trying to even reach, let alone clear, a higher bar than had ever been set before.

That's the kind of situation upon that Stephan Smith Collins found himself; after watching Doug Bradley raise all kinds of hell as Pinhead through nearly two decades' worth of *Hellraiser* films, Smith Collins was being asked to don the spikes.

However, up to nearly the minute he snared the part, even the actor was unaware of his new commitment.

"I'll never forget seeing the original *Hellraiser* when I was a kid," Smith Collins recalls of the 1987 film. "It was the first horror film I remember seeing and it terrified me! Pinhead was the most disturbing character I had ever seen—still is, actually."

A quarter-century later, Smith Collins was delighted at the irony of getting a shot at his first horror role.

"When I saw I had an audition for *Hellraiser: Revelations*, I about passed out with excitement," he recalls of the 2011 tale. "For the audition, I had no idea I was auditioning for the role of Pinhead, as the producers didn't want the public to know that the incomparable Doug Bradley was sitting this one out. You prepare for auditions by learning how to create a character with confidence that no one else could create it, as no one else is you."

Informed he'd be trying out for the role of Pinhead's own cenobite assistant (as was everyone else at the audition), Smith Collins got called back for a wardrobe test that night.

"Honestly, this meeting seemed like a scene from a horror film," Smith Collins says. "Walking into the warehouse, I saw everything *Hellraiser*: blood, guts, and gore galore—including a life-sized model of Pinhead himself."

He stepped into several outfits, including the legendary Pinhead regalia. Then Mike Reagan, gearing up to direct the film's special effects, asked if he could make a cast of Collins' face.

"He warned me that it would take over an hour," Smith Collins says, "and that once the plaster had been applied, my head would be encased in plaster with my mouth and eyes essentially glued shut, with small straws placed in my nostrils so I could breathe and small holes at my ears so I could hear." Many actors of every genre have a paid such a price and higher, and he eagerly agreed.

With his head encased in plastic, Smith Collins heard something he'd hoped for for decades, but not completely expected.

"(He) said 'So you must be pretty stoked to be playing Pinhead.'

"I panicked. I was thinking 'He's got the wrong guy! He's making a cast of the wrong face!' I started waving my arms and hands around, trying to tell him something was wrong. (He) thought I was getting claustrophobic. He started saying things like 'It's OK. Just relax. Breathe through your nose.' Because my eyes and mouth were glued shut, there was nothing I could do but wait until he was finished before I told him that he was casting the wrong face."

Soon enough, Smith Collins was sent to his cell phone.

"I realized I had turned off the ringer at the audition and forgot to turn it back on," he says. "When I pulled the phone out of my bag, I saw I had missed several phones calls both from casting and my agents. Yup, I was going to be playing Pinhead. Again, I nearly passed out." Indeed, there would be a new spike-headed representation of the underworld this time around, and Collins had gotten the call far, far from glory.

As had been the case when Bradley had originated the story back in 1987, Pinhead and his friends from way down where weren't in the film much, at least until the end. In self-filmed mode for a while, *Revelations* (2011) starts by discussing two youths who went down to Mexico and never returned. A video shows their inadvertent killing of a woman, but there's something else in their collection of returned belongings that's a bit more interesting to a sister of one guy, named Steven: an ominous-looking box that any *Hellraiser* fan will recognize.

Playing with the box, the sister suddenly finds her bro resurrected, but he's far from himself, covered in blood and babbling something about . . . *cenobites*?

Things go from uncertain to terrifying at high speed, as Steven suddenly blasts his dad with a shotgun and holds the rest of the family hostage, waiting for something. . . .

Another flashback shows that Steven's friend Nico diddled with the box just enough to open it wide, wide so that a select group could venture out of it, out of Hell, and visit Earth. The group, led by Pinhead, offers Nico a chance to feel a pleasure greater than anything in this universe, if he's just willing to walk through Hell first.

He agrees, but cenobites aren't always of their word, yanking him away and ripping off his skin, leaving him desperate for a chance to return. But the only way is for Steven to kill more women and feed him their blood, another plot flashback to the original flick.

Steven's not the type, so Nico kills him and takes his skin. Yes, it's him that just shot the dad—he just *looks* like Steven. Now he's got Steven's sister working on the box, hoping to trade her to those inside, that they'll let him live in return. But again, things don't go his way, and Pinhead and the gang are back.

"As an actor, I wanted to pay homage to the character that had found its way into so many nightmares including my own," Smith Collins says, "but I also wanted to try to make certain elements of Pinhead my own. Like James Bond, any actor who takes on playing 007 is taking on the challenge of living up to his predecessor. And even though every actor is bringing their own style and unique perspective to the role, the character is engrained into the fans' mind. Such is the case with Pinhead. I guess I'm the George Lazenby of Pinheads." Of the six actors who've played the world's greatest secret agent, as of 2016, Lazenby is the only one to do it just once (not counting David Niven in the 1967 spoof *Casino Royale*), appearing only in *On Her Majesty's Secret Service* of 1969.

"Clive Barker is to be credited with creating the role, and Doug Bradley is to be credited as bringing that incredible character to life in such a way as to become iconic," Smith Collins says. "In many ways, I was simply borrowing the character for *Revelations*."

But Pinhead doesn't just borrow souls, as Nico finds out the hardest of ways. He's got the strictest of no-return policies, ready to take Nico instead of the sister. Pinhead's eternal chain weapons roar from the walls, ensnaring the youth.

Before the cenobites can leave, however, the father gets revenge, blasting Nico away with his own gun. He can't know what a mistake it was—now Pinhead, angrier now than we ever (or at least rarely) saw him in Bradley's world, can't take his original victim alive. With the father on death's door, now he has to take Steven's mom.

The chains come back, the mother's captured, and the cenobites take her down. Her dad finally dies, and the sister's all alone—but she's still got the box. The *Hellraiser* saga looks to continue.

Jolene Andersen showed that lady cenobites can play just as dirty as the men in *Hellraiser: Revelations* (2011).

Off set, Smith Collins' work had been just about as tough as Nico's. "In my world, it was about the hours that went into applying the makeup and prosthetics that create Pinhead," he says. "All in all, it took about three hours every day to become Pinhead and about two hours to get back into my own skin, so to speak. But as long as you're doing what you love, you're in for an incredible ride."

Unlike Jason, Michael, and Freddy, Pinhead doesn't make it a habit of working alone. Bradley's creation wasn't there by himself for several of his first forays, and Smith Collins' man wouldn't have it any differently.

And while it's far past impossible to imagine a cenobite having much use for physical attraction, let alone love—you can't help but think that their reproductive habits are probably similar to the ones that Spock and the rest of the Vulcans painfully suffered through in the pon farr activities!—Pinhead seemed to, in some crazy way, always enjoy the company of a pretty lady; several supporting gals have shown up in cenobite form throughout the *Hellraiser* tales. In *Revelations*, Jolene Andersen got the new chance to play the pinned man's top hench(wo)man.

Although she *may* have dressed as one of the first cenobites during a trick-or-treating outing at some point, Andersen's career was rolling far before she decided to commence scaring.

"It started when I was really young," she remembers. "I always loved pretending. I loved stories and read a lot of books as a kid. I always had a wild imagination. I'm a very sensitive person, and it was easy for me to see and think my way through things. Bringing stories to life was very fascinating to me, which is probably why I ended up as an actor."

After spending a decade's worth of weekends in the theaters of New Jersey (though she's originally from Namibia), Andersen finally snared her own chance to perform, ironically as a dead woman in the 2003 thriller *Ocean Buzz*.

"I always loved horror films," she says. "I was really attracted to the weird and scary; I always had a thing for things that are kind of sick and wrong. I just find these stories and their characters so interesting, because they're kind of abnormal and so much fun to work on. It's different from watching them because you really get to be a part of all the things that you love: the gory effects, the costumes, everything."

As Pinhead and his not-so-merry band arrive on the strange new world of Earth, we see someone new lurking in the background. Her (or Its, depending on one's views) kind is called the chatterer for a reason—there are no eyes, a weird-looking cranium, only a small mouth filled with teeth that horrifyingly live up to the character's name. We've seen these creatures before in *Hellraiser* lore, but, if only based on the build, we can tell that there's something new: the chatterer's a lady.

Learning she might just have a shot at snaring the role, Andersen rushed around, checking out a few previous *Hellraiser* flicks, particularly the work of Barbie Wilde, Sarah Hayward, and others that had played Pinhead's female colleagues.

"It was really cool that the character was a woman," Andersen says. "When I went in for my fit in the costuming, I loved that they had her in this very sexy, S+M-type bondage outfit. For the casting, they wanted her to be really tall with this strong foreboding presence, and I loved that they wrapped this all into a woman. There's something about a female evil character that I really love. It goes against type. I like to see women be evil, be ruthless."

Still, the same sort of imagination that had helped Barker, Bradley, and others form Pinhead's tales, the same one that had carried him and his cronies to one of the longest-running epics in American film history, the creativity that brought together the balance between good and evil, Earth and hell, real and supernatural, turned out to be perhaps her biggest weapon (or asset, shall we say).

"These kinds of roles aren't too difficult to tap into, once you see the breakdown and you get a glimpse of what's interesting," says Andersen. "Your character is already written. You've got a character description, and it's very colorful. Then you go to the audition and you talk to the director and you go further with it and see what vision you have for the character.

"Then you go to the costuming and the special effects and those guys and you talk more about it. It's a big collaborative experience. When you go to sets, it's amazing that they've built this gory, creepy world. When you're in costume and on set, I don't find it very difficult at all to tap into it and just go for it. What I love about horror characters, especially evil characters, is that feeling that the sky's the limit. You have this freedom, like the whole world is created around you."

The new world wouldn't be the only thing around her, and in more than one kind of sense.

"I had to put my body into a glove," she equates of the chatterer's look. "It was difficult to be inside that mask and those clothes. Her mask, without a nose and with this little slit eyes. It was difficult to feel, to be disconnected from everyone around me. I had a team of people leading me around, telling me to breathe, keeping me calm. It got painful, confined, uncomfortable, a creepy place with blood and hooks hanging everywhere. I'd take a nap on a bed with blood all over it where everyone had died. You go to a dark place when you're stuck there for twelve or fourteen hours. It all lends itself to what's happening."

That ended up being quite a bit for the flick's two main women: Andersen's monster manhandles the sister throughout, effortlessly shoving her around while the other cenobites do their thing.

"It's a very physical thing," Andersen says. "You tap into your body. I loved that she was this big, silent, brooding thing with all this energy. Bringing the strengths to this character who isn't afraid of anyone, to what this monster is and how it would feel, you tap into the physicality of the character."

Once again, the humans all either die or are abandoned. The series' infamous box is shut, but the door is wide open for a *Re-Revelation*!

"I like it when everything's left in a big mess, without a happy ending." Andersen says. "You have no control, and you usually get defeated. It all goes wrong. When you have monsters and you have the supernatural and you have things that you can't explain and that you don't have any power over, when the bad guy is all powerful, I always found that so fascinating creatively. It tested the limits of the human psyche, when the whole universe was your playground. You can go anywhere with it."

Decades after Sissy Spacek (left) almost won an Oscar for playing Carrie White in 1976, Chloe Moretz followed in her terrifyingly bloody footsteps in 2013.

Sissy Spacek:

Carrie

WHEN WE CAN terrify a fellow who himself has induced millions to sleep with the light on, we've done our job at film fearing.

Over the next few decades, it would become a common occurrence for Stephen King. Sitting in a theater in the mid-1970s, however, this was a feeling of newness.

For the first time ever, the man who would set the standard for American horror writing was seeing his words brought to visual demonstration.

He watched the title character of one of his first literary creations get tortured by almost everyone. Her classmates, her teachers, even her own mother made this young woman's life a living hell.

But one day, it's all too much. One day (prom night, actually), she, in a victory for every bullied introvert everywhere, gets her slaughtering revenge on everyone who tormented her—and, for good measure, even a few that didn't. Unfortunately, her life is also lost, and many are joyed because of it.

In the film's final scene, we see one of the few people who didn't completely despise the girl walking up to the incinerated site of the victim's former home, marked subtly with a cross.

She leans over, willing to be one of the only ones to offer a peace offering, a final goodbye to a soul that few ever took the time to see the good inside of.

But she's not completely gone. As one of the most ominous tunes since the shower scene from *Psycho* hits, the victim reaches up from under the ground and beyond the grave, desperately reaching out for one last grasp at happiness, trying to hold on to one of the few good things in her life, one of the only people, the only things, that ever gave her anything but pain.

As the hand latches onto the visitor, she goes straight into hysterics—and good Lord, who wouldn't?—and we see that it was all in the subconscious; she's back in bed at home, in her mother's arms, temporarily, at least, far on the wrong side of mental stability.

In the audience, the man who invented the story was terrified by his own creation.

"I knew it was coming," King says of the last scene of 1976's *Carrie*, "and still felt as though I'd swallowed a snowcone whole."

After hitting it big in the supporting aspect with her role as a teenage murderess in *Badlands* in 1973, Sissy Spacek grabbed for another chance to scare audiences in a less realistic, but miles more over-the-top manner. Her husband Jack Fisk had gotten a job on Brian DePalma's new film, and De-Palma had mentioned that there might be a spot for Fisk's lady in front of the camera.

Spacek got her hands on King's novel, which had hit bookstores in 1974.

"I read it and got all into it," Spacek says of the book. "Two weeks later, (DePalma's) secretary called and said they wanted me to come in and read for it." She and Fisk acted out some scenes from the script.

Then de Palma decided to needle her a tad, telling her that another actress was the frontrunner for the role.

"It made me . . . really mad," Spacek says. "He was in essence saying, 'You don't have a chance, babe.' Hrrrrr, I'll show *him*."

With Vaseline in her hair, and wearing a pale blue sailor dress her mother had made for her in middle school ("I got all frumpy," she explains. "I looked like a total dork, and that was the point."), Spacek, nearly a decade out of high school, came in to try out for the role.

"The makeup people grabbed me as I walked in and said, 'Hey, we've got to work on you,' but I convinced them not to," she recalls. "I was told later that day that I'd gotten the part."

Unable to call upon her own past for the "social outcast" role (she'd grown up cheerleading and taking home the Homecoming Queen honor in Quitman, a small Texas town), Spacek looked instead to someone she'd known for inadvertent inspiration.

"She was from a poor family and wore weird clothes, but she was really beautiful," she explains.

"People made fun of her, but not as much as they did of Carrie. Dorothy filled the space in my class that Carrie did in hers, and I based a lot of the character on her. I tried to get friendly with her in school. She called me Elizabeth (Sissy's given name—the nickname came from her brothers) and we sat together in class. I did it out of curiosity to know what a person like that was like, and she was really neat. We just sort of had this little friendship that was apart from my other friends. At the end of the year, she wrote in my yearbook, 'Elizabeth, you're always so nice to me.' The words were misspelled, but I was really devastated, because our friendship had meant something to her."

We in the audience learn early on that Carrie's not exactly the most popular, outgoing girl in school. Sheltered from real life by her psycho-religious mother Margaret (Piper Laurie), Carrie's been taught, in a nutshell, that the human body is filthy, that humanity is evil, and that sexual love, even affection, doesn't exist. But she gets the worst of wakeup calls at the worst of times.

An early shower scene helped Spacek draw the line between nudity and sexuality, as Carrie experiences her first period in the midst of a post-gym class shower—she goes to Bates High School, a nod to another cinematic maternally ruined nut—and her classmates let her have it (the scene "was like getting hit by a mack truck," Spacek says).

"I knew it had to be horrendous and bigger than life," she recalls. "She had to give the girls a motive for being so weird. I used an etching from the Bible of a guy getting stoned to death." Her bugged-out eyes are introduced here and reappear throughout the film, never more prominent than in Carrie's final rampage.

"When the blood hits," Spacek explains, "it's almost like (Carrie) looks up to God. It's coming from the heavens, and that's where God lives. I wanted subtle touches like this."

There's another foreshadowing effect moments later: as Carrie strolls home, wearing the same dress that Spacek wore to her audition, a bratty snot-nose rolls up behind her on his bike. But he's suddenly thrown off the sidewalk and off balance, careening into an injury. Casting a darkly curious glance his way, Carrie lets us know that she had something secret to do with the "accident."

Soon we meet Margaret, and find that Carrie's by far the most stable woman in her family, with her mama ranting about the wrath of a God we should all be terrified of and smacking her around at every turn.

Unlike Spacek, Laurie didn't really have to worry about first impressions with acting; she was fifteen years past an Oscar-nominated performance alongside Paul Newman in *The Hustler*. But like Spacek eventually would with her character, she went all the way with Margaret, and then went a little farther.

"I wanted it to be raw," recalls Laurie, brought out of retirement for the role. "My take on Margaret's confession to her daughter is very different than how it was written in the script."

But despite Carrie's oft-sad, defeatist visage and slouched, introverted body movements, Spacek decided not to go too far with her pain—and it made her appear even more of a depressing character, as we know that the suffering Carrie felt at home and in school is now a sad state of normalcy.

"We played down the crying," Spacek says. "I didn't want Carrie to be a little wimp who cried all the time. So anytime she cried, it was like bottling it in. There was never any release; she would cry but always push it back, so that she was like a time bomb all the time. Finally, it all comes out and she explodes." That's one of the final scenes, but we're nowhere near that point just yet.

First, we've got to talk about the preparation that Spacek utilized throughout filming, subscribing to the same techniques that those making a horror flick often employ—as in, practicing self-sequestration from her co-stars.

"I hid out in my dressing room a lot," Spacek remembers. "I sort of lurked in dark corners of the soundstage, and peered out from behind things. My dressing room was filled with religious books and heavy classical music . . . I didn't want there to be anything reminiscent of Sissy's world to distract me."

Fisk, she remembers, "had a book of Gustave Dore's Bible illustrations that I pored over every day, studying the body language of people being stoned by their persecutors or tortured for their scenes." She'd incorporate these unnatural positions in just about every scene.

"Some of Dore's figures were looking up at the sky without lifting their heads, and I practiced staring up and down like that, so that only the whites of my eyes would show."

Through it all, she could find some kindred souls in nearly every audience. From the current teens searching for their own identity—keep in mind that America was hardly a year out of Vietnam at this point, and many of their parents, perhaps even their friends and former classmates, were still feeling the desert heat—to the adults that had long since grabbed their diplomas, but still may have had a sad memory or two waiting behind nightmare door number one, many saw a part of themselves in the sad recluse, and others secretly might have glimpsed themselves in her tormentors.

To their credit, a few students do appear to break with the maddening crowd. There's Sue (Amy Irving) and her boyfriend Tommy (William Katt), who decide that Tommy should take Carrie to the prom to make up for her bullied-ness.

Ignoring her mother's mindless rantings that "they're all gonna laugh at you!" Carrie makes her way there, and she's awakening feelings inside Tommy that he never dreamed he'd feel for anyone but Sue. There's a wondrous dancing sequence whose surrealness lends itself to a step into heaven for the young woman, or at least happiness, a true foreign land for her.

"The rhythm of the whole scene got me excited," Spacek says. "We were spinning on a circle, and the camera moved the other way. We had to be on camera every time we said a line. If anyone had explained it to me before we started, I would have said it was impossible! It worked, and I couldn't believe it . . . It's an exhilarating scene. You share Carrie's happiness." Then the pair is elected to educational royalty, and dreams might all be coming true.

But it can't last for her. Eventually, reality's going to come right back and steal back the show. It was all a setup. The voting was fixed, her preening placement determined earlier, a final act that the words "harassment" and "bullying" exponentially combined don't even come close to describing.

As Carrie basks in cheers she never thought she'd hear, a moment that would make her a trillionaire if she could keep the feeling inside forever, school bully-ette Chris (Nancy Allen, married to de Palma at the time) and her jockish jackass boyfriend Billy (John Travolta, far from *Grease*) unleash the ultimate prank on Carrie. Waiting until she's in the perfect position, they dump a pot of pig's blood on her head.

"I told them at first they could use real blood, I was so into the part!" says Spacek, who slept in the blood for two straight nights so it wouldn't have to be re-done. "It was actually a mixture of Karo syrup and food coloring. It was so sticky and I would freeze on the soundstage!"

Carrie's eyes hit the size of Thanksgiving plates, staring out to space and seeing very little. The crowd appears to be laughing at her, but whether it's real or her far-past-stable imagination we're not sure. They may have thought she'd run off in terror, but something new's going to happen now. Her mother was right, and now someone's going to pay.

Oh no. That's about enough. That's just not going to work anymore, to happen anymore. Looking into Carrie's eyes, we don't know who's looking back right now, but we do know that something's going to happen. Something bad. Something hurtful. People are going to suffer. People are going to meet some seriously violent ends on this one.

Things start to collapse from the ceiling, and one person dies *fast*. Fire breaks out behind Carrie, who's past the point of feeling. A fire hose smashes out of the wall and starts blasting people. As Chris and Billy scurry away, the fire starts to spread around, eventually engulfing the building. Dozens won't make it out alive. It's her doing. It's her doing hard.

"I had to stand on that stage while everything was on fire!" Spacek says. "I got all the hair on my body practically singed off! I got so involved in it! 'Fire? It can't hurt me! I'm Carrie, I'll flex!' While I was on the platform, my cue was 'Leave the stage only when you can't stand the heat anymore. But walk slowly!'" She was about ten feet from the flames, themselves leaping twelve feet high.

As Carrie steps away from the gym and wanders down the street, Chris and Billy, in his car, see their shot at revenge. But it's not going to happen: Carrie causes their car to swerve around her, flip over, burst into flames, and send them to the same fate that befell so many of their fellow tormentors.

"Because the film was so stylized, I wanted to do it, except I didn't want to get run over, of course!" she explains. "I worked with the stunt girl a lot because, at that point, I wanted Carrie's body movements to be so stiff. The car was rigged with a 'cannon.' When the stunt man got up to 60 miles per hour, he shot a two-foot telephone pole out of the bottom of the car which flipped it over! A second later, he blew up a gas can in the trunk, which flipped it over some more!"

Carrie makes it home, and her mother appears to welcome her. But as the two embrace, Carrie's mom, also insane in all kinds of different ways, plunges a knife straight into her daughter's back, sending her careening down the stairs, and once again necessitating a stuntwoman for the actress.

"They rigged a platform at the top of the stairs," she says. "When Piper stabs me, I fall back out of frame, foot last. It's so well cut that it looks like me. Poor (stuntwoman). She had to do it three times! It's one of my favorite sequences: the stabbing, the fall, the scooting across the floor. I just loved it."

The terror continues as Carrie kills Margaret, using her telekinetic powers to blast knifes and other sharp utensils into her, pinning her in a crucifixion position. With nothing else to live for, Carrie takes her mom down to the basement. Her powers are out of control, collapsing the house and killing them both.

Despite several weeks of preparation beforehand, much of Margaret's death scene wasn't rehearsed. "I wanted it not to be a sorrowful death," Laurie recalls. "I wanted it to be something that she exulted in, that she celebrated. It was great the way they made it all work. I thought the movie was better than the book."

"You may have noticed all the attic space between the stairs and Carrie's room?" asks Spacek, who ironically would play Laurie's sister two decades later in *The Grass Harp* (1995). "Well, the flooring wasn't finished and Carrie hid things down there, too. It was her own private world. I wanted to establish that because, at one time, we thought that Carrie could crash through the floor to the kitchen after being stabbed, so she would literally crash through her own little world, the one she had created."

But things aren't quite over. With the White house little more than an ash pit, Sue cautiously steps toward it, a bouquet in her hand, a funeral-esque peace offering.

But as she leans over to place the final farewell, someone comes from up from below. It's Carrie, somehow there, somehow around, desperately trying to hold on to one of the only people who ever cared about her, or maybe to take Sue along with her. . . .

Indeed, it's the final scene that still lives on today, three decades after it first hit the screens, as Carrie tries to hang on to one last glimpse of reality and happiness, and Sue may never be OK again.

Even though her arm is the only thing seen, a shot that many could have performed, Spacek couldn't let anyone else be Carrie again: she was underground during the scene, and it's her personal appendage that we see.

"Those rocks were pumice and they were heavy," Spacek says. "It was the last day of shooting and I was all dolled up and they wanted my stand-in to do it. But my hand is my hand! It was claustrophobic but very exciting. I couldn't see and what with the blood being slippery, I almost broke Amy Irving's arm! The rocks scratched my arms to bits all the way down, but I wouldn't have missed that for the world!"

As we see Sue at home in bed (but hardly safe), there's a bit of an inside joke to be had here: Irving's real-life mom, longtime actress Priscilla Pointer, played her mother in the flick.

The next spring, Spacek's trump card kept rolling, as she scored a Best Actress nod at the Academy Awards, although Faye Dunaway would win for *Network* (Dunaway's co-star Beatrice Straight beat Laurie for the Supporting trophy). Spacek's career wasn't defined by the scary genre—five other Best Actress nominations and a 1980 victory for the Loretta Lynn biopic *Coal Miner's Daughter* can have that effect.

"I don't want to live my life to be a movie star," she says. "That's a trap. Movie star is not a position in life. I keep telling myself, 'Sissy, life is not staying king of the mountain. You've just got to continue to grow and live your life purely.'

It took far too long, but the *Carrie* magic kept spreading; Emily Bergl played the girl's secret half-sister Rachel in 1999's *The Rage: Carrie II*, and Angela Bettis took the lead in a 2002 TV movie.

Emily Bergl's Rachel portrayed a family member of one of horror's most legendary victims in *Carrie II* (1999).

Rachel shows that Carrie might have gotten rocked from both sides when it came to heredity; in the first film, Carrie reminds her mom that Daddy ditched her for another lady.

Rachel's mom, perhaps? Looks like Carrie got mental illness from her mom and the telekinesis from her (and Rachel's) dad. Ouch!

For Bergl's screen debut, the actress used the same prepatory techniques she'd honed in years in stage work.

Before stepping into character, she explains, Bergl often decides to "wander the streets of New York as my character. Even though no one on the street could tell that I was doing anything, I just kind of like to walk in Rachel's shoes." She also read up on telekinesis, and checked over King's novelization and the first film (Irving revived Sue as a counselor trying to save Rachel from Carrie's fate—flashbacks included!—before becoming an inadvertent victim).

Rachel, Bergl explains, "knows whenever she opens up and becomes emotional, strange things start to happen." Her version ends at a high school party at a classmate's house, culminating in an inferno, with much more graphic death and gore than Spacek's story.

Like Bergl, Bettis spent the majority of her first acting years on the stage, with film and TV work here and there (she was in 1999's *Girl, Interrupted*, which landed Angelina Jolie a Supporting Actress Oscar). Then she hit it big alongside Lucky McGee in the title role of 2002's *May*, the story of a young veterinarian whose lack of socialization puts her over the edge, all the way to mass murder and Frankenstein-type work, even throwing in bits of comedy along the way.

Bettis was determined to make her version of Carrie White a remake, but not a copy.

"I tried to interpret the role differently, so they didn't end up with the same thing," she says. "Sissy

Carrie

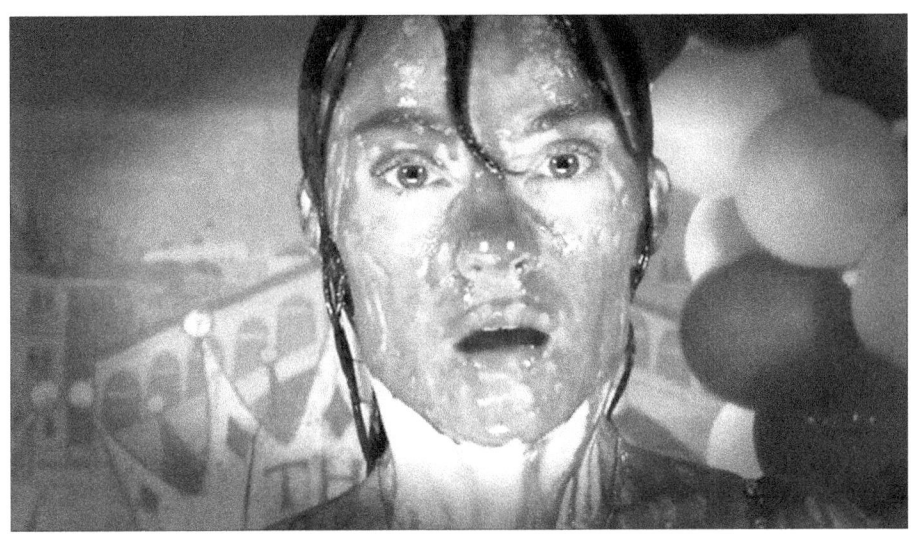

Carrie came to the small screen in 2002, with Angela Bettis in the lead.

Spacek's take was certainly correct, so I had to find another correct way to do it." With an extra hour of screen time to work with, the film had time for a bit more plot and character development, but a few changes were made, the most notable being that Carrie survives Bettis' version (it was hoped to make the flick the diving board for a full series, but it didn't get picked up).

In horror, Bettis explains, "Sometimes there are just places that you got to go. I'm the kind of the actor who, to do my job well, I actually have to go to that place. And after doing it and doing it and doing it, I can end up with a big, black hole in my heart." She'd work with McGee again for *The Woods* (2006) and *The Woman* (2011).

By the time a new *Carrie* came about in 2013, Chloe Moretz had long since established herself as the Queen (well, she was a teenager, so maybe Princess would be appropriate) of Horror Remakes: she'd appeared in the new version of *The Amityville Horror* (2005) and the 2010 vampire flick *Let Me In* (the Americanized version of *Let the Right One In*, 2008). She'd also gone werewolf in 2012's *Dark Shadows*.

So an old role was nothing new. Still, critics and fans tend not to take too kindly to remakes—but it's better to let them worry about that sort of thing. Moretz had a role to get ready for, and people were (and are) going to say about it what they want. If nothing else, her age was more realistic—unlike Spacek, Moretz actually was a teenager during filming.

"I loved the original movie," she says, "but you have to be completely secure in what you're doing and what you're putting on screen. I have to think about it like any other movie. It's a movie, a script, and a character you love and you really want to go into it, so you do the same you do on any other film, because that's just your process. You just have to be completely confident in what you're doing or else you'll tear yourself apart."

Moretz, and her character, are clearly living in a different world than from when Spacek carried off the role, and even a significant distance from Bergl's and Bettis's jobs as well. Film technology has shot forward like a crazed rocket in the past decade, but social media has also become an integral (albeit not always welcome!) aspect of American society. That, and bullying and the way it's handled—not nearly well enough—have changed as well.

"We have seen these kids who have been pushed so far and have been so isolated and so ostracized within their communities," Moretz explains, "that they eventually emotionally combust in several different ways: in suicide, in massacres, in whatever else. And the sadness about this movie is, it's what you've seen in real life; it's just portrayed on a screen. It's relevant because of the things that have been going on, and it strikes a deeper chord than it did in the '70s."

Having spent much of her own educational life in the home-schooling area, Moretz had to call on her friends to discuss the happenings of everyday public edification. Carrie herself certainly hadn't experienced much.

"What I really kind of attach to with Carrie was that she doesn't know that world of teenagers," Moretz says. "It's the one place where I don't feel comfortable in because when I'm with a bunch of teenagers, I don't know what I'm doing. And I'm like, 'This is not my safe zone. I don't know what I'm talking about.'"

Working alongside Kimberly Pierce, who'd directed Hilary Swank to an Oscar in 1999's *Boys Don't Cry*, Moretz elaborated on King's texts with her own.

"It was a lot of understanding emotions," says the actress, "which I think, at fifteen years old, I had been through a lot in my life because everyone has been through a lot in their life, but a whole lot of emotions that I haven't actually dealt with. She brought all the emotions out and honestly, by the end of the movie I became such an adult because I dealt with every vulnerability I've ever had in such an upfront manner."

She also visited some who find their everyday lives filled with more vulnerability than she or even Carrie ever did, a reality that's far too often even scarier than much of King's work: Moretz checked through several homeless shelters, filled with people who'd look at Carrie's life with envy.

"I've never done that before for a role and I learned so much," she says, " . . . to go meet these people who have never known any semblance of love and money and life; what we go through every day, being able to go out to Whole Foods if you want to and buy an all-organic meal, they have never lived that. And I talked to these women who have been sexually abused and physically abused and verbally abused, and they're so strong. Even though they've had so much done to them, they're so strong, and you look into their eyes and you learn so much just from talking to them . . . I laughed with them and I cried with them and I spent like a week with all of them, and I learned more than I've ever learned—even as Chloe."

Modernism kicks straight in quite early in Moretz's film, as Carrie's menstruation nightmare ends up not just on the school gossip networks, but the Internet, unheard of back in the 1970s.

Carrie

Piper Laurie (left) and Julianne Moore (right) became maternally evil in the *Carrie* films.

"It was having to jump into a world where, imagine going to seeing yourself being sad, you look down and you're bleeding out," Moretz says. "I can't stop the blood, I don't know where it's coming from. I'm terrified, I know I'm dying, I know blood means death and I don't know how to stop it. She reaches out for help, she's screaming and all she wants is for someone to help her. It's jumping into the space of that vulnerability and that terror is hard because you're doing it on a set where we had a lot of smoke on it that day and no one could breathe and coughing. It really was a horrible atmosphere to be in but I felt so uncomfortable, so cold and dirty from the ground, that it worked so well."

While Moretz's (admittedly much shorter) acting résumé might have made her an obvious pick at re-telling a tale of the scary type, Laurie's follower was a bit less expected; even after four Oscar nominations (and getting shafted out of a fifth for 1998's *The Big Lebowski*!), horror villainy was quite a new world for Julianne Moore—unless, of course, we jump back a quarter century to 1990 and *Tales from the Darkside*!

"The thing that interested me the most about her," Moore says of Margaret, "is . . . how tremendously isolated she was. She joined this religious sect and then found that they were not strict enough, they were not rigorous enough for her, so she ended up peeling off from them with this man that she met. They had their own church, they would preach to each other . . . So you think like, 'Oh, my gosh, here's this woman who has probably had like several psychotic breaks, who is completely socially isolated, who has no one—only had (Carrie's dad) who then dies, and is just left with this child.' So you think, this is her only relationship, this is her only community." Just as others we've heard from here did, she started with King's legendary words.

"I read the script and I read the book," says Moore, who'd finally win her Oscar in 2014 for *Still Alice*. The book was really most important to me . . . That's where it comes from for me, always. There have been things where maybe I've looked at film or music, but . . . it really was about what Stephen King had written."

Now let's go to the other side of the film, the infamous prom night. Once again, Carrie's doused in pig blood, and the falling pail kills her date (Ansel Elgort was the new Tommy). It's time for Carrie's infamous stare into the gleeful crowd—and now it's time for some to violently die.

It's often the subtleties that distinguish between trendsetters and remakes, and this happens here—unlike Spacek, who used her eyes and head jerks to show off her telekinesis, Moretz brings her hands and arms to bear. That, and the fact that she spares a teacher than was nice to her, shows that she might have a bit more stability than her predecessors.

But, aided by the film world's innovations, she gets to be quite a bit more violent with her powers. Once again, as Carrie's classmates burn to death in the gym, her main enemy and the girl's boyfriend attempt to run her down. But Moretz's character doesn't make them swerve past her and explode, like in the original; she stops the car short, the boyfriend's head fatally smashing the windshield. With her lady tormentor still alive, Carrie tosses the car into a gas station pump, then causes an explosion to blast the girl to bits.

Just as before, things end with Carrie and her mom buried under the wreckage of their home. But the film smartly doesn't copy the original ending—as we expect it, the impact would have been severely lessened. Instead, things finish with a close-up of Carrie's grave, which suddenly starts to shake and crack.

Is part two on the way? It would hardly be a surprise. But with Carrie gone, at least for the time being, Moretz could finally step out of the strange and terrifying world that she'd kept herself inside of since the first of filming.

"It was the first movie I ever did in which I wanted to try method (acting)," she says. "You know, trying to really breathe and live in (Carrie) because she is such a dark character you can't just cut and be like hee-hawing around."

Oakley Stevenson's Christine challenged the whole "Guns don't kill people. People do" theory in the opening moments of 2000's The Convent.

Oakley Stevenson:

The Convent

SHE KNEW IT would be intense. She knew it would be painful. She knew it would be tough to watch.

But could she be the one to pull it off? Well, Oakley Stevenson thought so.

"When I read the script," she recalls of 2000's *The Convent*, "I couldn't get rid of it. I'd read the script, and go back to the opening scene. I'd read twenty pages, and go back to the opening scene."

No one would envy the person who undertook the task. Stevenson wouldn't mind having to reach right out and yank in the confidence of those who didn't believe (of yet!).

If it was her, or whoever it was behind the role of young Christine, it was all the challenges in the acting world. The opening scene would be the lady stepping out of a car, striding her assertive self into a church. . . .

And pulling out a huge gun and blasting several people straight to the place they preached of. Then dumping a gallon of gasoline, tossing a match into it, and lighting something that would seem likely to burn for eternity for those with the misfortune to be standing near it.

"It was really intense, with fire all over the place," she remembers. "The 'gas' that I had was supposed to be water, but it smelled like gas. I knew I was doing something dangerous when I was doing it, and it was sacrilegious on top of it. It was a very intense role to play."

In a scene that got less and less entertaining as America was ravaged by one horrible mass shooting after another over the next decade and so forth, Christine would do it all (rare for a woman, both in the movies and reality) and then get away. Later on in the reel world, she—or rather, her portrayer—would get a chance to find likability in the audience.

"She was incredibly broken and misunderstood, scarred and scared," Stevenson says, "a character I felt, could be interpreted really, really interestingly. I also liked the revenge aspect, a loner, misunderstood. I loved the complexity of the character. I didn't feel like I'd seen anything like her before."

It was fortunate that Christine would so gorily and memorably debut, because *Convent* viewers wouldn't see her again for at least a reel. Twenty years later, the title place has become a happening place for the local juvenile delinquency core to break in and practice for their final exam in Vandalism 101. The newest group steps in, with impromptu leader Clorissa (Joanna Canton) and her pals, including the cheerleader that the crew had attempted to hand Stevenson.

"They wanted me to be the cheerleader, because I'm a tall blonde," she remembers. "I said absolutely not. I put on a dark wig, grabbed a broom, and acted out the scene. Who doesn't want to look badass? It was so cool." The crew agreed, handing her the role; Renee Graham ended up playing the cheerer Kaitlin.

Busted by a motley crew of lawmen consisting of longtime horror star Bill Moseley and '90s rap star Coolio, the group flees, but one's left behind. She's nabbed by a group of Satanists, a sacrifice to summon their person, Him.

It works, but it doesn't. Her killing turns her into a possessed entity that bloodily takes out almost all of them, and some of her former friends, including Kaitlin.

One of the few left, Clorissa escapes to the nearby hangout of Christine, now an adult in the gorgeous form of horror icon Adrienne Barbeau. Now we go back to the same opening scene that took such a strong grip on Stevenson's attention back at auditions.

"I put a little backstory to the way she was," she remembers. "I wanted the audience to give me empathy and like me. I was wanting the audience to feel for you, like you're going to get them. It was about becoming a numb character and getting other people to like you."

She also tried to get like Barbeau, or at least the Christine the elder lady was playing.

"I studied her for a bit," Stevenson remembers. "I wanted to get her mannerisms: the way she walked, her body movement. My dialogue was the body movement."

Barbeau told us, and Clorissa, the background that Christine had to embody. A pregnant student at the convent, she'd been forced toward a sacrifice, but of her unborn son. Christian nutcases of the time might have been able to find some kind of religious justification for such an act, but the priest and nuns doing this weren't doing the work of Anyone special—it was of the entity behind their possession.

Filming this had proved even tougher than momentary mass murder, Stevenson recalls.

"The abortion scene with the priest was the toughest scene," she says. "I'm deathly afraid of needles, and they knew that, so they played around with real and fake needles. I actually passed out." Christine was a bit tougher, fighting her way free and saving her boy. But the possession was still there, and it was her new responsibility to go in and exterminate it, just as she had back at the start. It was far from some random, senseless act.

Now into battle at least one more time, Christine and Clorissa go to the extreme side of Second Amendment rights, hauling huge guns into the convent to blast anything that doesn't speak right. With only one way to put it away together, Christine kicks Clorissa and her brother out, then gives her life for the place's own sins. Still, possessions don't die that easily in Hollywood, but we haven't seen a sequel yet.

Not long after, Stevenson went behind the camera almost for good.

"I was working on a project a few years ago," she says, "and the costume department fell apart. I stepped in to fix it, and it felt completely natural. I was very successful." She's costumed stars for Fox's *Castle* and *Raising Hope*, and for years for the stars of its *The Real* talk show, along with some films.

"I had the casting couch experience, and I really wasn't pleased with it," she explains. "Then reality TV came in, and I wasn't getting a sense of pleasure like I was when I was growing up."

Madison Stone went to the ground with demonic animation in 1992's *Evil Toons*.

Madison Stone:

Evil Toons

YOU'VE GOT TO hand it to horror movie monsters—they've got some seriously great taste in ladies.

From the creature that stalked stunner Julie Adams through some black lagoons to a great white shark chomping on beach babe Susan Backlinie to all those lovely ladies that Freddy Krueger went after, successfully or otherwise, the main bad guys have some high standards in their prey (we're not mentioning Michael Myers here—as lovely as Jamie Lee Curtis and Danielle Harris are, their playing his relatives would take this discussion in a direction it doesn't need to go).

So when a group of young beauties pulled up to the ominous-looking house early in *Evil Toons* (1992), it was pretty clear that the title character would have his supernatural selection. But what or who might he be?

After a tough day of cleaning and renovating the joint, it's time for the foursome to kick back and chill. The arrival of a strange fellow named Gideon (David Carradine) with a stranger book disrupts things, but soon they can celebrate a job pretty well done.

And if this is how women *really* hang out during slumber parties, they need to happen quite a bit more often!

Up to then in her career, Madison Stone, like some others in the cast—not Carradine!—had done the majority of her work in films with, shall we say, their own secluded area in the video store. Any who saw it would have trouble buying this, but *Toons* was actually a step down in the risqué department for several of its performers.

"As an actor, you do what you're told, and you assimilate," Stone says. "Acting is acting: you either have it or you don't. They told me how this girl was supposed to be, her character, her demeanor, her personality, and I became that." Her Roxanne would become a few things.

Her pals are ready to hit the sack, but Rox still has a bit of energy left, and she knows just who to use it on. Her boyfriend's about to show, and she's going to wow him in all sorts of ways—like, for example, the striptease she demonstrates for her friends. This after some breast-size comparison amongst the group.

Yeah, is this *really* what women do during a typical "Girls' Night Out"? A fellow can dream....

With her left alone, that book opens up, to a threatening cartoon. Since this is horror at the campiest of the campy, the drawing comes to life in a cartoon darker than anything you'd find on *South Park*! Actually, it looks more like an evil cousin of something from *Where the Wild Things Are*.

Perhaps a strange thing in a strange land, the creature glances around, unsure of what to do and where to go. Then it, just like the shark, the creature, and so many others, happens upon a breathtaking coincidence in the form of a lady!

Rox is still polishing up her dancing show, and it's a willing audience. Then it gets just a bit too hungry—for many things—and attacks. In the demonic form of *Who Framed Roger Rabbit!* (1988), Rox goes to the floor with an evil monster.

Acting out her brawl with the animated sort, she recalls, "was actually quite fun. I was told where I was to be. They had fishing wire to move my clothes. You hear something, and you turn your head and look for something behind you. If it's not there, you have to pretend it's there."

Rox is dead, but her body still lives, with a new owner, huge teeth, and a dark voice. One by one, her boyfriend (too late, dude!), the house owner, and her friends violently die, until Gideon returns to set the book aflame.

"That was hard," Stone admits. "When David Carradine and I were fighting, he wanted to switch the plastic knife with the real knife. Nobody got hurt, and it was very effective. It was humorous, like hearing yourself on an answering machine." With the book burned, everyone's alive again, and it's time to re-kick back with some Saturday morning cartoons. But perhaps those drawings will demonize as well....

"I can become anything," Stone explains. "Some shit's just natural!"

Even the practices of Nazi-ism became just a bit more evil in the hands of Ilsa (Dyanne Thorne) through three films in the 1970s.

Dyanne Thorne:

Ilsa series

AS THEY SEE you doing your thing on the screen, film audiences will judge you, or rather your character. They may like you, cheer for you, hate you, boo you, whatever. Let them; they paid for a ticket to see your work, they've earned the privilege to form an opinion.

As a performer, you've got a different job. You can look at the man or woman you'll be becoming for a few weeks (or days, as this subject did, at first) of work and a few hours on the screen, and you needn't worry about how you feel about your characters yourself. It's a different environment with a different objective.

She knew she'd be disliked, or even worse. That was OK. Playing a member of group that personified evil, a character specifically inspired by two of the worst of the worst of the worst, Dyanne Thorne's goal wasn't to get people to like (or even *not hate*, if you catch the drift there) her Ilsa character, only to want to watch her, even if they wanted to see her suffer. Had she allowed any of that personal opinion stuff to break through, it might have changed, probably lessened, Thorne's work. It might have made it less intense. It might have made it less realistic. It might be easy to forget, or gloss over to start with.

She didn't need that. Ilsa was a Nazi, based on actual women of the Holocaust, which was still on the world's mind, even as Vietnam's battles raged. No way was anyone in the seats going to get behind this title anti-heroine, so no reason for Thorne to worry about it.

"An actress doesn't judge her character," Thorne shrugs. "I know that's a generality. I presented it to my boyfriend, and he threw it across the floor (said boyfriend is now her husband and frequent co-star Howard Maurer)."

Then the two started to give 1975's *Ilsa: She Wolf of the SS* another thought. After a ton of mostly comedic work on stage, a plethora of one-shot TV showups, and the occasional cheesy turkey (like 1965's *Encounter*, where she played the crazy stepmom of a ludicrously young Robert De Niro), a sort-of biopic, even in the most explosive of senses, would certainly add a bit of . . . well, diversity is probably the only way to go with that, to Thorne's résumé.

"(Howard) said, 'Somebody's going to do it, so you have to think, as an actress, is this something you want to do?'" Thorney says. "At some point, you can't judge—you have to *do*. The truth is, if you don't act, you're not an actor. I wasn't getting offered anything else. I wanted to try it. Maybe you prostitute yourself like that, but the chance was to play a woman that nobody was doing. Maybe Joan Crawford or Bette Davis got to do (tough) roles before me, but women were not given any roles that allowed them to discipline a man, if you will."

As young performers are so often forced to do, Thorne made the best of a rough situation, trying to find the bright side of playing an evil villainess.

"I was doing comedy, and it was a role that was the antithesis of that," she says. "I had an opportunity to play a dominating women instead of the things I was used to doing. I like the idea that it was based on the life of a real person."

Actually, Ilsa had sprung from two Nazi-esses. Ilse Koch guarded at the Sachsenhausen and Buchenwald concentration camps, aiding in the deaths of countless victims—and she's best known for allegedly making lampshades out of their tattooed skin. Irma Ida Ilse Grese was a guard at Ravensbruck and Auschwitz, arguably the war's most well-known camp. For the last months of the war, Grese, at just twenty-one, moved up to warden of the female section of Begren-Belsen, hand-picking who she felt should be gassed.

Grese was hanged for her crimes in December 1945, while Koch gave herself the same punishment in prison in 1967. (Author's note: checking out *Ilsa* and its backstories, as well as 2008's *The Reader*, really shows you what an underrated role women played in the Nazi party. That's something that needs to get some more attention.)

In another familiar position for acting newcomers, Thorne had to move fast to prepare. She read up on Ilsa's "role models." She tried to find a German accent in her acting training memories.

"Speed reading doesn't give you all the facts, but it does give you an insight on the character to some degree," she recalls. "I pulled out my books on dialect and worked on my dialect. As an actor, you open your heart and your mind to step inside the other person, about to sit down and meditate and do the wonderful acting lessons that you're taught. At some point, you've prepared enough that you see a character and you move in, and you try to be what you think that character might have been, and at that point, you leave yourself behind." Far, FAR behind, she'd attempt!

Her title character lives straight up to her nickname right off the credits, having a man neutered for failing to satisfy her in the orgasmic sense. Ilsa then uses some female captives as lab rats, proving just how equally tough women can be by having them beaten to death in the same manner as so many men.

Ironically enough, shooting took place on the set of the recently ended *Hogan's Heroes* (1971), which spent seven years telling the tastelessly comedic tales of an Air Force colonel and his friends' adventures in a German POW camp. The demolition of the set at the end wasn't an act; with *Heroes* cancelled, the crew didn't mind sacrificing its set for cheap realism!

Roughly, but not ironically, everything (the whole film) had to get knocked out in all of *nine days*.

"There's a word in the dictionary for that, and it's spelled H-E-L-L," Thorne says, "but you're in the character, so you kind of let it go. We had one twenty-five-hour day. It wasn't an easy shoot, but when you're committed, you're committed. As Ilsa, I was in a war situation, and was totally committed. I was finding it exciting to portray this character."

Never one for the drinking or the smoking that filled up so many film sets of the times, Thorne had become acquainted with gun work during a 1968 appearance on *Star Trek*.

"I learned how to handle firearms, but realizing that a girl had to handle herself, I learned not only to be more physically active, but to do things like some basic martial arts," she says. "The thing was to keep yourself strong. Those kinds of things really prepared me early to become Ilsa. You have to be prepared, because you never know what's around the corner. The agent may say I'm not interested, but the producer and director will say 'You're the only one that I want.' That's what really happened to me."

In one final bit of unexpectedness, audiences loved *Ilsa*. Not Ilsa the lady, you see, but her story. It's why, despite dying in her first outing, Ilsa, in true Jason Voorhees/Michael Myers fashion, was resurrected a year later to become the *Harem Keeper of the Oil Sheiks*, finding slaves for her sheik-ish friend.

Now away from the male persuasion (being *killed* by them is probably something of a turn-off, isn't it?), Ilsa appears to be into her own, forcing her unwilling ladies to takes all *kinds* of care of Ilsa's lesbian bodyguards. She also patents explosive dildos, truly giving women the best of both worlds!

For the first time, however, Ilsa gets a bit of redemption. Charmed into bed by an American, she's soon raped by her former boss. With hell truly hathing no fury like her, she kills a guard and recruits the slaves to take him out. With him tied up, Ilsa has his mistress give him a taste of his own criminal bathwater—but only she knows that one of her bombs will take them both out.

"They tied me up, and I just freaked out," Thorne says. "I don't do well with being tied up! In the work I've done, either I get murdered, or I've murdered my husbands and killed everybody that's been in my path."

The Tigress of Siberia of 1977 started out with Ilsa plying her trade in a Gulag prison camp of 1953, taking out her frustration of the loss of her beloved Stalin by killing almost all the prisoners. But one survives, and a quarter-century later, he and the Soviet boxers he coaches find their way to a bordello—and guess who's the head madam? Filming took place in the midst of a blizzard, but the war between these two is going to be anything but Cold. . . .

"I had to be prepared before I ever got the first role," Thorne explains. "It was not a teenage role. They liked beautiful, young sweet girls, but you have to have a certain amount of life, and I had seen my share of life by the time I got to do the first *Ilsa*."

That same year, Thorne and Ilsa took one more trip together, as the character's now *The Wicked Warden*. While Thorne's lady tortures the patients in her mental ward, a reporter on the outside goes undercover to find out what happened to her sister.

"Each film was based on a truth," Thorne says. "The second one was about the oil sheiks in California and around the world, abducting beautiful young college girls. *Tigress* was based on the Stalin situation. Part four was based on sanitarium where women were being mistreated that was run by a woman who was found out by a journalist in Europe. It's hard to imagine that those things really happened. As the series went through, Ilsa was the same character, the same person under different circumstances."

Be honest—by this point in the profile, you're pretty much incapable of feeling shocked, right? Reading about all this, getting smacked by sardonicism over and time again, you're not going to be surprised anymore, are you?

Are you? Listen to this; all along the times she was playing Ilsa, and afterward, Thorne was a minister. Throughout her career, she studied and studied.

"You get lonely out there on the road, particularly if you're doing a two-character play," she recalls. "I'd be there for about a month, and I'd take a course at a local college, studying philosophy, psychology, and religion. I did that for my whole career. It was something to do when I didn't know what else to do in a town by myself."

A few years ago, Thorne snared a PhD. in religion, and she and Maurer have an alternative wedding company in Vegas: alternative meaning, well, individualized. Some even chose to do so with Ilsa's themes, albeit in a less brutal fashion.

"We don't get out whips and chains!" Thorne jokes. "It's more like 'This Is Your Life!' They review it with a lot of humor."

After bringing Ilsa to life, for all of her evil, murderous, bloody deeds, sometimes there's nothing else to do but look back on it and smile—especially if an impact made in such a short time carries on today for a special group of film fans. Thorne and Ilsa, together four times in three years, might have terrified and certainly disgusted us at times, but the simple fact that the two still stand together in their own spot in action acting four decades after we met them is a story few have earned the right to tell—in *any* genre.

"I don't think you can intellectualize it too much," Thorne says. "An actor acts. I'm an actress, and I was offered a role, a chance to do something new and different. I was not, in any way, promoting Nazisim. The things that came out for the films were always a complete surprise. I think it was in my guardian angel's hands. The things that came to me were things I never truly pursued; they just fell into my hands."

Young Rhonda (Samm Todd) doesn't know she's about to go up against tormentors factual and fake in 2007's *Trick 'r Treat*.

Samm Todd:

Trick 'r Treat

IT MIGHT NOT carry the same prestige as its December 25 counterpart, but Halloween has its own set of traditions.

First off, it's the respect. You're going to wear the costumes, and you're damned sure going to enjoy it. Secondly, if someone shows up at your house, you'd better have some candy ready—and we're not talking about apples or dental floss here. Chocolate, sweet tarts, something that teeth see and think, "Oh boy, this enemy's going to get us good."

And if you find yourself on the wrong side of "Trick or treat!" subscribing to the first option instead of the second, you're going to find yourself getting ten times the comeuppance.

All of this was learned, seen, and felt in blood-red living color in 2007's anthological *Trick 'r Treat*, and, so common in Hollywood, all in the same neighborhood! Like Michael Myers first did to it decades before, the holiday known for fear is taken to an all-time dangerous and often fatal level.

Like so many in single-digit grade school, Samm Todd had spent most Octobers looking forward to the month's last day, and with it a chance to become something that only exists in imagination, even of the nightmarish sort.

"I have one distinct Halloween memory of first grade," Todd recalls, "when I dressed up like a witch, and I was really into it. My mom put these warts all over my face, and gave me a fake nose."

Heading to school, she might have expected to not exactly stand out—those of the broom-riding pastime are quite common on Halloween. But stepping into her classroom, the youngster was surprised.

"I went into my first grade class, and all the other girls were Dorothy (Gale, of *Wizard of Oz* fame)," she says. "I was like this gargoyle witch. My teacher told me I was frightening. I definitely connected and learned a lot about Halloween." Nearly a decade later, she'd be in a similar position in a brand new setting.

Long before we get to Todd's *Trick* tale, we find out just how seriously her neighbors—well, some of them—take their Halloween. A local wife who badmouths the holiday is chopped to pieces and turned into a human decoration. The school principal poisons a kid who had the audacity to . . . *steal his candy*, then helps his own son turn the kid's head into a jack-o-lantern.

Then comes "The School Bus Massacre Revisited." Decades before, such a vehicle crashed into a nearby lake, killing all but the driver. Now an assertive young girl is taking her friends to the tragedy's site, giving everyone a too-close view of something that doesn't even happen that often in horror films.

Typical for this type of film, one group member is about the opposite of the leader, a model of introversion, intentionally and otherwise, trying to hold on to one of the first groups that's ever been friendly enough to reach out and welcome her.

The character's name was Rhonda. For the first audition of her new career, Todd hoped she'd be the performer behind her.

"My mother was an actress, and she was always against me going out for film or TV when I was a kid," Todd remembers. "We made an agreement in high school that if I got good grades, I could get an agent and make a career. It kind of fell into place really perfectly."

Rhonda's certainly not lacking intellectually, but that's not always the kind of thing that makes teenagers want to hang out with you socially. Todd studied up on the holiday's history to rattle off an impromptu lesson on it, using all kinds of scientific terms, to a fellow attendee, himself barely old enough to finish fifth grade.

"She's pretty smart and totally awkward and socially uncomfortable," Todd describes, "but at that age, you're going to be in and out of cliques and groups. It's a very surreal experience at that time, and most of time, I felt that way. It felt pretty good to research something that was a little bit different as well."

But again, Rhonda's social issues come probably as far from within as without, she continues.

The crew, she says, "wanted her to have some affiliation with Asperger's Syndrome or autism and be very socially uncomfortable in front of people." Asperger's, itself still relatively new to the mental health field, is a form of autism that often gifts its afflicted with amazing assets in the cerebral field, only to cheat them into social difficulty and trouble with non-verbal communication, making it quite easy for them to rub wrong the general public that too often misinterprets their conduct as disrespect.

Getting ready to be Rhonda, Todd went to a source that, like the character, became an impromptu role model.

"One of my best friends has a brother that is severely autistic, and we would be hanging out around this time," she says. "I would watch his mannerisms. I wanted to create something that was easily recognizable, but not offensive or gaudy." As is often the case with those afflicted, much of the youngster's communication came far from speech.

"When he was talking to people, he would be really subdued," Todd recalls. "He had a lot of activity going on with his hands and arms, and I think I've always held a lot of tension in my hands when I'm around people I don't know. I always feel very stuck and awkward. I focused on giving (Rhonda) certain mannerisms with her arms, her hands, her wrists, her legs, making her look uncomfortable. I did the things that I do when I'm uncomfortable." Todd was kept away from her co-stars during filming to keep anyone from building a real relationship.

And Rhonda would have all kinds of reasons to feel that way in abundance; soon enough, it's revealed that the whole thing's a trick. As Rhonda makes her way down the makeshift elevator and on to the swampy area near the bus' final destination, she finds she's just there to be a target: the rest of the little brats pretend to be the massacre's victims, pursuing the terrified youngster around the mud. With her glasses knocked off and broken and her dazed from being tripped too many times, the panicked girl's destined to live forever as a punchline.

"I didn't totally understand the physical demands of being in a horror film until I was in it," Todd admits. "The main sort of realization is the hard work, a lot of running and crawling. You definitely get scraped up, doing that for hours. They really pushed all of us to our breaking point by the time we finished those scenes."

Then, for the film's first time, the supernatural comes straight into deadly play. The "real" victims blast from the lake from whence they died, chasing the tormentors themselves. One after another is dragged away to be violently killed.

As the remaining make their horrified way back to the elevator to safety, Rhonda's already locked herself inside. They beg for help, for forgiveness (no one yells, "Help me, Rhonda! Help, help me, Rhonda!" which would have planted some impromptu comedy into a scene meant to scare). She slowly reaches for the key to unlock the device's door.

Then her hand falls away, and she gives an emotionless, revengeful wave. For probably the first time in her life, she's going to take some control and cause some deserved pain, as we hear the group becoming a meal of the newly undead.

"I felt that this was a bit more of an accomplishment on Rhonda's behalf," Todd says. "But it was difficult when we were filming to not feel a little guilty, going up the elevator and stoically waving goodbye. I felt a little guilt. Rhonda was pretty fed up by that point."

She makes it out, but not everyone will. The aforementioned principal finds himself at a party, suddenly surrounded by gorgeous, clothes-less women. Then things get too good to be true; the ladies suddenly transform into werewolves, devouring him and the rest of the fellows (Anna Paquin, who spent years battling vampires on *True Blood*, got a different taste of horror here, as a wolf-ess). The principal's next door neighbor is suddenly attacked by the same creature who killed the wife early on (the victim mumbles, "You gotta be fuckin' kidding me," during the battle, a line surprisingly not more common in battles with the supernatural), only to have the attacker leave when it obtains a chocolate bar. After all, remember, this holiday is all about the candy.

He steps outside, and notices Rhonda wandering down the street, nearly run down by the relapsed lady wolves. Then the same kids who inadvertently saved her show up at his door. He was the ill-fated driver. As Rhonda makes her way home, he finally pays.

"When you're on set, everyone's very professional. There's a kind of detachment from the actual thing you're producing," Todd says. "But at the same time, you're obviously getting very engulfed in the material. The dark humor really shined through."

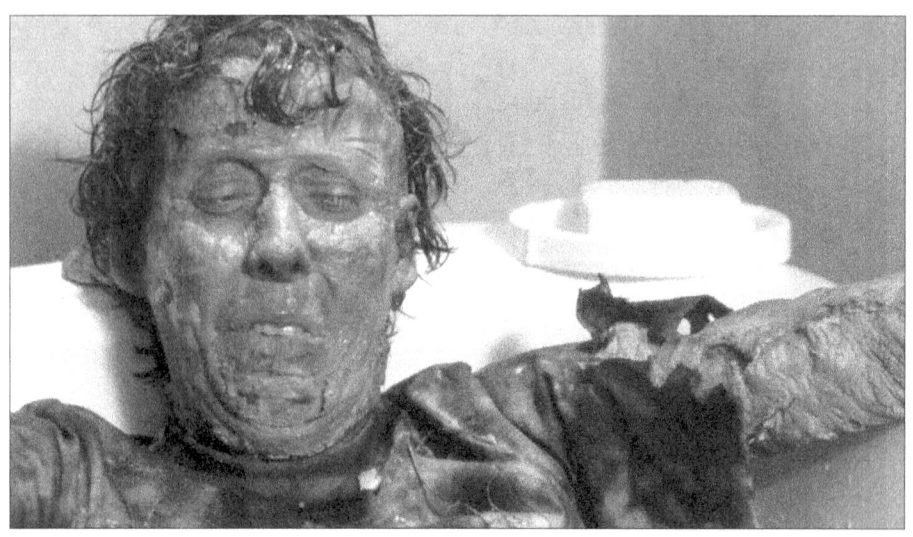

A bath of nuclear waste turned Mark Torgl into *The Toxic Avenger* (1984)

Mark Torgl:

Toxic Avenger series

Anyone, for anything, in any film, for any reason, doing whatever they want or can, at least with studio approval.

No matter who you are, no matter what you want, there will be a place for you at Troma Entertainment. It's the Utopia for those who will do whatever it takes and then even more to make it in horror.

"They'll put anyone in their movies who is willing to go to extremes," proclaims Mark Torgl, who's become living proof several times over, "to be ridiculous, naked, and bloody."

For about all of its first decade, the indie production company mainly stuck to comedy of the campy kind, like 1983's *The First Turn-On!!* (exclamation points part of the official title), the tale of a group of teens trapped in a cave by an avalanche, wiling away their lonely hours through deep discussions of virginity displacement.

A New York film student had shown up to smooth off the roughest draft parts. Then he'd been whacked into the cast. A top actor bailed, and Troma co-founder Lloyd Kaufman, whose name wasn't quite household among cult fans just yet (though he'd done supervisory work on 1976's top film *Rocky*), told Torgl to take over.

"It was an over the top, socially awkward nerdy role," Torgl recalls. "Lloyd says the dinner scene, where I wipe mashed potatoes through my hair and fellate a corn on the cob to impress my girlfriend's parents is classic film history." The next year, Kaufman's company would stake its first claim in horror legend.

Long before knocking out such cinematic masterpieces as *Killer Condom* (1996), *Surf Nazis Must Die* (1987), and, we couldn't possibly pass over, *Yeti: A Love Story* (2006), Troma took a bloody stab at horror, sort of a *Revenge of the Nerds* meets *Friday the 13th* runs into *Frankenstein* sort of thing! Kaufman watched one upcomer after another tried out for the man who'd become the title character of 1984's *The Toxic Avenger*.

He wasn't happy. Fortunately, Kaufman had a longer memory that it often seems in Hollywood.

"He said, 'What we need is what Torgl did . . . last year,'" Torgl says. "They called me and said if I wanted the role, it was mine." A huge fan of bizarre (or at least, they seemed so upon release, way, *way* back when) flicks like *Night of the Living Dead* (1968), *Basket Case* (1982), and 1977's *Eraserhead*—seriously, watch that and try to figure out how the *hell* that move got green-lighted and bankrolled at the time!—Torgl roared forth to list his own name on such a cast. Like most young men, though, he'd already had some practice.

"I've been acting like an idiot ever since I was a little kid," he admits.

To call Melvin Junko an idiot would be unfair; not entirely bright, the health club janitor is a bit too crazily optimistic to realize he's just there for bullying target practice by the jocks and jockettes (who, typically, are all just *so* fit and fine looking!). So when one of the gals appears to grow a heart, inviting him to go trysting in a dark room, it all seems too good to be true.

It is. He's tricked into making out with a sheep, exposed in front of everyone.

"The sheep scene was tough," Torgl remembers, "because the sheep was covered with gnats and they started jumping on me." That, combined with being loudly mocked, sends Melvin running to the second floor, and toppling out a window.

Right into a barrel of toxic waste, and catching fire. As he tries to recover in the tub, something starts to happen to Melvin.

"The tub scene was tough because the water was ice cold," Torgl says. "They could not warm it, no matter how much boiling water they poured into it. Lloyd even tried to warm it up by pissing into the tub. Nothing worked. Finally, I just went for it and used the discomfort to help with the scene."

In a scenario that, fortunately, viewers didn't try to imitate at home, the waste turns Melvin into a superstrong but facially deformed creature—much like Dr. Frank's monster—who finally gets revenge. Now played by Mitch Cohen and voiced by Kenneth Kessler, he bashes the brains from the heads of drug dealers, destroys some fast food robbers, whomps his healthy tormentors, and, finally, becomes a local hero for exterminating the crooked mayor.

In other words, he gets the ending that Frankenstein's monster deserved!

As much trouble as the crew had had picking just the right Melvin, things went their way in abundance on the other side; hundreds of potential Bozos showed up for casting.

No, this wasn't a biopic of the stereotypical clown—that's what the leader of the anti-Junko pack would be called. A recent graduate of an acting school near Broadway made the first cut.

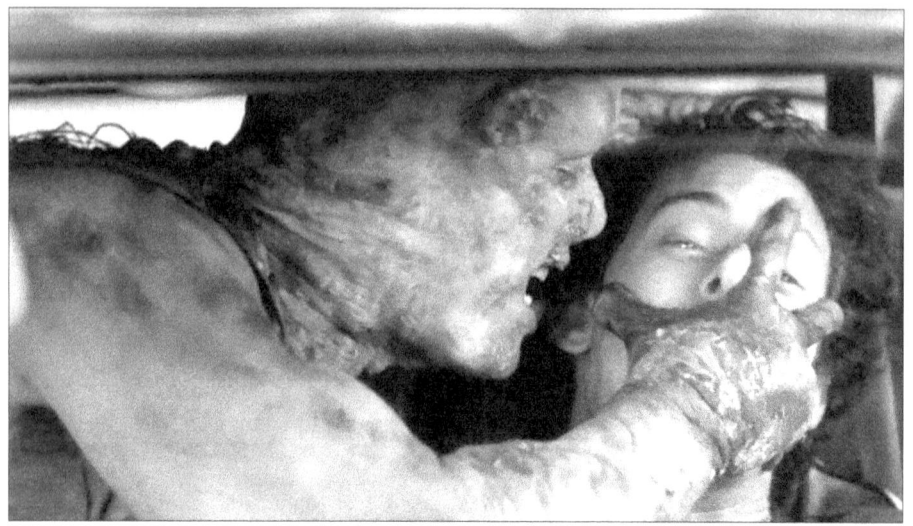

Bozo (Gary Schneider) tries to keep from becoming *The Toxic Avenger*'s latest victim (1984).

"Then the fun began," remembers Gary Schneider. "I think I got called back about eight times. It was emotionally exhausting." Finally, it was down to him and a fellow the crew knew from *The First Turn-On!!*

The person's name was Vincent D'Onofrio. Yes, the same fellow who'd show up in *Full Metal Jacket* (1987), *Men in Black* (1997), and enough other productions to make him a lasting household name decades later. But before he'd make Pvt. Gomer Pyle a landmark in *Jacket*, the crew picked D'Onofrio as their new Bozo.

"I was devastated," Schneider says. "I had put everything I had emotionally into that part."

Over the next few weeks, he searched for enough replenishment for his next tryout. Then Schneider's phone rang.

D'Onofrio was heading elsewhere. Schneider had a new chance to prove that no one was "settling" for him. He'd also have the challenge of taking a guy named Bozo and making him a nerd-terrorizing Lothario.

"It was pretty clear that Bozo was very angry on the outside," Schneider explains, "but I also saw him as having a lot of deep hurt on the inside. His biggest obstacle was in dealing with his rage and emotional pain underneath it." Melvin's hardly the guy's first victim; he and his pals run down pedestrians for points—scores get higher for those who take out both the rider *and* the bike!

"I thought of Bozo as being similar to a rabid dog," says his portrayer. "Whether he was running someone over with his car or eating breakfast, there was a lot of pain because he had a horribly abusive childhood. I tried to give him some depth, even though he was a very one-dimensional character."

As Toxie gives Melvin's pseudo-seducer an impromptu crewcut, Bozo and a friend try to steal away in a car. But the Avenger's upon them, firing the friend out a window and forcing Bozo towards a cliff, revealing his true self to his terrified enemy. As they drive off, it's starting to look like a Kamikaze mission on Toxie's part.

"This type of scene was, and still is, rare in low-budget films," Schneider says. "They obviously couldn't skimp on money." Even with a stuntman taking Bozo's dive, it was tough for the young performer to do the post-inferno accident scene. Upside down, he took Bozo's last breaths from under layers of latex cosmetics.

"I needed to lay in this burned mess and not move," he recalls, "as Toxie got up and walked away." The Avenger's not just strong; he's superhuman.

The film's locale being called Tromaville started as an inside joke and turned into a message of irony; the film bombed when it first arrived, but, as they usually do, become a cult classic with late-night showings to a legion that lives on today. Once the *Avenger* did its dirty work, Troma turned nearly exclusively to horror production, knocking out the titles we mentioned earlier and over a thousand more—including a few more rounds of the "man" soon known as Toxie.

In 1989, now hiding the face of Ron Fazio, the Avenger gets tricked into visiting Japan to see his fake father, while an evil company tries to take over his hometown (gee, the fact that it was *called* Apocalypse, Inc. didn't tip someone off that maybe these guys weren't all the way right?).

The same year (the films were shot together), Apocalypse blackmails him into working for them while it takes the whole town captive. Then he finds that the company head's moniker of Lou Sipher was a pretty sorry disguise; the guy's truly the devil, and the Avenger's got his biggest challenge yet.

At least, until part four showed up in 2000. When an explosion opens up a parallel universe (anyone who expected anything less clearly was watching the wrong series), Toxie's trapped in the dark lands of Armortville (backward and forward at the same time!) as his evil twin Noxie takes over his town; David Mattey played both roles. Desperate to do what so many couldn't, the sad town's mayor calls in every favor he can think of to stop Toxie.

Future horror directing household name Eli Roth shows up. Hugh Hefner plays the President(?!). And in the evil form of the man he'd been over a decade before, Torgl came back as Evil Melvin.

"I did it for the fun of it and to get a free trip to New York," he says. "I was living in L.A. at that point. I had to dig deep to my dark side, which many people have witnessed."

That's it for now. There have been comic books, cartoons, even a stage production of the Avenger's antics. Will there be another film? Maybe. The way horror's been going for the past decade or so, sequel rumors running all over the Internet and everywhere else, probably. So many in the horror film have come back from the dead when a new director takes charge; Toxie's still standing (and, some would say, better than he's ever been!).

"It's a live-action cartoon, nothing held back, and fans love to laugh through it," Torgl says. "It's a B-movie masterpiece. It's very easy to watch it over and over again. It even has an anti-bullying and anti-pollution message. The most offensive movie with a positive message ever made!"

Zombies come and go and live and die, but Allan Trautman's Tarman from *Return of the Living Dead* (1985) lives on, well after his violent on-screen passing.

Allan Trautman:

Return of the Living Dead

ON ONE SIDE, it's the easiest type of a role for a performer.

No backstory to create.

No lines to memorize.

What a piece of apple pie, right?

Then, however, we reach the other side of the flipped coin. There, we see the difficulty therein.

Having to act out thoughts and feelings without so much as a facial expression.

Spending the whole film buried inside a huge costume.

Trying to bring a living, although certainly not human, side to something FAR from humanity.

Yeah, that was going to be a bit more difficult, especially back in the mid-'80s, long before the glut of zombie films (and TV shows) that would engulf American cinema decades later. Yes, for his role in 1985's *Return of the Living Dead*, Allan Trautman couldn't look back to much—even the legendary *Night of the Living Dead* (1968) hadn't provided his creature a jumping-off point. But his education background had given him something.

"I loved a good horror movie, like *The Exorcist*, films that had a greatest appeal like that, but not really zombie films," Trautman admits. "(But) as an actor, what appealed to me was getting paid and getting a job. I told my agent I loved zombies and couldn't wait!"

No surprises about what was going on here. Trautman knew he wouldn't be the hero who saves everyone, the guy who sacrifices himself for the damsel in distress, even the jerk who becomes a zombie feast early on. He'd be one of the formerly deceased, back to feast upon the thinking organs that horror characters have a tendency not to use much.

Still, Trautman would have the distinction of being one of the few such creatures in zombie history to have a name worth a spot in the credits list. He'd be the Tarman.

Why the moniker? Keep reading.

"I figured there would be some heavy makeup things going on," Trautman recalls. "I'd been a puppeteer for a while, so I was familiar with that kind of work."

Catch that? Indeed, he'd been the man behind a few talking dolls and the like before.

"I started doing puppeteering when I was in college when I switched my major from physics to theater," he says. "I was looking for work in college, and I happened to see a notice for a public education station TV series, willing to train puppeteers."

He'd carry it into Hollywood on the small screen for years of *Unhappily Ever After* (1995) and the big one for *Babe* (1995) and the first two *Men in Black* films.

"I did puppets for the aliens in the *Men in Black* headquarters!" he remembers.

Still, the Tarman would be the first time he'd be covered head to toe and everything in between.

"Whenever you're doing a role in a suit like that," Trautman explains, "you need to be aware of how the suit is moving, and your body. Your movements have to be visible through the suit, just like puppeteering—when you put a puppet on, you need to make the puppet move. It's not just doing what you feel your hand is doing. You also have to be aware of what is behind the whole performance that you give to make it read through the suit."

As important as his character ended up, it takes a while for *Return* to reach him, so let's hit the background. It's the Day of Independence at a medical supply company in Louisville, and a few employees are going over the latest corpse supply before heading out to celebrate. But, per usual for these flicks, one bumbler crashes into a container full of mysterious green gas, which just *happens* to carry the right anecdote to cure death.

Meanwhile, a group of young punks are tearing around outside, partying in a graveyard. The aptly named Suicide (Mark Venturini), truly a rebel without a cause or clue, runs things from behind the wheel, with Trash (legendary scream queen Linnea Quigley) in full exhibition mode, entertaining with a cemetery striptease. Her pal Tina (Beverly Randolph), hiding her envy behind jealousy, storms off to find her friend at the supply house.

One corpse there has been killed (re-killed?), but the workers feel that cremation is necessary. It doesn't work—the fire helps the gas blast up the chimney and roar through gathering clouds. Then a storm breaks out, raining the resurrective material all over the graveyard—and forming an undead army of hundreds.

Meanwhile, Tina's down in the lower levels of the company, looking for her friend. Then she ventures into the basement—and our subject lumbers up behind her.

"They told me that they really wanted to see this creature thinking," Trautman says. "They didn't want some mindless, lumbering creature, like in previous zombie films. It was important to get across the fact that I was thinking, and the way you make creatures think is through eye focus. Where is he looking? What is his body language? What is going on his head? I was very aware of that."

Tina hides in a locker, her screams bringing the rest of the gang hauling in. One of them gives the creature his name, based on it appearing as though it was painted in the dark road adhesive material.

"I came up with the (Tarman's) walk on the spot," Trautman says. "That was what it would be like if you were about to fall apart and the only things holding you together were little bits of tar. The toughest thing to do was to not to fall down. I was so slimy that the floor got slimy underneath me. I let them glue the head on hours before they were ready to shoot my scene, and I just sat around."

Tina manages to make it away, but Suicide's not so lucky, as Tarman makes his brain into impromptu cuisine. But another fellow manages to knock its head clean straight off.

"It seemed pretty straightforward to me," Trautman says of the role. "Once you're in that kind of costume, you're doing the things in the script. As long as you're thinking, and you know what's going through his head, you're his vessel at that point."

When the zombies—including Trash, who forgot to put her clothes back on when she switched over—get too strong and high in numbers for the townsfolk, the military's forced to take the most drastic of actions, as a nuclear bomb blasts away thousands of both the current and formerly alive. But as the president prepares to visit the area, we see the rain waking up more corpses. . . .

For Part 2, of course! Three years later, the dead *Return*ed again, and guess who happened to be back in cannibalistic action? This time, however, the Tarman just showed up long enough to get smacked into a river.

"It's best not to ask too many questions," Trautman says of his second go-round. "You just go by it and move on. He was popular enough for them to bring him back. We tapped into something with that: people have finally embraced zombies as mainstream comfortable phenomenons, and movies like this that helped pave the way for that."

Further on in *Living Dead* action. . . .

As the film's first sequel arrived (or *Return*ed) in 1988, a group of boys, per usual for the age, decided that leaving well enough alone just wasn't good enough, releasing a barrel of toxicity into an unsuspecting town and causing an unwelcome increase in impromptu family reunions. Apparently, the whole "'Til death do us part" thing doesn't apply to the locale of Westvale.

With zombies on the mindless attack, Lucy Wilson and her little brother Jesse take over the few still unaffected, leading them to a plant to send a current straight through town and send these SOBs right back where they came from.

"When my agent called me with the audition, I just laughed," recalls Marsha Dietlein, the film's leading lass. "I was like, 'Oh, great, my first job will be starring in a horror film!' And then I got it! I was really excited. It was amazing to have the lead in a film and have that be your first experience. I have two little brothers and two little sisters, so I was very comfortable playing the older sister of a little kid."

Attempting to channel the "goddess of asskick" complex she'd seen Sigourney Weaver pull off in the first few *Alien* movies, Dietlein checked over the first *Return* film, and the original *Living Dead* piece. Watching other characters deal with the unimaginable, Dietlein felt herself stepping into their terrified, but eerily relatable, shoes.

"You put yourself in that stage when you're on the set," she explained. "You're shooting nights, all night long. You're shooting in graveyards, running around housing complexes that nobody lived in. I was just trying to get in the moment, to believe it in the moment . . . You just try to believe that you're really in that freaky situation. I was trying to get into the emotions of a life-or-death situation."

Like Ellen Ripley, Lucy knew her way around the shooting ranges. But like Weaver, Dietlein herself wasn't into the blasting weaponry, at least at first.

"I faked my way through it," she says. "I tried to act like I knew what I was doing. I never really liked shooting guns. It cracked me up in the movie knowing I would have to be a good marksman."

As expected, Lucy, her brother, and a couple of other good guys make it out alive as the military shows up to clean up the mess. But in the next film, it would be them that screwed things up. . . .

Walking into a zombie film, fans expect certain things. Large guns, earth-shattering makeup effects, and typically enough blood to overflow the Grand Canyon.

But *love*? That's a new one. That's a conundrum. That's all but a regular oxymoron: the words "zombies" and "adoration" go together like pumpkin pie and ketchup: two great tastes that don't taste great together!

That is, until the third *Return* put a brand-new spin on the retold-to-tears storyline in 1993. It gave us all the guns, all the gore that we expected and probably wanted, but it also showed that even in death and destruction, there's, God amazed, a bit of heart and hope.

As we've seen over the past few pages, women had carried the lead in zombie films before, and been on the evil side as well. Melinda Clarke, however, got to straddle the line between the two, and in the same film.

1993's *Return of the Living Dead 3* became a terrifying version of *Romeo and Juliet*, with Julie (Melinda Clarke) in the evilly seductive role.

With her living on the wild side and him just hoping he could find his own, Julie and Curt don't have much in life without each other. His mother's passed on and his dad's too drowned as a big wheel in the military to have much family time; her family functions disappeared long ago. And when people don't have much, they grab extra hard at what they've got.

"Julie's a rebellious teenager from a dysfunctional family," explains Clarke, who allegedly used actual vomit as a tool during her auditions, "and the only thing she has is her boyfriend, so they're really playing out that strange Romeo and Juliet/Sid and Nancy-type relationship. She turns into a zombie, but she's not a bad ghoul (a bad girl, maybe, but young men rarely mind that!) walking around moaning."

Paul Rudd, who'd eventually hit it big in *Anchorman* (2004), *The 40-Year-Old Virgin* (2005), *Monsters vs. Aliens* (2009), and other flicks, nearly got the leading man role until J. Trevor Edmond reached out and snared it.

"I had studied Shakespeare when I was studying drama," Edmond says, "and I just applied everything I had learned doing Romeo and Juliet and the character of Romeo—the emotional fabric of Curt was very similar to the Romeo character (of) William Shakespeare. So I just borrowed off a lot of the performance choices that I had made in doing that in my student acting and that actually translated very well. It's bizarre drawing parallels between William Shakespeare and a *Return of the Living Dead* movie, but it worked in this particular case."

Just off a play about the high lives and tragic deaths of shock-rocker Sid Vicious and his girlfriend Nancy Spungen, Clarke saw a bit of realistic parallel in their tale to her own.

"Nancy was literally psychotic," she recalls. "She went from one extreme to the other, as mentally ill people do. The producers wanted someone Julie has something happen to her that is inconceivable, reality wise. To make that believable as an actress, you use that parallel, the pain addicts feel."

Grossed out by watching Curt's dad and his colleagues attempt to chemically revive a dead person, only to have it go tragically wrong (Really? Get right out of town!), the two hop on Curt's motorcycle and spurt away. But Julie's still in the mood even after witnessing corpse resurrection, and her wandering hands throw Curt's balance way off.

There's a crash, and a huge pole's in the wrong place at the wrong time. Julie meets it head on, and she doesn't win the battle.

Now keep in mind that up to this point, not only in the film but the entire *Living Dead* series, we've seen one person after another deal with situations that no one in the entire world could ever really be ready for. When we sit back and say, "Well, they should or shouldn't have done that," about people in a *damned zombie movie*, it's not just the whole "hindsight 20-20 thing," it's surrealism with hypocrisy thrown into the equation.

So when we see the heartbroken young man pull his beloved back on the cycle and head back to the plant with the idea of resurrecting her with the chemical he just saw create a monster, before we laugh it off, we need to ask ourselves—no, we'd never be in that situation, but if we were, might we actually do the same thing?

Taking a few moments to consider, we'd probably hit the affirmative response. So maybe unthinkable and unrealistic aren't exactly synonyms after all.

The experiment works, and Julie's back. But not quite to normal. First off, she's starving—and not for the good stuff this time. No, this hunger is a bit more common. But after tearing through a stack of snacks at a local convenience store, and taking a chomp out of a gangster looking to throw his weight on the weaker sex (or so he was dumb enough to believe!), Julie realizes that culinaries won't quench her pangs.

But something else will. Something else not entirely unrealistic in society today, and quite a bit more common than we all wish it was. Granted, most people who try it don't get anywhere near the level that Julie tries—over one hundred prosthetics that at times took her nine hours of makeup to get into—but pain, self-inflicted pain, the release of inner pain by forcing ourselves to feel it on the outside. . . .

"Her spirit's intact, and at times she struggles with the fact that she's in danger of attacking her boyfriend," Clarke says. "She doesn't know how to handle it, so she goes through stages of extreme mental torture. It's wonderful to play, because there's a lot involved doing a scene that is entirely Julie struggling through this situation. She finds that inflicting pain brings her back to reality; then she gets to the point where even that doesn't curb the horrific hunger for brains, so she breaks down and eats someone." As Julie pierces parts of her body that even the hole-pokers of the world wouldn't touch, we see close-ups of her wide eyes, opening and closing in something not entirely unlike pure ecstasy.

But even that doesn't become enough, and Julie indeed allows her cannibalistic urges to win the battle, chowing an innocent homeless man who'd helped the pair escape the bad guys—and focusing on his brain matter.

"It's a very selfish thing—Curt doesn't want to go on without her," Clarke says. "We joke about the fact that Trevor's character sees me kill people and eat their brains, yet he keeps saying, 'I'm not going on without you!' When we talk about it like that, it's very funny, but they're kids, so they can get away with it—they're naïve, and they act without thinking."

She's right—after so much death, after bringing her back, and after seeing her take a guiltless life, Curt *still* can't let go. And after seeing Julie, now recaptured by the military and destined to be used as a guinea pig, he fights in to save her, endangering her own life and demonstrating a feeling towards her that most of us spend our entire lives dreaming about winning from another person.

"Here's this little seventeen-year-old with this complete animalistic urge going on a killing spree—and she's a good guy," Clarke says. "But she hates what she does and she wants to die, so there's a human factor in the zombies this time. I'm not just a monotone, 'I'm going to eat your brains' girl. She was fully intact when she became the living dead, so she's struggling with that, and there are a lot of dynamics that she goes through."

Love can rule the heart, the mind, and, in some cases, the sanity. People will go to immeasurable lengths not only to obtain it, but to maintain it. To stay with the person that will accept them for who they are, even sometimes it appears that there may just be one such person in the entire world, will push a person to sometimes unthinkable lengths. The love we might feel both for and from another . . . well, that can mean more than money, fame, any other material possessions. It can make us go farther, be stronger, be more than we ever thought possible. Sometimes we fight. Sometimes we kill. Sometimes we die, and all for love.

Unlike most zombie films—although its trendsetter, the original *Night of the Living Dead*, broke our hearts in the same way—the new *Return* doesn't end with a new couple walking off into the sunset towards a lifetime of love. Curt protects Julie from another zombie, but gets chomped by it himself, and there's no going back for him. He sadly opens a fire pit, then takes his final walk inside with one he couldn't live or die without.

As the Blue Oyster Cult mentioned in "Don't Fear the Reaper," not even death could stop the love of Romeo and Juliet. Some say that Vicious and Spungen might be experiencing the same thing. And as corny as it may seem, for the few moments after the credits role, as Curt and Julie go out together into darkness through the flames, the audience might just feel that they may die . . . but their love won't.

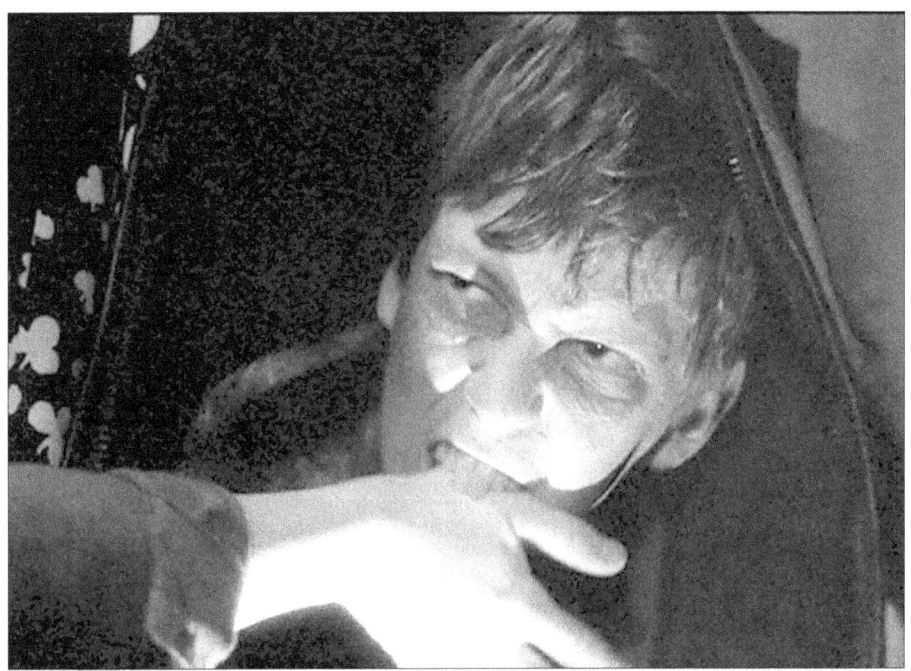

He was nearly turned into a cannibalistic monster in 1987's *The Gate* before Terry's (Baph Tripp) friends saved him from the demons below.

Baph Tripp:
The Gate films

HE COULD HAVE done some research. Envisioned each step and scene in the film. Autobiographied a backstory for the character.

But it just wasn't necessary. Baph Tripp had been ready for his first big role before he'd even auditioned.

By living

"My life as a normalish, somewhat nerdy kid *was* my preparation," Tripp recalls. "To a responsible adult with a work ethic, that maybe sounds like a lazy cop-out, but at the time I was a kid having an experience, and I didn't even know that preparation was a thing that actors did. It never occurred to me to do any, that I can recall. I learned my lines and I hit my marks."

And why make things harder than he felt they needed to be?

"I had always acted in school plays and things, as lots of kids do," he recalls, "but I have no recollection of a burning drive to 'be' an actor . . . Other kids got whatever jobs for pocket money that they got: mine just happened to include a couple of horror films."

After a short stint in acting school, he got a shot to be in a scary movie, before even having seen one in his life. Before Tripp (his first name was Louis at the time) even tried out for 1987's *The Gate*, its director knew he'd found his guy.

"(Director) Tibor Takacs would sit in the casting room and watch as auditioning actors arrived and waited to go in and read for him and the casting agent," Tripp says. "When I showed up, so the story went, he turned to someone and said, '*That's* Terry. I just hope he can act.'" As it turned out, once again, Tripp just had to be himself, with a few small modifications.

"Basically, Terry was in many ways *me*," he says, "and kind of an archetype of any number of awkward pre-teen boys." Some backyard construction leaves a huge hole in the existence of Terry's friend Glen (Stephen Dorff, who'd eventually make the jump from child to grownup star), but there's a huge, lovely geode rock that science geeks like these guys just love.

However, there's already serious tragedy in the times: Terry's mother has recently passed, and Glen's dog suddenly passes as well. Glen's folks are out of town, with his sister Alexandra (Christa Denton) running things— in typically annoying youngster mode, the guys just love to label her "Al."

In true *Amityville* fashion, ghosts and bugs start tormenting the youths, but Terry's into high-speed action, bringing out his interests in the occult and heavy metal music (and people have the *nerve* to blame those things for juvenile delinquency!) to figure this mess all out.

It doesn't really work, so everyone turns to a certain other Book. But this isn't *The Exorcist*; Christianity doesn't hurt these critters. Terry topples into the hole, where mini demons, who'd be cute if they weren't so bloodthirsty, try to make him a meal before Glen and Al save him.

"Ask any twelve-year-old boy if he wants to take a couple of months off school," Tapp pontificates, "and be in a movie where he gets to raise demons from the depths of Hell and be kidnapped by a zombie and then come back as a demon himself, growling and biting the other actors.

"Or, you know, you can stay at home and do your math homework. Are you kidding me?"

Terry's soon kidnapped by the bad guys and turned into one, trying to chew off Glen's hand before Al jams a Barbie doll through his eye. But she's soon taken too, and pretty soon it's down to Glen and a demon the size of the entire house, a four-eyed ugly SOB who looks like a crossbreed of Godzilla and one of the title characters from *Aliens* (1986).

But he's got one chance left, and it's the giant rocketship his sister gave him. Glen fires it up, blasting the . . . thing with it.

It explodes. Terry, Al, and the dog show up unharmed. Still, explaining the totaled house to their folks might open the door to another horrifying experience.

Takacs added a new chapter to his tale in 1990 and handed Tripp and Louis the lead. With his dad falling into the clutches of the demon known as Booze, Terry goes back to the portal, hoping it might just give him the power to save his father.

"I had a good time on the set of the first one," Tripp recalls. "It was relatively successful . . . the question isn't why did I do another, but why *wouldn't* I?"

His wish comes true, but this is a *Monkey's Paw* kind of situation; each wish brings harm somewhere else. Soon, the demons are running rampant.

Just as before, becoming Terry was just about looking back at the life he'd lived.

"Since I had already played Terry, I felt I had a good handle on him," Tripp says. "Again, he was largely me, as far as I was concerned. There was no need to go hang out with disaffected teenagers to learn their behavior; I already was one." Still, that made things a bit tough for a scene where Terry cries over his daddy, kept alive by machines.

"People made suggestions to try to help me get in touch with some inner sadness that would allow the tears to flow, but it just wouldn't physically happen," Tripp recalls. "Eventually, we cheated by spraying some kind of irritant in my eyes. Up until that point, I hadn't felt like I had ever necessarily failed as an actor; I was no Canadian Brando, but it seemed like people were happy enough with what I was able to provide. I was disappointed and irritated that I just didn't know how to access that kind of emotional reaction on command, but not disappointed enough to cry about it, obviously."

But he certainly felt redeemed getting to check out his and everyone else's work in the flicks—and getting to make out with flick bombshell Liz didn't hurt too much either (ironically, Liz portrayer Pamela Adlon would later win an Emmy for voicing Hank Hill's son Bobby!).

"Watching the effects in the films was the best part for me," Tripp remembers, "because I'm too self-conscious about what I'm doing on the screen when I'm in the shot otherwise. The effects guys on both films were amazing."

Ana Turpin's Ana hangs on to the closest thing she's ever had to a friend in *Para Elisa* (2012).

Ana Turpin:

Para Elisa

SOME OF US might be ashamed of this, but we shouldn't be. We have taken the notes and orchestra of one of history's greatest composers, one around long before heavy metal and shock rock, and associated it with violence, murder, even rape.

We shouldn't feel bad about that. It's only human. It says something strong about the nature of film fans that so many of us enjoyed 1971's *A Clockwork Orange* as a film, that we stepped beneath the surface of the Kubrickian world to feel its effects. We watched its characters do the worst of humanity's bottom levels, along with the notes of a man named Beethoven.

Granted, if the composer knew what we were doing and thinking about his music right now, he'd probably wake up and somersault in his grave. Sorry, Ludwig! But these things happen, and we shouldn't look within and find fault for doing this.

When another film emerged from far from America or Beethoven's German homeland, one many felt was even darker than *Clockwork*, things went in a new direction. Far from the then-universe-shattering special effects and large budget that Kubrick and his merry crew enjoyed, 2012's *Para Elisa* (itself translated into "For Elisa" or "Fur Elise," arguably Beethoven's greatest tune) went straight into horror, and of the realistic kind, which many consider scariest of all.

"As an actress, I like to bring to life characters and enjoy genre films," remembers Ana Turpin, prepping for Elisa herself. "*Para Elisa* was a wonderful experience, a dip in the terror. Doing such extreme characters allows you to delve into the psychology of the characters and that's the most fun part of my job!"

Looking for some green to celebrate her post-graduation outside of her home of Spain, college lass Ana (Ona Casamiquela) finds an ad for a babysitter, ready to take care of a young innocent girl.

That's not entirely true or false: the charge in question is indeed young, but only in mentality. Her innocence comes from never being allowed outside her mom's apartment. And the mother in question is looking for a sitter, a playmate for Elisa . . . one that never leaves.

A sedative puts Ana down, and now she's Elisa's new plaything. But trapped in the mentality her mom would never allow to mature, Elisa can't really tell that her doll is alive. It can talk, it can move, and it feels pain when she drops or hits it.

"Giving life to this character was a challenge for my career," Turpin explains. "I had to work in a very delicate line, where I could get a very credible persona, or the opposite. I always like to take risks in my profession and Elisa was one of them!"

Perhaps Elisa's mental challenges aren't caused by her mom, at least not all of them. Her self-imposed isolation and lack of speech may be from elsewhere. And if we're wondering about the piano connection, it has to do with the tranquility in which her mind drowns itself when her mom raises the title tune's notes from the family instrument.

"Elisa's character was one of the gifts of my career," says Turpin, who took several months to get ready for the lady. "Giving life to this kind of wonderful monster was a very hard work. I studied the behavior of children with bipolar disorder, drug taking at the time and secondary effects that could develop. I also worked the body because she is a girl who has never left home and she has no relationship or references from abroad. Her world is a bubble, and she copies the pattern of the mother: love/hate."

Not surprisingly, Elisa finds herself tormented by the dream worlds, half-awake in hysterics. Her mom rushes in to wake her (Ana's still incapacitated, outside and in), but Elisa inadvertently hits her too hard in the wrong spot, sending her mom down for good, choking on her own blood.

On her own and out of control, with no one, even Ana, able to take care, Elisa screams and stumbles around, begging her mom to wake up and play the soothing song. The she finally realizes that her mom can't ever come back, and turns to the only even remote link of contact she has left, smashing Ana's legs to make sure she doesn't try to leave too.

"The scene where I wake up screaming and I end up killing my mother was very complex, as it required a high level of madness while much accuracy level," Turpin says. "Also, scenes where I have to drag other characters required great strength, and I ended up exhausted!"

That's an understatement for how Ana ends up. Hardly able to move, she still manages to whack out Elisa with a crucifix and crawl away, trying desperately to ignore the mom's body. But just as she appears to be home free, Elisa recovers in the last moments, not ready to say her own goodbye . . .

"When you see the finished film with all effects, is when it all makes sense," Turpin says. "It's exciting to see the work of all departments together. That's the magic of cinema! The characters need to be understood, and it is advice that can be applied to life, and it is wonderful!"

Kevin Van Hentenryck spent three *Basket Case* films alongside and sometimes up against the puppeted Belial.

Kevin Van Hentenryck:

Basket Case series

SOMETIMES, AN ACTOR just has to go for it. Go for it all, broke or fixed.

There's no one to ask, and there's nothing to say anyway. He (in this case, our subject is male) needs to just charge straight into a new situation, one that could only come from the creatively deviant mind of horror, and somehow find a way to make it . . . let's stick with "credible" here; "realistic" isn't even an appropriate term.

It's not a time to worry too much about what others might think, because chances are that viewers probably never considered this sort of thing's existence at all, so they certainly haven't established rules of realism on this role. In that as well, there's no justification for anyone to downgrade an actor's performance.

"You get to split up the normally complicated and interwoven human psyche into two distinct parts: good and evil," Kevin Van Hentenryck explains of his roles in the *Basket Case* films. "You get to play with that. You have two characters there, even if one is in the film is just a little rubber guy. That was it, primarily." Yes, that was it—he was playing Siamese twins, one lacking deep development, but equipped with quite the temper and libido. Just stick with us for a while here.

Back in the mid-1970s, Van Hentenryck's girlfriend told him of a fellow named Frank Henenlotter looking to put together some features of Frank's own. Van Hentenryck sat down with Frank, and things got going fast—Frank gave Van Hentenryck, count 'em, *three* separate parts in his upcoming feature *Slash of the Knife*, bound to blast the horror film world off its hinges.

It never came out. Then, six months later, Frank called Van Hentenryck with a new idea, one named after a slang insult for people that we only imagine might have some mental difficulties.

"I was on his case about using student actors because you get better results and we could use the experience," Van Hentenryck recalls. "He told me the story of *Basket Case*. I said, 'Sign me up!' It was a unique opportunity for an actor to get to play two roles within one. We love that shit!"

As is often the case with horror flick protagonists, the main character sees what we consider normal as intimidating, even frightening. We look at those like him and run; he looks at us as just as far out there. He might be as terrified of us as we are of him—why *don't* we have a separated and severely underdeveloped Siamese twin in the basket we have to carry around? It's his everyday life!

It's Duane Bradley's existence, and it's perfectly average for him, so how could anyone else not follow in his lifestyle, or at least embrace it like he does. Even when little Belial emerges from his basket to let the world know just how pissed he is at being cut off (literally, in the surgical sense) from his bro, there's nothing unusual about this.

"Duane is kind of the straight man," Van Hentenryck says. "He think he's normal, and you're starting off with one screw loose right from the get-go, and the relationship he has with his brother always appealed to me."

Indeed, the brothers are more than a bit upset at those that had the nerve to un-conjoin them, and they're in the Big Apple for revenge in the 1982 series opener.

"Most of my preparation was regarding Belial, the brother," Van Hentenryck says. "I wrote out lines for my brother. All his lines were going through my head, as if he were really saying them to me. At one point, we weighed the basket after we dumped (Belial) out. It's very important that the basket have a feel when the weight jumps out. It's about the specific details of such a weird situation."

As twins, perhaps even more so than "regular" siblings, so often do, these fellows have more than just a physical connection. Once in a while, they find a way inside each other's heads.

"There's one scene in a bar where I say, 'Duane and I were so messed up,'" recalls Van Hentenryck (remember, he was playing Duane against his puppeteered brother). "Frank said that people would think it's a mistake. I said, not anyone who knows anything about filmmaking. That was my approach to the character. They are so interlinked, it's like sometimes I can't tell which voice is mine."

Belial eventually gets an attitude with his brother's friendship towards a nurse, attacking and killing her. Duane finally loses it on his bro, sending both of them flying from a window. But not fatally—in 1990, Frank brought everyone back for a sequeled shot, as the brothers join a group of fellow ... interesting individuals.

"It was more of a friend's project than a job," Van Hentenryck says of *Case*. "We worked weekends and nights when people and locations were available, and we managed to stumble onto an archive that people identify with. I am classically trained as an actor. Everything has to come from the script. That's how I work. You start trying to figure out how you can make this into the character."

A year after the first sequel came another—1991's Part Three had Belial becoming a dad, with everyone on the run from the law. Things boil down to the monstrous twin against a crooked sheriff—both of whom had lost kids by this point—with Belial's remaining babies helping him to escape. Everyone winds up on a talk show, and the world finds out that these people will be treated just a bit better from now on—or else.

"We stumbled onto an archive that everyone understands," Van Hentenryck explains of the series. "We all have this good and evil within us and with Duane, there's a clear-cut difference. That fascinated people. That's why fantasy is so big in the movies, because the bad guys are so clearly defined. In real life, things that should be good, like our government, are in fact the bad guys, so it's much less clear. The solutions are less obvious. So when you take the Bradley brothers, you have such a clear-cut split between them. That's wonderful to play with. Duane is the perennial outsider, the nerd. People identify with this. We've all felt something like that."

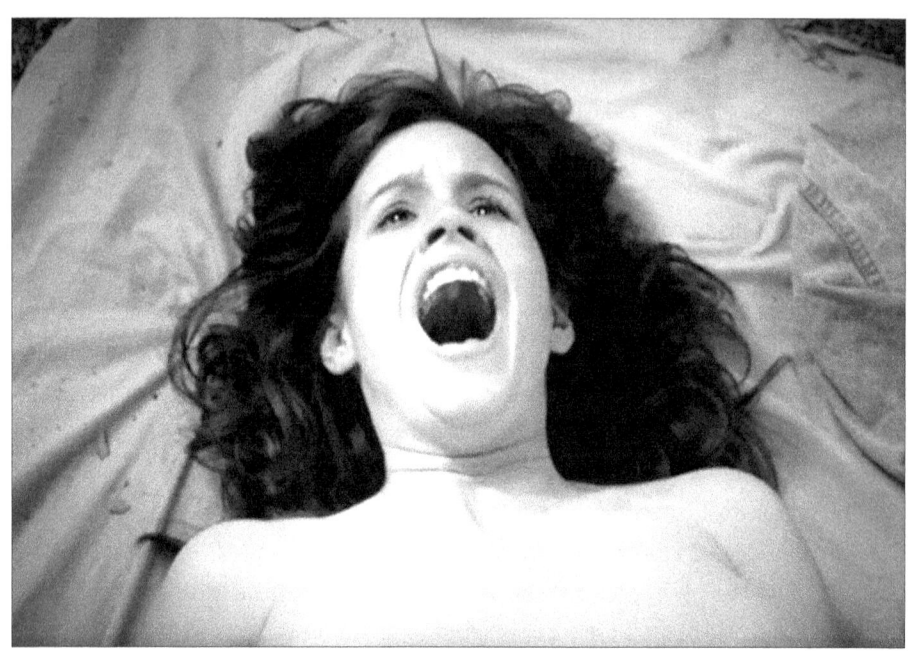

Debi Sue Voorhees' Tina finds out too late that she's about to become the next victim in *Friday the 13th: A New Beginning* (1985).

Debi Sue Voorhees:

Friday the 13*th* V: A New Beginning

WHEN IT COMES to American last name commonality, certain monikers have always been at or near the top of the list. Just about all of us probably know a few someones named Smith, Jones, Davis, even Zombrofski (OK, the last one might be a stretch!).

Then, however, there are those that reach landmark status among certain groups. Generations of horror fans can all instantly form associations to Krueger, Myers, Bates, and others.

For the *Friday the 13th* community, thy title be Voorhees. First came Pamela. Then her son Jason. And, as the fifth edition of the series showed up in 1985, Debi Sue arrived with it.

Pamela's sister? Jason's cousin? An adoptee that no one knew about, created, in true horror form, just to have a sequel excuse?

No, the truth's much simpler, although coincidental to the extreme. She'd actually be the latest member of the monster's prey group—but only in character form.

"I decided to go into acting when I was about nineteen," recalls the Dallas native. "I was looking for something fun and adventurous, and it was." While Voorhees served drinks at her local Playboy Club in the first years of the '80s, Pamela and her son wrote (in blood!) the first few chapters of *Friday the 13*th. But 1984's *The Final Chapter* failed to live up to its title, with *A New Beginning* forming just a year later.

Far from the old slaughtering ground of Camp Crystal Lake, this saga moved to Pennsylvania, complete with a new villain, although we wouldn't know that until the end. With formulae similar to that used two years later by *Nightmare on Elm Street*'s group of *Dream Warriors* (1987), the background's now a halfway house for who've let the typical young adult issues like anger management and eating disorders get out of control.

"I don't like horror films," Voorhees admits. "I'm a big chicken! (But) when you're working as an actress, you get yourself out there. You're blessed when you're given an opportunity to perform. If you've got any smarts, you grab those opportunities, and you learn and you keep moving forward, and you keep going for something else. The woman who called me about the film said my name made them sure that they'd better see me!" As it turned out, they and the millions who went to the *Beginning* would end up seeing quite a bit of her. . . .

One house resident after another was being turned into sliced sirloin, but Tina and her boyfriend Eddie couldn't worry about that. The two were too busy doing what had landed them there to begin with, what they did best.

Each other. Anytime, anywhere. In horror films, that's all but begging for violent death.

"I just thought Tina was fun and lighthearted," recalls Voorhees. "The biggest thing the director (Danny Steinmann) and I had talked about was that he liked my audition because I understood that she was playful and fun. When she says 'fuck you,' she's not mad at her boyfriend. She's having fun with him. She's a light teen, having a good time. It wasn't about her being mad or anything."

She and John Dixon sat down to lay out Tina and Eddie's romps.

"We met ahead of time to be a little more comfortable with each other," Voorhees remembers. "We met at the beach and just visited and chatted for a while. It's just nudity, hardly anything to bat an eye at." As those in his position have done for legions of horror cinema, the killer here took things just a *bit* more seriously.

Resting between rounds, Tina finds herself taken by a new fellow, and not in pleasurable manner, as a pair of shears make her blind, and then dead. Eddie doesn't fare much better, his cranium losing a collision contest with a tree.

"The hardest thing (about filming) was the blood in my eyes, because it just burned so much," Voorhees remembers. "You just go with the moment and be as realistic as possible."

As it turns out, the guy behind it all isn't the same one who hacked his way through the first few films; it's actually Dick Wieand's Roy, whose son's early murder at the axe-wielding hands of another resident sent him over the mental edge and into Jason's persona. Sadly, like the *Halloween* series found out with *Season of the Witch* (1982), horror fans don't really adapt well to change, as *Beginning*'s quiet work at the box office brought back Jason and the lake the next year in *Jason Lives*.

Still, while roles like Tina gave Voorhees a quick, easy, and certainly longtime spot of reverence among the horror film world, the far too serious and not nearly enough humorous world of education couldn't wait to look down upon her past: robbing students of a new chance to believe in the eternal words of "Hot For Teacher," school officials in Voorhees' homeland dismissed her from two high school teaching jobs.

"What can you say?" she rhetorically ponders. "It was a life change, it was different, and it brought me right back to film. So it was a good thing."

In 2012, she wrote, helped produce, and appeared before and behind the cameras of *Billy Shakespeare*, updating the legendary Bard and the tales he wrote to the modern worlds of struggling in the Hollywood play and screenwriting roles, with a love triangle and a few drag queens in the mix. But the last name that bridged the gap between her reality and horror creativity will forever solidify an easy spot amongst the horror genre.

"I get contacted by fans every day," says Voorhees, who's also banged out a novel and few other scripts along the way. "When you're doing it, you don't really see the scope of what it's going to be. I didn't know it was still going to be popular now."

Possession and addiction teamed up against and inside Carson Morris (Lara Vosburgh) in 2014's *Inner Demons*.

Lara Vosburgh:

Inner Demons

IT'S SCARIER THAN all the movies outlined in this book put together. It's about going against an opponent that adds more sequels to its evil deeds than any saga in film history.

Drug abuse. Heading down the dark path ourselves, or watching another, someone we love, take it, it's a terrifying view. More and more chapters are added to the same stories in horror (part two, part three, part nineteen) because we want them made; we feel we can add something special to an old story. But that's voluntary—drugs are things that we *can't* escape, because there's nowhere truly safe from them. They keep coming back. They're never too far away, and always willing to be our unwelcome visitor—it's just what they do. Escape only becomes permanent when we pass away. We wish they could be un-invented.

You might be thinking I'm leading into an episode of *Intervention* here. Viewers of 2014's *Inner Demons* might have felt the same way. Not that this would be a negative—it's one of the best shows on TV. For over eight years, the show helped hundreds of people battle opponents that would *love* to come back for another fight. The show went off the air in the summer of 2013, but (hopefully due to ticked-off loudmouth fans like me!), switched networks and came back less than two years later.

No, this isn't that. *Demons* didn't have the happy ending that *Intervention* usually enjoys (well, at the end of the episode, at least. We'll never know if things will stay that way). Self-filmed movies like this rarely come to an upbeat conclusion, and *Demons* wasn't an exception.

"Conflicts in screenplays often deal with obstacles we face in reality, and can also introduce us to possible resolutions," explains Lara Vosburgh. "As an actor, you must try and resolve the conflict in the play and find different tactics to do so. It is very empowering. It gives me faith that man can make the world a better place." Vosburgh's film debut came as Carson Morris, a former churchgoing honor student now snatched up in the worlds of goth dressing and makeup and pipe and smoke to take her down with them.

"From a young age, I developed a love for people and diversity and acting, fascinates me because it allows me to explore a variety of identities, time periods and geographical locations," she continues. "The more people I meet and characters I play, the more I find meaning in my own life and learn about myself."

That's a quest upon which almost all of us start in the teenage years, and there are usually a few pits and traps to catch us along the way. Maybe more than a few.

"This film talks about some really important issues," Vosburgh says, "such as the deadly effect drug and alcohol addictions have on families, about how terrible it is when somebody 'cries wolf' and no one believes them, so they are left to struggle alone. It also shows how some entertainment shows will endanger its participants just for the sake of good ratings." With nowhere else to turn—at least, that's the reason they give—Carson's family puts her in front of cameras and millions of viewers, convincing her that this problem can be solved if she just lets others watch her fight it. It sounds like Vosburgh and Carson weren't all that far apart—notwithstanding their, ahem, afflictions!

"I knew this role would challenge me and require me to expand my comfort zone by sharing my darker sides with others," explains Vosburgh. "More so than it is hard to channel your darker sides, it is hard to share them with others. Oddly enough, sometimes it's easier to share hardships with strangers than with your loved ones with whom you are most vulnerable. Carson participates in a reality TV show in order to share her process of getting off of heroin and it is ultimately revealed that she is dealing with demonic possession."

As horrible as the drug needle and pipe are, they're at least part of a familiar issue. People are trained to deal with this, and do so every day all over the country. That's not to say it's an easy problem to fight or that every treatment works—that's ludicrous. This only means that we have some ideas as to where to *start* when we're around someone in the midst of war. There's a Plan A, Plan B, and however many letters we need.

But being possessed? There's no rehab centers for that. Few people (at least, here in America) believe it exists, and even fewer take it too seriously. Try saying to someone, "Hey, let's get a priest to come by with holy water and a Bible and yell, 'I cast thee out, demon!'" and see if they don't walk away laughing—or run off in terror. But this is horror, and we have different normalcy standards here.

"I believe audiences of horror films consist mostly of sophisticated cinefiles who not only have a love for gore, but also an acute understating of the art of film," Vosburgh explains. "Horror fans don't just want to be scared—they want a good film that will challenge them and be emotionally compelling. On a less cerebral level, I just love being scared and feeling the adrenaline rushing through my body. When I am scared, it connects me to something primal and shifts me into a survival mode that sharpens all my senses and makes me feel super alive and part of nature." Whether possessed by the demons or the powder, fear goes into overdrive for those with monsters on the inside, and it's often covered up with anger, as we see in the temper and strength that roars from Carson upon anyone unlucky enough to be sitting nearby or making eye contact.

"I watched videos of hyenas to prepare for the physicality of demonic possession and connect to places that were emotionally scary," she says. "Also, my background as a dancer really helped me with the physical aspect of the role." However, she finally makes it to treatment, but the crew is still in tow (*Intervention* doesn't go this far). The group meetings that show her—or the thing within her—as just as omniscient as any idol or power of worship took Vosburgh back to another of her prep methods.

"I went to observe Alcoholics Anonymous and Narcotics Anonymous sessions," she explains. "I was truly inspired by their bravery to stand in front of strangers and talk about their biggest struggles." Revealing everyone else's sins in public doesn't quite endear her to everyone else, but it's not all her fault. But only we know that; we're the only ones who saw Carson get out of bed, only to have a clone-like form of her still there. We're the only ones who saw her reflection stand still as she turned away from a mirror, then go into demonic mode. Even doctors and nurses with years of experience have no clue how to handle this.

"Carson is a sixteen-year-old, which can be a challenging age for any kid, because you are still figuring out at that stage who you are and what values are important for you," Vosburgh explains. "A sixteen-year-old searching for her voice is almost like dealing with a demon from within—the personality demon, especially if the kid is living in an environment that does not respect what the kid stands for." Disrespect doesn't even begin to describe this place, this family, this atmosphere. It might just be the saddest part of the film.

She's soon kicked out of rehab, and forced back home with a family that's just about out of hope—and, per far too usual for such cases, her dad looks for answers inside a bottle. Her mom, one of those stereotypical self-righteous religious types we so often see in films like this, admits that violence was everyday stuff for the Morrises. Now the show cameraman is about the only one who feels that anything can be saved here.

"I loved the fact this horror film is a great story of human connection," Vosburgh says. "It talks about love and how true love can save us, and how sometimes even if the entire world doesn't believe you, it's enough to have one person who does. Carson as a character was somewhat broken, and yet very self-aware and resilient—just very real. Sharing her story on national television was not the hard part for her, it was the fact that she had to ask for help from her love interest." But they can't end up together, for no reason other than Carson's still a teenager, and he's, well, a bit older. Even in gory horror there's a place for morality.

Even with in-family massacring going on. Carson methodically slits her mom's throat. Just as her only remaining ally looks to have the inside trespasser out, her dad walks in with a huge gun and blasts her brains to the outside. Then his own.

The only one left, Carson's former savior turns to one of the many cameras that's been filming this whole mess. As he yanks it out, we see black spots where his eyes were. Just as they were moments ago in Carson's. Looks like whatever had her now has him, just like what Father Damian put himself through in the last moments of *The Exorcist* (1976). Unlike that story, though, this one ends with the creature still alive.

"Doing *Inner Demons* helped me overcome my fears of what others might think about the more private sides of me that I bring out while acting, and allowed me to fully commit to the task of being a good storyteller," Vosburgh remarks. "Whenever I do a role that changes my perception, I get all excited like a kid in Disneyland and run to speak about it with my friends. I love hearing from others what new things they learned from a performance, or how they felt a connection with one of the characters or specific parts of the storyline. These connections are exactly why I love acting, because to me acting, film, and theater are all collaborative arts based on creating meaningful connections. Not only do these mediums connect me to other people, but also to a variety of stories and ideas that need to be talked about. Of course acting is make believe, but when an audience member watches a film or a play it can give them a spark of inspiration to change something within themselves, their communities, or the global community."

As far too many probably did in reality, Eileen Walsh's Chrispina went for the self-inflicted release from the pain, inside and out, of asylum "life" in 2002's *The Magdalene Sisters*.

Eileen Walsh:

The Magdalene Sisters

IT WASN'T EASY. It *shouldn't* have been easy. Acting out horrible stories like those depicted in *The Magdalene Sisters* (2002) should be hard. For an experienced actress or a rookie, it's a job that must carry some difficulty. Especially when performing the sort of horror that our subjects actually went through—and far too many still go through today—difficulty helps us find a way into their position. Feel the pain, inner and outer, that they felt. A tough job doesn't only help an individual performer improve; it helps capture the mindset of someone who was really there, facing the realistic side of something we have the luxury of only having to perform.

For centuries, tens of thousands of young women were institutionalized in Magdalene asylums (some called them "laundries," probably because it sounds lighter), there to, ideally, follow in the footsteps of the places' namesake, a former prostitute who mended her ways. England and Ireland started the first few in the late 1700s, and America followed around the turn of the century. Soon Australia and Canada followed, anxious to give women who'd stepped out of line or been pushed a new direction, a manner and means to take their natural gifts and use them for the right reasons.

But for some, what they found was scarier than any brothel or street corner—and those are just the women who actually did the criminal stuff; many residents, like the ones we'll meet here, were forced there just for breaking imaginary religious rules. The nuns and clergymen there weren't always role models or mentors. They were something else, something that pitch-blackened the goal of the establishments and the Person of whom they preached. It was darker than anything one might find in the horror film section, because it happened. Many were abused. Some were killed.

And, sadly enough, not enough people, even today, cared enough to give a damn. Films like *One Flew over the Cuckoo's Nest* (1975) were credited with opening America's eyes to the plight of the mentally ill; *Magdalene* showed the terrifying inside of the worst the asylums did, for far too long and until recently, as the last such place closed only in 1996.

No, acting in films like this should require a little extra effort, and maybe even some suffering. Others went through much worse, so some agonizing devotion, it's what they deserve from us.

A year after wowing (and depressing hell out of) America with *Leaving Las Vegas* (1995), Mike Figgis was telling the story of *Miss Julie* (1996) and a young actress named Eileen Walsh had been lucky enough to snare a small role. That's when she ran into Peter Mullan.

He'd had a small role in *Braveheart* (1995), and now Mullan was working on a screenplay that went in the far other direction of the Scottish story's uplifting message.

"He mentioned his script in development and from that moment I chased it," Walsh says. "Every audition I had, I would ask if they were casting it or knew who would be." Along the way, she picked up a few more roles, then "happened" to run into Peter's brother Lenny, casting for the film one afternoon in Dublin.

"My audition itself was rigorous with a lot of improvising," she remembers, "and even then Peter had Chrispina earmarked for me." His brother's 2002 film would show and tell just one of the horrifying stories of what exactly went on behind the thick wooden doors of the laundries.

As was the case with *Cuckoo's Nest*, many of the committed (they were called "fallen" at the time) had done nothing even law enforcement of the 1960s would worry about. Some had gotten pregnant without marriage. Some were just a bit too flirtatious with the opposite sex, even if not even intending to act on anything. One had been blamed for her own rape.

Walsh's role model had a few strikes against her: a young unmarried mom, her mind had kept her in the set of a child—which, back then and probably to an extent today, many thought could be overcome ("cured," as the hypocrites say) by religion.

"All my focus went on her mental age/capacity," Walsh says. "It was important not to get nervous in the meeting, but keep reacting like an eight-year-old: open, honest, eager to please, and quick to a wobbly lip and tears, needing her mum. We all know these qualities, so suddenly she wasn't that different from me. I just had to be brave enough to present myself in such a fragile way."

It would be about a year before she'd head to Scotland to film the story, just time enough to get familiar with the history of the asylums themselves. In Ireland in the early 2000s, the Internet hadn't really taken off yet, so Walsh was left to do her own research in the anciently fashioned way.

She hit the library hard to read the scary tales. She looked for newspaper clippings that told the hard truth in black and white, and read them all over. She hunted down documentaries that showed the story.

"But then I found this book called *A Light in the Window*," she asserts, "and that became my go-to Bible." The 1994 novel (it was republished in the early 2000s as the asylum history stepped into the public eye) explains things through the life of a midwife in such a place, who, between delivering the babies that had landed the girls there to begin with, witnessed the cruelty and abuse they suffered at the hands of the religious wrong. Forced to give up kids that were sold to adoption agencies, the prisoners were beaten, humiliated, and abused until they left—alive or otherwise.

Walsh took it all in. Then she tried to put it all inside the approaching mindset of Chrispina's single-digit-age mind.

"I felt I then had to approach it from my eight-year-old person," she explains.

Now came the tougher part. As in, the entire job.

She and others are whipped repeatedly, with head nun Sister Bridget both ordering it and dishing it out herself (late great Geraldine McEwan has the role, and she's even scarier than playing the witch in 1991's *Robin Hood: Prince of Thieves*!). Chrispina tries to hang herself. She's being abused by a priest, punctuated by a darkly funny scene in which he's humiliated in front of everyone, her blasting him with shouts of, "You're not a man of God!"

All along, Walsh and her colleagues kept their end goal in mind: paying tribute to those that had gone through this in reality. "Every scene was hard," she claims. "There wasn't an easy one."

Eventually came the toughest of all.

We see the girls exercising, but only from the knees down. We don't think much of it just yet.

Then we see what makes this so tough. They're all unclothed, in a huge group. And there's two nuns there, loving every second of their abuse, wondering why the girls don't find it as funny as they do. There's an impromptu contest over whose body parts stand out most. It's very tough to believe how women like these nuns, these evil games(wo)men, managed to sneak their way into the cleric.

"But Peter and his team did a wonderful job on what was as a group the toughest day," Walsh remembers of the scene. "Peter ensured that bottles of fizz were all opened at the end of the day, no doubt paid for from his own pocket."

Some of the women escape, but Chrispina becomes the sad ending that occurred so often in reality: her already addled mind ruined forever, she's locked in a mental institution, away from her friends, her son, and reality until she dies young.

"Watching the film for me was awful," Walsh says, "and full of pride and sadness and everything in between. It's hard seeing your face, but I'm sure I'm not the only actor ever to say that!"

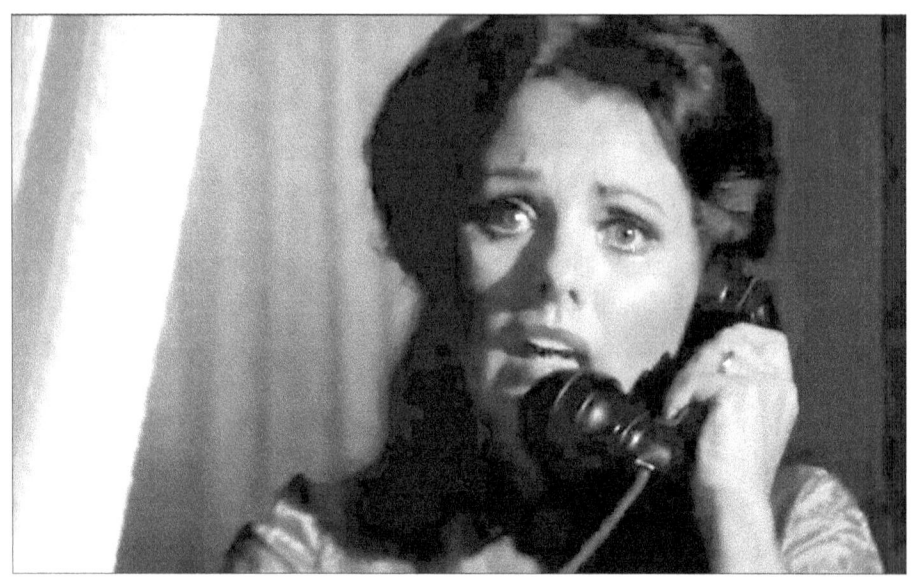

Dawn Wells stepped away from Gilligan's Island to act out horror in 1976's *The Town that Dreaded Sundown*.

Dawn Wells:

The Town That Dreaded Sundown

GO AHEAD AND admit it. Let's just get this right out into the open.

You saw the name at the top of this profile, and right away thought, "What? Why is this lady in a piece on horror? Isn't that Mary Ann? The *Gilligan's Island* gal, one of my first schoolboy crushes, right next to Wonder Woman, all three of Charlie's Angels, and Winnie Cooper from *The Wonder Years*?"

Probably. But now that that wave has risen and crashed as much as Dawn Wells caused so many young men's hormones to do so back during her *Island* times, let's look at one of the (*so* many!) other things she did, as overlooked as so many other works you'll see in these books.

Just about a decade after the castaways left the island for the "last" time (nearly all of them would reprise their respective roles in one form or another for the rest of their performing careers; as of 2016, Wells and Tina "Ginger" Louise are the only two still around), Wells had just finished up narrating and performing her way past the cameras of the Western *Winterhawk* (1975), Charles Pierce cheering her on from the director's chair.

Pierce had shifted gears and genres after that, stepping straight into real-life horror to tell one of the most underreported tales in American history. Back home just after her country celebrated its two hundredth birthday on Independence Day 1976, Wells hoped her own next job would show up soon.

But even she hadn't anticipated this sort of speed.

Well into filming *The Town That Dreaded Sundown*, Pierce wasn't satisfied.

"He called me and told me he had an actress that couldn't chew gum, carry groceries, and walk at the same time," Wells remembers. "He asked if I'd helped him out. He told me the whole story, and I said sure."

The very next day, she was on a plane to Arkansas.

"I got off the place, and they costumed me into the 1940s," Wells remembers. "While I was preparing physically, Charles told me the story of the film."

She learned the legend of a spree that terrified Texas and Arkansas, themselves still recovering from the world war that had ended the previous summer. From February to May 1946, eight people were attacked, five shot to death. Less than a week after the fifth shooting victim died, another man was found dead on railroad tracks a few miles north of the town. Still today, speculation abounds as to whether his death was an accident, the killer's work . . . or a suicide from shame of being the murderer himself.

That's right; films have been made based (very, *very* loosely) on the crimes of Ed Gein, Ted Bundy, and many others. But the difference between them and the man who made the Texarkana area dread the night (when all of his crimes were committed) is simply this: they paid, albeit too late and not enough, for their crimes.

He never did. He was never caught. Like Jack the Ripper before and the Zodiac later, his (or hers, anything's possible) identity is still today an official mystery. He's still referred to as just the Phantom.

And, just as many from the area probably still feel today, those of the area of the mid-'70s still lived in a certain degree of fear, even decades after the nightmare. Wells' character would be named Helen Reed, but everyone who knew the first bit about the case was aware of her basis on Katie Starks, who'd seen her husband become the Phantom's final "official" victim and barely managed to escape herself.

Preparing at high speed for the first "real person" (instead of fictional character) role of her career, Wells asked if she could meet Katie, who still lived nearby. Like most residents of the time, Katie wasn't interested.

"I didn't pry," Wells says. "It didn't matter who the character really was when I was asked to do the role. My character was scared to death, trying to fight for your life. If there had been scenes where I was relating to someone, like her husband or whoever, there would have been more background of who she was. But all we knew what that she got shot and tried to survive, which applies to any human being."

Surrounded by many locals on and off the crew, Wells found her way around 1940s Texarkana, along the border between the states (Pierce played a cop in his own film).

"As we went from scene to scene, I got a feeling for the atmosphere," says Wells, who shot all her scenes in one twenty-straight-hours day of filming. "I learned about where it happened right away. There was time to get inside myself, of feeling the fear of being in that city, that little town where the murders happened. I got the feeling of the atmosphere."

Then came her toughest moment, one both horrifying and miraculous that she, and formerly Katie, had escaped from alive.

On the night of May 3, 1946, Katie and her husband Virgil were listening to their radio. From another room, she heard glass break, the sounds of bullets tearing apart windows and through her husband's head. Katie ran to the phone to call for help, but more bullets blasted forth. One went straight through her head; another broke her jaw.

She fell. Then she got right back up and ran straight through and out of the house, blood splashing everywhere. She made it to a neighbor's house and eventually to the hospital.

Now Wells had to act it all out.

"You're always prepared (as an actress)," explains Wells. "You always have something inside of you, ready to create. Your job is to do the best you can under the circumstances."

As her husband sits in the living room reading the paper, Helen brushes her hair. The Phantom's bullets break the window and take his life. She calls for him softly, clearly expecting him to answer, not knowing he never will again. Imagine waiting those moments, hoping to hear a response, not knowing the person we called for is already dead.

"I was shot twice in the face, and it was all about the special effects," she remembers. "Getting shot in the face and trying to escape was a natural human emotion. The preparation time wasn't there, and I don't think it mattered." The Phantom, armed with a picaxe and gun, pursues Helen across a cornfield, a killer who'll stop at nothing to commit murder, even without motive.

Wells tried to keep her mind on her fearful performance (Bud Davis, who played the Phantom, later helped with the stunt work on 1994's *Forrest Gump*, 2009's *Inglourious Basterds*, and many other films). It wasn't easy, because reality was right in front of her, barking its insanely powerful head off.

A pit bull had been assigned to witness Helen's escape and vocally awaken the neighbors that would save her. But these breeds aren't known for their heroism or dramatic talent, and Wells feared she might experience the brutal stereotype often—and unfairly—labeled to such canines.

"The dog was barking, all riled up," she recalls. "It was growling, teeth bared, and I'm on my face in the grass. The crew was there, and they told Charlie that if it went after me, they'd have to shoot it."

As her Helen crawled forth, the dog did its work. Then it yanked its stake from the ground.

"I've got my face down and my hands over my head, and the dog pulls the stake out!" Wells recalls. "Guns went off everywhere, missed the dog, but they got the dog in tow."

After nearly a full day and night straight of shooting, Wells stumbled back to her hotel. The clerk took one look at her and fainted dead away.

Then she realized her pseudo gunshot wounds and fake blood were still all over her face and head.

Katie, who eventually remarried, passed away in July 1994, about three months shy of her 85th birthday. That September, Youell Swinney died as well. If the man who died on the tracks wasn't the Phantom, Swinney may well have been.

A longtime criminal, he was caught driving a car stolen during the spree. He'd owned a gun similar to the type used in at least some of the killing. His wife claimed that he'd told her he'd committed the crimes, and gave some info not even the police knew at the time, though she later recanted. He had no alibi for the times of the murders.

But there was never enough to prosecute, although many involved with the case still believe Swinney did it (a lifelong criminal, he went to jail for the car theft in 1947 and stayed for over a quarter-century. The killings stopped when he was off the streets.).

As remakes started piling up (some, like me, call it "overtaking") in the horror world in the 2000s, it wasn't any big surprise that a new version of *Sundown* came along in 2014. To its credit, the film put a different spin on the whole "redo" attempt.

It starts at the film's real-life annual Halloween showing near Texarkana, where a girl and her boyfriend are suddenly attacked in a car, much like the actual Phantom's first victims. She escapes, but he's killed. Soon more and more people are violently dying in similar ways, and the original gal keeps getting messages from the Phantom, demanding she make people "remember."

As it turns out, a local deputy is the killer, helped along by her boyfriend, whose murder was a fake. As it turns out, he's the grandson of Hank McCreedy, the Phantom's "forgotten" victim (apparently based on Earl Cliff McSpadden, the man whose body was found on the railroad tracks).

Of course, she kills him. And, of course, the final scene has a shadow following her down a hallway, suggesting there will someday be another *Sundown*.

In 1972, Pierce had directed *The Legend of Boggy Creek*, a slightly less serious jaunt to folklore. It's the docu-dramedy about the Fouke Monster, a Bigfoot colleague said to hang out in a small town in Arkansas. Doing the whole self-filmed thing *decades* before any *Blair Witch* or *Paranormal* ideas, the tale, like *Sundown*, eventually pulled in a cult classic following.

The year after making *Sundown*, Wells headed back to the neck of the woods for *Return to Boggy Creek* (Tom Moore directed this one). She'd play the mom of three kids who get lost in the title area until the Monster shows up to save them. A year before she hit it big on *Diff'Rent Strokes*, Dana Plato was Wells' daughter.

"With Dana Plato, our relationship was very motherly," remembers Wells, who never became a mom herself. "I was playing the mother in a fantasy, but the circumstances were kind of dangerous, with water moccasin, cockfights around the corner, good ol' boys. When you're playing fantasy with a monster, you try to personalize it. There's no such thing as a monster, so what would bring the most fear to you? Would it be somebody hopped up on something with weapons in their hands, or would it be something you wouldn't believe, like ghost stories and hearing noises?"

It's questions like that that Wells never stopped asking, through half a century on screens big and small, through hundreds of stage productions, and even while instructing new members of the acting business at Idaho's Film Actors Boot Camp, which she founded in 1988.

"At one point, as actors, we all want to try everything," she explains. "We all want to stretch and grow and do as much as we can. It's much more difficult to fool a camera that's focused on you from chin to forehead than it is to fool somebody twenty to thirty feet away in a theater. It's the technique: your ability in the theater is to project it to the balcony, and in film, the audience can see the subtleties in your eyes and on your face, and you hope you exude the truth."

Liz White helped the title character of *The Woman in Black* (2012) get revenge for her kid's death.

Liz White:
The Woman in Black

THEY WERE GOING to pay—through the nose, eyes, mouth, and everywhere else.

For her entire life, one horror film after another had tapped its way all the way through Liz White's subconscious and gleefully tormented her from the inside out.

"I could never watch horror," White recalls. "Anything that combined shock with the supernatural sent me into a world of the worst imaginings. I couldn't bear the lack of control. The director has you strapped to their waterboard: each shock and gasp as inevitable as the next, but nevertheless painful. I could never understand why people would watch it for pleasure."

It would be ironic that the role that launched White straight into America film fans' eyes and minds would be of the genre that had turned her into an impromptu insomniac, but it was certainly welcome.

Now she could dish it out. Now others could feel her pain. It was time for her to scare.

That the ones she'd be terrifying had nothing to do with her earlier trepidation . . . well, that was just the most minor of inconveniences. As it turned out, the character she'd become had some motivations that weren't entirely different.

She almost didn't get the title role in 2012's *The Woman in Black*, and neither did anyone else. Some of the crew wanted the distress-causing damsel to be played by a fully costumed background performer, which would have saved some green. But James Watkins finally had a shot at putting his own name in the annals of horror directing, and he wasn't going to leave it to a living prop.

"I am really glad that James opted for an actor," White says. "There was no dialogue and scant interaction, but there was a story locked in Jennet. I was hungry for it and James seemed like a really exciting, young, bright director."

Bright, however, would the last adjective anyone could apply to the final filmed project, and that's driven home with an explosive sledgehammer in the first moments. The first people we see are three little girls having a friendly attic tea party.

Suddenly, everything stops. The girls stand up and slowly walk toward an entrancing object in the corner that only they can see. With as little emotion as the dolls they were just playing with, the girls walk straight to a window . . . and jump right out. Clearly this isn't going to be the realistic sort of horror.

That, even after pouring her way through the script and Susan Hill's 1983 novelization, made things even tougher than White had expected to locate the lady named Jennet, and, even more elusive, her reasons. The film's characters didn't have the simplest of times either.

Trying to help his son heal from the tragic loss of the boy's mom, young lawyer Arthur Kipps (Daniel Radcliffe) works his way through the sale of an old Edwardian house. But the old owner, recently passed, doesn't appear to have left the place empty. Arthur's tormented by the sounds of a wrecking carriage. He hears a young boy crying desperately to be saved.

Then a terrifying dark being, attired in funeral clothing, roars toward him—and no one believes that it happened. But he already has more to worry about: a young girl, having swallowed some poison, dies before him, and now we find out about the woman that White was working toward.

"The props guy had disappeared with a camera dolly and come back with a 'ghost dolly,'" she remembers of the swooping scene. "I was instructed to lurch forward as several men pushed me to the other side of the room on what was a essentially a tray with wheels. James was waiting for the take that had the optimum speed combined with the scariest scream. It was difficult because if my concentration lapsed I wouldn't feel scary; I would feel highly ridiculous. As ever, time was of the essence so that would snap me back into killer-ghost mode."

We now know *who* the lady is . . . but why? What could entice anyone, even the most evil of humans, to cause this behavior? That was still the most elusive answer to locate, and even when it was, nothing could even be remotely justifying to these actions.

Still, *something* needed to be found, and it finally was. As more and more local children follow in the fatal footsteps of the first ones we saw, astoundingly dying from their own doings, we and Arthur find out the tragically sad truth that the locals desperately tried to conceal; that everything is from the supernatural actions of Jennet, the sister of the lady who owned the house. After adopting Jennet's son, the woman had been in a carriage crash with the young boy, then disregarded his pleas for help—hence what we and he heard earlier—saving only herself. Jennet had taken her own life with a noose's help, but vowed that her work wasn't through.

White was using the vehicle to turn the tables on a genre that had terrified her; Jennet slammed her unthinkable pain down on others who had no right to enjoy the parental privileges that she'd been denied. Once again, there was the slightest commonality between them.

"Losing her son and indeed her sense of family as she witnessed that no one helped to save her boy had removed any empathy she had in her," White says, "and to express her pain without compromise became her *raison d'etre*. Her revenge tactic, to kill children, was hard to swallow, but thank goodness it's just make-believe."

Ironically, her co-workers quite often forgot that during filming, even far from the cameras. With little dialogue—except one part that we'll hit *hard* in a few moments—much of White's work was done through Jennet's look and action.

"The makeup and the costume combined made for such an imposing figure that on my first day on set, and many subsequent ones, people found it very difficult to talk to me," she remembers. "We would begin a polite conversation, as you do when you first meet your colleagues, and in mid-sentence they would say something along the lines of 'I'm sorry, Liz, I can't talk to you anymore. You are freaking me out.'"

Jennet only real speech—well, "speech" would be more appropriate—came in the scene where White could show her as an innocent lady in agony that no parent should ever be shoved toward, the witnessing of her child's death. It would be one of her only chances to inject the monster Miss with an ounce of humanity, and White went at high effort and volume to take advantage of Jennet's little dialogue.

Its entirety would be a scream, an expression of the terror of seeing one's child die.

"I was encouraged that much of the work had been done for me and all that remained to do was to perfect the thousand-yard stare and the scream," she says. "I hadn't practiced it because there aren't many places you can get away with it. I remember doubting my lack of preparation and being scared that I wasn't good enough, so when James asked me to do a scream, I just went for it. People were suitably freaked out. I was relieved."

Trying to save his son from Jennet's black magic, Arthur finds her child's body and buries it with Jennet, going the appeasement route. Things seem to calm down, but, hey, this is a horror movie—we can't shut the door to potential sequels!

Waiting for a train ride back home, Arthur sees his boy on the tracks, strolling forward in a similar mindset that we saw in the girls way back at the start. Arthur jumps down to save him, but Jennet's face glares at him from the upcoming train.

He braces for impact, but it doesn't happen. Opening his eyes, Arthur sees his dead wife, and his son asks about Jennet. Looks like her evil ploy worked again—and, as the family strolls off together, Jennet takes one more terrifying look.

This time, it's toward us. This isn't over.

She was right—part two arrived in 2014, with Leanne Best in the new title role.

"I am very proud of what everybody achieved on *The Woman In Black*, particularly the final shot," White says. "If you knew how many hot water bottles were stuffed up my dress on the shot railway platform at 3:30 on a November morning, it might ruin the impact for you."

But not for her, and not for the rest of the *Woman*'s workers; all that pseudo-revenge White looked to grab over the audience might have been just an illusion after all.

"To play the part of the ghost was no threat at all. I had all the control," she says, "or so I thought; at the premiere, when I saw the film for the first time, flanked by my agent, my father, and my best friend, I screamed louder than the rest combined!"

For much of America, the tale that White, Watkins, Ratcliffe, and the rest would tell may have been their first interaction with Hill's tome. It was indeed the first time the story had hit the big screen.

But the saga had been shown before. Before the 1980s were even finished, British audiences took a walk down the dark streets of England's east coast in a TV movie. After spending years in the musical spotlight, rocking across the United Kingdom as a member of the band She Trinity, Pauline Moran answered her true calling.

"After five years with the group," she recalls, "I obtained a grant from the Inner London Education Authority and won a place at the Royal Academy of Dramatic Art (RADA)." After spending much of the 1970s and '80s on stages and screens of all sizes, Moran got the title role in 1989's *The Woman in Black*.

"To be involved in acting is to be involved in all genres if you are genuinely committed to the profession," she says, "and a role in a horror film would be approached in the same way as any other. According to my then agent, my physical appearance rendered me more suitable for period drama and for many years I found this to be an accurate observation."

Kipps was now Arthur Kidd, and Adrian Rawlins was the man behind the character. Unlike Radcliffe's Kipps, he has no wife or son. But he's still in England, a solicitor sent to handle the estate of a recently deceased widow. Ironically enough, a few years later, Rawlins would play James Potter, pappy to Radcliffe's boy wizard!

After noticing a strange lady near the back of the funeral and within the graveyard, Kidd's left alone in the house. But strange noises, sounding like a horse and scared child, start to torment him. He soon learns that the lady was Jennet, that the recently passed widow was her sister, and that the sister had abducted Jennet's son.

Still, there's another difference here, far from the 2012 tale; this time around, Jennet stole back her boy, only to perish right next to him in a marsh carriage crash.

"I have a great fondness for gothic literature and drama," Moran remembers, "and had little trouble projecting myself into the role." Like White would later, she studied hell out of the Woman's parts of Hill's book. "The locations were superbly appropriate and underpinned the most chilling scenes so well."

Nearly overcome with it all, Kidd faints away. But this Woman's here to haunt straight to the extreme; she's no kindly spirit.

With the young boy's apparition hovering alongside his mom, she screams straight into Kidd, knocking him back unconscious and just about over the dark edges of sanity. It was one of Moran's favorites, a feeling that spread amongst the critics as the show sneaked around the globe. With the help of the same techniques utilized by a fellow named Hitchcock, Moran was transformed into something far scarier than humanity, a hell of a lot harder than getting stabbed in a shower!

"With a wind machine blowing against me at full force," she recalls, "I was placed on a dolly which was pulled towards the camera. At the same time, the camera was pushed towards me whilst it focused slowly away from me, which gave an unearthly and disorientating effect on screen. I managed to sustain the malevolent piercing scream without damaging my voice, so my RADA training came in very useful."

The American versions were still decades away, as were the special effects advances that have roared through Hollywood on an almost daily basis for the past years. Finances weren't exactly a luxury for the *Woman* TV crew either; small screen shows don't get anywhere near the budget help that the big screen projects do.

But something else showed up to help. Something unpredictable and certainly uncontrollable, but natural. Maybe even an intervention in a divine sort of way. England's winters tend to go straight to the freezing extreme, and getting ready to film the finale on the waters of Osea Island in East England, the crew felt Mother Nature step in and give them the seriously cold shoulder.

"It was bitterly cold with searing winds, which added to the atmosphere but not to the comfort of the actors," Moran recalls. Even with layer of thermal suiting under the costumes, the performers could feel chills making their way through to living marrow.

"There was also very fine rain driving through my clothes which made it necessary for me to be wrapped in cling-film over the thermal suit underneath the costume," Moran continues. "After one day's filming on the island, we were taken back to the mainland by boat just at that time of day when twilight makes the horizon seem to disappear. We were some way out in the estuary when we discovered that the engine had failed and there was only one oar on the boat. We had to improvise with a broom and an oar to get us back to the island, whilst we continued to drift further out to sea; it seemed to take forever."

Other differences between the writing and the showing show up. At the end of the book, Kipps's wife and daughter are at a fair, the ladies on a leisurely carriage ride. Suddenly, the Woman steps out and spooks the horse. It bashes the carriage into a tree, killing the daughter instantly and the wife eventually, and leaving Kipps alive but alone.

Is that worse that what we saw? It's a matter of opinion, but Watkins' version was, well, a *bit* more upbeat than how things concluded in the first version. As the small-screen version rolls near the credits, Kidd and his family are on a boat when he sees the Woman casting a pitch-black stare at him . . . while she's standing in the midst of the waves.

"The scene where The Woman appears to walk on water was filmed on a day with a high wind, and I was standing in the middle of a lake on a platform no bigger than a chopping board just beneath the water level," Moran remembers. "The wind created a vortex of waves on the surface of the lake which swirled in the opposite direction to the physical force of the wind, creating an optical illusion which made it extremely difficult to avoid falling into the water."

Kidd's too terrified to so much as open his mouth. But Moran's version gets even more involved, and to an even grander, albeit darker effect, than White or her literary counterpart had.

Suddenly, a tree falls on the boat. Everyone dies. The woman's pain is spread about, several fold over.

"Literature is not drama and changes have to be made in order for it to work on screen," Moran explains. "Even to this day, our low-budget version has acquired many devotees who discuss the film avidly online. When the 2012 version was released, a whole new audience was found for both versions and much online debate followed. Hatred and grief beyond the prison of the grave is a powerful hook for a gothic tale, and this story has it all."

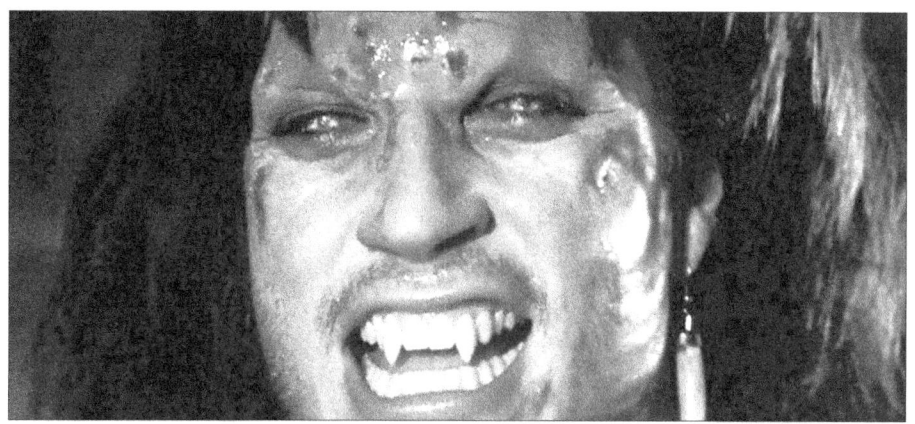

Dwayne (Billy Wirth) clearly enjoyed being one of 1987's *The Lost Boys*, perhaps a bit much!

Billy Wirth/Jamison Newlander:

The Lost Boys

YOU GET TO stay up all night, and sleep during the day, which is, of course, hours longer. You can traipse around all night, doing anything and going anywhere, without the slightest danger from the evil authority. After all, just a few things can even hurt you, let alone finish you for good.

Super speed and strength? The ability to fly? A hypnotic mental power that can subliminally order around those not in the know, or even seduce a gorgeous woman and make her think it's all too good to be true!

Sounds like life's dream coming true, doesn't it? Especially for the young, oftentimes lazy hormone machines known as young adult males, right?

No wonder vampires only allow a certain select and very special few to become a part of their jolly old fraternity, is it? Well, there is the whole "must kill to live" thing. . . .

The way Billy Wirth describes it, you'd have no idea that bloodsuckers were even part of 1987's *The Lost Boys*, at least at first.

"I bonded with Kiefer (Sutherland) and Brooke (McCarter) and Alex (Winter)," Wirth recalls of getting ready for the flick with his co-stars. "We got the regular connection, like we were a family. It added to us feeling comfortable with each other. It was a really cool environment to hang out on the boardwalk."

Of course, the group also had to spend quite a bit of time hidden away, and not just in the chairs in which they were caked with all kinds of makeup.

Yes, a person unfamiliar with the storyline wouldn't realize the horror aspect for quite some time. Emerson brothers Michael (Jason Patric) and Sam (Corey Haim) and their mom Lucy (Dianne West), fresh off a divorce, arrive in Santa Clara, CA, a cozy summer town known for being the murder capital of the planet—which obviously has nothing to do with anything else in the plot, not at all!

Both fall in with their respective cool age crowds, Sam with Frog brothers Edgar and Allen (perhaps their parents were at home trying to make a third one they could call Poe!), Michael with Wirth's Dwayne and his pals. As is usually the case with vampires in the movies, there just happens to be present a clan member who's hotter than the fire that vampires must avoid, and here it's Jamie Gertz's Star. But while Michael's trying to woo her in the group's hideout, Sutherland's David, apparently the leader of the fanged pack, tricks him into drinking red stuff that he only thinks is wine.

Yes, it's plasma, and Michael's heading down the path to (un)death.

Unlike an adult-oriented horror flick, like *The Exorcist*, might have done, the movie doesn't get the adults involved much. Had Lucy known more than she does, we might have seen Michael get taken to hospitals and psychiatrists, tested and analyzed by everyone with a MD of any kind.

Not here. He's a vampire, and that's all we need. Skip the seriousness and get straight to the fun part of saving him. Even if it might mean killing him. Even if that's what he wants.

That's the tale of the Frogs, Corey Feldman's Edgar and Jamison Newlander's Allen, seemingly the only pair in town willing to accept the reason for the rising death count. Getting ready for the roles, the two played the same game as Wirth and his new pals.

"I met (director Joel Schumacher), and we hit it off," Newlander remembers. "Then I came back and read with Feldman and we hit it off. But I wasn't a big enough star for them at the time." While Feldman's star had already risen from hits like *The Goonies* (1985), *Gremlins* (1984), and *Stand by Me* (1986), Newlander hadn't landed a smash of yet.

But even after a search that made extensive seem understated, the crew remembered the fellow who'd established a sibling-like bond, if not the strongest physical resemblance, to Feldman.

"I came back, and we had some good chemistry," Newlander recalls. "I was a little more straightlaced, and (Feldman) was more outspoken. I have two sides as an actor. I can be a comedic actor, and I can have a serious side. It was deadpan. It's not like jerky comedy. I worked on there being very little movement, really focused."

Wirth, Schumacher, and the rest of the group went shopping up and down the legendary Melrose Avenue, checking out the leather and pitch-black clothes that show that their wearers want very much to show everyone that walks by just how wild and rebellious they are.

"We stayed up late," Wirth remembers. "Schumacher wouldn't let us go into the sun. He didn't want us to get tan. We had a lot of night shoots." Getting a chance to roar around on some souped-up cycles (they learned from some stunt drivers) was probably a pretty big incentive as well!

While Lucy falls into a whirlwind romance with video store owner Max (Edward Herrmann), Sam

Against warriors like Allen Frog (Jamison Newlander), *The Lost Boys* (1987) didn't have a chance in the hell he hoped to send them to.

and the Frogs take advantage of daylight to surprise the sleeping vamps, but only kill Winter's Marko with a spike. David's on their tail, and he knows where they live.

Like most vampire films, *Lost Boys* gives its own interpretation of the creatures' "rules." First off, Michael's only a half-vampire at first—you don't get all the way in until you actually kill somebody—so he can go into the light. Also, while some vampires in the film (like the head one we'll meet later) need to be invited in before they can do anything, others don't, especially those on the attack. But this isn't time to be too serious about this stuff.

"I had an idea that we were into something cool, but we didn't have any idea that it would stand the test of time," Newlander admits. "It's violent at times, but not compared to the horror films of today. People appreciate the story and the good filmmaking."

With the enemy troops advancing, the two brother teams are ready, complete with sharpened stakes, enough garlic to take out a football team, and bathtubs and water guns full of holy water.

And as inexperienced as they are in actual hand-to-clawed-hand combat, the Frogs manage to take out McCarter's Paul, helped along by the family dog, always known for having a sixth sense toward evil in horror movies. Downstairs, Sam faces the flying sadist that Dwayne has become. It takes a crossbow and some electricity, not to mention quite a bit of time, but he comes out alive.

David doesn't—Michael slams him through a superhuman pair of deep antlers. But another vampiric rule for this flick is that killing the head vamp makes everyone else turn back to normal (as normal as humans can ever be). Michael doesn't do so. David wasn't the main bad guy.

That just happened to be mom's new man, Max—and anyone who spent watching the late, great

Hermann as the kindly grandpa on *Gilmore Girls* was undoubtedly knocked for three loops and a somersault. But just as he's about to make Lucy his eternal bride, her dad, who's been hiding a secret all film, barrels in with a car loaded up with wooden stakes and sends Max to eternity. Clearly, the Frogs weren't the only ones in the know about locals living forever.

"We were the Lost Boys!" Wirth proclaims. "The story was about the brothers, their friendship, one of them growing up, the love story between Jason and Jamie Gertz. Then you had the story of the Lost Boys and their living on the boardwalk forever. All these different stories made it a really dynamic story." *Note: Sadly, McCarter passed away of liver disease on December 22, 2015, just before this book went to press.*

The very next year, Newlander showed up in *The Blob* remake. Surprisingly, however, it took over two decades to try to recapture the *Lost* magic.

2008's *Lost Boys: The Tribe* revolved around Michael's kids (he and Lucy have both passed by now) hanging out in a similar town, trying to get to the surfing scene. When the sister falls for the same trick as her dad, Edgar shows up to do his thing. Her brother ends up switching over to save her, and the head vamp is destroyed to save them all.

But after all of that, even after the credits get going, things are still happening. Edgar's accosted by Sam himself, who's now himself sucking blood for a living. Just as the two roar into battle, things end.

Newlander's scenes in *Tribe* were cut, but he managed to show up two years later for *The Thirst*, which has his bro starting a full-blown army against an even larger group of undead. Newlander even switches to the evil side for a time, but makes it back to good in the end (the film came out just after Haim's sad, untimely passing).

"I was happy to just have a part," Newlander says. "Feldman and I worked together to get all that chemistry back! In this kind of film and this kind of acting, some actors were really deep in character, and I wasn't really like that. I just *did* it."

Mary Woronov's knowing smile has shined through and darkened horror films for decades.

Mary Woronov

WHEN LEARNING ONE'S own methods of preparing to portray, it's important to experiment—and since it's better to go too far than not far enough, especially early on, we *might* want to spend some extra time there. Doing research. Writing backstories. Formulating who we'll be becoming long before we even reach the set, let alone get into the scene work.

Still, there might come a point where we might just be better off going straight for broke. At some time, it may be better to just try leaving it all to chance and hope.

Because some people skip all the stuff we've been discussing all book long and just go right into it. They do something you can't really teach. It's something you can't really learn.

It just happens. She steps onto set and into character, and it's just right there. Mary Woronov glances or even gazes into a co-star's eyes and hears the words wafting or even blasting from somebody's vocal cords, and she just becomes *it*.

Whether her own personal *it* is what everyone is looking for, however, well, that's a question she's been leaving up to the debates of horror film fans for decades.

"Once I see the person opposite me and I understand what he's doing," Woronov tersely describes, "it's very simply to counterbalance him. Not just counterbalance him in the story, but counterbalance him as an actor, helping him to do more of what he needs to do, according to me. You work with the director, and sometimes he gets it and sometimes he doesn't."

Woronov's career rolled long before she took too huge of a step into horror, mainly because of a pair of fellows who certainly *got* her, just as generations of fans of every genre have grabbed hold of them. Still, her reason for taking up owned residence (as opposed to the leased kind!) into the terrifying cinema category was pretty simple and sad at the same time.

"There was nothing else left to me," she glooms. "I had finished all my movies with (Roger) Corman (that wasn't entirely true, she'd happily discover), who I loved working for. I had finished all my movies with (Andy) Warhol, who was fabulous, and I was only trying to pay the rent, which I don't have to do anymore. I never really looked for (horror films), but they are very attracted to me."

Her film debut came in 1966's *Chelsea Girls*, Warhol's own mainstream debut; the same year, the two worked on *Superboy*.

"In the beginning, when I was working with Warhol, there was no acting," she says. "Then I did all these plays in New York, and it all happened instantaneously. It wasn't about working your role out and feeling it; it was about going with the flow. No one knew what you were going to do. That's the way I learned to do it."

Woronov's then-husband Ted Gershuny directed her through her horror debut in 1972 as she battled an escaped mental patient on Christmas Eve of *Silent Night, Bloody Night*, and he fixed her up the next year in *Sugar Cookies*, as she avenged the death of her lesbian lover (an up-and-comer named Oliver Stone produced the film).

"My characters were great, but I always played the mean girl," Woronov says. "I never got the 'Lassie-come home' moms. I played gay a lot, back when you weren't even allowed to mention that there were lesbians around."

She considers her own unofficial Hollywood debut to be 1975's *Death Race 2000*, a depiction of the kind of event that many of the time probably thought would be true by now, just as many of today see *The Hunger Games* saga as something that will be a real show someday, tuned to the competitive action/violence-obsessed society that America has been becoming for quite some time. Woronov was Calamity Jane, one of the few ladies to compete in the title race, where only the winner gets out alive and so many viewers and gamblers spend all kinds of money.

"That movie was very relevant and very funny," Woronov says. "It had the sense of humor that I like. I was really nervous and I didn't know how to prepare. I very intimidated for the first half of filming—I was OK for the second half." Perhaps Jane helped lay the seeds for the preparatory techniques that would carry Woronov through the next few decades.

Up against David Carradine's Frankenstein (far from the legendary scientific creation!) and Sylvester Stallone's Machine Gun Joe, Jane's taken out by an all-too-conveniently placed land mine. Joe suffers the same fate at the exploding pieces of a grenade—as of 2016, after about four decades of films, Stallone has only died in *Death Race* and 1978's *F.I.S.T.*, giving him one of Hollywood's best "survival" records—leaving the Frank man to win the race, and, soon after, the country.

"I didn't know how to drive," Woronov admits. "The car was driven by someone else. They had to pull me around in the car when the camera was doing close-ups." Her character wasn't resurrected for the 2008 *Death Race* remake, although Carradine came back for Frankenstein to be tragically killed early on.

Many consider Woronov's top role to be the curmudgeonly Miss Togar of 1979's *Rock 'N Roll High School*, but horror fans prefer *Eating Raoul* three years later. After directing her in *Death Race*, Paul Bartel turned himself and Woronov into a married couple in his *Raoul* screenplay (he'd also direct the dark tale).

The two are the Blands, a broke couple dreaming of a career in restaurateur-ism. Then one day, a drunk breaks into their apartment and tries to rape Mary (the actors used their real first names), only to have Paul blast him to eternity with a frying pan. The two steal his money, toss him into a trash compactor, and see a new road to success.

A few killings later, the Blands are getting almost all the way along, but the title character breaks into their house and finds their secret, forcing them to cut him in on the deal. He tries to win Mary's heart, but she's playing him all along, taking him out at the end. Forced to toss together a dinner with no food, the two suddenly discover the tastes that Hannibal Lecter would show us nearly a decade later, living up to the film's title and the realization of the dream that will cornerstone their restaurant.

"It was written for me, and that's usually why I go for roles," Woronov says of Mary. "Paul wrote it for me and him, because both of us had worked quite extensively in Corman movies, and they always wrote us together for some reason. We became a sort of team. When we started acting in it, I loved it." So successful was it that the Blands showed up for a quick cameo in 1986's *Chopping Mall*, their new location part of the background that would soon be overtaken by evil robots.

Three years later, Woronov would help Julian Sands' title character communicate with the dark forces in *Warlock*, her channeler suddenly overtaken by his friends, in both the physical and mental sense.

"Working with Julian was wonderful," Woronov says. "I usually don't get ready for roles; people want me because of certain things, and they always want me to overact, and it's always the same story."

She stepped far from horror in 1990 with a small role in *Dick Tracy*, and light years from it alongside some animated household names in 2003's *Looney Tunes: Back in Action* (playing, what else, the vice president of Acme's Bad Ideas!). But two years later, Woronov helped another young director get started in horror, stabbed to death in the opening moments of Rob Zombie's *Devil's Rejects*.

"(Zombie) was a good director because he never told me what to do," she explains. "The first time I got stabbed, the actor missed all the pads, so it's a good thing that knife was retractable, or I'd be dead!"

Obviously, her character wouldn't be so lucky—and neither would she in a slightly bigger role in *The House of the Devil* (2009).

In typical horror fare, the story begins with a college student low on funds, impulsively agreeing to babysit for a strange couple nearby. She's Samantha (Jocelin Donahue) and they're the Ulmans. Woronov is the Mrs., and her husband is longtime horror star Tom Noonan (fellow scaring legend Dee Wallace has an early cameo as Samantha's landlord).

Tricked into staying alone at the Ulman house, Samantha's drugged and finds herself in the midst of a ritual, Mr. Ulman's own mom using her blood to draw art on Samantha, soon forcing the young woman to drink it. As things move scarily forward, Mrs. Ulman begins an ominous chant, and we're not sure who she's actually conversing with.

Per usual for her, "I didn't really know what I was going to do until I hit the set," Woronov says. "The costume matters to me once I get into it. The reaction of the other people matters to me. It all happens really instantaneously, and if it doesn't happen, I'm in trouble. Usually, it does happen. I turn into that person. I understand what I need to do in order to fit in to what is going on, and I can do it. It's just being able to act. I don't sit around and plot it out; you could plot something out and it might be entirely wrong, because it's only from your head. Once I hit the set, that's when I start."

Samantha escapes, takes out Mrs. Ulman, and plants a gun to her own head to escape the mental torture her world has become. But her aim is off, and the final scene is her in a hospital, a nurse assuring her that both of them will be OK—she and the far-from-immaculate conception that's now on her inside.

"People keep picking me for the roles, and I kept on getting horror movies," Woronov says. "It was just the way my career went."

And while Warhol's passing put a sad end to the partnership the two had enjoyed, she'd get at least one more round with Corman, cameo-ing in his 2012 spoof *Attack of the 50-Foot Cheerleader*.

"There's no more pleasant way to pay your rent than doing a movie," Woronov exclaims. "It's all been a *lot* of fun!"

Scary kids

EVER SINCE I had grade-school nightmares about Drew Barrymore in *Firestarter* (1984) and *Poltergeist*'s Heather O'Rourke (1982)—not to mention sleeping with the lights on in my twenties after Dakota Fanning turned all our vertebrae to ice in *Hide and Seek* (2005) and Daveigh Chase made us all afraid to use our VCRs in *The Ring* (2002)—I've often wondered: what is it about kid actors that makes them so scary? Why are the scary kids the thing that we so often remember most about horror films? What about the pint-sized horrors so curdles our plasma?

Well, I think I've finally come to a conclusion. When we see adult actors playing horror movie villains, we might stop and think—OK, these people have had YEARS to hone their craft. They're scary because they've been learning it for a long while. An adult has had all kinds of time to find the skills to transform into the most frightening beings on screen.

But the kids? They haven't had that period to develop those skills. They don't have the experience that comes from years of instruction that so many professional actors enjoy. They haven't been *alive* long enough. Unless they started acting school in the nursery, their ability to make us double-check the door locks before we go to sleep at night has come from within.

So maybe they aren't really acting. Maybe their ability to pretend to be so scary isn't an ability after all; it might be natural. It might be who they truly are. This forbidding brood isn't really so much talented as acting so much as they might be . . . just being themselves!

"Whether she was a good person or a bad person, I played her as just a person involved in those activities, which was probably even more frightening to watch," said Patty McCormick, whose portrayal of eight-year-old murderess Rhoda Penmark in 1956's *The Bad Seed* was one of the first films to explore the "evil child" premise. In McCormack's Oscar-nominated performance, Rhoda kills a young classmate, then burns alive a witness to the crime.

In the days before ratings came about, children were banned from seeing the film in America (even McCormack herself had trouble getting in, often having to explain that she was actually in the film to be able to check herself out on screen).

"What motivated Rhoda was a sense that her own morality was about taking care of herself," explains McCormack, seemingly showing that such acts can't always been considered evil if they're committed by one too young to know the difference between right and wrong.

"She had no sense of not being good or not being bad; she just took care of business."

OK, I've got to stop this before I swear off horror and convert to Disney flicks for the rest of my life. But let's find out how some of these other kids got so horrifying. . . .

Even history's most evil were young once, as Ella-Maria Gollmer showed us in 2009's *The Countess*.

Ella-Maria Gollmer:

The Countess

As we've seen through this project, many horror performers can move forward quickly, leaping towards the front of the genre with little experience. Many of the ones we'll meet here, though, were able to do so without the strong hands of realism holding them back, doing the kinds of horror that either can't actually happen, or probably won't.

Some, however, have to take a different kind of chance. Others, like the lady we're about to hear from, are tasked with overcoming experience and moving into the type of reality we only wish came from horrifying fiction. This type of horror may be unlikely, as we've seen—but we know it already occurred.

Most people who know just about anything about Elizabeth Bathory go straight to her deeds, which get almost as much credit as Vlad the Impaler for inspiring Dracula's bio. Her violent murders, torture as both a participant and eager viewer, of a number of innocent women that we'll never truly be able to fully certify. The beatings, mutilations, and long, slow draining of their blood, which Bathory, in the most infamous action of her regime, bathed in, her deranged mind believing it held in her youth.

That's enough for many people—just paint someone as a monster, justify it with a glance at their lives, and walk away. But while films like *The Countess* (2009) are some of the most difficult stories to tell, and for many of us to watch, they're also some of the most important to make. Because they tell us more of the truth than we were really interested in knowing, and show how important it is for stories like Bathory's to tell the whole truth. It's how we learn and don't forget, even continents away and centuries later.

Again, though, they're pretty tough to depict, especially for those as new to the acting world as Ella-Maria Gollmer was.

The acting world had long been aware of Julie Delpy's talent before the camera, but the film gave her a shot at new cinematic credibility, writing and directing it as well (note: don't mistake it for the action-packed biopic *Bathory* of the year before. *Fright Night II* also told Bathory's tale in 2013, throwing realism out the window). Delpy would also carry the bulk of the acting load, playing the cold, malevolent title madam through her older years.

But as wonderful an actress as Delpy is, she didn't have to ability to morph off a few years and play the gal that Bathory was before she fully became a monstrous mistress.

Paula Hartmann played the child before she reached royalty through an arranged marriage, as many did back in Hungary in the late 1500s. Once that period arrived in Bathory's life, and the film, Gollmer stepped in.

Again, like many, she knew a bit of the dark, bloody side of Bathory beforehand.

"I had heard stories from the spooky Middle Ages," Gollmer recalls. "In Germany (her homeland), lots of fairytales play in this era, so of course I was interested in the life of the medieval people. I had seen medieval towns with their castles and their scary torture chambers and had heard stories about burning witches. It really fascinated me. And how could you possibly have the idea to bathe in the blood of virginal women to stay young? It sounds made up, but it is not. It is inspired by Ms. Bathory's story."

She wouldn't have to tell that part of Bathory's bio, but there were still some aspects that the then-pre-teen was far from in reality (*fortunately!*).

Like the engagement the young woman was forced into before her teenage years. And the pregnancy and childbirth she went through at thirteen.

"The set design and the wardrobe put me in the place so I could feel closer to the character," Gollmer says. "You immediately start to behave differently, especially if you have a pillow underneath your skirt. There was not much more of a preparation for that. I mean, how would you prepare being pregnant as a thirteen-year-old kid?" Bathory did in fact become expecting at that age—by one of her servants, rather than her future husband!

"I enjoyed the training," Gollmer says. "Everything was a game for me, playing around, being in nice places, surrounded by all these grownups making a movie. That was pretty exciting by itself back then."

Acting out the birth, Gollmer looked back to what she'd seen far from in person.

"I was not nervous at all," she asserts. "I just had fun with my skirt and all the fake blood, and the crew was really nice so I felt comfortable. I had seen movies that show women giving birth and I just tried to imitate them. So I screamed and followed the instructions of the director. I guess the newborn baby was more nervous than I was."

The baby, named Anastasia far before the Romanov princess made the name household, was taken away from Bathory soon after her birth, and no one will probably ever know what happened to her.

"I just followed my intuition, acting as if I would become a mom," Gollmer says. "That is pretty much how acting started for me. I just followed my intuition and my imagination that came from books, stories, costumes, and the dancing classes I took. When looking back, I am astonished by myself. As an adult you always want to do a good job, make the scene or the moment work, and as a kid you just play, because it is too much fun to worry about doing it right."

Even enveloped in times far past and surrounded by blood and death, though faked, she somehow knew she'd be OK, even so early in her new career. "In a bizarre way, I never feel more safe than when performing in front of the camera," Gollmer says, "being surrounded by creative and inspiring people. If being in the moment is the answer to everything, for me, there is no better way to get there than by acting."

Her betrothed, with whom Bathory would have five more children, made both his future wife and her servant pay: his ordered fatal torture of the young man took place right in front of Bathory's eyes (calls up images of that evil little shit Joffrey on *Game of Thrones*, doesn't it?). Doing that scene forced Gollmer's imagination to work in an even more different way.

"There is one moment when I look out of the window, watching my boyfriend being killed brutally," she remembers. "I could not really see him; the set was built in a studio, so all I could see were paper walls and light bulbs. I was thinking that I should be very sad or even cry, but I was afraid that I would not be able to produce tears. I had no idea that they use eyedrops to make you look like you cried."

Still, she never expected, in a strange kind of a way, to be given just a little say, a bit of authority as to how her character came off in the film.

"We did three takes," Gollmer says. "In some way, I managed to produce tears by myself. The second take was the one we used eyedrops, and in the third one, we left the tears out. That´s the take they took. I learned a great lesson that day. Do not be afraid of emotional scenes. Those ones are the best. And do not pressure yourself with the fact that you should be able to cry on spot. It is not about that. Being a good actor, your emotions will show anyways."

Still, some of the toughest parts for the then-newcomer came when she had to speak a new and very strange language, one known worldwide as one of the most difficult for non-natives to learn.

"Since lots of the actors, including me, on the set, were Germans," she says, "we needed to have a coach to help us with the correct English pronunciation. If I look at the lines I said now, I am pretty surprised that the English came out that well, especially now since I am taking speech classes to lose my German accent."

It's been those tools, and many more she's picked up since, that have kept Gollmer's career going strong.

"I always try to keep some of this natural behavior that I had as a child when I act, although I am preparing my parts much more carefully now," she explains. "I try to find out as much information as I can get about the character. If she existed in real life, that is even better, because there is concrete material that you can be inspired by. If it is a fictional character, I think of famous people that are living or I take people I know as an inspiration. Not only women, just people that I know in general. It is more about the mannerisms and how they appear. But the preparation of every character varies. There is no recipe. But I think every character you are playing is a specific note of your own character. So you have to find the parallels between you and the fictional character, so you better have to know what is up with you."

Led by Mara (Lindsay Haun), a group of strange- looking and -acting kids turned a small California town into a *Village of the Damned* in 1995.

Lindsey Haun:

Village of the Damned

WAS SHE BORN to be bad? Bad to the bone?

Maybe, maybe not, but Lindsey Haun certainly couldn't wait to find out.

Before elementary school, she'd already been through years of acting. She'd been next to some of the biggest names in the acting game.

Still, "I got tired of doing commercials," she recalls. "Having to just sit around and smile was not interesting to me. (On shows) I was playing little girls who were crying, kidnapped, or sick."

So perhaps it was time to go in a different and much darker direction. Time to take the frightful offensive. Some preparation in that regard had been by her home, in a much more welcoming sense than usual.

If children are in a movie, the flick must be appropriate for youths, no matter the subject or rating, right? It had seemed so in her household. Her dad Jimmy, between guitar gigs for Air Supply, had followed the philosophy straight home.

"He loved horror movies, especially if they had a kid in them," Haun remembers. "He'd say, hey, you'll like this, because they have a kid too! I saw *The Shining* when I was four, and I grew up on *Poltergeist*, *The Omen*, and *The Exorcist*. I grew up terrified of horror movies, but I also loved them, like a comforting fear sort of thing."

Clearly, the market for terrifying kids has been around for decades in American cinema. Haun knew she wanted to be next.

"When I was around eight or nine, I started saying to my mom that I really wanted to play a bad guy," Haun recalls. But neither her previous work nor her father's show business contacts could guarantee her spot there. Haun thought of someone (Someone) that just might be able to help.

"My mom was a Christian and I grew up going to church, believing," she says, "so I started praying to Jesus for help." Maybe it was the most ironically divine of interventions that came next; maybe not, but something happened.

A quarter century before Haun was even born, Englishman John Wydham had novelized the story of *The Midwich Cuckoos*, the tale of a British township overtaken by a collective coma. Soon after, all of the women there left with the ability suddenly turn up expecting and give birth just a few months later, all on the same day.

The offsprings develop at high speed, but there's a downside: all that mental ability was exchanged with a complete lack of emotion. Then the adults start dying, seemingly by their own hand. One of the kid's fathers tries to show them a way to live, but he finds out that this has happened before: a small Soviet town was forced to blast a group of unwelcome additions to oblivion when things started going the wrong way. Soon after, he's forced to follow suit.

Just to stop any conclusion-jumping before it starts, the title's use of the word "cuckoo" had nothing to do with mental deficiency slang; it referred to the fact that the cuckoos' eggs hatch sooner and its descendants develop faster than most of the birds' feathered colleagues. Still, in any case, the moniker's certainly inappropriate for something that's supposed to scare holy hell out of us—when the film version came about in 1960, it was re-named *Village of the Damned*, which makes the point like the bomb that would come in play later.

Now we can see the children grow at high speed and evolve into something away from human, as if they're all members of a different family that's far from Earth. Telepathic towards each other and the adults, it's clear that world domination is their goal, and their ability to turn the big, mean adults who just want to kill them against each other shows that they won't be stopped.

Until Professor Gordon Zellaby, the "father" of kids leader David (Martin Stephens) figures out a way. Once again, the kids are wiped out, with Zellaby with them.

The film had been a surprise hit in both its British beginning land and here in America, and efforts had been made in the past to redo it (remember, this was *long* before the 2010s, where remakes are about as commonplace as originals in horror movies!). Now the time had come again, and Haun happened to be in the right place and time.

In the 1990s, a few modifications could be made to the story. First off, more violence—a *hell* of lot more violence.

Secondly, audiences would be more likely to accept a lady leading the kids. Her name would be

Mara. Her "father" would become the kids' strongest opponent. The two would end up at mental warfare—but only after Mara's strength had overtaken much of the land, now in California, although it was still called Midwich.

That's where Haun wanted to land.

"She was so freakin' cool," she says of Mara. "I thrived in that kind of environment. Little kids have egos, and I liked being their leader, their head honcho. For three months, you get to pretend that you were the most powerful being ever and there's a whole host of adults to cater to you. That's pretty powerful."

However, she still actually had to, you know, *get the role*! Haun read down *Cuckoos* and watched the first *Village* (one of the few her dad hadn't happened upon!). A slightly larger name in Hollywood would be on the other side of the camera, and Haun looked over some of his work, like *The Thing* (1982), an old favorite of hers.

Indeed, it would be none other than John Carpenter; Haun's first acting job had been on the TV series *Anything but Love* alongside Jamie Lee Curtis, whose star had been launched along with Carpenter's in the original *Halloween* (1978).

She also worked with a few coaches.

"At nine, I'd like to say I was hyper-intelligent and hyper-mature, but it was my relationship with my two coaches who taught me how to be an adult inside a little kid, which is weird to a child," Haun says. "It requires extreme discipline. One told me I should stare at him and not blink for as long as possible as I was saying my lines. As I was saying lines, he would take on other shapes—I started to imagine that he was Whoopi Goldberg, because I really loved her!"

But love was something that she'd have to leave behind, back in Lindsey, as Haun morphed into Mara.

"I grew up being really into aliens," she says, "and this hint that she might be an alien was exciting, Some of the other kids in the audition room were crying as we were memorizing each of the lines, pages and pages of monologue, because Mara could read people's minds. We were learning words that we didn't know, like 'inevitable.' We were supposed to be these advanced, possibly alien beings, inhabiting the bodies of these children, and it was a really, really hard audition. But I really liked it; I like stuff that's challenging." Instilling intimidation, fear, even terror into others much older, larger, and stronger, all without showing the first shred of emotion—it's tough to imagine a tougher task, especially for one with so little life experience, let alone acting ability. But Haun and eight others passed all the "audtionary" tests and got to placing the finishing, personal touches on Mara and the rest.

"My mom hadn't really been into horror movies," she remembers. "We'd watch horror films while I was getting ready, and she'd say things like 'What are you thinking about? How does this make you feel?' It really helped me get into the headspace of what I wanted and who I wanted the character to be. She had this stonewall strength that was really intimidating, probably really unnerving."

Things are unnerving in Midwich long before Mara or the others show their silver heads. In the midst of a wild town fair, dark clouds pass overhead. We see one lady collapse, and we only wish it had been a freak occurrence; soon, *everyone* in the area, even the dogs and cows, is feeling a collective narcolepsy attack. Everyone, that is, except Dr. Alan Chaffee, lucky enough to be driving out of town at the time.

In his last full-length film before the horseback riding tragedy that ultimately ended his life, Alan was the former Superman himself, Christopher Reeve. In a similar switch from a legendary role, Mark Hamill showed up as Rev. George, who's about to be presiding over quite a few more funerals.

Soon, Alan's delivering some unexpected and oft-unwelcome news to several fertile women. Even when government scientist Dr. Susan Verner (Kirstie Alley, in another role a woman wouldn't have gotten in the original) shows up to help him break the news, no one's sure what the hell's going on.

Still, Alan and his main lady Barbara are one of the ten couples to obtain (not *welcome*!) a new addition a few months later; they name the young beauty . . . Mara.

But another new girl doesn't make it past birth, which causes some trouble later on. We're not to it yet.

Aging far beyond their years both physically and mentally, the children, long before they really mean to, instill more than one sense in the town, and through it, the audience. There's fear, yes, but also a certain degree of awe. Awe and perhaps even jealousy that we weren't so lucky, not enough to be born like this. Naturally impugned with this kind of intellect, this dehydrated-esque thirst for learning. Many adults in the film and many viewers out of it (and probably their parents and teachers!) *wish* they could have gotten this kind of start, wishing they could be so damned *Damned* in every right way!

Then the people start to die. Mara's mom suddenly leaps off a cliff, another person off a roof. One man drives his truck into a gas tank. It's full chaos, and no one, except the infamous nine, has the first clue. When a bright glow erupts from a pair of their eyes, they've got the adults by the mind.

"Every time that they did a close-up of my eyes glowing, they had me strapped into a contraption like a wooden cross to hold me completely still to do the visual effects," Haun says. "That was really uncomfortable, because I was in there for a really long time."

In the midst of acting out the death and destruction, she stayed in Mara's world, much more so than her co-stars. Perhaps Mara's powerful intimidation was starting to make its way from the outside in.

"It was really tough," she says. "Other kids would go out and play and be in the sun, and I would sit in my trailer, rehearsing and rehearsing and rehearsing. It made me a little bit of an egomaniac. At nine, it's hard to completely separate from the character, because of how much of an impact she made and how much I had to be her."

Too smart for the "regular" schoolkids, the group forms its own school, with Alan as the improvised instructor. He all but begs his pseudo-daughter to stop or at least explain the tragedies, and she coldly describes its necessity—the survival of her and the rest is far more important than any mere human. Soon enough, they and theirs forming elsewhere will own the globe.

"The scenes between me and Christopher Reeve in the barn were tough," Haun says. "I had a really hard time keeping a straight face. His strength shocked me every time, and my reaction to being shocked was to laugh. It was the first time I'd really experienced that as an actor."

The town tries to clear, but Verner's not fast enough; the kids force her to show them the body of their partner that died, then to gut herself with her own scalpel.

A lynch mob forms to capture the group. A woman is made to burn herself alive, causing everyone else to flee. The reverend attempts to blast the youths away, only to find his gun underneath his chin and the trigger pulled.

Police. The National Guard. Everyone attacks the nine in the barn. No one's faster than the children's brains. The cops are mind-tricked into shooting each other, the soldiers following suit with machine guns. A helicopter attack becomes a mass suicide.

But there's one chance left, and it's Alan, who might just have a way past their psychic sickening. The boy who was left without a mate when the original girl died has shown the slightest bit of concern for others, and Mara's mind is on him. Until it's on Alan, alone with the kids in their makeshift school.

With a bomb in his bag.

The other kids distracted by their partner's escape, Alan forces his thoughts on a brick wall around the bomb's image. Mara's onto him, her eyes suddenly glowing. Then her whole face is overtaken as Alan's in mental agony.

Finally, Mara's too strong for Alan. His mind goes to the bag, and the kids all see it.

But it's too late. Everyone knows what hit them, but not for long; the explosion gives the town the ultimate cure. The last boy and his mom drive away—and his eyes *don't* suddenly start glowing! A horror movie that *doesn't* end with foreshadowing!

"I didn't expect my performance to be as successful as it was," Haun says, "not that I was beating myself up, but I didn't realize how strong the character was. I was really surprised by it and really proud of it. I felt like a professional for the first time. Not just for the result, but the work that went into it. It impacted the way that I approached any work in my entire life."

Over a decade later, she'd take things in a new horrifying direction.

"The interesting thing about horror to me in not the slasher thing, but the question of is it real or is it not?" Haun explains. "The horror films that I really loved are more psychological than really bloody."

Its title may sound comedic, but *Shrooms* was anything but. In a horror not too far from the veins of *Reefer Madness*, the 2007 film showed what can happen when the wrong drugs fall into the wrong places. Off in Ireland, her Tara and friend searches the world's greenest fields and hills for mushrooms, and not the kind one would use to decorate a pizza!

She and the crew got together to authorize Tara's pseudo-autobiography.

"She'd grown up with a militant father in a very Catholic family, the male version of the mother in *Carrie*," Haun theorizes. "Tara had become an A-type, overachiever trying to appease her father, become the perfect girl."

Under the influence of the title "characters," Tara starts to see her friends violently dying. Perhaps at the hands of woodsmen like in the *Texas Chainsaw Massacre* series. Maybe a mythical creature from the abandoned children's home nearby never went all the way away. Then her friends start to turn on her, and she's not sure what's going on.

Tara's soon enough the only one left, and she may not make it. Then her phone rings, and shoves her straight through an awakened flashback.

"I was really excited about playing a character that had this kind of duality," Haun says. "You love her, and then you realize that you've been rooting for the wrong person."

Yep—all those visions that she thought were imaginary weren't. Though it wasn't totally her fault (much less malicious that Mara!), Tara's the very one that carried out every single bloody deed.

"That's how we figured out how she would be capable of these acts, that she had this violence stored up in her," Haun says. "Being betrayed by her best friend is the kind of thing that throws her whole world into a loop. She's looking for a world that's kinder, a world outside of her father's world, trying to create this new family, and when she realizes that they hurt her too, she snaps."

Though, as we've been over, TV work was nothing new for Haun, she hadn't done much scaring there during the first few decades of her career. Then came a phone call from her agent.

The year before, HBO had grabbed hold of America's eternal fixation on vampires with *True Blood*, and it was time for the second season of the serials of Sookie Stackhouse (Anna Paquin) and her friends' wars with the fanged ones of the Deep South.

In the second go-round's second offering, Sookie's boyfriend Bill Compton's hanging out at the pseudo palace of Sophie-Anne Leclerq (Evan Rachel Wood), the vampire queen of the Big Easy. Then he happens to run into Hadley, the queen's girlfriend—and Sookie's cousin, unseen since she wasted a ton of her grandmother's money by running away from rehab.

"I was originally supposed to be in just a few episodes," Haun recalls. "I went in one morning, and two hours later, I'd booked it."

The next season, Hadley gave up her cousin to save her own life, just before she was "plasmatically" emptied by Eric Northman (Alexander Skarsgård). She makes amends with Sookie, takes her son away, and, in the fifth season, helps Sookie and her brother find that their parents were murdered by vampires—not, as they thought, as accidental drowning.

With roles like Hadley, Haun explains, "I draw from people I know, especially if I don't have a lot of time. I had some family members that weren't necessarily making the right choices, but were making choices to survive. I based (Hadley) off one of my cousins who had had a very rough time."

Back to all that power, all those assets, everything we talked about *way* back at the beginning, it all came real for Haun, just as with her colleagues that made the so-often-damned-difficult transition from child to grownup horror stars (like fellow *Village* star Thomas Dekker, who showed up in the highly acclaimed first two *Chromeskull* films and the . . . well, not as admired 2010 *Nightmare on Elm Street* remake). It's something that hit her quite a bit harder than expected—not quite like the bomb that took Mara out, but pretty strong!—just after visiting the *Village*.

"The first time I saw it was with a real audience, when I went with my Girl Scout troop," she recalls. "Somehow, people realized I was in the audience." Hopefully taking into account the young girl's age, the crowd didn't get near the line between the lady and the character.

"When I left, people lined the walkways and clapped," Haun recalls. "It was awesome, but very weird. Getting that kind of attention is strange. There have been times in my career when I haven't been able to go out in public." Once she, as far from Mara as inhumanely possible, stepped into the Disney Channel spotlight with *The Color of Friendship* flick in 2000, things started getting even more intrusive, and it's all too easy for us all, even those of us that feel our fan devotion is beneficial to our favorites, to see the issues that can get dangerous all too quickly.

"I've had people look under stalls to see if it was me in the bathroom," remembers Haun. "As a kid, I probably loved it, but now I look at it in a different light. It's weird to give a child that much power. People think that you're giving a child a really good thing by applauding, and not to say that you shouldn't applaud a child for doing a good thing, but it's a strange thing, being a child actor and performer. It's a strange tightrope to walk and become a complete person on the other side."

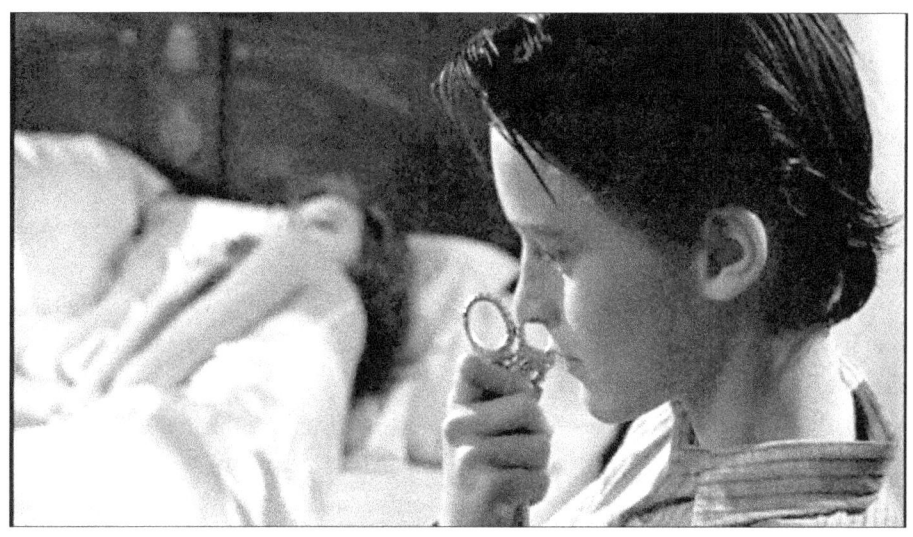

Franklyn Madson prepares to get his mom's revenge on an innocent lady in 1991's *Dead Again*.

Gregor Hesse:

Dead Again

MURDER, EVEN OF the violent, gory kind, never tasted so good. Even if a kid was doing it.

No, this isn't about *Silence of the Lambs VII: Hannibal's Childhood*, or anything like that. It's just a kid-ish spin on a scene that was far from humorous when viewers saw it.

"I was amazed that the fake blood tasted like sugar," Gregor Hesse recalls. "It made me very happy to taste blood that was really sugar. It wasn't awful at all." Again, though, those who watched one of Hesse's roughest scenes back in *Dead Again* came away with a vastly different impression.

Probably just one of many they'd felt throughout the flick. As far as possible from his usual preaching of the words of Shakespeare, Kenneth Branagh yanked his audience from thriller to romance to fear, even depression, through the 1991 film, and maybe that's appropriate: a film that ends like *Dead Again*, a storyline deeper that Mount Everett's crevasses, perhaps shouldn't be easy to classify. It's how we go about plunging far beneath the superficial. But even in the flick's final tragedy, there's a certain degree of honor, even redemption.

It was certainly far from the few roles Hesse himself had stepped into beforehand, such as a small persona two years before in the underrated *The Wizard*, a glorified Nintendo advertisement in which child household name Fred Savage and his younger brother travel the nation for a video game tournament and learn much about themselves and the world in the bargain. Ironically enough, Hesse's last acting role would be alongside Savage on a 1993 episode of *The Wonder Years*.

But all that was years away. It was time for something twenty shades darker and fifty feet deeper.

"You can't tell by the way I look if I'm German or Spanish or French," explains Hesse, "but because I'm German, I felt I related to the role. I've always been a fan of getting dressed in old clothes and stuff like that, so it wasn't hard at all for me to do a period piece."

Both behind and before the *Dead Again* cameras, Branagh starts in eerie black and white as Roman Strauss, a composer ready for execution for the brutal scissors stabbing death of his fellow musician wife Margaret (Emma Thompson).

But that happened long ago; now it's then-present-day, and Branagh's now detective Mike Church, trying to find out the background of this beauty who stumbled into the orphanage in which he grew up.

The actress is Thompson. The character . . . well, we don't know, because she's forgotten. And the connection between this lighter storyline and the gore we just saw, that's also going to be tough to decipher.

Until trusty hypnotist Franklyn Madson (Derek Jacobi) pushes her mind back to the past, a journey that finds recollections of Margaret and Roman, like their wedding day, when Margaret met Roman's housekeeper Inga and her son Frankie, trying to overcome the stuttering issue that bullies today still love to target.

After four months of prepping for the young fellow, it was time for Hesse to shine in the flick's black and white.

"I can memorize really well," he recalls. "I memorized my lines and started acting it out. I would rehearse in front of the mirror and remember my lines. I did countless different ways of doing it, really deepening myself into the role and being German and evil and jealous like Frankie was, which is not my character at all."

The film lightens up a bit, with Mike courting the gal he's nicknamed Grace—Branagh and Thompson being married at the time probably helped, although not to the hilarious extent they'd go in 1993's Bardish comedy *Much Ado About Nothing*, as the headstrong, outspoken Beatrice and Benedick, who can't stand each other and end up married. Sadly, the pair broke up in 1995.

Back in the past, Margaret, her relationship with Roman going the wrong way, sees Frankie searching her jewelry box. It was Hesse's toughest scene . . . to that point.

"There was never a moment I was intimidated by Kenneth Branagh, except for one moment," he remembers. "I had to do a scene so well. The scene where I steal the jewelry, had to do it over and over and over, and we worked until midnight. It was kind of intimidating, but I did it and got congratulations and round of applause."

Finally, things fall together for *Again*; under Madison's techniques, Mike realizes he's Margaret's reincarnation, and Grace is the former Roman. He also finds Inga (German acting legend Hanna Schygulla), who wistfully recalls her loving plight to Roman, his spurning of her for his wife, and her tearful reminiscence to her son, the only one she could ever truly open up to.

And here's where Frankie truly shows the jealousy and anger that Hesse referred to a few paragraphs ago.

It was him. Barely into his teen years. A young boy had stolen into Margaret's room, found her in bed, and, blaming her for his mom's pain, brutalized her with the cutting tools.

"The murder scene was one of the biggest scenes," Hesse says. "It took forever to film, with the steady camera operator and crane operator. It was a very hard scene to do. I had to do it over and over, with fake blood. It came out a success because of the choreography." And, of course, the cuisine-esque plasma flavor he'd surprisingly enjoy.

"There was some question as to why I should murder her," he continues. "The reality is that love conquers all in the film, so it didn't seem harmful."

There's one more epilogue to Inga's sad story: Madson is Frankie. He knew from the start that Margaret and Roman's spirits would come back for him.

He kills his mom. Back in Grace's apartment—her amnesia took away her memories of her original name of Amanda and painting skill, a different artistic talent than she'd enjoyed as Roman—she accidentally shoots Mike, leaving her easy prey for Madson.

Or so he thinks. Mike stabs him and stumbles away. Madson charges, but Mike grabs a huge sculpture of scissors (Amanda's fixation on them is now sadly clear), and gets revenge for the woman he once was, impaling her killer upon them.

The next year, Thompson would grab an Oscar for her work in *Howard's End*.

"She said I was the nicest murderer she'd ever been killed by!" Hesse proudly asserts.

Timmy (Bret Lehr) caused one hell of an *Identity* crisis in 2003.

Bret Loehr:

Identity

IT WOULD BE difficult for anyone. Hell, it would be brutally painful.

Being asked to imagine your own *mother* dying? Being asked to imagine her dropping right in front of you? Trying to think of what it might be like to, out of nowhere, see her victimized by a shocking tragedy and watch her pass when, seconds before, nothing whatsoever was wrong?

Putting oneself in that position would be difficult for those with decades on the planet, even for people with tons of acting experience. Asking someone else to do it might be considered borderline abusive—especially to a *child*!

But that was the cornerstone of one of the new millennium's first "scary kid" performances, and the start of a career.

"I was very young, only about ten when I made it," Bret Loehr remembers of *Identity* (2003). "I went into the audition, and (director) James Mangold was there. The whole audition process was symmetry; I got it into my head, how would you react if your mother died, if you saw your mother get hit by a car, if you saw your mother laying on the side of the road, dying? It was mostly facial reaction. I just had to use my face." His character wouldn't speak much—but when he did, it would complete the film's last twist.

"With a horror film, what you see is just what's portrayed on the screen," Loehr explains. "Behind the scenes, it's really just a bunch of actors working together and having a fun time with a script that they love. It's not all scary and whatnot. It was fun working with some high-quality actors."

At the outset, *Identity* appears to be two films with little in common. On one side, we see an oversized, sinister fellow whose outset pretty much begets his past. He's Malcolm Rivers (Pruitt Taylor Vince), and the system's about ready to cash the bill he rang up, taking a host of innocent lives. He's got one chance left, and it's in the form of his shrink, who believes that it wasn't Malcolm who did it, but a personality who stole his mind and took evil control. It's up to the impromptu team to convince a group of law men (not lawmen!) that said entity can be erased if Malcolm gets a little more time.

Then the other tale starts to spin. A group of people happen to arrive together at a middle-of-nowhere motel, flooded in by rain, the remnants of which will probably never dry. There's an actress from the past and a pair of newlyweds. The actress is driven by Ed (John Cusack), a former man of the law. Amanda Peet is Paris, a lovely lady of the streetwalking night. Ray Liotta is Officer Rhodes, transporting Jake Busey's Robert Maine, who may have killed as many as Malcolm. And then there's George and Alice York, too distracted by Alice's injuries from a car wreck to pay much attention to their little boy Timmy.

Is it a flashback to Malcolm's crimes? Is he suddenly going to appear and wipe everyone out? Will one of the characters confess to being the actual perpetrator, or happen upon evidence that clears him (probably just as an innocent man is executed, per Hollywood)?

Well, not quite, or at least not yet. Calamity starts knocking them all over. The actress' head is found, her body elsewhere. The new husband gets killed. His wife escapes with Timmy, but their car explodes. The kid's mom dies of her injuries. His stepdad gets hit with a car.

Is it Maine's doing? Perhaps he's Malcolm's long-lost partner.

Nope; he's found with his head in a U-shape behind his neck, a baseball bat slammed down his throat to close the deal.

Then all the bodies suddenly vanish. Here's where we start to get the idea.

"It was hard," recalls Loehr. "I left some days crying. Not really crying because I was sad, but because James did such a great job of putting these ideas inside my head to get this reaction from me. Sometimes I felt very calm in doing this, like someone was talking through the story. But I was just a kid who did what I was told."

Meanwhile, Ed finds that Rhodes was actually Maine's pal, having done just as bad. Rhodes kills someone else. We're not *quite* sure what's up with this.

Back at Malcolm's hearing, his doctor suddenly calls for someone else.

It's Ed. Cusack's face appears where Vince's was just moments ago.

Then it hits us like one of the lightning bolts landing all over the motel residents: the whole hotel story is in Malcolm's head. The dying are his personalities taking one another out, perhaps the killer, apparently Rhodes, looking to run the show alone.

"When you come on a movie set, it's not a scary place to be," Loehr says, "but I was given good imagery and find a place to lose myself in the environment of my mom dying, my dad dying. As a young kid, it's very hard, really getting in the idea of getting into the circumstances of the situation. That's what you have to do in horror: you see someone dying, you have to relate it to someone close to you to get your reaction."

Now knowing that Ed is on to him, Rhodes goes for one last victim. But Ed seems to know that he's not fighting for his life, as he doesn't have one. All that matters is taking out the villain and leaving Paris alone to do right. He takes a bullet from Rhodes but manages to blast him away before dying.

Rhodes was hardly Liotta's first time as a villain, but, Loehr claims, it's an even better act than what we saw on the screen.

"Ray Liotta was, by far, the nicest guy on that set," recalls the kid who was Timmy. "He was the most helpful, offering any kind of help. With all these actors around, I was just a little sponge, learning all this cool information and weird things that were going on." Hey, for those not in the know, can you guess why I'm still writing about someone whose character had little to do with the storyline and has been gone for a while? You will.

The law convinced that Malcolm's bad sides are terminated, his sentence gets commuted to institutionalization. As we see him and the doctor driving away, Paris joyfully tends to an orange grove back in her Florida homeland. For a film so full of death, this one might just have a happy ending.

Then she notices an ominous shadow. Glancing up, we see the mistake we made.

We all thought Rhodes was running the Malcolm Show. We were totally wrong.

It's Timmy, ominously tapping a hatchet in his hand like he does this all the time.

Now it does become flashback time. In machine gun mode, we see Timmy smothering his mom to death. He jammed the bat down Maine's throat. He caused his stepdad to step in front of the car. He scurried off after rigging the wife's car to blow.

And he's got one more death, and his only line to go along with it.

"Whores," he coldly explains to Paris, "don't get a second chance." She's terrified. She's helpless. What is a personality to do?

Nothing. Timmy chops her to bits. He was the true killer, Malcolm's true controller, and the killer won.

And it's not over for the man, either: he suddenly grabs the shrink, unable to wait another second for at least one last victim.

Again, doing this sort of thing would be tough for anyone to act out, let alone one making his film debut, and Loehr felt it throughout, he says.

"I'm killing someone, covering my mother's mouth and nose, especially having my mother on set with me," he says, "it was a hard thing to think about. It wasn't so much emotional as it was interesting. Killing my mom was very interesting."

Identity comes across as both a psychologist's dream and nightmare, every reason to be both joyful and heartbroken that what it depicts can't happen, at least not in any recorded case. Having all of your client's personalities kill each other until only the good one is still around . . . wouldn't that just make every brainpeeker's job quite a bit easier? But the possibility that good doesn't always win in the end, that evil always finds a way to sneak back through, that the form that Timmy ends up representing is left standing after everything else, well, let's just be glad that *Identity*'s story can't (or *hasn't*) found its way out of the supernatural realms.

Ironically enough, Timmy's murder of Paris occurred on Loehr's first day on the set; his toughest parts truly came at the start.

"I remember driving to the orange fields, knowing I had to do this," he says. "I had an idea what was going on—not putting that much emphasis on 'Wow, I'm going to get to kill someone,' but more of just going to work and doing what I was told to do. I got there, met Amanda Peet for the first time, and then I had to kill her. It was the first time I ever had to play this sort of thing, so that kind of got me the intensity for doing it."

It was tough to leave Timmy behind, and not just for Loehr, he jokes.

"None of my friends wanted to sleep at my house for a little bit!" he says. "But it was cool because it's a hard thing to grasp, the whole idea of it. I had to watch it a few times to really get the full idea of it, but people still remember this movie."

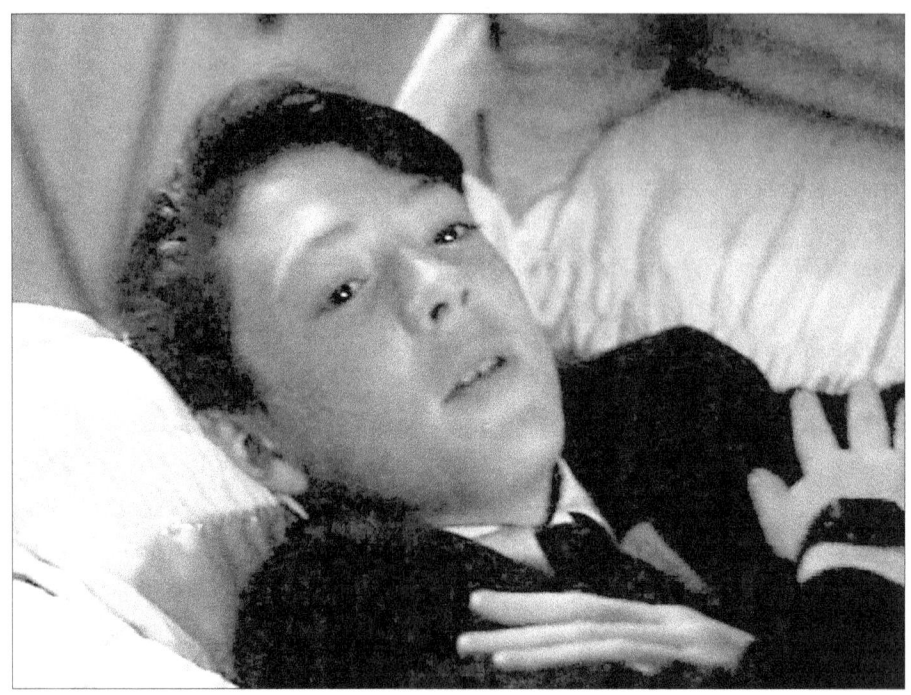

Marc Marut's Johnny McFarley contemplates his next move, and potential murder, in *The Paperboy* (1994).

Marc Marut:

The Paperboy

HORROR FILMS AREN'T really known for depth, and that might be in part because we might not really like what we'd find there. It's the same thing that's oftentimes so depressing about true crime (aside from the violence and death, of course).

Thinking about some of the most evil people society has ever seen—on the real-life news or the cinematically crafted films—we might just consider all of the goods that were there for their using. Intelligence, charisma, friendliness, thinking far outside the box . . . these qualities were there. They existed in everyone who got away with serial murder for years, everyone who persuaded millions of their countrymen (and women) to genocide and suicide, everyone known for showing the "darkest weapon" instead of the "moral asset" side of these techniques.

Basically, they could have used their tools for good and come out as ethical landmarks. But they didn't. They showed us everything that could be done wrong with those techniques, often in violent and fatal ways. And that just depresses the holy hell out of us.

Watching horror films, we tend to push that sort of thing to the back of our mind; because if we start to think about it, about why characters like Johnny McFarley do what they do (even murder!), we might get too sad to get scared.

"In order to understand a character, I have to first understand his motivation," explains Marc Marut of his first full-length cinematic lead. "Once I understand WHAT the character is trying to accomplish, then I think about HOW he tries to accomplish it and WHY he does it that way, that's how I got into Johnny's head . . . The thing about Johnny, though, is when he decided to make something happen, he set out to do it by any means necessary. He's kind of the ultimate go-getter."

Sounds like quite the strong (and, sadly enough, unusual!) quality for the typical teenage boy, doesn't it? After all, it was that sort of thing, teamed with irony, that started off Marut's acting career itself.

"I think every kid wants to be an actor (at least to some extent), but I completely fell into the business by accident," he recalls. "It was all because of Cub Scouts: I was nine years old, and there was a party at the end of the year for all the kids who had ten skill badges or more. All the cool kids were going, so I desperately wanted to go too."

Unfortunately, he was a few skills short. Desperately searching for the marks that would gain him entrance, Marut learned of an upcoming visitor to the stages of his Toronto homeland.

Les Misérables was coming to town, and trying out for its leading (pre-teen) male role would score the youngster that elusive badge.

He tried out. He got the badge—and, out of nowhere, the role of Gavrosh, the youngest leader of the French Revolution that helps whip up his countrymen with tunes like the aptly named "Little People" and helps end the tale with "Do You Hear the People Sing" (Daniel Huttlestone grabbed the role when the Oscar-winning musical moved to theaters in 2012).

"I never did get to go to the (scouting) party," Marut recalls sadly, "but I did get to be one of the original cast members of the first Canadian production of *Les Misérables*. It was a phenomenal experience for me, and I've been an actor ever since." Several short roles in TV and film followed, including the futuristic sci-fi *TekWar* series (1994) that William Shatner sketched out between turns as Captain Kirk.

"I immediately bought all the books and got immersed in the story," Marut recalls of his role as Danny Cardigan, son of Greg Evigan's protagonist Jake, tracking down the drug lords that unfairly put him in jail (Shatner played Jake's boss).

"I've always loved the horror and sci-fi genres, especially as a kid. I remember feeling euphoric after watching movies like *Superman*, and I used to run around the house pretending I could fly. There's a fantasy aspect to those genres that allows me to enter a completely different world that's unrestricted by reality, and controlled entirely by the filmmaker's imagination. It's complete freedom as far as filmmaking goes, and I love being swept away."

Also in 1994, Marut finally got his own main man role. In the world of *The Paperboy*, he'd be the titular lead, and, in a sense, step even farther from reality than Danny had allowed.

"I was intrigued by the fact Johnny McFarley's character was a complete psychopath and could go from being a sweet and charming boy to a psychotic murderer at the drop of a hat," Marut says. "I wanted to take on a role where the mood changes could be so sudden, and so extreme. I also just thought it would be fun to pretend to go around killing people!" Of course, getting to work alongside the kind of gorgeous older gal that kicks a young man's hormones into overdrive wouldn't hurt much either, and his co-star Alexandra Paul beautifully fit that role.

"I find that although it can take some work to get into a character," Marut says, "once I'm there it becomes effortless. At the audition I really felt like I owned the part. When we started filming it was easy for me because I already had Johnny established in my mind, so everything came together on set."

The Paperboy doesn't wait too long putting its youngster in the evil side: the title character's film debut is the theft of an elderly lady's oxygen. As it turns out, she's the mom of Paul's Melissa, who arrives home for the funeral with her own young daughter, welcomed by the seemingly friendly Johnny.

Here's where we get just a bit of sympathy for the kid, or at least some reasoning. Johnny's mom's long dead, and his dad's just too busy with work to bother with fatherhood. But we won't find out for a while just what happened to not-so-dear Mommy.

"As a child, Johnny had been severely abused by his mother," Marut says, "but when he finally stood up for himself and killed her, he really took control of his own life. He finally saw that by taking action he had influence on his surroundings, and was able to change things for the better. With his mother dead and his father neglecting him, who could blame the kid for wanting a new family?" That, he hoped, would be Melissa and her little girl, the mom and sister he'd never known.

Even if he has to take out his old group to have them. Melissa's friend catches Johnny spying on her; he causes her to wind up paralyzed. Johnny's dad gives him a set of golf clubs to say he's sorry for not being there, and that the pair will get closer when they move away. But it's too late, as Johnny beats his dad to death with a putter.

"The toughest scene to film was when Johnny kills his father," Marut says, "simply because there was an accident on set. The golf club in the movie was a retractable putter, the shaft being made up of three sections held together only by an elastic string in the middle . . . When I swung the club hard the string snapped, sending the club head flying right into (actor Barry Flatman's) hand! Despite having two broken knuckles, he insisted on finishing the scene before going to the hospital. What a trouper!"

Just about all the way on his own now, Johnny lays out Melissa's boyfriend, but he's not as badly hurt as the kid had hoped. Finally alone with the older lady, Johnny reveals that, despite the most unconventional of methods, his goal really wasn't unreasonable.

"What really tied Johnny together as a character was false hope," Marut explains. "He truly believed that his plan would unfold exactly the way he intended, and then when it didn't, he thought that he could just force it back on course by killing anyone who stood in his way. All he really wanted was to be accepted and loved, and what he didn't realize is that you can't force people to love you."

And despite all the pain he's caused, Johnny's heartbreak is real. With nothing else, he tries to take Melissa out as her little girl escapes. When the cops arrive, it looks like he may get away with everything, blubbering that she, perhaps spurred on by so much sudden loss, went nuts and aimed for his life. But the boyfriend shows up, and lets Johnny and the cops know what we the audience so sadly found out long ago. Johnny's going away for a long time.

"I think if you boil it down," Marut says, "he's not a bad kid: Johnny McFarley's just a naïve twelve-year-old boy—with some serious psychotic tendencies!"

As zombie films roared to the mainstream in the 2000s, many performers probably based their work around Heather Mazur's "modeling" in the *Living Dead* remake of 1990.

Heather Mazur:

Night of the Living Dead

WHAT WOULD THEY think of her? What would they say?

The critics, who'd be gauging Heather Mazur's first trudgings before a camera? Important, but not at the top.

The audiences, sure to compare her work with someone who'd set the hell out of a trend in horror cinema, along with the rest of the crew of 1990's *Night of the Living Dead* remake?

Of course, Mazur was thinking about her viewers. Still, there was a group of someones just a *tad* more important to the then-teen, a crowd that, in all fairness, gets much more credit than it should in the opinionative sense!

"It was really hard to look ugly at a time when I was *really* into boys!" Mazur remembers. "I was mortified at the fact that they had to make me look so horrible at that age, using all that gruesome makeup to turn me into a zombie."

Just as had been the case a quarter-century before when George Romero and the rest of the first *Living Dead* crew got their hands bloody in dying colors of black and white, the new *Dead* show kicked off in America's steel capital, eventually moving about half an hour south to Washington, Penn. for filming.

"I was living in Pittsburgh, part of a singing and dancing group," Mazur remembers. "A few of us got calls from a local agent, and I went in and auditioned for a movie that I didn't know much about at the time."

That's fortunate; middle-schoolers *shouldn't* know much about zombie flicks! Far from the musical worlds she'd been exploring up to then, Mazur stepped into the tryout room. She was asked to desperately call for her mom, then improvise passing out and staying unconscious for a while. She showed them how a member of the undead might "awaken."

It meant more than enough to the right person. A fellow named Tom Savini was already moving toward legendary levels in the special effects world, but in his directing debut, he knew he'd found his new Sarah.

It was established early on that this *Dead* would be different than its predecessor, and not just because it was in color. Just as before, young beauty Barbara (Pat Tallman) and her brother Johnny visit their mom's grave. But we know right away that this Barbara's going to be tougher than the one Judith Ridley became in the original, particularly because she's adorned in a darker bowlcut hairstyle, rather than Ridley's blonde flowing locks that always just scream, "I'm a damsel in distress! Get a man over here to save me!" That, and the impromptu whaling she lays on a couple of living impaired critters, one of which took out her brother.

She, a fellow named Ben (Tony Todd, far from the evil he'd soon use to make *Candyman* into a household horror name two years later), and others soon gather at a nearby farmhouse—and in the basement, there's the Cooper family, despairing over their daughter Sarah, in a coma after being chomped by one of those . . . things.

The first time around, it had been Kyra Schon, who at least got to say a line along the way: her, "I hurt. . . ." was two more words than Mazur would utter.

"That was a bummer," she says. "Back then, I didn't know it was OK to stop filming and say, 'I need to go to the bathroom!' I was doing something for the first time, and I was really nervous that I would screw it up."

While her dad Harry (Tom Towles) starts arguing with everyone, her mom Helen can't accept that the world's greatest team of doctors couldn't save her little girl. The zombies stay on the attack, and it's soon down to the Coopers, Ben, and Barbara. Then Helen sees that the table upon which her daughter lay is empty.

Did she wake up? Has she recovered? Will she be OK?

Then Sarah steps around a corner, and it's clear this isn't a miracle. Stalking her mom, her facial features in horrifying mode, her mouth suddenly resembling that of a starved cobra, there's nowhere for Helen to go. Pinning her against a wall, Sarah gives her the same treatment the young girl herself received, sinking her teeth slam into her mom's jugular.

And as an inside joke, Helen's plasma spatters across a wall, hitting a trowel that just happens to be hanging there—the same kind of weapon that Schon had used to methodically stab her mom to death in the original.

Sarah makes her way upstairs, advancing on Ben and Bobbie. For the first time all film, Harry shows an ounce of humanity, unable to blast away the thing that was his little girl. Ben tries, but a shootout erupts between the men, and Bobbie's left to whack Sarah back to where she once was and where she's much better off.

"The first thing I shot was my last shot in the movie, where I get shot down," Mazur remembers. "It was the first shot in my life. It was my first time getting movie blocking and cues and it was a bit overwhelming to me."

Unlike the first Bobbie, this one manages to escape, and finds some help along the way (Russell Streiner, who played Johnny the first time, cameos as a sheriff being interviewed; he also produced the film). Making her way back, she sadly discovers that Ben didn't make it. And someone's going to pay.

Harry's there. He made it through the night. But he won't escape this time—Bobbie stoically plants a round through his cerebellum.

Ironically enough, Towles and Bill Moseley, who played an early *Dead* victim, teamed up nearly three decades later for another remake when Rob Zombie put out an updated *Halloween* in 2007 (the pair had previously worked for Zombie in 2003's *House of 1000 Corpses* and 2005's *The Devil's Rejects*). Towles passed away in April 2015.

For her part, Mazur vanished from the film world for over a decade, but she was certainly busy; it might be worth taking time off the screen for a Bachelor's from Carnegie Mellon—and a Master's from the drama school at *Yale*!

Along the way were spots on and off Broadway, including a nationwide theater production of *Jolson*, in which Mazur played the legendary title performer's wife Ruby Keeler, herself a name in singing, acting, and tap dancing, Mazur started showing back up to TV in the first few years of the 2000s.

For all that time, however, Mazur never checked back over her work as Sarah. But as zombie films started dominating horror screens small (*Walking Dead*) and large (WAY too many to list!) over the new millennium, she took another look at her debut.

And that's when she realized that the young fellows she'd worried about way back in 1990 were probably Sarah's biggest fans, then and now.

"When the movie came out, I was terribly nervous because I was just boy crazy," she admits. "Now, in retrospect, the boys probably thought it was the coolest thing in the world."

Addy Miller introduced America to TV's newest sensation as *The Walking Dead*'s first victim in 2010.

Addy Miller/Madison Lintz:

The Walking Dead

IT'S DIFFICULT ENOUGH to keep the attention of horror film fans of any kind for very long, which is why these sorts of films rarely last even two hours. Zombie films are no exception; things happen at high speed, full of gunshots, zinging one-liners, and gory deaths.

Indeed, in all fairness, it's tough to get such viewers to sit still and focus for very long, and many don't even try. So when AMC announced it was releasing an entire TV series on the topic, many thought it couldn't be done.

Fortunately, they still tuned in; *The Walking Dead* would set viewership records for basic cable by its second season. But right off the bat, as is so often the case with horror flicks, we get one of the biggest scares from one of the smallest sources, a tradition that would continue a year later.

First impressions are of the utmost importance in any aspect of society, and the entertainment world demonstrates this like crazy—changing the channel is much quicker and easier than finding an excuse to end a bad first date! As the series began on Halloween 2010, lost policeman Rick Grimes (Andrew Lincoln) stared off into a strange land.

It's not entirely unfamiliar; we can tell he's been here for a while, but still hasn't fully adjusted. This is not the world he's used to living in. These are not the people he's used to looking after, as a father, and husband, and a cop.

He's at an abandoned gas station. There's tons of broken-down cars around.

Then he sees their drivers. Or, who used to be their drivers. Bodies everywhere. Many of them decaying, insects already enjoying their new home.

Once again, he doesn't look entirely surprised. This might be the worst thing he's seen, but not the first example of this sort of thing.

Suddenly, he hears something. Glancing under a car, he sees the bottom half of a figure, adorned with a pair of bunny slippers.

Surely, this couldn't be one of the villains, right? Just maybe, there's someone here who can still be saved.

His instincts as an officer still sort of hanging around, Rick calls to her. Then she turns around, and this new dark reality blinds him once again.

He can't believe his eyes—or hers, or any other parts of her. This child, with almost every youngster's prized possession of a teddy bear still clutched in her arms, isn't a child anymore. Normal kids, normal people, don't walk around with their facial features distorted like this. She's one . . . of THEM.

Spotting her new prey, the youngster goes on the attack, the only thing her kind's addled mind can comprehend. Police officers know that they could be shoved into a "kill or be killed" situation every minute of every day; it's never supposed to be like this.

Silently consoling himself that this isn't a child, not a human, not anything but a monster with no thoughts other than a destruction of humanity that continues with him, Rick sadly draws his pistol and blasts her right between the eyes. Both the girl and the bear go flying to the ground. Both he, and we the viewers, have been taken to the extreme as to what we can expect from this series.

We never find out anything else about the first member of *The Walking Dead* (at least, through the first five seasons), and maybe it's better that way. Seeing a child die by any means is never an easy thing to watch, make believe or otherwise, and the less we know about her, the better. We don't want to feel sympathetic here. It's easier to accept that Rick had to commit a certain deadly deed for the greater good. And getting something so shocking out of the way so early in a series did a great job steeling us toward what was to show up later. Much more death. Much more destruction. Many more zombies of all ages that just had to be killed. Those that we'd come to know and fear as . . . *Walkers*!

But who was the first *Dead* girl? Addy Miller had shown up before the cameras in the past, playing the younger version of Dakota Fanning's Lily in 2008's *The Secret Life of Bees* (truly one of the signs that a person is making the jump from child to grownup star is even having a "younger self" in a film!). Of course, she'd looked quite a bit different back then—and looks would become one of the toughest areas of getting ready to play that little zombie.

When Addy and her colleagues first heard of the role, they didn't hear much at all.

"They just said, 'Act like a zombie and move towards the camera a little bit,'" she recalls. "When we were auditioning, they wouldn't tell us one thing, what the name of it was, or anything. They were really secret. We didn't know if it was a prank or anything."

Soon after, she learned the story of the *Walking Dead* and got into character.

"We went to 'Zombie School,'" says Addy, who calls 1982's *Poltergeist*, also featuring a frightening young girl ("They're heeeeeeere!"), her favorite horror flick. "We had to practice walking like a zombie. They'd put a chair in your way, and you'd go right through it, because you're lifeless." The opening *Dead* scene that featured her approaching the audience nearly head on, evoking memories of the scene in 1968's *Night of the Living Dead* when undead youngster Karen Cooper lurches toward her disbelieving mother, soon to be a victim. Addy watched *Living Dead* and other George Romero films to get ready for the role.

Filming it would get done in a few hours. The cosmetic readiness, however, would take slightly longer.

Molds of her teeth and hair were made. Addy's mouth was stretched sideways and outwards to high heaven, her lips hidden. Contacts were jammed into her eyes to make them look a bit . . . spacey.

"They were a little scratchy at first, but then I got used to them," she says of the eye aids. "It was kind of hard to see out of the contacts, but I didn't mind wearing them."

Then came the matter of acting out getting shot in the head (hey, off topic here, but can anyone possibly imagine what a surreal conversation this must be? Addy probably gets asked a lot by fans, "Hey, what was it like getting shot like that?" and "That guy who killed you, was he nice?" or some things along the same lines. How strange it must be, not only to have that chat, but to have it enough to get used to it! That's out there. . . .). Addy calls her death scenes some of the highlights of filming.

"I had to do two stunts," she says, "and I didn't realize how much fun they would be! The stunt coordinator taught me how to fall without getting hurt."

Meanwhile, one of her colleagues, early in the acting world herself, stuck around long enough to help her co-stars knock back the walker attack a few episodes in, then JUST escape the season-one culminating explosion at the Center for Disease Control lab.

The young girl we'd soon know as Sophia was Madison Lintz. If the last name sounds familiar, it's because her family peppers the acting landscape—in just a pair of generations, she's one of five "Lintzes" to reach the big screen.

That's where it all started for Madison—her mom Kelly had worked with Frank Darabont on *The Mist* in 2007 and figured that her youngest daughter would be perfect for a role on his new zombie show (in 2013, Madison's sister Mackenzie would become the next family member to show Stephen King's work, snaring a role on the TV series *Under the Dome*).

In her family's studio basement, Madison became the newest audition addition to Darabont's newest creation. Her tape sent in, it worked.

Over the last weeks of the first season and first of the second, Madison turned Sophia into a small, significant part of the *Dead* group, on the run from something(s) they thought only existed in imagined horror.

"The first time I saw the zombies, I was like, 'Gross!'" recalled the youngster. "But I was astounded that someone could do makeup that good. It was amazing." She'd soon get a closer look and feel for that action, but we're not quite there.

Sophia's (Madison Linz) degenerative transformation into a Walker, and requisite murder, was truly one of *The Walking Dead*'s saddest moments.

With her dad dead in the attack (hardly a loss, as he abused both the women in his family), Sophia's alone with her mom Carol—until she gets close to Rick's son Carl and the other kids.

But early in the second season, she, Rick, Carol, and the rest are happened upon by a group of walkers, eager to add to their brood. Chased by two of them into the woods, she hides next to a creek while Rick can hunt down and take them out . . . but when he returns, she's gone.

Still, there's hope. Perhaps she was wandering back to the hideout and got lost. Maybe she's found a better hiding place. With Carl and Carol at the unofficial helm, the group spends the next month of shows searching for her. But the seventh episode's title, "Pretty Much Dead Already," let viewers know that everything wasn't going to be OK.

On the sidelines and in the game, Madison had been readying herself for the final scenes.

"As an actor, your job is to serve the story and I knew this outcome for Sophia would be the best way to do that," she recalls. "On the other hand, as Madison, I was sad to leave my *Walking Dead* family. I'll always cherish them as my first TV family."

Commandeering a huge barn, Rick and the rest of the group gun down a group of walkers that wander out the door. One undead creature after another wanders out, but our humans have been here so many times before, blasting them down with discipline like a military formation.

With dozens of them enemy laying all over the ground, the group sits back and takes a long collective breath. There will be many more battles to fight, but this one's been won.

But Rick's law enforcement instincts keep kicking in, and he senses that things aren't quite over. Everyone's ready to shoot a bit more.

Then, from inside, we the audience see a familiar shape—but just from behind, so there's still hope here. Maybe the person we're seeing was kept captive, but not turned.

She steps outside. There's a huge bite mark on her shoulder. Her eyes are rolled back, unrecognizable. Madison spent about two hours in the makeup chair for this performance, and we can tell that both she and the cosmetic crew went far to show the walker Sophia now is.

A denying Carol rushes forward, but she's stopped. Once again, Rick steps forward, gun drawn. One blast later, Sophia, or the non-human she became, is out for good.

The crew "hid me from the cast so that their reactions could be even more genuine when they did see Sophia come out of the barn," Madison recalls. About being a walker, "I'd been seeing it for two summers, so it came naturally." Just as Addy's death set the tone for the series' opening, this one reinforced it for the next season—and, to an extent, the remainder of the series. Not only is Rick now hardened to the reality that this is neither the first nor last time, but the others have gotten a closer, more painful look at what's in store for them, and what they'll have to do to get there.

Killing kids. Shooting family members, or at least being there to watch it. It's an impossible storyline, but still a depressing one. Addy's death started the series; Sophia's ends "Already."

But while Sophia's end brought all the pain, Madison wasn't quite finished. One quick Internet-led glance behind the scenes shows us just what an act the whole thing was.

Still in character, Sophia lays dead, shows the viral video. Then a "Cut!" call roars, and everyone steps out of character and into celebratory mode, giving her the kind of thanks that she, Addy, and other *Dead* stars still get at conventions and other appearances today.

As Madison rises, fellow cast and crew fill the air with congratulatory shouts. Several raise her hand. She steps into one embrace after another.

"Everybody was cheering and hugging me," she says. "It was the best day of my life!"

The Cell (2000) gave us at least sort of a reason for one to become a serial killer in the background of Carl Rudolph Stargher (Jake Thomas).

Jake Thomas:

The Cell

PUTTING JAKE THOMAS in this section of the book caused a series case of the qualms.

His character in *The Cell* (2000) is hardly evil, but more of the opening act to the main attraction. By the time Thomas shows up, we've long since known that the adult he'll become is hardcore pitch. The young version of Carl Rudolph Stargher (adulted by Vincent D'Onofrio), however, helps explore the premise that horror films rarely explore to a large degree: *why*.

"The character, at that age, was a regular, slightly scared kid," Thomas remembers of his big screen debut. "It wasn't super difficult to get into the mindset. I was just playing a version of myself. My preparation was mainly running lines with my parents so I understood what we'd be doing and what I'd have to do."

The film goes in a different direction quite early; rather than spending a big chunk on Stargher and his deeds—kidnapping, mental torture, and eventual drowning of women, then bleaching them into doll-ish playthings—he's snared less than a third of the way in, though suddenly comatose.

Hey, don't worry: the good thing about horror is that reality doesn't have to apply, and there's a new treatment allowing shrinks like Jennifer Lopez's Catherine Deane to wander through his psyche (think she'd need a search warrant in real life?) and get a few questions answered. Like, where is his last victim?

And, what in the hell makes a man *do* this?

We see some of his victims, and others he'd like to make into realism, helped along by some demonic makeup effects that almost won the flick as Oscar.

Soon, it's just her and a terrified youngster in a room with a gorgeous horse. The simple fact that a guy within sight of puberty doesn't enjoy spending time alone with a lady as lovely as Lopez in and of itself is a sign of a problem!

"Nothing on the set was scary or too intense or anything," Thomas remarks. "The people on set were creepy, but even the women in the scary costumes were all very nice to me. Jennifer Lopez was great."

We're in a place where destruction is the rule. Just as the smaller Stargher shoves the doc out of the way, a huge set of razors plummets down to slice the horse neatly into bits, even more graphic than the first *Saw* film that would hit in 2004.

Lopez herself wouldn't become a mom for a few more years, but Deane goes maternally nurturing here, giving Stargher a comfort he never had. But that's why so many have suffered at his hands.

We see his dirtbag dad beating him, all the women in his life doing nothing about it. He was just a fellow without a chance or a choice. Some of us are just born with a mind that outdoes us, overpowers us, and hurts us. It fights us every time we try to help, to heal, to do right, and eventually we decide that doing right just isn't worth the effort. You have a father that abuses you, sometimes you give up trying to be unlike his worthless ass because it's too tough and may not even be worth the effort.

I guess that's why his character ended up in this section of the tome. Evil, just like every other human emotion, isn't black and white. No one goes a hundred percent either way, and probably doesn't even come close. This isn't a reasonable doubt situation, but a "more of one than of the other" decision. Stargher's not all bad, just more bad than good (Weird, but D'Onofrio was more of a jerk as a misogynist husband in *Men in Black* [1998] and a greedy businessman in *Jurassic World* [2015] than here as a serial killer!).

His adult form ruling within like a king, his darkness even takes over Deane and makes her his slave. Fortunately, she escapes and tries to save his young innocence (Thomas says Lopez and D'Onofrio didn't interact on set, not wanting to get friendly with a cinematic enemy).

Even two years before she turned into a fighting machine in *Enough*, Lopez whomps the bad guy and gets ready to send him to hell. But even as he begs her to do so, she realizes she can't kill one Stargher without the other.

The first time we saw young Stargher was his baptism. Now he'll leave in a similar way, Deane (now clad in a nun's habit) holds him beneath the waves of a small pool in her mind. As Deane's colleagues save Stargher's last victim, he becomes hers, albeit in a much cleaner and more justified way.

"That was intense for me," Thomas remembers of the scene, "because she had to hold me under water." Watching it, as well as the rest of *The Cell*, wouldn't be quite as tough, he remembers with a laugh.

"At the premiere," he says, "my father took me in and out of the theater during the most graphic scenes. I actually didn't see the movie until I was much older."

Wes Craven, a legend in horror filmmaking, passed away during the completion of this book.

Epilogue

THIS BOOK BEGAN with a tribute, and now it ends with another . . . although I certainly wish I didn't have a reason to write this.

On August 30, 2015, before this book went to press, the horror world (screw that, the film world) suffered an immeasurable loss when Wes Craven took his final bow.

I could be selfish and say that without Craven, this book, and so many others like it, wouldn't be written. I wouldn't be wrong. But that's not important enough. Without him, an entire genre of film wouldn't have reached the levels it did. His work on *Last House on the Left* introduced a new form of horror to audiences of the '70s. The *Nightmare on Elm Street* series became its own entity in the '80s. And when viewers of the '90s started to find something new to watch, something outside of scarers, Craven's work brought them right back with *Scream*.

You could say that no other director has done so much for his or her specific genre alone, and you'd have a rock-solid leg to stand on. Craven gave several different generations a motive to care about the horror genre, and showed those that had left it behind a reason to start caring again.

There's nothing that can heal the pain of a lost loved one, but there's certainly quite a bit that can improve it, if only a few degrees. And the same loyalty that brings people to those conventions I've been writing about, the ones that dress and act like their favorite characters, extends over into being there for each other when someone's in need.

Epilogue

Like I said back at the beginning, it's easy to get a sense of camaraderie amongst the fans at all those conventions. And as I've seen since Craven died, that fraternizing nature has gone even farther. It's about saying thanks, and going out of your way to do so. It's about finding new and special ways to give your own tribute to people that made their own special difference for you. All over the 'Net, all over social media, and at the same conventions and the like that I've written so much about, a community now says thanks so much to someone who deserves it (just as we all did to Christopher Lee, Gunnar Hansen, Betsy Palmer, and so many others stolen from the horror world in 2015)—and it wasn't just the fans; we've seen the fellow performers and directors pay their own tribute to those lost as well. This book was my way of paying tribute to the genre's underrated, and I hope this epilogue says my own thanks to someone that enough praise to fill a hundred books this size wouldn't be enough for.

For the past few years, there's been a building buzz amongst the horror community about Craven getting a Lifetime Achievement Oscar. Sadly, he won't be around to receive it, and to give it posthumously might even be considered a bit petty. But every time we see a new filmmaker with a special set of guts and imagination try something new in horror, and hopefully succeed, we'll see a bit of Wes Craven. We'll forever be seeing certain things, big or small, in the horror world that will make us say, "Hey, they learned that from Craven!"

And if we still want to see a special part of Wes Craven, well, we've got all sorts of films that will always be credited for setting the standards in a genre. The films that have stood the test of time, and will continue to live on.

Throughout his life, Wes Craven's films made history, again and again. Now his name and his legacy will be a part of it—because while no man lives forever, his work, the memories he created and gifted to millions, certainly will.

References

Aarons, Bonnie. Phone interview. March 25, 2016.

Abramsohn, Roy. Phone interview. May 15, 2014.

Adair, Gene. (2002). *Alfred Hitchcock: Filming Our Fears*. Oxford University Press: New York.

Adler, Page. Phone interview. Jan, 26, 2014.

Adrienne, Amanda. E-mail interview. May 30, 2015.

AHS Poland. (2014, Oct. 9). American Horror Story Freak Show—Interview with Ben Woolf. Retrieved on March 19, 2015, from https://www.youtube.com/watch?v=4dnqjGsrlbk

Alex, Rob. (2011). Addy Miller of 'The Walking Dead': Dragon*Con 2011. *The Backstage Beat*. Retrieved on May 1, 2012, from http://atlanta.thebackstagebeat.com/2011/09/addy-miller-dragoncon-2011/

Allen, Eva. E-mail interview. Nov. 19, 2015.

AMC. (2012, January 26). Making of the Barn Scene: Inside The Walking Dead. YouTube. Retrieved on October 7, 2013, from http://www.youtube.com/watch?v=xaKNtt8WVFc

Amge, Jyoti. E-mail interview. Feb. 27, 2015.

Andersen, Jolene. Phone interview. Feb. 25, 2015.

Anderson, Philip. (1999, August 14). Heather Donohue - Blair Witch Project. *Kaos2000*. Retrieved on May 26, 2014, from http://www.kaos2000.net/interviews/heatherdonohue/heatherdonohue.html

Andrews, Leslie. E-mail interview. Sept. 16, 22, 2014.

Azzopardi, Chris. (2013, October 29). 'Carrie' star Chloe Grace Moretz: The (spooky) gay interview. *Dallas Voice*. Retrieved on July 3, 2014, from http://www.dallasvoice.com/carrie-star-chloe-grace-moretz-spooky-gay-interview-10160390.html

Baker, Amanda. E-mail interview. Nov. 18, 2014.

Bearse, Amanda. Q+A session, Scares that Care horror movie convention, Williamsburg, VA., June 22, 2014.

Beer, Daniel. Personal interview. Oct. 17, 2015.

Biodrowski, Steve. (1993/4 Winter) Living Dead: Part III. *Imagi-Movies 1(2)*. 16-17, 19-20, 25, 27.

Biodrowski, Steve. (1993/4 Winter) Living Dead: Part III, Zombie Makeup. *Imagi-Movies 1(2)*. 24

Biodrowski, Steve. (1993/4 Winter) Living Dead: Part III, Cool Ghoul Girl. *Imagi-Movies 1(2)*. 26

Bishara, Joseph. Phone interview. April 8, 2015.

Blake, Edith. (1975). *On Location on Martha's Vineyard*. Ballantine Books: New York.

Blay, Zeba. (2012, Nov, 6). Scarlett Johansson 'terrified shooting Hitchcock Psycho shower scene.' *Digital Spy*. Retrieved June 4, 2013, from http://www.digitalspy.com/movies/news/a436254/scarlett-johansson-terrified-shooting-hitchcock-psycho-shower-scene.html

Boulton, Caroline. E-mail interview. July 28, 2015.

Bova, Nate. E-mail interview. Jan. 19, 2016.

References

Boylan, Krew. E-mail interview. Jan. 15, 2016.

Brian S. (2011, January 21). Exclusive Interview: Actress Rodleen Getsic. *Geek Tyrant*. Retrieved on January 22, 2013, from http://geektyrant.com/news/2011/1/21/exclusive-interview-actress-rodleen-getsic-the-bunny-game-vs.html

Brown, Raine. E-mail interview. Aug. 15, 2014.

Butler, Sarah. Q+A session at horror movie convention, Virginia Beach, VA. Nov. 11, 2012.

Buza, George. E-mail interview. Jan. 11, 2016.

Campanella, Roberto. Phone interview. Sept. 3, 2015.

Campbell, Neve. Q+A session at Monster Mania horror movie convention, Cherry Hill, NJ. August 1, 2015.

Calautti, Katie. (2012, November 13). Carrie's Julianne Moore Discusses Tapping into Margaret's Madness. *Spinoff Online*. Retrieved on July 3, 2014, from http://spinoff.comicbookresources.com/2012/11/13/carries-julianne-moore-discusses-tapping-into-margarets-madness

Carmean, Karen, and Gaston, Georg. (1994). *Robert Shaw: More Than a Life*. Lanham, Md.: Madison Books.

Carmelo, Tonantzin. Phone interview. March 6, 2015.

Carter, Lauren Ashley. Phone interview. Aug. 31, 2015/April 1, 2016..

Chaw, Walter. (2013, July 12). Witchy Woman: FFC Interviews Heather Donahue. *Film Freak Central*. Retrieved on May 26, 2014, from http://www.filmfreakcentral.net/ffc/2013/07/witchy-woman-ffc-interviews-heather-donahue.html

Childs, Mike & Alan Jones. (1999, December 3). Carrie: Sissy Spacek. *Femme Fatales, 8 (8)*. 48-50, 61.

Chilton, Melinda. Phone interview. June 12, 2014.

Chitwood, Adam. (2013, July 16). Chloe Grace Moretz Talks Playing with Telekinetic Powers, the Grueling Audition Process, Preparing for the Role, and More on the Set of 'Carrie.' *Collider*. Retrieved on July 3, 2015, from http://collider.com/chloe-grace-moretz-carrie-interview/

Chuang, Juju, & Pinedo, Aristides. (2013, October 17). Chloe Grace Moretz Was 'Intimidated' to Take on 'Carrie,' Tried to Never Break Character on Set. *ABCNews*. Retrieved on July 3, 2014, from http://abcnews.go.com/Entertainment/chloe-grace-moretz-intimidated-carrie/story?id=20597776

Church, Ellie. E-mail interview. July 27, 2014.

Cobb, Julie. Phone interview. Feb. 4, 2014.

Colloca, Silvia. E-mail interview. March 16, 2016.

Coulter, Jean. Phone interview. June 22, 2015.

Crowe, Tonya. Phone interview. Dec. 7, 2015.

Cunningham, Sean (Producer) & Craven, Wes (Director). (1972). *Last House on the Left*. [DVD]. Los Angeles, CA.: MGM/UA Home Entertainment.

Cunningham, Sean & Craven, Wes (Producers). Iliadis, Dennis (Director). (2009). *Last House on the Left*. [DVD]. Los Angeles, CA.: Rogue Pictures

Dawson, Vicky. E-mail interview. Feb. 17, 2016.

De Luca, Danielle. E-mail interview. Oct. 24, 2014.

De Rousse, Marcia. Phone interview. Aug. 25, 2014.

DeVasquez, Devin. E-mail interview. Feb. 14, 2015.

DiBella, Joe. Phone interview. June 5, 2014.

Dietlein, Marsha. Phone interview. Jan. 12, 2012.

Douglas, Edward. (2012, October 15). NYCC Exclusive: Chloe Moretz Talks to Us About 'Carrie.' *Shock Till You Drop*. Retrieved on July 3, 3015, from http://www.shocktillyoudrop.com/news/170455-nycc-exclusive-chloe-moretz-talks-to-us-about-carrie/

Drummond, Alice. E-mail interview. May 10, 2015.

Ervin, Erica. E-mail interview. March 18, 2015.

Everson, Amy. Phone interview. March 12, 2016.

Exclusive: Riki Lindhome on Playing the Sadistic Sadie in 'Last House on the Left'! (2009, February 11). *Fearnet*. Retrieved on July 16, 2013, from http://www.fearnet.com/news/news-article/exclusive-riki-lindhome-playing-sadistic-sadie-last-house-left

Exclusive Video: 'I Spit on Your Grave' Interviews. (2011, Feb. 8). *Fangoria*. Retrieved on April 20, 2012, from http://www.fangoria.com/index.php/moviestv/fangoria-tv/3443-exclusive-video-i-spit-on-your-grave-interviews

Farrands, Daniel, & Andrew Kasch. (2010). *Never Sleep Again: The Elm Street Legacy*. DVD.1428 Films.

Ferrante, Anthony C. (1993, May) Return of the Living Dead: Part III, Zombiepunk. *Fangoria (127)*. 44-50.

Franich, Megan. E-mail interview. March 12, 2016.

Fraser, Mat. Phone interview. Jan. 20, 2016.

French, John. (1993). *Robert Shaw: The Price of Success*. London: Nick Hern Books.

Fuller, Jonathan. Phone interview. March 18, 2015.

Gastini, Marta. E-mail interview. June 7, 2014.

Geretta, Geretta. Phone interview. Dec. 10, 2014.

Getlen, Larry. (2014, January 19). Christina Ricci gets a grip on Lizzie Borden. *New York Post*. Retrieved on Jan. 28, 2015, from http://nypost.com/2014/01/19/christina-ricci-gets-a-grip-on-lizzie-borden/

Getsic, Rodleen. Phone interview. Feb 23, 2013.

Getsic, Rodleen. (2013). My Monsterpiece: An Art Film. *Cine-Excess eJournal*. Retrieved on Sept. 13, 2014 from http://www.cine-excess.co.uk/my-monsterpiece.html

Gibson, Leah. Phone interview. Jan. 15, 2014.

Giovinazzo, Buddy. Phone interview. March 11, 2016.

Goethals, Angela. Phone interview. April 14, 2014.

Goldman, Carole. Phone interview. Dec. 16, 2015.

References

Gollmer, Ella-Maria. E-mail interview. May 20, 2015.

Gomez, Macarena. E-mail interview. Sept. 15, 2014.

Gower, Andre. Phone interview. Oct. 8, 2015.

Goodson, William Wilson. (1999, February 12). Carrie II. *Femme Fatales*. 8-11.

Graham, Holter. E-mail interview. Nov. 21, 2014.

Graysmith, Robert. (2010). *The Girl in Alfred Hitchcock's Shower*. Berkley Books: New York.

Griffin, Lynne. Phone interview. Oct. 19, 2015.

Grote, Steffi. E-mail interview. Jan. 14, 2015.

Haun, Lindsey. Phone interview. Feb. 11, 2015.

Hawker, Luke. E-mail interview. Jan. 22, 2016.

Hayward, Lindsay. Phone interview. June 3, 2015.

Hayes, Britt. (2002, May 5). Interview: Cast of 'I Spit On Your Grave.' *Brutal as Hell*. Retrieved on April 20, 2012, fromhttp://www.brutalashell.com/2010/05/interview-cast-of-i-spit-on-your-grave/

Herbert, Christopher. (2011, March 5). Garret Dillahunt Interview—Last House on the Left. *Jolly Good Show*. Retrieved on July 16, 2013, from http://www.jollygoodshow.net/reviews/index.php/features/interviews/267-garret-dillahunt-interview-last-house-on-the-left?showall=&start=1

Hertford, Whit. Phone interview. April 3, 2009.

Hesse, Gregor. Phone interview. Oct. 1, 2015.

Hitchcock, Alfred. (2008). *Psycho: Special Edition*. DVD. Universal Studios.

Hubatsek, Andrew. E-mail interview. April 4, 2016.

Huck, Amy. E-mail interview. March 22, 2016.

I Spit on Your Grave: Exclusive: Sarah Butler Interview. *Movie Web*. Retrieved on April 20, 2012, from http://www.movieweb.com/movie/i-spit-on-your-grave/exclusive-sarah-butler-interview

Interview: Rodleen Getsic. (2012, August 3). *Horror News*. Retrieved on Sept. 13, 2014 from http://horrornews.net/54871/interview-rodleen-getsic-the-bunny-game/

Interview: Slavitza Jovan. Aug. 27, 1998. *ProtonCharging.com*. Retrieved on April 15, 2010, from http://proton-charging.com/gb/1998/08/27/interview-slavitza-jovan/

Interview with Addy Miller.(2011). *ARG Zombies*. Retrieved on May 1, 2012, fromhttp://www.argzombies.com/blog/products-interviews/interview-with-addy-miller/

It DVD

Jackson, Roger. Q+A session at Monster Mania horror movie convention, Cherry Hill, NJ. August 1, 2015.

Jacobs, Jay. (2009). Sara Paxton Takes a Sharp Left Turn to the Last House. *Pop Entertainment*. Retrieved on July 16, 2013, from http://www.popentertainment.com/sarapaxton.htm

Jankiewicz, Patrick. (2009). *Just When You Thought it Was Safe: A Jaws Companion*. Albany, Georgia: Bear Manor Media.

Jarratt, John. E-mail interview. July 30, 2014.

'Jaws' Actress Lee Fierro. (2008, July 22). *PlumTV*. Retrieved on Nov. 2, 2011, from http://www.plumtv.com/videos/vineyard-jaws-actress-lee-fiero

Jelinek, Tobias. E-mail interview. March 24, 2016.

Jennifer. (2014, April 4). Interview. *Christina Ricci*. Retrieved on Jan. 28, 2015, from http://www.christinaricci.ws/category/interviews

JimmyO. (2010, October 6). Exclusive Interview with 'I Spit on Your Grave' Star Sarah Butler. *I Am Rogue*. Retrieved on April 20, 2012, from http://www.iamrogue.com/news/interviews/item/1188-exclusive-interview-with-i-spit-on-your-grave-star-sarah-butler.html

Jones, Gene. Phone interview. Sept. 3, 2014.

Kamin, Dan. E-mail interview. March 21, 2014.

Kavadas, Andrew. E-mail interview. March 8, 2016.

Keaton, Camille. Personal interview. April 20, 2012.

Keeping, Daisy. E-mail interview. June 18, 2015.

Kelegian, Sylva. E-mail interview. Jan. 22, 2016.

Kerswell, J.A. (2012). *The Slasher Movie Book*. Chicago Review Press: Chicago.

Kinkade, Amelia. E-mail interview. Aug. 21, 2015.

King, Nick. Phone interview. Sept. 14, 2015.

Kirk, James. E-mail interview. June 14, 2014.

Laliberte, Nicole. Phone interview. April 4, 2016.

Langenkamp, Heather. Q+A at 'Scares that Care' Horror Movie Convention. June 22, 2014.

Larson, Jill. Phone interview. Jan. 9, 2015.

The Last House on the Left. (2013). *Tribute Entertainment*. Retrieved on July 16, 2013, from http://www.tribute.ca/interviews/garret-dillahunt/starchat/537/

The Last House on the Left's Krug. (2009, March 10). *Ain't it Cool News*. Retrieved on July 16, 2013, from http://www.aintitcool.com/node/40382

The Last House on the Left—Garret Dillahunt Interview. (2013). *Movie Web*. Retrieved on July 16, 2013, from http://www.movieweb.com/movie/the-last-house-on-the-left/garret-dillahunt-interview

Laurie, Piper. Q+A session at Scares that Cares horror film convention, Virginia Beach, VA, July 25, 2015.

LeboFilms. (2011, Oct. 13). Addy Miller Interview from The Walking Dead. *YouTube*. Retrieved on May 1, 2012, from http://www.youtube.com/watch?v=ngXH-HMjfWI

Lebofilms. (2012, July 9). Madison Lintz, Sophia from 'Walking Dead.' Y*outube*. Retrieved on October 7. 2013, from http://www.youtube.com/watch?v=-fa1LPh-SYI

Leigh, Janet and Christopher Nickens. (1995). *Psycho*: *Behind the Scenes of the Classic Thriller*. Harmony Books: New York.

References

Leemans, Kimberly. E-mail interview. Feb. 19, 2016.

Lintz, Madison. Personal interview. Oct. 5, 2013.

Llao, Ramon. E-mail interview. March 28, 2016.

Loehr, Bret. Phone interview. Jan. 12, 2015.

Lynch, John Carroll. Phone interview. March 13, 2015.

MacKay, Michael Reid. Phone interview. Oct. 9, 2015.

Mad, Bad, and Dangerous to Know. (2011, February). *The Terror Trap*. Retrieved on July 13, 2013, from http://www.terrortrap.com/interviews/davidhess/

Madison Lintz (Sophia) Interview. (2012, January 23). *YouTube*. Retrieved on October 7, 2013, from http://thewalkingdeadrumors.com/from-the-cast/madison-lintz-sophia-interview/

Marut, Marc. Phone interview. Nov. 26, 2014.

Mazur, Heather. Phone interview. Aug. 26, 2015.

McCall, Joan. E-mail interview. Oct. 8, 2015.

McGilligan, Patrick. (2003). *Alfred Hitchcock: A Life in Darkness and Light*. Regan Books: New York.

McKinney, Jennifer. Phone interview. Feb. 26, 2016.

McMinn, Teri. Phone interview. Oct. 19, 2015.

Meyers, Jeffrey. (2009). *The Genius and the Goddess*. University of Illinois Press: Chicago.

Miller, Addy. Q+A session at "Blood at the Beach" horror movie convention, Virginia Beach, VA. April 20, 2012.

Miller, Victoria Leigh. (2014, October 3). "'AHS: Freak Show' Star Rose Siggins on Her Real Life Without Legs: 'This is my Normal." *Yahoo TV*. Retrieved on December 13, 2015, from https://www.yahoo.com/tv/bp/american-horror-story--freak-show-legless-suzy-rose-siggins-200324891.html

Miner, Rachel. Phone interview. July 2, 2014.

Molina, Melissa. (2013, October 18). Interview: Chloe Grace Moretz On Becoming 'Carrie.' *Movie Pilot*. Retrieved on July 3, 2015, from http://moviepilot.com/posts/2013/10/18/interview-chloe-grace-moretz-on-becoming-carrie-1147733?lt_source=external,manual,manual

Moran, Pauline. E-mail interview. Sept. 15, 2015.

Mortimer, Ingrid. Phone interview. Oct. 23, 2015.

Movie Geeks United. (2012, Jan. 13). MGU Interview: Riki Lindhome. *YouTube*. Retrieved on July 16, 2013, from http://www.youtube.com/watch?v=8Pdl5pbK_W4

Murray, Rebecca. (2013). Last House on the Left- Riki Lindhome Interview. *About*. Retrieved on July 16, 2013, from http://video.about.com/movies/Last-House-Riki-Lindhome.htm#vdTrn

Murray, Rebecca. (2013). Sara Paxton Talks About 'Last House On the Left.' *About*. Retrieved on July 16, 2013, from http://movies.about.com/od/thelasthouseontheleft/a/sara-paxton.htm

MutantVille Players. (2011, June 9). The Walking Dead Addy Miller "Little Girl." *YouTube*. Retrieved on May 1, 2012, from http://www.youtube.com/watch?v=w8oc0P2BRq0&feature=related

Naughton, David. Phone interview. Nov. 19, 2009.

Naughton, David. Q+A session at Scares that Cares horror/charity convention, Williamsburg, VA, July 25, 2015.

Nelkin, Stacey. Phone interview. Feb. 25, 2015.

Newlander, Jamison. Q+A session, Four State Slasher Convention. Winchester, VA. Oct. 16, 2015.

Newton, Steve. (1990, December). Clowning Around With Tim Curry. *Fangoria*. 28-31.

Norton, Al. (2009, March 13). Interview with Last House on the Left Star Riki Lindhome, *411 Mania*. Retrieved on July 16, 2013, from http://www.411mania.com/movies/columns/99113/411Mania-Interviews-Last-House-on-the-Left-star-Riki-Lindhome.htm

Nutman, Philip. (1990, December). King Talks. Fangoria. 22-26, 59.

Palmer, Randy. (1999, April). There's Something About Carrie. *Fangoria, 181*, 26-28, 30-31, 76.

Perkins, Amber. Phone interview. July 23, 2014.

Perkins, Emily. E-mail interview. Jan. 15, 2015.

Peters, John. (2011, Feb. 28). Sarah Butler Talks 'I Spit on Your Grave.' *Killer Film*. Retrieved on April 20, 2012, from http://www.killerfilm.com/interviews/read/sarah-butler-talks-i-spit-on-your-grave-65305

Poirier, Denise. Phone/E-mail interview. Feb. 28, 2016.

Powers, Andy. E-mail interview. August 22, 2015.

Quigley, Linnea. E-mail interview. March 21, 2016.

Quinn, Rachel. Phone interview. July 1, 2014.

Ragsdale, William. Q+A session, Scares that Care horror movie convention, Williamsburg, VA., June 22, 2014.

Rebello, Stephen. (1990). *Alfred Hitchcock and the Making of* Psycho. Dembner Books: New York.

Regehr, Duncan. E-mail interview. Sept. 13, 2015.

Risk, Tristan. E-mail interview. Jan. 11, 2015.

Roberts, Conrad. Phone interview. March 25, 2016.

Roberts, Sheila. Sara Paxton Interview, Last House on the Left. *Movies Online*. Retrieved on July 16, 2013, from http://www.moviesonline.ca/movienews_16453.html

Rochon, Debbie. E-mail interview. January 7, 2015.

Rodriguez, Perla. E-mail interview. May 1, 2014.

Rogak, Lisa. (2008). *Haunted Heart: The Life and Times of Stephen King*. St. Martin's Press: New York.

Rothman, William. (1982). *Hitchcock: The Mysterious Gaze*. Harvard University Press: Cambridge, Mass.

Rothrock, Richard. (1995 Winter). "Shark Bait." *Femme Fatales.(3)*3. 6-7, 62.

Sanchez, Victoria. E-mail interview. Feb. 10, 2015.

Sarandon, Chris. Q+A session, Scares that Care horror movie convention, Williamsburg, VA., June 21, 2014.

References

Scapperotti, Dan. (1999, December 3). Fatale Attractions. *Femme Fatales*. 8(8). 5-6

Scarlett Johansson Interview For 'Hitchcock.' (2012, Nov. 20. *Zimbio*. Retrieved June 4, 2013, from http://www.zimbio.com/Sir+Anthony+Hopkins/articles/5XyUOgPOcFG/Scarlett+Johansson+Interview+Hitchcock

Scarlett Johansson Talks 'Hitchcock,' New Tattoo on 'Today.' (2012, Nov. 12). *Hollywood Reporter*. Retrieved June 4, 2013, from http://www.hollywoodreporter.com/live-feed/scarlett-johansson-talks-hitchcock-new-394442

Schirmer, Chason. Phone interview. July 16, 2014.

Schneider, Gary. E-mail interview. Dec. 2, 2015.

Sexton, Tobe. Phone interview. July 2, 2014.

Shepis, Tiffany. E-mail interview. March 31, 2016.

Silvaggio, Joe. Phone interview. Jan. 11, 2016.

Simmons, Chelan. Personal interview. July 24, 2015.

Sizemore, James. E-mail interview. March 9, 2016.

Smith, Rachele Brooke. E-mail interview. May 22, 2014.

Smith Collins, Stephan. E-mail interview. Feb. 19, 2015.

Spacek, Sissy. (2012). *My Extraordinary Ordinary Life*. Hyperion: New York.

Spielberg, Steven. (2005). *Jaws: 30th Anniversary Edition*. DVD. Universal Studios.

Spoto, Donald. (2008). *Spellbound by Beauty: Alfred Hitchcock and his Leading Ladies*. Harmony Books: New York.

Spry, Bailey. Phone interview. Aug. 10, 2015

Stehlin, Andrew. E-mail interview. April 8, 2016.

Stevenson, Oakley. Phone interview. Dec. 26, 2015.

Stone, Madison. Phone interview. March 20, 2016.

Szulkin, David A. (2000, June.) *Wes Craven's* Last House on the Left: *The Making of a Cult Classic*. FAB Press: England.

Tanamor, Jason. (2011, April 14). Heather Donahue Talks Marijuana and the Possibility of Another 'Blair Witch Project' Movie. *Yahoo!* Retrieved on May 26, 2014, from http://voices.yahoo.com/heather-donahue-talks-marijuana-possibility-8291875.html

Taylor, Alison. Phone interview. June 12, 2014.

Taylor, Matt. (2011). *Jaws: Memories from Martha's Vineyard*. Moonrise Media: Martha's Vineyard, Mass.

TCFan123. (2008, Jan. 17). Tim Curry Interview from 1997. YouTube. Retrieved from http://www.youtube.com/watch?v=Wu0mJakYzow

Thomas, Jake. Phone interview. March 24, 2016.

Thorne, Dyanne. Phone interview. May 20-21, 2015.

Todd, Samm. Phone interview. Oct. 8, 2014.

Topel, Fred. (2015). Chloe Moretz Talks About 'Carrie.' *About. Entertainment*. Retrieved on July 3, 2015, from http://movies.about.com/od/carrie/fl/carrie-moretz-interview.htm

Torgl, Mark. E-mail interview. Nov. 17, 2015.

Trautman, Allan. Phone interview. Jan. 23, 2015.

Tripp, Baph. E-mail interview. Oct. 4, 2015.

Turpin, Ana. E-mail interview. Feb. 15, 2016.

Van Hentenryck, Kevin. Phone interview. Jan. 23, 2015.

Voorhees, Debi Sue. Phone interview. August 4, 2015.

Vosburgh, Lara. E-mail interview. April 9, 2016.

Walsh, Eileen. E-mail interview. Jan. 21, 2016.

Wakkechinsky, David, and Amy Wallace. (1993). *The Book of Lists: The '90s Edition*. Little, Brown, and Company: New York.

Webb, Haley. E-mail interview. June 26, 2014.

Wells, Dawn. Phone interview. June 24, 2015.

White, Liz. E-mail interview. Feb. 10, 2015.

Wieselman, Jarett. (2009, July 13). Get To Know: Riki Lindhome. *New York Post*. Retrieved on July 16, 2013, from http://www.nypost.com/p/blogs/popwrap/item_41mTNqSNGTO2txGRScl5UP#axzz2QC13R8TR

Wilson, Staci Layne. (2009, March 6). Garret Dillahunt. *Horror*. Retrieved on July 16, 2013, from http://www.horror.com/php/article-2297-1.html

Wilson, Staci Layne. (2009, March 6). Sara Paxton- Interview. *Horror*. Retrieved on July 16, 2013, from http://www.horror.com/php/article-2299-1.html

Winecoff, Charles. (1996). *Split Image: The Life of Anthony Perkins*. Penguin Group: New York.

Wirth, Billy. Q+A session, Four State Slasher Convention. Winchester, VA. Oct. 16, 2015.

Woronov, Mary. Phone interview. Feb. 24, 2015.

Worland, Rick. (2007). *The Horror Film*. Blackwell Publishing: Malden, MA.

Wright, Tom. Personal interview. Oct. 17, 2015.

About the Author

A LIFELONG FILM fan, Jason Norman is a college English teacher in Chesapeake, Virginia. The winner of two Virginia Press Association awards, he lives with his amazing wife Jennifer, who, through the course of his writing, acts as his researcher, editor, photographer, and official film convention partner (all working for free!). This is his second book.

www.ingramcontent.com/pod-product-compliance
Lightning Source LLC
Chambersburg PA
CBHW070158240426
43671CB00007B/486